FOURTH EDITION

Market-Based Management

Strategies for Growing Customer Value and Profitability

Roger J. Best

Emeritus Professor of Marketing
University of Oregon

PEARSON

Prentice
Hall

Upper Saddle River, New Jersey 07458

Library of Congress Cataloging-in-Publication Data

Best, Roger J.
  Market-based management: strategies for growing customer value and profitability/
Roger J. Best.--4th ed.
    p. cm.
  Includes bibliographical references and index.
  ISBN 0-13-146956-8
  1. Marketing—Management. I. Title.

  HF5415.13.B46 2004
  658.8--dc22   2004040085

Acquisitions Editor: Katie Stevens
Editorial Director: Jeff Shelstad
Assistant Editor: Melissa Pellerano
Editorial Assistant: Rebecca Lembo
Executive Marketing Manager: Michelle O'Brien
Marketing Assistant: Nicole Macchiarelli
Senior Managing Editor: Judy Leale
Production Editor: Kelly Warsak
Permissions Supervisor: Charles Morris
Manufacturing Buyer: Michelle Klein
Design Manager: Maria Lange
Art Director: Janet Slowik
Interior Design: Karen Quigley
Cover Design: Karen Quigley
Cover Illustration: Dennis Harms/Stock Illustration Source/Images.com
Illustrator (Interior): BookMasters, Inc.
Manager, Print Production: Christy Mahon
Composition: Laserwords
Full-Service Project Management: Jennifer Welsch/BookMasters, Inc.
Printer/Binder: Phoenix Color Corp.
Cover Printer: Phoenix Color Corp.
Typeface: 10.5/12 Times

Credits and acknowledgments borrowed from other sources and reproduced, with permission, in this textbook
appear on page 496.

Pearson Education LTD.   Pearson Education Australia PTY, Limited
Pearson Education Singapore, Pte. Ltd   Pearson Education North Asia Ltd
Pearson Education, Canada, Ltd   Pearson Educación de Mexico, S.A. de C.V.
Pearson Education–Japan   Pearson Education Malaysia, Pte. Ltd

10 9 8 7 6 5 4 3 2
ISBN 0-13-146956-8

To my toughest critics — Robin, Mary, and Oliver

BRIEF CONTENTS

CONTENTS

PART I ■ MARKET ORIENTATION AND PERFORMANCE 3

PART II ■ MARKET ANALYSIS 61

CHAPTER 6   COMPETITOR ANALYSIS AND SOURCES OF ADVANTAGE 169

PREFACE

> ■ **Gains in marketing knowledge without application are missed learning opportunities.**
> — *Dr. Roger J. Best*

This fourth edition of *Market-Based Management* is built around a performance orientation and the belief that real learning occurs only with application of knowledge. As shown in the following figure, marketing knowledge is the driver of improved marketing performance but this can only be achieved with marketing application and experience.

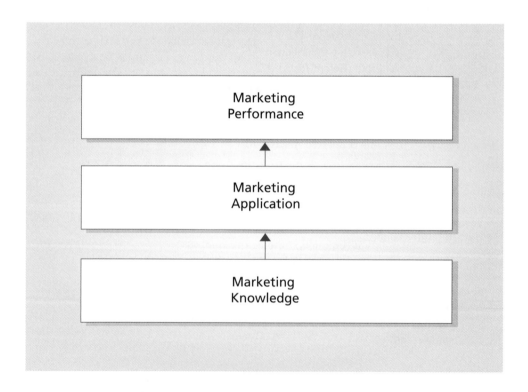

Based on positive feedback from students, professors, and those working in the field of marketing, I was encouraged to continue to build on this philosophy with this fourth edition of *Market-Based Management*. The strength of the book retains its focus on market orientation and the processes and tools for building marketing strategies that deliver superior levels of customer satisfaction, value, and profitability. The differentiating feature of this book is its focus on marketing performance and marketing profitability and the role marketing strategies play in building the profits of a business. The best way to accomplish this is with market-driven strategies that attract, satisfy, and retain target customers with a value that is superior to competing products or services.

The fourth edition builds on this continuing theme in several ways. A special effort was made to include more coverage of customer loyalty, marketing performance metrics, customer relationship marketing, and brand and product-line strategies. Perhaps even more important is the addition of the Marketing Performance Tools at the end of each chapter. These online tools will allow users of *Market-Based Management* the opportunity to apply their marketing knowledge and develop further marketing insights. For instructors, the Marketing Performance Tools can be used to create additional assignments.

Market-based management is intuitively easy but deceptively difficult. The reason marketing students and marketing professionals like this book is because it is readable, and because it presents the tools and processes needed to actually build a market-driven strategy. The concepts, by themselves, are important and are the backbone of market-based management. However, they are of limited value if they cannot be applied in a way that delivers superior customer value and profitability. Those in marketing need to take a greater level of responsibility for managing profits and the external performance metrics of a business. This is an important benefit of this book. It is my hope that this book will help you in your understanding of, commitment to, and practice of market-based management.

Roger J. Best
Emeritus Professor of Marketing
University of Oregon

INSTRUCTIONAL SUPPORT

Various teaching supplements are available to accompany this textbook. They consist of the following:

- Instructor's Manual with Test Item File
- Instructor's Resource CD, which includes the Word files for the above mentioned items, plus PowerPoint files and TestGen EQ software
- Web site with student resources (*www.prenhall.com/best*)

Please contact your Prentice Hall sales representative to obtain these materials.

These items may also be found for download at *www.prenhall.com*, the homepage for Prentice Hall's online Instructor's Resource Center (IRC).

In order to access these materials, please follow the instructions below.

- Go to *www.prenhall.com*
- Use the "Search our Catalog" field across the top to search for this textbook.
- Once you locate the book's catalog page, locate the "Instructor" link on the left menu bar and click on it.
- Scroll down the Instructor Resources page and you will see supplement download links. (Look for the small disk icons.)
- Click on any download link; you will be taken to a login page. Follow the instructions to register if you have not already done so. Once your status as an instructor has been validated (allow 24–48 hours), you will receive an e-mail message confirming your username and password. You only need to register once to access any Prentice Hall instructor resource.

Dr. Roger J. Best is an emeritus professor of marketing at the University of Oregon and president and owner of the Marketing Excellence Survey. He earned a bachelor of science in electrical engineering from California State Polytechnic University in 1968. Following graduation, he joined the General Electric Company where he worked in both engineering and product management. While at GE, he received a patent for a product he developed. Dr. Best completed his MBA at California State University, Hayward in 1972 and received his doctorate from the University of Oregon in 1975. He taught at the University of Arizona from 1975 to 1980 and the University of Oregon from 1980 to 2000. He currently teaches part-time in the University of Oregon MBA program where in 2004 he won the Outstanding MBA Teacher Award.

Over the past 25 years, he has published over 50 articles and won numerous teaching awards. In 1998, he received the American Marketing Association Distinguished Teaching in Marketing Award. In 1988, the Academy of Marketing Science voted an article on marketing productivity by Del Hawkins, Roger Best, and Charles Lillis the Outstanding Article of the Year. Dr. Best also developed the Marketing Excellence Survey (*www.MESurvey.com*), a benchmarking tool for assessing a manager's marketing knowledge and market attitudes based on a worldwide database of over 25,000 managers and MarkProf (*www.MarkProf.com*), a marketing profitability program to help marketing managers better manage the profit impact of marketing strategies.

Over the past 20 years, Dr. Best has been active in working with a variety of companies in both marketing strategy consulting and management education. These companies include 3M, General Electric, Dow Chemical, Dow Corning, DuPont, Eastman Kodak, MediaOne, Lucas Industries, Tektronix, ESCO, Pacific Western Pipe, James Hardie Industries, Sprint, and US West. Dr. Best has also taught many executive management education programs at INSEAD Fontainebleau, France.

ACKNOWLEDGMENTS

A book such as this is an assimilation of knowledge from many sources. It is an integration of perspectives intended for a particular audience. An author's added value is in the focus, integration, and presentation, but the basic knowledge is derived from many sources. I would like to acknowledge specific individuals whose knowledge contributed to my understanding of marketing and shaped many of the ideas presented in this fourth edition of *Market-Based Management*. These individuals include Stewart Bither, John Cady, George Day, Del Hawkins, Thomas Kinnear, Jean-Claude Larreche, Charles Lillis, Joseph Newman, and Donald Tull.

Second, I would like to acknowledge the valuable feedback I received from the following reviewers for the fourth edition. Their thoughtful reviews and suggestions for improvement are appreciated and greatly enhanced this edition.

- Jacqueline Callery, *Robert Morris College*
- Laura Leli Carmine, *Lewis University*
- Anthony DiBenedetto, *Temple University*
- Betsy Gelb, *University of Houston*
- Ronald Goldsmith, *Florida State University*
- Regina McNally, *Michigan State University*
- Rex Moody, *Central Washington University*
- Kim Nelson, *University of South Florida–St. Petersburg*
- Cynthia Sadler, *Mount Mercy College*
- Donald Self, *Auburn University Montgomery*
- Susan Spiggle, *University of Connecticut*

Finally, I would like to thank marketing managers from 3M, Dow Chemical, Dow Corning, and DuPont for their comments and encouragement. Their real-world perspective and feedback help me continue to pursue a more applied approach in presenting *Market-Based Management*. Also, the fourth edition would not have been possible without the support of Dr. Bruce Cooley, Thitapon Ousawat, and the careful proofreading of Santwana Singh. Their participation and contributions were critical to every aspect of this edition and are greatly appreciated. I also owe a special thanks to my editors, Katie Stevens and Melissa Pellerano, who encouraged me to write the fourth edition and dogged me until it was finished. They and my wife, Robin, deserve a great deal of credit for enduring my ups and downs in the writing of this edition.

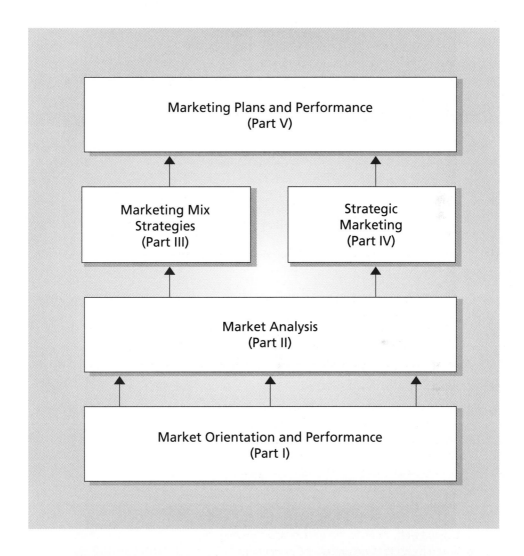

This model represents both the logic of market-based management and the organization of this book. Market Orientation and Marketing Performance (Part I) are the bedrock of market-based management and fosters a Market Analysis (Part II) built around customer needs, market trends, and competition.

A commitment to a market orientation and ongoing market analysis allows the development of focused Marketing Mix Strategies (Part III) and Strategic Marketing (Part IV), long-run marketing strategies. Marketing Plans and Performance (Part V) are the culmination of this process.

Successful implementation of this process is designed to create and deliver higher levels of customer value that enhance customer satisfaction and contribute to higher levels of profitability.

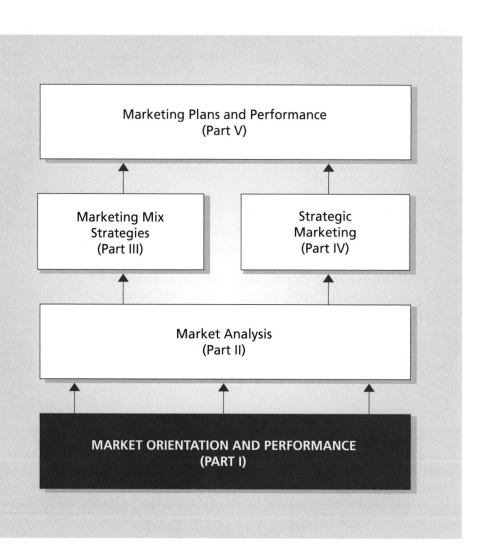

Market Orientation and Performance

■ Marketing isn't somebody's responsibility; marketing is everybody's responsibility.
 — *Jack Welch, CEO, 1981–2001*
 General Electric Co.

A market-based business has a strong market orientation that permeates all functions and employees of an organization. While those in marketing have the primary responsibility to lead marketing excellence, in a market-based business, all members of the organization have a strong market orientation. This means all members of the organization are sensitive to customers' needs, are aware of competitors' moves, and work well across organizational boundaries toward a timely market-based customer solution. What's the payoff? Market-based businesses with a strong market orientation are more profitable.

Part I demonstrates the connectivity between market orientation, customer satisfaction, market-based management, and profitability. In Chapter 1, we examine the fundamental components of market orientation and how each is related to customer satisfaction and retention. From this perspective, we will calculate the profit impact of a lifetime customer as well as the high cost of customer dissatisfaction. Although a strong market orientation enhances a business's chances for long-run survival, short-run profits can also be increased with marketing efforts to increase customer satisfaction and retention.

A strong market orientation cannot be created by mere proclamation. To attain a strong market orientation, a business needs to adopt a market-based management philosophy. This means restructuring an organization around markets rather than products or factories and creating an employee culture that is responsive to customers and changing market conditions. Market-based management also requires businesses to measure profits at the market level and to track external, market-based performance metrics. These topics, and their relation to marketing strategies and profitable growth, are discussed in Chapter 2.

CHAPTER 1

Customer Focus and Managing Customer Loyalty

I n today's globally competitive world, customers expect more, have more choices, and are less brand loyal. Businesses such as Sears, Kodak, and General Motors at one time seemed invincible in terms of their market domination. However, in each case, these companies have had to restructure (reengineer) their organizations to address changing customer needs and emerging competitive forces. In the long run, the survival of every business is at risk. Although companies such as Dell Computer, Microsoft, and Wal-Mart were business heroes of the 1990s, there is no guarantee that these same companies will continue to dominate over the next decade. The only thing that is constant . . . is *change*.

- Customers will continue to *change* in needs, demographics, lifestyle, and consumption behavior.
- Competitors will *change* as new technologies emerge and barriers to foreign competition shift.
- The environment in which businesses operate will continue to *change* as economic, political, social, and technological forces shift.

The companies that *survive* and *grow* will be the ones that *understand change* and are out in front leading, often creating change. Others, slow to comprehend change, will follow with reactive strategies, while still others will disappear, not knowing that change has even occurred.

CUSTOMER FOCUS AND PROFITABILITY

A sports reporter once asked Wayne Gretzky what made him a great hockey player. Gretzky's response was, "I skate to where the puck is going, not to where it is." In other words, Wayne Gretzky has a tremendous instinct for change. He is able to position himself as change is occurring in such a way that he can either score a goal or assist in scoring a goal. Businesses that can sense the direction of change, and position themselves to lead in the change, can prosper and grow. Those that wait to read about it in the *Wall Street Journal* are hopelessly behind the play of the game and, at best, can only "skate" to catch up.

Businesses that are able to skate to where the puck is going have a strong (external) market orientation. They are constantly in tune with customers' needs, competitors' strategies, changing environmental conditions, and emerging technologies, and they seek ways to continuously improve the solutions they bring to target customers. This process enables them to move with—and often lead—change.

One of the benefits of a strong customer focus is long-run survival. Western cultures have long been criticized for being extremely short term in perspective. Consequently, long-run survival of a business may not be a strong management motive in developing a strong customer focus that strives to build long-term customer relationships. Managers are often judged on last quarter's results and not on what they are doing to ensure the long-run survival of the business. Likewise, shareholders can be more interested in immediate earnings than in the long-run survival of a business.

Although the long-run benefits of a strong customer focus are crucial to business survival and the economic health of a nation, the purpose of this chapter is to demonstrate both the *short-run* and *long-run* benefits of a strong customer focus. Businesses with a strong customer focus not only outperform their competition in delivering higher levels of customer satisfaction, they also deliver higher profits in the short run. A customer-focused business creates greater customer value and manages customer loyalty as a way to create greater shareholder value. However, perhaps the best way to understand the marketing logic that links customer focus to shareholder value is to examine the sequence of events that evolves when a business has little or no customer focus.

How to Underwhelm Customers and Shareholders

Businesses with a weak customer focus underwhelm both customers and shareholders. A business with a weak customer focus has only a superficial or poor understanding of customer needs and competition. Moving clockwise from the top in Figure 1-1, little or no customer focus translates into an unfocused value proposition and minimal customer satisfaction.[1] This results in low levels of customer loyalty because customers are easily attracted to competitors. Marketing efforts to hold off customer switching are expensive, as is the cost of acquiring new customers to replace lost customers. Low levels of customer loyalty and higher marketing costs contribute to disappointing business profits. In response, short-term sales tactics and accounting maneuvers are used to bolster short-run financial results. However, investors and Wall Street analysts are able to see through this facade, and shareholder value generally stagnates. Perhaps even worse, as shown in the scenario described in Figure 1-1, management is now under even greater pressure to produce short-run profits. This means that there is not the time, the inclination, or the motivation to understand customer needs and to unravel competitors' strategies, so the vicious circle of poor performance displayed in Figure 1-1 continues.

Customer Focus and Customer Satisfaction

Contrary to the scenario presented in Figure 1-1, a business with a strong customer focus stays in close contact with customers in an effort to deliver high levels of customer satisfaction and build customer loyalty. Marketing strategies in these businesses are built around customer needs and other sources of customer satisfaction. The strength of a business's customer focus also relies on how well it *understands key competitors* and evolving

FIGURE 1-1 UNDERWHELMING CUSTOMERS AND SHAREHOLDERS

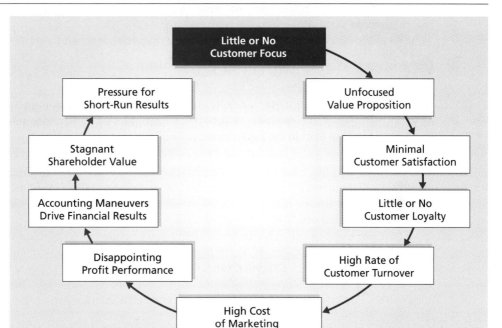

competitive forces. This aspect of customer focus enables a business to track its relative competitiveness in such areas as pricing, product quality and availability, service quality, and customer satisfaction.

The primary benefit of a strong customer focus and higher levels of customer satisfaction is a higher level of customer loyalty.[2] Keeping good customers should be the *first priority* of market-based management. As shown in Figure 1-2, a business with a strong customer focus is in the best position to develop and implement strategies that deliver

FIGURE 1-2 CUSTOMER FOCUS, CUSTOMER SATISFACTION, AND PROFITABILITY

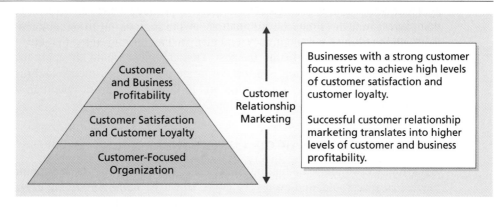

high levels of customer satisfaction and loyalty. In turn, customer satisfaction and loyalty drive customer profitability. We will show that very satisfied, loyal customers are the ones who shape the profitability of a business.

Customer Satisfaction: A Key Marketing Performance Metric

Although a market-based business will use several external metrics to track market performance, an essential performance metric is customer satisfaction. Many marketing strategies can be developed to attract customers, but it is the business that completely satisfies customers that gets to keep them. This viewpoint may sound philanthropic to those who do not accept the whole concept of market orientation and market-based management. We will demonstrate in this chapter the tremendous leverage a business can create in growing profits from a base of "very satisfied" customers and proactive management of dissatisfied customers.

There are many ways to measure customer satisfaction. One common measure is a customer satisfaction index (CSI) derived from customers' ratings of their overall satisfaction on a six-point scale that ranges from very dissatisfied to very satisfied. As shown, each level of customer satisfaction is given a rating that ranges from zero for very dissatisfied customers to 100 for very satisfied customers.

Very Dissatisfied (0)	Moderately Dissatisfied (20)	Somewhat Dissatisfied (40)	Somewhat Satisfied (60)	Moderately Satisfied (80)	Very Satisfied (100)

To create an overall CSI for a given sample of customers, a business simply computes the average of those customers' satisfaction ratings.

Assume, for example, that an interview with 100 Hewlett-Packard (HP) printer customers produced an average CSI of 72. By itself, an overall average customer satisfaction level of 72 does not tell us much and is not likely to get management's attention. Is a CSI of 72 a good level of performance? That depends on the business's overall CSI in earlier measurements, its target objective, and the overall CSI given to a leading competitor. Let's assume that an overall CSI of 72 is an improvement over earlier measures and that the average CSI of a leading competitor is 62. Those numbers would lead many businesses to feel pretty good about their level of performance and perhaps become complacent in their pursuit of customer satisfaction. Also, efforts to increase customer satisfaction require time and money, and many managers may argue that the incremental benefit is not sufficient to justify the cost. That argument would *not* apply to a business where customer satisfaction is a top corporate performance metric and priority.[3] To really understand customer satisfaction and to leverage its profit potential, we need to expand our view of customer satisfaction.

A Wide-Angle View of Customer Satisfaction

An average customer satisfaction index of 72 (where 100 is the maximum) may be viewed as acceptable, and even very good. However, *managing to the average* masks our understanding of customer satisfaction and opportunities for increased profits.[4]

FIGURE 1-3 CUSTOMER SATISFACTION: A WIDE-ANGLE VIEW

If we expand our view of customer satisfaction by reporting the percentage for each category on our customer satisfaction scale, a more meaningful set of insights emerges. As illustrated in Figure 1-3, the average CSI of 72 was derived from 83 percent who reported varying degrees of satisfaction and 17 percent who reported varying degrees of dissatisfaction. The 22 percent who were somewhat satisfied in their customer satisfaction are certainly vulnerable to competitor moves, but it is the 17 percent categorized as dissatisfied who are serious candidates for exit as customers. Thus, our immediate concern should be our dissatisfied customers.

Customer satisfaction is an excellent market-based performance metric and barometer of future revenues and profits, as stated here.

> Customer satisfaction is a forward-looking indicator of business success that measures how well customers will respond to the company in the future. Other measures of market performance, such as sales and market share, are backward-looking measures of success. They tell how well the firm has done in the past, but not how well it will do in the future.[5]

Thus, customer satisfaction is a good leading indicator of operating performance. A business may have produced excellent financial results while underwhelming and disappointing a growing number of its customers. Because customers cannot always immediately switch to alternative solutions, customer dissatisfaction often precedes customer exit and reductions in sales and profitability.

For many businesses, quarterly measures of customer satisfaction provide an excellent way to anticipate future performance. If customer satisfaction is on the decline, an early warning signal is given, providing the opportunity to correct the problem before real damage is done. Of course, if a business does not track customer satisfaction, it forgoes the opportunity to correct problems before sales and profits decline.

De-Averaging Customer Satisfaction and Customer Profitability

De-averaging the CSI to a wide-angle view of customer satisfaction allows managers to see more completely the opportunities for improvement. De-averaging, however, is even more important in understanding customer profitability.[6] As shown in Figure 1-4, the average customer revenue is $630 dollars in our example. However, "very satisfied" customers spend an average of $1,500 per year—roughly two and a half times the average. Even more impressive is the role that "very satisfied" customers play in profitability.[7]

Although the average customer profitability is $250 per year, "very satisfied" customers produce $800 per year in customer profit. "Very satisfied" customers not only buy more, they buy higher-margin products and services as illustrated in Figure 1-4.

When we chart customer profitability against customer satisfaction as illustrated in Figure 1-5, we can clearly see that "very satisfied" customers drive profitability. Dissatisfied customers buy in smaller amounts and often buy lower-margin or promotional products. After considering the cost of marketing, we can see that these customers lose the company money in this example. "Somewhat satisfied" and "satisfied" customers are profitable but are below the overall average customer profitability that is largely determined by the profit impact of "very satisfied" customers. De-averaging customer satisfaction clearly demonstrates the importance of "very satisfied" customers to the overall profits of a business.

We have shown the importance that "very satisfied" customers have in the profitability of a business, but "dissatisfied" customers are equally important. Attracting a new customer costs considerably more than retaining a customer. When a customer is dissatisfied and leaves, a business suffers several economic consequences, which lower the business's profits.

Dissatisfied customers often do not complain to a manufacturer, but they do walk and they *do* talk.[8] Well-documented studies show that out of 100 dissatisfied customers, only 4 will complain to a business.[9] Of the 96 dissatisfied customers who do not complain, 91 will exit as customers, as shown in Figure 1-6. Exiting customers directly erode market position, but they also make it more difficult to attract new customers because each dissatisfied customer will tell 8 to 10 other people of his or her dissatisfaction.

The market impact is enormous. For example, assume that a business has captured 10 percent of a 2-million customer market, or 200,000 customers. If 15 percent of those 200,000 customers were dissatisfied, this business would have 30,000 dissatisfied

FIGURE 1-4 DE-AVERAGING CUSTOMER SATISFACTION AND CUSTOMER PROFITABILITY

Customer Satisfaction	Customer Percent (%)	CSI Score	Annual Sales ($)	Percent Margin (%)	Gross Profit ($)	Retention Cost ($)	Customer Profit ($)
Very Satisfied	25	100	1,500	60	900	100	800
Satisfied	36	80	500	50	250	100	150
Somewhat Satisfied	22	60	250	50	125	100	25
Somewhat Dissatisfied	10	40	150	40	60	100	(40)
Dissatisfied	5	20	75	40	30	100	(70)
Very Dissatisfied	2	0	50	40	20	100	(80)
	100	72	$630		$350		$250

**FIGURE 1-5 DE-AVERAGING CUSTOMER SATISFACTION
            AND CUSTOMER PROFITABILITY**

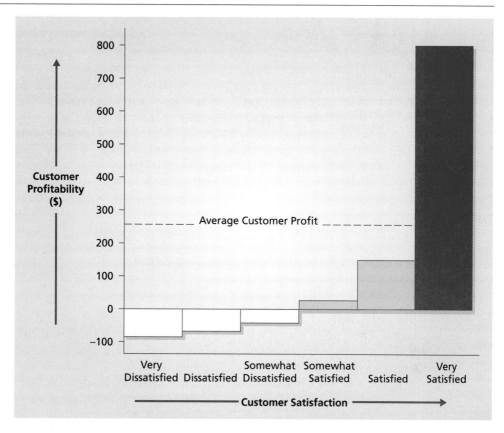

customers. The statistics presented in Figure 1-6 indicate that the business would lose 92 percent of those dissatisfied customers—each year. The 27,600 lost customers translate to a 1.4 point reduction in market share. To hold its 10 percent share of the market (customers), the business would have to attract 27,600 new replacement customers. This is a very expensive way to hold market share.

It gets worse.[10] Many dissatisfied customers become "customer terrorists"; they vent their dissatisfaction by telling others about it. Recall that each dissatisfied customer tells 8 to 10 other people. This means that the 30,000 dissatisfied customers will communicate their dissatisfaction to approximately a quarter of a million other individuals. These may not all be potential customers, but this level of negative word-of-mouth communication makes new customer attraction much more difficult and more expensive.[11]

This kind of market behavior has led some businesses to develop programs to encourage dissatisfied customers to complain. For example, Domino's Pizza instituted a program that simply encouraged dissatisfied customers to complain rather than just leave.[12] Their marketing efforts succeeded in getting 20 percent of their dissatisfied customers to complain. For those who complain, Domino's can resolve 80 percent of the problems within 24 hours. When complaints can be resolved quickly, 95 percent of those customers can be retained. When complaints cannot be resolved within 24 hours, the customer retention rate falls to 46 percent.

FIGURE 1-6 CUSTOMER DISSATISFACTION AND CUSTOMER EXIT

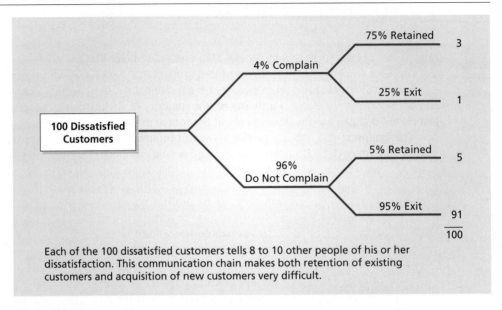

Each of the 100 dissatisfied customers tells 8 to 10 other people of his or her dissatisfaction. This communication chain makes both retention of existing customers and acquisition of new customers very difficult.

Not surprisingly, if customers do not complain, the odds of retention drop below 40 percent. Thus, while it may seem odd at first, one of the jobs of market-based management is not only to track customer satisfaction but also to *encourage dissatisfied customers to complain*. Only with the specific details of a customer complaint and the source of dissatisfaction can a business take corrective action.[13] Companies such as AT&T proactively address potential customer dissatisfaction by encouraging customer complaints through full-page ads with toll-free telephone numbers. Their proactive marketing efforts have two important effects. First, they address problems as they occur, greatly reducing potential customer dissatisfaction and exit. Second, communicating their proactive services reinforces customer satisfaction by communicating the importance of their efforts to provide maximum customer satisfaction.[14]

Profit Impact of Customer Dissatisfaction

MBNA America is a Delaware-based credit card company that, in the early 1990s, became frustrated with customer dissatisfaction and defection. All 300 employees were brought together in an effort to understand the problem and develop methods of delivering greater levels of customer satisfaction with the intent of keeping each and every customer. At the time, MBNA America had a 90 percent customer retention rate. After several years of dedicating themselves to improved customer satisfaction and retention, they raised customer retention to 95 percent. That may seem like a small difference, but the impact on their profits was a *sixteen-fold* increase, and their industry ranking went from 38th to 4th.[15] Thus, their marketing efforts to satisfy and retain customers paid off in higher levels of profitability.

As shown in Figure 1-6, most dissatisfied customers do not complain; they just walk away. To hold market share in a mature market, a business must replace its lost customers. Let's examine a business that is in a mature market with 200,000 customers and has a

75 percent rate of customer retention. Each year this business loses 50,000 customers and, to hold a customer base of 200,000, must replace those customers with 50,000 new customers. However, before we look at the profit impact of this level of customer satisfaction and retention, let's look at how this business got to a level of 75 percent customer retention. A closer look at customer satisfaction, complaint behavior, and customer retention enables us to build the customer retention tree in Figure 1-7. As shown, the business is operating at a 70 percent level of customer satisfaction. Of the 30 percent who are dissatisfied, 24.9 percent are lost. Furthermore, the majority of dissatisfied customers who are lost do not complain to the business about the source of their dissatisfaction.

The customer profitability profile shown in Figure 1-8 reflects the information presented in Figure 1-6. It shows the average annual revenue, margin, and marketing expense per customer for retained customers, lost customers, and new customers. As shown, retained customers are the profit driver of this business, producing 80 percent of the sales revenue and 89 percent of the gross profit.

Lost customers are generally dissatisfied or somewhat satisfied customers. Because they are not with the business for the whole year or are in the process of reducing their purchases from the business, the annual revenue per customer is much lower. However, retaining dissatisfied customers is also expensive because they require the business to expend extra resources in an attempt to keep them. These extra efforts often mean additional work for the sales force, price concessions, adjustments to inventory or terms of sale, and greater customer service. The net result of losing dissatisfied customers in this example is a negative *net marketing contribution* of $2.5 million per year. The net marketing contribution shown in Figure 1-8 is the total revenue received from customers less the variable costs of producing those revenues less the direct marketing expenses needed to serve this level of customer volume. This concept will be discussed in detail in Chapter 2.

FIGURE 1-7 CUSTOMER SATISFACTION AND RETENTION

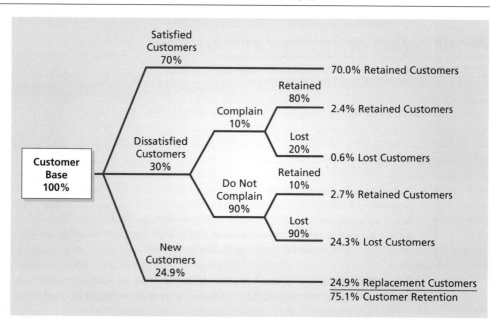

FIGURE 1-8 PROFIT IMPACT OF 75 PERCENT CUSTOMER RETENTION

Customer Performance	Retained Customers	Lost Customers	New Customers	Overall Performance
Number of Customers	150,000	50,000	50,000	250,000
Revenue per Customer	$800.0	$200.0	$400.0	
Sales Revenue (millions)	$120.0	$ 10.0	$ 20.0	$150.0
Variable Cost per Customer	$400.0	$150.0	$300.0	
Margin per Customer	$400.0	$ 50.0	$100.0	
Gross Profit (millions)	$ 60.0	$ 2.5	$ 5.0	$ 67.5
Marketing Expense per Customer	$ 60.0	$100.0	$300.0	
Total Marketing Expense (millions)	$ 9.0	$ 5.0	$ 15.0	$ 29.0
Net Marketing Contribution (millions)	$ 51.0	−$ 2.5	−$ 10.0	$ 38.5
Operating Expenses (millions)				$ 30.0
Net Profit Before Taxes (millions)				$ 8.5
Return on Sales				5.67%

New customers are also less profitable. Advertising and sales promotion dollars have to be spent to generate sales leads and produce trial purchases. This raises the marketing expenses associated with attracting, qualifying, and serving new customers. New customers also generally buy less because they are in the evaluation stage and have not yet fully committed themselves to the business or its products. This lowers both the annual revenue and margin produced by each new customer. The net result in this example is that the business actually loses $10 million in net marketing contribution each year in its efforts to replace lost customers.

PROFIT IMPACT OF CUSTOMER RETENTION

For the business situation presented in Figure 1-8, overall sales revenues of $150 million produce a net profit of $8.5 million, for a 5.67 percent return on sales—but what would be the profit impact of improved customer satisfaction? Let's assume that $1 million were dedicated to reducing the number of dissatisfied customers so that 80 percent of the business's customers could be retained each year. The marketing logic and profit impact of this strategy can be summarized as follows:

> If the business can retain 80 percent of its customers each year instead of 75 percent, the business will reduce the cost associated with customer dissatisfaction and exit and will not have to spend as much on marketing efforts to attract new customers. Also, because retained customers produce a higher annual revenue and margin per customer than do lost or new customers, the total profits of the business should increase.

This effort would produce only a slight increase in sales revenues, as shown in Figure 1-9. However, there would be a tremendous improvement in marketing efficiency

FIGURE 1-9 PROFIT IMPACT OF 5 PERCENT IMPROVEMENT IN CUSTOMER RETENTION

Customer Performance	Retained Customers	Lost Customers	New Customers	Overall Performance
Number of Customers	160,000	40,000	40,000	240,000
Revenue per Customer	$800.0	$200.0	$400.0	
Sales Revenue (millions)	$128.0	$ 8.0	$ 16.0	$152.0
Variable Cost per Customer	$400.0	$150.0	$300.0	
Margin per Customer	$400.0	$ 50.0	$100.0	
Gross Profit (millions)	$ 64.0	$ 2.0	$ 4.0	$ 70.0
Marketing Expense per Customer	$ 62.5	$100.0	$300.0	
Total Marketing Expense (millions)	$ 10.0	$ 4.0	$ 12.0	$ 26.0
Net Marketing Contribution (millions)	$ 54.0	−$ 2.0	−$ 8.0	$ 44.0
Operating Expenses (millions)				$ 30.0
Net Profit Before Taxes (millions)				$ 14.0
Return on Sales				9.2%

and profitability. Because retained customers are more profitable than new customers, the overall gross profit derived from retained customers would increase from $60 million to $64 million. The overall marketing expenses would go up because of the $1 million that was added to the marketing budget to achieve an 80 percent customer retention. The net result would be a $3 million improvement in net marketing contribution derived from retained customers.

More important, the net loss of managing dissatisfied customers who exit and the net loss associated with attracting new customers would be reduced by a total of $2.5 million in this example. The cumulative impact of increased customer satisfaction and retention is an increase of net profits from $8.5 to $14 million. This incremental gain in net profits is derived from a larger number of retained customers, the reduced cost of serving dissatisfied customers, and reduced expenses associated with acquiring new customers to maintain the same customer base. This is a 64 percent increase in net profits with essentially *no change in market share or sales revenue*.

One can readily see the enormous potential for increased profits and cash flow that centers around customer satisfaction and retention. For each additional customer that is retained, net profits increase. Inefficient costs associated with serving dissatisfied customers and the cost of acquiring new customers to replace them are reduced. Thus, there is tremendous financial leverage in satisfying and retaining customers.

Customer Satisfaction and Customer Retention

The relationship between customer satisfaction and customer retention is intuitively easy to discern. However, different competitive conditions modify this relationship.[16] For example, in less competitive markets, customers are more easily retained even with poor levels of customer satisfaction because there are few substitutes or because switching costs are high. In markets where there are relatively few choices, such as phone service, water companies, or hospitals, customers may stay even when dissatisfied. In these types of markets, where choice is limited or switching is costly, higher levels of customer retention are achievable at relatively lower levels of customer satisfaction.

However, in highly competitive markets with many choices and low customer switching costs, even relatively high levels of customer satisfaction may not ensure against customer defection. Grocery store, restaurant, and bank customers can switch quickly if they are not completely satisfied. Although the time between purchase events is longer, personal computer, automobile, and consumer electronics customers can also easily move to another brand if not completely satisfied. In these markets, customer retention is much more difficult. As a result, it takes higher levels of customer satisfaction to retain customers from one purchase to the next.

Customer Retention and Customer Life Expectancy

Customer satisfaction and retention are important linkages to a market-based strategy and profitability. The ultimate objective of any given marketing strategy should be to attract, satisfy, and retain target customers. If a business can accomplish this objective with a competitive advantage in attractive markets, the business will produce above-average profits.

The customer is a critical component in the profitability equation but is completely overlooked in any financial analysis or annual reports. Customers are a *marketing asset* that businesses have yet to quantify in their accounting systems, yet the business that can attract, satisfy, and keep customers over their lifetime of purchases is in a powerful position to deliver superior levels of profitability. Businesses that lack a market orientation look at customers as *individual purchase transactions.* A market-based business looks at customers as *lifetime partners.* The *New York Times* tracks its customer retention and the retention rates of competing newspapers by length of subscription.[17] Among *mature subscribers* (those who have had subscriptions longer than 24 months), the *New York Times* has a retention rate of 94 percent. Their closest competitor has an 80 percent retention rate.

The higher the rate of customer retention, the greater the profit impact for a given business. In the short run, we showed this to be true on the basis of increased profits from retained customers, reduced losses from lost customers, and a lower cost of attracting new customers in order to maintain a certain customer base. However, there is also a longer-term profit impact of higher levels of customer retention because a higher rate of retention lengthens the life of a customer relationship.

A business that has a 50 percent rate of customer retention has a fifty-fifty chance of retaining a customer from one year to the next. This fact translates into an average customer life of 2 years, as shown in Figure 1-10. The average life expectancy of a customer is equal to one divided by one minus the rate of customer retention. Therefore, as customer retention increases, the customer's life expectancy increases. However, more important, customer life expectancy increases exponentially with customer retention, as illustrated in Figure 1-10.

For example, the average level of customer retention among health care providers is 80 percent.[18] This translates into an average customer life of 5 years. If a health

FIGURE 1-10 CUSTOMER LIFE EXPECTANCY AND CUSTOMER RETENTION

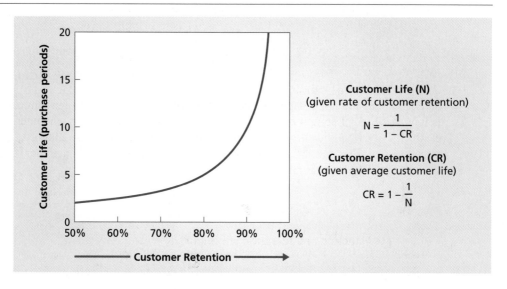

Customer Life (N)
(given rate of customer retention)

$$N = \frac{1}{1 - CR}$$

Customer Retention (CR)
(given average customer life)

$$CR = 1 - \frac{1}{N}$$

care provider could manage to increase its customer retention to 90 percent, that increase would produce an average customer life of 10 years. Thus, the life expectancy of a customer grows exponentially as a business moves to higher levels of customer retention.

The Lifetime Value of a Customer

The Cadillac division of General Motors estimates that a Cadillac customer will spend approximately $350,000 over a lifetime on automotive purchases and maintenance. If Cadillac loses that customer early in this customer life cycle, it loses hundreds of thousands of dollars in future cash flow. To replace that lost customer, Cadillac has to attract and develop a new customer, which is an expensive process. Thus, the cost of marketing efforts to ensure customer satisfaction is small in comparison with both the current and future benefits of customer purchases, as well as the cost of replacing customers if they become dissatisfied and leave. In general, it costs five times more to replace a customer than it costs to keep a customer.

Figure 1-11 illustrates the average profit per credit card customer generated over a 5-year period. Acquiring and setting up accounts for new credit card customers nets an annual loss of $51 per customer. Newly acquired credit card customers are also slow to use their new cards; they produce an average profit of $30 the first year, $42 the second year, and $44 the third year. By year 5, the average profit obtained from a credit card customer is $55. Thus, the value of a credit card customer continues to grow over time. Of course, if a credit card company loses a customer after year 4 because of customer dissatisfaction, the process of replacing him or her is expensive. This cost in the first year following customer exit is $106 ($55 in lost profit from the exiting customer and the $51 loss associated with attracting a new customer to replace that customer).

FIGURE 1-11 LIFETIME VALUE OF A CUSTOMER

Period	Cash Flow	Present Value of $1*	Present Value of Cash Flow
0	−$51	1.000	−$51.0
1	$30	0.909	$27.3
2	$42	0.826	$34.7
3	$44	0.751	$33.0
4	$49	0.683	$33.5
5	$55	0.621	$34.2
Net Present Value of Cash Flow			$111.7

* Appendix 1.1 provides a table of present values.

In this example, the average customer life is 5 years. Working backward, we can estimate the customer retention to be 80 percent, as shown here.

$$\textbf{Customer Retention} = 1-\frac{1}{N} = 1-\frac{1}{5} = \textbf{0.80 (or 80\%)}$$

To estimate the lifetime value of a customer at this rate of customer retention, we need to compute the *net present value* of the customer cash flow shown in Figure 1-11. The initial $51 that it cost to acquire this customer is gone immediately. However, it takes a year to achieve the first year's revenue of $30. The present value of $30 received a year in the future is less than $30 received immediately. In this example, the business has a discount rate of 10 percent. Therefore, the present value of $1 received after 1 year is $0.909 (the rate at which $1 is discounted for 1 year at 10 percent). Thus, $30 to be received 1 year later is $27.3 ($30 × 0.909). This discounting is performed for each year's receipts, and the values are totaled to arrive at the net present value of this cash flow. When each year's cash flow is properly discounted, the net present value of the sum of these cash flows is equal to $111.70. This is what this customer is worth in today's dollars. If the customer life expectancy was only 3 years, the customer value (net present value) would be considerably smaller. The longer the rate of customer retention, the longer the average customer life expectancy and the greater the customer value.

To better understand this concept, let's look at the customer value (net present value) over a 3-year period for online shoppers for consumer electronics, groceries, and apparel[19] as illustrated in Figure 1-12. The cost of acquiring a grocery customer is almost twice the cost of acquiring a consumer-electronics customer. After 3 years, the online consumer-electronics customer has a negative net present value of −$15.36. The average online grocery customer produces a net present value of $58.43 in 3 years. The average online apparel customer is even more profitable, producing a net present value of $126.99 in 3 years.

FIGURE 1-12 NET PRESENT VALUE OF ONLINE CUSTOMERS

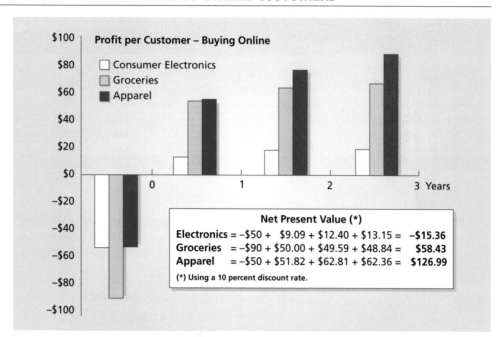

CUSTOMER LOYALTY AND MANAGING CUSTOMER LOYALTY

Although customer satisfaction and customer retention are important marketing performance metrics that are linked to customer profitability, customer loyalty requires another level of customer commitment. Many ways exist to measure the psychological commitment a customer has to a brand or a company, but a recommendation to others stands as the highest form of emotional endorsement. When customers recommend a product or service, it means they have the utmost confidence in the value created and delivered by the brand or company they recommend.

Measuring Customer Loyalty

Recognizing customer satisfaction, customer retention, and customer recommendation as components of customer loyalty, we can combine the three to form a customer loyalty index (CLI):

CLI = (Customer Satisfaction) × (Customer Retention) × (Customer Recommendation)

For example, a "somewhat satisfied" customer (CSI equal to 60) may have a high customer retention value (.90) when switching costs are high or there are no attractive alternatives. Multiplying customer satisfaction by customer retention yields an index of 54. This high level of customer retention could lead a company to believe all is well despite a weak level of customer satisfaction. However, if the customer is asked:

"What is the probability you would recommend this brand or company to others?"

FIGURE 1-13 MEASURING CUSTOMER LOYALTY

Customer Satisfaction	Customer Percent (%)	CSI Score	Planned Repurchase (%)	Who Would Recommend (%)	Customer Loyalty
Very Satisfied	25	100	0.95	0.90	86
Satisfied	36	80	0.80	0.75	48
Somewhat Satisfied	22	60	0.50	0.50	15
Somewhat Dissatisfied	10	40	0.10	0.00	0
Dissatisfied	5	20	0.10	0.00	0
Very Dissatisfied	2	0	0.00	0.00	0
	100	72	0.65		42

The customer may say 10 percent, which paints a completely different picture. A low level of customer recommendation signals a lower level of customer loyalty. When this customer recommendation of 10 percent is taken into account, the CLI drops from 54 to 5.4:

$$\textbf{Customer Loyalty Index} = 60 \times .90 \times .10 = \textbf{5.4}$$

This should send at a red flag to management and any business managing customer loyalty. Clearly, this is a "captured customer." With a relatively low level of customer satisfaction, this customer would "exit" if given the choice. Customer loyalty is actually quite low, and the customer retention is a false sense of accomplishment.

We can see in Figure 1-13 how customer loyalty varies for the sample of HP printer customers we have been tracking. As one would expect, very satisfied customers have a high rate of planned repurchase and a high rate of recommendation. This yields a CLI of 86 for very satisfied customers. Satisfied customers are less loyal, with a CLI of 48. Somewhat satisfied customers are clearly less loyal due to a lower rate of planned repurchase and a lower rate of recommendation. The dissatisfied customers have a CLI equal to zero based on zero or low levels of planned repurchase and recommendation. Thus, the overall average CLI of 42 provides a benchmark from which HP can judge its overall customer loyalty and track how customer loyalty changes with efforts to improve customer satisfaction and loyalty.

Customer Loyalty and Customer Relationship Marketing

Although we have shown customer satisfaction and retention to have a positive impact on profitability, a business can have customers it *wants to keep* as well as customers it should *strive to abandon*.[20] Likewise, with the acquisition of new customers, there are customers the business *should pursue* and customers the business *should avoid*. This is part of a process called *customer relationship marketing*, which is addressed in Chapter 5.

To manage customer relationships effectively with regard to retention, it is useful to classify customers on the basis of customer loyalty and profitability.[21] Not all customers are the same. Some may be loyal and profitable, others profitable but not loyal, some loyal but not profitable, and others neither loyal nor profitable. One goal of customer relationship marketing is to manage these differences in an effort to obtain higher levels of loyalty and profitability. The four customer types described are shown in Figure 1-14.

FIGURE 1-14 STRATEGIES FOR MANAGING CUSTOMER LOYALTY AND PROFITABILITY

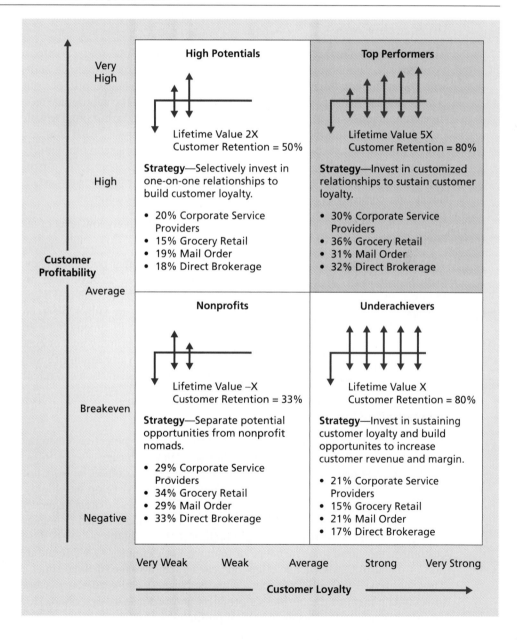

Top Performers

These customers are the "golden nuggets" or "crown jewels" for any business. The combination of above-average loyalty and customer profitability creates a majority of a business's profits.[22] The primary objective of customer relationship marketing is to develop sustainable, long-term, one-on-one relationships with these customers using customized programs that deliver superior levels of customer satisfaction. As shown in Figure 1-14, 30 to 36 percent of the customers for the types of businesses shown are top performers in their customer portfolio.[23]

Underachievers

These customers are the "unpolished gems" of a business's customer portfolio. They are loyal but not highly profitable, some even unprofitable. The business is underachieving with respect to the profit potential of these customers, who make up 15 percent to 21 percent of their customer portfolios, as shown in Figure 1-14. The appropriate customer relationship marketing strategy is to invest in customer relationship programs that provide more buying opportunities for these customers. For example, PearlParadise.com offers special sales to underachievers to build their customer revenue and profitability.[24] Instead of offering special sales to the general public, PearlParadise.com sends e-mail messages to loyal customers with a special link created just for their loyal customers. The bottom line is, this company grew the sales and profits of its loyal customers.

High Potentials

These are the "rough-cut diamonds" of a business's customer portfolio. They have high profit potential but are not loyal customers. For the types of businesses presented in Figure 1-14, high potentials are often mismanaged opportunities that make up 15 percent to 20 percent of their customer portfolios. These customers are vulnerable to competitors' efforts and can easily be lured away. An effort to build loyalty among these customers is important to retain them and the profits they produce. The primary goal of customer relationship marketing is to invest in building customer loyalty among these customers through customized offerings that will enhance customer satisfaction and retention.

Nonprofits

These customers include a wide range of customers from potential "customer gems" to "fools gold." As shown in Figure 1-14, this portion of a business's portfolio comprises 29 percent to 34 percent of its customers. These are new customers who are not profitable and not loyal. Many new customers have the potential to develop into highly profitable and loyal customers; others could simply buy and exit. These exiters generally do not fit the business's offerings and are unlikely to be satisfied and retained no matter how hard the business tries.[25] Although it would be best to avoid these customers,[26] as first-time customers, they need to be managed differently. For example, AT&T found that 1.7 million of its customers switched telephone carriers an average of three times per year.[27] These customers lack any experience with the business and need above-average service to acclimate them to the business's products and services as described. How they are managed greatly influences their level of profitability and loyalty.

New Customer Acquisition

Acquiring new customers is a tricky process that requires careful customer relationship marketing. It is common to think of every new customer as beneficial to the business. When the phone rings and someone wants to buy, it takes a rare individual to say "no." Dr. Charles Lillis, former CEO of MediaOne, once said:

> "I will know when our businesses have done a good job of market segmentation when they can tell me who we should not sell to."

Unrestrained acquisition of new customers can result in customers who are neither loyal nor profitable. This results in an even higher loss given the cost of customer acquisition with little or no offsetting income. Thus, it is important to understand the differences between target customers and nontarget customers. A customer profile of who is *not* a good target customer is just as valuable as a profile of who *is* a good target customer. A customer-acquisition process that can identify *nonprofits* and avoid them can lower the total cost of acquisition and raise customer retention rates. To the degree a business can attract target customers and avoid nontarget customers, the business can reduce the overall cost of new-customer acquisition and achieve higher rates of customer retention.

Win-Back Customers

New customers may also be *win-back customers*. These are customers who switched to a competing alternative because they were "mismanaged." Win-back customers need special attention that addresses the dissatisfaction that caused them to leave in the first place. If the customer relationship marketing program is working effectively, both types of new customers can evolve to the level of *top performers*.

Win-back customers are already familiar with the company and its products and services. As a result, they are likely to start where they left off. In Figure 1-15, this would be the level of profitability shown in year 3 for the "mismanaged opportunities." Because of a higher rate of initial purchase, when these customers are won back and retained, they yield a higher lifetime customer value as illustrated in Figure 1-15. The "second lifetime value" in this example yields a net present value almost three times higher than the average first-time customer after 5 years.

Managing Customer Exit

Every business loses customers at one time or another, however, customers are lost for different reasons. Some are profitable customers that a business would like to win back. These were mismanaged customers who left the business due to dissatisfaction and/or low loyalty. Lost customers can also include abandoned customers who were unprofitable and successfully abandoned.

Customer relationship marketing is an important aspect of managing customer retention and profitability. Successful customer relationship marketing involves managing all customers relationships based on their level of customer loyalty and profit potential. Careful management of all customer relationships starts with identifying target customers to acquire and retain, and includes managing new customers and abandoning unprofitable customers. Each customer relationship has an impact on overall retention levels and profitability.

FIGURE 1-15 LIFETIME VALUE OF WIN-BACK CUSTOMERS

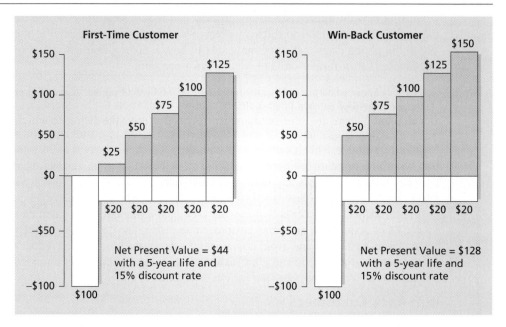

BUILDING A MARKETING ORIENTATION

Although we have stressed the importance of customer focus and customer relationship marketing, a strong market orientation goes beyond customer focus to include a strong competitor orientation and a strong team approach in building customer solutions.[28]

- **Customer Focus:** An obsession with understanding customer needs and delivering customer satisfaction.
- **Competitor Orientation:** Continuous recognition of competitors' sources of advantage, competitive position, and marketing strategies.
- **Team Approach:** The ability to work in cross-functional teams dedicated to developing and delivering customer solutions.

Businesses that achieve levels of excellence in all three areas of market orientation have been shown to be more profitable. A strong *customer focus* enables a business to keep close tabs on customers and to develop marketing strategies around customer needs and other sources of customer satisfaction. The strength of a business's market orientation also relies on how well it *understands key competitors* and evolving competitive forces. This aspect of market orientation enables a business to track its relative competitiveness in such areas as pricing, product quality and availability, service quality, and customer satisfaction. A business with a strong market orientation also *works well as a team across functions*, thereby leveraging cross-functional skills and business activities that affect customer response and satisfaction.

The real benefits of a strong market orientation are higher levels of customer satisfaction and a higher level of customer retention. Keeping good customers should be the first priority of market-based management. A business with a strong market orientation is in the best position to develop and implement strategies that deliver high levels of customer satisfaction and retention. In turn, customer satisfaction and retention drive customer revenue and the cost of marketing. Ultimately, they are key forces in shaping the profitability of a business. So—how does a business build a strong market orientation? Why do some businesses have a strong market orientation while others cannot seem to develop one? There are three fundamental forces that drive the degree to which a business has a market orientation:

1. **Marketing Knowledge:** The degree to which managers and employees have been educated and trained in marketing directly affects the market orientation of a business.
2. **Marketing Leadership:** The market orientation of a business starts at the top. If senior management and the key marketing managers of a business do not have a strong market orientation, it is difficult for a business to establish any level of marketing excellence.
3. **Employee Satisfaction:** If employees are unhappy in their jobs and uninformed as to how they affect customers, the business's market orientation will never achieve even minimal effectiveness regardless of senior management speeches and market-based statements of mission and philosophy.

Marketing Knowledge

The extent to which a manager has a strong market orientation is directly related to his or her level of marketing knowledge[29]: the higher one's level of marketing knowledge, the stronger that individual's customer focus, competitor orientation, and marketing team orientation as shown in Figure 1-16. This graphic was built from a database of over 30,000 managers from 90 countries.[30] Further analysis of these data also found that marketing knowledge and market-oriented attitudes are strongly correlated to marketing education, marketing experience, and participation in marketing training programs. Marketing excellence requires more than words. Businesses seeking to build a strong market orientation need to invest in building their marketing knowledge.

Measures of marketing knowledge and marketing attitudes before and after corporate marketing education programs demonstrate that meaningful improvements in marketing knowledge can be obtained as illustrated in Figure 1-17. This has training implications for businesses wanting to build their marketing knowledge in pursuit of marketing excellence. Masters of Business Administration (MBA) marketing education can also make a difference. Measures of marketing knowledge and marketing attitudes before and after a first-year MBA marketing course for over 1,500 MBA students at Northwestern University, Penn State University, and the University of Oregon demonstrated a significant gain in marketing knowledge and attitudes as shown in Figure 1-17. This has obvious recruiting and hiring implications for companies interested in building marketing excellence.

Although formal marketing education and training are absolutely essential for those in marketing and higher-level positions of leadership, market orientation is also

FIGURE 1-16 MARKET-ORIENTED ATTITUDES AS A FUNCTION OF MARKETING KNOWLEDGE

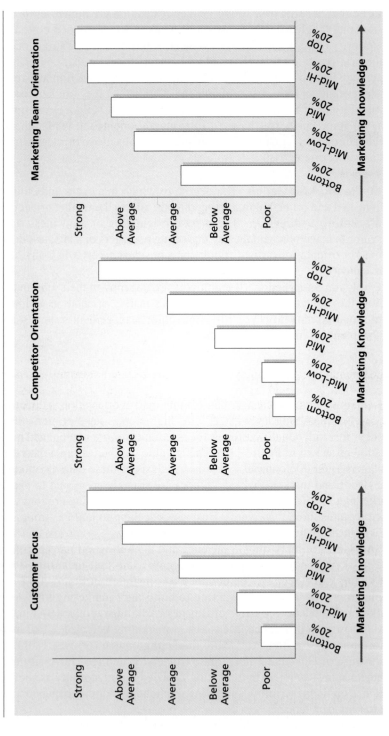

FIGURE 1-17 IMPACT OF MARKETING EDUCATION ON MARKETING KNOWLEDGE AND MARKET-ORIENTED ATTITUDES

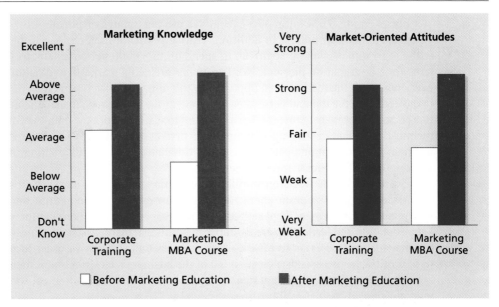

fundamental to every employee of the organization. For example, Disney spends 4 days training the personnel who clean their theme parks.[31] They train what they call the "popcorn people" to be information guides because they are the first to be asked where something is located. These "popcorn people" are also trained to treat customers as guests and to consider themselves as cast members on stage at all times. Naturally, the individual marketing orientation of these employees plays a key role in creating a Disney company market orientation that delivers high levels of customer satisfaction.

Marketing Leadership

A marketing leadership audit conducted for a mid-sized electronics company involved assessing marketing attitudes and practices across several layers of the business's management hierarchy. The following comments were given in response to the question, "How often do you see customers?"

> **Company CEO:** "I really don't have too much time for that. I have many financial issues, administrative tasks, and many meetings. So I leave it to my vice president of marketing."
>
> **Vice President of Marketing:** "Well, I have a rather considerable staff and many responsibilities with regard to marketing plans and day-to-day decisions regarding our sales force and advertising. So I really don't have the time. But we have a very highly trained sales force, and they are talking to customers all the time."
>
> **Sales Force:** "We are in continuous contact with our customers and we bring back new ideas all the time. But nobody in management has the time to listen."

Obviously, this business lacks marketing leadership at the top. To build a strong market orientation, all levels of management—and senior management in particular—need to have a strong customer focus. Market orientation and marketing leadership start at the top.

For example, IBM's top 470 executives are personally responsible for more than 1,300 customer accounts.[32] In addition, IBM gives frontline employees the authority, without prior management approval, to spend up to $5,000 per complaint to solve problems for a customer on the spot. Nordstrom has created a market-based culture in which every customer interaction is an opportunity to build customer satisfaction.[33] This initiative is led from the top and permeates all levels of the Nordstrom management hierarchy. Starbucks senior management believes that the first 4 hours of new employee training are the most important in shaping an employee's market orientation. To the degree that management fails to communicate its customer orientation during this training, it will have failed to shape Starbucks' market orientation.

Every marketing decision implicitly or explicitly sends a message to employees about management's commitment to a market orientation. The actions and words of senior and middle management set the tone of a business's market orientation. Their market orientation and leadership are essential in building a market-based business culture. A top management decision to raise customer prices unjustifiably in order to meet short-term profit objectives sends a clear signal of the business's lack of commitment to a market orientation. Thus, consistent market-based leadership is a requirement for building a market-oriented business culture.

Market Orientation and Employee Satisfaction

Think about calling a business with a complaint and interacting with a person who hates his job and the company where he works. What kind of reception do you think you will get? Employee satisfaction is a key factor in delivering customer satisfaction.[34] Employee satisfaction affects customer service, which in turn influences customer satisfaction and retention—and as we have already shown, higher levels of customer satisfaction result in higher levels of customer retention and profitability. Sears found that in all of its many stores, there was a high correlation between customer satisfaction, employee satisfaction, and store profitability.[35] NCR found that, among 12 manufacturing operations, higher levels of employee job satisfaction corresponded with higher levels of customer satisfaction.[36] Thus, building a strong market orientation requires a healthy business environment in which employees like their jobs and enjoy working for the organization.

■ Summary

The strength of a business's customer focus is directly related to its ability to develop market-based strategies that deliver high levels of customer satisfaction. For years, many observers would have considered that statement to be a nice academic philosophy that had little to do with a company in business to make a profit. Today, however, considerable evidence exists that businesses that operate with higher levels of customer satisfaction are more profitable. They are more profitable because they are able to retain a high percentage of customers, have less rework as a result of poor product or service quality, and need to spend less time and money attracting new customers to replace lost customers. Thus, businesses with a strong customer focus are able to deliver higher levels of both customer satisfaction and profitability.

A closer look at customer profitability takes us to customer loyalty. Retained customers who are not loyal will eventually leave the company for a competing alternative. To fully leverage the profit impact, a business must engage in customer relationship marketing to address different combinations of customer loyalty and profitability. Not all new, retained, or lost customers are the same in profitability and loyalty. Customer differences need to be managed effectively in order to achieve high levels of customer retention and profitability. To the degree that a business can manage customer relationships, it can build customer loyalty and profitability.

Finally, a business with a strong market orientation will complement its customer focus with a strong competitor orientation and a team approach to creating and delivering customer solutions. We demonstrated that marketing knowledge is a key correlate of a strong market orientation and customer focus. Efforts to improve marketing knowledge have been shown to improve market-oriented attitudes. Marketing leadership is also critical. Senior management and marketing managers play key roles in leading marketing excellence. Their marketing knowledge and market-oriented attitudes set the tone for a strong customer focus. Employee satisfaction is also critical. A business with unhappy employees will simply not be able to deliver levels of customer satisfaction that achieve high levels of profitability.

■ Market-Based Logic and Strategic Thinking

1 How would a business with a strong customer focus differ from one with a weak market orientation?

2 How does a strong customer focus impact profitability and shareholder value?

3 Why are very satisfied customers critical to the overall profits of a business?

4 Why are customer satisfaction and customer retention important drivers of profitability?

5 Why are average measures of customer satisfaction misleading indicators of market-based performance?

6 How does the mix of customers who are satisfied, neutral, and dissatisfied affect a business's net profits?

7 Using the Customer Satisfaction and Retention diagram in Figure 1-7, determine how customer retention would change if the business increased its percentage of satisfied customers from 70 to 80 percent.

8 Why do high levels of customer dissatisfaction make attracting new customers more difficult?

9 How do high levels of customer dissatisfaction increase the cost of marketing and hence decrease net profits?

10 Why are satisfied customers crucial to a business's net profits?

11 If the average customer life of a credit card customer (see Figure 1-11) was extended 1 year, what would be the level of customer retention required? Also, if the profit obtained in the sixth year is the same as that in the fifth year, what is the net gain in customer value (net present value)?

12 How does customer selection affect customer retention?

13 Why is customer recommendation of a brand or company an important element of customer loyalty?

14 How could a business have high customer retention and a low customer loyalty index?

15 Why are some loyal customers not profitable?

16 Why is marketing knowledge an important element in building a strong market orientation?

17 What role do marketing education and employee training play in building market orientation?

18 Why is market orientation important at all levels of an organization?

19 What role does marketing leadership play in building the market orientation of a business?

20 How can the senior management of an organization destroy a business's market orientation?

21 How does employee satisfaction impact customer satisfaction?

22 Why is it difficult to build customer satisfaction when employee satisfaction is low?

Marketing Performance Tools

The ultimate test of one's knowledge and understanding of market-based management is application of these marketing concepts and tools. The **marketing performance tools** presented here are based on marketing concepts presented in Chapter 1. Each is provided with data to facilitate experiential learning as you address the questions that follow. You may also input your own data to further extend your use of these marketing performance tools.

Each of the following marketing performance tools can be accessed by going to *www.rogerjbest.com* or *www.prenhall.com/best*. The shaded cells are input cells. The nonshaded cells are computed information based on your input.

MARKETING PERFORMANCE TOOL—Customer Satisfaction and Customer Profitability

Customer Satisfaction	Customer Percent (%)	CSI Score	Customer Revenue ($)	Percent Margin (%)	Gross Profit ($)	Retention Cost ($)	Customer Profit ($)
Very Satisfied	25	100	1,500	60	900	100	800
Satisfied	36	80	500	50	250	100	150
Somewhat Satisfied	22	60	250	50	125	100	25
Somewhat Dissatisfied	10	40	150	40	60	100	(40)
Dissatisfied	5	20	75	40	30	100	(70)
Very Dissatisfied	2	0	50	40	20	100	(80)
	100	72	630		350		250

This **marketing performance tool** allows you to evaluate how changes in customer satisfaction impact customer revenue and profitability.

Application Exercise: How would the average revenue per customer and average customer profit change if a strategy were implemented to increase "very satisfied" from 25 percent to 30 percent while "satisfied" customers decrease from 36 percent to 31 percent?

MARKETING PERFORMANCE TOOL—Customer Retention and Customer Loyalty

Customer Satisfaction	Customer Percent (%)	CSI Score	Planned Repurchase (%)	Who Would Recommend (%)	Customer Loyalty
Very Satisfied	25	100	0.95	0.90	86
Satisfied	36	80	0.80	0.75	48
Somewhat Satisfied	22	60	0.50	0.50	15
Somewhat Dissatisfied	10	40	0.10	0.00	0
Dissatisfied	5	20	0.10	0.00	0
Very Dissatisfied	2	0	0.00	0.00	0
	100	72	0.65		42

This **marketing performance tool** allows you to evaluate how changes in customer satisfaction impact customer retention and customer loyalty.

Application Exercise: How would customer retention and customer loyalty change given the same improvement in customer satisfaction described in the previous exercise?

MARKETING PERFORMANCE TOOL—Lifetime Value of a Customer

Customer Retention	67%										
Customer Life	3.0										

Year	0	1	2	3	4	5	6	7	8	9	10
Customer Margin		$250	$250	$250							
Acquisition Cost	($350)										
Retention Cost		($70)	($70)	($70)							
Net Profit	**($350)**	**$180**	**$180**	**$180**	**$0**	**$0**	**$0**	**$0**	**$0**	**$0**	**$0**
Discount Rate	20%										
Present Value Multiplier	1.000	0.833	0.694	0.579	0.482	0.402	0.335	0.279	0.233	0.194	0.162
Net Present Value	($350)	$150	$125	$104	$0	$0	$0	$0	$0	$0	$0
Lifetime Value of Customer	**$29.17**										

This **marketing performance tool** allows you to evaluate the lifetime value of a customer based on variations in retention, customer margin, retention costs, acquisition costs, and discount rate.

Application Exercise: How would the lifetime value of the average customer change with the new level of customer retention estimated in the preceding exercise? You will need to modify the average annual customer profit and average customer retention in order to estimate the new lifetime value of a customer. Use the same average cost of retention ($70 per year), customer acquisition cost of $350, and discount rate of 20 percent.

Notes

1. Bradley Gale. *Managing Customer Value* (New York: Free Press, 1994): Chapter 2.
2. Frederick F. Reichheld and W. Earl Sasser Jr. "Zero Defections: Quality Comes to Services," *Harvard Business Review* (September–October 1990): 106–111; and Frederick F. Reichheld, "Loyalty-Based Management," *Harvard Business Review* (March–April 1993): 64–73.
3. M. Menezes and J. Serbin. "Xerox Corporation: The Customer Satisfaction Program," Boston, MA: Harvard Business School Publishing.
4. Patrick Byrne. "Only 10% of Companies Satisfy Customers," *Transportation and Distribution* (December 1993); and Tom Eck, "Are Customers Happy? Don't Assume," *Positive Impact* (July 1992): 3.
5. Steven Schnaars. *Marketing Strategy* (New York: Free Press, 1998): 186–205.
6. Larry Seldon and Geoffrey Colvin. *Angel Customers and Demon Customers* (Portfolio, 2003): 45–59.
7. Peter Doyle. *Value-Based Marketing* (Wiley, 2000): 8–85.
8. Valarie Zeithaml, A. Parasuraman, and Leonard Berry. *Delivering Quality Service* (New York: Free Press, 1990): Chapter 1; and John Goodman, Ted Mama, and Liz Brigham, "Customer Service: Costly Nuisance or Lower Cost Profit Strategy?"*Journal of Bank Retailing* (Fall 1986): 12.
9. TARP. "Consumer Complaint Handling in America: An Update Study," White House Office of Consumer Affairs, Washington, DC, 1986; TARP. "Consumer Complaint Handling in America, Final Report," U.S. Office of Consumer Affairs, Washington, DC, 1979; and Kathy Rhoades, "The Importance of Customer Complaints," *Protect Yourself* (January 1988): 15–18.
10. J. Singh. "Consumer Complaint Intentions and Behavior," *Journal of Marketing* (January 1988): 93–107; Jack Dart and Kim Freeman. "Dissatisfaction Response Styles Among Clients of Professional Accounting," *Journal of Business Research* 29 (January 1994): 75–81.
11. A. M. McGahan and Pankaj Ghemawat. "Competition to Retain Customers," *Marketing Science* 13 (Spring 1994): 165–176; Mark H. McCormack. "One Disappointed Customer Is One Too Many," *Positive Impact* 4 (September 1993): 7–8: Jeffery Gitomer. "Customer Complaints Can Breed Sales If Handled Correctly," *Positive Impact* 5 (February 1994): 10–11; Financial Services Report. "Most Popular Trends in Retention—Appealing to Your 'Best' Customers," *Positive Impact* 5 (May 1994): 24; and Sreekanth Sampathkumaran. "Migration Analysis Helps Stop Customer Attrition," *Marketing News* 28 (August 1994): 18–19.
12. T. Lucia. "Domino's Theory—Only Service Succeeds," *Positive Impact* (February 1992): 6–7.
13. Bernice Johnston. *Real World Customer Service—What to Really Say When the Customer Complains* (Small Business Source Books, 1996).
14. See the following articles in *Positive Impact*: Debbie Mitchell Price. "More Than Ever, It Pays to Keep the Customer Satisfied," 3 (February 1992): 7–8; Rosalie Robles Crowe. "Customer Satisfaction Paramount," 5 (April 1994): 7–8; Rod Riggs. "More-Than-Satisfied Customer Now the Goal," 5 (January 1994): 4–5; Peter Larson. "Customer Loyalty Is a Commodity Worth Fighting For," 4 (November 1993): 4; and Julie Bonnin. "L.L. Bean Keeps Its Customers Returning," 5 (January 1993): 7–8.
15. Reichheld and Sasser. "Zero Defections: Quality Comes to Services," 106–111; and Reichheld. "Loyalty-Based Management," 64–73.
16. Thomas Jones and W. Earl Sasser Jr."Why Satisfied Customers Defect," *Harvard Business Review* (November–December 1995): 88–89.
17. Frederick Reichheld and Phil Schefter. "E-Loyalty: Your Secret Weapon on the Web," *Harvard Business Review* (July–August 2000): 105–113.
18. Roberta Clarke. "Addressing Voluntary Disenrollment," *CDR Healthcare Resources* (1997): 10–12.
19. Michael Johnson and Anders Gustafsson. *Improving Customer Satisfaction, Loyalty, and Profit* (New York: Jossey-Bass, Inc., 2000).
20. Paul Nunes and Brian Johnson. "Are Some Customers More Equal than Others?" *Harvard Business Review* (November 2001): 37–50.
21. Jill Griffin and Michael Lowenstein. *Customer Winback* (Jossey-Bass, 2001).
22. Melinda Nykamp. *The Customer Differential* (AMACOM, 2001).
23. Werner Reinartz and V. Kumar. "The Mismanagement of Customer Loyalty," *Harvard Business Review* (July 2002): 86–94.

24. Melissa Campanelli. "Happy Returns," *Entrepreneur* (January 2004): 39.

25. Werner Reinartz and V. Kumar. "On the Profitability of Long-Life Customers in a Noncontractual Setting: An Empirical Investigation and Implications for Marketing," *Journal of Marketing* (October 2000): 17–35.

26. Ravi Dhar and Rashi Glazer. "Hedging Customers," *Harvard Business Review* (May 2003): 86–92.

27. Steve Schriver. "Customer Loyalty—Going, Going . . . ," *American Demographics* (September 1997): 20–23.

28. Ajay K. Kohli and Bernard J. Jaworski. "Market Orientation: The Construct, Research Propositions, and Managerial Implications," *Journal of Marketing* 54 (April 1995): 1–18; Bernard J. Jaworski and Ajay K. Kohli. "Market Orientation: Antecedents and Consequences," *Journal of Marketing* 57 (July 1993): 53–70; Ajay K. Kohli, Bernard Jaworski, and Ajith Kumar. "Markor: A Measure of Market Orientation," *Journal of Marketing* 30 (November 1993): 467–77; John C. Narver and Stanley F. Slater. "The Effect of a Market Orientation on Business Profitability," *Journal of Marketing* 54 (October 1990): 20–35; and Stanley F. Slater and John C. Narver. "Does Competitive Environment Moderate the Market Orientation-Performance Relationship," *Journal of Marketing* 58 (January 1994): 46–55.

29. Roger Best. "Determining the Marketing IQ of Your Management Team," *DriveMarketing Excellence* (November 1994), New York: Institute for International Research; and Roger Best and JoDee Nice. "Building Marketing Excellence," *Marketing Excellence Survey* (2001): 1–13.

30. Roger J. Best, *Marketing Excellence Survey*, *www.mesurvey.com*, 2004.

31. Mary Connelly. "Chrysler Adopts Disney Mindset for Customers," *Automotive News* (February 1992).

32. Robert Hiebeler, Thomas Kelly, and Charles Ketteman. *Best Practices: Building Your Business with Customer-Focused Solutions* (New York: Simon and Schuster, 1998): 167–200.

33. Rosalind Bentley. "The Name Nordstrom—Aim to Keep Customer Happy Is Legendary," *Positive Impact* (July 1992): 5.

34. Jack W. Wiley. "Customer Satisfaction and Employee Opinions: A Supportive Work Environment and Its Financial Costs," *Human Resource Planning* 14 (1991): 117–23; Anita Bruzzese. "Happy Employees Make Happy Customers," *Positive Impact* 4 (November 1993): 8–9; Jim Cathcart. "Fill the Needs of Employees to Better Serve Customers," *Positive Impact* 5 (November 1994): 7–8; and Peter Lawson, "Studies Link Customer-Employee Satisfaction," *Positive Impact* 3 (March 1992): 11–12.

35. Anthony Rucei, Steven Kirin, and Richard Quinn. "The Employee-Customer Profit Chain at Sears," *Harvard Business Review* (January–February 1998): 82–97.

36. Leonard A. Schlesinger and Jeffery Zomitsky. "Job Satisfaction, Service Capability, and Customer Satisfaction: An Examination of Linkages and Management Implications," *Human Resource Planning* 14 (1991): 141–149.

Present Value Table

Period (N)	DR = 8%	DR = 9%	DR = 10%	DR = 11%	DR = 12%	DR = 13%	DR = 14%	DR = 15%
0	1.000	1.000	1.000	1.000	1.000	1.000	1.000	1.000
1	0.926	0.917	0.909	0.901	0.893	0.885	0.887	0.870
2	0.857	0.842	0.826	0.812	0.797	0.783	0.769	0.756
3	0.794	0.772	0.751	0.731	0.712	0.693	0.675	0.658
4	0.735	0.708	0.683	0.659	0.636	0.613	0.592	0.572
5	0.681	0.650	0.621	0.593	0.567	0.543	0.519	0.497
6	0.630	0.596	0.564	0.535	0.507	0.480	0.456	0.432
7	0.583	0.547	0.513	0.482	0.452	0.425	0.400	0.376
8	0.540	0.502	0.467	0.434	0.404	0.376	0.351	0.327
9	0.500	0.460	0.424	0.391	0.361	0.333	0.308	0.284
10	0.463	0.422	0.386	0.352	0.322	0.295	0.270	0.247
11	0.429	0.388	0.350	0.317	0.287	0.261	0.237	0.215
12	0.397	0.356	0.319	0.286	0.257	0.231	0.208	0.187
13	0.368	0.326	0.290	0.258	0.229	0.204	0.182	0.163
14	0.340	0.299	0.263	0.232	0.205	0.181	0.160	0.141
15	0.315	0.275	0.239	0.209	0.183	0.160	0.140	0.123
16	0.292	0.252	0.218	0.188	0.163	0.141	0.123	0.107
17	0.270	0.231	0.198	0.170	0.146	0.125	0.108	0.093
18	0.250	0.212	0.180	0.153	0.130	0.111	0.095	0.081
19	0.232	0.194	0.164	0.138	0.116	0.098	0.083	0.070
20	0.215	0.178	0.149	0.124	0.104	0.087	0.073	0.061

Present Value Formula

$$PV = \frac{1}{(1 + DR)^N}$$

PV = Present Value of $1.00
N = Number of periods before the $1.00 will be received
DR = Discount Rate (cost of borrowing or desired rate of return)

Example I: N = 5 periods and Discount Rate (DR) = 10%

$$PV = \frac{1}{(1 + 0.10)^5} = \frac{1}{1.611} = 0.621 \ (\$1.00 \text{ received in 5 years is worth } \$0.621 \text{ today})$$

Example II: N = 2.33 periods and Discount Rate (DR) = 10%

$$PV = \frac{1}{(1 + 0.10)^{2.33}} = \frac{1}{1.249} = 0.801 \ (\$1.00 \text{ received in 2.33 years is worth } \$0.801 \text{ today})$$

CHAPTER 2

Marketing Performance and Marketing Profitability

CommTech is a $454 million business that manufactures a wide range of imaging and data transmission products for medical, industrial, and business-to-business markets. Five years ago, a new management team was put in place after several years of disappointing performance. The new management team reorganized the business and designed programs to lower unit costs, control overhead expenses, and facilitate better management of assets. In addition, the new management team put in place an extensive sales training program that enabled the sales force to improve its sales productivity from $1.4 million to $2.2 million per salesperson.

The results were sensational! In 5 years, the new management team almost doubled sales and more than tripled net profits. As shown in Figure 2-1, CommTech's return on sales grew from 6.3 percent to 12.1 percent, and its return on assets increased from 11.3 percent to 26.7 percent. On the basis of this information,

- How would you rate CommTech's performance over the last 5 years?
- What aspects of CommTech's performance were most impressive?
- Should CommTech follow the same strategy for the next 5 years?

FIGURE 2-1 COMMTECH'S 5-YEAR FINANCIAL PERFORMANCE

Performance (millions)	Base Year	1	2	3	4	5
Sales Revenues	$254	$293	$318	$387	$431	$454
Cost of Goods Sold	$183	$210	$230	$283	$314	$331
Gross Profit	$ 71	$83	$ 88	$104	$117	$123
Marketing and Sales Expense	18	23	24	26	27	28
Other Operating Expense	37	38	38	41	40	40
Net Profit (before taxes)	$ 16	$ 22	$ 26	$ 37	$ 50	$ 55
Return on Sales (%)	6.3	7.5	8.2	9.6	11.6	12.1
Assets (millions)	$141	$162	$167	$194	$205	$206
Return on Assets (%)	11.3	13.6	15.6	19.1	24.4	26.7

MARKET VERSUS FINANCIAL PERFORMANCE

Most of us would be quick to conclude that CommTech's performance over the last 5 years was outstanding. Who would not like to have run a business in which sales almost doubled and profits more than tripled over a 5-year period?

Despite those impressive increases, it is probably a mistake to evaluate CommTech's performance in such rosy terms when all the criteria used to arrive at this judgment are *financial* measures of performance. Sales revenues, net profits, return on sales, assets as a percentage of sales, and return on assets are all excellent measures of internal financial performance. These measures, however, do not provide an *external or market-based view* of performance. As a result, we do not know how CommTech has performed relative to external benchmarks such as market growth, competitive prices, relative product and service quality, and satisfying and retaining customers. Therefore, following the same strategy for the next 5 years may or may not be the best strategy for achieving profitable growth.

Using traditional methods of tracking performance, most would judge CommTech to be a real success story. However, it can be demonstrated that, in reality, its efforts represent a cumulative loss to the corporation and its shareholders of $122 million in net income and cash flow over the 5-year period. This difference in performance is due largely to a lack of market-based performance metrics and an over-reliance on traditional financial measures to guide strategic thinking and performance evaluation.

Marketing Performance

To complement a business's internal financial performance, a business needs a parallel set of external metrics to track market-based performance.[1] Although these measures may not have the additive elegance of financial accounting, individually and collectively they provide a different and more strategic view of business performance. In Figure 2-2 is a set of market-based performance metrics that paints a different picture of CommTech's

FIGURE 2-2 COMMTECH'S 5-YEAR MARKET-BASED PERFORMANCE

Performance Metric	Base Year	1	2	3	4	5
Market Growth (% dollars)	18.3	18.3	18.3	18.3	18.3	18.3
CommTech Sales Growth (%)	12.8	17.8	13.3	24.9	18.2	7.7
Market Share (%)	20.3	18.3	17.5	16.2	14.4	13.0
Customer Retention (%)	88.2	87.1	85.0	82.2	80.9	80.0
New Customers (%)	11.7	12.9	14.9	24.1	22.5	29.2
Dissatisfied Customers (%)	13.6	14.3	16.1	17.3	18.9	19.6
Relative Product Quality (*)	119	120	117	120	109	107
Relative Service Quality (*)	100	100	95	93	89	87
Relative New Product Sales (*)	108	108	103	99	95	93

(*) Relative index where 100 is equal to competition, greater than 100 ahead of competition and below 100 behind competition.

performance over the past 5 years. One can readily see several strategic flaws in CommTech's market-based performance. First, CommTech sales, while showing impressive growth, were increasing at a rate less than the market growth rate. This analysis shows that CommTech was actually losing market share over the past 5 years. New-product sales, product quality, and service quality each eroded *relative to competition.* Declines in relative product and service quality do not necessarily mean that CommTech's actual product or service quality declined. In many instances, the competition simply moved ahead in delivering a higher level of product and service quality. On a relative basis, the competition's more rapid progress caused CommTech to lose ground to competitors in these areas.

Declines in quality, along with declines in relative new-product sales, made it more difficult to hold customers as customer satisfaction declined and the percentage of dissatisfied customers grew. The net results were an eroding market-based performance, high levels of customer turnover, and a steady decline in market share.

A Market-Based Strategy

What would have been the impact of a strategy to hold market share? To hold a 20 percent share in a growing market, Commtech's marketing budget and product research and development would have needed to keep pace with market demand and the competition. At this level of investment and a 20 percent market share, the results presented in Figure 2-3 would have been plausible.

Although the market-based strategy to hold share would have delivered approximately the same return on assets as the internally driven strategy, it would have produced an additional $122 million in net profit (before taxes). Thus, over the 5-year period, the business gave up $122 million in bottom-line cash. Furthermore, CommTech's lost income will be greater over the next 5 years, even if share erosion is halted and market growth completely subsides. If the market continues to grow and market share continues to erode, CommTech's lost profit opportunity could easily approach $500 million over the next 5 years.

FIGURE 2-3 MARKET-BASED STRATEGY TO HOLD A 20 PERCENT MARKET SHARE

Performance (millions)	Base Year	1	2	3	4	5
Sales Revenues	$254	$312	$363	$477	$596	$697
Cost of Goods Sold	$183	$216	$251	$339	$415	$484
Gross Profit	$ 71	$ 96	$112	$138	$181	$213
Marketing and Sales Expense	18	24	27	32	41	50
Other Operating Expense	37	41	45	52	59	66
Net Profit (before taxes)	$ 16	$ 31	$ 40	$ 54	$ 81	$ 97
Return on Sales (%)	6.3	9.9	11.0	11.3	13.6	13.9
Assets (millions)	$141	$172	$196	$253	$310	$355
Return on Assets (%)	11.3	18.0	20.4	21.3	26.1	27.3
Last Income (before taxes)*	$ 0	$ 9	$ 14	$ 17	$ 31	$ 42

*Difference in Net Profits in Figures 2-3 and 2-1.

It is clear from the CommTech business situation that market-based management has the potential to dramatically improve profits. The foundation of market-based performance is a commitment to metrics that track marketing performance and marketing profitability.

The CommTech situation underscores the importance of market-based performance metrics. Most business systems are set up to track revenues, costs, factory overhead, accounts receivable, operating expenses, and profits—yet a business's customers are its most important asset and the only significant source of positive cash flow. Giving up customers in a period of growth simply means that the business has to work harder and spend more in order to replace each lost customer.

MARKETING PERFORMANCE METRICS

Marketing performance metrics provide a powerful complement to conventional measures of financial performance. Marketing performance metrics allow marketing managers to understand, track, and manage the market-based performance of a marketing strategy.[2] Shown in Figure 2-4 are three classes of marketing performance metrics.

1. **Market Performance Metrics**—These metrics gauge external market conditions and the attractiveness of markets. Market performance metrics include market growth, market share, market attractiveness, industry attractiveness, and market demand to potential.
2. **Competitive Performance Metrics**—These external metrics track the competitiveness of a business's products. Competitive performance metrics include a business's performance relative to competition with respect to price, product quality, service quality, brand, and cost.

FIGURE 2-4 FINANCIAL PERFORMANCE METRICS VERSUS MARKETING PERFORMANCE METRICS

Financial Performance Metrics	Marketing Performance Metrics
Cost Metrics • Average cost per unit • Marketing & sales expenses • Operating expenses	**Market Metrics** • Market growth rate • Market share • Market demand to potential
Productivity Metrics • Inventory turnover • Sales per employee • Days of accounts receivable	**Competitiveness Metrics** • Relative product quality • Relative service quality • Relative price and value
Profitability Metrics • Return on sales • Return on assets • Return on invested capital	**Customer Metrics** • Customer satisfaction • Customer retention • Customer loyalty

3. **Customer Performance Metrics**—These external metrics track customer performance. Customer performance metrics include measures of customer satisfaction, customer retention, customer loyalty, customer awareness, and customer value.

Each of these marketing performance metrics plays a critical role in taking a business to a higher level of marketing effectiveness and profitability. Each metric will be presented and operationalized in subsequent chapters of this book. In Chapter 1, we have already operationalized measures of customer satisfaction, customer retention, customer loyalty, and the lifetime value of a customer. Throughout the book we will build a marketing performance metrics and demonstrate how they track marketing performance and show how they impact a business's profitability.

Internal Versus External Performance Metrics

To be successful, a business needs both internal and external performance metrics.[3] As presented in Figure 2-4, internal measures are critical for tracking unit costs, expenses, asset utilization, employee and capital productivity, and overall measures of profitability. Market-based performance metrics are equally important for providing an external view of the business's market-based performance. Although CPA firms have done an excellent job in developing procedures for internal measures of a business's performance, the next frontier for either CPA firms or market research firms will be the development of standardized procedures for external measures of a business's market-based performance. With both sets of performance metrics, managers as well as financial analysts and shareholders will be in a much better position to evaluate a business's marketing effectiveness and business performance.

In-Process Versus End-Result Performance Metrics

The primary purpose of market metrics is to maintain an ongoing measure of market performance—and, because many market metrics precede financial performance, they are critical to strategy implementation and financial performance. However, not all market metrics are leading indicators of business performance. There are *in-process market metrics* and *end-result market metrics*.[4] Both are important, but in-process market metrics are particularly important because they are also leading indicators of financial performance. End-result metrics correspond more closely to financial performance.

Product awareness, intentions to purchase, product trial, and customer satisfaction and dissatisfaction, along with customer perceptions of relative product quality, service quality, and customer value, all serve as in-process market metrics. Changes in each, positive or negative, generally precede actual changes in customer purchase behavior. As a result, these in-process measures of customer thinking and attitude are important leading indicators of future purchase behavior and, hence, of revenue and profit performance.

For example, perhaps customers are satisfied, but they perceive the value they derive from your product, relative to competing alternatives, is steadily diminishing. You may well have done nothing to dissatisfy customers; the competition may have simply improved in delivering customer value based upon a combination of total benefits in comparison to total cost. However, the net effect is that customer perceptions of the value derived from your product have diminished. This change in customer perceptions, in

FIGURE 2-5 INTERNAL VERSUS EXTERNAL AND IN-PROCESS VERSUS END-RESULT PERFORMANCE METRICS

	Time Perspective	
Measurement Perspectives	**In-Process Metrics**	**End-Result Metrics**
Internal (in company)	Product Defects Late Deliveries Billing Errors Accounts Receivable Inventory Turnover	Net Profit/Earnings Return on Sales Margin per Unit Return on Assets Asset Turnover
External (in market)	Customer Satisfaction Relative Product Quality Relative Service Quality Intentions to Purchase Product Awareness	Market Share Customer Retention Relative New-Product Sales Revenue per Customer Market Growth Rate

turn, opens the door to competitors' products that your customer may be inclined to try or purchase. With an early warning signal, a market-based business can take corrective action before customers switch their purchases to a competitor. Without in-process market metrics, problems may go undetected and unresolved until after declines in financial performance make it clear that something went wrong.

External end-result market metrics include market share, customer retention, revenue per customer, and others, as shown in Figure 2-5. End-result market metrics are likely to occur at the end of a financial performance period, and each provides a different set of performance diagnostics and insights.

For example, let's assume that sales revenues are increasing and are ahead of forecast, and that financial performance is also better than expected. Most businesses would feel pretty good about this performance. However, if end-result market metrics show that the business is losing share in a growing market and that poor customer retention is masked by new customer growth, there is cause for concern. Without end-result market metrics, the business has only the limited insights of an internal perspective on end-result performance.

MARKETING PROFITABILITY

Although market-based performance metrics are essential to understanding external performance, it is also important that a business be managed to grow and to produce profits and shareholder value. Consider, for example, the Santa Fe Sportswear Company. The company's sales of $125 million were built around five product lines. The company was profitable overall, but two of the product lines had not performed well. In response, the senior management team of Santa Fe Sportswear met to review product line performance. In preparation for the senior management review, the finance manager prepared the product line profitability summary presented in Figure 2-6.

FIGURE 2-6 SANTA FE SPORTSWEAR PRODUCT LINE PROFITABILITY

Santa Fe Sportswear Performance (millions)	Khaki Pants	Wind Breakers	Classic Polo	Casual Shorts	Knitted Sweaters	Company Total
Sales Revenues	$60.0	$25.0	$15.0	$10.0	$15.0	$125
Cost of Goods Sold	$37.5	$16.0	$ 7.5	$ 8.0	$11.0	$ 80
Gross Profit	$22.5	$ 9.0	$ 7.5	$ 2.0	$ 4.0	$ 45
Operating Expenses	$17.0	$ 7.0	$ 4.0	$ 3.0	$ 4.0	$ 35
Net Profit (before taxes)	$ 5.5	$ 2.0	$ 3.5	($ 1.0)	$ 0.0	$ 10

Using this information, the finance manager argued the following:

> "We are wasting resources on the casual shorts and knitted sweaters product lines. One makes no money and the other loses money. I recommend we drop both product lines and refocus our efforts on the profitable product lines."

Would this be a good decision? How should the marketing manager present her interpretation of the profit performance of the casual shorts and knitted sweaters product lines? A measure of marketing profitability is needed to help gauge the degree to which a marketing strategy contributes to a business's profits. However, what is marketing profitability? How is it measured? How is it managed? How would it shed light on the profitability of the casual shorts product line?

Measuring Marketing Profitability

To create a measure of marketing profitability, we need to examine more closely the elements of profitability and determine which of them come under the influence of the marketing function. To do this, we need to systematically break down the elements of profitability and marketing strategy and examine how they interact.[5] The best method is to start with a broad definition of net profit and then expand the profit equation into a definition that encompasses a market-level measure of profitability. In its most basic terms, a business's net profit is simply its revenues minus its expenses:

$$\textbf{Net Profits }(\text{before taxes}) = \text{Revenues} - \text{Expenses}$$

The casual shorts product line produces $10 million in sales revenues as shown here. The cost of goods sold is $8 million. Various expenses that make up the cost of goods sold are summarized in Figure 2-7. After deducting operating expenses of $3 million, net profit before taxes is −$1 million. From the finance manager's perspective, eliminating this product line's apparent loss would improve overall profits by $1 million.

$$\textbf{Profits }(\text{Casual Shorts}) = \frac{\text{Sales}}{\text{Revenues}} - \frac{\text{Cost of}}{\text{Goods Sold}} - \frac{\text{Operating}}{\text{Expenses}}$$
$$= \$10 \text{ million} - \$8 \text{ million} - \$3 \text{ million}$$
$$= - \$1 \text{ million}$$

FIGURE 2-7 COST OF GOODS SOLD, MARKETING EXPENSES, AND OPERATING EXPENSES

Cost of Goods Sold—The total cost of producing a product that varies with volume sold	
Variable Cost	Includes purchase of materials, direct labor, packaging, transportation costs, and any other costs associated with making and shipping a product.
Manufacturing Overhead	This is an allocated cost based on usage of the fixed manufacturing plant, equipment, and other fixed expenses needed to run the production operation.
Marketing and Sales Expenses*—Direct expenses that vary with a marketing strategy	
Marketing Management	Expenses associated with marketing management and resources needed to support this function.
Sales, Service, and Support	Expenses associated with the sales force, customer service, and technical and administrative support services.
Advertising and Promotion	All expenses associated with the marketing communications budget.
Operating Expenses—Indirect expenses that do not vary with the marketing strategy	
Research and Development	Expenses for developing new products and/or improving old products.
Corporate Overhead	Overhead expenses for corporate staff, legal council, professional services, corporate advertising, and the salaries of senior management and their staff.

*Marketing and Sales Expenses are traditionally a part of Sales, General, and Administration (SG&A) reported in most annual reports.

However, to understand marketing profitability and how it contributes to a business's profits, we need to isolate marketing and sales expense. When this is done as shown, we can see that the casual shorts product line actually produces $1 million in net marketing contribution.

$$\begin{array}{l}\underset{\text{(CasualShorts)}}{\textbf{Profits}} = \underset{\text{Revenues}}{\text{Sales}} - \underset{\text{GoodsSold}}{\text{Cost of}} - \underset{\text{Expenses}}{\underset{\text{\& Sales}}{\text{Marketing}}} - \underset{\text{Expenses}}{\underset{\text{Operating}}{\text{Other}}}\\[2mm] -\$1\text{ million} = \$10\text{ milllion} - \$8\text{ million} - \$1\text{ million} - \$2\text{ million}\\[2mm] -\$1\text{ million} = \underset{\underset{\text{Contribution}}{\text{Net Marketing}}}{\$1\text{ million}} \quad - \underset{\underset{\text{Expenses}}{\text{Operating}}}{\$2\text{ million}}\end{array}$$

The $1 million in net marketing contribution from the casual shorts product line is a measure of marketing profitability. If the casual shorts product line were eliminated, Santa Fe

Sportswear would reduce its overall profits by the $1 million marketing profit produced by the casual shorts product line. The marketing and sales expenses associated with the casual shorts product line would eventually go to zero because there would be no purpose for these expenses. However, $2 million of operating expenses were allocated to the casual shorts product line. If the casual shorts product line were eliminated, those $2 million would have to be reallocated to the other product lines, making them appear less profitable. To make effective market-based decisions, we need to separate marketing and sales expenses from overall fixed operating expenses.[6] Net marketing contribution does this, capturing the actual profitability of a product line without including any allocated overhead not directly related to the product line itself.

Net Marketing Contribution—Product Focus

Using net marketing contribution (NMC) as a measure of marketing profits, we can better understand how marketing strategies contribute to the overall profits of a business as shown in Figure 2-8.

Profits (before tax) = [All Product Net Marketing Contributions] − Operating Expenses

$$= [\text{NMC}(1) + \text{NMC}(2) + \text{NMC}(3) + \text{NMC}(4) + \text{NMC}(5)] - \text{Operating Expenses}$$
$$= [\$15.5 + \$6.0 + \$5.5 + \$1.0 + \$2.0] - \$20.0$$
$$= \$10 \text{ million}$$

The portion bracketed as NMC is our measure marketing profitability. These are the components of profitability that are largely under the control of the marketing function, whereas operating expenses are generally under the control of those in general management. Thus, we can rewrite the net profit of a business as shown, where marketing controls the NMC component of net profit:

$$\textbf{Net Profit} \text{ (before taxes)} = \text{NMC} - \text{Operating Expenses}$$

From this perspective, a marketing strategy produces a net marketing contribution.[7] This NMC has to cover the business's operating expenses and more in order for the business to make a profit.

FIGURE 2-8 PRODUCT LINE—NET MARKETING CONTRIBUTION

Santa Fe Sportswear Performance (millions)	Khaki Pants	Wind Breakers	Classic Polo	Casual Shorts	Knitted Sweaters	Company Total
Sales Revenues	$60.0	$25.0	$15.0	$10.0	$15.0	$125
Cost of Goods Sold	$37.5	$16.0	$ 7.5	$ 8.0	$11.0	$ 80
Gross Profit	$22.5	$ 9.0	$ 7.5	$ 2.0	$ 4.0	$ 45
Marketing & Sales Expenses	$ 7.0	$ 3.0	$ 2.0	$ 1.0	$ 2.0	$ 15
Net Marketing Contribution	$15.5	$ 6.0	$ 5.5	$ 1.0	$ 2.0	$ 30
Operating Expenses	$10.0	$ 4.0	$ 2.0	$ 2.0	$ 2.0	$ 20
Net Profit (before taxes)	$ 5.5	$ 2.0	$ 3.5	($ 1.0)	$ 0.0	$ 10

Using net marketing contribution as a measure of marketing profitability, the marketing manager can more readily evaluate the profit impact of a marketing strategy. Each product or market should be managed to produce a *positive* NMC. In this way, marketing decisions can be evaluated with respect to not only revenue and share gains but also how they affect the profits by the level of NMC they produce.

If we break down NMC into gross profit and marketing expenses, we have one level of marketing profitability. Gross profit can be further broken down into volume and margin and volume broken down into market demand and market share. If we further break down margin into price minus variable cost, we can see how pricing can impact marketing profits. Finally, deducting the marketing expenses needed, we can see how different elements under the control of the marketing manager can impact marketing profitabililty.

$$\begin{aligned}\textbf{NMC} &= \text{Gross Profit} - \text{Marketing Expenses}\\ &= (\text{Unit Volume}) \times (\text{Margin per Unit}) - \text{Marketing Expenses}\\ &= \frac{\text{Market}}{\text{Demand}} \times \frac{\text{Market}}{\text{Share}} \times \frac{\text{Price}}{(\text{per Unit})} - \frac{\text{Variable Cost}}{(\text{per Unit})} - \frac{\text{Marketing}}{\text{Expenses}}\end{aligned}$$

Using this breakdown of net marketing contribution as a way to examine marketing profitability, we need to reexamine Santa Fe Sportswear's product line profitability. Santa Fe Sportswear's marketing strategy for khaki pants currently produces an NMC of $15.5 million, as shown in Figure 3-8. This level of marketing profitability is the result of a 12.5 percent share of 12 million units of market demand, a price of $40 per unit, a variable cost of $25 per unit, and marketing expenses of $7 million.

$$\begin{aligned}\textbf{NMC} \text{ (khaki pants)} &= (12 \text{ million} \times 0.125) \times (\$40 - \$25) - \$7 \text{ million}\\ &= (1.5 \text{ million}) \times (\$15) - \$7 \text{ million}\\ &= \$22.5 \text{ million} - \$7 \text{ million}\\ &= \$15.5 \text{ million}\end{aligned}$$

To demonstrate how the profit impact of a marketing strategy can be assessed, assume that the marketing manager of Santa Fe Sportswear's khaki pants line proposed to cut prices by 10 percent in order to grow share from 12.5 to 15 percent. This marketing strategy would produce 300,000 more units in sales volume, but at a lower margin ($15 vs. $11). The net result of this marketing strategy would be a decrease in NMC from $15.5 million to $12.8 million and, therefore, a decrease in net profits of the same amount.

$$\begin{aligned}\textbf{NMC} \text{ (khaki pants)} &= [12 \text{ million} \times 0.15 \times (\$36 - \$25)] - \$7 \text{ million}\\ &= [1.8 \text{ million} \times \$11 \text{ per unit}] - \$7 \text{ million}\\ &= \$19.8 \text{ million} - \$7 \text{ million}\\ &= \textbf{\$12.8 million}\end{aligned}$$

Net Marketing Contribution and Business Unit Profitability

When a business has several product lines, it produces several sources of net marketing contribution. The sum of the NMCs of all these product lines is the only source of cash flow produced by the business; everything else is expense, as shown:

$$\underset{\underbrace{}_{\textbf{NMCs from all served markets}}}{\begin{array}{cccc} \text{Net Profit} & \text{NMC} & \text{NMC} & \text{NMC} \\ \text{(before taxes)} & \text{Product (1)} & \text{Product (2)} & \text{Product (n)} \end{array}}$$

Net Profit (before taxes) − NMC Product (1) + NMC Product (2) + ⋯ + NMC Product (n) − Operating Expenses

NMCs from all served markets

Now, let's return to the question raised earlier: Would eliminating the casual shorts and knitted sweaters product lines be a good idea? And would such a decision improve the net profits of Santa Fe Sportswear?

First, Figure 2-9 presents a market-based view of Santa Fe Sportswear's product line profitability and overall company net profits (before taxes). As shown, each product line produces a positive net marketing contribution, which means each product line is making a positive contribution toward operating expenses and net profit (before taxes). If we assume that the operating expenses of the business would not change with the elimination of the casual shorts and knitted sweaters product lines, then net profit before taxes would actually decrease by the amount of the NMC these two product lines were producing. Eliminating the casual shorts and knitted sweaters product lines would reduce sales revenues by $25 million, and net profit would fall from $10 million to $7 million:

$$\begin{array}{lllll} \text{Net Profit} & \text{NMC} & \text{NMC} & \text{NMC} & \text{Operating} \\ \text{(before taxes)} = & \text{(Khaki Pants)} + & \text{(Wind Breakers)} + & \text{(Classic Polo)} - & \text{Expenses} \\ = \$15.5 \text{ million} & + \$6.0 \text{ million} & + \$5.5 \text{ million} & - \$20 \text{ million} \\ = \$7.0 \text{ million} \end{array}$$

FIGURE 2-9 SANTA FE SPORTSWEAR—PRODUCT-FOCUSED MARKETING PROFITABILITY

Santa Fe Sportswear Performance (millions)	Khaki Pants	Wind Breakers	Classic Polo	Casual Shorts	Knitted Sweaters	Company Total
Market Demand (million units)	12	10	15	20	5	62
Market Share	12.5%	5.0%	3.3%	2.0%	4.0%	5.0%
Volume Sold (million units)	1.5	0.5	0.5	0.4	0.2	3.1
Average Price per Unit	$40.00	$50.00	$30.00	$25.00	$75.00	$ 40.33
Sales Revenues	$60.0	$25.0	$15.0	$10.0	$15.0	$125.0
Average Cost per Unit	$25.00	$32.00	$15.00	$20.00	$55.00	$ 25.81
Average Margin per Unit	$15.00	$18.00	$15.00	$ 5.00	$20.00	$ 14.52
Gross Profit	$22.5	$ 9.0	$ 7.5	$ 2.0	$ 4.0	$ 45.0
Marketing & Sales Expenses	$ 7.0	$ 3.0	$ 2.0	$ 1.0	$ 2.0	$ 15.0
Net Marketing Contribution	**$15.5**	**$ 6.0**	**$ 5.5**	**$ 1.0**	**$ 2.0**	**$ 30.0**
Operating Expenses	$10.0	$ 4.0	$ 2.0	$ 2.0	$ 2.0	$ 20.0
Net Profit (before taxes)	**$ 5.5**	**$ 2.0**	**$ 3.5**	**($ 1.0)**	**$ 0.0**	**$ 10.0**

FIGURE 2-10 SANTA FE SPORTSWEAR—PRODUCT LINE MARKETING PROFITABILITY

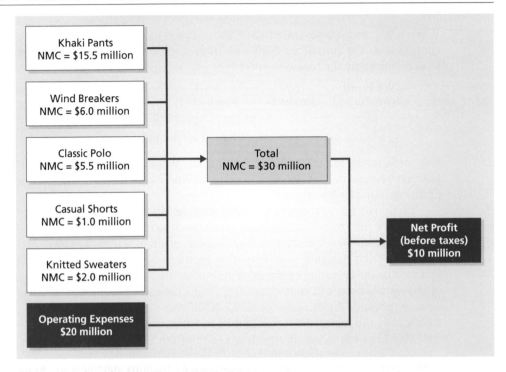

Another way for the marketing manager to demonstrate visually how each product line contributes to overall net profits is presented in Figure 2-10. As shown, each product line is producing a positive NMC. As a result, each makes a contribution toward covering operating expenses and producing net profit. Eliminating any of these products without a commensurate reduction in operating expenses would result in a reduction in net profits.

Marketing Profitability—A Customer Focus

Accounting systems are generally built around production. Revenues and costs are directly associated with producing something, whether it be a product or a service. Costs that are not directly related to production are allocated to products or services using some agreed-upon accounting rules that have nothing to do with satisfying customers or making money. To develop marketing strategies that satisfy customers and grow profits, we need to extend the accounting unit of analysis to better assist the marketing function in managing marketing profitability. To accomplish this, we need an alternative way to track a business's revenues, variable costs, fixed expenses, and net profits.

It is convenient to report performance by product, but there are several reasons we should also track performance by markets and customers. Regardless of the technical or psychological appeal of a business's products or services, cash flow is produced only when a customer buys a business's product or service. There are many products and services a business may produce, but there is only a finite number of actual and potential customers in any given market. The objective of a marketing strategy should be to attract, satisfy, and retain target customers in a way that grows the profits of the business.

FIGURE 2-11 SANTA FE SPORTSWEAR—CUSTOMER-FOCUSED MARKETING PROFITABILITY

Santa Fe Sportswear Performance (millions)	Traditional Buyer	Fashion Buyer	Trend Setter	Company Total
Market Demand*	6,800,000	6,000,000	8,000,000	20,800,000
Market Share	9.00%	3.50%	6.00%	6.23%
Customer Volume*	612,000	210,000	480,000	1,302,000
Average Revenue per Customer	$90.00	$180.00	$65.00	$95.31
Sales Revenues	$ 55.1	$37.8	$ 31.2	$124.1
Average Cost per Unit	$55.00	$124.50	$40.00	$60.75
Average Margin per Unit	$35.00	$ 55.50	$25.00	$34.56
Gross Profit	$ 21.4	$ 11.6	$ 12.0	$ 45.0
Marketing & Sales Expenses	$ 6.0	$ 4.5	$ 4.5	$ 15.0
Net Marketing Contribution	$ 15.4	$ 7.1	$ 7.5	$ 30.0
Operating Expenses	$ 8.0	$ 6.0	$ 6.0	$ 20.0
Net Profit (before taxes)	$ 7.4	$ 1.1	$ 1.5	$ 10.0

* Number of customers

Using customers and the market segments they belong to as the accounting units, we can create a more insightful understanding of market-based profitability and ways to grow it. However, let's first see what a market-based profitability statement would look like.

In Figure 2-11, we have rebuilt the performance of Santa Fe Sportswear around the three markets served. One can quickly observe that the product-based and market-based accounting approaches produce the same total revenue, gross profit, net marketing contribution, and net profits. However, each presents a different insight into market-based management. Both are important and meaningful. The product-focused accounting statement (Figure 2-9) helps us understand product unit volume, product price, and product unit margin. Customer-focused accounting (Figure 2-11) helps us understand customer demand, customer share, customer volume, revenue per customer, and variable cost per customer. In this case all three market segments produce a positive net profit. In Figure 2-9, casual shorts and knitted sweaters did not produce positive net profits, but in Figure 2-11 we can see that each segment makes a meaningful NMC. Eliminating any of these products would result in lower segment profits and lower overall profits for Santa Fe Sportswear.

MARKETING STRATEGIES AND PROFITABLE GROWTH

Recognizing the product or customer as the unit of analysis, we can evaluate different aspects of net marketing contribution in order to gain better insight into the development of marketing strategies designed to grow profitability.[8] As shown in Figure 2-12, each element of the NMC equation offers the potential to create a marketing strategy that will affect profits. In each case, the NMC of a proposed strategy must exceed the current NMC in order to grow the net profits of the business. In light of this fact, there is a limited number of fundamental marketing strategies that a business can consider in order to grow NMC.

FIGURE 2-12 FUNDAMENTAL MARKET-BASED STRATEGIES AND PROFITABLE GROWTH

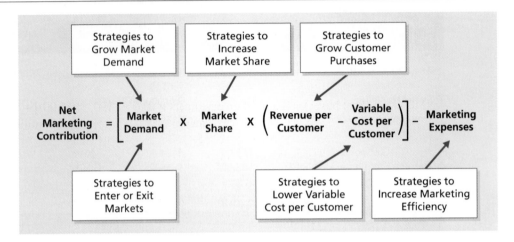

Consider, for example, Santa Fe Sportswear's performance among traditional buyers, as presented in Figure 2-11. As shown here, traditional buyers currently produce an NMC of $15.4 million. This is derived from a 9 percent share of a market demand of 6.8 million customers, revenues of $90 per customer, variable costs of $55 per customer, and marketing expenses of $6 million.

NMC (Traditional Buyer) = [6.8 million customers × 0.09 × ($90 − $55)] − $6 million
= [612,000 customers × $35] − $6 million
= $21.4 million − $6 million
= **$15.4 million**

Marketing strategies to grow the marketing profitability of this segment could address market demand, market share, revenue per customer, variable cost per customer, or marketing expenses. In the remainder of this section, we will discuss the market-based strategies suggested in Figure 2-12 and assess how selected strategies in each area might affect the profits of Santa Fe Sportswear.

Strategies to Grow Market Demand

In many markets, a large part of the marketing challenge is to bring more customers into the market. If you think about portable music players, cellular telephones, and personal computers, you may realize that a good portion of the profitable growth comes from new customers. Thus, marketing strategies to attract more customers and grow market demand offer one way to grow the net profits of a business. If a business is able to hold or grow share while attracting new customers to the market, there is a potential to grow profits. Profits will grow, however, only when the NMC produced by the proposed marketing strategy exceeds the current NMC.

For example, the Santa Fe Sportswear's traditional buyer marketing manager believes that segment demand could be grown from 6.8 million customers to 8.0 million customers with a 50 percent increase in marketing effort. If this increase could be achieved, and Santa

Fe Sportswear were able to maintain a 9.0 percent share, volume would increase by 108,000 customers. However, would this proposed strategy improve the traditional buyers' segment marketing profitability and increase the business's overall profitability?

We can see from the following calculations that this would be a worthwhile marketing strategy. NMC would increase by $0.8 million (from $15.4 to $16.2 million). The gain of 108,000 new customers would produce enough additional total contribution to cover the additional $3 million in marketing expenses required to achieve this growth.

$$\begin{aligned}
\text{NMC (traditional buyer)} &= [8.0 \text{ million customers} \times 0.09 \times (\$90 - \$55.00)] - \$9 \text{ million} \\
&= [720{,}000 \text{ customers} \times \$35.00 \text{ per unit}] - \$9 \text{ million} \\
&= \$25.2 \text{ million} - \$9 \text{ million} \\
&= \mathbf{\$16.2 \text{ million}}
\end{aligned}$$

In some instances, a business may actually take lower the NMCs in the short run in order to build demand and future profits. However, the discounted cash flow from the long-term strategy has to exceed that of the current strategy in order for this approach to be viable.

Strategies to Increase Market Share

Perhaps the most common marketing strategy to grow revenue and profits is market share penetration. For any served market, a strategy is developed to grow the business's share of its served market. The same rules apply: a market penetration strategy is likely to cost money, margin, or both, and the NMC of the penetration strategy needs to exceed the current NMC for the business to improve profitability. For example, in the traditional buyer segment, Santa Fe Sportswear could consider a strategy to increase its market share from 9.0 to 11 percent by lowering its prices 10 percent. As the following shows, the additional 136,000 customers would not be sufficient to offset the lower margin that would result from a 10 percent price decrease. The net result is a projected decrease in net marketing contribution from $15.4 million to $13.45 million.

$$\begin{aligned}
\text{NMC (traditional buyer)} &= [6.8 \text{ million customers} \times 0.11 \times (\$81 - \$55.00)] - \$6 \text{ million} \\
&= [748{,}000 \text{ customers} \times \$26.00 \text{ per customer}] - \$6 \text{ million} \\
&= \$19.45 \text{ million} - \$6 \text{ million} \\
&= \mathbf{\$13.45 \text{ million}}
\end{aligned}$$

Strategies to Increase Revenue per Customer

In a mature market with a strong share position, a business may not find it feasible or profitable to grow market demand or market share. However, the business's customers still remain its best strategic asset, and an examination of customer needs might reveal new products and services to better serve those needs and grow revenues. To evaluate the overall profit impact of such a marketing strategy, a business would have to project what higher prices could be attained and what increases in the average cost per unit would be required.

Also to be considered are potential additional marketing expenses, such as the additional advertising dollars that would be necessary to make existing customers aware of product or service improvements. Thus, it is important to examine all aspects of the strategy to ensure that a strategy to increase price per unit leads to an increase in net marketing contribution. To illustrate the profit impact of a strategy to build revenue per customer, consider that in the traditional buyer segment, a major product-line improvement would be able to raise average revenue per customer from $90 to $100. However, this improvement would also raise the average variable cost per customer by $5.00 because of increased materials costs. In addition, another $2 million in marketing expenses will be needed to introduce the improved product line and to communicate its benefits. As shown here, this marketing strategy would produce an incremental gain of $1.1 million in NMC when compared with the current NMC of $15.4 million.

$$
\begin{aligned}
\text{NMC (traditional buyer)} \quad &= [6.8 \text{ million customers} \times 0.09 \times (\$90 - \$50.00)] - \$7 \text{ million} \\
&= [612{,}000 \text{ customers} \times \$40.00 \text{ per customer}] - \$7 \text{ million} \\
&= \$24.5 \text{ million} - \$7 \text{ million} \\
&= \mathbf{\$17.5 \text{ million}}
\end{aligned}
$$

Strategies to Lower Variable Cost

Another way to grow net profits is by lowering the variable cost per unit. For example, perhaps transportation costs and sales commissions could be lowered with a new distribution strategy for a given market or market segment. This strategy would lower variable expenses per unit and increase margin per unit, but the business has to be concerned about the level of customer satisfaction that will be delivered by this alternative distribution system. If customer satisfaction drops, so will customer retention—and in the long run, net profits will erode even though the business has achieved a lower variable cost and higher margin per unit. Thus, a successful marketing strategy must hold or increase customer satisfaction while growing net profits through increases in NMC.

Continuing with the Santa Fe Sportswear example, the marketing manager for the traditional buyer segment is evaluating a new order entry and billing system that would improve customer satisfaction and lower the variable cost of serving a customer by $5 per customer. However, this new system will add $1 million per year in fixed marketing expense. The system would improve customer satisfaction and lower variable costs, but would it improve profitability? As shown, the proposed order entry and billing system would improve the net marketing contribution by $2.1 million, improving both customer satisfaction and profitability.

$$
\begin{aligned}
\text{NMC (traditional buyer)} \quad &= [6.8 \text{ million customers} \times 0.09 \times (\$90 - \$50.00)] - \$7 \text{ million} \\
&= [612{,}000 \text{ customers} \times \$40.00 \text{ per customer}] - \$7 \text{ million} \\
&= \$24.5 \text{ million} - \$7 \text{ million} \\
&= \mathbf{\$17.5 \text{ million}}
\end{aligned}
$$

Strategies to Increase Market Efficiency

Another way to improve the profitability of a marketing strategy is to lower fixed marketing expenses; that is, to be more efficient in the use of marketing expenses to achieve a particular performance objective. The more focused a business is with respect to target customers, the fewer marketing dollars it has to expend in order to achieve a desired marketing objective. Likewise, alternative forms of distribution can affect the fixed marketing expenses needed. For example, a business short on financial resources may elect to use a distributor rather than incur the fixed cost of direct selling and distribution. Santa Fe Sportswear currently uses a direct sales force for traditional buyers and, as we have seen, spends $6 million in marketing expenses to obtain a market share of 9.0 percent. The business is considering shifting to manufacturers' representatives as a way to lower marketing expenses. The reps would be paid a 10 percent sales commission, and the business could reduce its marketing expenses by $2 million. However, as shown here, the 10 percent sales commission would be too costly in terms of reduced margin. As a result, the business is better off with its current marketing strategy because the current NMC ($15.4 million) is greater than the NMC of the projected marketing strategy.

$$
\begin{aligned}
\text{NMC (traditional buyer)} &= [6.8 \text{ million customers} \times 0.09 \times (\$90 - \$9 - \$55.00)] - \$4 \text{ million} \\
&= [612,\!000 \text{ customers} \times \$26.00 \text{ per unit}] - \$4 \text{ million} \\
&= \$15.9 \text{ million} - \$4 \text{ million} \\
&= \$11.9 \text{ million}
\end{aligned}
$$

MARKETING PROFITABILITY METRICS

Although net marketing contribution allows us to measure the profit impact of a marketing strategy, it does not provide any insight into the relative marketing efficiencies of various NMCs. For example, in a recent year Frito-Lay produced an NMC of $4.0 billion and Nokia produced an NMC of $6.9 billion as shown here.

Net Marketing = SalesRevenue × % Gross Margin − Marketing & Sales Expenses
Contribution   = $14.2 billion ×   46%   − $2.5 billion
 (Frito-Lay)   = $4.03 billion

Net Marketing = SalesRevenue × % Gross Margin − Marketing & Sales Expenses
Contribution   = $22.6 billion ×   39%   − $1.9 billion
 (Nokia)   = $6.9 billion

Because the sales revenues of each company are quite different ($14.2 billion vs. $22.6 billion), it is difficult to judge which company was more efficient in producing marketing profits. To address this issue, we will examine two marketing profitability metrics that allow us to evaluate the marketing profitability of a business and its marketing strategies. These metrics will also help us better understand how marketing profitability impacts the overall financial performance of a business.

Marketing Return on Sales

The first marketing profitability metric we will examine is market return on sales (marketing ROS). By dividing the NMC by sales, we can control for the size of sales revenues.

Although Frito-Lay and Nokia were quite different in level of sales revenues, both companies produced marketing ROS close to 30 percent.

Marketing ROS = Net Marketing Contribution / Sales Revenues × 100%

Marketing ROS (Frito-Lay) = $4.0 billion / $14.2 billion × 100% = **28.2%**
Marketing ROS (Nokia)   = $6.9 billion / $22.6 billion × 100% = **30.5%**

What level of marketing ROS indicates good performance? Let's examine the marketing ROS and the overall financial performance of four competing firms to better gauge a good marketing ROS from an average or poor marketing ROS. Figure 2-13 shows the sales, gross profit, and marketing profitability for four competing companies in the sports equipment market. Rossignol, although not the largest in sales, produced the best marketing ROS at 44 percent. At the other extreme was Head with a 14 percent marketing ROS. In between were Salomon (Marketing ROS = 21 percent) and K2 (Marketing ROS = 15 percent). When we compare the respective marketing profits of four well known competitors, we can readily see that overall profitability follows closely and corresponds with Marketing ROS. In each case, the higher the Marketing ROS, the higher the financial performance as measured by overall return on sales, return on equity, and return on invested capital.

Marketing Return on Investment

A second marketing profitability metric assesses the marketing productivity of an investment in marketing. Recognizing NMC as the measure of marketing profitability, we can standardize this marketing profitability metric by dividing the NMC by the investment in marketing, which is the marketing and sales expenses as presented here. This creates a measure of marketing return on investment (ROI) that allows the manager to evaluate the efficiency of the marketing expenses used to produce a given level of

FIGURE 2-13 MARKETING ROS AND OVERALL PROFITABILITY

Performance (millions)	Rossignol	Salomon	K2	Head	Average
Sales Revenue	$558	$807	$582	$388	$584
Percent Margin (%)	64	41	30	40	44
Gross Profit	$357	$331	$175	$155	$255
Marketing Performance					
Marketing & Sales (% Sales)*	19.9	19.8	14.8	26.5	19.9
Net Marketing Contribution	$246	$171	$ 88	$ 52	$140
Marketing Return on Sales	**44%**	**21%**	**15%**	**14%**	**24%**
Financial Performance					
Return on Sales (%)	11.3	4.8	2.7	−0.7	5
Return on Equity (%)	61.7	30.3	6.9	−1.1	24
Return on Invested Capital (%)	28.5	12.3	5.2	−0.8	11

*Based on sales, general & administrative expenses

marketing profitability. Marketing ROI also allows us to compare the marketing efficiency of different strategies, or compare one company to another.

$$\textbf{Market ROI} = \frac{\text{Net Marketing Contribution}}{\text{Marketing \& Sales Expenses}} \times 100\%$$

The ratio of NMC to marketing and sales expenses provides a measure of how efficient a given marketing budget is in producing marketing profits. For example, Frito-Lay produces an overall NMC of $4.0 billion with a marketing budget of $2.5 billion. This is a market productivity of 160 percent, which means that each dollar of marketing budget produces $1.60 in NMC. However, Nokia is even more efficient in producing marketing profits with a marketing productivity of 363 percent as shown next.

Marketing ROI = (Net Marketing Contribution / Marketing & Sales Expenses) × 100%
   (Frito - Lay)   = ($4.0 billion / $2.5 billion) × 100%
               = **160%**

Marketing ROI = (Net Marketing Contribution / Marketing & Sales Expenses) × 100%
   (Nokia)   = ($6.9 billion / $1.9 billion) × 100%
               = **363%**

Although each of these companies produced excellent measures of marketing ROS, Nokia also produces this level of return with over twice the efficiency. In other words, Nokia is able to produce a similar Marketing ROS with proportionately fewer marketing resources.

Returning to our analysis of the four sports equipment manufacturers, in Figure 2-14 we can see how marketing productivity corresponds to different measures of overall financial performance. As with Marketing ROS, companies with higher levels of marketing productivity produce higher levels of return on sales, return on equity, and return on invested capital. As shown, Rossignol leads in both marketing profitability metrics and

FIGURE 2-14 MARKETING ROI AND OVERALL PROFITABILITY

Performance (millions)	Rossignol	Salomon	K2	Head	Average
Marketing Performance					
Marketing & Sales (% sales)	19.9	19.8	14.8	26.5	19.9
Marketing ROS (%)	44	21	15	14	24
Marketing ROI (%)	233	108	102	51	123
Financial Performance					
Return on Sales (%)	11.3	4.8	2.7	−0.7	5
Return on Equity (%)	61.7	30.3	6.9	−1.1	24
Return on Invested Capital (%)	28.5	12.3	5.2	−0.8	11

FIGURE 2-15 FINANCIAL PERFORMANCE AND MARKETING PROFITABILITY METRICS

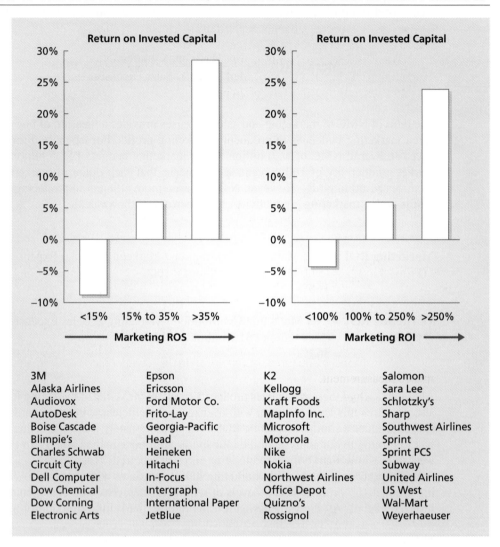

3M	Epson	K2	Salomon
Alaska Airlines	Ericsson	Kellogg	Sara Lee
Audiovox	Ford Motor Co.	Kraft Foods	Schlotzky's
AutoDesk	Frito-Lay	MapInfo Inc.	Sharp
Boise Cascade	Georgia-Pacific	Microsoft	Southwest Airlines
Blimpie's	Head	Motorola	Sprint
Charles Schwab	Heineken	Nike	Sprint PCS
Circuit City	Hitachi	Nokia	Subway
Dell Computer	In-Focus	Northwest Airlines	United Airlines
Dow Chemical	Intergraph	Office Depot	US West
Dow Corning	International Paper	Quizno's	Wal-Mart
Electronic Arts	JetBlue	Rossignol	Weyerhaeuser

all three overall financial performance metrics. Head is last in both marketing profitability metrics and last in all three overall financial performance metrics.

Profit Impact of Marketing Profitability Metrics

To further validate the profit impact of Marketing ROS and marketing productivity, we created the graphs shown in Figure 2-15 for the sample of companies shown. In most cases, marketing and sales expenses were not available. We had to use sales, general and administrative (SGA) expenses, of which marketing and sales expenses are the majority. Using this data, the bottom third in Marketing ROS achieved less than 15 percent ROS and earned an average return on invested capital (ROIC) of -9 percent. The middle third in Marketing ROS had an average ROIC of 4 percent. However, the top third in Marketing ROS produced an average ROIC of 28 percent corresponding to their average Marketing ROS greater than 35 percent.

ROIC also varied with different levels of marketing productivity. The bottom third in Marketing ROI (less than 100 percent) had a negative ROIC while the top third (greater than 250 percent) had an ROIC of 24 percent.

■ Summary

A market-based business engages in three important distinguishing practices:

1. It tracks market-based measures of marketing performance.
2. It measures marketing profits by product, market, or both.
3. It organizes around markets rather than products.

Without an external set of market-based performance metrics, a business will never know its market performance. For CommTech, an over-reliance on traditional measures of internal performance cost the business and its shareholders $122 million in net profits. Thus, an important step in becoming a market-based business is to develop a key set of external market-based measures of performance. These external market metrics can include in-process metrics, which typically precede financial performance measurement, and end-result market metrics, which are more likely to coincide with financial performance measurement.

To develop and implement marketing strategies that are going to increase customer satisfaction and grow profits, a business needs to be able to measure the profitability of a marketing decision. This means understanding the revenues that result from serving a target market of customers and all the costs associated with serving that market. A common problem that often arises in most accounting systems is the need to allocate overhead costs. This has the potential to distort profitability and can lead to erroneous decisions that actually reduce profitability. To grow profits, a business needs to grow net marketing contribution. Allocating overhead costs will distort the profitability picture. If the accountants persist in allocating overhead costs, simply ask that they be allocated after the NMC has been computed so that market-level profitability can be clearly observed.

Marketing strategies for growing net marketing contribution include growing market demand, increasing market share, lowering variable cost, and increasing market efficiency. To address the efficiency of marketing strategies, we introduced two marketing profitability metrics. Marketing ROS (NMC divided by sales) helps in evaluating the marketing profitability of alternative strategies or businesses when there is a large difference in sales. Marketing ROI (NMC divided by marketing and sales expenses) allows us to evaluate the productivity of different marketing strategies with respect to marketing profits and marketing investment. Both marketing profitability metrics were shown to have a strong relationship with financial performance as measured by a business's return on invested capital.

■ Market-Based Logic and Strategic Thinking

1 Why are market-based measures of performance critical to achieving profitable growth?
2 How do market-based measures of performance differ from internal measures of performance? Why are both necessary?
3 Why does a business need both internal (financial) measures of performance and external (market-based) measures of performance?
4 What roles do market-based measures of performance play in achieving profitable growth?
5 Why are performance metrics important?
6 What is the fundamental difference between a market performance metric and a financial performance metric?
7 Why are in-process metrics an important part of a successful marketing strategy? What is the relationship between in-process metrics and end-result metrics?
8 What are some of the fundamental differences between product-based accounting and customer-based accounting?
9 How does net marketing contribution enable a business to better understand the profit impact of a marketing strategy?
10 What is the difference between a variable cost and a fixed expense?
11 Why are marketing expenses considered semi-variable expenses and cost of goods sold a variable expense?
12 How can treatment of operating expenses distort interpretations of profitability?
13 How can one assess the profit impact of a specific marketing strategy?
14 Under what conditions would you expect operating expenses to change with changes in marketing strategies?
15 What fundamental marketing strategies can a business pursue to grow marketing profits?
16 Explain how any given marketing strategy might affect different components of net marketing contribution.
17 Why would a business want to measure its profitability by market segment?
18 How does a marketing profitability metric such as marketing ROS help in comparing the marketing profits of two competitors?
19 What does a Marketing ROS of 20 percent mean?
20 What does it mean when a competitor with approximately the same sales has a Marketing ROI of half as large?
21 Using Figures 2-12 and 2-13 explain how marketing ROS and marketing ROI relate to financial performance.

Marketing Performance Tools

Each of the following **marketing performance tools** can be accessed by going to *www.rogerjbest.com* or *www.prenhall.com/best*. The shaded cells are input cells. The non-shaded cells are computed information based on your input.

MARKETING PERFORMANCE TOOL—Marketing Profitability: A Product Focus

Product Name Area of Performance	Current Performance	Alternative Strategy	Difference
Market Demand	20,000,000	20,000,000	0
Market Share (%)	2.0	2.0	0.0
Unit Volume	400,000	400,000	0
Price per Unit ($)	25.00	25.00	0.00
Sales Revenues	10,000,000	10,000,000	0
Cost per Unit ($)	20.00	20.00	0.00
Margin per Unit ($)	5.00	5.00	0.00
Gross Profit ($)	2,000,000	2,000,000	0
Marketing & Sales Expenses ($)	1,000,000	1,000,000	0
Mktg & Sales Expenses (% Sales)	10.0	10.0	0.0
Net Marketing Contribution	$1,000,000	$1,000,000	0
Marketing ROS (%)	10.0	10.0	0.0
Marketing ROI (%)	100	100	0.0

This **marketing performance tool** allows you to evaluate marketing profitability dynamics from a *product-volume* perspective. Changes in any of the gray cells allow you to evaluate the performance impact of these changes or an alternative strategy. Outlined here is an application exercise to help you get started in using this marketing performance tool.

Application Exercise: How would the marketing profitability change if marketing and sales expenses rose to 12 percent in an effort to grow market share from 2 percent to 3 percent? Would it be more profitable to lower price by 10 percent (to $22.50) to grow market share to 3 percent?

MARKETING PERFORMANCE TOOL—Marketing Profitability: A Customer Focus

Market Segment Area of Performance	Current Performance	Alternative Strategy	Difference
Market Demand (customers)	8,000,000	8,000,000	0
Market Share (%)	6.0	6.00	0.0
Unit Volume	480,000	480,000	0
Revenue per Customer ($)	65.00	65.00	0.00
Sales Revenues ($)	31,200,000	31,200,000	0
Average Cost per Customer ($)	40.00	40.00	0.00
Margin per Unit ($)	25.00	25.00	0.00
Gross Profit ($)	12,000,000	12,000,000	0
Marketing & Sales Expenses ($)	4,500,000	4,500,000	0
Mktg & Sales Expenses (% Sales)	14.4	14.4	0.0
Net Marketing Contribution	$7,500,000	$7,500,000	0
Marketing ROS (%)	24.0	24.0	0.0
Marketing ROI (%)	167	167	0.0

This **marketing performance tool** allows you to evaluate marketing profitability dynamics from a *customer* perspective. Changes in any of the shaded cells allow you to evaluate the performance impact of these changes or an alternative strategy. Outlined here is an application exercise to help you get started in using this marketing performance tool.

Application Exercise: What would be the marketing profit impact of a strategy to increase marketing and sales expenses to 12 percent in an effort to grow market share from 6 percent to 7 percent? Or, would it be more profitable to lower prices by 10 percent (hence revenue per customer) to grow share to 7 percent?

Notes

1. Bradley Gale. "Tracking Competitive Position Drives Shareholder Value," *Global Management* (1992): 367–71.
2. Yuxin Chen, James Hess, Ronald Wilcox, and Z. John Zhang. "Accounting Profits Versus Marketing Profits: A Relevant Metric for Category Management," *Marketing Science*, 18, no. 3 (1999): 208–229.
3. Robert Kaplan and David Norton. "The Balanced Scorecard—Measures That Drive Performance," *Harvard Business Review* (January–February 1992): 71–79; and Robert Eccles. "The Performance Measurement Manifesto," *Harvard Business Review* (January–February 1991): 131–37.
4. George Cressman. "Choosing the Right Metric," *Drive Marketing Excellence* (November 1994), New York: Institute for International Research.
5. John Shank and Vijay Govindarajan. *Strategic Cost Analysis* (New York: Irwin, 1989): 99–112.
6. John Shank and Vijay Govindarajan. "The Perils of Cost Allocation Based on Production Volumes," *Accounting Horizons* 4 (1988): 71–79; and John Shank and Vijay Govindarajan. "Making Strategy Explicit in Cost Analysis: A Case Study," *Sloan Marketing Review* (Spring 1988): 15–30.
7. Michael Morris and Gene Morris. *Market-Oriented Pricing* (New York: NTC Business Books, 1990): 99–100; and Don Schultz, "Spreadsheet Approach to Measuring ROI for MCI," *Marketing News* 28 (February 1994): 12.
8. William Christopher. "Marketing Achievement Reporting: A Profitability Approach," *Industrial Marketing Management* (New York: Elsevier North Holland, Inc. 1977): 149–62; Patrick Dunne and Harry Wolk. "Marketing Cost Analysis: A Modularized Contribution," *Journal of Marketing* (July 1977): 83–94; Stanley Shapiro and V. H. Kirpalard. *Marketing Effectiveness: Insights from Accounting and Finance* (Needham Heights, MA: Allyn and Bacon, 1984): 377–424; and Jean-Claude Larreche and Hubert Gatignon. *MARKSTRAT* (New York: Scientific Press, 1990): 22–23.

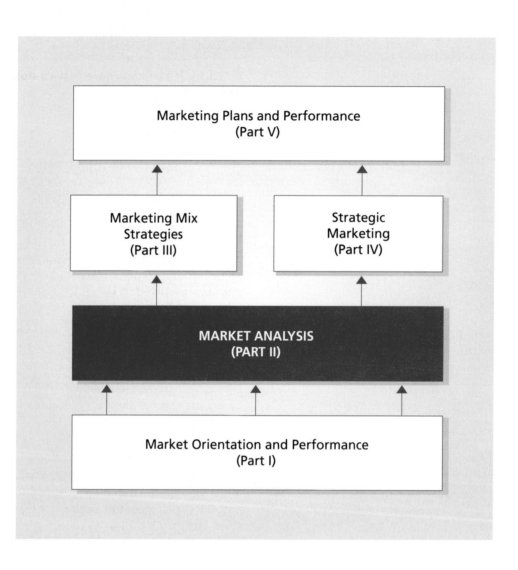

PART II

Market Analysis

■ "I made it a policy to never leave a store without talking to a customer."
— *James Cantalupo, CEO McDonald's*

■ "Everyone in business pays lip service to customer wants but Cantalupo attached to it an unwavering obsession with quantifying them. With a zeal for measuring the customer experience and sharing the data freely with store operators, he has pulled off a turnaround that has stunned everyone in the business with its speed and scope. In one year same store sales increased 20 percent, net profits increase 65 percent and McDonald's stock price doubled."*
— *Daniel Kruger*

Market analysis is an essential input to the development of market-based management strategies that deliver superior levels of customer satisfaction and profitability. The continuous pursuit of customer needs, ongoing monitoring of competitors' moves and capabilities, and tracking of market-based performance are the core competencies of market-focused business.

Part II includes four chapters that are built around the fundamental inputs of market analysis: market demand, customer analysis, market segmentation, and competitor analysis. Chapter 3 focuses on market definition, market potential, market demand, and market growth opportunities. However, markets do not buy products; customers buy products. Chapter 4 covers customer analysis and the discovery of benefits that deliver a superior value.

Because customers in any market differ in many ways, rarely can one marketing strategy adequately serve all their needs. Chapter 5 addresses needs-based market segmentation and the development of segment strategies. Finally, Chapter 6 focuses on competitor analysis, competitive position, and sources of competitive advantage.

*Daniel Kruger, "You Want Data With That?" *Forbes* (March 29, 2004): 57–60.

Market Potential, Market Demand, and Market Share

Perhaps the biggest threat to business survival, and a major cause of missed market opportunities, is a narrow focus on existing product-markets. Businesses that are unable to see the broader picture of customers, market demand, and the forces that shape unserved market demand are exposed to this risk.[1] Theodore Levitt's timeless perspective on marketing myopia applies today as well as it did when he first wrote on the subject more than 40 years ago:

> "A myopic vision of the potential markets a business might serve translates into a narrow product-focused market definition."[2]

Marketing leaders with a broad market vision usually see the world differently. Their view of market demand goes beyond a view of existing products and customers and enables them to see untapped or emerging market opportunities that others overlook or ignore. With unrestricted market vision, these businesses can move quickly to control their own destinies.[3]

In 1846 Church & Dwight Co. began selling sodium bicarbonate to help with cooking. For 120 years they developed *vertical market demand* with their Arm & Hammer brand Baking Soda, until they finally discovered its first *lateral market* application as a refrigerator deodorizer. Later they developed the vertical market demand for this application with packaging innovations that further improved product usage and stimulated demand.

Further product applications of Arm & Hammer Baking Soda were developed over the last 25 years in other lateral markets: carpet deodorizers, cat litter deodorizers, personal products, and household products as well as industrial and agricultural products. Shown in Figure 3-1 are product applications they have developed for lateral market applications of the basic Arm & Hammer Baking Soda. A broad view of their potential markets and sustained efforts to develop vertical and lateral market demand for their products has allowed the Church & Dwight Co. to enjoy long-term sales growth.

MARKET DEFINITION

At any point in time, there are *existing* customers who make up current market demand and *potential* customers who provide the opportunity for growing market demand. Over time the overall demand for a product or service is finite. A fixed number of customers buy at a certain rate of purchase; thus, there is a certain level of market demand, whether for fast food, personal computers, or automobiles.

FIGURE 3-1 ARM & HAMMER—VERTICAL AND LATERAL MARKET DEMAND

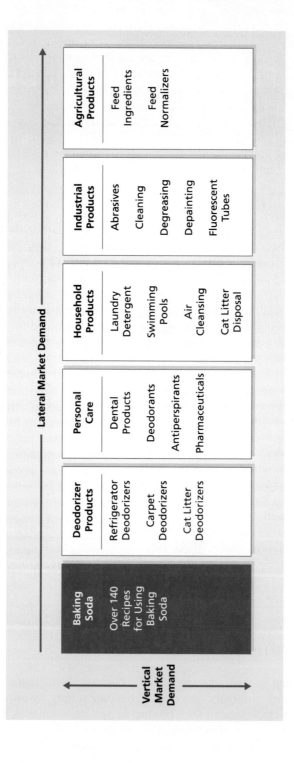

Potential customers help define the level of future market demand. In mature markets, the market potential (maximum number of customers) is close to the market demand (existing number of customers). In emerging or growing markets, market demand will grow as more customers enter the market. However, for a business to achieve a desired level of performance in a market, it needs to obtain a desired share of that market. To manage performance over time, a business needs to understand both vertical and lateral market demands for their products.

The cola wars of the 1980s lured soft drink manufacturers into a limited vision and, hence, a limited definition of their markets. Strategies to hold share and grow market demand in an intensely competitive market blurred their market vision. Although there is nothing inherently wrong with a narrow product-market focus, a restricted product-market focus limits a business's view of other market opportunities and competitive threats.

Many observers would agree that this limited focus was the only choice these manufacturers had because the loss of one market share point in the soft drink market is worth almost $600 million in retail sales. Losing one share point in this market has to hurt profits because marketing and overhead expenses are not likely to go down in the midst of a battle to hold market share. Thus, their aggressive moves to hold share could be legitimately defended.

The battle to hold share in the soft drink market, however, represents only one portion of the battlefield. Adjacent to this battlefield is a whole new set of competitive threats and market opportunities that have emerged over the last 25 years. As illustrated in Figure 3-2, these new product-markets include mineral waters, sports drinks, fruit juices, fruit drinks, and specialty tea and coffee products.

FIGURE 3-2 MARKET DEFINITION AND MARKET OPPORTUNITIES

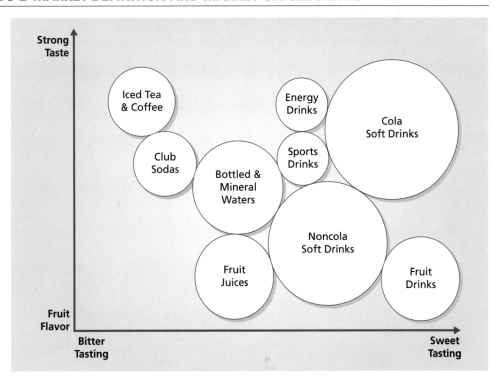

Because of their focus on the soft drink market, soft drink manufacturers were late to react to these new forms of competition. So where did the consumers of Perrier, Gatorade, Snapple, Ocean Spray, and New York Express Iced Coffee come from? Many came from the soft drink market into these new product-markets while others were drawn away from alcoholic beverages and hot-served coffees and teas. Collectively, these substitute products produce $30 billion in annual retail sales, approximately half that of the soft drink market. In response to these new market opportunities, Coca-Cola and Pepsi have aggressively entered these markets. They are working to better position themselves to gain share as these markets continue to grow at twice the rate of the soft drink market.

Broad Market Vision

The first step in understanding market demand is to develop a broad vision of what the market is. A market definition that is limited to a particular product focus maintains the status quo. A business with a narrow market focus sees only the *articulated needs* of served customers.[4] As shown in Figure 3-3, this will result in a limited level of full market potential as the served market moves left to right to penetrate the *unserved* portion of the narrow market definition. Businesses have an inclination to define their market based on the customers they see. This limits their thinking and the potential to grow their business outside their narrow view of served customers with an articulated need, leaving a vast untapped market opportunity.

A broad market vision encourages discovery of *unarticulated needs* and uncovers new *unserved* opportunities as illustrated in Figure 3-3. For Fred Smith, founder of Federal Express, a broad market focus meant a vision of overnight mail, new choices for customers,

FIGURE 3-3 MARKET DEFINITION AND UNTAPPED MARKET OPPORTUNITY

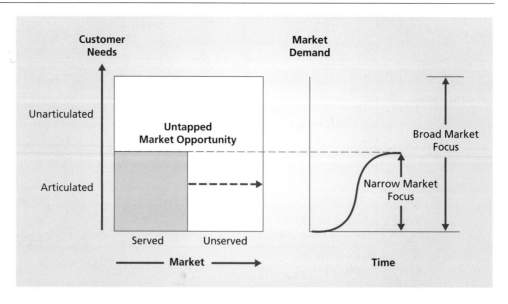

and a profitable business opportunity that bankers, professors, and industry experts could not envision and said would not work. For Phil Knight, founder of Nike, it meant a market vision for running and sports footwear as well as sports clothing—and for Bill Gates, cofounder of Microsoft, it meant a market vision of people using computers in a variety of ways.

To avoid a narrow market definition and the potential to restrict discovery of new market opportunities, a business needs a broad *strategic market definition*. This includes a broader definition of all product-markets that are potential substitutes for the product-markets currently served by the business. For example, the market definition for soft drinks could be limited to the soft drink product domain and not include important substitute product-markets.

A broader strategic market definition would include all relevant substitute products. The degree of substitutability in a broad strategic market definition is represented by the distance between markets.[5] The closer one market is to another, the greater the likelihood that customers will substitute one product for another. A broad strategic market definition enables managers to see a broader set of customer needs and potential new market opportunities. This ability, of course, provides a wider range of market-based strategies as management assesses which markets it would like to participate in, recognizing its own core competencies and capabilities.

Thus, a broad strategic market definition provides three key benefits to a market-based business:

- It opens the window of opportunity to a broader set of customer needs.
- It provides better understanding of potential substitutes and competitive threats.
- It helps a business better understand fundamental customer needs.

Vertical Versus Lateral Market Demand

With a broader market vision, a business is able to see more opportunities for growth. These broader market opportunities often exist within a *vertical* market and in adjacent *lateral* markets. Vertical markets represent market opportunities within a product-market definition.[6] For example, Nike started its company with a running shoe focused on amateur and professional runners. This narrow market definition allowed Nike to focus its efforts while a small start-up company. But as Nike penetrated this market they saw new vertical opportunities for apparel and equipment. They further advanced their vertical market definition of the running shoe market to include footwear, apparel, and equipment for women and kids as illustrated in Figure 3-4.

Lateral market opportunities in training and walking footwear, apparel, and equipment for men, women, and kids were a nature lateral market opportunity for the Nike product. However, subsequent moves into lateral markets such as baseball, basketball, football, golf, hiking, soccer, and tennis provided new market opportunities for sales growth as shown in Figure 3-4. Again, within each lateral market there were many vertical served market opportunities in footwear, apparel, and equipment for men, women, and kids. For women this even included products for pregnant women and women doing yoga exercises.

Lateral market demand serves as a complement to vertical market demand.[7] In fact, lateral market development cannot be fully developed without vertical market demand because vertical product line extensions will produce more product variations as lateral markets are developed. For example, Hero is a leading brand of cereal in Europe. With the cereal market fully developed, Hero developed a cereal bar by combining cereal with

FIGURE 3-4 VERTICAL AND LATERAL MARKET DEMAND

	Lateral Market Demand									
Markets	**Running**	**Training**	**Walking**	**Baseball**	**Basketball**	**Football**	**Golf**	**Hiking**	**Soccer**	**Tennis**
Men's										
Footwear										
Apparel										
Equipment										
Women's										
Footwear										
Apparel										
Equipment										
Kid's										
Footwear										
Apparel										
Equipment										

Vertical Market Demand (axis label, left side)

chocolate and caramel. Today, the Hero cereal bar is the market leader in this lateral market. For soft drink manufacturers, the various lateral markets in sports drinks, fruit juices, fruit drinks, energy drinks, and bottled water represent many opportunities for growth. For a computer company such as Dell, this has led to lateral market development in printers, software, storage devices, and services. For Honda, lateral market development led to snow blowers, jet skis, all-terrain vehicles, lawn and garden equipment and many other product-markets that extend beyond their core business in automobiles and motorcycles. However, companies without a broad market vision rarely take such opportunities seriously.

Served Market Definition

With a broad market definition, a business is in a better position to define the market domains in which it will compete. Recall that the primary determinant of market vision is the *fundamental customer need* being met. This fundamental customer need has a tremendous impact on how the business defines its market and the size of the market it will develop and serve. A *served market* is defined as the market in which a business competes for target customers.[8] It includes both the business's and its competitors' customers.

For example, the served market for Lexus is much different from that for Tercel, though both are Toyota products. Each has a separate and distinct set of customers and competitors that make up unique served markets. The automotive market, while broadly defined as a transportation market, is made up of many smaller served markets based on the unique needs of customers for price and car benefits. Likewise, a broad market definition of the beer market has enabled Anheuser-Busch to create several served market definitions. As the beer market matured, it fragmented into many new market opportunities along with new types of customers and competitors. It required a broad market vision and more than one served market definition to effectively manage penetration of these new market opportunities.

MARKET POTENTIAL

Once a served market definition has been established, a business is in a better position to understand several important aspects of market demand. The first, and most crucial, is how many customers make up the maximum potential for this market definition.[9] This perspective creates a sharp contrast between a product-focused and a market-based business.

> A product-focused business is interested in product volume, whereas a market-based business is interested in how many customers make up a market.

Product volume and sales revenues can vary with customer behavior and competitive strategies. However, the potential number of customers within a market domain is a finite number of great strategic significance because it places the true upper limit on the number of consuming units.

For example, what is the market potential for disposable diapers? The number of babies between newborn and 2 years of age might be a reasonable estimate of the maximum number of consuming units. However, do all households with children in this age bracket purchase disposable diapers? No! Some cannot afford them; others oppose them because of their negative environmental impact; still others may simply prefer the advantages they see in cloth diapers. Thus, the number of consuming units is almost always less than the maximum market potential (maximum number of customers).

Untapped Market Opportunities

Many new markets and most global markets are well below their full market potential; that is, there are large numbers of possible customers who have not yet entered the market. For example, the market potential (maximum number) for personal computers is estimated to be 250 million per year, and the market is expected to reach saturation by 2010. At this time there will be an estimated installed base of one billion personal computers. In 2001, the level of market penetration (131.5 million PCs) was slightly over 50 percent, as illustrated in Figure 3-5—but, one could ask, why will it take so long for this market to reach its full market potential? There are five major forces that can restrict a market from reaching its full potential, as illustrated in Figure 3-6.

Awareness

This means not just *product awareness* but *complete comprehension of benefits.* If potential customers are unaware of a product or do not fully or accurately understand its benefits, then they will not be fully informed and they will be unable to discern the product's potential value to them. For the personal computer, most potential customers in a worldwide market would be aware of the product, but many may not fully comprehend the benefits. Because the product is complex and experiential, many of the benefits are understood only after a period of use.

FIGURE 3-5 PERSONAL COMPUTER MARKET DEVELOPMENT

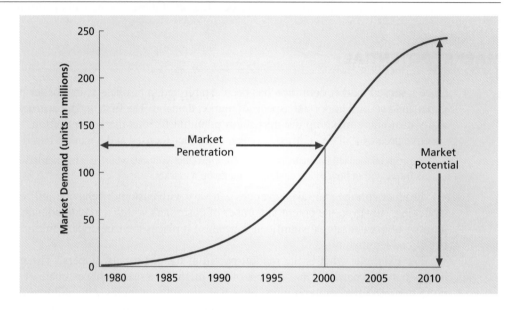

Availability

A second force that can restrict market demand is *availability*. For most mature markets, product availability is not a significant force that restricts market demand. However, lack of availability of products in short supply, difficulties in making products available, or a lack of services to support their use, can all contribute to reduced market demand. Many people can readily purchase personal computers, but services to support them might not be available in many geographic markets.

Ability to Use

The inability to use a product can also restrict expansion of a market to its full potential. People in many parts of the world would benefit from the use of a personal computer, but if you do not have electricity, you cannot use one even when the product is available. Perhaps more important, the ability to use a personal computer requires a certain level of specialized education. In response to this need, businesses such as Apple Computer and Microsoft have funded educational programs that should contribute to the market development of the personal computer market.

Benefit Deficiency

For some consumers, the benefits of a given type of product are not attractive or compelling enough for them to enter the market. For others, such as those consumers who oppose disposable diapers for environmental reasons, the benefit proposition is simply deficient and not strong enough to stimulate purchase even if the product is available and affordable and a proper use situation exists. Because consumers have a wide range of

FIGURE 3-6 MAXIMUM MARKET POTENTIAL AND CURRENT MARKET DEMAND

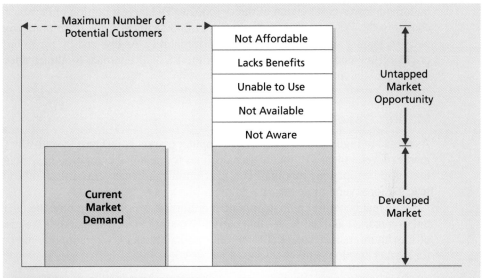

FORCES THAT LIMIT MARKET DEMAND

- *Awareness:* These potential customers would buy the product if they knew it was available and accurately understood its benefits.
- *Availability:* Potential customers are aware, able to buy, and have the desire to buy, but this product or service is not available in their geographic market.
- *Ability to Use:* Although the product is affordable and attractive, customers are not able to use it because of the use environment in which they operate. These customers lack the knowledge, other resources, and/or requirements to make the product or service workable.
- *Benefit Deficiency:* The key benefits of the product or service are not important (or are even unattractive) to a subset of potential customers.
- *Affordability:* Regardless of product attractiveness or perceived benefits, the cost is simply too high for some consumers.

product and lifestyle needs, it may be difficult to accommodate all the needs and desired benefits in any given market, so there is a practical limit that may restrict any market from reaching its maximum market potential. For example, many older people may not see a benefit in owning a personal computer (PC). However, with the expansion of e-mail and Internet home shopping, this growing segment of the population could become an important source of new customer growth that would contribute to further development of the PC market.

Affordability

Finally, many of the products some people take for granted are simply not affordable for others. Although the benefits are known and attractive, the product is too expensive given the income available to many potential customers. Once again, businesses with narrowly focused product orientation will never see beyond their current customer market. As a result, they will never challenge their engineers and production managers with the task of building a lower-cost version of their products. The largest portion of new customer purchases in the PC market is in the under $1,000 segment. This price point triggered the entry of a new group of buyers based on affordability. As low-end PC prices approach the prices of low-end televisions and VCRs, the PC will continue to attract price-sensitive buyers into the market.

Market Development Index

As shown in Figure 3-5, the personal computer market is just past the halfway point in its market development. Although price declines for personal computers have contributed to market development, this market's maximum market potential probably will not be reached for several more years.

The real benefit of a broader market definition is in knowing both the overall potential of a market and the forces that currently restrict market demand. If we create a ratio of maximum market potential to current market demand, we can index the opportunity for market development.

$$\textbf{Market Development Index} = \frac{\text{Current Market Demand}}{\text{Maximum Market Demand}} \times 100$$

A market development index (MDI) of less than 33, for example, would suggest that there is considerable growth potential.

The first third of the market potential can generally be served with higher prices and basic benefits. To bring more customers into the market, businesses have to lower prices, offer a wider range of product alternatives, and expand distribution to increase availability. When the market development index is between 33 and 67, development of the market is based on addressing benefit deficiencies and price reductions that bring more customers into the market at a more affordable price.

When the market development index rises above 67, there is still considerable opportunity for growth. However, the task will be more difficult because the business faces the more difficult causes that restrict full market development. These forces are likely to include affordability, benefit deficiency, and inability to use. Overcoming these hurdles requires real market-based, customer-focused solutions. Though a tougher marketing task, developing this untapped portion of customers provides a more differentiated position and one that competitors may find hard to copy. While the challenge may be greater, the rewards of market ownership could also be greater.

Market Potential and Market Growth

Recognizing that every market has some upper limit (its market potential), marketing people are intrigued by the question of how fast the market will grow as it expands to its full potential. Shown in Figure 3-7 are the market growth curves for several products. The upper limit in each case represents the market potential for each product-market. The rate at which customers enter a market is a market-specific phenomenon based on product

FIGURE 3-7 MARKET PENETRATION AND MARKET DEVELOPMENT INDEX

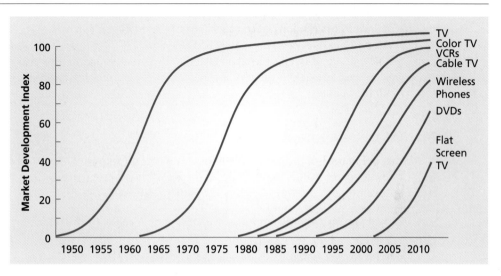

attractiveness, customer characteristics, and marketing efforts.[10] However, the early pattern established by the rate of customer entry into a market provides sufficient information to project the market growth rate accurately in most instances.[11]

Three fundamental forces capture the shape of the market growth curve and hence the rate of market growth:

1. **Market Potential:** The maximum number of customers who can enter the market given a specific served market definition.
2. **Market Penetration:** The total number of customers who have entered that market at a specific point in time.
3. **Rate of Entry:** The rate at which new customers enter the market.

These three forces define the shape and parameters of a market's customer attraction and growth. Some markets grow faster and reach their full potential much faster than others, but why? What would make some product-markets grow at a fast rate and others at a comparatively slow rate? The next section addresses these questions and provides marketing strategies that can be developed to accelerate market growth.

Rate of Market Development

New markets depend on finding new customers. Most potential customers are not going to be the first to buy a new product. New products are often higher priced, more complex, and less accepted by mainstream society than are established products. As a result, a variety of risks are associated with being among the first buyers of a new product or technology. Emerging markets are initially relatively small and made up of *innovators* and *early adopters*, as shown in Figure 3-8. In general, customers who make up the *early market* possess more knowledge, are less price sensitive, more benefit driven, and less dependent on what others do or think than most people. These *lead customers* are critical. If they

FIGURE 3-8 CUSTOMER ADOPTION AND MARKET DEVELOPMENT

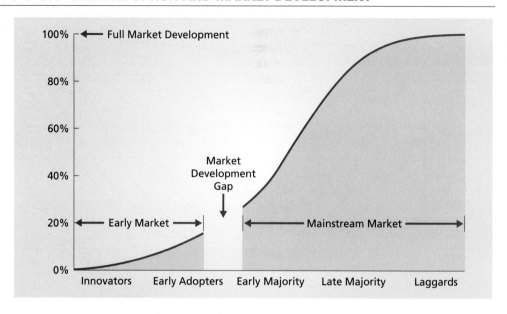

cannot be attracted, satisfied, and retained, the market is likely to die because the main-stream market will not buy if the lead customers do not. The first job in successfully developing a new product-market is to identify lead customers and penetrate the early market.

For a new market to move from the *early market* to the *mainstream market* requires the development of *complete solutions*.[12] Although customers in the early market are willing to struggle to make new products workable, those in the mainstream market are less willing to put up with less-than-complete solutions; they want a 100 percent solution. To successfully reach the mainstream market, a business needs to create a complete solution—one that has all the necessary features, functions, and supporting products and services.[13]

Unfortunately, there is one more challenge. The mainstream market comprises many segments, and each has a different view of what it considers a complete solution.[14] To successfully reach the mainstream market, a business must carefully identify its target customers and focus on the delivery of what those target customers consider a complete solution. However, just as there are lead customers in the early market, there are *lead segments* in the mainstream market. As a result, further success in the mainstream market is partially dependent on the influence of one segment over another. The more quickly businesses address the complete solution needed to close the *market development gap* shown in Figure 3-8, the faster the market grows.

Accelerating Market Growth

Developing and delivering a complete solution requires more than further product development. The rate at which the mainstream market adopts a new product also depends on customer characteristics, product positioning, and market influences. Given adequate product awareness and availability, a number of forces can act to accelerate or slow customer attraction and the rate of market growth.[15] As shown in Figure 3-9, there are 6 customer adoption forces and 6 product adoption forces affecting new product-market penetration.

Customer Adoption Forces

Customer adoption forces are one dimension of the forces that shape the rate at which customers enter a market. First, customers must feel a need for the product, and the strength of that felt need can vary. When the *felt need* for a product is low, customer attraction will be slow. For years, many potential customers simply did not feel a strong need to have a microwave oven and the lack of a felt need slowed the rate at which customers entered this product-market. Also, many people perceived a safety risk with microwave ovens, and this perception also slowed market growth. Customer perceptions of risk can include a variety of *perceived risk* factors such as perceived safety, social, and economic risk.

A third customer factor is the nature and size of the *decision-making unit*. Group decisions, whether in a business or in a family, slow the rate of customer entry. Individual decision makers are less likely to be inhibited by others and are freer to make decisions quickly. In addition, the market demand for products that are *easily observed*, such as a Walkman, color TV, or fashionable sunglasses, grows faster than for products that are less observable, such as household cleaners, insurance programs, or bed sheets. Also, the easier it is to try a product without buying, the faster its rate of market penetration. The Walkman is both *observable* and *easy to try*. Insurance programs are difficult to observe and cannot be tried without purchasing the product. When the product is easily observed and it is easily tried or sampled, market penetration is accelerated. Finally, when word-of-mouth communication is positive and users are inclined to recommend the product, market penetration is also accelerated.

We can develop a customer adoption index by estimating the market penetration for each of the customer forces outlined in Figure 3-9. This helps gauge the rate of market penetration. Naturally, the higher the overall percentage, the more rapid the market penetration. In our example, the customer adoption forces for flat-panel displays are favorable (63 percent). This will contribute to an above-average rate of market penetration should the product adoption forces not offset this rate of market penetration.

Product Adoption Forces

The strength of a product's positioning (its relative benefits) also plays a key role in the rate of market growth. The stronger the *relative advantage* and the more *affordable the price*, the greater the customer value created by the product and the faster the rate of customer market entry. However, this is the point at which many businesses stop. They do not follow through and examine more closely the *perceived complexity* and *ease of use* perceived by potential customers. If the product is not compatible with the way things are normally done or it is difficult to use, customers may be reluctant to try or purchase the product.

FIGURE 3-9 MANAGING THE RATE OF MARKET—FLAT PANEL DISPLAYS

Percent	Customer Influence	Customer Forces Affecting the Rate on New Product-Market Penetration Percent of Customers Who . . .
80	Felt Need	Have a strong, recognized need for this product
90	Personal Risk	Perceive little or no economic, social, or safety risk associated with owning or using this product
30	Buying Decision	Can buy the product relatively easily with little or no input from others
67	Observable	Can easily observe this product in use prior to purchase
30	Trialability	Can try or sample the product prior to purchase
80	Recommend	Who would recommend this product to others
63	Average	Customer Adoption Score

Percent	Product Influence	Product Forces Affecting the Rate on New Product-Market Penetration Percent of Customers Who . . .
90	Product Advantage	Believe this product offers a discernable advantage over existing products
20	Affordable Price	Feel the price of the product is affordable given their buying power
60	Easy to Use	Feel this product is not overly complex and would be easy to use
60	Performance Risk	Feel there is little or no chance the product will fail to perform as advertised
80	Availability	Feel the product is readily available at the point of purchase preferred by customers
20	Customer Service	Feel there is sufficient after-sales services in place to support any after-purchase problems
55	Average	Product Adoption Score

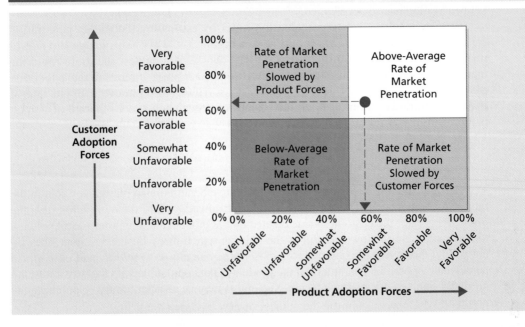

When first introduced, the microwave oven had some attractive benefits although it was expensive. However, many people did not buy a microwave oven because they thought they were too complex and hard to use—they required a different way of cooking. For many high-tech products, the relative advantages are enormous, but the perceived complexity and the difficulty in using them can deter customers and hinder market demand. If a product does not offer a complete solution, potential customers are reluctant to enter a market. To accelerate customer market entry, a business needs to ensure that all related products and services are available to create a complete solution. Mainstream customers want "plug-in" solutions that are easy to use. Finally, lack of product availability and after-sales customer service can be *product-adoption killers*. Products must be available where target customers prefer to buy, whether at specialty stores, department or wholesale stores such as Costco or Wal-Mart, or Internet store sites. Also, new products present new customer challenges. Without sufficient after-sales customer support, a new product could be doomed by bad word-of-mouth communication when customers encounter problems or cannot achieve desired product performance.

In Figure 3-9 we projected the customer adoption forces for flat-panel displays at an overall index of 63 percent. The product adoption index is estimated to be 55 percent. Both are above average, which may help explain the annual rate of new-product adoption of 65 percent per year. Unit sales of 4 million displays in 2003 are projected to grow to 30 million in 2007. Although this is above-average growth, market penetration could be accelerated at an even higher rate by addressing "trialability" and "customer service." Marketing strategies to encourage in-store viewing could improve trial usage, while a more extensive after-sale customer service program could also accelerate market penetration.

Market Demand

Based on the rate of market development, at any point in time the market demand for a product is made up of new customers to the market and existing customers who continue to purchase the product. For example, the market demand for PCs in any given year is a combination of first-time customers and existing customers. Existing customers repurchase at an average rate of every 4 to 5 years. As shown, in 2005 the total market demand for PCs is projected to be 200 million units. Market demand in 2005 is made up of 125 million replacement purchases from existing customers and 75 million first-time PC buyers. Five years earlier (in 2000), half of the purchases were replacement purchases and half were first-time buyers. Thus, we can sense that the market growth is slowing. In fact, by 2010 the PC market is projected to reach maturity at a market demand of 275 million units per year.

$$\frac{\text{Market Demand}}{\text{(year 2005)}} = \frac{\text{Replacement Purchases}}{\text{(average 1999 and 2000)}} + \frac{\text{New Customer Purchases}}{\text{(entering market in 2005)}}$$
$$= \qquad 125 \text{ million} \qquad + \qquad 75 \text{ million}$$
$$= \qquad 200 \text{ million}$$

Projecting Future Market Demand

Market demand in 2010 will be the result of repeat purchases made in 2005 and 2006. Using the estimates of replacement purchases and projected market demand in 2010 shown in Figure 3-10, we can estimate the number of new customer purchases by computing the

FIGURE 3-10 MARKET DEMAND FOR PERSONAL COMPUTERS

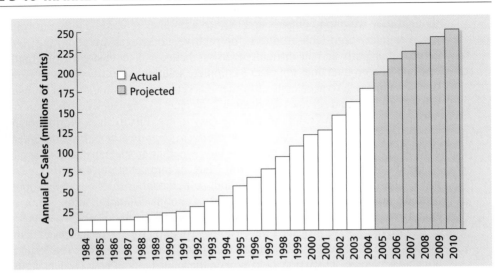

difference between the projected volume to be sold and the projected replacement purchases. This is estimated to be 40 million new customer purchases. When combined, the replacement market demand in 2010 will be estimated to equal the market potential of 250 million units per year. As the PC market demand approaches its market potential, the number of new customers will diminish until the market demand is almost entirely replacement purchases.

Combining the number of existing customers, their rate of repurchase, and new unit sales, one can create the market demand forecast shown in Figure 3-10.

Market Demand	Replacement Purchases		New Customer Purchases
(year 2010)	= (average 2005 and 2006)	+	(entering market in 2010)
	= 210 million	+	40 million
	= 250 million		

PRODUCT LIFE CYCLE

In Figure 3-11 we can clearly see the introductory and growth stages of a product life cycle. As the market demand approaches the market potential, growth will slow. Eventually the market will become a mature market with little or no growth, as shown in Figure 3-11. This is critical because the volume in any given year of the product life cycle is derived from both market demand and market share. When market demand ceases to grow, gains in volume can only be achieved with gains in market share. When a market enters the decline phase of the product life cycle, declining volumes are inevitable.

FIGURE 3-11 PRODUCT LIFE CYCLE AND MARKETING PROFITABILITY

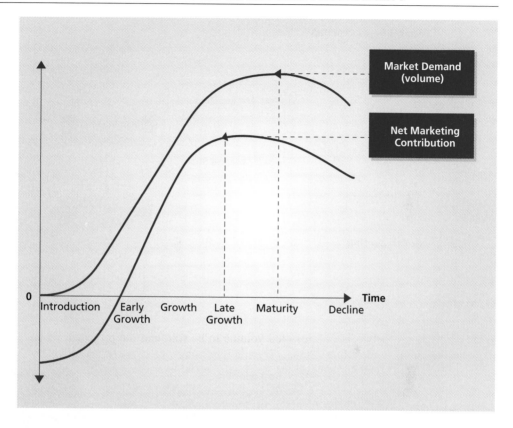

In addition to changes in volume over the product life cycle, there are important changes in the average selling price and average cost per unit. As shown in Figure 3-12, prices, unit costs, and margins per unit decline over the product life cycle. In general, market demand and volume are increasing faster than margins are decreasing. This allows gross profit to grow during the growth stage of the product life cycle.

Market Demand, Prices, and Marketing Expenses

Although a business's volume is the result of market demand and market share, a business has to spend money on marketing and sales to achieve a market share. In the early stages of the product life cycle, the marketing and sales expense is greater than the gross profit because volumes are small. This results in a negative net marketing contribution, as shown in Figure 3-11. As the business moves into the growth stage, it is able to reach a breakeven NMC (where gross profit equals marketing and sales expenses). Beyond that point, NMCs grow and normally peak in the late growth stage of the product life cycle.

As a market matures, the combination of flat market demand, lower margins, and high marketing and sales expenses results in a lower NMC, as Figure 3-11 showed. In the decline stage, marketing profits will continue to decline with decreases in market demand despite efforts to milk the product for profits while reducing marketing and sales expenditures.

FIGURE 3-12 PC MARKET DEMAND, PRICES, AND MARKETING PROFITABILITY

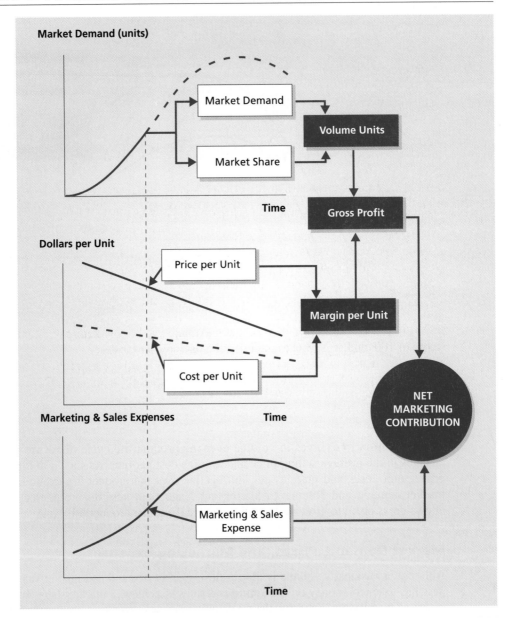

Product Life Cycle and Marketing Profitability

Figure 3-13 provides a good illustration of how profits vary over the product life cycle. We can see the impact market growth had on marketing profits throughout the 1990s despite price erosion and increased spending on marketing and sales. Profits in the PC market are projected to peak in 2005 in the late stages of growth. This is when PC manufacturers

FIGURE 3-13 PC MARKET DEMAND, PRICES, AND MARKETING PROFITABILITY

PC Market Performance	1990	1995	2000	2005	2010
Market Demand (units)	24,000,000	58,000,000	128,000,000	197,000,000	250,000,000
Average Selling Price	$2,971	$2,690	$1,938	$1,675	$1,450
Industry Sales (millions)	$71,304	$156,020	$248,064	$329,975	$362,500
Average Margin (%)	45	30	22	18	15
Industry Gross Profit (millions)	$32,087	$46,806	$54,574	$59,396	$54,375
Marketing & Sales (% Sales)	25	20	15	12	10
Net Marketing Contribution (millions)	$14,261	$15,602	$17,364	$19,799	$18,125

should experience their best profits. As the PC market moves into maturity, demand will grow much more slowly and price competition to hold or gain market share will cause marketing profits to decline.

To recognize how marketing profits vary over the product life cycle, it is useful to have an index of product life cycle profitability to help gauge current and future product life cycle profits. In Figure 3-14, we have created a marketing profitability score for each of six stages of the product life cycle based on marketing profitability illustrated in Figures 3-11 and 3-12. A single product would obtain a single score. For example, if a product were in its growth stage, it would get a score of 60. As this product moves into its late growth, the product would reach its maximum level of marketing profitability with a score of 100, and as it reaches maturity, the profit index would drop to 80.

For a business with several products at different stages of the product life cycle, we can use the percentage of sales at each stage to compute an overall product life cycle

FIGURE 3-14 PRODUCT LIFE CYCLE PROFITABILITY INDEX

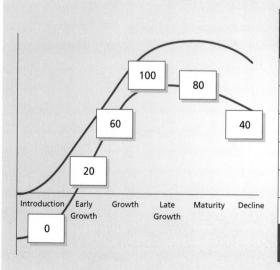

Stage of Product Life Cycle	Profit Index	Percent of Sales	Weighted Average
Decline	40	10	4
Maturity	80	45	36
Late Growth	100	10	10
Growth	60	15	9
Early Growth	20	10	2
Introduction	0	10	0
Product Life Cycle	Profit	Index	61

profit index. In Figure 3-14 we have a distribution of sales that covers all but six stages of the product life cycle. The weighted average based on percent of sales yields product life cycle profit index of 61. As product sales change over the product life cycle, the product life cycle profit index will shift. Using the product life cycle profit index, businesses can better plan profits and manage new product introductions to meet both short- and long-run profitability objectives for their business or product lines.

Generic Product Life Cycle Versus Individual Product Life Cycles

The PC market demand we have described outlines the generic product life cycle for a product-market category such as personal computers. This is by no means the same as the average product life cycle for a given product. For example, as the PC market grew, Intel has gone through entire product life cycles for several products as illustrated in Figure 3-15.

As markets evolve, they are supported by an evolution of products that also go through a life cycle. Shown in Figure 3-15 is the PC market demand over the product life for six generations of Intel products. In each case, there was an emerging market period followed by a period of rapid growth. New customers entering the market plus expanding purchase amounts by existing customers in this case drove growth. In this example, each product life cycle had a very rapid growth phase followed by a very short mature stage and then a stage of rapid decline in market demand.

All of these product life cycles had similar durations (less than 10 years), and each subsequent product achieved a higher level of life cycle demand. Furthermore, there was an overlap between product life cycles. This type of market growth and product life cycle behavior is typical of many high-tech product-markets. However, many more mature markets, such as the automotive, commercial aircraft, and housing markets, have much longer product life cycles. Growth in these markets is largely dependent on increases in the population and favorable economic factors that affect customer purchase behavior.

**FIGURE 3-15 INTEL PRODUCT LIFE CYCLES VERSUS GENERIC LIFE CYCLE
FOR MICROPROCESSORS**

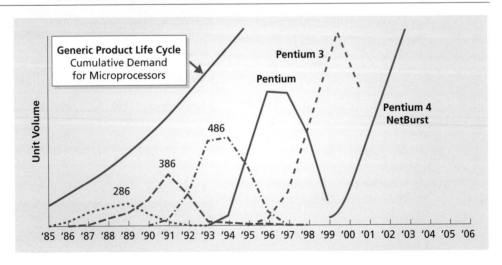

MARKET SHARE AND SHARE POTENTIAL

The potential of a market, its growth rate, and the shape of the product life cycle provide key insights into current and future market demand. A business needs to translate this information into a sales forecast of unit volume. Somebody has to decide how much to produce and how big a manufacturing operation to build. A business's estimate of sales volume can have a dramatic impact on profitability. If the unit volume forecast is correct and a plant with the right level of capacity is built, total production volume will be near plant capacity, and the best production economies will be achieved. On the other hand, if a business overbuilds capacity, manufacturing overheads will be higher and lower overall profits will result. If the business under builds capacity because of poor sales planning, it will forgo a great deal of potential profit due to lost customer sales.

A first step in developing a good estimate of sales is to develop a good estimate of market demand. The market demand sets an upper limit on sales. If a business had a 100 percent market share, then its sales would equal the total market demand. Following this logic, a business's sales are equal to the product of its market share and market demand, as shown here:

$$\text{Volume (units)} = \text{Market Demand(units)} \times \text{Market Share}$$

As an example, Dell Computer sold approximately 14.5 million PCs in 2000. This was based on Dell's 11.2 percent share of a market demand of 130 million PCs. Over the next 3 years, the market grew to 160 million units while Dell grew its market share to 14.2 percent. The combination of market growth and share growth produced 22.7 million units in 2003 as shown here.

$$\text{Dell Unit Sales (2000)} = 130 \text{ million} \times 11.2\% = 14.5 \text{ million units}$$
$$\text{Dell Unit Sales (2003)} = 160 \text{ million} \times 14.2\% = 22.7 \text{ million units}$$

Dell's future sales will depend on the same two factors: market demand and market share. If Dell can hold market share as market demand grows to 200 million by 2005, Dell's unit sales will increase to 28.4 million. To the degree that Dell can also grow market share over this period of time, Dell will exceed this level of unit sales.

$$\text{Dell Unit Sales (2005)} = 200 \text{ million} \times 14.2\% = 28.4 \text{ million units}$$

Share Development Tree

Although market share estimation can involve a complex set of mathematical propositions, there is a simple marketing logic that provides a reasonable estimate of what a business's market share should be. Figure 3-16 shows how market share can be estimated from a set of hierarchical market share effects. Each step along the *share development path* indicates how customer response influences market share.[16] Because many other factors can also affect actual market share, the market share index is simply an indicator of what market share *should* be given certain expected levels of market performance.

FIGURE 3-16 MARKET SHARE DEVELOPMENT TREE

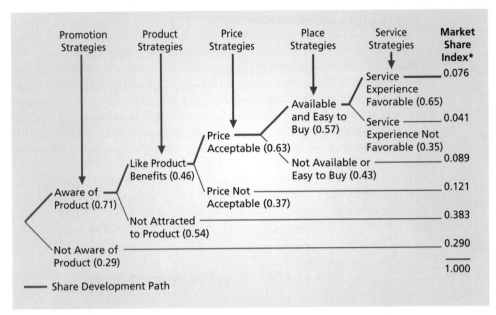

* The Market Share index is derived by multiplying all terms along a given path.

Each step along the share development path and its impact on share are explained in the remainder of this section.

As shown in Figure 3-16, the share development path traces a hierarchy of market share effects that leads to a particular level of indexed market penetration. Perhaps most important is that the overall share index is the interaction between effects. Should one perform poorly, the overall index will perform poorly. Further, each share effect is derived from a particular component of what we call the "marketing mix." The marketing mix for a given group of target customers includes:

Market Share = Promotion × Product × Price × Place × Service

- **Promotion** strategies intend to create awareness of a product and its benefits.
- **Product** positioning strategies build around benefits designed to create product attractiveness and preferences.
- **Price** strategies are designed to enhance intentions to buy based on a price that creates an attractive customer value.
- **Place** strategies ensure that there is adequate availability and service to facilitate purchase.
- **Service** strategies are intended to enhance customer satisfaction and retain customers.

As shown in Figure 3-16, each of these marketing mix factors creates a different impact on target customer response and share development. In managing market share, a business must develop a successful strategy for each element of the marketing mix.

Product Awareness

The first share effect in the share development tree is product *awareness*: the percentage of the market that is aware of the product. For mature products such as Coca-Cola, Kodak film, or Ford cars, product awareness is not an issue because virtually all target market customers know about the company's product. However, if a business has low awareness, then its market share is limited by a marketing communications problem.

In the early 1980s, Hewlett-Packard began to think about products such as computers and printers for the consumer market. HP had already established its name in the consumer market to some degree with HP calculators, so it thought awareness would not be an issue. However, a survey of U.S. households in the early 1980s showed that less than 10 percent had any awareness of Hewlett-Packard.

Awareness is a particular problem for many industrial and commercial businesses. They rely mostly on specialized advertising, trade shows, sales promotions, and sales calls to communicate their product positioning and generate awareness. Consumer goods manufacturers are better able to utilize a variety of mass media and in-store merchandising techniques to build awareness of their products. Nevertheless, the first marketing challenge in building market share, whether as a consumer goods business or as a manufacturer of capital equipment, is to build a broad base of product awareness among target market customers.

Product Attractiveness

Even if target customers are aware of a product, the product needs to be *attractive* to target customers; that is, target customers have to have favorable attitudes and interest in the product and the benefits it offers at a particular price. If customers are indifferent or negative, the purchase path is short circuited and market share is dramatically reduced, as illustrated in Figure 3-16. When this is the case, there is little chance of gaining market share from these customers. In the example presented in Figure 3-16, 71 percent of the target market customers are aware of the product, but only 46 percent of these customers prefer it (find it attractive). As a result, a significant portion of the business's share potential is lost.

This marketing problem is most likely a product-positioning problem. Well-positioned products with attractive benefits and price are likely to be in the customer's choice set; products that are not well positioned are simply not considered in a purchase decision. Of course, if there are few close substitutes, then it is easier to capture a higher percentage of favorable predispositions. For IBM in the personal computer market, the product differentiation between IBM and competitors decreased and the number of competitors increased throughout the late 1980s and into the 1990s. As a result, it was difficult to hold a dominant position as the most favored PC manufacturer. The percentage of customers preferring IBM over other personal computers declined, as did IBM's market share.

Price Acceptable

While a product can be attractive, its price also has to be at an *acceptable* level for customers to have high intentions to purchase. When intentions to buy are low, this could mean the price is too high or there are factors other than price that lower intentions to purchase. Even when prices are acceptable, customers are not always able to switch or to buy immediately. Understanding why these customers have low intentions to buy when interested in a product could uncover a creative marketing solution that would help grow share. In the example shown in Figure 3-16, 63 percent of the customers who are aware of the product and are attracted to it also intend to purchase. Those customers who do not intend to purchase cost the business another 12 percent of its potential market share. To stimulate intentions to purchase, a business may have to give the customers extra incentives to purchase its product. This is a situation where sales promotion programs can be a valuable marketing tool to offset high price barriers and to stimulate trial usage. Once customers have tried the product, we would hope that they would be able to more fully comprehend the product's benefits. In addition, buy-back programs, rebates, and customer financing could provide customer solutions when attractiveness is high but intentions to buy are low.

Product Availability

A fourth share management factor in building market share is product *availability*. If potentially interested customers seek a product and cannot find it at their preferred point of purchase, there is a loss of potential market share. As shown in Figure 3-16, the lack of product availability results in an 8.9 percent reduction in potential market share. If a business could succeed in building its availability to customers intending to buy from 57 percent to 70 percent, it could increase its overall market share index from 7.6 percent to 9.3 percent.

Service Experience

Finally, while the share development path shown in Figure 3-16 takes a customer to the point of purchase, a bad *service experience* can negate the entire marketing effort. Most banks and grocery stores have high awareness, the same products, similar prices, and convenient locations, so service is often the determining factor in customer purchase. Most customer dissatisfaction occurs as a result of poor customer service. As shown in Figure 3-16, only 65 percent of the potential customers who could buy this product had a positive service experience. Increasing this market metric to 80 percent would improve the company's market share index from 7.6 percent to 9.4 percent.

Market Share Index

If we follow the share development path from awareness to product preference, intention to purchase, product availability, and actual purchase, we can create a *market share index*. The market share index is the product of these five share performance factors along the share development path shown in Figure 3-16. In this example, a market share index of 0.076 is derived as follows:

$$\begin{aligned}
\begin{matrix}\textbf{Market}\\ \textbf{Share}\\ \textbf{Index}\end{matrix} &= \begin{matrix}\textbf{Product}\\ \textbf{Awareness}\end{matrix} \times \begin{matrix}\textbf{Product}\\ \textbf{Preference}\end{matrix} \times \begin{matrix}\textbf{Intention}\\ \textbf{to Buy}\end{matrix} \times \begin{matrix}\textbf{Product}\\ \textbf{Availability}\end{matrix} \times \begin{matrix}\textbf{Product}\\ \textbf{Purchase}\end{matrix}\\
&= \quad 0.71 \quad \times \quad 0.46 \quad \times \quad 0.63 \quad \times \quad 0.57 \quad \times \quad 0.65\\
&= 0.076 \ \ (7.6\%)
\end{aligned}$$

Although a business's actual market share may be slightly higher or lower, this market share index is a reasonable approximation. It provides us three important benefits:

1. It helps identify important sources of lost market share opportunity.
2. It provides a mechanism to assess the market share change when a certain level of improvement is directed in a key area of poor performance.
3. It enables us to estimate what might be a reasonable market share potential, given reasonable levels of performance in each area along the purchase path.

Share Potential and Market Share Management

Summarized in Figure 3-17 are the marketing performance gaps between actual customer response and *desired* customer response along the share development path. For each area of performance, the performance gap highlights the degree to which market share is lost along the purchase path. On the basis of the performance gaps shown in Figure 3-17, a business could estimate the share and revenue loss due to below-expected levels of share performance. For example, assume that a business serves a $500 million market and has a 7.6 percent market share index based on the actual response in each area of performance shown in Figure 3-16. If the business can improve product awareness from 71 percent to 80 percent, it should increase its market share and revenue. We cannot determine the exact extent of the impact on share, but a reasonable estimate can be made based on the planned improvement, as shown:

$$\begin{matrix}\textbf{Market Share Index}\\ \text{(current awareness)}\end{matrix} = 0.71 \times 0.46 \times 0.63 \times 0.57 \times 0.65 = 0.076 \ (7.6\%)$$

$$\begin{matrix}\textbf{Market Share Index}\\ \text{(improved awareness)}\end{matrix} = 0.80 \times 0.46 \times 0.63 \times 0.57 \times 0.65 = 0.085 \ (8.6\%)$$

This is an estimated increase of 0.9 percent market share in a $500 million market, amounting to a $4.5 million incremental gain in sales revenue. If the business focused instead on the performance gap created by product availability, increasing actual availability from 57 to 70 percent, it could improve its market share index by 1.7 percent, as shown:

$$\begin{matrix}\textbf{Market Share Index}\\ \text{(improved availability)}\end{matrix} = 0.71 \times 0.46 \times 0.63 \times 0.70 \times 0.65 = 0.093 \ (9.4\%)$$

This level of share impact would increase sales revenue by $8.5 million. In each case, of course, management must assess the cost of marketing efforts needed to produce these changes in order to estimate the profit impact (change in net marketing contribution).

FIGURE 3-17 CURRENT VERSUS POTENTIAL MARKET SHARE INDEX

Share Performance Factor	Current Response	Desired Response	Performance Gap*
Product Awareness	0.71	0.80	−0.09
Product Attractiveness	0.46	0.60	−0.14
Price Acceptable	0.63	0.80	−0.17
Product Availability	0.57	0.70	−0.13
Service Experience	0.65	0.75	−0.10
Market Share Index	0.076	0.202	−0.126

*Performance Gap = Current Response − Desired Response

Market Share Potential

Establishing a *desired level of response* at each step along the share development path provides a basis for estimating a business's market share potential. For example, in Figure 3-17, if we compute the market share index on the basis of desired response, we can estimate our share potential as shown here.

$$\underset{\text{(potential)}}{\textbf{Market Share Index}} = 0.80 \times 0.60 \times 0.80 \times 0.70 \times 0.75 = 0.202 \ (20.2\%)$$

This means that if the business achieves the desired level of performance at each step along the customer purchase path, it should achieve a share index considerably greater than the current share index. In this way, a business can assess its actual share relative to its share potential and can assess the degree to which further growth can be achieved with market share gains.

Share Development Index

Having determined its market share potential, a business is now in the position to assess its opportunity for market share development. In our example, the business's current market share index should have been 7.6 percent. However, owing to a variety of other factors, the actual market share was only 6.3 percent. Furthermore, we estimated that the business's market share index potential would be 20.2 percent if the business achieved the desired level of customer response along the share development path. A ratio of actual market share to potential market share provides a share development index (SDI), as shown:

$$\text{SDI} = \frac{\textbf{Actual Market Share}}{\textbf{Potential Market Share}} \times 100$$

$$= \frac{6.3\%}{20.2\%} \times 100 = 31$$

FIGURE 3-18 MARKET DEVELOPMENT–SHARE DEVELOPMENT MATRIX

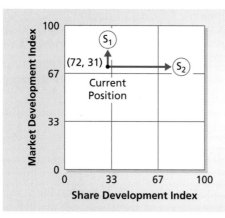

Market Development Index (MDI)

Market Demand (current) = 180 million units
Market Potential (maximum) = 250 million units
MDI = (180 million/250 million) x 100 = 72

Share Development Index (SDI)

Market Share (current) = 6.3%
Market Share (potential) = 20.2%
SDI = (6.3%/20.2%) x 100 = 31

In this case, the SDI is 31; that is, the business has achieved only 31 percent of its potential market share performance given full effectiveness of its delivered marketing strategy at each step along the share development path.

If we combine the MDI presented earlier with the SDI, we are able to create an important planning matrix that can help uncover opportunities for growth as illustrated in Figure 3-18. On the vertical axis is the MDI, the degree to which the market has been developed. On the horizontal axis is the SDI, the business's level of market share development. When combined, this graphic provides a way to evaluate growth opportunities. Depending on the situation, the business may find one of several strategies to aid it in its development of marketing strategies that will contribute to profitable growth. As illustrated in Figure 3-18, further growth could be best achieved with share development strategy.

■ Summary

A critical first step in any marketing strategy is to determine the size of the market. A business with a narrow product focus will see only the products it sells in its current market. Therefore, it is important to start this process by developing a broad, strategic view of the market that encompasses a wide range of substitute products. From a broad market vision, a business can begin to see more of its markets, as well as adjacent markets that might serve as new opportunities for growth.

With a broader market definition, a business can begin to understand the maximum potential of the market it intends to serve. In some instances the market may be underdeveloped and well below its maximum potential demand. When this is the case, it is important to determine the sources of lost market demand; that is, what is preventing customers from entering the market? Factors such as a lack of awareness, preferences, price, availability, and service can all contribute to lost market opportunity. A market development index helps quantify when efforts should be made to improve market development.

Market demand over time is an important aspect of market planning and strategy development. In many of today's markets, market demand is made up of both new customers and existing customers making replacement purchases. Based on the rate at which new customers come into the market, the time it takes for all potential customers to enter the market, and the rate of product replacement, a unique market demand occurs over time. The rate at which a market approaches its full potential is a function of target customer characteristics, product positioning, and marketing effort. Each of these factors can be influenced by the marketing strategies developed by a firm and its competitors.

Over time, market demand emerges from small volumes in the introductory stages to rapidly accelerating growth in volume. During this stage of the product life cycle, prices and margins decline while marketing expenses increase. However, the combination of volume, margins, and marketing expenses produces increasing net marketing contribution throughout the fast growth phase of the product life cycle. As growth slows, net marketing contributions typically peak and start to modestly decline as the product life cycle enters a mature stage with little or no market growth.

The demand for a business's products is also based on the share of market it can extract from a given level of market demand. Market share is simply the proportion of sales a business can obtain from the total market demand at any given point in time, but a business needs to know if its share performance is at, above, or below what it should expect. Five marketing mix factors (promotion, product, price, place, and service) are used to create an index of market share response. The market share index helps a business understand its share potential.

Combining the market development index with a share development index allows us to better discover sales volume and opportunities to grow sales volume. For a given segment or geographic market, we can determine what our best opportunities for sales growth are. In instances where the market is fully developed and we have achieved the full potential of our market share performance, defensive strategies can be developed.

■ Market-Based Logic and Strategic Thinking

1 How does a product-focused market definition differ from a broad, strategic market definition?

2 What are some of the benefits of a broad, strategic market definition?

3 Why is market vision an important element of market demand?

4 What is the difference between vertical and horizontal market opportunities?

5 Why is it important to establish the maximum potential for market demand?

6 What would be the maximum market potential for disposable diapers?

7 What forces would restrict today's market demand for disposable diapers from reaching the maximum market demand?

8 What factors help accelerate market growth? How can a business affect these factors to accelerate market growth?

9 How does a market development index help a business in its market planning?

10 How do customer adoption forces accelerate or impede market penetration?

11 How do product adoption forces accelerate or impede market penetration?

12 How could a business accelerate the rate of market penetration?

13 Why is it important to decompose market demand into replacement and new purchases?

14 Why do volumes, prices, and margins vary over the product life cycle?

15 In Figure 3-11, why is the net marketing contribution negative in the introductory stage of the product life cycle?

16 Why does the net marketing contribution peak during the late growth stage of the product life cycle?

17 What performance factors underlie market share performance?

18 How would a business use an index of its current and potential market share?

19 What are the advantages of computing a market share index?

20 Why might a business's actual market share be different from its market share index for a given target market?

21 How could the market development–share development matrix be used to develop international marketing strategies?

Marketing Performance Tools

Each of the following **marketing performance tools** can be accessed by going to *www.rogerjbest.com* or *www.prenhall.com/best*.

The shaded cells are input cells. The non-shaded cells are computed information based on your input.

MARKETING PERFORMANCE TOOL—Market Demand and Unit Sales Volume

Market Development	Base Year	Year 1	Year 2	Year 3	Year 4	Year 5
Calendar Year	2004	2005	2006	2007	2008	2009
Market Potential (units)	250,000,000	250,000,000	250,000,000	250,000,000	250,000,000	250,000,000
Market Demand (units)	180,000,000	197,000,000	215,000,000	230,000,000	240,000,000	245,000,000
Market Growth Rate (%)		9.4	9.1	7.0	4.3	2.1
Market Development Index	0.72	0.788	0.86	0.92	0.96	0.98
Market Share (%)	5	5	5	5	5	5
Volume Sold (units)	9,000,000	9,850,000	10,750,000	11,500,000	12,000,000	12,250,000

This **marketing performance tool** allows you to evaluate how changes in market potential, market demand, and market share impact the volume sold.

Application Exercise: Shown in the table above is the forecast for the PC market demand and a business with a 5 percent market share. Evaluate how this business's volume would change for each of the following market conditions (separately):

■ A change in market potential from 250 million to 300 million.

■ A one-point increase in market share over each of the next 5 years (from 5 percent to 10 percent).

■ A market growth rate of approximately half of what is projected.

MARKETING PERFORMANCE TOOL—Customer Adoption and Product Adoption

Percent	Customer Influence	Customer Forces Affecting the Rate on New-Product-Market Penetration Percent of Customers Who. . .
80	Felt Need	Have a strong, recognized need for this product
90	Personal Risk	Perceive little or no economic, social, or safety risk associated with owning or using this product
30	Buying Decision	Can buy the product relatively easily with little or no input from others
67	Observable	Can easily observe this product in use prior to purchase
30	Trialability	Can try or sample the product prior to purchase
80	Recommend	Would recommend this product to others
63%	Average	Customer Adoption Score

Percent	Product Influence	Product Forces Affecting the Rate on New-Product-Market Penetration Percent of Customers Who. . .
90	Product Advantage	Believe this product offers a discernable advantage over existing products
20	Affordable Price	Feel the price of the product is affordable given their buying power
80	Easy to Use	Feel this product is not overly complex and would be easy to use
60	Performance Risk	Feel there is little or no chance the product will fail to perform as advertised
80	Availability	Feel the product is readily available at the point of purchase preferred by customers
20	Customer Service	Feel there is sufficient after-sales services in place to support any after-purchase problems
58%	Average	Product Adoption Score

This **marketing performance tool** allows you to estimate the rate of market penetration for a new product by estimating the percent for each category of influence. Separate indexes are created for each of the forces. A matrix built with the two will allow you to evaluate the relative speed of market penetration and to identify which adoption forces are slowing the rate of market penetration.

Application Exercise: Assess the rates of new product adoption for homeopathy medicines and Viagra. Which has a faster rate of market penetration? Which forces could be better managed by manufacturers to accelerate new product-market penetration? What event or events could slow or accelerate the rate of market penetration for each product?

MARKETING PERFORMANCE TOOL—Market Share Index and Share Development

Market Share Performance Metrics	Current Performance	Achieveble Performance	Performance Gap
Percent of target customers who are sufficiently aware of product and benefits	60.0	60.0	0.0
Percent of aware customers who prefer product benefits over competing product offerings	40.0	40.0	0.0
Percent of customers who are not deterred by the price of the product given its benefits	60.0	60.0	0.0
Percent of customers who can readily purchase the product at their preferred point of purchase	30.0	30.0	0.0
Percent of buying customers who are retained and continue to purchase the product	80.0	80.0	0.0
Market Share Performance Metrics	**3.5%**	**3.5%**	**0.0%**
Market Share Development Index	**100**		

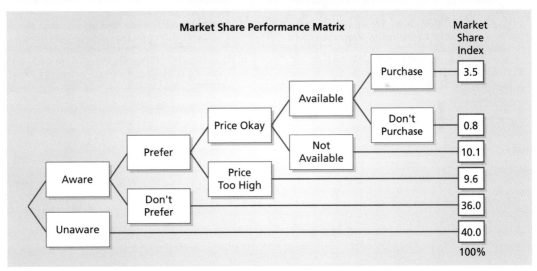

Market Share Performance Matrix

This **marketing performance tool** allows you to estimate a product's market share index based on five market share performance metrics, each of which can be traced to promotion, product, price, place, and service, in that order. The "achievable performance" is what a business believes it could obtain with a successful marketing effort in a given area of market share performance.

Application Exercise: A glaring shortcoming in current performance is "Percent of customers who can readily purchase the product at their preferred point of purchase." What would be the estimated market share impact if this market share performance metric were improved from 30 percent to 70 percent? Given this impact, how would the market share index be further improved with an increase in customer awareness from 60 percent to 70 percent? Input these changes under achievable performance.

Notes

1. Noel Tichy and Stratford Sherman. *Control Your Destiny or Someone Else Will* (New York: Harper Business, 1993); and Richard Ott, "The Prerequisite of Demand Creation," in *Creating Demand* (Burr Ridge, IL: Business One Irwin, 1992): 3–10.
2. Theodore Levitt. "Marketing Myopia," *Harvard Business Review* (July–August 1960): 45–56.
3. Jerry Porras and James Collins. "Successful Habits of Visionary Companies," *Built to Last* (New York: Harper Collins, 1994); and Burt Nanus, *Visionary Leadership* (San Francisco: Jossey-Bass, 1992).
4. Gary Hamel and C. K. Prahalad. *Competing for the Future* (Cambridge, MA: Harvard Business School Press, 1994): 103.
5. R. E. Bucklin and V. Srinivasan. "Determining Interbrand Substitutability Through Survey Measurement of Consumer Preference Structures," *Journal of Marketing Research* (February 1991): 58–71; "Car Makers Use Image Map as Tool to Position Products," *Wall Street Journal* (March 22, 1984): 33; and "Mapping the Dessert Category," *Marketing News* (May 14, 1982): 3.
6. Michael Porter. *Competitive Advantage* (New York: Free Press, 1985): 37; and Jeffrey Rayport and John Sviokla. "Exploiting the Virtual Value Chain," *Harvard Business Review* (November–December 1995): 75–85.
7. Philip Kotler and Fernado Trias de Bes. *Lateral Marketing* (Wiley, 2003).
8. Derek Abell and John Hanunond. *Strategic Market Planning* (Upper Saddle River, NJ: Prentice Hall, 1979): 185–86.
9. Philip Kotler. *Marketing Management,* 7th ed. (Upper Saddle River, NJ: Prentice Hall, 1991): 240–60.
10. Roger Calantorte, Anthony di Benedetto, and Sriraman Bhoovaraghavan. "Examining the Relationship Between the Degree of Innovation and New Product Success," *Journal of Business Research* 30 (June 1994): 143–48; and Fareena Sultan, John Farley, and Donald Lehmann. "A Meta-Analysis of Applications of Diffusion Models," *Journal of Marketing Research* (February 1990): 70–77.
11. Frank Bass, Trichy Krishonan, and Dipak Jain. "Why the Bass Model Fits Without Decision Variables," *Marketing Science* 13 (Summer 1994): 203–223.
12. Geoffrey Moore. *Inside the Tornado* (New York: Harper Collins, 1985): 11–26.
13. William Davidson. *Marketing High Technology* (New York: Free Press, 1986).
14. John Naisbitt. *Global Paradox: The Bigger the World Economy, the More Powerful Its Smallest Players* (New York: Morrow, 1994).
15. Delbert Hawkins, Roger Best, and Kenneth Coney. *Consumer Behavior—Implications for Marketing Strategy*, 8th ed. (New York: Irwin, 2001): 250–251.
16. Doug Schaffer. "Competing Based on the Customer's Hierarchy of Needs," *National Productivity Review* (Summer 1995).

Customer Analysis and Value Creation

In developing a customer strategy for the Lexus, the Lexus marketing team starts with current customers. They conduct in-depth interviews with current customers—many in the homes of the customers—to determine their likes and dislikes as well as their lifestyles. From this customer input and comparisons with competing luxury cars, the Lexus team identifies product improvements that range from more leg room to better fuel economy to a longer coat hook (customers complained that the conventional coat hook was not long enough to carry dry cleaning). They believe that product improvements that enhance product benefits are critical to delivering a superior customer value. To further build customer value, the Lexus marketing team seeks to also find a price that enhances customer value, as illustrated in Figure 4-1.

FIGURE 4-1 LEXUS'S CUSTOMER VALUE CREATION PROCESS

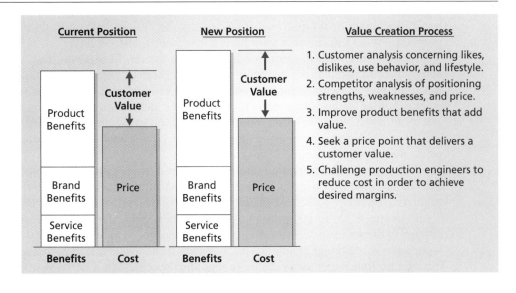

DISCOVERING CUSTOMER BENEFITS

The Lexus marketing team does more than just survey target customers. They try to understand all aspects of the customers' product usage, lifestyles, and demographics. Gathering this information requires more than a survey of customer perceptions and preferences. To discover customer benefits, one needs to understand the total customer environment, not simply the product features customers like or do not like. What we really need to find out is what the customers want but cannot get from the products they purchase.

A Day in the Life of a Customer

One way to better understand customer needs is to become the customer.[1] Although customers' descriptions of their needs are important, customers do not always reveal (or think of) the frustrations they encounter in the purchase, use, and disposal of a product when asked. For example, to better understand how customers used their car trunks, Honda employees videotaped people loading groceries. Different cars, different consumers, and different grocery bags all affected how much car owners had to struggle to get the bags into their car trunk. Some arranged their plastic bags to keep them from tipping over; others paused to rest a bag on the edge of the trunk wall and then had to lift the lid again after it partly closed. Watching the videos, Honda engineers put themselves in the customers' shoes. They could see and feel users' experiences and envision better trunk designs.

Empathic Design

Videotaping customer product use is one form of the *empathic design*.[2] This is an observational approach to understanding customer needs and discovering customer problems and frustrations that arise when acquiring, using, and disposing of a product. Intuit, the maker of the personal-finance software Quicken, has a Follow-Me-Home program. Product developers gain permission from first-time buyers to observe their initial experience with the software in their own homes. In this way, they learn what other software applications are running on the customer's system and how that software can interfere with or complement Quicken. Product developers can also see what other data files the customer refers to and accesses and whether they are on paper or in electronic form. From in-home observations, Intuit designers discovered that many small-business owners were using Quicken to keep their books; that discovery led to a whole new product line called Quick Books.

Although actual observation might be preferred, it may not be possible to observe customers in many consumer, business, or industrial markets. As an alternative, one could develop two hypothetical videos.[3] Video I requires a customer to describe the product he or she wants to buy and, in a sequence of scenes, the process he or she goes through in the acquisition, installation, use, maintenance, and disposal of this product. It is particularly important to note the parts of each scene that create customer problems or frustrations. Remember that Video I is not product specific; it is a narrative of the process the customer goes through in acquiring and using the product of interest. Video I describes a typical day in the life of a business's customer.

VIDEO I—THE CURRENT PROCESS

Customer Use Process	Customer Frustration	Cost to Customer
Cut the particleboard	Saw blades wear out quickly from excess grit	Production downtime and saw blade sharpening and replacement
Build furniture	Need to use thicker pieces	Lamination process to glue pieces
Produce finished product	Desired finish not achieved	Requires sanding for desired finish

In the ideal situation in this example the solution was pretty obvious. The customer wanted particleboard with less grit and available in thicker pieces. Less grit would significantly lower the associated cost of saw blades and sanding. Thicker pieces would eliminate the lamination process. The combined benefits of this customer solution would significantly reduce the furniture manufacturer's costs as Video II summarizes.

VIDEO II—THE DESIRED PROCESS

Customer Process	Ideal Solution	Benefit to Customer
Cut the particleboard to size	Saw blades last longer	Less production downtime lower saw blade expenses
Build furniture	Buy thicker pieces	Eliminate lamination process
Produce finished product	Smoother finish	Less sanding required for finish

Video II requires the customer to re-describe the scenes of Video I with improvements they would desire in each scene. This video provides the opportunity to discover new customer benefits. For example, a marketing team from the Weyerhaeuser Corporation visited a large furniture maker to better determine what they wanted when they purchased particleboard. The furniture maker made it clear that what they wanted was a low price with reliable quality. Weyerhaeuser presented a compelling case for higher quality, but the customer was not swayed. Weyerhaeuser was left with no basis for creating customer value because they could not compete on price against a competitor that had a considerable cost advantage.

This is where most businesses would stop in their analysis of customer needs. However, Weyerhaeuser put together a multifunctional team to revisit the furniture manufacturer to gain a more complete picture of how the manufacturer purchased, inventoried, used, and processed particleboard in making furniture (Video I). This time they wanted to understand the customer process in using the product, not just product-specific purchase criteria.

By focusing on the *process* of using a product, and not just the *product*, Weyerhaeuser discovered important customer frustrations in using particleboard. One frustration centered on the grit found in most particleboard. More grit led to more production downtime to sharpen saw blades and more expense due to shorter blade life. Grit also resulted in an unsatisfactory finish in many instances. When this occurred the furniture piece had to be sanded to obtain the desired level of smoothness. Another customer frustration was the thickness of the particleboard. The customer had to laminate pieces of particleboard to get the thickness required for certain furniture. The following summarizes the customer frustrations and their associated cost uncovered in customer visits used to create a hypothetical Video I.

With these customer insights, Weyerhaeuser responded with thicker, cleaner (less grit) particleboard. Although more expensive per unit, the new product saved the customer money; thicker pieces of particleboard eliminated the laminating process, and less grit reduced tool wear, each providing significant savings. These product features translated into meaningful customer benefits, as presented in Figure 4-2.

Lead User Analysis

Not all customers use products the same. Some may be new users and lack experience with the product. Others may be occasional users and have a limited base of experience. Observing or probing these customers for sources of dissatisfaction or opportunities for improvement will most often result in limited insight. However, for most products there are *lead users*—customers who are more knowledgeable users and who often extend the application of the product to solve other problems or achieve a more complete customer solution.

Studying the behavior of lead users can provide valuable insights into how a product can be improved and the process of using the product made easier. A deeper understanding of lead users' needs and desired solutions can lead to significant incremental improvements in products and customer value. For example, lead users of cell or wireless phones devised ways to extend the capabilities of the phone beyond its intended application by using them to access the Internet—a technology that is spawning new products and new companies.

FIGURE 4-2 WEYERHAEUSER VALUE-ADDED CUSTOMER BENEFITS

FIGURE 4-3 LEAD USER CUSTOMER ANALYSIS

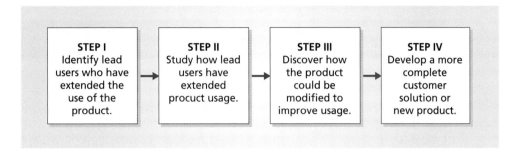

STEP I
Identify lead users who have extended the use of the product.

STEP II
Study how lead users have extended procuct usage.

STEP III
Discover how the product could be modified to improve usage.

STEP IV
Develop a more complete customer solution or new product.

Identifying lead users of a product is Step I in the process of uncovering lead-user solutions as outlined in Figure 4-3.[4] Discovering how lead users use the product to solve their own problems (Step II) opens the door to uncovering new insights into how a product is used or enhanced by lead users to create a more complete customer solution. With these insights, a business can better understand how they can add value-added features, functions, and services (Step III). Step IV involves engineering products based on these insights to enhance existing products or develop completely new products that offer more complete customer solutions.

In applying this process, 3M identified lead users in museum transportation. The need to carefully pack valuable and often extremely delicate museum pieces led these users to develop many innovative packing solutions. By studying how these lead users adapted conventional packing material for museum pieces, 3M was able to develop a new line of off-the-shelf packaging materials.[5] Furthermore, 3M has found that refining or building off of "lead user" applications of existing products produces eight times more revenue than new products generated by more conventional analysis of existing customer needs.[6]

Staple Yourself to an Order

Another way to expand a business's insight into how products are acquired and used is the process of following the steps a customer takes in purchasing a product. By taking a detailed look at the customer order process, a business can discover problems and sources of frustration in the customer buying process. This day-in-the-life-of-a-customer process is called "staple yourself to an order."[7]

This customer analysis process, outlined in Figure 4-4, involves tracking the customer order process from the early stages of order planning to the resolution of claims when after-purchase problems arise. Each step of the customer order cycle presents potential customer problems and frustrations we have all experienced. The earlier these problems occur in the cycle, the less likely a customer is to buy from a business. Problems or frustrations that occur later in the process hurt the chances of repurchase and, hence, lower customer retention.

One way to operationalize this process is to ask, what are the worst things we could do to a customer at each stage of the customer order cycle? On the basis of the level of customer frustration these problems create and the frequency with which they occur, a market-based business would identify the opportunities to build customer value by improving the customer buying process. While product-oriented competitors are focused

FIGURE 4-4 STAGES IN THE CUSTOMER ORDER CYCLE AND OPPORTUNITIES TO BUILD VALUES

Stage in the Customer Order Cycle	Potential Problems, Customer Frustrations, and Opportunities to Build Value
Order Planning	Customers do not recognize your solution in solving a problem
Order Development	Insufficient or incorrect information on your solution
Order Evaluation	Misperceptions or incomplete information limit fair evaluation
Order Placement	Difficulties in placing order with your business
Order Entry	Order recorded or priced incorrectly
Order Processing	Order in process but customer not aware of order status and delivery
Order Delivery	Product delivered late or damaged; wrong product delivered
Customer Invoice	Bill has errors, no one to contact, and calls lead to voice-mail hell
After-Sale Services	Problems after purchase with no one to call; calls not returned
Product Usage	Inadequate instructions; no hot-line offered
Product Problems	Product does not work and must be returned at customer's expense
Returns and Claims	Customer has to fight to get warranty claim resolved

on product features and price, a market-based business focusing on product benefits and the customer order cycle can develop important sources of customer value competitors will never see.

Kano Method

Building customer solutions also involves understanding the expectations customers have for a product or service. Customer expectations have a complex influence on the relationship between product quality and customer satisfaction or dissatisfaction. With a good grasp on customer requirements, a business is in a good position to create and position a product that adds higher customer value. The *Kano method* was developed by Professor Kano and has been used primarily in concept engineering.[8] This section is devoted to a discussion of the Kano method and how it can be used in marketing to discover which product features drive customer satisfaction and which cause customer dissatisfaction as well as to identify new product features and product features that could be eliminated.

Customers have explicit and implicit requirements and expectations that influence their satisfaction or dissatisfaction. Some product features are expected and taken for granted, and customers become extremely dissatisfied if a product fails to meet these minimum expectations. Other well intentioned design features can be inherently dissatisfying for many customers. For example, Microsoft's "Office Assistant" paperclip was so irritating to so many of its customers that the company added a menu option to hide it. Product features can also be unexpected but highly desirable, adding greatly to customer satisfaction. The Kano method is a concept engineering tool that was developed to help design engineers better understand what customers want and don't want as well as what influences their satisfaction and dissatisfaction. Summarized below are five types of product features measured using the Kano method:

1. **Must-Be Features:** These are called must-be features because they must be there for the customer to have any interest in the product at all. If they are not a part of the product, it results in customer dissatisfaction. However, because they are expected, must-be features will not cause high levels of customer satisfaction.
2. **One-Dimensional Features:** These product features have a direct impact on customer satisfaction. To the degree they are present, the customer will be satisfied, and to the degree they are absent, the customer will be dissatisfied.
3. **Attractive Features:** These are customer requirements that are not expected or expressed by customers, but when fulfilled they contribute to customer satisfaction. When they are absent, customers are not dissatisfied. Attractive features are the real hidden drivers of improved customer value.
4. **Reverse Features:** These are features that a customer doesn't want. Their presence causes some level of dissatisfaction but will not increase customer satisfaction when they are removed. You could call these *frustration features* that the customer does not want and only interfere with the use of the product. Many over-engineered products are more complicated than desired by the customer. Eliminating these features would lower dissatisfaction but not increase satisfaction with the product.
5. **Indifferent Features:** These are product or service features that the customer does not really care about. Their presence is cause for neither customer satisfaction nor dissatisfaction. If they were not there, neither customer satisfaction nor customer dissatisfaction would change. Removing indifferent features could lower the cost of the product without affecting customer satisfaction or dissatisfaction.

Analyzing these five different types of customer features can create a complex set of product design criteria. However, when applied correctly, the Kano method can lead to a product design that is focused on the areas of highest impact for customer satisfaction. Products can be differentiated in terms of how well they fulfill different attractive requirements. Businesses can identify and avoid product features that fail to meet customers' must-be requirements. Products can also be more closely tailored to customers in identified segments to provide them the highest customer value.

The Kano Measurement Process

After identifying as many customer requirements as possible from surveys, focus groups, or other in-depth methods, each current or possible product feature is presented in a pair of questions—one *functional* and one *dysfunctional*—as shown in Figure 4-5. Each question in the pair has five possible answers. In Figure 4-5 we created pairs of questions for each of eight product features that could be created for skis.

A customer's results are tabulated in a 5 by 5 matrix, with the five rows being the five possible answers to the question *positively worded* in terms of satisfaction, and the columns being the five possible answers to the question *negatively worded* in terms of dissatisfaction. Depending on the customer's answers to the functional and dysfunctional feature, that customer's requirements for each feature fall into one of the 25 cells of the matrix. Figure 4-5 also shows which cells correspond to attractive, must-be, one-dimensional, reverse, and indifferent requirements. Some of the combinations are somewhat illogical and therefore unlikely to occur. For example, two of the cells are labeled "Questionable" because these combinations of ratings make no sense and have questionable value.

FIGURE 4-5 KANO METHOD QUESTIONNAIRE

Customer Response to Performance: Using the "How Do You Feel" scale on the right, answer both the positive and the negative questions, for each product feature.

Customer Response: How Do You Feel?
1. I like it that way.
2. It must be that way.
3. I am neutral.
4. I can live with it that way.
5. I dislike it that way.

Functional Form of Question: *"If the edges of your skis grip well on hard snow, how do you feel?"*

Dysfunctional Form of Question: *"If the edges of your skis do not grip well on hard snow, how do you feel?"*

INDIVIDUAL CUSTOMER'S RESPONSES

Feature Number	Ski Performance Features, Functions, or Services	Customer's Response
F1	If the edges of your skis grip well on hard snow, how do you feel?	1 (like)
	If the edges of your skis *do not* grip well on hard snow, how do you feel?	5 (dislike)
F2	If your skis have a scratch-resistant surface, how do you feel?	1 (like)
	If your skis *do not* have a scratch-resistant surface, how do you feel?	4 (live with)
F3	If your skis are very light, how do you feel?	3 (neutral)
	If your skis *are not* very light, how do you feel?	5 (dislike)
F4	If we provide a trade-in offer for old skis, how do you feel?	1 (like)
	If we *do not* provide a trade-in offer for old skis, how do you feel?	5 (dislike)
F5	If your skis come with an integrated antitheft device, how do you feel?	2 (must be)
	If your skis *do not* come with an integrated antitheft device, how do you feel?	5 (dislike)
F6	If your ski design matches ski boots and bindings, how do you feel?	1 (like)
	If your ski design *does not* match ski boots and bindings, how do you feel?	2 (must be)
F7	If the manufacturer puts its 800 number on your ski, how do you feel?	5 (dislike)
	If the manufacturer *does not* put its 800 number on your ski, how do you feel?	1 (like)
F8	If the manufacturer provides a free ski video, how do you feel?	3 (neutral)
	If the manufacturer *does not* provide a free ski video, how do you feel?	3 (neutral)

Functional Performance	Dysfunctional Performance				
	1. Like	2. Must Be	3. Neutral	4. Live With	5. Dislike
1. Like	Questionable	Attractive (F6)	Attractive	Attractive (F2)	One Dimensional (F1, F4)
2. Must Be	Reverse	Indifferent	Indifferent	Indifferent	Must Be (F5)
3. Neutral	Reverse	Indifferent	Indifferent (F8)	Indifferent	Must Be (F3)
4. Live With	Reverse	Indifferent	Indifferent	Indifferent	Must Be
5. Dislike	Reverse (F7)	Reverse	Reverse	Reverse	Questionable

The next step in the Kano method is to combine the results for a sample of customers from a given market segment. A list is made up that shows what type of customer requirement is needed for each feature for each customer surveyed, and responses from many customers combined into a table of percentages as illustrated in Figure 4-6A. For each of the eight ski product features, we can see which ones are attractive, one-dimensional, must-be, reverse, and indifferent. This summary provides valuable insight into customer requirements, allowing product and marketing efforts to be highly focused. If there is a great disparity in how customers respond to these questions, then one could further segment this data based on these differences to better understand the product requirements of each segment.

Managing Customer Satisfaction/Dissatisfaction

The Kano method also includes a way to compute the potential for customer satisfaction and the potential for customer dissatisfaction. As shown in Figure 4-6, *one-dimensional* features F1 and F4 can influence both customer satisfaction and dissatisfaction based on the customer's performance experience. Features F2 and F6 are *attractive* features, which if present, can increase customer satisfaction but if they are not present, they do not cause customer dissatisfaction. Features F5 and F3 are *must-be* features. If they do not perform as expected, they will cause customer dissatisfaction. However, if they do perform as expected, they have little or no influence of customer satisfaction. F7 is a

FIGURE 4-6A KANO METHOD CUSTOMER SATISFACTION/DISSATISFACTION

Feature Number	Performance Feature	Attractive (%)	One Dimensional (%)	Must Be (%)	Indifferent (%)	Reverse (%)	Question (%)	Customer Sat.	Customer Dissat.
F1	Edge Grip		67	26	7			67	-93
F2	Scratch Resistant	63	23	10	4			86	-33
F3	Weight		2	82	16			2	-84
F4	Trade-In		57	18	23		2	58	-77
F5	Antitheft Device	12		54	34			12	-54
F6	Design Fits Equip.	73	4	21	2			77	-25
F7	Manufacturer's 800 No.		10	10	10	70		10	-90
F8	Manufacturer's Video	10		10	75	5		10	-15

$$\frac{\text{Potential for}}{\text{Customer Satisfaction}} = \frac{(\text{Attractive} + \text{One Dimensional}) \times 100}{(\text{Attractive} + \text{One Dimensional} + \text{Must Be} + \text{Reverse} + \text{Indifferent})}$$

$$\frac{\text{Potential for}}{\text{Customer Dissatisfaction}} = \frac{(\text{One Dimensional} + \text{Must Be} + \text{Reverse}) \times -100}{(\text{Attractive} + \text{One Dimensional} + \text{Must Be} + \text{Reverse} + \text{Indifferent})}$$

FIGURE 4-6B MANAGING CUSTOMER SATISFACTION/DISSATISFACTION

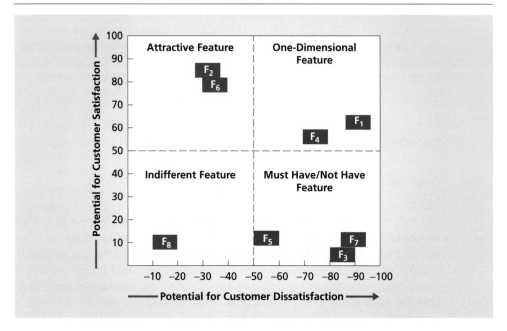

reverse feature. It appears in the must-have/not-have quadrant. This feature has the potential to cause some level of customer dissatisfaction. Eliminating it would reduce customer dissatisfaction but not increase customer satisfaction. Finally, F8 is an *indifferent* feature. It has little influence on customer satisfaction or customer dissatisfaction. If this is an expensive product feature, it could be eliminated to reduce the product cost without influencing customer satisfaction or dissatisfaction.

Customer Benefits and Customer Value

Weyerhaeuser's, Intuit's, Honda's, and 3M's efforts to create increased customer benefits went beyond product-specific thinking. They each engaged in an analysis of the customer situation and the various problems customers encountered. With a deeper understanding of the use situation, they were able to engineer customer solutions that went beyond those provided by currently available products.[9] Had Weyerhaeuser focused only on the product features and not on the customer needs, they would not have discovered their customer solution. If Intuit had only sold its product but not sought to understand how it was used, they would not have discovered a need for new products.

All customers have problems that require solutions. The more help a business's product or service provides to customers, the more value it adds to a customer solution. A business should view itself as a *provider of solutions* rather than a *seller of products and services*. To accomplish this requires a much broader view of the customers' underlying problems that goes beyond products or services and achieves a more comprehensive understanding of customer needs and use situations. This provides a business with a better opportunity to create customer benefits that add value for customers. A business that builds customer solutions will be in the best position to discover new opportunities to add more value.[10]

LIFE CYCLE COSTS AND VALUE CREATION

Customers are willing to pay more for products and services that add value. However, the overall value derived from customer benefits needs to exceed the costs of acquiring those benefits:

Customer Value = Customer Benefits − Cost of Purchase

Creating attractive benefits at a high cost could result in negative customer value. Thus, a business needs to be sensitive to both the benefits it creates in response to customer needs and the total cost of acquiring those benefits. In the following sections, we will examine several ways in which a business can create customer benefits and deliver a greater value to target customers.

To deliver a customer value that creates a superior *economic value* requires that the customer achieve a *net economic gain* over the user life cycle. For example, Weyerhaeuser created an economic value for furniture manufacturers even though the cost of the purchased product was higher than the cost of competing products. The savings created by eliminating the need for lamination to make thicker furniture legs and the reduced cost of saw blade wear more than offset the higher price of the new, improved product. Thus, the customer value created was greater than that of competitors' products, and it was measurable in actual savings (economic value).

There are six primary sources of life cycle costs that create economic value as outlined in Figure 4-7. The price paid for a product or service stands out as the most obvious cost of purchase to most customers. As a result, a business with a lower price and the same quality can easily communicate its economic value to target customers. Because

FIGURE 4-7 ECONOMIC BENEFITS AND VALUE CREATION

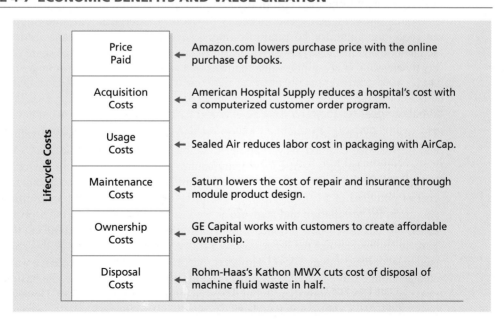

Lifecycle Costs	
Price Paid	Amazon.com lowers purchase price with the online purchase of books.
Acquisition Costs	American Hospital Supply reduces a hospital's cost with a computerized customer order program.
Usage Costs	Sealed Air reduces labor cost in packaging with AirCap.
Maintenance Costs	Saturn lowers the cost of repair and insurance through module product design.
Ownership Costs	GE Capital works with customers to create affordable ownership.
Disposal Costs	Rohm-Haas's Kathon MWX cuts cost of disposal of machine fluid waste in half.

customers may not look beyond a product's price, other sources of economic value may go unnoticed. However, other sources of value creation can include costs associated with acquisition, usage, maintenance, ownership, and disposal of a product. Discovering these value creation opportunities is marketing's job and one of the key benefits of spending a day in the life of a customer.

Low Price

Quite often, price or terms of payment can destroy customer value. Regardless of benefits and potential economic value, the product may simply be unaffordable, or the price may be too high relative to the benefits provided. For example, DuPont found that for more expensive blood analyzers, large hospitals could justify a high price based on overall benefits. Smaller hospitals simply did not have the volume of blood chemistry work to justify purchasing a higher-priced, more sophisticated blood analyzer. As DuPont rolled out subsequent new-product improvements, they met resistance from large hospitals that wanted to buy the newer products but could not economically justify the purchase because the existing product worked well and was still relatively new. This situation led to a strategy in which DuPont bought back the old blood analyzers from the large hospitals, refurbished them, and then resold them to smaller hospitals. In this way, DuPont created an affordable combination of benefits and price for both large and small hospitals.

Acquisition Costs

With respect to acquisition costs, American Hospital Supply found that one-half of every dollar spent by hospitals on pharmaceuticals, chemicals, and hospital equipment went to the acquisition and inventory of such products. As identified in Figure 4-7, acquisition costs are a part of the total cost of purchase. By putting computers in hospitals to streamline order entry, logistics, and inventory procedures, American Hospital Supply created an economic value for hospital customers, saving them a significant portion of their acquisition and inventory costs. American Hospital Supply won a large share of this market by creating an economic value that was real and measurable by hospital customers.

Usage Costs

The cost associated with using a product is an obvious area of potential value creation and the one that enabled Weyerhaeuser to deliver a greater economic value even with a higher price. The same is true for a manufacturer's telecommunications switch, as shown in Figure 4-8. The customer's current telecommunications switch had a total (life cycle) cost of purchase of $1,000. The purchase price was only $300, but an additional $200 was spent for installation and start-up, as well as $500 in usage and other post-purchase costs. The business's new product offered customers a solution that could cut the start-up costs in half and reduce the usage cost by $100. As shown in Figure 4-8, this solution created an economic value of $500. However, the product had to be priced in a way that created economic value for both customers and the business. In response, the business set its price at $375, $75 more than the existing customer solution of $300. However, at this price, it created a solution that added $125 per switch to the customer's bottom line.[11]

FIGURE 4-8 ECONOMIC VALUE OF A TELECOMMUNICATIONS SWITCH

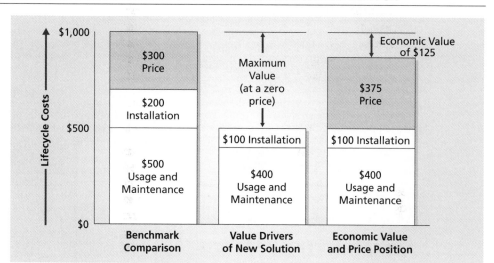

A second example is presented in Figure 4-9. Sealed Air's AirCap provided an economic value of $0.65 even though its price was $0.25 higher than the price of the competition's product. The $0.65 economic value was made possible by reduced costs of labor and freight relative to those for the competing product.

Ownership Costs

Some products are simply more expensive to own than others. These products often have purchase prices that require financing or higher insurance costs or both. General Electric, many years ago, developed GE Capital to create affordable ownership with GE financing. GE Capital has been very successful and is today a large business, serving both GE and non-GE customers.

Ownership also has the risk of dissatisfaction. What happens after a product warranty expires? Copiers, for example, have potentially high ownership cost if the product goes bad. As response to this risk, Xerox created a customer satisfaction program that guarantees product performance for an extended period of time.

Maintenance Costs

The cost of repair and maintenance can be expensive for both customers and businesses. The cost of repair for products under warranty is generally the responsibility of the business that sold the product. After warranty, repair and normal maintenance are costs to the customer. As presented in Figure 4-7, General Motors designed the Saturn to be easily repaired in the event of an accident. This design saves both customers and insurers potentially millions of dollars. The savings are so significant over the life of the car that the customer's cost of insurance for a Saturn can be hundreds of dollars lower than for a comparable car.

FIGURE 4-9 LOWER LABOR AND FREIGHT COSTS DRIVE AIRCAP'S ECONOMIC VALUE

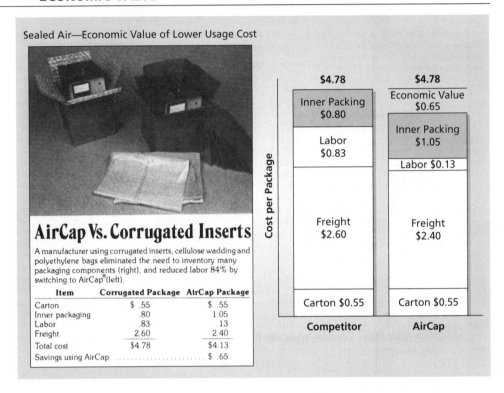

A second example is Loctite's Quick Metal. Quick Metal can be applied to worn or cracked machine parts during routine maintenance to prevent an extended shutdown. Quick Metal's value proposition, *"Keep the machinery running until the new part arrives,"* tells customers how Quick Metal can create an important savings (economic value) for them.

Disposal Costs

The way products are disposed of offers another important source of economic value creation. FP International (FPI) manufactures styrene packaging materials from waste styrene packaging that it picks up from its customers. FPI then sells its recycled styrene packaging back to the customer at a premium price. Because FPI lowers the total cost of the product by solving the customer's disposal problem, it is able to charge a higher price for its product.

A second example is described in Figure 4-10. Kathon MWX is a product that creates a significant economic value for machine shop owners by extending the life of metal-working fluids. The net result is a significant reduction in the cost of disposing these fluids. Finally, in Figure 4-11 we can see the total cost of purchase for three models of competing Honda and Ford automobiles. Although Ford offers a lower price paid after cash rebates in two of the three examples, the total cost of purchase for Ford is higher than Honda in all three

FIGURE 4-10 LOWER COST OF DISPOSAL IS THE VALUE DRIVER

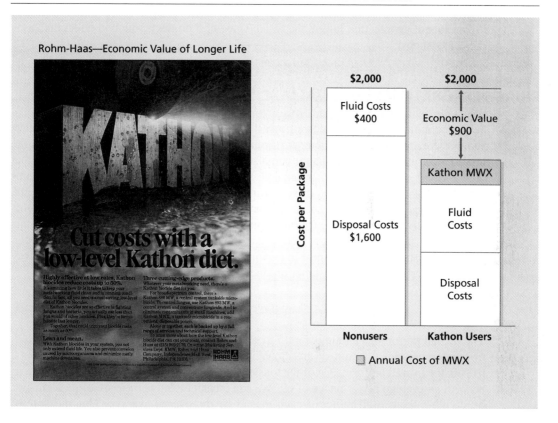

FIGURE 4-11 LIFE CYCLE COST FOR COMPETING AUTOMOBILES

Type of Automobile Manufacturer & Model	Transaction Price	Cash Rebate	Net Price	Cost to Own	Life Cycle Cost
Small Sport Utility					
Honda (CRV EX AWD)	$21,165	$0	$21,165	$7,775	$28,940
Ford Escape (XLT AWD)	$24,539	($2,000)	$22,539	$14,423	$36,962
Honda Value (Savings)			($1,374)	($6,648)	($8,022)
Midsize Sport Utility					
Honda Pilot (EX 4WD)	$28,865	$0	$28,865	$9,735	$38,600
Ford Explorer (XLS 4WD)	$31,720	($4,000)	$27,720	$13,934	$41,654
Honda Value (Savings)			$1,145	($4,199)	($3,054)
Midsize Sedan					
Honda Accord (EX V 6)	$24,410	$0	$24,410	$6,920	$31,330
Ford Taurus (SE)	$19,649	($3,000)	$16,649	$18,725	$35,374
Honda Value (Savings)			$7,761	($11,805)	($4,044)

cases. Insurance costs for Ford are generally lower, but the cost of maintenance and higher rate of depreciation increase the total cost of ownership over a 5-year period.[12] A higher rate of deprecation lowers the resale value of a product, which in effect increases the disposal cost.

PRICE-PERFORMANCE AND VALUE CREATION

While economic value provides a powerful basis for creating a cost-based customer value, there are aspects of product performance that are more difficult to quantify in the total cost of purchase. Performance can also include product features and functions that do not save money but enhance usage and, in that way, create customer value. For example, a car has cost-based value drivers in its fuel economy, maintenance requirements, insurance, and resale value. A car also offers safety, reliability, design, and other features such as front-wheel drive, luggage racks, and comfort. Although these latter components of customer value are difficult to quantify with respect to the total cost of owning a car, they can be evaluated with respect to performance. *Consumer Reports* provides one way to rate the performance of consumer products.

Relative Performance

The overall performance ratings for 15 toasters based on the *Consumer Reports*' evaluations of eight product features[13] are shown in Figure 4-12a. On a scale that ranged from 0 to 100, the overall performance of the toasters listed ranged from a low of 55 to a high of 88 with an average performance of 69. We can create a relative measure of performance by dividing the overall rating of each toaster by the overall average. This measure of product performance will help us more readily assess performance around a benchmark average of 100, as shown here.

$$\text{Relative Performance} = \frac{\text{Product Performance}}{\text{Average Performance}} \times 100$$

$$\text{Relative Performance} = \frac{82}{69} \times 100 = 119$$

When each toaster's *Consumer Reports* rating is divided by the average of all ratings (69) and multiplied by 100, we have a measure of relative performance in which the average performance is equal to 100. Now we can readily assess performance as it varies from a low of 80 to a high of 128, where 100 is average. Sunbeam, for example, has a relative performance of 119. This means that Sunbeam's overall performance is 19 percent better than the average of the 15 toasters evaluated.

Relative Price

To acquire Sunbeam's above-average relative performance requires paying a certain amount of money. Their price is reported as $28, but it is difficult to readily infer the attractiveness of this price in absolute dollars. Thus, a measure of relative price is also

FIGURE 4-12a TOASTER RELATIVE PRICE-PERFORMANCE AND RELATIVE VALUE

Number and Name of Toaster	Overall Performance	Relative Performance	Toaster Price	Relative Price	Relative Value
1 Cuisinart CPT-60	88	128	$70	215	−87
2 Sunbeam	82	119	28	85	33
3 KitchenAid	81	117	77	237	−120
4 Black & Decker	77	112	25	77	35
5 Cuisinart CPT-30	75	109	40	123	−14
6 Breadman	74	107	35	108	−1
7 Proctor-Silex 22425	72	104	15	46	58
8 Krups	70	101	32	98	3
9 Oster	65	94	45	138	−44
10 Toastmaster B1021	63	91	16	49	42
11 Proctor-Silex 22415	60	87	35	108	−21
12 Toastmaster B1035	58	84	21	65	19
13 Betty Crocker	58	84	25	77	7
14 Proctor-Silex 22205	57	83	11	34	49
15 Rival	55	80	13	40	40
Average	**69.0**	**100.0**	**$32.50**	**100.0**	**0**

important in understanding value creation. For the 15 toasters evaluated, the overall average price was $32.50. When the average price is used as a performance benchmark, Sunbeam's relative price is 86, as shown.

$$\text{Relative Price} = \frac{\text{Product Price}}{\text{Average Price}} \times 100$$

$$\text{Relative Price (Sunbeam)} = \frac{\$28}{\$32.50} \times 100 = 86$$

This means that the price of Sunbeam's toaster is 14 percent lower than the average price of the 15 toasters evaluated. As shown in Figure 4-12a, the relative prices of the 15 toasters ranged from a low of 34 to a high of 237. At the lowest price, a customer could buy a toaster 67 percent below the average price, and at the high end a customer would pay 137 percent more than the average price. Thus, the Sunbeam relative price, although attractive, is not the lowest relative price of the 15 toasters considered.

Customer Value

With measures of relative performance and relative price, we can readily identify products that are above or below average in performance or price. However, to infer customer value we need to compute the difference in these two relative measures, as shown here for Sunbeam.

Customer Value = Relative Performance − Relative Price
Customer Value (Sunbeam) = 119 − 86 = **33**

In this example, Sunbeam has a positive customer value of 33. A customer value of zero would mean that the relative performance was offset by the relative price. This off-set could occur for a product with above- or below-average performance. For example, the Breadman toaster has an above-average relative performance (107) that is almost entirely offset by an above-average relative price (108). The net difference is a customer value of −1.

Using this measure of customer value, we can assess the value of different combinations of performance and price. As shown in Figure 4-12a, the customer value for these 15 toasters ranges from a low of −120 to a high of +58. To better understand this range of customer value, we need to examine these results a little further.

Value Map

A graph of relative performance versus relative price allows us to create a *value map*, as illustrated in Figure 4-12b. As shown, all the toasters to the right of the diagonal line have positive customer values. However, four of the nine toasters that stand out as having above-average performance have below-average price. For these four brands, customer value is created with very attractive prices. Thus, price-sensitive customers might find alternative 7 the most attractive value, because it has both a low relative price and slightly above-average relative performance. A performance-oriented customer would probably find Sunbeam (alternative 2) particularly attractive, because it offers above-average performance with a lower-than-average price.

Alternatives 1 and 3 may seem to be overpriced relative to performance. This method of inferring customer value, however, does not take into account the perceived status or

FIGURE 4-12b PRICE-PERFORMANCE VALUE MAP

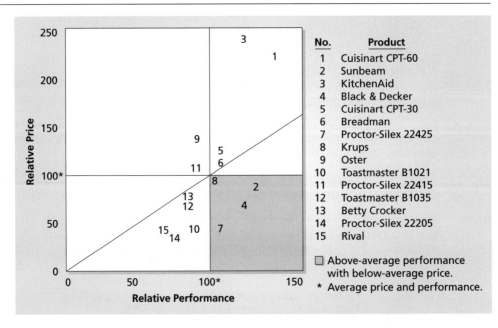

No.	Product
1	Cuisinart CPT-60
2	Sunbeam
3	KitchenAid
4	Black & Decker
5	Cuisinart CPT-30
6	Breadman
7	Proctor-Silex 22425
8	Krups
9	Oster
10	Toastmaster B1021
11	Proctor-Silex 22415
12	Toastmaster B1035
13	Betty Crocker
14	Proctor-Silex 22205
15	Rival

☐ Above-average performance with below-average price.
* Average price and performance.

reputation of a brand, which can also be an important source of value creation and one that we can include in a measure of customer value.

PERCEIVED BENEFITS AND VALUE CREATION

Economic value and price-performance relative value provide excellent measures of customer value. However, our evaluation of products often needs to go beyond economic and price-performance measures of customer values. Customer *perceptions* of service quality, brand reputation, and costs other than price also affect customer value. This next section examines how we can utilize customer perceptions of a broader range of benefits and costs to infer the level of customer value for a business's products or services.

Product Benefits

Value creation is logically affected by perceptions of product benefits. These perceived benefits are not easily translated from economic benefits or objectively rated measures of product performance, yet, it is customer perceptions of product benefits that drive purchase behavior.[14] We need a method for measuring customer perceptions of product benefits and the relative value derived from them when compared with a competitive benchmark.[15]

Shown in Figure 4-13 are four product benefits sought in the purchase and use of a commercial copier. Each product benefit is weighted with respect to relative importance. For instance, in this example, Machine Uptime is weighted twice as important as Image Quality, four times as important as Ease of Use, and so on. To determine the degree to which a relative advantage in delivering these product benefits is created by a business, the business needs to evaluate each customer benefit relative to competing products. In this case, three competitors were used to benchmark the business's perceived performance and overall relative advantage.

The ratings shown for the business and each competitor are ratings of perceived machine uptime that range from 0 (disastrous) to 10 (outstanding). If the business outperforms a competitor by more than one point, it receives a portion of the importance allocated to that customer benefit. For example, in Figure 4-13, competitor A is rated only

FIGURE 4-13 MEASURING PERCEIVED PRODUCT BENEFITS

Customer Determined Company Benefits	Relative Importance	Business Rating	Competitor A	B	C	Relative Advantage
Machine Uptime	40	8	7	5	6	27
Print Speed	30	9	8	5	5	20
Image Quality	20	7	7	7	6	0
Ease of Use	10	4	6	7	6	−10
	100					37

Relative Product Benefits: 100 + 37 = 137

one point lower than the business, whereas competitors B and C are rated more than one point lower. As shown, the business derives no perceived advantage over competitor A and, hence, gets zero points. However, because the business is perceived to be better than competitors B and C (by more than one point), it receives the 40 points attached to perceived machine uptime from each competitor. When these three perceived performance impacts are averaged, an overall relative advantage of 27 is obtained:

$$\frac{\text{Machine}}{\text{Uptime}} = \frac{0+40+40}{3} = \frac{80}{3} = 27$$

For print speed, the business also outperformed two of the competitors by more than one point and, therefore, received two-thirds of the relative importance allocated to print speed. However, the business achieved no relative advantage in image quality and was hurt by being rated more than one point below each of the three competitors with respect to ease of use.

When the relative advantage is added up for all four product benefits, this business produces an overall relative advantage of 37. This means that, on the basis of perceived ratings of product benefits relative to the competition, the business produces 37 percent greater benefits. When this overall relative advantage is added to a base index of 100, a relative product benefit index of 137 is produced.

Service Benefits

For many markets (or segments), product differentiation may be minimal, because competitors are able to emulate the best features of each other's products. When this is the case, service quality can be a crucial source of differentiation and competitive advantage.[16] To measure a business's perceived service benefits, we can use the same approach we used for perceived product benefits.

Shown in Figure 4-14 is a measure of perceived service benefits for the same business as that evaluated in Figure 4-13. In this case, the business is roughly equal to two and behind one of its benchmark competitors with respect to repair time. This position detracts from its overall perceived service benefits because 60 percent of the importance is attached to this aspect of service benefits. With respect to response to problems, the business roughly matches competitor A and competitor B, and outperforms competitor C.

FIGURE 4-14 MEASURING PERCEIVED SERVICE BENEFITS

Customer Determined Company Benefits	Relative Importance	Business Rating	Competitor A	B	C	Relative Advantage
Repair Time	60	5	7	6	5	−20
Response Time to Problems	30	5	5	6	2	10
Quality of Service	10	7	7	6	8	0
	100					−10

Relative Service Benefits: 100 − 10 = 90

The net result is a slight relative advantage. However, there is an excellent opportunity to move ahead of fairly average competitor performance, as illustrated:

$$\frac{\text{Response to}}{\text{Problems}} = \frac{0 + 0 + 30}{3} = \frac{30}{3} = 10$$

With respect to quality of service, the business failed to capture any relative advantage. Overall, the business produced a service benefit index of 90. This implies that the business is 10 percent less attractive than its competitors in delivering service benefits to target customers.

Company or Brand Benefits

A third source of customer benefit is a business's brand or company reputation. Whether a brand such as Lexus or Perrier, or a company such as Nordstrom or Hewlett-Packard, the company or brand name itself provides potential benefit to some customers. For Lexus and Perrier, the name adds social status to the product. This is an intangible benefit that could be of great importance to many customers. For Nordstrom, the reputation for customer service creates an added company benefit that goes beyond actual customer service. For HP, its reputation for innovation is valued by many customers and creates a customer benefit that is neither product nor service specific.

To measure a business's perceived brand or company benefits, we can use the same method we used for measuring perceived product or service benefits. As shown in Figure 4-15, the company benefits for this copier company was driven by two factors: customer commitment and reputation for quality. In this case, the business leads two benchmark competitors in customer commitment and has no relative advantage in reputation for quality. The net result of these customer perceptions is an overall index of 140 with respect to company benefits.

Overall Customer Benefits

To arrive at an overall measure of perceived customer benefits, we need a way to combine these three key sources of customer benefits. Combining them requires weighing the relative importance of each of these major sources of customer benefit. In this example, the majority of the weight was given to product benefits (0.60), and smaller amounts to service (0.30) and company (0.10) benefits, as illustrated in Figure 4-16. When the relative

FIGURE 4-15 MEASURING A BUSINESS'S BRAND OR COMPANY BENEFITS

Customer Determined Company Benefits	Relative Importance	Business Rating	Competitor A	B	C	Relative Advantage
Customer Commitment	60	8	7	6	4	40
Reputation for Quality	40	9	8	9	8	0
	100					40
Relative Company Benefits: 100 + 40 = 140						

FIGURE 4-16 MEASURING OVERALL PERCEIVED CUSTOMER BENEFITS

Customer Determined Benefits	Relative Importance	Relative Advantage	Overall Benefits
Product Benefits	0.60	137	82
Service Benefits	0.30	90	27
Company Benefits	0.10	140	14
	1.00		123
	Overall Relative Benefits = 123		

advantage is weighted by the relative importance shown in Figure 4-16 an overall index of perceived benefits can be obtained. In this case, the overall perceived benefit score of 123 can be interpreted to mean that the business is 23 percent ahead of the competition in delivering perceived customer benefits—but has the business created a superior customer value? We don't know. The level of perceived customer value cannot be determined until we also determine the perceived cost of acquiring these benefits.

Perceived Cost of Purchase

Before we can determine the overall level of value created for customers, we need to determine the perceived cost of purchase. The first step is similar to computing overall perceived benefits. We have to first determine the cost components considered by the customer in a purchase decision and the relative importance of each component. In Figure 4-17, there are four sources of cost to be considered in the customer's total cost of purchase. The purchase price carries the majority of the relative importance. Other factors, such as service and repairs, toner, and paper are also significant cost components of the customer's total perceived cost of purchase.

In this case, the business is perceived to be 15 percent higher in purchase price, and, as a result, the competitive position multiplier is 1.15 (a constant of 1 plus the relative position). By simply multiplying the relative importance for price (40) by the competitive position multiplier (1.15), we can index the overall perceived position of the business on

FIGURE 4-17 MEASURING THE TOTAL COSTS OF PURCHASE

Customer Determined Cost of Purchase	Relative Importance	Competitive Position (%)	Cost Multiplier	Overall Cost of Purchase
Purchase Price	40	15	1.15	46
Service and Repair	30	10	1.10	33
Toner	20	0	1.00	20
Paper	10	−20	0.80	8
	100			107
	Overall Relative Cost of Purchase = 107			

purchase price as 46. Note that a cost multiplier greater than one increases the total cost of purchase, whereas a cost multiplier less than one reduces the total cost of purchase.

The business's competitive position with respect to service and repair is perceived to be higher than the competitors', which increases the perceived total cost of purchase. However, the business is perceived to be less expensive with regard to the cost of paper, which decreases the perceived total cost of purchase. Because there is no perceived difference in the cost of toner between this business and its competitors, the cost multiplier is 1.00 and the relative weight of 20 translates to a value of 20 for the overall perceived position on this factor.

The sum of these four areas of perceived cost produces an index of overall perceived cost of purchase, which in this case is 107. This can be interpreted to mean that the business is perceived to be 7 percent more expensive to do business with than its competitors; the difference can be traced back to its higher prices and higher service and repair costs, despite a lower cost of paper.

Perceived Customer Value

Once customers' perceptions of overall benefits and total cost of purchase have been obtained, a business can evaluate the degree of value it creates for its customers. Shown in Figure 4-18 is the customer value created by the copier company. Each area of perceived benefit and perceived cost is graphed using the results presented in Figures 4-16 and 4-17. The difference between the overall customer benefits (123) and the total cost of purchase (107) creates an index of perceived customer value score of 16. This means that the business has been able to create a superior customer value while commanding a 15 percent price premium. If a business wanted to further improve its perceived customer value without lowering price, it could strive to improve key weaknesses in areas of

FIGURE 4-18 CUSTOMER VALUE AND VALUE MAP

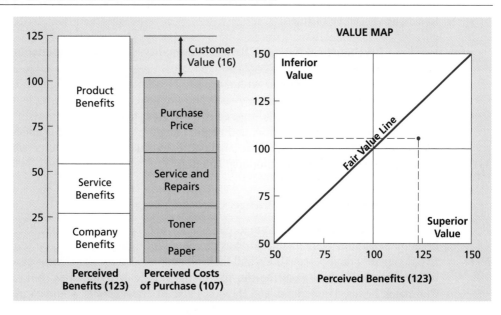

importance to customers. Ease of use, repair time, and service and repair are all areas that detract from customer value. To the degree that these areas could be improved, the business could improve the value it creates for customers while maintaining a price premium.

EMOTIONAL BENEFITS AND VALUE CREATION

So far, we have looked at customer benefits that could be described largely as *rational* benefits. The rational appeal of an automobile includes gas economy, maintenance cost, insurance, resale value, size, and price. Less tangible rational benefits might include quality of repair service, friendliness of service personnel, and manufacturer reputation. For many customers there are also *emotional* benefits that are tied to psychological needs that are more personal in nature.[17] The same can be true in many business-to-business purchases, in which emotional benefits could be tied to security, reputation, or friendship. Thus, to be complete in our understanding of customer benefits and value creation, we need to also understand sources of emotional customer benefits and how they contribute to customer value.

Emotional Benefits and Psychological Value

Each of us has both physical and psychological needs. Physical needs such as hunger, thirst, sleep, and safety generally come first. However, as those needs are met, our psychological needs such as the need for warm relationships, affiliation, status, recognition, respect, fun, enjoyment, excitement, and self-fulfillment become more important to us. Because many products have personalities with psychological meanings, our psychological needs can be served with the purchase of products that offer a set of emotional benefits that are consistent with those needs. As shown here, our psychological needs will draw us to products with a brand personality that satisfies our psychological needs. To the degree that a product's brand personality delivers desired emotional benefits, our psychological needs can be fulfilled.

Psychological Needs → Brand Personality → Emotional Benefits

As an example, a consumer with a need to be seen as rugged, tough, and self-sufficient might be attracted to a Chevy truck and the advertising that positions the Chevy truck as strong, independent, and rugged. On the other hand, consumers with a need for status, recognition, sophistication, and respect might be attracted to a Mercedes. Thus, for products that project a "brand personality," there is the opportunity to create customer value through the delivery of emotional benefits.

Brand Personality and Value Creation

In a comprehensive study of human personality and brand personality, five dominant brand personalities were identified,[18] as presented in Figure 4-19. As you look over the five dominant brand personalities and their related personality traits, ask yourself which of the five would best describe the following brands or companies: Nike, Gateway Computer, Lexus, Timberland, and Hewlett-Packard. Most people would align Nike with

FIGURE 4-19 BRAND PERSONALITY AND PERSONALITY TRAITS

Brand Personality	Personality Trait	Not at All Descriptive				Extremely Descriptive
Sincerity	Down to earth	—	—	—	—	—
	Honest	—	—	—	—	—
	Wholesome	—	—	—	—	—
	Cheerful	—	—	—	—	—
Excitement	Daring	—	—	—	—	—
	Spirited	—	—	—	—	—
	Imaginative	—	—	—	—	—
	Up-to-date	—	—	—	—	—
Competence	Reliable	—	—	—	—	—
	Intelligent	—	—	—	—	—
	Successful	—	—	—	—	—
Sophistication	Upper class	—	—	—	—	—
	Charming	—	—	—	—	—
Ruggedness	Outdoorsy	—	—	—	—	—
	Tough	—	—	—	—	—

excitement. Nike's brand personality has been carefully honed to exemplify daring, spirit, imagination, and being ahead of the crowd (up-to-date). Betty Crocker, on the other hand, projects an image of being down-to-earth, honest, and wholesome, which translates into sincerity. Timberland footwear has a brand personality that projects ruggedness. Lexus seeks to project sophistication. Hewlett-Packard products project an image of competence built around intelligence, success, and reliability.

In each case, consumers with psychological needs that match well with the brand personality of a product will be drawn to that product. This conclusion assumes that other product benefits, service benefits, and price needs are adequately met. To the degree that the brand delivers these emotional benefits, it will contribute to the overall value a customer derives from the purchase of one product over another.

For example, what if Nike had used John Wooden (a famous college basketball coach) instead of Michael Jordan to endorse Nike Air basketball shoes (later named Air Jordan)? The personality of the Nike brand would be different, and the emotional benefits created by the product would be considerably less for the target customers. Products have personalities. The spokesperson and ad copy used to promote a product help create the product's brand personality and emotional benefits.

TRANSACTION COST AND VALUE CREATION

A customer buying a refrigerator would be interested in product features such as size, storage configuration, color, freezer capacity, and operating efficiency, as well as the costs and benefits associated with the price paid, delivery, terms of payment, return policy, and warranty. In contrast, a channel intermediary is less interested in end-user customer benefits and more interested in the value created by the sales transaction.

Whether a Kool-Aid stand or Wal-Mart, the basic purpose of a channel intermediary is to connect producers with consumers. To accomplish this channel, intermediaries must invest in space to provide products, marketing resources to promote products, and people to facilitate customer transactions. Value for the channel intermediary is derived from a combination of (1) profitable use of space, (2) inventory turnover (the rate at which merchandise in that space is sold), and (3) the marketing expenses needed to promote the merchandise held in that space.

Space Value

In Figure 4-20, let's assume that a channel intermediary has 5,000 square feet of space (each square is 100 square feet). The four gray squares amount to 400 square feet that an intermediary such as Home Depot has allocated to the sale of major appliances. The first aspect of managing value in this situation is to know how much potential value the intermediary can obtain from 400 square feet of major appliances. Let's assume that for major appliances the average margin per square foot is $25. This means that space is worth $10,000 if customers bought the entire inventory of major appliances in that space.

$$\textbf{Space Value} = \text{Margin per square foot} \times \text{Inventory (square feet)}$$
$$= \textbf{\$25} \text{ per square foot} \times \textbf{400} \text{ square feet}$$
$$= \textbf{\$10,000}$$

   If the channel intermediary had the option of placing another line of merchandise in the same 400 square feet at $30, that space has a value of $12,000. All things being equal, the alternative at $30 per square foot offers a better space value.
   However, overall value to the intermediary depends on the rate at which this inventory sells and the marketing expenses associated with selling it. It may be that merchandise with a higher margin per square foot does not sell as fast as the lower margin merchandise, or perhaps the higher margin merchandise requires more marketing expenses to attract and serve customers. Thus, the overall transaction value has to take into account all these factors.

FIGURE 4-20 INTERMEDIARIES USE SPACE TO CONNECT MANUFACTURERS WITH CUSTOMERS

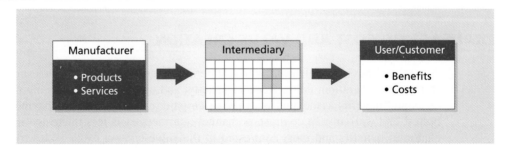

Transaction Value

The $10,000 of profit potential for the intermediary's space will be converted into gross profit based on the rate at which the intermediary can sell the major appliance inventory. If the inventory can be sold five times per year, then 400 square feet of space allocated to major appliances can produce $50,000 in gross profit per year. For this level of sales transaction to occur, the intermediary has to invest in marketing. Marketing expenses typically include displays, advertising, product literature, sales training, and promotional samples when applicable. For major appliances, let's assume that the channel intermediary spends $10,000 per year marketing its major appliances. The net result is a transaction value of $40,000 that the channel intermediary derived from the use of 400 square feet of space.

Transaction Value = Margin per square foot × Inventory (square feet) × Inventory Turnover − Marketing Expenses

= $25 per square foot × 400 square feet × 5 turns per year × $10,000

= **$50,000 − $10,000**

= **$40,000**

Thus, the transaction value for an intermediary is going to vary based upon margins, efficient use of space, inventory turnover, and marketing expenses. Each of these areas of transaction value can be affected by the manufacturer's product, market demand, margins, and marketing policies.

For example, The Home Depot wanted to sell large appliances but did not want to carry a large inventory of different sizes and colors of various large appliances. Carrying this type of inventory is expensive in terms of retail floor space, warehouse space, and financing costs. To create an attractive transaction value, GE offered to hold the inventory and take over the responsibility of delivering the appliances from GE warehouses. The Home Depot would keep a few floor models for display, and GE would operate a computer kiosk in the Home Depot store from which customers could make color and size selections. The net result was less space allocated to the sale of major appliances, less investment in inventory, no delivery expense, and reduced marketing expenses at the point of sale. Each of these contributed to a tremendous increase in transaction value for Home Depot while GE benefited by gaining access to the millions of consumers who shop at Home Depot.

Value Creation Across the Supply Chain

In many markets, the supply chain involves more than one intermediary. For most building products the supply chain includes a channel intermediary, builder, and owner. As shown in Figure 4-21, each of these is a customer with different needs and unique ways of determining customer value.

The Silent Floor is a building product that creates different types of customer value across the supply chain. The Silent Floor is a partially assembled flooring system that will not squeak or bounce when someone walks across it. In focus-group interviews, home owners indicated they would pay more for a floor that didn't bounce or squeak. Although the product could be developed to achieve success for these consumers, the

FIGURE 4-21 THE SILENT FLOOR: CUSTOMER VALUE CREATION ACROSS THE SUPPLY CHAIN

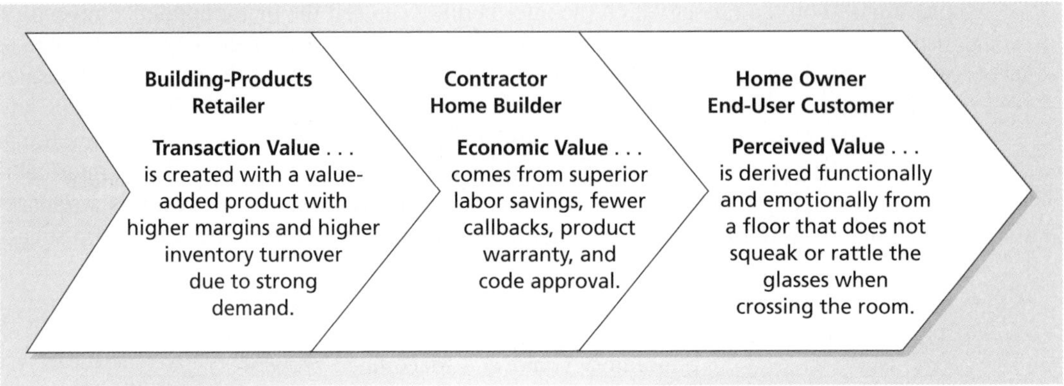

Building-Products Retailer	Contractor Home Builder	Home Owner End-User Customer
Transaction Value . . . is created with a value-added product with higher margins and higher inventory turnover due to strong demand.	**Economic Value . . .** comes from superior labor savings, fewer callbacks, product warranty, and code approval.	**Perceived Value . . .** is derived functionally and emotionally from a floor that does not squeak or rattle the glasses when crossing the room.

manufacturer also had to address the needs of the other customers in the value chain shown in Figure 4-21.

The value drivers that influenced retailers and builders were less focused on the product itself and more on the process of selling and using it. For building-product retailers, transaction value was derived from margin per square foot, inventory requirements, inventory turnover, and marketing expenses. Value for contractors and home builders was created by the economic value derived from lower installation costs, fewer callbacks for rework, a manufacturer's product warranty that limited liability, and a code-approved product that accelerated the completion process. As shown in Figure 4-21, The Silent Floor created an attractive customer value for each of these different types of customers in the supply chain.

IDENTIFYING VALUE DRIVERS

We have shown that there are several ways to create customer value, but it can be challenging to determine which aspects of customer value are the key value drivers. Asking customers directly is one approach, but when asked in this way, customers tend to think everything is important. We can more accurately determine what a customer values when they make product choices involving several alternative product-price configurations. In the process of making trade-offs between different combinations of price and benefits we can create a set of preference curves using *conjoint analysis*.[19]

Using The Silent Floor as an example, nine hypothetical flooring systems created from four dimensions of potential value are presented in Figure 4-22.[20] Each alternative shows a different combination of labor savings, product warranty, price, and callbacks. In this case, home builders would be asked to rank these nine alternatives in order of preference as a purchase alternative. Shown in Figure 4-23 are the preferences curves derived from a conjoint analysis of the rank order preferences that were also shown in Figure 4-22.

FIGURE 4-22 HOME BUILDER'S TRADE-OFF ANALYSIS FOR NINE FLOORING SYSTEMS

Flooring System A
Labor Savings..............None
Product Warranty.......5 years
Delivered Price..........Competitive
Customer Callbacks....None
| Customer Ranking: 5 |

Flooring System B
Labor Savings..............None
Product Warranty.......10 years
Delivered Price..........+20%
Customer Callbacks....Frequent
| Customer Ranking: 6 |

Flooring System C
Labor Savings..............None
Product Warranty.......None
Delivered Price..........+40%
Customer Callbacks....Some
| Customer Ranking: 8 |

Flooring System D
Labor Savings..............20%
Product Warranty.......10 years
Delivered Price..........Competitive
Customer Callbacks....Some
| Customer Ranking: 1 |

Flooring System E
Labor Savings..............20%
Product Warranty.......10 years
Delivered Price..........+20%
Customer Callbacks....None
| Customer Ranking: 7 |

Flooring System F
Labor Savings..............20%
Product Warranty.......5 years
Delivered Price..........+40%
Customer Callbacks....Frequent
| Customer Ranking: 9 |

Flooring System G
Labor Savings..............40%
Product Warranty.......None
Delivered Price..........Competitive
Customer Callbacks....Frequent
| Customer Ranking: 3 |

Flooring System H
Labor Savings..............40%
Product Warranty.......5 years
Delivered Price..........+20%
Customer Callbacks....Some
| Customer Ranking: 2 |

Flooring System I
Labor Savings..............40%
Product Warranty.......10 years
Delivered Price..........+40%
Customer Callbacks....None
| Customer Ranking: 4 |

Builder's Preference Ranking: D, H, G, I, A, B, E, C, F
Conjoint Analysis used in this ranking to create the preferences curves.
(See Appendix 4.1 for details)

Customer Preferences

In this example the preference curves represent how the homebuilder values the different performance features and price for a flooring system. The higher the number on each preference curve, the more important that level of performance was in creating customer value.[21] A 40 percent labor savings (1.00) is considerably more important than a 20 percent labor savings (0.33). The larger the range from low to high on a performance feature or price, the more important that aspect of value was to the customer when ranking the alternatives. The percentages shown in the preference curves represent the importance of each performance feature and price. In this example, price accounted for 34 percent of the overall influence in preferences ranking influence, while the other 66 percent was influenced by the three performance features. Labor savings was the most important performance feature at 28 percent, while warranty and callbacks each accounted for 19 percent in the ranking of these alternative flooring systems.

FIGURE 4-23 HOME BUILDER'S TRADE-OFF ANALYSIS FOR FLOORING SYSTEMS

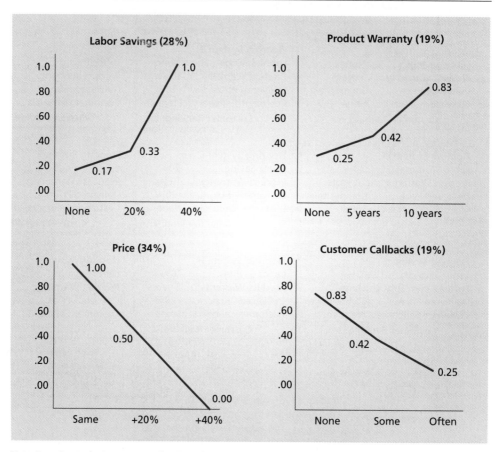

Note: To estimate the importance of each preference curve, the low to high score is summed for each of the preference curves (2.99) and then each low to high range is divided by this sum. When each is expressed as a percent, it represents the importance that performance feature had on the ranking of alternatives.

Customer Value

To determine the value driver of any flooring system we need to build a *customer value index* (CVI) for a specific flooring system. This can be done by using the preference curves shown in Figure 4-23. For example, the conventional flooring system has a CVI of 1.67. This score is derived from the performance and price of this flooring system and how the home builder valued the performance features and price as shown here. For the conventional flooring system, price is clearly the value driver (1.0 of 1.67) because it makes up 60 percent of the total CVI.

Customer Value Index = Labor Savings + Warranty + Price + Callbacks

CVI of Conventional
   Flooring System   = None (.17) + None (.25) + Commodity (1.0) + Often (.25)

                   = 1.67

A flooring system with 40 percent labor savings and no customer callbacks could be positioned in two ways. As shown in Figure 4-24, Strategy A offers the full labor savings

FIGURE 4-24 CUSTOMER VALUE: CONVENTIONAL AND VALUE-ADDED FLOORING SYSTEMS

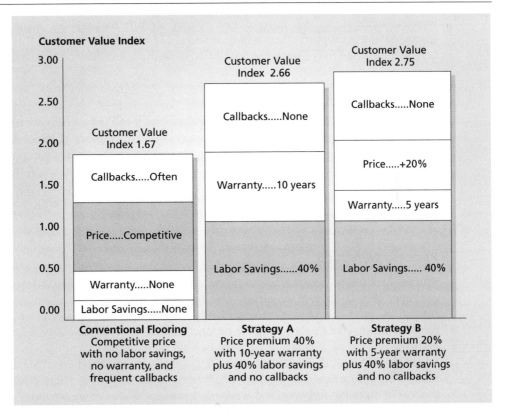

and customer callback benefits along with a 10-year warranty and a price that is 40 percent higher than the current flooring system. This combination produces a customer value index of 2.66, which is 59 percent higher than the customer value index produced by a conventional flooring system. Thus Strategy A should be more attractive to home builders than the conventional system. The value driver for this strategy is the labor savings (1.0 of 2.66) because it is the largest contributor to the overall customer value index.

Strategy B shown in Figure 4-24 provides the same labor savings and customer callback performance as Strategy A, but is priced only 20 percent higher than the current flooring system and offers only a 5-year warranty. The customer value index for this combination of performance and price is 2.75, which is 65 percent higher in value than the current flooring system. The value driver for Strategy B is also a labor saving. Strategies A and B are both superior to the conventional flooring system in terms of customer value. Strategy A, however, is likely to be more profitable, given a much higher price premium.

CUSTOMER ANALYSIS TOOLS

A passion for creating customer value is at the heart of market-based management, and that passion demands customer analysis—not as an occasional project but as an ongoing process that is a regular part of doing business, much like accounting. Many methods and tools can help us better understand customer needs, problems, relative performance, and factors that influence performance and customer satisfaction. Figure 4-25 lists a number of customer-analysis methods and tools that are used for different purposes. Some have been discussed in this chapter; others will be discussed in subsequent chapters. It is important here to understand the primary focus of different methods and customer-analysis tools.

Discovery Methods

Discovery methods are largely *observational*, as shown in Figure 4-25. Sometimes customers cannot articulate their needs or they may not be fully aware of the problems they encounter in the use of a product. Watching customers use a product can provide new insights for how a product could be improved. In this chapter we discussed four discovery tools for customer analysis: empathic design, a day in the life of a customer, the Kano method, and lead user analysis. Each of these tools is useful in seeing new ways to enhance customer value.

Process Methods

Process methods go beyond the product in an attempt to better understand the *process* a customer goes through in acquiring, owning, using, and replacing a product. Looking beyond the product provides the opportunity for a business to see a broader set of customer problems and thereby improve product benefits to help solve a broader problem. For example, life cycle cost analysis goes beyond the purchase of a product in an effort to understand the customer's cost over the life cycle of use and ownership. "Staple yourself to an order" is particularly good for uncovering opportunities for value creation in the process of ordering, shipping, and receiving a product. Focus groups of target customers are also used to obtain a broader understanding of the process customers use in using a particular product.

Tracking Methods

Tracking methods are used to *track* (monitor) consumption and performance. Surveys allow a business to track product awareness, intentions to purchase, and ratings of product

FIGURE 4-25 CUSTOMER ANALYSIS TOOLS

Methods	Primary Focus	Customer Analysis Tools
Discovery	Observing Usage	Empathic Design, A Day in the Life, Lead User Analysis
Process	Understanding Process	Staple Yourself to an Order, Focus Groups, Life Cycle Cost Analysis, Kano Method
Tracking	Measuring Performance	Customer Surveys, Customer Panels, Scanner Data
Testing	Testing Features/Price	Conjoint Analysis, Multidimensional Scaling, Experimental Design
Analysis	Analyzing Relationships	Regression, Discriminant, Factor, and Cluster Analysis

and service performance relative to competing products. Tracking tools are not particularly good for discovering unmet customer needs or problems encountered in the process of using a product. However, tracking consumption with scanner data or customer panels provides valuable insights into product consumption. In this chapter we used tracking methods to evaluate the performance ratings of toaster ovens and discover how customers rate the product, service, and company benefits of four competing printers.

Testing Methods

Testing methods go beyond observation and tracking in an attempt to *test* how customers will react to different marketing offerings. Customer trade-off analysis (also called conjoint analysis) allows a business to test new product features within the context of other product features and different levels of price. Test results help a business understand the level of importance or impact a particular change is likely to have on customer preferences. Multidimensional scaling (discussed in Chapter 6) can be used to test how customers perceive the competitive position of a product relative to competing products and substitutes. Research using experimental design allows a business to test the impact of a marketing effect such as price or advertising in comparison to a control group that is not exposed to the experimental treatment effect. Testing methods are critical in evaluating the potential impact of a change in a product, price, promotion, place, or service.

Analysis Methods

Finally, *analysis* methods are more complex statistical tools that allow us to examine relationships between variables. For example, in Chapter 5 we will illustrate how cluster analysis is used in market segmentation to group customers with similar needs. Discriminant analysis, which seeks to find variables that differentiate one group from another, can be used to determine which demographic characteristics differentiate needs-based market segments. Regression analysis is commonly used to understand how a response variable such as sales or product awareness is affected by variations in several influence variables such as price, advertising, and sales promotions. Factor analysis seeks to find a set of underlying dimensions among highly correlated variables. For example, factor analysis of car performance ratings may reduce the data to a few important dimensions of performance. This enhances a business's understanding of what drives customer perceptions of car performance. Although analysis methods are important customer analysis tools, they are more statistical in nature and the detail of their use is beyond the scope of this book. Each of the customer analysis tools listed in Figure 4-25 is defined in the glossary.

■ Summary

A strong customer focus and an ongoing commitment to understanding customers' needs and the problems customers encounter are at the core of any market-based strategy. Too often, businesses oversimplify the analysis of customer needs by narrowly focusing on specific product features and price. Although this assessment is important, it is perhaps more important for a business to look beyond current product features and price to see more broadly and understand the complete process or cycle the customer goes through in acquiring and using a product. Spending a day in the life of a customer or lead user provides a practical way for managers to more fully understand customers' needs and discover new opportunities to improve customer value and satisfaction. The Kano method analyzes customers' expressed and latent requirements for product features that lead to customer satisfaction and dissatisfaction.

End-user customers are interested in product benefits, service benefits, brand image (emotional benefits), and the cost of purchase. In contrast, channel intermediaries who sell manufacturers' products to these customers have a different way of assessing customer value. Intermediaries are attracted, satisfied, and retained with a superior transaction value. Transaction value is the economic value derived from marketing a product based on the margin it produces per square foot of space, required inventory (square feet of space), inventory turnover (the number of times per year the inventory sells), and marketing expenses associated with promoting the product. Any one of these components can be modified to improve an intermediary's transaction value. When we look across the entire supply chain, we may find that different members of the supply chain have different ways of inferring customer value. This presents an additional challenge to manufacturers who rely on others to reach and serve end-user customers.

We examined three areas of customer analysis that influence customer benefits (economic benefits, perceived benefits, and emotional benefits) and the way customers derive value from these benefits. Economic benefits are a measurable difference in savings that enables a business to create an economic value greater than that of competing products. A lower price is an obvious source of economic value, but there are also non-price areas from which economic benefit can be created. Savings derived from lower acquisition, usage, ownership, maintenance and repair, and disposal costs offer ways to lower the total cost of purchase for a target customer and thereby create more customer value. However, not all benefits can be quantified into an economic value expressed in dollar savings.

Customer benefits derived from a product's appearance, exceptional service, or reputation are more difficult to put a dollar value on. Likewise, customer perceptions of performance have a strong influence on product preference and purchase behavior. By measuring customer perceptions of product benefits, service benefits, and brand benefits relative to competition, we are able to develop an overall index of total benefits derived from a particular business's product. By also measuring perception of price and non-price costs of purchase relative to competition, we can develop an overall index of the total cost of purchase. The difference between total perceived benefits and cost provides a measure of perceived customer value. The larger the customer value, the greater the potential to attract, satisfy, and retain customers.

A third area of customer benefit and value creation is emotional benefits. Products that serve an underlying psychological need, type of personality, or personal values are creating emotional benefits that add value for the customer. Understanding these aspects of a target market is important in positioning a product and enhancing its perceived value. Products, like people, have personalities, and the closer we are able to position the product with respect to the target customer's emotional needs, the greater potential value we will be able to create with a given product.

Finally, trade-off analysis was introduced to help us better quantify the value created by different combinations of price and product positioning. The customer trade-off process enables us to uncover the degree to which different aspects of a product are driving customer preferences. This analysis in turn enables a business to index the value it creates relative to key competitors and to evaluate the impact alternative positioning strategies would have on customer preference and relative value. Overall, customer analysis and value creation are important inputs in developing marketing strategies designed to yield high levels of customer satisfaction.

■ Market-Based Logic and Strategic Thinking

1 What is the danger in asking customers what is important to them in a particular product purchase?
2 How do product features differ from customer benefits?
3 What is meant by "staple yourself to an order"? How would this process increase opportunities to improve customer value?
4 How does empathic design help a business discover customer problems and new opportunities for value creation?
5 What is the purpose of spending a day in the life of a customer?
6 How would the Kano method help identify new product features? How would the Kano method identify features that cause customer dissatisfaction?
7 How could Microsoft use the Kano method to improve customer satisfaction with their Windows operating system?
8 Why should the scenes in each videotape of a day in the life of a customer go beyond the use of our product or service?
9 What is economic value to the customer?
10 What are the ways in which a business can create a more attractive economic value?
11 Why is it important to measure perceived benefits and perceived costs?
12 What are the ways in which a business can improve the perceived value of its product?
13 How should customer preference and purchase behavior change as a function of different levels of perceived customer value?
14 Why are emotional benefits important?
15 How do psychological motives help shape emotional benefits and customer perceptions of value?
16 How does the personality of a spokesperson help shape the emotional benefits of the product being endorsed?
17 Using Figure 4-18, discuss the brand personalities of Kodak film, Mountain Dew, and Prudential Insurance and how these brand personalities were created.
18 What is transactional value?
19 Explain how a convenience store could estimate its transaction value in selling Coca-Cola products.
20 How could Coca-Cola improve the convenience store owner's transaction value?
21 What is trade-off analysis? How does it help us understand customer preferences?
22 How could a business determine if customers would prefer a new service?

Marketing Performance Tools

Each of the following **marketing performance** tools can be accessed by going to *www.rogerjbest.com* or *www.prenhall.com/best*. The shaded cells are input cells. The non-shaded cells contain values computed from your input.

MARKETING PERFORMANCE TOOL—Life Cycle Cost Analysis

Cost of Purchase Generic Category	Specific Cost	Product A AirCap	Product B Competitor	Life Cycle Cost
Price Paid (after discounts and rebates)	Packing Material	$1.05	$0.80	$0.25
Shipping Cost	Shipping Cost	$2.40	$2.60	($0.20)
Installation/Handling	Packing Box	$0.55	$0.55	$0.00
Inventory (holding costs)				$0.00
Financing Costs (loan interest)				$0.00
Owning Costs (insurance)				$0.00
Usage Costs (cost to use)	Labor to Pack	$0.13	$0.83	($0.70)
Maintenance (cost of routine maintenance)	Breakage/1000	$0.05	$0.10	($0.05)
Disposal Cost (cost to get rid of product)				$0.00
Resale Value (input as a negative number)				$0.00
Life Cycle Cost and Economic Value		$4.18	$4.88	($0.70)

This **marketing performance tool** allows you to evaluate the life cycle cost and economic value for your product (or other reference product) and a competing product. Enter data or change data in the shaded cells.

Application Exercise: This example is taken from Figure 4-7 with the addition of an estimated cost due to breakage in shipping. How much economic value would AirCap create if it (1) sold at the competitor's price; (2) split the potential savings?

MARKETING PERFORMANCE TOOL—Customer Benefits
Product Benefits

Customer Determined Product Benefits	Relative Importance	A	Competitor B	C	Relative Advantage
Machine Uptime	40	0	40	40	27
Print Speed	30	0	30	30	20
Image Quality	20	0	0	0	0
Paper	10	−10	−10	−10	−10
	100				37
Relative Product Benefits					137

SERVICE BENEFITS

Customer Determined Service Benefits	Relative Importance	Competitor A	Competitor B	Competitor C	Relative Advantage
Repair Time	60	−60	0	0	−20
Response Time to Problems	30	0	0	30	10
Quality of Service	10	0	0	0	0
	100				−10
Relative Service Benefits					90

COMPANY BENEFITS

Customer Determined Company/Brand Benefits	Relative Importance	Competitor A	Competitor B	Competitor C	Relative Advantage
Customer Commitment	60	0	60	60	40
Reputation for Quality	40	0	0	0	0
	100				40
Relative Company/Brand Benefits					140

This **marketing performance tool** allows you to evaluate the customer benefits for your product relative to three competing products. Enter data or change data in the shaded cells.

Application Exercise: This example is taken from Figures 4-13 to 4-16. To use this application tool, follow these instructions for each customer benefit:

■ Input the relative importance under a competitor for a product when it is rated two or more points higher than a competing product.

■ Input a zero value under the competing product when the product is rated within plus or minus one point of the competing product.

■ Input a minus relative importance under the competing product when your product is rated more than two points lower than a competing product.

The relative advantage and overall benefits scores are computed automatically. For an overall estimate of customer benefits, you will need to input the relative importance of each category of customer benefits as shown here:

OVERALL PERCEIVED CUSTOMER BENEFITS

Customer Benefits	Relative Importance	Relative Advantage	Overall Benefits
Product Benefits	0.60	137	82.2
Service Benefits	0.30	90	27.0
Company/Brand	0.10	140	14.0
	1.00		123.2

MARKETING PERFORMANCE TOOL—Customer Cost and Customer Value
Overall Perceived Cost of Purchase

Customer Perceptions Total Cost of Purchase	Relative Importance	Competitive Position (%)	Cost Multiplier	Overall Cost of Purchase
Purchase Price	40	15	1.15	46
Service and Repair	30	10	1.10	33
Toner	20	0	1.00	20
Paper	10	−20	0.80	8
	100			107

This **marketing performance tool** allows you to evaluate the customer benefits for your product relative to three competing products. Enter data or change data in the shaded cells.

Application Exercise: This example is taken from Figure 4-17. To use this application tool, vary the perceived cost (shaded cells) in order to change the overall perceived cost of purchase. Use this result and the overall perceived benefits to construct a value map as illustrated in Figure 4-18. You may want to copy the following chart to graph your results.

CUSTOMER VALUE AND VALUE MAP

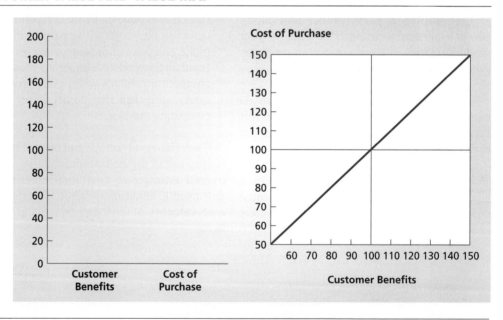

Notes

1. Readings in *Positive Impact*: William Henry Jr. "Walking in the Customer's Shoes" (November 1994): 6–7; Paul Tulenko. "It's Important to Know What Customers Want" (August 1994): 9–10; American Marketplace, "Author Says Success Lies in Customer Value Management" (August 1994): 11–12.

2. Dorothy Leonard and Jeffrey Rayport. "Spark Innovation through Empathic Design," *Harvard Business Review* (November–December 1997).

3. Michael Lanning. *Delivering Profitable Value* (Reading, MA: Perseus Books, 1998): 228–253.

4. Eric von Hippel. "Lead Users: An Important Source of Novel Product Concepts," *Management Science* 32, no. 7 (July 1986): 791–805.

5. Craig Henderson. "Finding, Examining Lead Users Push 3M to Leading Edge of Innovation." In Practice Case Study Series, *American Productivity & Quality Center*, 2000.

6. Gary Lillien, Pamela Morrison, Mary Sonnack, and Eric von Hippel. "Performance Assessment of the Lead User Idea Generation Process for New Product Development," working paper ISBM No. 4-2001, The Pennsylvania State University.

7. Benson Shapiro, V. Kasturi Rangan, and John Sviokla. "Staple Yourself to an Order," *Harvard Business Review* (July–August 1992): 113–122.

8. Elmar Sauerwein, Franz Bailom, Kurt Matzler, and Hans Hinterhuber. "The Kano Model: How to Delight Your Customers," *International Working Seminar on Production Economics*," Innsbruck, Austria, February 19–23, 1996, 313–327.

9. Robert Yeager. "Customers Don't Buy Technologies; They Buy Solutions: Here's How Five Advanced Technology Marketers Saw the Light and Avoided Becoming High-Tech Commodities," *Business Marketing* (November 1985): 61–76.

10. Michael Hammer. *The Agenda*, Crown Business (2001).

11. John Forbis and Nitin Mehta. "Value-Based Strategies for Industrial Products," *Business Horizons* (May 1981): 32–42.

12. David Kiley. "On Cars, Big Rebates Aren't Always Big Savings," *USA Today* (August 5, 2003); also visit ***www.edmounds.com*** for other total cost of purchase comparisons.

13. "Ratings and Recommendation: Toasters and Toaster-Oven/Broilers," *Consumer Reports* (August 1998): 42–43.

14. "Perceptions of Quality," *Journal of Marketing* (October 1993): 18–34.

15. Bradley Gale. *Managing Customer Value* (New York: Free Press, 1994).

16. Morris Holbrook. "The Nature of Customer Value: An Axiology of Services in the Consumption Experience." In *Service Quality: New Directions in Theory and Practice*, Roland Rust and Richard Oliver, ed. (London: Sage Publications, 1991): 21–71.

17. Delbert Hawkins, Roger Best, and Kenneth Coney. "The Changing American Society: Values and Demographics," in *Consumer Behavior: Implications for Marketing Strategy*, 6th ed. (New York: Irwin, 1995): 66–88.

18. Jennifer Aaker. "Dimensions of Brand Personality," *Journal of Marketing Research* (August 1997): 347–356.

19. Donald Tull and Delbert Hawkins. *Marketing Research: Measurement and Method*, 6th ed. (New York: Macmillan, 1993): 406–418; and M. Agarwal and P. Green. "Adaptive Conjoint Analysis Versus Self-Explicated Models," *International Journal of Research* (June 1991): 141–146.

20. John Morton and Hugh Devine. "How to Diagnose What Buyers Really Want," *Business Marketing* (October 1985): 70–83.

21. J. Axelrod and N. Frendberg. "Conjoint Analysis," *Marketing Research* (June 1990): 28–35; P. Green and V. Srinivasan. "Conjoint Analysis in Marketing Research," *Journal of Marketing* (October 1990): 3–19; D.Wittink and P. Cattin. "Commercial Use of Conjoint Analysis," *Journal of Marketing* (July 1989): 19–96; and A. Page and H. Rosenbaum. "Redesigning Product Lines with Conjoint Analysis," *Journal of Product Management* (1987): 120–137.

APPENDIX 4.1

Trade-Off Analysis Computations

Step 1. Determine individual scores for each attribute (factor/level) by summing the scores for that attribute.

Labor Savings	Price		
	Same	+20%	+40%
None	Some 5 years (A) [5]	Often 10 years (B) [6]	None None (C) [8]	= 19
20%	None 10 years (D) [1]	Some None (E) [7]	Often 5 years (F) [9]	= 17
40%	Often None (G) [3]	None 5 years (H) [2]	Some 10 years (I) [4]	= 9

= 9   = 15   = 21

Product Warranty

None	= 8 + 7 + 3	= 18
5 years	= 5 + 9 + 2	= 16
10 years	= 6 + 1 + 4	= 11

Customer Callbacks

None	= 8 + 1 + 2	= 11
Some	= 5 + 7 + 4	= 16
Often	= 6 + 9 + 3	= 18

Step 2. Rank attributes and summed attribute scores from lowest to highest. (X's below)

	X	Y
+40% Labor Savings	9	1.00
Same Price	9	1.00
10 Years Product Warranty	11	0.83
No Call	11	0.83
Price +20%	15	0.50
5 Years Product Warranty	16	0.42
Some Call Backs	16	0.42
+20% Labor Savings	17	0.33
No Product Warranty	18	0.25
Often Call Backs	18	0.25
None Speed	19	0.17
Price + 40%	21	0.00

Step 3. Determine the maximum score, minimum score, and difference between the maximum and minimum scores.

Step 4. Rescale the raw scores, (X's) using the following Normalization Formula:

Normalization Formula:

$$Y = \frac{X_{max} - X}{X_{max} - X_{min}}$$

$$Y = \frac{21 - X}{21 - 9}$$

$$Y = \frac{21 - X}{12}$$

Now, all scores will vary between zero and one, depending on their overall attractiveness to this customer segment.

CHAPTER 5

Market Segmentation and Customer Relationship Marketing

Hardiplank is the market leader in fiber-cement siding, with a 13 percent share of all siding sold in the United States. While cultivating the market for fiber-cement siding in the 1990s, James Hardie relied on a mass-marketing strategy. The company assumed that siding was a commodity that had to be price competitive with conventional siding materials such as wood, stucco, vinyl, and aluminum. However, fiber cement siding has valuable benefits that other siding products do not have. It is resistant to fire, rot, and bug infestation. Because of this, James Hardie provides a 50-year warranty. Although builders are cost sensitive, they found that home owners with higher-quality homes would pay more for a higher-quality product that had these benefits.

This knowledge led James Hardie to segment the siding market into two broad segments. Roughly 30 percent fell into a quality segment and 70 percent into a price segment as illustrated in Figure 5-1. In addition to the normal product benefits offered by fiber cement, the quality segment wanted a high-quality appearance. In response to this need, James Hardie created a pre-painted fiber-cement siding to ensure a finished appearance and branded it "Color Plus" to provide further differentiation. They also introduced a trim kit that would enhance the overall appearance for the quality-conscious customer. This allowed quality-conscious architects and home builders the opportunity to enhance the quality appearance of a home. These value-added products were sold at higher prices and higher margins.

The price segment was primarily focused on builders of tract homes, manufactured homes, and multiunit housing. The total cost of purchase was the key need, and material was a major portion of this cost. To better serve the price segment, James Hardie modified the product to make it easier and faster to install. This multiproduct segmentation strategy allowed James Hardie to grow its average price per thousand square feet from $419 in 1999 to $471 in 2003, even while more than doubling the volume sold. The bottom line: This segmentation strategy allowed James Hardie to grow profits from a pretax return on sales of 19.9 percent in 1999 to 25 percent in 2003.

Market segmentation is the cornerstone of a market-based strategy and a powerful driver of improvements in marketing profitability and marketing productivity. It involves identifying specific groups of customers with unique customer needs and purchase behaviors and identifying the relevant demographic characteristics associated with each segment. Market segmentation opens the door to multiple market-based strategies and greater marketing efficiency. It creates opportunities for sales and profit growth.

FIGURE 5-1 MASS MARKET STRATEGY VERSUS MULTI-SEGMENT STRATEGY

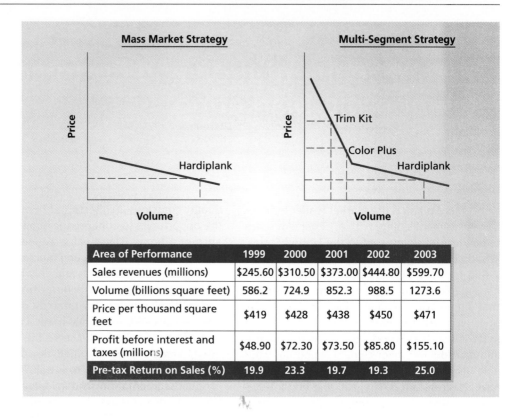

Area of Performance	1999	2000	2001	2002	2003
Sales revenues (millions)	$245.60	$310.50	$373.00	$444.80	$599.70
Volume (billions square feet)	586.2	724.9	852.3	988.5	1273.6
Price per thousand square feet	$419	$428	$438	$450	$471
Profit before interest and taxes (millions)	$48.90	$72.30	$73.50	$85.80	$155.10
Pre-tax Return on Sales (%)	19.9	23.3	19.7	19.3	25.0

CUSTOMER NEEDS

Understanding customer needs is the first step in successful market segmentation. A business with a strong market orientation will seek to understand customer needs and develop strategies to attract, satisfy, and retain target customers. Because potential customers will rarely all have the same needs, a business with a strong market orientation will divide its served market into segments as described below.

> A market segment is a specific group of customers with similar needs, purchasing behaviors, and identifying characteristics.[1]

Both consumers and businesses have market needs, but the factors influencing their needs differ in important ways. Understanding why customers have different needs is helpful in determining how to divide up a market into useful needs-based market segments.

Forces That Shape Consumer Market Needs

Consumers differ in a great many ways. Obviously people have different preferences for automobiles, toothpaste, and entertainment. Not so obvious are the factors that influence their preferences. Although there are many factors that contribute to these differences[2], there are three primary forces that shape the needs of consumers, as summarized in Figure 5-2.

**FIGURE 5-2 FUNDAMENTAL FORCES THAT SHAPE DIFFERENCES
IN CONSUMER NEEDS**

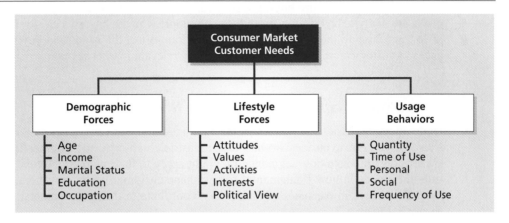

Demographic Influences

Needs and preferences often shift as a person moves *demographically* from one life situation to another. Changes in income, occupation, and educational status all contribute to a changing set of customer needs for a variety of products. Consider how customer needs and preferences for an automobile change as one moves from college student to management trainee. A few years later, the same person may get married and start a family, and changes in marital status and household will once again shift automobile needs and preferences. Because of the variety of demographic differences among individuals and households, we should expect a large array of differences in what these consumers need, can afford, and buy. To the extent that demographics reflect the needs and preferences of customers, they can be used to identify market segments.

Lifestyle Influences

Demographics are not alone in shaping customer needs and market demand. *Lifestyle forces* created by differences in values, attitudes, and interests also contribute to differences in customer needs. Two consumers who are demographically the same may differ significantly in their attitudes and value orientations. A consumer with strong environmental values is likely to prefer a different type of car than a demographically identical person whose values are more focused on fun, enjoyment, and personal gratification. These differences, as well as differences in preferred activities and interests, contribute to lifestyle forces that shape customer needs and product preferences. To the extent that lifestyle attributes reflect the needs and buying preferences of customers, they can be used to identify relevant market segments.

Usage Behaviors

A third major force in shaping customer needs is *usage behavior*. How the product is used, when it is used, and how much it is used are likely to shape customer needs for certain products. A family with two or three children under 10 will have a different set of usage behaviors for an automobile than a family with two children over the age of 16. In addition, if parents are buying a first car for their child as a graduation gift, their needs are likely to be different from those of people who are buying a car for the family or for business. To the extent that usage behaviors reflect the needs and buying preferences of customers, they can be used to identify relevant market segments.

Forces That Shape Business Market Needs

Quite often, discussions of market segmentation are limited to consumer markets, and as a result, managers in business-to-business, industrial, high-tech, and commercial markets are left to extrapolate how segmentation might apply to their markets. Actually, there is little difference in how fundamental forces shape customer needs, but there are fairly large differences in the types of factors that contribute to these fundamental forces, as shown in Figure 5-3.

Firmographics

In consumer markets, one of the key forces is demographics. A more appropriate term in business-to-business markets would be *firmographics*. Differences in the size of a commercial or industrial business in both employees and sales are likely to contribute to differences in customer needs. Industries can also be identified by the Standard Industrial Classification (SIC) code. These industry differences often correspond to different product applications and different needs for products. Likewise, the newness of a business, number of locations, and financial stability are also important firmographics that may play a role in shaping customer needs in nonconsumer, business-to-business markets.

FIGURE 5-3 FUNDAMENTAL FORCES THAT DRIVE DIFFERENCES IN BUSINESS-TO-BUSINESS CUSTOMER NEEDS

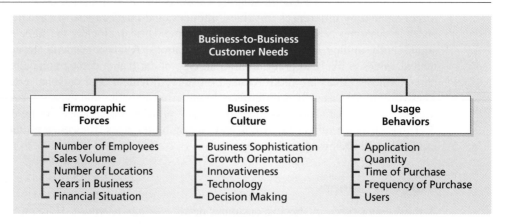

Business Culture

Just as consumer markets have lifestyles, businesses have *cultures* (styles) that can have a profound impact on their needs. Two firms that are similar in firmographics may have different needs due to major differences in their corporate style or culture. A firm with a strong technological base and growth orientation is going to have a different set of needs from a commodity business with no aspirations for growth. Other differences in attitudes with respect to innovation and risk and centralized versus decentralized decision making are also likely to shape the customer needs and requirements in a purchase decision.

Usage Behaviors

Finally, as in consumer markets, usage behavior can play a role in shaping business customer needs. How much a business buys, how often it purchases, who uses the product, and how it is used all influence the specific needs a business-to-business customer will have in selecting one vendor or product over another. Quite often, it is not simply the product a customer is buying but the support, service, and integrity of the company from which it is buying. For example, though there are several million small businesses in the United States, they can be divided into two core segments: *growth-oriented entrepreneurs* and *cost-focused sustainers*. As shown in Figure 5-4, each segment is different in business need, firmographics, and purchase behavior. Growth-oriented entrepreneurs are better educated, more sophisticated, better organized, and have a passion to grow their business. By contrast, cost-focused sustainers are more centered on maintaining the status quo at the lowest cost. These small businesses also tend to be less sophisticated in their operations, have a lower level of formal education, and are less likely to have a working financial plan. To sell successfully in either segment requires a strategy that recognizes the unique needs and behaviors of each segment.

FIGURE 5-4 MARKET SEGMENTATION OF THE SMALL-BUSINESS MARKET

Growth-Oriented Entrepreneurs

Core Business Need
  Ways to invest and grow

Firmographics
  Medium size
  More sophisticated
  Higher in education
  Ongoing financial plan

Purchase Behavior
  Products that enhance productivity
  High revenue per customer
  Willing to buy value-added solutions

Value Proposition
  Solutions that help you grow
  your business

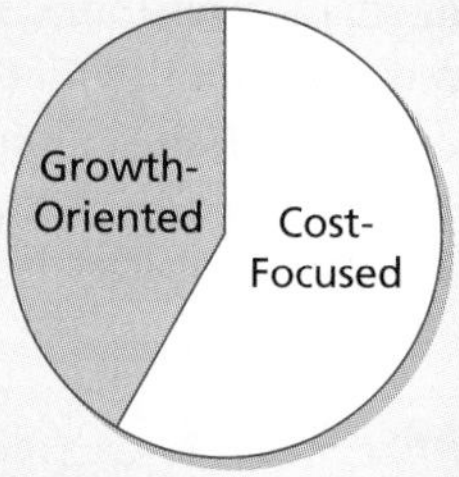

Cost-Focused Sustainers

Core Business Need
  Ways to continue and save

Firmographics
  Small in sales/employees
  Less sophisticated
  Lower in education
  Limited or no financial plan

Purchase Behavior
  Products that lower cost
  Low revenue per customer
  Confused by value-added solutions

Value Proposition
  Solutions that save your
  business money

NEEDS-BASED MARKET SEGMENTATION

Understanding customer needs is a basic tenet of market-based management. Although demographics, lifestyle, and usage behaviors help to shape customer needs, they are not always the best ways to identify groups of similar customers. Simply too many variables and too many meaningless combinations exist. Instead, the market segmentation process should start with customer needs as described here:

> First, group customers with like needs and then discover which of the many demographics, lifestyle forces, and usage behaviors make them distinct from customers with different needs.

In this way, we are able to let customer needs drive the market-segmentation process and let the unique combination of external forces that shaped them follow. This approach reduces the chance of an artificial segmentation of the market based on a combination of demographics and usage behaviors that are *not* the key forces that shape customer needs. However, before we proceed with the process of needs-based segmentation, let's first examine the demographic trap.

The Demographic Trap

Marketers new to market segmentation will often fall into the *demographic trap*. Given the strong role demographics, lifestyle, and usage play in shaping customer needs, it would seem logical to segment a market on the basis of these differences. For example, in the consumer financial services market, we could segment the market on the basis of differences in income, education, and age, as well as differences in amount invested, frequency of transactions, and type of investments purchased. If we created three meaningful categories for each of these six variables, we would have over 700 possible market segments!

$$\text{Number of Segments} = (3 \text{ categories per variable})^6 = 729$$

This is too many segments to consider if we are to develop a meaningful marketing strategy for each customer group. Perhaps even more important, it is possible that none of these 729 segments has anything to do with customer needs. It may be convenient to group customers into demographic, lifestyle, or usage categories, but the demographics selected may or may not be relevant in shaping customer needs. Although markets are heterogeneous, and people differ from one another by demographics, personal attitudes, and life circumstances, demographic segmentation seldom provides much guidance for product development or message strategies.[3] It makes more sense to start the market-segmentation process with customer needs and group customers on the basis of similar needs.

Needs-Based Market Segments

To illustrate the importance of needs-based segmentation, consider again how we might segment the market for investment services. Relevant demographics that might be considered to cause differences in needs could include income, assets, age, occupation, marital status, education, and perhaps, others. Relevant use behaviors might include experience with investments, size of investment portfolio, portfolio diversification, and

FIGURE 5-5 KEY STEPS IN A NEEDS-BASED MARKET SEGMENTATION PROCESS

Steps in Segmentation Process	Description
1. Needs-Based Segmentation	Group customers into segments based on similar needs and benefits sought by customer in solving a particular consumption problem.
2. Segment Identification	For each needs-based segment, determine which demographics, lifestyles, and usage behaviors make the segment distinct and identifiable (actionable).
3. Segment Attractiveness	Using predetermined segment attractiveness criteria, determine the overall attractiveness of each segment.
4. Segment Profitability	Determine segment profitability (net marketing contribution).
5. Segment Positioning	For each segment, create a "value proposition" and product-price positioning strategy based on that segment's unique customer needs and characteristics.
6. Segment "Acid Test"	Create "segment storyboards" to test the attractiveness of each segment's positioning strategy.
7. Marketing Mix Strategy	Expand segment positioning strategy to include all aspects of the marketing mix: product, price, promotion, and place.

amount of average transaction. Each of these influences could legitimately be argued to be an important force in shaping customer needs. However, attempting to segment this market on the basis of all of these differences would be a hopeless task. Instead, the first step in the market segmentation process outlined in Figure 5-5 is to determine customers' investment needs and the benefits they hope to derive from their investment decisions. A study of female investors' needs might produce three *needs-based segments*:[4]

- **Segment A:** Investors who seek investments that outperform inflation with minimum tax consequences.
- **Segment B:** Investors who seek investments that provide appreciation with limited risk.
- **Segment C:** Investors who seek investments that produce high levels of current income with minimal risk.

It would not take much of a financial adviser to figure out which type of investments would best suit each segment of investors. However, on the basis of needs alone, we do not know who these customers are. The primary benefit of needs-based market segmentation is that segments are created around specific customer needs. The primary disadvantage is that we do not know who these customers are. We need to determine what observable demographics and behaviors differentiate one segment from another in order to make a needs-based segmentation actionable.

Segment Identification

After grouping customers into needs-based segments, step 2 in the segmentation process is segment identification. For a segmentation scheme to be actionable, it must characterize segments by demographics or other measurable variables for purposes of targeting and positioning.[5] For each needs-based segment, we need to determine the demographics, lifestyles, and usage behaviors that make one segment meaningfully different from another. The key descriptive factors that make Segment A distinct from the other segments are career orientation, occupation, college education, and above-average income, as shown in Figure 5-6. Women in this segment are also more likely to be self-confident and individualistic, and to have interests outside the home. On the basis of these characteristics, this segment is labeled the *Career Woman*. With accurate delineation of segment needs and identification, one can begin to visualize a self-confident career woman who has discretionary income to invest but wants her investments to grow at a rate greater than inflation without the burden of additional taxes.

Although Segment B is in the same general age category as Segment A, customers in Segment B have lower incomes, are more likely to have young children, and are less likely to be married. They have less experience with investments and are more likely to be fearful of investment decisions. This segment is labeled the *Single Parent*, given both the unique family situation and lifestyle orientation.

Segment C is called the *Mature Woman* because of age, conservative outlook, and wealth position. These investors want investments that deliver high levels of current income with limited risk. Thus, all three segments have unique needs and identities that enable us to successfully accomplish the first two steps in the needs-based segmentation process outlined in Figure 5-5.

FIGURE 5-6 SEGMENT IDENTIFICATION: FEMALE INVESTOR MARKET SEGMENTS

Core Need: Segment Profile:	Growth Without Taxes Segment A	Appreciation with Minimal Risk Segment B	Income with Minimal Risk Segment C
Demographics			
Age	35–45	35–55	55–75
Income > $50,000	86%	3%	63%
Working	100%	43%	17%
Professional	83%	9%	13%
Married	56%	13%	35%
Youngest Child < 5	24%	83%	5%
College Educated	78%	23%	17%
Lifestyle			
Investment Attitude	Confident	Concerned	Conservative
Interests	Sports/Reading	Family	Leisure
Entertainment	Concerts	Movies	Television
Key Value	Individualistic	Cooperative	Traditional
Usage Behaviors			
Experience	Some/Extensive	None/Limited	Limited/Moderate
Risk Preference	Moderate/High	Low	Low/Moderate
Net Worth	Growing	Fixed	Fixed

Segment Attractiveness

What makes one segment attractive and another not attractive? Although every business might answer this question somewhat differently according to its industry perspective, when we step back and look more broadly at the factors that make a market attractive, we find few differences. Common to most assessments of segment attractiveness would be measurements of *market growth*, *competitive intensity*, and *market access*.

Market Growth

As shown in Figure 5-7, forces that shape market growth include the size of the segment, rate of growth, and market potential. Large, growing segments with potential for future growth are more attractive than combinations of small segments without potential for growth. Each of these forces directly affects the opportunity for profitable growth. A first step in assessing segment attractiveness is to identify the key market forces that contribute to an attractive market opportunity for growth.

Competitive Intensity

The number of competitors, the number of substitutes, and the competitive rivalry among competitors affect the attractiveness of a segment. Even if the market growth for a segment is attractive, the competitive intensity could more than offset its attractiveness and opportunity for profitable growth. If there are many competitors and market entry is relatively easy, market attractiveness diminishes because it becomes more difficult to achieve market share and margin objectives. In addition, if there are many substitute products and limited product differentiation, margins will be further compressed. An attractive segment is one with relatively few competitors, little price competition, very few substitutes, and high barriers to competitor entry.

Market Access

To be attractive, a segment has to be accessible. The first requirement is access to channels that reach target segment customers. Without customer familiarity and channel access, there is little opportunity for success. Market access also requires a good fit

FIGURE 5-7 FORCES THAT SHAPE SEGMENT ATTRACTIVENESS

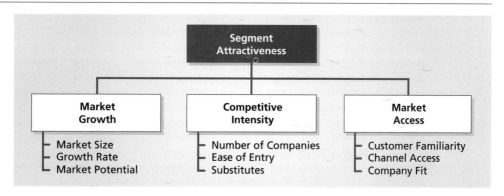

between a business's core capabilities and target segment needs. The better the match between customer needs and a business's sources of advantage, the easier it is to access markets. Without sufficient marketing resources, market access is greatly impeded. Segment attractiveness is greatly enhanced when a business has good customer access, sufficient marketing resources to access customers, and a good fit between business capabilities and customer needs.

The importance of market segmentation and segment attractiveness is highlighted in Figure 5-8. Without a segmentation of customers, this health insurance business attempted to sell to all willing buyers. However, customer segmentation based on insurance needs

FIGURE 5-8 MARKET SEGMENTATION OF THE BUSINESS INSURANCE MARKET

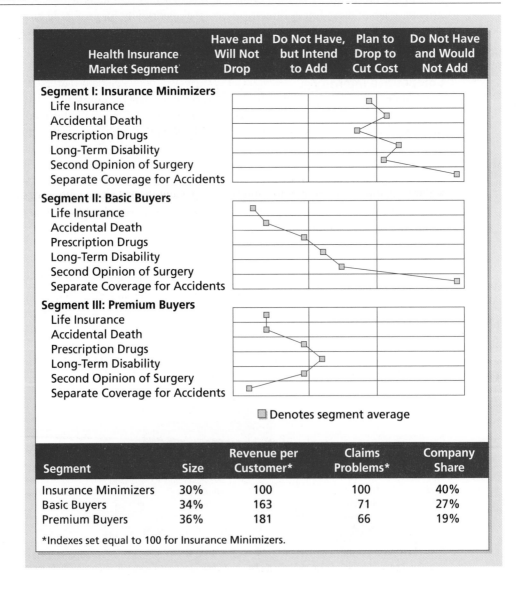

Segment	Size	Revenue per Customer*	Claims Problems*	Company Share
Insurance Minimizers	30%	100	100	40%
Basic Buyers	34%	163	71	27%
Premium Buyers	36%	181	66	19%

*Indexes set equal to 100 for Insurance Minimizers.

revealed that their greatest market penetration was in the smallest and least profitable segment, segment I. Given the relative attractiveness of the other two segments because of their revenue per customer and claims problems, the health insurance provider revised its marketing efforts around segments II and III. A key benefit of market segmentation is identifying segments that should *not* be pursued. As Chuck Lillis, the CEO of MediaOne Group, put it, "I will know when our businesses are doing a good job of market segmentation when they can articulate who we should *not* sell to." Businesses that do not segment their markets generally sell to everyone, and in doing so may hurt profits without even knowing it.

Segment Profitability

Although the market attractiveness of a segment may be acceptable, a business may elect not to pursue that segment if it does not offer a desired level of profit potential. To estimate segment profitability, we can estimate the net marketing contribution expected with a certain level of segment market penetration.

For example, the market for silicon sealants can be segmented into segments based on customer needs and product-market application, as illustrated in Figure 5-9. Although the silicon base product is the same in each market segment, the segment strategies are customized around different customer needs for (1) product amount, (2) product package, (3) product applicator, (4) engineering support, (5) technical service, (6) availability, and (7) price.

The *Engineered Solutions Segment* buys 100 million pounds per year and a silicon-sealants manufacturer is able to capture a 20 percent market share with a segment strategy designed for this segment. This segment is served with different size and packaging, a special silicon applicator, and a full technical-service solution provided through a one-on-one relationship between the company and the customer. Based on this level of product customization and service, a price of $10.00 per pound is obtained in this segment of the market. At this price level, margins are 60 percent and the cost of marketing expenses are 20 percent of sales. As shown here, this segment strategy yields a net marketing contribution of $80 million, a Marketing ROS of 40 percent, and Marketing ROI of 200 percent.

$$\begin{array}{c}\text{Net}\\ \text{Marketing}\\ \text{Contribution}\end{array} = \left[\begin{array}{c}\text{Segment}\\ \text{Demand}\end{array} \times \begin{array}{c}\text{Segment}\\ \text{Share}\end{array} \times \left(\begin{array}{c}\text{Price per}\\ \text{Unit}\end{array} - \begin{array}{c}\text{Percent}\\ \text{Margin}\end{array}\right)\right] - \begin{array}{c}\text{Marketing}\\ \text{Expense}\end{array}$$

$$= (100 \text{ million} \times .20 \times \$10.00 \times 60) - \$40 \text{ million}$$
$$= (20 \text{ million} \times \$6.00) - \$40 \text{ million}$$
$$= \$120 \text{ million} - \$40 \text{ million}$$
$$= \$80 \text{ million}$$

Marketing ROS = ($80 million / $200 million) × 100% = 40%

Marketing ROI = ($80 million / $40 million) × 100% = 200%

The *Service Solutions Segment* strategy is differentiated based on size of package, applicator, and direct sales and support. To enhance the *Service Solution Segment* strategy, industrial distributors are used to provide local availability and delivery. In this

FIGURE 5-9 SEGMENT MARKETING PROFITABILITY

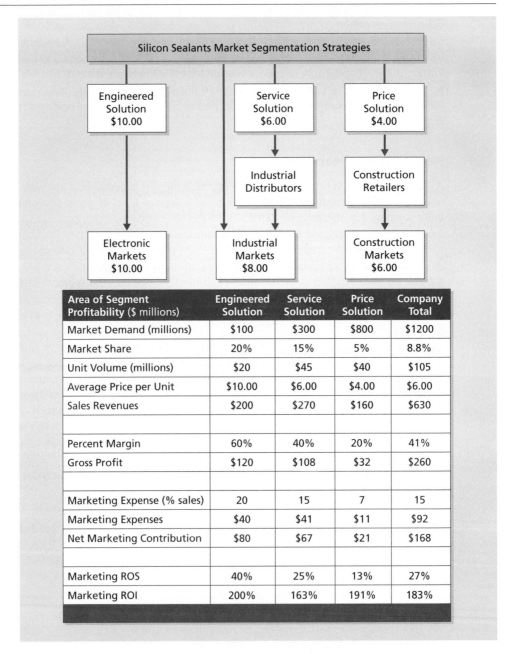

Area of Segment Profitability ($ millions)	Engineered Solution	Service Solution	Price Solution	Company Total
Market Demand (millions)	$100	$300	$800	$1200
Market Share	20%	15%	5%	8.8%
Unit Volume (millions)	$20	$45	$40	$105
Average Price per Unit	$10.00	$6.00	$4.00	$6.00
Sales Revenues	$200	$270	$160	$630
Percent Margin	60%	40%	20%	41%
Gross Profit	$120	$108	$32	$260
Marketing Expense (% sales)	20	15	7	15
Marketing Expenses	$40	$41	$11	$92
Net Marketing Contribution	$80	$67	$21	$168
Marketing ROS	40%	25%	13%	27%
Marketing ROI	200%	163%	191%	183%

segment, the net price is $6.00 per pound and the margin is 40 percent of the selling price. Marketing expenses in the Service Solution Segment are 15 percent of sales. As shown in Figure 5-9, this yields a Marketing ROS of 25 percent and a Marketing ROI of 167 percent.

The *Price Segment* is served with a large size package sold indirectly through construction retailers with no end-user sales or support. The net price in the *Price Segment* is $4.00 per pound with a margin of 20 percent of sales. The marketing expenses in the *Price Segment* are 7 percent of sales. This yields a marketing profit of $21 million. The *Price Segment* Marketing ROS is 13 percent and Marketing ROI 186 percent. Although the segment strategies vary considerably across these three segments based on customer needs, each segment strategy is profitable and contributes to the overall marketing profits of $168 million for all three segments.

Segment Positioning

For each target segment, a new set of marketing challenges needs to be addressed. A business needs to develop a customized *value proposition* for each positioning strategy that delivers value to target customers in each segment.[6] A value proposition includes all the key elements of the situation and the benefits the target customer is looking for in this purchase. For the female investor market described in Figure 5-6, Segment A included middle-aged professional women who were seeking investments that would have above-average growth with minimal tax consequences. The value proposition developed for this segment was: "*How to beat inflation and taxes with thoughtful investment planning.*" Ideally, the value proposition for a segment should be built around the key benefits sought by the target customer. As a result, the value proposition for Segment B and Segment C would be radically different because the needs, benefits, and purchase behaviors of these segments are radically different.

To develop a segment positioning strategy for each of the three segments, we need to return to Figure 5-6 as a guide. Because the three segments differ in primary needs, demographics, lifestyle, and purchase behaviors, it is important to use all this information in developing a customized positioning strategy for each segment.

Although there could be many possible strategies for each segment, Figure 5-10 outlines a value proposition and positioning strategy designed to meet the unique needs of each of these three segments. Product differences based on segment needs are relatively easy to determine. This is the first sign of a good segmentation program. If a business can readily link customer needs to specific product features and benefits, then it is on the right track in developing a successful segment strategy. If this linkage is difficult or arbitrary, target customers will be less likely to recognize a segment strategy as being unique. Because pricing is less important in the investment market than in, for example, the retail market, it is not a key part of the segment positioning strategy for any of the three segments. Had a segment emerged as price sensitive, then pricing may have become a critical issue in both the value proposition and the segment positioning strategy.

Promotion is critical in delivering the value proposition and communicating the identity of the customer target. Thus, both the ad copy and the media selected for advertising communications are crucial. For Segment A, the ad copy would portray a career woman in a business setting; potential media could include *Business Week*. Segment B requires a different approach because the family plays a larger role, as does limited experience in financial planning. Likewise, the promotion strategy for Segment C has to be carefully customized to the needs, lifestyles, and usage behaviors of mature female investors.

To reach customers in each of these segments, a business has to again be sensitive to the needs and lifestyle of the target customer. For the Career Woman, lunchtime seminars

FIGURE 5-10 SEGMENT STORYBOARDS FOR ACID TEST OF SEGMENT STRATEGIES

Investment Program A	**Investment Program B**	**Investment Program C**
How to Beat Inflation and Higher Taxes	*Special Help for Women with Special Money Problems*	*Safe Investment Solutions That Pay Good Income*
Key Benefits	**Key Benefits**	**Key Benefits**
• Capital Appreciation • Minimal Taxation	• Growth/Appreciation • Safety	• Safety • Income
Products	**Products**	**Products**
• Growth Stocks • Municipal Bonds • Growth Funds	• Growth Mutual Funds • Blue-Chip Stocks • High-Grade Bonds	• Utility Stocks • High-Grade Bonds • High-Dividend Stocks

Potential customers are instructed to examine each "segment storyboard" and select the one that best fits their investment needs. The degree to which target segment customers select the storyboard designed for them determines the degree to which the segment positioning strategy would be judged to be working.

at or near her place of work are used to more effectively deliver the value proposition and product portfolio that would best serve her needs and desired benefits. Morning or evening seminars at local schools are more likely to meet the place needs of the Single Parent Segment. A convenient location would be a key consideration in drawing mature women to a seminar customized to their needs. Interestingly, seminars targeted at the mature segment are given on cruise ships, where participants are able to write off a portion of their trip by attending a short seminar each day.

Segment Strategy Acid Test

To test our understanding of segment needs and our ability to translate that understanding into a value proposition, the next step in the segmentation process is an acid test of our strategy.[7] To conduct an acid test, we need to create at least three distinct segment storyboards, each of which delineates a different value proposition and segment positioning strategy. We would then ask potential customers to examine the segment storyboards and to select the one that best meets their needs. Figure 5-10 illustrates a sample storyboard for each of the female investor segments. A sample of female investors would be asked to evaluate each value proposition and each segment storyboard and to select the one that most appealed to them and their situation. If the strategy is successful, the majority of the potential customers from any given target segment will select the segment storyboard created for them. The higher the percentage of correct classification, the better the chance the business has of delivering a meaningful segment strategy. Of course, if target segment customers indicate that none of the segment storyboards fits their needs, then the business has failed to translate segment needs into a meaningful value proposition and segment positioning strategy. A telecommunications business found in an acid test that five segments found the storyboard created for them attractive, though they had suggestions on how to improve them, while one segment failed to find any of the segment storyboards attractive.

The business had to do more research, probing deeper into the overall needs of customers in the segment that failed to find an attractive segment storyboard. After additional customer research, and a second time through the acid test, the business was able to attract enough target segment customers to a revised storyboard to warrant moving forward in the segmentation process.

In another acid test, a segment of bank customers rejected a segment storyboard designed for them because it did not include the cost of a new service. A revised value proposition included both the benefits and the cost of this new service. In all cases, an important part of the acid test is to ask customers for ways in which the value proposition can be modified to better fit their needs, usage behavior, and lifestyle.

Segment Marketing Mix Strategy

Although this last step may seem a bit trivial given the preceding steps, a major cause of failure is ineffectively executing the segment strategy. To be successful, the segment strategy next needs to be expanded to include all elements of the marketing mix. The segment positioning strategy may include both product and price, but a complete marketing mix strategy needs also to include promotion (communications) and place (sales and distribution) strategies.[8] If target segment customers are not adequately aware of the segment value proposition or cannot acquire the product at preferred points of purchase, the segment strategy will fail.

For example, in Figure 5-11 we can see how DuPont developed different advertisements to execute a multi-segment strategy for Kevlar. Note the attention to distinct segment value propositions and product positioning differences that are unique to each target segment.[9] A generic ad highlighting product features would not have the impact that each segment-specific ad was designed to have.

SEGMENTATION STRATEGIES

On the basis of segment attractiveness, profit potential, and available resources, there are several segment strategies a business could pursue. As shown in Figure 5-12, segment strategies can range from a *mass market* strategy with no segment focus to *sub-segment strategies*, with numerous niche segments within segments. This section discusses these various segment strategies and the circumstances under which they are used.

Mass Market Strategy

When differences in customer needs are small or demographics are not distinctive, a business may elect to use a mass market strategy. This strategy presents a generic value proposition built around the core customer need and the business's generic positioning strategy.

FIGURE 5-11 DUPONT SEGMENT VALUE PROPOSITIONS AND POSITIONING STRATEGIES

Commercial Fishing

Value Proposition: *This boat hull of Kevlar saves fuel, gets there faster, and can carry more fish.*

Aircraft Design

Value Proposition: *Our L-1011 is 807 pounds lighter because of Kevlar 49.*

Wal-Mart, for example, pursues a mass market strategy built around a low-cost value proposition that has worked effectively for 30 years. Coca-Cola, Caterpillar, Sony, Marlboro, Phillips, Toyota, Volvo, and Kodak are some of many well-recognized global brands that use a global marketing strategy, while sometimes modifying their products and market communications to meet specific customer needs in specific international markets.

Large Segment Strategy

When a market is segmented and marketing resources are limited, a business could elect to pursue a large segment strategy. As illustrated in Figure 5-12, a mass market strategy could be segmented into three core segments. A large segment strategy would focus on segment A, because it is the largest, representing 50 percent of the market. Unlike a mass market strategy, a large segment strategy addresses one set of core customer needs. Thus, a large segment strategy engages the benefits of market segmentation while also providing a relatively large market demand. Chevy's truck strategy is a large segment strategy. Because market demand is somewhat limited and a large segment exists, this large segment strategy provides a cost-effective way to reach a large number of target customers.

FIGURE 5-12 MARKET SEGMENTATION STRATEGIES

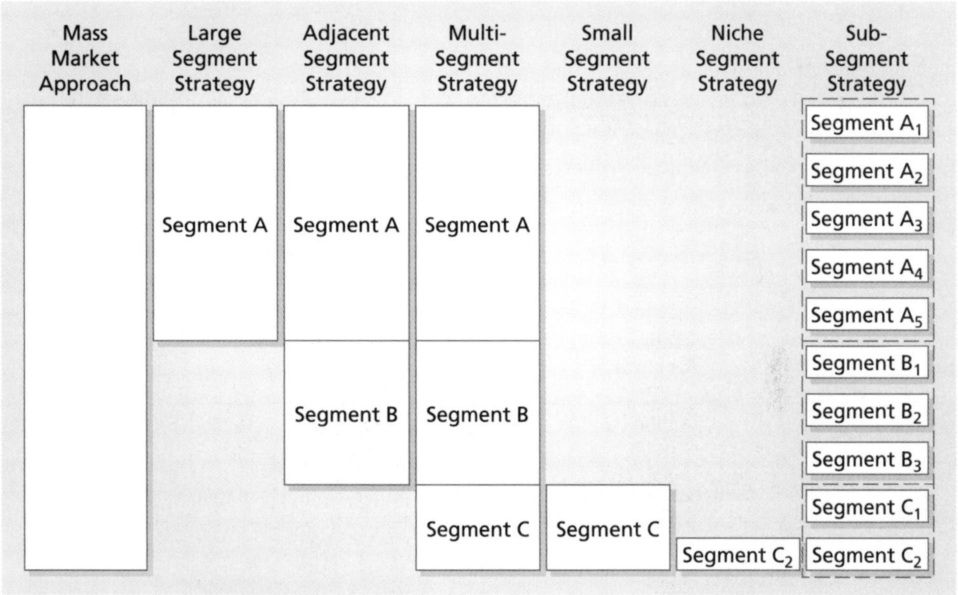

Mass Market Approach	Large Segment Strategy	Adjacent Segment Strategy	Multi-Segment Strategy	Small Segment Strategy	Niche Segment Strategy	Sub-Segment Strategy
						Segment A_1
						Segment A_2
	Segment A	Segment A	Segment A			Segment A_3
						Segment A_4
						Segment A_5
		Segment B	Segment B			Segment B_1
						Segment B_2
						Segment B_3
			Segment C	Segment C		Segment C_1
					Segment C_2	Segment C_2

Adjacent Segment Strategies

Quite often, businesses find themselves in a situation in which they have pursued a single segment focus but have reached the point of full market penetration. When this is the case, an adjacent segment strategy offers an attractive opportunity for market growth. Because resources are limited, a closely related attractive segment is tackled next. With profits derived from the primary target segment, the next most attractive adjacent segment is addressed.

In Figure 5-12, Segment B is profiled to be the next most similar to Segment A. When a business has reached full penetration of Segment A with a large segment strategy, it may pursue new growth by entering Segment B, an adjacent segment with respect to product and price needs.

An example of this segmentation strategy is Toyota's adjacent segment strategy in the U.S. car market. Toyota entered the U.S. market with the Corona at the low-price end of the market (today the Tercel serves this segment). As Toyota penetrated this segment, it moved to an adjacent segment in terms of price and quality by adding the Paseo, as shown in Figure 5-13. By the late 1980s, additional products were developed for higher price-quality segments. Next came entry into the luxury car segment with Lexus and an adjacent segment for the Supra and Avalon. Over a 40-year period, Toyota effectively used an adjacent segment strategy and today has a strong market position in each segment.

Multi-Segment Strategies

Market segmentation opens the door to multiple market-based strategies and greater marketing efficiency. For example, many retail gasoline companies operated for more than

FIGURE 5-13 TOYOTA'S ADJACENT SEGMENTATION STRATEGY

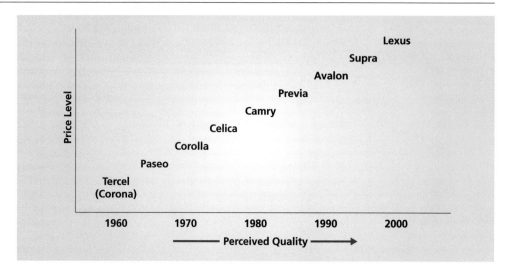

30 years on the fundamental belief that gas purchases were made primarily on the basis of price. This marketing belief guided their marketing strategy. However, a study of gas station customer needs uncovered five distinct segments, only one of which would be described as price shoppers.[10] The top three segments illustrated in Figure 5-14 are more concerned with quality, service, and the availability of other products such as coffee, soft drinks, sandwiches, and snack foods. In addition, each of the top three segments in the figure (Road Warriors, Generation F3, and True Blues) produced more revenue per customer than Home Bodies (convenience buyers) and Price Shoppers. These three target segments, which make up 59 percent of the gas customers, produce higher revenue per customer because they buy more gas, premium products, and food products. In addition, the average margin per customer in each of these segments is also higher than in the other two groups because the products they buy often have higher margins. By focusing on these three segments, a gas retailer could implement a series of marketing strategies to better serve the needs of these target segments and, if successful, grow its revenues and profits.

Perhaps an even more challenging multi-segment marketing strategy was one developed by an electric equipment manufacturer. The power generation and distribution market in the United States includes 7,000 entities. A segmentation study of this market produced 12 distinct needs-based segments that differed in customer needs, firmographics, and usage behavior,[11] as shown in Figure 5-15. At one extreme was a segment that included large, publicly owned utilities that had large engineering and maintenance staffs, and at the other extreme were small rural co-ops that produced electricity for small farming communities. Another segment actually included businesses that produce electricity for their own consumption and sell excess power to the local utilities. The Los Angeles Performing Arts Center is a customer in this segment. The electric equipment manufacturer found each of the segments attractive and already had sales to customers in each of the segments. The only difference was that before the segmentation study the business used a mass market strategy and treated all customers roughly the same. On the basis of the unique needs of

FIGURE 5-14 SEGMENTATION OF GASOLINE CUSTOMER MARKET

Segment	Size (%)	Core Customer Needs	Use Behavior	Key Demographics
Road Warriors	16	Premium Products and Quality Service	Drive 25,000 to 50,000 miles a year; buy premium gas, drinks, and sandwiches.	Higher income, middle-aged men.
Generation F3	27	Fast Fuel, Fast Service, and Fast Food	Constantly on the go; drive a lot, snack heavily, and want fuel and food fast.	Upwardly mobile men and women, half under 25.
True Blues	16	Branded Products and Reliable Service	Brand- and station-loyal; buy premium gas, pay cash.	Men and women with moderate to high income.
Home Bodies	21	Convenience	Use whatever gasoline is conveniently located.	Usually housewives who shuttle children during day.
Price Shoppers	20	Low Price	Neither brand nor station loyal.	Usually on tight budget.

each segment, 12 separate marketing programs were designed. Designing them required 12 different segment product-positioning and marketing approaches in order to build a strong value proposition for each segment.

The year the multi-segment strategy was implemented, the entire market experienced a decline of 15 percent in sales. In addition, one regional vice president had elected not to participate in the implementation of the multi-segment marketing strategy. Despite the market's decline, there were significant increases in sales in regions A and B and a smaller increase in region C, the control group, as shown in Figure 5-15. Overall, the business achieved a sales growth of more than 10 percent in a year that the market declined by 15 percent in sales volume. It is also important to note that this increase was achieved with essentially no change in marketing budget—simply better market focus and reallocation of marketing resources.

Small Segment Strategy

Although a market may provide three segment opportunities, a business with limited resources and certain capabilities may elect to compete in the smallest segment. The smallest segment, as represented by segment C in Figure 5-12, is often ignored by large competitors, who may use mass market or large segment strategies. Even businesses with a multi-segment strategy may not be able to compete effectively with a business that has a singular-focus small segment strategy. For example, Mercedes for many years used a small segment strategy to stay focused on the luxury car market. Having built a certain prestige in this market, Mercedes was reluctant to move into lower price-quality adjacent

FIGURE 5-15 MULTI-SEGMENT POWER GENERATION MARKET STRATEGY

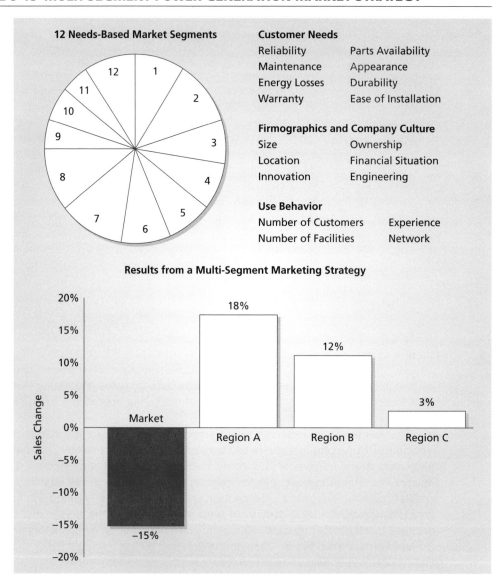

12 Needs-Based Market Segments

Customer Needs

Reliability	Parts Availability
Maintenance	Appearance
Energy Losses	Durability
Warranty	Ease of Installation

Firmographics and Company Culture

Size	Ownership
Location	Financial Situation
Innovation	Engineering

Use Behavior

Number of Customers	Experience
Number of Facilities	Network

Results from a Multi-Segment Marketing Strategy

segments. However, because of the increased attractiveness of adjacent segments, Mercedes is now pursuing a dual-segment strategy.

Niche Segment Strategies

Dividing a market into *homogeneous segments*—groups of customers with like needs—is never a perfect process. Even when customers in a given segment share common needs, there are still differences in demographics or usage behaviors that cannot be fully addressed with a single segment strategy. As a result, there is the opportunity for a business to carve out a niche within a segment and further customize its marketing effort to that group of target customers.

Consider the case of Sub-Zero refrigerators.[12] This business, with less than a 2 percent share of the U.S. refrigerator market, competes with industry giants who have large economies of scale and marketing resources. However, Sub-Zero holds 70 percent of the "Super Premium" segment, a niche market segment in the refrigerator market. Sub-Zero specializes in very expensive built-in refrigerators that start at $3,500. Target customers claim, "to own a Sub-Zero refrigerator is to have something special." It is hard to outperform niche competitors such as Sub-Zero because they have all their marketing resources focused on the specific needs of a certain type of customer. Within that segment, Sub-Zero can focus on a *niche market* that includes only high-end customers who are seeking a super premium refrigerator. For Sub-Zero, a needs-based market strategy is customized to the specific needs, lifestyle, and usage behavior of their niche customer.

Sub-Segment Strategies

Whether a market is segmented into 2 segments or as many 12, as in Figure 5-15, further customer differences could always be recognized. This often leads to confusion and to the following question: *How many segments are enough?* A better question is: *Are there meaningful differences in customer needs within segments that are not being met with the current market segmentation?* When the answer is yes, then further needs-based segmentation is warranted. If the answer is no, and core needs are met, then no further needs-based segmentation is required. However, it is possible that sub-segments within a core segment could be addressed with more precise marketing strategies to further serve customer needs within that segment.

Figure 5-12 shows a market divided into three needs-based segments: A, B and C. Within each core segment there are sub-segments that could be served with more customized marketing programs based on differences in product use or demographics. In this illustration, the segment A core segment strategy could be further customized to the use situation experienced for each of five sub-segments (A1, A2, A3, A4 and A5). Each of these sub-segments represents an opportunity to refine the core segment marketing strategy and tailor it to the individual needs of customers in these sub-segments.

For example, in Figure 5-16 we have expanded the two needs-based segments of the fiber-cement market presented in Figure 5-1 to include sub-segments within each of the two core segments. Within the quality segment, the "custom home" buyers and "spec home" builders generally have greater need for high-quality appearance. Because architects and custom home builders are important members of this sub-segment, a sub-segment strategy could be developed to better serve their application needs. James Hardie developed the Color Plus product and Trim Kit to better serve the needs of these sub-segment customers. Also within the same quality segment are "remodels" done by both builders and home owners who want a quality appearance but have slightly different problems in using fiber cement siding. Sub-segment strategies could be developed to further serve the unique needs of this "remodel" sub-segment.

The price segment is also divided into three sub-segments. Although driven primarily by price and the cost to install, these sub-segment customers differ in the problems they encounter in using fiber cement siding in tract homes, manufactured homes, and in

FIGURE 5-16 CORE AND SUB-SEGMENTS IN THE FIBER-CEMENT SIDING MARKET

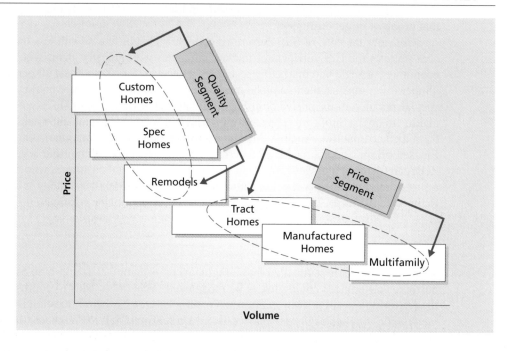

the construction of multifamily housing units. Appropriate sub-segment strategies could be developed to meet the needs of each of these smaller customer groups. Any sub-segment that does not warrant a specific marketing strategy is served with the core strategy for the price segment.

The addition of sub-segment customization allows a business to add further value and build customer loyalty. However, there is a trade-off between the cost of extending extra benefits to sub-segments of a market segment and the incremental financial benefit to the company. In some instances, the customer profitability and loyalty may be sufficiently low that a sub-segment strategy cannot be justified. When this is the case, the sub-segment customers would be served with the core segment strategy created for that segment's needs and use behaviors. As the profit potential for any given sub-segment increases, it becomes more attractive for a business to extend more personalized user communications to these sub-segment customers.

CUSTOMER RELATIONSHIP MARKETING

Many businesses work hard to acquire new customers, but this is where the customer relationship often stops. By contrast, customer relationship marketing is more focused on what happens after a customer is acquired in an effort to build a customer relationship that benefits both the customer and the company. For example, consider how Wells Fargo looks at individual customer relationships.[13]

"Much of the time, the opening of a new customer account is simply an opportunity to lose money. Most single-account households are unprofitable. We have to build a relationship to make a profit. If we can build a relationship, then we can keep customers through relationship building—not pushing products. They will reward us by buying more, buying profitably, and keeping more of their money with us."

—Terri Dial, CEO, Wells Fargo

As the potential for greater company value and customer value increases to higher levels, the opportunity exists to extend a business's market segmentation to individual customers. As shown in Figure 5-17, customer relationship marketing has different strategies based on different levels of value (benefits minus cost) for the company and its customers.

However, before we discuss these different individualized marketing strategies, it is important to understand the difference between customer relationship marketing and customer relationship management. To make this distinction clear, each is defined:

> *Customer relationship marketing* includes a range of one-on-one relationship marketing programs based on the level of company and customer value, as illustrated in Figure 5-17.
>
> *Customer relationship management* is a high-level customer relationship marketing program that attempts to build one-on-one relationships with certain customers when both company and customer value are high enough to warrant this level of marketing effort.

Customer Value Versus Company Value

Before going any further, we should define company value and how it differs from customer value in building a one-on-one customer relationship. Customers achieve greater customer value when the overall perceived benefits derived from products, services, and brand exceed by a meaningful margin the cost of obtaining these benefits (see Perceived Customer Value in Chapter 4). Customer relationship marketing attempts to create additional customer value through personalized communications, extra services, customized products, and special price offerings. Of course these added customer benefits come at some cost to the customer. When the customer perceives the overall benefits exceeding the overall costs by a meaningful margin, there is an attractive level of customer value in the one-on-one customer relationship.

Companies view value in more economic terms. As we saw in Chapter 1, higher levels of repeat purchase extended over longer periods of time create a higher lifetime customer value. As customer loyalty grows and customer retention increases, the lifetime value of the customer relationship also increases. Highly satisfied loyal customers have been shown to be more profitable. They typically buy more and often buy premium-priced products and services. The combination of higher customer profitability and higher customer loyalty creates a higher lifetime customer value based on the discounted cash flow over the life of the customer (see Lifetime Customer Value in Chapter 1).

FIGURE 5-17 CUSTOMER RELATIONSHIP MARKETING STRATEGIES

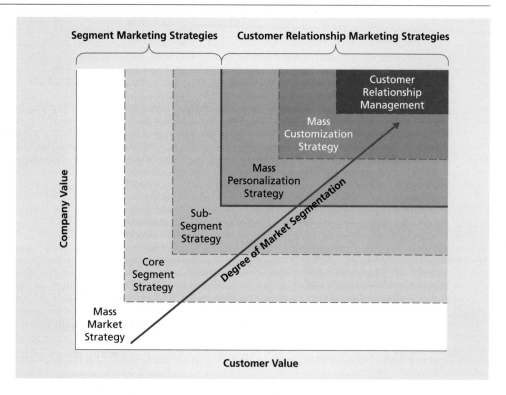

In Figure 5-17 we have indicated that as customer value and company value grows to the mutual benefit of both, a business may engage in higher levels of customer relationship marketing. Within any given segment or sub-segment, not all customers will have the potential for a high level of company value and customer value. For example, perhaps only 10 percent of all the builders and architects in the "custom home" sub-segment of the fiber cement siding quality market segment will offer the right combination of company value and customer value to warrant a customer relationship management program. The other 90 percent of the "custom home" sub-segment could be served with a mass personalization program customized for the "custom home" sub-segment, as shown in Figure 5-17.

Customer relationship marketing requires a higher level of marketing effort and marketing expense. As a result, it is important the company's extra marketing efforts warrant the cost. When both customer value and company value are favorable, a business can justify a one-on-one customer relationship marketing program. It is also possible that customers can migrate in customer loyalty and profitability and thereby receive different customer relationship marketing programs over time. A mass-customization customer could increase customer purchases and customer profitability to a level that a customer relationship management program of individualized customer services is developed for that customer to further build customer loyalty. However, before we discuss the three customer relationship marketing programs presented in Figure 5-17, we need to first discuss the role and importance of database marketing.

Database Marketing

At the core of customer relationship marketing is *database marketing*.[14] In customer relationship marketing, each customer is treated as unique and the goal is to build a more personal relationship between the business and the customer. The only difference in these customer relationship marketing programs is the level of company effort and customer benefit. As a result, it is necessary to have enough customer data to identify this customer individually by name, needs, buying behavior, and individual product preferences.

The rapid growth of database marketing technologies has lured many businesses down a side road to where technology is seen as the solution instead of a tool for building a solution. Without a solid commitment to serving individual customer needs, these businesses can fall into a *technology trap*. Many millions of dollars have been wasted implementing technological solutions without first strategizing a customer relationship marketing program.

The level of customer data required depends on the customer relationship marketing strategy to be used. Some customers may be targeted with a *mass-personalization* program that relies on largely personalized communications. Others may be served with a *mass-customization* strategy based on their buying behavior and individual needs for product and service customization. Still others, based on high levels of customer value and company value, may be good candidates for an individualized *customer relationship management* program.

It could be that certain customers across segments are excellent candidates for different types of customer relationship marketing programs. For example, referring to Figure 5-16, it is possible that certain contractors in the "tract home" building sub-segment would be best served with a mass-personalization strategy while others warrant a customer relationship management program. The overall goal of customer relationship marketing for a business is to serve customer needs as much as possible, subject to the cost of serving these needs (extra marketing expenses) and the benefits (customer loyalty and long-term customer profitability). The remainder of this chapter is devoted to a discussion of each of these customer relationship database marketing programs.

Mass Personalization

The first level of customer relationship marketing is a mass-personalization strategy that recognizes individual customers by name and buying behavior. This means the business recognizes the customer by name, buying behavior, and segment needs. Of course, a certain level of database marketing is needed to track individual customers and their buying history, segment needs, and segment value proposition. This information is then used to build personalized marketing communications for target customers.

For example, American Express has a core market segment labeled "Zero Spenders."[15] Zero Spenders are customers who hold an American Express Card and pay the annual fee but rarely or never use the card. These customers are marginally profitable and the most likely to defect. However, not all customers in this segment are the same. Some are not using the card because they can't afford much discretionary spending, but others are using cash or a competitor's card. To identify these sub-segments American Express developed a mass-personalization promotional program for these customers in the hope of attracting the high potential sub-segment customers. High potential customers attracted to these promotions self-select to participate in these attractive programs, which helps America Express better identify this sub-segment for future promotions in an effort to build American Express Card usage and customer loyalty.

A second example is United Airlines Frequent Flyer Mileage Plus program. This mass-personalization program allows customers to extend their involvement with United Airlines by joining the Frequent Flyer Program. This allows United to establish personalized communications and mileage awards based on level of customer travel. Customers who travel more are given more customer benefits. Frequent flyers can migrate to United Premium, Executive Premium, and 100K customer status. At each level, customer personalization increases with respect to mileage bonuses, ticket class upgrades, and personalized services provided, including exclusive 800-numbers for quicker customer reservations and problem solving.

In each case, United Airlines is striving to build customer retention and customer profitability with mass-personalization programs that add value for its frequent flyers. The goal is to personalize the customer interaction between the company's products and service, extending benefits to target customers based on the company's opportunity to grow customer loyalty, and customer profitability. As United expands these marketing efforts to include extra services or modified product offerings in building one-on-one marketing relationships, United is moving closer to a mass-customization program.

Mass Customization

Although market segmentation and sub-segmentation recognize that customers value a product's benefits differently, some customers within a segment are willing to pay more for extra benefits,[16] however, it is difficult to offer customers in the same segment different product-price configurations. Mass customization allows for this because the marketing mix is customized to level individual customer product preferences, extended services, and prices. Mass customization allows each customer to build a custom product to meet his or her specific needs, personal constraints, and price considerations. For example, Sun Microsystems allows for individual customer price customization and product configuration of their computer network solutions as described by Scott McNealy, CEO of Sun Microsystems[17]:

> We still have a price list here at Sun, but in the long run, we won't. We'll let our customers set prices in the online marketplace.

At Sun, mass-customization strategy treats every customer as a separate market segment in that individual customers are able to build the mix of product functions and service features that works best for their needs, product preferences, and the price they want to pay. With mass customization, customers build the product around their needs and the company delivers it to their specifications. This marketing strategy can only be done effectively when the incremental value is greater for the customers and the company. Ford, for example, expects mass customization to significantly reduce the $10 billion it spends on promotional pricing each year. Efforts like discount financing and cash-back programs have historically been offered to all customers on a broad range of models over a specific period of time. Mass customization allows Ford to finely target the price promotions for specific models and the customers who would most likely respond to a certain type of price promotion.[18]

Perhaps the most successful example of mass customization is Dell Computer. On Dell's web site, customers can choose from a variety of options to create their own computer configurations, which are then built to order and shipped within a short time. Figure 5-18 illustrates how mass customization works on Dell's web site.

Customers start with a base model and can then choose to customize it. Dell provides guidance on how to choose many options and in some cases gives recommendations. Considering a multitude of possible product configurations for Dell's Latitude D600 notebook computer, such guidance plays a vital role in helping customers not become overwhelmed to the point of indecisiveness. Once the options are set, clicking a button

FIGURE 5-18 MASS CUSTOMIZATION FOR ONLINE PURCHASE OF DELL NOTEBOOK COMPUTERS

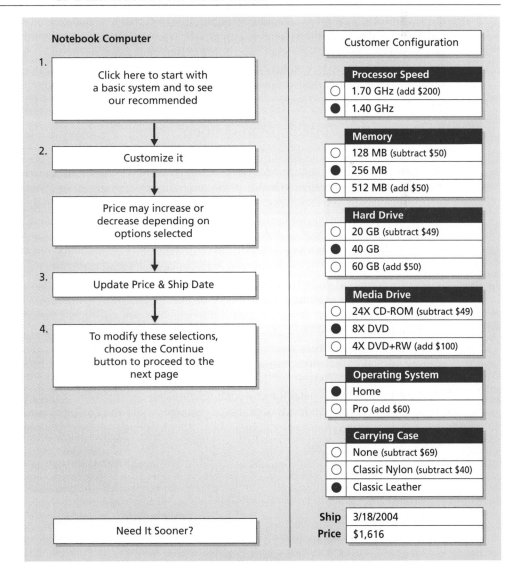

updates the price and shows the shipping date. Where delivery time is crucial, Dell even shows customers which options have the longest delay times, thus allowing them to factor in speed of delivery as another price-option.

Not only does a mass-customization marketing strategy allow Dell to provide customers with products that meet individual specifications, it also provides the company with important information about which features customers prefer, how preferences differ across demographic market segments, and how they change over time. This information is of paramount importance in a successful program of customer relationship marketing.

The use of mass customization essentially allows customers to become their own individual market segments. This is good for the customer as well as the business, because even the same customer may shift buying needs based on a changing situation. A number of companies are launching programs of mass customization, giving some validity to the word "custom-er". Products ranging from a Lexus to a Barbie Doll can now be individualized to suit a buyer's unique tastes. The whole point of mass customization is to let customers "build their product" according to their individual needs and price sensitivity. Mass customization combines the advantages of a niche-segment strategy with the breadth of opportunity available with multi-segment marketing strategies.

Customer Relationship Management

When the potential exists for high levels of both customer value and company value, a customer relationship management (CRM) program could be justified. Although needs-based market segmentation strives to build programs around target customers' needs in an effort to satisfy and retain customers, the ultimate goal of customer relationship management to build one-on-one customized relationships between a business and individual customers.[19]

The first step in building a successful customer relationship management program is to identify the level of company value and customer value for each customer. This requires a complete understanding of individual customer needs, product preferences, buying behaviors, customer loyalty, and customer profitability. A database marketing program is a key tool in developing this understanding, but customer relationship management is much more than just technology. Successful CRM actually develops and maintains one-on-one relationships with key customers.[20] Outlined here are four steps that are critical to the success of any customer relationship management program.

Step I: Qualify potential customer relationship management customers based on attractive levels of potential customer value and company value.

Step II: Understand individual customer needs, product preferences, and use behaviors.

Step III: Build an individualized customer solutions based on individual customer needs and establish one-on-one customer touch points in building and sustaining this relationship.

Step IV: Track customer experiences and all aspects of customer satisfaction to ensure high levels of customer satisfaction and customer loyalty are achieved.

To better understand this process let's examine how Marriott uses customer relationship management to better serve its Top Performers and High Potential customers. Marriot serves a segment they term the "Business Traveler." The Business Traveler customer has unique needs and travel patterns that require they be served with a different customer solution. In Step I, certain business travelers were identified as potentially profitable and loyal customers. Step II involved building a Marriott customer database of target customer profiles based on customer requests and stored preferences from past visits when a business customer calls to make a reservation at Marriott. Based on individual customer needs, tee times are scheduled, dinner reservations arranged, and recreation itineraries are created (Step III). With this individualized customer relationship solution in place, Marriott carries out Step IV by maintaining individual contact with customers to measure all aspects of their customer experience. This level of customer interaction facilitates the process of building customer loyalty and tracking customer performance.

For Marriott, high customer-satisfaction scores have translated into higher levels of repeat business and customer loyalty. Marriott has learned that customers who participate in their Personal Planning Service (a one-on-one marketing program) produce significantly higher customer-satisfaction scores and spend an average of $100 per day *more* on services beyond the room rate. This higher revenue per customer and higher levels of loyalty have translated into a hotel occupancy rate 10 percentage points higher than the industry average.

An important concept in customer relationship management is *customer touch points*. Every interaction with a customer or a potential customer is a *touch point*. Customer touch points include obvious interactions such as storefronts, Web sites, voice mail systems, direct mail advertising, mass e-mail messages, order desks, return counters, and service calls. Indirect customer touch points are less obvious, but sometimes even more important in developing potential customers into actual customers. These are often informational contacts such as news articles and word-of-mouth advertising, yet they shape the beliefs and attitudes of potential customers toward the business and its products and services.

At every point of contact—before, during, and after a sale—the way a business communicates shapes its relationships with customers and potential customers. The way a business manages each customer relationship from the first touch point determines the long-run profit potential of that customer.

■ Summary

At the heart of market-based management is a skillful execution of market segmentation. It is the core of a market-based strategy because it is built around customer needs, unique lifestyles, and usage behaviors. To the degree to which a business understands differences in customer needs, it can translate them into actionable segment strategies.

A specific segmentation process was presented with special emphasis on creating needs-based segments. Although it may be easy to create segments on the basis of differences in demographics or behavior, doing so may lead to a marketing strategy that does not deliver a needs-based customer solution. Demographics shape customer needs, and demographics also serve as a measurable way to identify needs-based market segments, but not always. The first step is to identify segments based on needs. Then needs-based segments must be demographically identified so that actionable strategies can be created for each segment.

These first two steps are crucial. The next steps in the segmentation process require that we index overall segment attractiveness and estimate segment profit potential to select target segments. A value proposition and marketing mix strategy must be developed for each target segment selected. To ensure that we have accurately translated target customer needs and identity characteristics into our positioning strategy (value proposition and marketing mix), a segment acid test is carried out. This enables a business to determine if customers are adequately attracted to the combination of a target segment value proposition and segment strategy designed for them. On the basis of customer feedback, a revised strategy can be finalized and implemented.

In some instances, resources may be limited and only a single segment or niche (sub-segment) within a segment may be pursued. In other instances, a multi-segment strategy may fit the resources and capabilities of a business. Of course, the more segment strategies a business has, the more difficulty it encounters in maintaining a distinct marketing strategy for each segment. With the use of database marketing, a business can actually take either a segment strategy or a multi-segment strategy one step further with mass customization. With mass customization, a business is able to further customize its value proposition and segment positioning through customized product positioning and communications. Mass customization enables a large business to obtain the advantages of a niche marketer while also serving many segments and niches within segments. A logical extension of mass customization is customer relationship management.

The ultimate goal of customer relationship management is an ongoing individual relationship between a business and individual customers. Because not all customers can be served by CRM, a critical first step is market segmentation. Once target customers are profiled, customized solutions can be built through individual customer touch points in an effort to satisfy and retain target customers.

■ Market-Based Logic and Strategic Thinking

1 How did market segmentation help James Hardie in its marketing strategy?
2 Why should customer needs be the driving force in segmenting a market?
3 What kind of problems can occur if a business segments a market on the basis of demographics or usage?
4 How are customer needs shaped and what role do these forces play in the segmentation process?
5 What happens when a business is able to segment a market on the basis of needs but unable to demographically or behaviorally identify the segments?
6 How does firmographics help shape business-to-business customer needs?
7 What forces shape market attractiveness and how should they be measured in order to develop an overall index of market attractiveness?
8 What criteria should be used in determining which segments a business should pursue?
9 What is a segment value proposition? Why is it a crucial part of the segmentation process?
10 How would you develop a value proposition for a retail gasoline business's target customers?

11 What is a segment marketing mix strategy? How did the marketing mix strategy differ for each of the three segments of the female investor services market?

12 What is an "acid test"? What are the advantages of performing an acid test?

13 How did DuPont create an effective multi-segment strategy for Kevlar?

14 What is an adjacent-segment strategy? Why would a business pursue an adjacent-segment strategy when more than one segment of the market is attractive and offers good profit potential?

15 When would a business pursue a single-segment market strategy?

16 Why is a niche strategy often difficult for competitors to outperform?

17 What is mass customization? How could a business using a mass-customization strategy match the effectiveness of smaller niche competitors?

18 What is customer relationship marketing? How should it improve customer satisfaction and retention?

19 Why is market segmentation a critical first step in building a customer relationship marketing program?

20 What are "customer touch points" and what role do they play in customer relationship management?

Marketing Performance Tools

Each of the following **marketing performance tools** can be accessed by going to *www.rogerjbest.com* or *www.prenhall.com/best*. The shaded cells are input cells. The non-shaded cells contain results calculated from your input values.

MARKETING PERFORMANCE TOOL—Profit Impact of Segment Strategy

Marketing Strategy	Mass Market Strategy	Quality Segment	Price Segment	Segment Strategy
Market Demand	3,000,000,000	900,000,000	2,100,000,000	3,000,000,000
Market Share (%)	67.0	67.0	67.0	67.0
Unit Volume	2,010,000,000	603,000,000	1,407,000,000	2,010,000,000
Average Price	$0.55	$2.00	$0.50	$0.95
Sales Revenues	$1,105,500,000	$1,206,000,000	$703,500,000	$1,909,500,000
Percent Margin (%)	30.0	60.0	25.0	47.1
Gross Profit ($)	331,650,000	723,600,000	175,875,000	899,475,000
Marketing & Sales (% sales)	12.0	20.0	8.0	15.6
Marketing & Sales Expenses	$132,660,000	$241,200,000	$56,280,000	$297,480,000
Net Marketing Contribution	$198,990,000	$482,400,000	$119,595,000	$601,995,000
Marketing ROS (%)	18.0	40.0	17.0	31.5
Marketing ROI (%)	150	200	213	202

This **marketing performance tool** allows you to estimate the sales and marketing profitability of a mass-market strategy and a strategy that segments the mass market into two needs-based market segments. The data is from an electronics company that could not compete effectively in the price segment of its market. Management shifted more marketing resources (15% of sales) to the quality segment and was able to raise prices to $2,500. This raised margins to 40 percent. For the price segment, they lowered the average price to $1,250 but reduced marketing resources to 5 percent of sales.

Application Exercise: How low would the price in the quality segment have to drop for the segment strategy to produce the same net marketing contribution as the mass-market strategy?

Holding price in the quality segment at $2,500, how much would the marketing and sales expenses in the price segment have to increase to achieve the same net marketing contribution as the mass-market strategy?

MARKETING PERFORMANCE TOOL—Profit Impact of Customer Relationship Marketing

Annual Customer Performance	Segment Average	Mass Personalization	Mass Customization	Customer Relationship Mgmt
Revenue per Customer	$1,000	$1,000	$1,200	$1,500
Percent Margin (%)	40	40	50	60
Gross Profit per Customer	$ 400	$ 400	$ 600	$ 900
Acquisition Cost	$ 500	$ 500	$ 500	$ 500
Retention Cost	$ 100	$ 150	$ 200	$ 250
Customer Profits	$ 300	$ 250	$ 400	$ 650
Customer Retention	0.60	0.67	0.75	0.80
Customer Life (years)	2.5	3.0	4.0	5.0
Discount Rate (%)	20	20	20	20

Customer Cash Flow Year	Cash Flow	Cash Flow	Cash Flow	Cash Flow
0	-$500	-$500	-$500	-$ 500
1	$300	$250	$400	$ 650
2	$300	$250	$400	$ 650
3	$150	$250	$400	$ 650
4			$400	$ 650
5				$ 650
6				
7				
8				
9				
10				
Lifetime Value	$ 45.14	$ 26.62	$535.49	$1,443.90

This **marketing performance tool** allows you to evaluate the customer profitability and lifetime value of different customer relationship marketing programs.

Application Exercise: For the previous customer relationship marketing situation, address the following questions:

■ How would the customer profitability and lifetime value change for the mass-person-alization program if the customer retention dropped from .67 to .60?

■ At what level of percent margin would the mass-customization program no longer produce a positive customer profit?

■ At what level of revenue per customer would the customer relationship management program not produce a positive lifetime value?

Notes

1. Wendell Smith. "Product Differentiation and Market Segmentation as Alternative Marketing Strategies," *Marketing Management* (Winter 1995): 63–65.
2. Delbert Hawkins, Roger Best, and Kenneth Coney. *Consumer Behavior: Implications for Marketing Strategy*, 6th ed. (New York: Irwin, 1995): 4–25.
3. Marshall Greenberg and Susan McDonald Schwartz. "Successful Needs/Benefits Segmentation: A User's Guide," *Journal of Consumer Marketing* (Summer 1989): 29–36.
4. "Merrill Lynch Campaign Targeted at Women Stresses Investment Options," *Marketing News* (November 30, 1979): 11.
5. Sachin Gupta and Pradeep Chintagunta. "On Using Demographic Variables to Determine Segment Membership in Logit Mixture Models," *Journal of Marketing Research* (February 1994): 128.
6. Michael Lanning. *Delivering Profitable Value* (Reading, MA: Perseus Books, 1998): 39–88.
7. William Band. "Customer-Accelerated Change," *Marketing Management* (Winter 1995): 19–33.
8. P. Dickson and J. Ginter. "Market Segmentation, Product Differentiation, and Marketing Strategy," *Journal of Marketing* (April 1987): 1–10.
9. G. Coles and J. Culley. "Not All Prospects Are Created Equal," *Business Marketing* (May 1986): 52–59.
10. Allanna Sullivan. "Mobil Bets Drivers Pick Cappuccino Over Parties," *Wall Street Journal* (January 30, 1995).
11. Dennis Gensch. "Targeting the Switchable Industrial Customer," *Marketing Science* (Winter 1984): 41–54.
12. J. Levine. "Cool!" *Forbes* (April 1996): 98.
13. Melinda Nykamp. *The Customer Differential* (New York: Amacom, 2001): 11.
14. Stan Rapp and Tom Collins. *MaxiMarketing* (New York: McGraw-Hill, 1987); Jonathan Berry. "Database Marketing—A Potent New Tool for Selling," *Business Week* (September 5, 1995): 56; Robert Buzzell and Rajendra Sisoda. "Information Technology and Marketing," in *Companion Encyclopedia of Marketing*, Michael Baker, ed. (Los Angeles: Rutledge, 1995).
15. Louise O'Brien and Charles Jones. "Do Rewards Really Create Loyalty," *Harvard Business Review* (May–June, 1995): 75–82.
16. James Gilmore and Joseph Pine II. "The Four Faces of Mass Customization," *Harvard Business Review* (January–February 1997): 91–103.
17. Scott McNealy. "Welcome to the Bazaar," *Harvard Business Review* (March 2001): 18–19.
18. Walter Baker, Mike Marn, and Craig Zawada. "Price Smarter on the Net," *Harvard Business Review* (February 2001): 122–127.
19. Don Peppers and Martha Rogers. *The One-On-One Future: Building Relationships One Customer at a Time* (Doubleday, 1997).
20. Don Peppers and Martha Rogers. *One to One B2B: Customer Development Strategies for the Business to Business World* (Doubleday, 2001).

Competitor Analysis and Sources of Advantage

Almost 2,500 years ago (510 B.C.) Sun Tzu, a Chinese general, wrote a military manual called *The Art of War*.[1] General Sun Tzu concluded that the out-and-out destruction of an enemy resulted in greater *losses* than the *gains* achieved. General Sun Tzu believed that deception, restraint, and minimalism were the best ways to defeat an enemy. Though it may seem paradoxical in competition and warfare, the major premise in *The Art of War* is neutralizing and subjugating a competitor into following without fighting. This is why *The Art of War* is a best seller today and its principles of competition are studied in many major corporations.[2]

KNOWLEDGE IS A SOURCE OF ADVANTAGE

In his manual, General Sun Tzu presents competitive strategy as a process of developing a *knowledge advantage* and then attacking *obliquely* in a way that is less noticed but in the end causes your competitor to follow you. With a less confrontational approach, General Sun Tzu believed that better results could be achieved without significant losses. Focused on a knowledge advantage, General Sun Tzu built competitive strategies based on superior knowledge of both the terrain (customers) and the enemy (competition).

In any competitive environment, knowledge is the key source of competitive advantage. In business, customers are what a business is trying to win, and competitors are the forces it is fighting to achieve that same goal. Without adequate knowledge of both customers and competitors, a business is severely handicapped in developing strategies to gain customers or grow market share. A knowledge advantage is necessary to develop a winning oblique strategy. Partial knowledge may seem like an advantage, but it often results in *reactive strategies* as depicted in Figure 6-1. A business with excellent customer knowledge but limited competitor knowledge is likely to overreact to customer demands. Likewise, having excellent competitor knowledge without adequate customer knowledge is likely to result in an overreaction to competitors' moves.

As shown in Figure 6-1, businesses that lack both customer knowledge and competitor knowledge are working with an *inside the box strategy* as they drive competitive moves from an internal perspective with minimal or limited market knowledge. Such a business can only make blind attempts at success that usually end up losing more ground than they gain.

FIGURE 6-1 COMPETITIVE STRATEGIES BASED ON LEVELS OF KNOWLEDGE

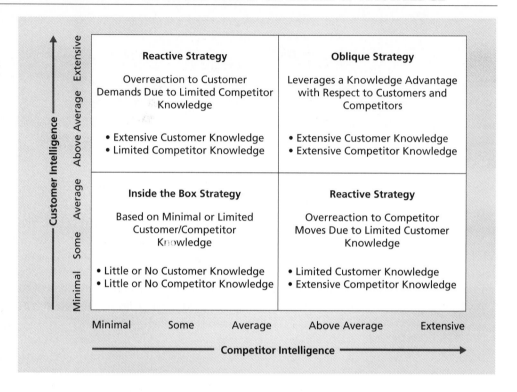

Others, with partial intelligence with respect to customers or competitors are likely to employ reactive strategies. These are normal responses to customer or competitor pressures when a business only sees one aspect of the marketplace. An oblique strategy requires superior customer intelligence and superior competitor intelligence as depicted in Figure 6-1.

With a knowledge advantage, a market-based strategy can be devised to achieve desired gains without sustaining excessive losses. Following Sun Tzu's general approach, market-based strategies that leverage a knowledge advantage with respect to both customers and competitors can be implemented with a nonconfrontational approach that minimizes losses. We have labelled this an oblique strategy because it seeks to gain a competitive advantage without direct confrontation. A competitive strategy with limited or partial customer and/or competitor knowledge could be more easily drawn into a frontal attack strategy—a direct attack on a competitor's position. To illustrate each type of competitive strategy, let's examine both types of competitive strategies.

Frontal Attack Strategy

A *frontal attack strategy* occurs when a business directly challenges a competitor in a battle for market share. In this battle for volume, sales, and market share, a frontal attack strategy often results in a "win/lose" outcome; the business achieves its marketing objective (wins the battle), but ends up with less profits (loses the war). To illustrate this, consider two frontal attack strategies, each in a blind pursuit of market share as illustrated in Figure 6-2.

FIGURE 6-2 FRONTAL ATTACK STRATEGIES OFTEN WIN THE BATTLE FOR MARKET SHARE BUT RESULT IN LOWER PROFITS

Area of Performance	Pre-Battle Performance	Price Battle Performance	Marketing Battle Performance
Market Demand (units)	1,000,000	1,000,000	1,000,000
Market Share (%)	40	50	50
Volume Sold (units)	400,000	500,000	500,000
Price per Unit	$100	$90	$100
Sales Revenues	$40,000,000	$45,000,000	$50,000,000
Cost per Unit	$70	$70	$70
Margin per Unit	$30	$20	$30
Gross Profit	$12,000,000	$10,000,000	$15,000,000
Marketing Expenses (% sales)	15	15	20
Marketing Expenses	$6,000,000	$6,750,000	$10,000,000
Net Marketing Contribution	**$6,000,000**	**$3,250,000**	**$5,000,000**

The first frontal attack strategy used a 10 percent price reduction to grow market share from 40 percent to 50 percent. As shown in Figure 6-2, this frontal attack produced a 25 percent increase in volume and a $5 million increase in sales. Goals were achieved, except that the approach resulted in a 46 percent reduction in marketing profits. Of course, losses in profits could be even greater when competitors retaliate and market gains are only marginally achieved.

A second frontal attack strategy used an increase in marketing expenses from 15 percent of sales to 20 percent in order to grow market share from 40 percent to 50 percent. Again the goal was achieved with volume increasing 25 percent and sales growing by $10 million, as shown in Figure 6-2. However, the cost of gaining 10 market share points was not worth the expense because marketing profits dropped by 16.7 percent. In these two examples, the business won sales and market share in a head-to-head battle with competitors, but in the end they lost more than they gained. They may have won the battle for market share and sales growth, but they lost the battle in terms of lower profits, and thus achieved a "win-lose" outcome.

Oblique Strategy

An oblique strategy is an indirect attack on a competitor's position in an attempt to win market share with minimal expenses. The goal is to achieve the objective in a battle for market *share* but do it in a way that creates the lowest cost and minimal competitor response. An oblique strategy is best achieved when a business leverages a source of advantage valued by customers (customer knowledge) that is not easily seen, understood, or copied by competitors (competitor knowledge). The goal of an oblique strategy is to gain market share and customers in a way that minimizes competitor response but achieves the desired marketing objective. This type of strategy does not directly attack competitors. Oblique strategies are more covert or tangential, focused more on the customers, and ideally end up confusing and baffling competitors. Oblique strategies can include subtle but important product innovations, improved product and/or service quality, innovative marketing programs, lowered costs of acquiring, using and disposing of products, and new marketing channels with more efficient supply-chain customer benefits. Each of these oblique strategies has the potential to build customer value and loyalty without directly confronting competitors and thus lower the cost of gaining market share.

To better understand oblique strategies, let's examine how they were used in three businesses. Anixter is a distributor of electronics parts that include the cables and connections to hook computers up to the Internet. They do not make the products; they are simply a distributor of commodity-type electrical and electronic peripheral parts. In a highly price-competitive environment, Anixter commands a price premium for its products. What their competitors see (with limited knowledge) is a high price. However, what their customers see and get is a lower total cost of purchase because Anixter works to reduce the customer's cost of acquisition and installation. Anixter's competitive tactics are under the radar screen for most competitors. Because most are in the dark with respect to extensive customer and competitor knowledge, Anixter leverages a source of knowledge advantage not seen by competitors. The net result is a high market share, higher margins, and higher profitability.

Dell Computer launched its company with an oblique strategy. Rather than confronting the competitive PC industry head-on, Dell's oblique leverage strategy went around retailers and distributors with a new direct marketing channel strategy. Part of Dell's approach was to remind customers every time they could of how Dell is different from its competitors and how they, the customers, can benefit from that differentiation. Dell grew this strategy into a dominant share position while some competitors watched and others eventually followed and tried to compete with Dell's strategy.

Google also used an oblique strategy to grow market share with product innovation that provided Internet customers with greater speed, accuracy, and ease of use. An important part of Google's oblique strategy and sustainable competitive advantage is based on a knowledge advantage. Almost 10 percent of Google's employees are Ph.D.s who are encouraged to come up with new innovative solutions. Google has also created innovative marketing solutions such as AdWords to further leverage its knowledge advantage. As shown in Figure 6-3, Google's oblique strategy increased its relative market share and profits as managers prepared to take their company public in 2004.

COMPETITION AND COMPETITIVE POSITION

Although the successes of Google, Dell, and Anixter are impressive, it is often difficult to hold a competitive advantage because competition and the competitive environment are always changing. To stay ahead, these companies must continuously update their customer and competitor knowledge and monitor their level of competitive advantage. Think about General Motors, NBC, or Sears; it was not so long ago that the competitive position of each of these market leaders changed dramatically. For General Motors, it was foreign competition that eroded its competitive position—first with lower prices, and then with higher levels of product quality. For NBC, CBS, and ABC, it was first ESPN, CNN, and Fox and then a multitude of cable networks and the Internet. For Sears, and others, it was Wal-Mart, Target, and Costco.

FIGURE 6-3 COMPETITIVE ADVANTAGE, RELATIVE MARKET SHARE, AND PROFITABILITY

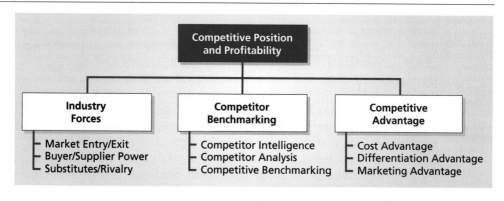

Competitor	1999 (%)	2003 (%)
Google	29.1	40.0
Yahoo!	27.3	27.1
MSN	18.2	15.9
AOL	14.5	11.4
Relative Share	48	74

$$\text{Relative Market Share} = \frac{40\%}{27.1\% + 15.9\% + 11.4\%} \times 100 = 74$$

Google has continued to improve its relative market share from 48 to 74 with product and marketing innovation. Relative market share has been shown to be correlated with profitability.

Profit Impact

0 10 20 30 40 50 60 70 80 90 100

→Relative Market Share Metric →

In each case, the market leader once held a strong, almost impenetrable competitive position. In each case, when new competitive forces emerged, the competitive position of the market leader was seriously eroded. It is important to recognize that in each example, the market leader had not lowered quality, raised prices, or cut back on marketing efforts. On the contrary, each had made serious efforts to improve products, reduce prices, and expand marketing efforts to retain customers. However, in each case, the competitive forces brought to bear on its market first challenged, and then eroded, the market leader's competitive position.

Three important aspects of competition affect a business's competitive position and profitability, as outlined in Figure 6-4. The first, industry forces, has to do with the

FIGURE 6-4 COMPETITIVE FORCES THAT SHAPE COMPETITIVE POSITION AND PROFITABILITY

Competitive Position and Profitability

Industry Forces
- Market Entry/Exit
- Buyer/Supplier Power
- Substitutes/Rivalry

Competitor Benchmarking
- Competitor Intelligence
- Competitor Analysis
- Competitive Benchmarking

Competitive Advantage
- Cost Advantage
- Differentiation Advantage
- Marketing Advantage

competitive forces within an industry. These competitive forces shape a market's attractiveness and profit potential. An important step in market analysis is to conduct an industry analysis of markets in order to select those markets that offer the best profit potential.

Second, within an industry or market, it is important for a business to benchmark its competitive position. External market measures of relative product quality, service quality, customer satisfaction, brand awareness, and market share are crucial market metrics that benchmark the strength of a business's competitive position. Internal metrics such as unit cost, order cycle time, delivery costs, accounts receivable, and sales per employee are equally important in benchmarking and managing competitiveness. However, to improve on an important competitive weakness, a business needs to benchmark world-class performance outside its industry in order to gain a competitive advantage.

Finally, to achieve a superior level of profitability, a business needs to attain a source of sustainable competitive advantage. This could be a cost advantage that yields more attractive prices, a differentiation advantage that enhances product preference or price premiums, or a marketing advantage that achieves greater customer awareness and availability. The purpose of this chapter is to examine each of these areas of competition and explore how it is used in the development of market-based strategies.

INDUSTRY ANALYSIS

A first step in industry analysis is to determine the attractiveness of the competitive environment. Developing a strong competitive position in an unattractive market has the potential to lessen profitability even when a business's competitive position in that industry is relatively strong.[3] Picking the right markets (industries) in which to compete is a crucial step in market analysis and strategy development.

Shown in Figure 6-5 are industry forces that shape the attractiveness of a competitive environment. Each of these industry forces can be evaluated along a continuum from unfavorable to favorable. As the sum of these forces favors a more attractive competitive environment, there is greater profit potential. A business in a market with low entry barriers, high exit barriers, high levels of customer and supplier power, many substitutes, and intense rivalry among competitors will have a lower profit potential than a business with a more favorable set of competitive forces.

Barriers to Entry

Market entry can be blocked in many ways. Many international markets are blocked by political barriers. These barriers reduce competition and enhance profit potential for protected competitors. Technology or low-cost manufacturing can also create entry barriers. Businesses with a superior cost or technological advantage create a market entry barrier that discourages competitors from entering a market. In addition, the resources needed to compete in a given market could be so great that entry is limited. High advertising expenditures, R&D spending, and sales force expenditures can each require resource levels that can block market entry for businesses with limited resources. For example, barriers to entry in the pharmaceutical industry are relatively high. Patents on prescription drugs, high R&D investments, and large sales forces needed to contact physicians deter competitor entry and contribute to the attractiveness of this competitive environment.

FIGURE 6-5 INDUSTRY ANALYSIS: INDUSTRY FORCES AND PROFIT POTENTIAL

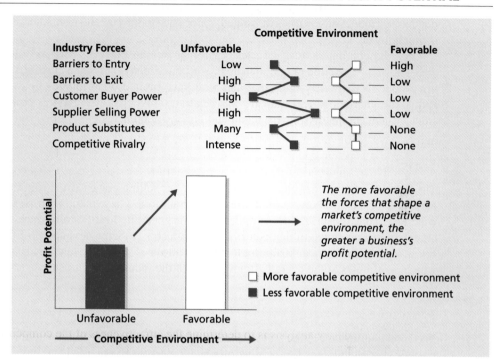

Barriers to Exit

The competitive environment is also enhanced when weak competitors can easily exit a market. Legal barriers, specialized assets, or the strategic importance of a business often prevent businesses from exiting markets when they should. A pharmaceutical company that is losing money on a particular prescription drug may want to exit, but legal, political, or social forces could create an environment in which market exit would be very difficult. The struggle to survive can lead to competitive practices that adversely affect industry profits.

Likewise, a business that has invested in specialized assets (capital or people or both) may find it difficult to exit a market because these assets are not easily sold or transferred to another business application. Businesses that have specialized in nuclear fuel reprocessing may find market exit difficult because of their specialized assets. Finally, a business that is dependent on products that are strategically important to its image or ability to market other products may not exit a market even though it is producing less-than-desired levels of profitability.

Customer Buying Power

When relatively few customers buy in large quantities and can easily switch suppliers, there is considerable customer buying power, which lowers market attractiveness. Large, concentrated groups of customers possess a buying power that enables them to negotiate lower prices or better terms and conditions of sale. Likewise, when customers can easily switch from one supplier to another, they force increased competition, which can lower prices as well as raise the cost of serving customers. In addition, when the purchased product or service is of limited importance to the customer, supplier dependence is much lower.

For the pharmaceutical industry, customer buying power is relatively low. Many well-known prescription drugs, such as Prozac, have many individual customers to whom the product is extremely important and who have limited opportunities to switch. As a result, the pharmaceutical industry has relatively low customer buying power, which enhances the competitive environment and profit potential.[4]

Supplier Selling Power

The flip side of customer buying power is supplier selling power. If a business is a large purchaser of a commodity product (less important to the buyer) and is in an industry in which switching costs are low, supplier power is generally low. For a business, this is an attractive market situation that contributes to industry attractiveness and profit potential. For many pharmaceutical businesses, supplier power is relatively low for these reasons, which contributes to the overall attractiveness of the industry.

Product Substitutes

The more substitute products available to customers, the easier it is for them to switch. Ease of switching intensifies competition and lowers profit potential and industry attractiveness. For example, in the soft drink industry, there are many product substitutes, so premium pricing is impossible. However, if the market definition is broadened to include non–soft drink substitutes, such as mineral water, fruit drinks, fruit juices, and sports drinks, one can begin to understand the enormous pressure this level of choice brings to bear on competitors serving these markets. It is important to have a broad market definition as presented in Chapter 3 in order to understand the full impact of substitutes in evaluating industry attractiveness. For example, in the pharmaceutical industry, there are fewer substitutes than in the beverage or automobile industry.

Competitive Rivalry

The more competitors in an industry, the lower the differentiation between competitors; the larger the excess industry capacity, the more likely the industry will engage in intense competitive rivalry. More intense competitor rivalry tends to lower prices and margins and raise marketing expenses in the battle to attract and retain customers. The net effect is a less attractive competitive environment in which the profit potential is lower.

The personal computer industry is an industry that is becoming increasingly more competitive due to price rivalry. The market has attracted many competitors with considerable capacity. In addition, product differentiation among personal computer products has become minimal. These factors, along with slower market growth, have intensified competition. By contrast, the pharmaceutical industry has fewer competitors for specific drugs, and product differentiation is much greater. As a result, the pharmaceutical industry is less likely to engage in intense competitive rivalry.

FIGURE 6-6 PERFORMANCE IMPACT OF PRICE RIVALRY AND PRISONER'S DILEMMA

Business's Marketing Strategy	Competitor's Marketing Strategy	
	Hold Price	Cut Price 5%
Hold Price	Market Share = 10% Volume = 1 million units Price = $100 per unit Margin = $40 per unit Total Contribution = $40 million	Market Share = 8% Volume = 800,000 units Price = $100 per unit Margin = $40 per unit Total Contribution = $32 million
Cut Price 5%	Market Share = 12% Volume = 1.2 million units Price = $95 per unit Margin = $35 per unit Total Contribution = $42 million	Market Share = 10% Volume = 1 million units Price = $95 per unit Margin = $35 per unit Total Contribution = $35 million

Prisoner's Dilemma

Intense competitive rivalry can evolve into what is known as a *prisoner's dilemma*.[5] In such situations, downward price moves by one competitor force "follower moves" by other competitors in order to minimize lost profits. Actually, all competitors would be better off if none cut prices to begin with.

Consider the example presented in Figure 6-6. The current scenario with both the business and its competitor holding price yields a total contribution (margin per unit multiplied by unit volume) of $40 million. If the competitor cuts price by 5 percent and the business holds price, the business will lose two share points and $8 million in total contribution. Of course, if the business were to lead with a price cut against a competitor who did not follow, the business could gain two share points and $2 million in total contribution. The worst effect of the prisoner's dilemma occurs when one competitor cuts price and the other matches that price in order to minimize losses. As shown in Figure 6-6, this combination results in no share gain or loss and a total contribution $5 million lower than when the two competitors both held at the higher price.

COMPETITIVE POSITION

Although selecting competitive environments that favor profit potential is an important aspect of competitive analysis, it has been shown that it is equally important for businesses to develop a strong competitive position in the markets in which they compete.[6] To understand the degree to which a business has a position of competitive advantage, we need to engage in a detailed analysis of competitors. An important question is "Which competitors should a business analyze?" We want to maintain a broad market definition to include all meaningful competing substitutes, however, at the same time, a business cannot engage in a detailed analysis of every competitor.[7] Thus, we need a mechanism to help us identify a relevant competitor set that will help prioritize which competitors to analyze and benchmark.

Benchmark Competitors

A variety of ways exist to identify a business's competitors. Perhaps the best is to have customers evaluate the degree to which they consider competitors as interchangeable substitutes. The closer customers perceive two competitors to be, the more likely they are to switch from one to the other. Likewise, the more dissimilar customers perceive any pair of competitors to be, the less likely they are to switch from one to the other. In addition, customers can rate each competitor on the basis of how far that competitor is from their ideal product or supplier. From these customer perceptions we can create a *perceptual map,* which is useful in gaining a better understanding of both the competitive position and key competitors to benchmark.

Perceptual mapping is a technique used to capture customer perceptions of competing products or services.[8] Without specifying criteria for evaluating differences between competing products, customers are simply asked to rate the degree to which they perceive each pair of competitors to be different from one another. For example, in the luxury car market, the Volvo 700, Mercedes 420, BMW 525, Lincoln Towncar, Buick Regal, and Honda Prelude are competing substitutes. As shown in Figure 6-7, the Volvo 700 and BMW 525 were rated very close in *perceived* similarity, whereas the Lincoln Towncar and Honda Prelude were rated as very dissimilar.

By asking customers to also rate each car shown with respect to how close it is to their ideal car, we can gain a better understanding of competitive position and key competitors. In the example presented in Figure 6-7, the customer ratings of the cars shown relative to the ideal car produced two different segments. There were two different sets of customer needs and product preferences operating in this sample market. The ideal car for segment A is almost equidistant from the Honda Prelude, Buick Regal, BMW 525, and Volvo 700. Thus, these four competitors would be the most likely choices for customers in segment A. If you were on the marketing team for Buick Regal, you should view Honda, Volvo, and BMW as your key competitors in serving segment A, even though Mercedes and the Lincoln Towncar are equally close to the Buick Regal. However, if Buick Regal were more interested in serving segment B, then Lincoln Towncar and Mercedes would be their competitors to benchmark.

A variety of multidimensional scaling programs can be used to create a perceptual map,[9] such as the one shown in Figure 6-7. In this example, a graphical representation of inter-brand differentiation was created in two dimensions.[10] In most applications, over 90 percent of competitor differentiation can be captured in two dimensions. With a perceptual map of competition, a business can easily discern two things: (1) which competitors it will compete against in a particular market segment and (2) its competitive position relative to these competitors in attracting and satisfying customers in this segment. However, to improve or maintain a position relative to competitors and the customer's ideal car, a business must also know on what basis target customers are differentiating competing products.

Competitor Analysis

Once a business has identified which competitors it should benchmark, the business now has to engage in a more detailed analysis of these competitors. A competitor analysis such as this is difficult to conduct and something a business may do only periodically. However, a market-based business with a strong market orientation is gathering competitor intelligence all the time and, as a result, has continuously evolving competitor profiles from which to evaluate its own competitiveness and competitive advantages.[11]

FIGURE 6-7 CUSTOMER PERCEPTIONS OF INTERBRAND DIFFERENTIATION

Competing Alternatives	← Degree of Perceived Differentiation →										
	Very Similar									Very Different	
Mercedes–Volvo	0	1	2	3	4	5	(6)	7	8	9	10
Mercedes–Lincoln	0	1	(2)	3	4	5	6	7	8	9	10
Mercedes–Honda	0	1	2	3	4	5	6	7	8	(9)	10
Mercedes–Buick	0	1	2	3	4	5	(6)	7	8	9	10
Mercedes–BMW	0	1	2	(3)	4	5	6	7	8	9	10
Mercedes–Ideal A	0	1	2	3	4	5	(6)	7	8	9	10
Mercedes–Ideal B	0	1	(2)	3	4	5	6	7	8	9	10
Volvo–Lincoln	0	1	2	3	4	5	6	(7)	8	9	10
Volvo–BMW	0	1	2	(3)	4	5	6	7	8	9	10
Volvo–Buick	0	1	2	3	(4)	5	6	7	8	9	10
Volvo–Honda	0	1	2	3	4	(5)	6	7	8	9	10
Volvo–Ideal A	0	1	(2)	3	4	5	6	7	8	9	10
Volvo–Ideal B	0	1	2	3	4	(5)	6	7	8	9	10
Lincoln–Honda	0	1	2	3	4	5	6	7	8	9	(10)
Lincoln–BMW	0	1	2	3	(4)	5	6	7	8	9	10
Lincoln–Buick	0	1	2	3	4	5	(6)	7	8	9	10
Lincoln–Ideal A	0	1	2	3	4	5	6	7	(8)	9	10
Lincoln–Ideal B	0	1	(2)	3	4	5	6	7	8	9	10
BMW–Honda	0	1	2	3	4	5	6	7	(8)	9	10
BMW–Buick	0	1	2	3	4	(5)	6	7	8	9	10
BMW–Ideal A	0	1	2	3	4	(5)	6	7	8	9	10
BMW–Ideal B	0	1	2	(3)	4	5	6	7	8	9	10
Buick–Honda	0	1	2	3	4	(5)	6	7	8	9	10
Buick–Ideal A	0	1	(2)	3	4	5	6	7	8	9	10
Buick–Ideal B	0	1	2	3	(4)	5	6	7	8	9	10
Honda–Ideal A	0	1	2	3	(4)	5	6	7	8	9	10
Honda–Ideal B	0	1	2	3	4	5	6	7	8	(9)	10

Perceptual Map

Dimension II
+10

• Volvo 700

• Honda Prelude

• BMW 525

• Ideal Car Segment A

−10   • Buick Regal   0   • Mercedes   +10   Dimension I

• Ideal Car Segment B

• Lincoln Towncar

−10

Competitor Intelligence

A great deal of competitive intelligence is public and readily available from dealers, trade press, business press, industry consultants, trade shows, financial reports, industry reports, general press, government documents, and customers.[12] However, unless a business has created a market-based culture in which everyone in the organization is an information gatherer, sources of competitive intelligence that are more valuable and difficult to find will slip by unnoticed.

For example, shown in Figure 6-8 is a list of competitor behaviors that signal when a competitor is in trouble or lacks marketing leadership. This type of competitor intelligence is readily available through published articles, financial reports, and information that salespeople could observe in customer visits or while talking with distributors. In each case, the competitive behavior opens the door to marketing strategies that could be implemented at a time when it would be difficult for the competitor to respond. For example, if a competitor is investing less in research and development, it would be an excellent time to accelerate new-product introductions. If they were changing ads and ad agencies often, that would be a good time to further promote your own value proposition to customers.

In today's expanding information age, information on markets and competitors is becoming rapidly more available. For example, the reference librarian at Multnomah County Library in Portland, Oregon, was challenged to see how much competitor intelligence he could gather in 1 hour. Five questions were posed with respect to the Merix Corporation, a small circuit board manufacturer. Outlined in Figure 6-9 is a summary of the competitive information and sources used to answer the questions posed. As shown, all five questions were adequately answered in 1 hour by a skilled person.[13]

FIGURE 6-8 KNOWING WHEN A COMPETITOR IS IN TROUBLE

Behaviors exhibited by a competitor *under pressure to improve profits/cash* flow:

- Laying off employees and closing plants or sales offices
- Across-the-board price increases without market justification
- Reducing advertising and not attending trade shows
- Cutting investment in research and development
- Increasing the average days in accounts payable
- Taking on more debt/increasing debt-to-equity ratio
- Tightening the terms of sale and payment conditions
- Not recruiting new people as employees retire; shrinking work force
- Pay sales people to collect unpaid bills

Behaviors exhibited by competitors that *lack marketing leadership/market focus*:

- Frequent changes in advertising message; change ad agencies often
- Lower-than-average sales per salesperson
- Higher-than-average marketing expenses as a percent of sales
- Frequent new-product failures
- Hollow/vague value proposition
- Uses cost-based pricing/does not understand the value of their products
- Frequently cutting prices to increase volume
- Frequent changes in senior management/marketing management

FIGURE 6-9 COMPETITOR INFORMATION SEARCH

Outlined here are the questions posed and the sources of information from which competitive intelligence was gathered in 1 hour by a research expert.

1. How big is the circuit board market served by Merix, and what is its current market share?

The *Market Share Reporter* gives market size and share of hundreds of sectors in the economy, but Merix did not appear. *Predicast* provides market sizes and reference to *SMT Trends* (a trade journal) that reports the market share statistics of the top 10 circuit board producers, but not Merix. However, the *CorpTech Dictionary of Technology Companies* turned out to be the mother lode. It gives Merix's SIC (standard industrial classification) and lists other companies in that sector. From this information, an estimate of market size and share was computed.

2. Merix has been dependent on a few large customers. Is it adding to its customer base?

A search of a local newspaper uncovers an article "Merix Wants More Customers." It quotes the company as saying 70 percent of revenues come from its top five customers. Merix's most recent annual report also states that 69.3 percent of revenues come from four customers. In addition, the SEC Edgar Web site reports Merix's 10K and states that not much progress has been made in adding new customers to its customer base.

3. Develop a biographical profile of Merix's CEO and her approach to business.

Standard and Poor's *Register of Directors and Executives* provides a short bio on the CEO, Debi Coleman, and her e-mail address. The *Biography and Genealogy Master Index, Dun & Bradstreet Reference Book of Corporate Management, Who's Who,* and *Who's Who of American Women* provide no details. However, *Who's Who in Finance and Industry* provides a detailed resume.

4. Will Merix have a booth at any upcoming trade shows? If so, where and when?

Trade Shows Worldwide and the current editions of *Trade Show and Exhibits Schedule* and *Trade Show Week Data Book* provide the answers needed.

5. Merix hired a new chief operating officer. What biographical information is available?

Predicast reported that a chief operating officer was hired, and *Business Wire* press releases provided a bio on the new COO.

Other sources considered but not used included *Business News Bank* (a CD-ROM database), *Business Index* (another CD-ROM database), *Value Line,* and *Red Chip Review.* Had time permitted, the *Manufacturers Register* (every state has one) and trade magazines would have been used.

A Sample Competitor Analysis

Rossignol is tied for second place behind Salomon, market leader in the recreation snow sports equipment market. Although there are many other competitors in this market, it is important that Rossignol understand its strengths and weaknesses relative to its three largest competitors, Salomon, K2, and Head. Using publicly available information, Rossignol can create a competitor analysis that benchmarks its performance against these three competitors.

Shown in Figure 6-10 are 11 performance metrics for Rossignol, Salomon, K2, and Head for 2002. Salomon has a higher market share and sales but slightly lower gross profit. However, Rossignol has a margin advantage based on percent of sales. Relative to K2, Rossignol has more that twice the percent margin. Although K2 has the lowest cost

FIGURE 6-10 COMPETITOR ANALYSIS (2002) OF ROSSIGNOL VERSUS BENCHMARK COMPETITORS

Performance (millions)	Rossignol	Salomon	K2	Head	Advantage
Relative Market Share	31	53	33	20	Salomon
Sales Revenue	$558	$807	$582	$388	Salomon
Percent Margin (%)	64	41	30	40	Rossignol
Gross Profit	$357	$331	$175	$155	Rossignol
Marketing Performance					
Marketing & Sales (% Sales)*	19.9	19.8	14.8	26.5	K2
Net Marketing Contribution	$259	$172	$ 88	$ 52	Rossignol
Marketing ROS (%)	46	21	15	13	Rossignol
Marketing ROI (%)	364	263	341	126	Rossignol
Financial Performance					
Return on Sales (%)	11.3	4.8	2.7	−0.7	Rossignol
Return on Equity (%)	61.7	30.3	6.9	−1.1	Rossignol
Return on Invested Capital (%)	28.5	12.3	5.2	−0.8	Rossignol

*Based on sales, general and administration expenses reported.

of marketing as a percent of sales, Rossignol outperforms K2 and the other competitors in all three marketing profitability metrics. As shown in Figure 6-10, Rossignol also outperforms these three competitors in three financial performance metrics.

The level of detail included in a competitor analysis can vary considerably from what is shown in Figure 6-10. In the example shown in Figure 6-11, the competitor analysis is broken down into two categories: Market-Based Performance and Operating Performance. As shown, each area is further broken down into more specific performance metrics that are measured for the business and a benchmark competitor. In this example, the business has almost one-third of the market share of the benchmark competitor. This competitive gap corresponds closely with similar competitive gaps in number of distributors, number of distributor locations, and sales force coverage. To close its share gap, the business undoubtedly needs to address adverse competitive gaps in distribution and sales coverage.

Overall, the business is behind its benchmark competitor in most aspects of market-based performance. The competitive gaps shown help create performance targets and management incentives to close these gaps. This, of course, is a key input into the development of a successful market-based strategy. From an internal perspective, this business is also poorly positioned in almost all areas of operating performance. Higher overhead costs and accounts receivable and lower return on sales per employee contribute to lower profitability and productivity. Each of these gaps may be difficult to close, and competitors are not likely to help. Thus, to successfully close important competitive gaps, a business may have to go outside its industry to find better competitive practices.

FIGURE 6-11 COMPETITOR ANALYSIS FOR AN INDUSTRIAL BUSINESS

Dimension of Competitiveness	Business Performance	Competitor Performance	Performance Gap*	
Market-Based Performance				
Market Share (%)	6	17	11	behind
Relative Price	115	100	15	higher
Relative Product Quality	115	105	10	better
Relative Service Quality	93	113	20	worse
Number of Distributors	87	261	174	fewer
Sales Force (number)	36	60	24	fewer
Advertising & Promotion (% of sales)	2.0	2.0	0	equal
Sales, General and Administration (% of sales)	16.0	17.0	1.0	lower
Operating Performance				
Cost of Goods Sold (% of sales)	48.0	50.8	2.8	lower
Direct Materials (% of sales)	26.0	17.6	8.4	higher
Overhead (% of sales)	12.0	10.0	1.0	higher
Return on Assets (%)	17.1	19.5	2.4	lower
Return on Sales (%)	7.4	11.1	3.7	lower
Asset Turnover	2.3	1.6	0.7	higher
Accounts Receivable (days)	46	38	8	higher
Sales per Employee	$1.5 mil	$2.1 mil	0.6	lower

*Performance Gap = Business Performance − Competitor Performance

Competitive Benchmarking

Sometimes a business needs to go outside its industry to benchmark a business known to be superior in a particular business process. General Mills, for example, uses the same production lines to make a variety of related food products. For example, the same production line used for scalloped potatoes is used for au gratin potatoes. To change over from one production run to another requires as much as 12 hours. Although there were ongoing efforts to reduce downtime during the production changeover, only small incremental improvements could be achieved. Recognizing that NASCAR pit teams have to change equipment during a race with minimum loss of time, General Mills decided to benchmark NASCAR pit teams' process of changing equipment when a race car came off the track for servicing. What they learned allowed them to implement a new process that reduced production change time to as little as 20 minutes.

Competitive benchmarking is a process developed initially at Xerox to improve its competitive position relative to key competitors. The idea is for a business to identify a key area of competitive weakness, such as billing errors in Figure 6-12, and then benchmark a company, outside its industry that is recognized as a world-class performer in this area.[14] In this way, a business can hope to gain access to the underlying processes that produce this best practice and develop a system that, when successfully implemented, has the potential of being better than that of its key competitors.

FIGURE 6-12 COMPETITIVE BENCHMARKING: XEROX BILLING ERRORS

Competitive Benchmarking	Xerox: Billing Errors
1. Identify a key area of competitive weakness.	1. Xerox found billing errors were more frequent than those of competitors.
2. Identify a benchmark company.	2. Xerox looked at Citicorp, AT&T, and American Express.
3. Track the benchmark company's process advantage.	3. With the cooperation of American Express, Xerox developed new systems to reduce billing errors.

The first step in competitive benchmarking is to identify a key area of competitive weakness that affects customer satisfaction or profitability or both. For Xerox, a large number of billing errors was an annoying competitive weakness, as outlined in Figure 6-12. This was a source of considerable customer frustration and hurt overall perceptions of performance and customer satisfaction. The second step was to identify several companies that would be recognized as among the best in the world in this area of performance. Xerox identified Citicorp, American Express, and AT&T. After talking with these companies, Xerox selected American Express and gained the cooperation of American Express in order to study its billing systems, which had a significantly lower error rate and many more transactions.

Once inside American Express, Xerox could observe the systems and processes that led to a more error-free billing system. This knowledge was transferred into several programs to begin the process of becoming more competitive in this key area of competitive weakness. Performance benchmarks were set in an effort to work toward decreasing billing errors. These efforts took time, but Xerox reached its goal and turned a competitive weakness into a competitive strength. Xerox had a similar success story in competitive benchmarking of order cycle time (the time it takes to deliver the product after the customer places the order), using L.L. Bean as a benchmark company.

SOURCES OF COMPETITIVE ADVANTAGE

As a business begins to more fully grasp its position relative to key competitors, it gains better insight into potential sources of competitive advantage. For a source of relative advantage to be a competitive advantage requires (1) that the area of relative advantage be meaningful to target customers and (2) that the relative advantage be sustainable (not easily copied by competitors).

Wal-Mart, for example, has developed a low-cost advantage that has enabled it to attract and satisfy target customers by offering lower prices. Hewlett-Packard, by contrast, has built a differentiation advantage with product innovation and quality, and Nordstrom has built a differential advantage with service quality. Each attracts and satisfies customers with differentially superior products or services. Nike, on the other hand, has developed a marketing advantage with creative and aggressive marketing efforts and with retailing that attracts and satisfies target customers.

In each case, the business developed a source of competitive advantage that is meaningful to target customers. It becomes an area they work on each day in order to sustain

FIGURE 6-13 MAJOR SOURCES OF COMPETITIVE ADVANTAGE

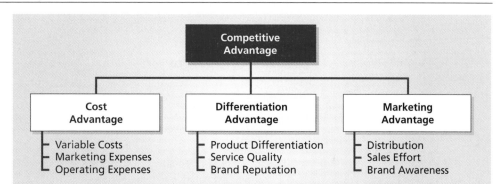

their level of competitive advantage. Although there are potentially many areas of competitive advantage, the three primary areas are described next and in Figure 6-13.

- **Cost Advantage:** A significantly lower cost position from which to create lower prices while still achieving desirable profit margins.
- **Differentiation Advantage:** A meaningful differentiation that creates desired customer benefits at a level superior to competition.
- **Marketing Advantage:** A marketing effort that dominates the competition in sales coverage, distribution, or brand recognition, or some combination of the three.

COST ADVANTAGE

A business can achieve three different types of cost advantage, as outlined in Figure 6-13. It can achieve a lower variable cost per unit sold, a lower level of marketing expenses, or a lower level of operating and overhead expense. Each of these cost advantages is achieved in different ways.

Variable Cost Advantage

Businesses with a lower unit cost are able to achieve the same (or better) unit margin at lower prices than competing businesses. Unit or variable costs include manufacturing costs and variable costs associated with distribution, such as discounts, sales commissions, transportation, and other variable transaction costs. As demonstrated in Figure 6-14, a unit cost advantage relative to competition contributes to higher levels of profitability.

But how does a business achieve a low variable cost advantage? Volume is a key factor. Businesses with a substantial market share (volume) advantage can generally achieve a lower unit cost.[15] As volume increases, the cost per unit generally decreases. For example, as demonstrated in Figure 6-15, the cost of cellular phone service decreases at the rate of 18 percent every time the volume of customers in a geographic market doubles. Thus, when a cellular business in a given market doubles its customer base from 400,000 to 800,000, the unit cost decreases by 18 percent. In this case, the business that attains the largest customer penetration (volume) achieves a lower unit cost.

FIGURE 6-14 PROFIT IMPACT OF A VARIABLE COST ADVANTAGE

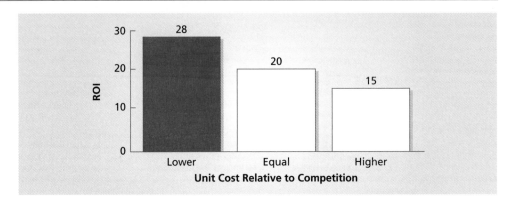

FIGURE 6-15 UNIT COST ADVANTAGE DUE TO VOLUME ADVANTAGE

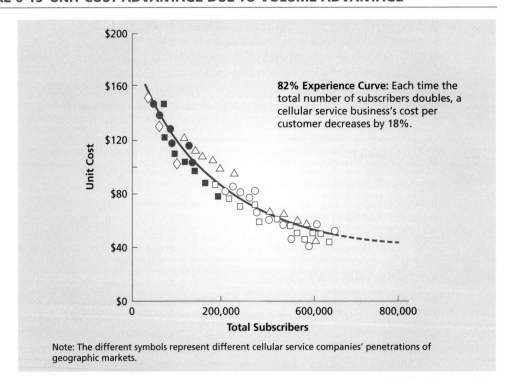

Note: The different symbols represent different cellular service companies' penetrations of geographic markets.

A larger production volume allows for production and purchasing economies that lower the unit cost of a product, thereby creating a *scale effect*. With volume purchases, Wal-Mart has been able to negotiate a lower cost of goods. The same scale effect would occur for a manufacturer who had twice the production capacity. For example, as Honda has moved from one level of production capacity to an increased capacity, there has been some reduction in unit cost due to a scale effect for certain a component product, as illustrated in Figure 6-16.

FIGURE 6-16 IGNITION SWITCH COST ADVANTAGE DUE TO SCALE AND SCOPE EFFECTS

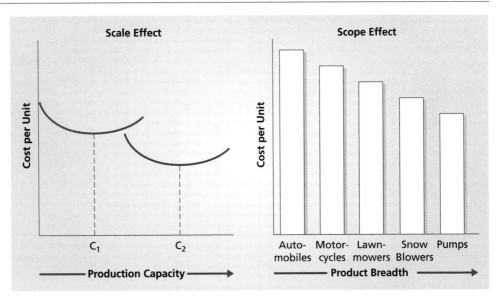

Likewise, as a business adds products to its product line that have similar purchased materials and manufacturing processes, it is able to lower the average unit cost of all products. This is a *scope effect*. For Honda, the cost of ignition switches is lower because the same ignition switch components are used in cars, motorcycles, lawnmowers, all-terrain vehicles, snow blowers, snowmobiles, jet skis, and generators, as illustrated in Figure 6-16. In each case, the addition of another product line provides a volume-cost advantage across product lines for common component parts such as ignition switches, spark plugs, carburetors, and so on.

Finally, as a business builds more of the same product, there is a greater opportunity for *learning effects*. These non-scale, non-scope effects contribute to lower costs through process improvements that are the result of learning. Each unit produced provides additional learning and the opportunity to build the next unit more efficiently. Naturally, the business with more production experience has the best opportunity to learn from experience. This learning normally leads to improvements in processes that result in a lower cost per unit.

Marketing Cost Advantage

Quite often, businesses may not look beyond variable costs for sources of cost advantage. However, marketing cost efficiencies can be derived from product line extensions.

For example, it takes a certain number of salespeople to adequately cover a target market. As the sales force is given more products to sell to the same customers, a *marketing cost scope effect* is created. As illustrated in Figure 6-17, Procter & Gamble sales force expense per pound of soap detergent sold should decrease as more brands of soap detergent are added to its product line. A competitor with far fewer brands

FIGURE 6-17 PRODUCT SCOPE AND MARKETING COST ADVANTAGE

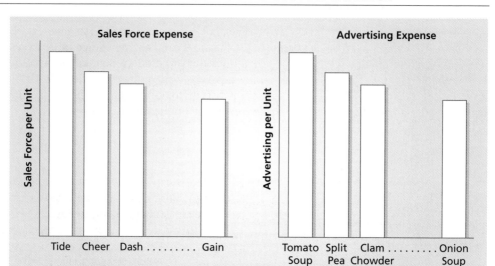

would have to have the same sales-call frequency to adequately serve retailers and, therefore, would experience a higher cost per pound sold because it had fewer brands to sell.

Another area of marketing cost advantage is derived from the advertising cost efficiency of a brand extension strategy. For example, Campbell's Soup is the banner brand from which a whole line of soup brands has been created. Each time an individual soup is advertised, it is reinforcing top-of-the-mind awareness of Campbell's Soup and each soup in the product line. In this way, the scope effect created by additional soups should lower the advertising dollars spent per ounce of soup sold.

Operating Cost Advantage

Although an operating cost advantage is generally outside the control or influence of the marketing function, lower operating expenses relative to competitors contribute to a low-cost advantage. For example, Wal-Mart achieves an operating-expense-to-sales ratio under 20 percent of sales; many of its competitors' operating expenses are well over 20 percent. This difference gives Wal-Mart another source of cost advantage from which to create greater customer value with lower prices and greater shareholder value with lower operating expenses.

Likewise, McDonald's has been able to cut the cost of construction of new McDonald's restaurants by 50 percent since 1990 by sticking to standardized building designs. Because the building is an asset that needs to be depreciated, this source of operating expense is drastically lower than it would be if each building had a unique design. Using a standardized design, along with rapid store expansion, has contributed to McDonald's earnings and shareholder value.

DIFFERENTIATION ADVANTAGE

Every business must manage its costs, but not every business can have a cost advantage. To achieve above-average profits, a business needs some source of competitive advantage. A differentiation advantage with respect to product, service, or brand reputation is a potential source of competitive advantage as outlined earlier. However, as do all sources of competitive advantage, a differentiation advantage has to be meaningful to target customers and sustainable (not easily duplicated by competitors).

Product Advantage

There are many aspects of a product around which a business can build a differentiation advantage. A product's durability, reliability, performance, features, appearance, and conformance to a specific application each has the potential of being a differential advantage.[16] For example, the ESCO Corporation is a manufacturer of earth-moving equipment parts that are used in very demanding mining and construction applications. The company has developed a differential advantage in the wear life of its products due to proprietary steel chemistry and product design. The end result is that its products last longer and are less likely to break than are the products of its competitors.

   Both of these customer benefits save the customer money even when its products are sold at a higher price. Overall, businesses with a relative advantage in product quality produce higher levels of profitability, as illustrated in Figure 6-18.

Service Advantage

A business can achieve a differentiation service advantage in the same way it can achieve a differential product advantage.[17] The same baseline conditions are required: First, the service advantage has to be meaningful and important to target customers,

FIGURE 6-18 PROFIT IMPACT OF A DIFFERENTIATION PRODUCT AND SERVICE ADVANTAGE

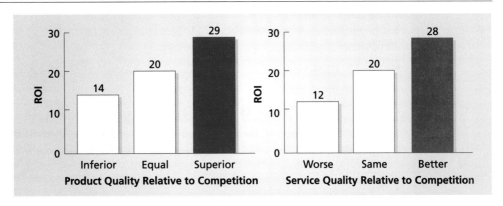

and second, it has to be sustainable. FedEx tracks its performance each day on 10 service quality indicators (each weighed by the customer pain a failure creates). This service quality index is carefully monitored each day to help FedEx maintain a service quality advantage. As its service quality index improves, customer satisfaction improves and the overall cost per package decreases. Thus, on the days that its service quality is at its highest level, FedEx is able to create greater overall customer satisfaction with fewer errors, lower costs, and greater profits for shareholders. As shown in Figure 6-18, businesses with a service quality advantage produce higher levels of profitability.

Reputation Advantage

Another source of differential competitive advantage is brand reputation. Although competing watchmakers may match the quality of a Rolex watch, they cannot easily match Rolex's brand reputation advantage. Products such as Chanel, Nikon, and Perrier have built successful brand reputations that provide a source of competitive advantage in their ability to attract target customers. Their reputation or status adds a dimension of appeal that is an important customer benefit to many less price-sensitive, more image-conscious consumers.

A brand reputation advantage can be measured in the same way as a product or service differential advantage. We find that businesses with an advantage in brand reputation are able to both attract customers and obtain a price premium. As shown in Figure 6-19, the reputation of a consumer product or service can have a bigger impact on price premiums than a product advantage. Even in business-to-business markets, an advantage in brand or company reputation helps to support price and, hence, margins.

FIGURE 6-19 PRICE IMPACT OF RELATIVE QUALITY AND REPUTATION

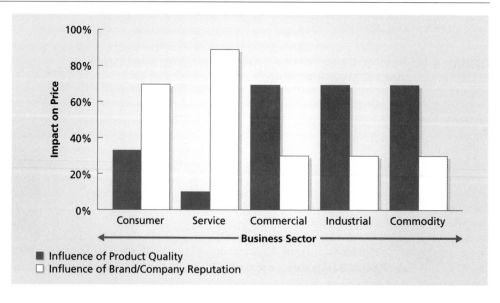

MARKETING ADVANTAGE

A business that dominates markets with a relative advantage in distribution, sales coverage, or marketing communications can control (and often block) market access. This is also a source of competitive advantage. Whether through sales and distribution or marketing communications, Eastman Kodak, Procter & Gamble, Campbell's Soup, and many others have developed a source of competitive advantage around their marketing expertise.

Channel Advantage

In all markets in which distribution is required for market access, there is a finite number of distributors, whether retailers in consumer markets or dealers in business-to-business markets. Furthermore, there are even fewer top-notch distributors. Therefore, a business that is able to dominate these distributors can control channels in a given market and, to some degree, control market access. This is a source of competitive advantage independent of cost or differential advantage.

Shown in Figure 6-20 is the relationship between distributor share and market share, along with the impact of market share advantage on profitability. What this suggests is that as a business is able to dominate the channels to market, it is able to achieve a higher relative market share. As shown, larger relative shares tend to correspond with greater levels of profitability.[18]

Sales Force Advantage

In both consumer and business-to-business markets, certain levels of sales call frequency and after-sale service are required. Because there is a limit to how many sales calls a salesperson can make in a given time period, a business with more salespeople will simply be able to reach and serve more customers. For example, on the basis of a certain call frequency and purchase behavior in a given industry, assume that the sales per salesperson is $2 million per year. If one business has 100 salespeople, it is able to achieve sales

FIGURE 6-20 DISTRIBUTION OUTLET SHARE VERSUS MARKET SHARE

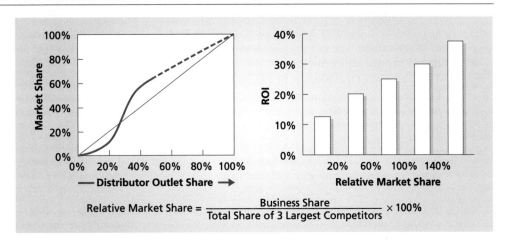

of $200 million. A business with 20 salespeople would achieve an estimated sales level of $40 million, assuming equal sales force capabilities and competitive products in terms of price and quality. Thus, the business with a sales force that is five times larger has a marketing advantage. For the competing business to neutralize this advantage, it would have to increase its sales coverage, assuming no change in price or differentiation advantage.

Brand Awareness

Nike has very good products with attractive prices. However, what makes Nike a tough competitor is the level of market awareness and identity it has been able to develop with creative ad copy, pervasive promotion of the Nike swoosh, careful selection of product spokespersons, and heavy advertising. This level of competitive advantage makes it difficult for competitors who may in fact have a better product or lower price with comparable quality. Nike's name, logo recognition, and top-of-the-mind awareness make it easier for Nike to attract customers for existing products and to launch line extensions or entirely new product lines under the Nike name and logo.

This type of competitive advantage, like all others, is relevant only when the communications created are meaningful and important to target customers. To obtain and sustain a marketing communications advantage takes more than advertising dollars. It goes right to the core of market-based management. Who are our customers? What do they want? And how do we communicate our product in a way that best serves their needs?

■ Summary

Competitive analysis is an important aspect of marketing strategy and market orientation. A marketing knowledge advantage with respect to customers and competitors is a source of a competitive advantage. With a knowledge advantage, a business can pursue an oblique, indirect competitive attack that forces competitors to follow. An oblique strategy is more profitable than a direct frontal attack which requires more resources and may or may not result in a market share gain.

There are three primary dimensions to competitor analysis: industry forces, competitor benchmarking, and competitive advantage. The first aspect of competitive analysis is an analysis of industry forces. Industry forces such as competitor entry and exit, number of substitutes, buyer and supplier power, and competitive rivalry each affect profit potential. When the collective sum of these forces is favorable, the profit potential is greater. Thus, to obtain the best profit potential, a business needs to assess its industry forces. Competitor analysis is a way of bringing all these sources of competitiveness together to help understand a business's competitive position in a given market. A complete competitor profile enables a business to better understand its key strengths and weaknesses.

Quite often, a business may be overlooking several fundamental weaknesses in its competitive makeup. A competitor gap analysis is intended to expose these major weaknesses. Often, a competitor analysis will lead to an area of weakness that needs to be further examined and better understood. Competitive benchmarking is a process in which a business identifies a business outside its industry that is known for excellence in a given area. By studying a world-class business, a business can hope to not only improve in its area of weakness but to also improve to the extent it could gain a competitive advantage over its competitors.

There are three primary sources of competitive advantage: cost advantage, differentiation advantage, and marketing advantage. A cost advantage in either variable costs, marketing expenses, or overhead expenses enables a business to price more aggressively in building customer value. Share leaders often have a cost advantage due to economies of scale, economies of scope, and experience curve effects. Niche businesses can also achieve a cost advantage with lower overhead and lower marketing expenses.

Differentiation is a second major source of advantage. An advantage in product quality, service quality, or reputation (image) provides a unique source of differential advantage. In each case, a business with a differential advantage that is meaningful to target customers is in a position to charge more for its products and enhance profitability through higher margins. For markets in which service quality is more important than product quality, profitability is even greater. In some industries, particularly service industries, a business's reputation for quality has a large impact on its price positioning.

A third major source of advantage is a marketing advantage. A business with a strong distribution system can control market access and limit competitors' ability to reach target customers. Likewise, a business with a large, well-trained, and well-supported sales force is able to better serve customers and respond more quickly to their problems or changing needs. This again is a considerable source of market-driven advantage. Finally, businesses that have a core competency in marketing communications are able to build and sustain market awareness and customer preference effectively and cost efficiently. Again, this is a tremendous source of advantage because these businesses will be able to more easily attract new customers and maintain a presence with existing customers.

■ Market-Based Logic and Strategic Thinking

1 How would a marketing knowledge advantage be a source of competitive advantage in the cell phone market for a company like Nokia?
2 How would Nokia use an oblique competitive strategy versus a frontal attack competitive strategy in a battle to win the cell phone market share?
3 Why is competitor orientation an important element of a business's market orientation?
4 How could the industry forces for a regional phone company be different from the industry forces for a regional bank?
5 How will the industry change as competitors enter the regional phone market? How will profit potential be affected?
6 What impact would Procter & Gamble's everyday low price strategy have on competitive rivalry and the prisoner's dilemma?
7 How will the Internet affect competitor intelligence gathering? What traditional sources of competitor intelligence will most likely be available on the Internet?
8 What is the benefit of a competitor gap analysis? How would the results be used in strategy development?
9 When should a business do a competitive benchmarking study?
10 What are the benefits of competitive benchmarking?
11 Cost and differentiation are well known sources of competitive advantage, but why is a marketing advantage also a potential source of competitive advantage?
12 What are the various ways a business can achieve a cost advantage?
13 Why do share leaders often have a cost advantage?

14 What areas of relative advantage does Wal-Mart use to drive its competitive position? How should Kmart and Sears drive their competitive positions?

15 Why are businesses with a relative advantage in either market share, unit cost, or product quality more profitable than businesses that have no advantage in any of those areas?

16 Identify for each area of differential advantage a business that uses this as a source of competitive advantage. Explain how each source of differential advantage helps the business attract and satisfy target customers.

17 Identify businesses that have developed different types of marketing advantage, and explain for each how this advantage affects profitability.

18 How could a business with a niche market strategy develop a marketing advantage as a source of competitive advantage?

Marketing Performance Tools

Each of the following **marketing perfor mance tools** can be accessed by going to *www.rogerjbest.com* or *www.prenhall.com/best*. The shaded cells are input cells. The non-shaded cells contain results calculated from your input values.

MARKETING PERFORMANCE TOOL—Industry Analysis

Industry Forces	Unfavorable to Favorable					Index
	−100	−50	0	50	100	
Barriers to Entry	None	Low	Some	Mod.	High	50
Barriers to Exit	High	Mod.	Some	Low	None	50
Customer's Buyer Power	High	Mod.	Some	Low	None	−50
Seller's Selling Power	High	Mod.	Some	Low	None	50
Product Substitutes	Many	Mod.	Some	Few	None	0
Price Rivalry	Intense	Mod.	Some	Low	None	50
Industry Structure Metric						**25**

Note: Mod. = Moderate

This **marketing performance tool** allows you to assess the attractiveness of an industry, market, or market segment. Each of the six forces shown are assessed using a scale that varies from −100 (very unfavorable) to 100 (very favorable). In this example, the barriers to entry are moderately high, thus a somewhat favorable score of 50. On the other hand, customer buyer power was rated somewhat unfavorable (−50) because buying power was assessed as moderately high. The overall score of 25 is positive and suggests that this industry or market is somewhat above average (zero) in overall favorableness with respect to competitive forces and profit potential. Answer the application exercise questions presented below. The shaded numeric input cells can be changed in doing the following application exercise. However, you can create an entirely new example of your own by using all the shaded input cells.

Application Exercise: Using the data provided, estimate the industry attractiveness of the personal computer industry. There is no right or wrong answer—simply your assessment of the six competitive forces based on your understanding of the personal computer market. Then, estimate the industry attractiveness of the specialized retailer of fashion clothes.

MARKETING PERFORMANCE TOOL—Cost Advantage

Cost Advantage	Company	Leading Competitor	Relative Position	Competitive Advantage
Cost of Goods Sold (% sales)	48.0%	50.0%	96	4.0%
Sales, General, and Adm Expenses (% sales)	16.0%	17.0%	94	5.9%
Overhead Expenses (% sales)	10.0%	12.0%	83	16.7%

Note: Because marketing expenses are rarely reported we are using SG&A which includes all marketing and sales expenses. Overhead expenses are the remaining expenses used to compute operating income (income before taxes and interest).

This **marketing performance tool** allows you to assess the business's cost advantage relative to a leading competitor. The shaded cells are data obtained from the income statement for business and a leading competitor. Percent of sales data is used to control for difference in size. In this example, the Company has a cost advantage in all three areas of cost. Answer the application exercise questions presented below. The shaded numeric input cells can be changed in doing the following application exercise.

Application Exercise: Using performance tool, obtain the cost data needed from the income statement for a company of interest. For public companies this can be obtained online. Input the percent of sales for the three areas of cost. Obtain the cost data needed from the income statement for one of the company's leading competitors. For public companies this can be obtained online. Input the percent of sales for the three areas of cost. Assess the degree to which the company has a cost advantage over its leading competitor.

MARKETING PERFORMANCE TOOL—Differentiation Advantage

Differentiation Advantage	Company % Behind	Compared to % Equal	Competitor % Ahead	Competitive Advantage
Product Differentiation	0%	85%	15%	15%
Service Differentiation	20%	80%	0%	-20%
Brand/Company Reputation	10%	80%	10%	0%

Note: The percentage for each source of differentiation advantage should sum to 100%.

This **marketing performance tool** allows you to assess a business's differentiation advantage relative to a leading competitor. The shaded cells are data normally obtained from customer surveys. However, in many instances management has to make these assessments based on their perceptions of competitive performance. Because you do not have survey data, the application exercise questions will only require your opinion. Answer the application exercise questions presented below. The shaded numeric input cells can be changed in doing the following application exercise.

Application Exercise: Using this performance tool, for a company of interest (or the one selected in the previous application exercise) estimate the percentage of customers that would rate company's product performance as behind their leading competitor, the percent that would rate them equal in product performance, and the percent that would rate the company ahead of their leading competitor. Repeat this process for service performance and brand image (reputation). Assess the degree to which the company has a differentiation advantage over its leading competitor.

MARKETING PERFORMANCE TOOL—Marketing Advantage

Marketing Advantage	Company	Leading Competitor	Relative Position	Competitive Advantage
Market Share	6%	17%	0.35	−65%
Awareness (% target market)	57%	84%	0.68	−32%
Distribution (% market coverage)	43%	67%	0.64	−36%

This **marketing performance tool** allows you to assess a business's marketing advantage relative to a leading competitor. The shaded cells are data normally obtained from company data and customer surveys. However, in many instances management has to make these assessments based on their perceptions of competitive performance. Because you do not have survey data, the application exercise questions will only require your opinion. Answer the application exercise questions presented below. The shaded numeric input cells can be changed in doing the following application exercise.

Application Exercise: Using this performance tool for a company of interest (or the one selected in the previous application exercise) estimate the company's market share and the share of its leading competitor. Repeat this assessment with respect to brand awareness and distribution. Assess the degree to which the company has a marketing advantage over its leading competitor.

Notes

1. Sun Tzu. *The Art of War*, A Reader's Companion (Spark Publishing, 2003).
2. Gary Gagliardi. *The Art of War Plus the Art of Marketing,* 2nd ed. (Clearbridge Publishing, 2002).
3. Michael Porter. *Competitive Strategy* (New York: Free Press, 1980): chapter 1.
4. Anita McGahan. "Industry Structure and Competitive Advantage," *Harvard Business Review* (November–December 1994): 115–124.
5. Sharon Oster. "Understanding Rivalry: Game Theory," in *Modern Competitive Analysis,* 2nd ed. (Kinderhook, NY: Oxford 1994): 237–251.

6. George Day and Prakash Nedungadi. "Managerial Representations of Competitive Advantage," *Journal of Marketing* (April 1994): 31–44; Richard Rumelt, "How Much Does Industry Matter?" *Strategic Management Journal* (March 1991): 67–86; and Ralf Boscheck, "Competitive Advantage: Superior Offer or Unfair Dominance," *California Management Review* (Fall 1994): 132–151.

7. Joseph Porac and Howard Thomas. "Taxonomic Mental Models of Competitor Definition," *Academy of Management Review* 15 (1990): 224–240.

8. Hugh Devine Jr. and John Morton."How Does the Market Really See Your Product?" *Business Marketing* (July 1984): 70–79.

9. Donald Tull and Delbert Hawkins. *Marketing Research: Measurement and Method,* 6th ed. (New York: Macmillan, 1993): 431.

10. Glen Urban and Steven Star. *Advanced Marketing Strategy* (Upper Saddle River, NJ: Prentice Hall, 1991): 144.

11. Stanley Slater and John Narver. "Does Competitive Environment Moderate the Market Orientation– Performance Relationship?" *Journal of Marketing* (January 1994): 46–55; and John Narver and Stanley Slater, "The Effect of Market Orientation on Business Profitability," *Journal of Marketing* (October 1990): 20–35.

12. Leonard Fuld. *The New Competitive Intelligence—The Complete Resource for Finding, Analyzing, and Using Information about Your Competitors* (New York: John Wiley & Sons, 1995).

13. "Intelligence," *Oregon Business* (May 1988): 28–32.

14. Robert Camp. *Benchmarking—The Search for Industry Best Practices That Lead to Superior Performance* (Milwaukee, WI: Quality Press, 1989); Kathleen Leibfried and C. McNair, *Benchmarking: A Tool for Continuous Improvement* (New York: Free Press, 1992); Jeremy Main, "How to Steal the Best Ideas Around," *Fortune* (October 9, 1992): 102–106; Gregory Watson, *Strategic Benchmarking* (New York: Wiley, 1993); and Gregory Watson, *Benchmarking for Competitive Advantage* (Portland, OR: Productivity Press, 1993).

15. William Boulding and Richard Staelin. "A Look on the Cost Side: Market Share and the Competitive Environment," *Marketing Science* (Spring 1993): 144–166.

16. David Garvin. "Competing on the Eight Dimensions of Quality," *Harvard Business Review* (November– December 1987): 101–109.

17. Bradley Gale. *Managing Customer Value* (New York: Free Press, 1994): 309.

18. Robert Buzzell and Bradley Gale. *The PIMS Principles: Linking Strategy to Performance* (New York: Free Press, 1987).

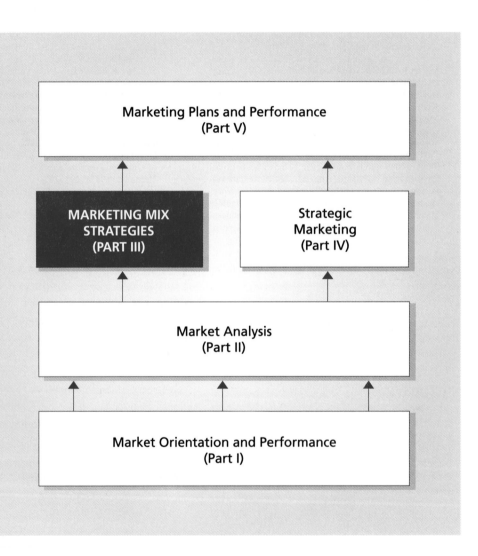

PART III

Marketing Mix Strategies

■ "Price is only relevant in the context of the value of what it is you're offering. If you've got a really good product, people will afford it. Whereas if you've got a product nobody wants, it doesn't matter how cheap you make it."
    —*Joel Hoesktra*
        CEO, General Mills

Businesses that lack a market orientation are likely to price their products by simply checking the competition or marking up their costs to achieve a desired profit margin. Odds are good that these businesses will hurt their customer value, market share, and profit margins. A market-based business will set prices based on customer needs and the strength of its product position relative to competitors.

Part III focuses on short-run tactical marketing strategies designed around the marketing mix for a particular target market. The market analysis presented in Part II is a prerequisite for the development of a tactical marketing strategy because these strategies are built around market demand, the needs of a target segment, and within the context of a competitive environment. Chapter 7 is devoted to product positioning and differentiation, branding and brand management, and product-line strategies. Chapter 8 presents alternative market-based pricing strategies. The combination of product and price creates a certain level of customer attractiveness for a business's product position. Without a strong marketing effort in terms of sales effort, distribution, advertising, and promotion, however, the share potential of a business cannot be fully realized. Chapter 9 examines the various marketing systems (channels and sales) that can be used to effectively reach target customers, and Chapter 10 focuses on the role marketing communications play in delivering a successful marketing mix strategy.

Product Positioning, Branding, and Product-Line Strategies

At an Intel conference Paul Otellini, president and chief operating officer, began with a story about Wayne Gretzky and his famous quote: *"I skate to where the puck is going, not to where it is."* Building on this theme, Otellini handed out a hockey puck to each Intel manager in attendance. On one side of the puck was written *"Follow Me"* and on the other side was the Intel logo and trademark slogan *"Intel Inside"* as shown in Figure 7-1. The "Intel Inside" slogan has allowed Intel to build a flagship brand for a product no one sees, touches, or even knows how it really works. The Intel brand is one of the top 10 global brands, with a brand equity valued at over $30 billion.[1] With this flagship umbrella brand, Intel has been able to grow its sales with product line additions and sub-brand names.

FIGURE 7-1 INTEL INSIDE

PRODUCT POSITIONING

During the 1980s, Intel used numbers to brand further innovations to their microprocessor lines. The Intel 286, 386, and 486 gave way to the Intel Pentium Processor by the early 1990s, as illustrated in Figure 7-2. By the mid 1990s, there were new opportunities for more powerful processors at higher prices, which led Intel to design and brand the more powerful Intel Xeon Processor for the PC server market. The Xeon was positioned at a higher price-performance point than the Pentium, offering more customer value at a higher price. By the late 1990s, the lower-priced PC market was emerging with the aid of Intel's competitor Advanced Micro Devices. Intel could have responded by lowering the

FIGURE 7-2 INTEL PRODUCT POSITIONING, BRANDING, AND CUSTOMER VALUE

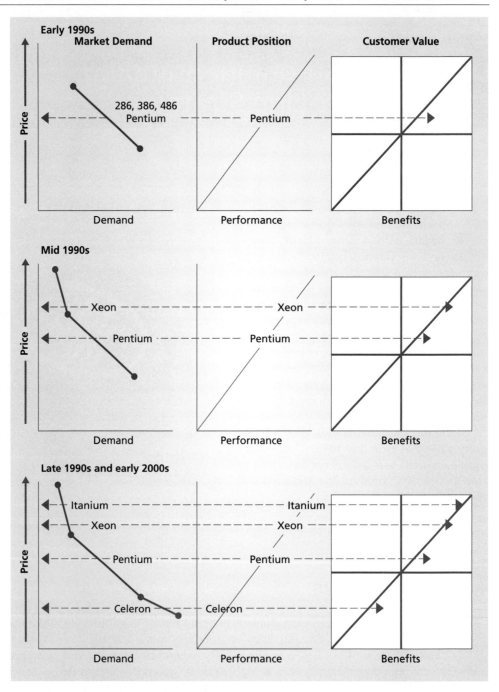

price on Pentium processors. Instead, Intel held the Pentium's price position and launched the Intel Celeron processor at a lower price-performance point to compete with Advanced Micro Devices in the lower price segment of the PC market. In the early 2000s, Intel also released the more powerful Itanium processor at a higher price point than the Xeon. This product-line and brand-management strategy has enabled Intel to grow with market demand while maintaining an 85 percent market share.

The cordless drill market is partitioned into five needs-based product segments, as illustrated in Figure 7-3.[2] At the low end are light-duty cordless drills, which are relatively low in power, torque, and endurance (time to a battery change). At the other extreme are heavy-duty power cordless drills, which are high in power, torque, and endurance. Sears has elected to position products in each of the price-performance segments. Black & Decker, on the other hand, has positioned itself in four of the five cordless drill segments at much lower prices. DeWalt (a Black & Decker brand) is positioned higher than Sears in four of the five segments.

Although Sears' product positioning strategy covers all five price-performance segments, its relative position is not the same in all five segments. At the low-price end of the market (light duty), Sears is higher-priced than Black & Decker for roughly the same performance. At the high-price end of the market (heavy-duty power), Sears is priced just below DeWalt. In the mid-price segments (medium duty, all purpose, and heavy duty), Sears faces both brands. In these segments, Sears is rated and priced slightly lower than DeWalt. Black & Decker is rated and priced significantly lower in the all-purpose and heavy-duty segments.

Although the primary purpose of an expanded product line is to attract more customers, product line variations can also allow existing customers to trade-up to higher-quality,

FIGURE 7-3 PRODUCT-LINE POSITIONING—CORDLESS DRILLS

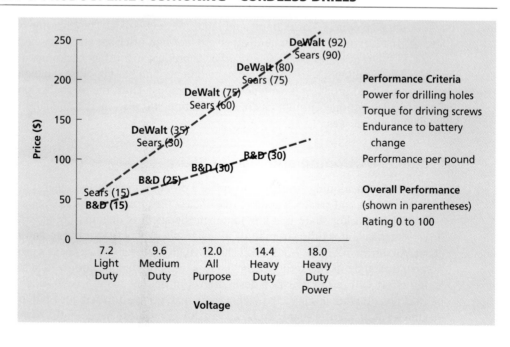

FIGURE 7-4 STARBUCKS PRODUCT LINE AND TRADE-UP OPPORTUNITIES

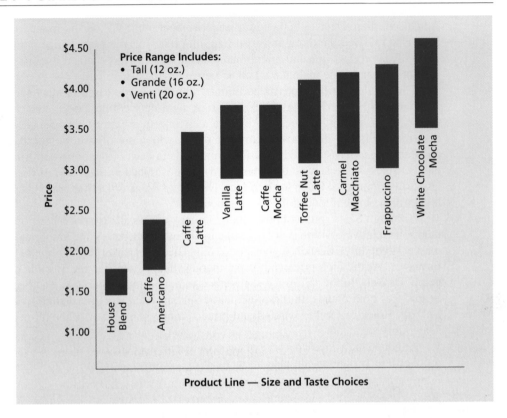

higher-priced products. For example, in Figure 7-4 the Starbucks product line offers three size alternatives for each of nine distinct product-line offerings that vary in price from below $1.50 to just over $4.50. The Starbucks product line offers customers variety and choice but also allows Starbucks to grow margin per purchase because the higher-priced, more-specialized products have much higher margins. Thus, the Starbucks product line impacts sales volume through customer attraction and also increases margins through product line trade-ups.

Product Positioning and Market Share

The goal of a positioning strategy is to create a product-price position that is attractive to target customers and creates a good source of cash flow for the business. Achieving a certain level of market share is a key factor in the success of a marketing strategy and directly dependent on the strength of a business's product positioning and marketing effort. As shown in Figure 7-5, market share is represented as the business's product position multiplied by its marketing effort. Thus, a weak product position with a strong marketing effort will fail to deliver a desired level of market share. Likewise, an attractive product position that is supported with a weak marketing effort will also fail to achieve a desired level of market share. To be successful, a business needs both. Also shown in

FIGURE 7-5 PRODUCT-PRICE POSITION, MARKETING EFFORT, AND MARKET SHARE

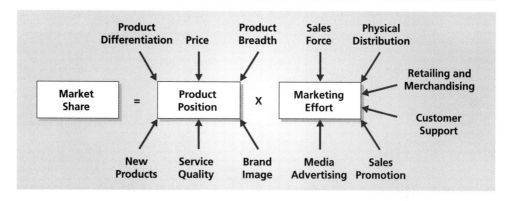

Figure 7-5 are the various factors that contribute to a business's product position and marketing effort. Product differentiation, price, product breadth, new products, service quality, and brand image each contribute to the strength of a business's overall product position. As these inputs to product positioning outperform those of competitors, the strength of a business's product position increases and becomes more attractive to target customers.

To illustrate how product positioning impacts marketing and profit performance, consider how Samsung repositioned its consumer electronics. Samsung had traditionally positioned its consumer electronics products at lower prices. Product quality and performance were lower, and products were sold through discount retailers such as Wal-Mart. In 1999, sales were $27 billion and profits after tax were $1.5 billion, 5.6 percent of sales. However, Samsung senior management put in place a strategy to re-position Samsung as a higher-quality, higher-priced brand of consumer electronic products. All aspects of product positioning and marketing effort, shown in Figure 7-6, had to be changed in order to accomplish this repositioning objective. This required a massive investment in product development as research and development increased from $1 billion in 1999 to $3 billion in 2003. It also required new channels as Samsung abandoned low-price retailers for higher-priced retailers. Marketing expenses also grew from $4.9 billion in 1999 to $6.6 billon in 2003, and the strategy paid off. Samsung's repositioning increased sales by $20 billion in the same time period and profits (after tax) increase more than three fold. This strategy also paid off in terms of marketing productivity as Marketing ROI increased from 71 percent in 1999 to 171 percent in 2003.

Product Positioning Strategies

To create an attractive product position and achieve a desired level of market share and profitability requires several ongoing product management efforts. The first is to develop a positioning strategy designed around target customers' needs. Several key questions must be answered before it is possible to create a positioning strategy: Who is our target customer? What is our positioning strategy? Will the positioning strategy create a superior value for target customers? For a particular target price, a business needs to develop a position based on either a low price or some source of differentiation and product positioning that is meaningful to target customers. As shown in

FIGURE 7-6 SAMSUNG PRODUCT REPOSITIONING AND PERFORMANCE

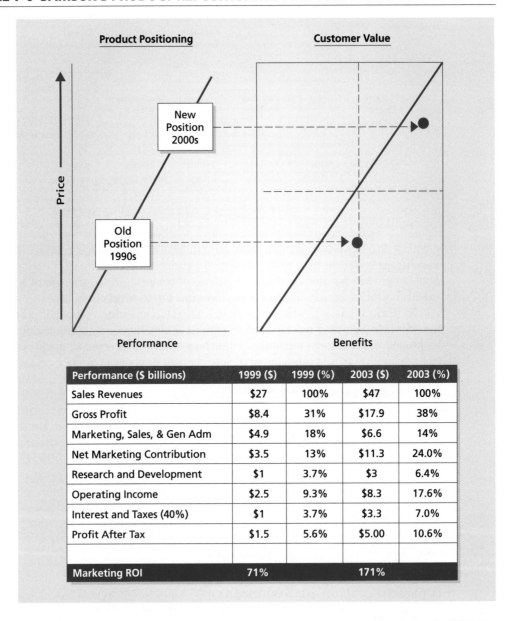

Performance ($ billions)	1999 ($)	1999 (%)	2003 ($)	2003 (%)
Sales Revenues	$27	100%	$47	100%
Gross Profit	$8.4	31%	$17.9	38%
Marketing, Sales, & Gen Adm	$4.9	18%	$6.6	14%
Net Marketing Contribution	$3.5	13%	$11.3	24.0%
Research and Development	$1	3.7%	$3	6.4%
Operating Income	$2.5	9.3%	$8.3	17.6%
Interest and Taxes (40%)	$1	3.7%	$3.3	7.0%
Profit After Tax	$1.5	5.6%	$5.00	10.6%
Marketing ROI	71%		171%	

Figure 7-7, a differential advantage could be built around some combination of cost, product, service, and brand.

A second important area of product management involves branding and brand management strategies. How broad should the product line be? How should brands be created to communicate a consistent image and desired target market identity? How can a brand's assets and potential liabilities be managed to create higher levels of brand equity?

FIGURE 7-7 PRODUCT POSITIONING STRATEGIES

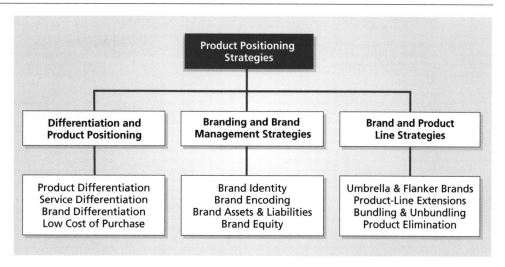

Finally, a third area of product management includes brand and product-line strategies. To what degree should flanker brands be added as extensions of a strong umbrella brand? And when should a business bundle or unbundle products in order to attract and satisfy target customers? From a core product positioning strategy, these types of product line strategies need to be developed in order to fully leverage a business's capabilities and profit potential. The remainder of this chapter is devoted to the three areas and specific topics identified in Figure 7-7.

PRODUCT POSITIONING AND DIFFERENTIATION

On the basis of target customer needs, a business must develop a product position that is in some way differentially superior to competitors' product positions. In a price-sensitive market, product positioning generally requires a lower price, because other sources of differentiation are not valued by target customers. For markets in which differentiation is possible and valued by target customers, a variety of strategies are possible. Product, service, and brand image differences that are meaningful to target customers and differentially superior to those of competitors offer the potential to create a more attractive product position. Regardless of the product-positioning strategy pursued, the goal is to create a customer value superior to that offered by competitors, as illustrated in Figure 7-8.

Product Differentiation

Many customers are not seeking the lowest price, and many are willing to pay a higher price for products that deliver important customer benefits. Differences in product quality, reliability, and performance can attract customers who are seeking products that perform better than average. There are eight dimensions of product quality that can serve as

FIGURE 7-8 DIFFERENTIATION AND CUSTOMER VALUE

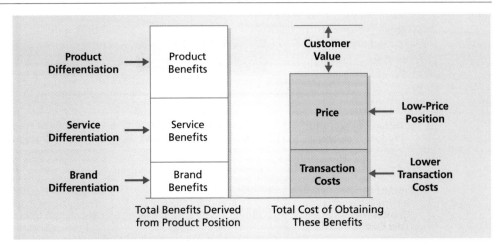

basis for product differentiation.[3] These dimensions can be arranged into four hierarchical categories of product quality, as shown in Figure 7-9. If a business fails to deliver acceptable or expected levels of reliability and conformance, an advantage in other dimensions of product quality will not matter. At the other extreme, quality aesthetics as a source of differentiation are of value only when all other aspects of quality are met with respect to customer quality expectations.

FIGURE 7-9 DIMENSIONS OF PRODUCT QUALITY

Quality Killers

Reliability	Time to failure or malfunction for a given product
Conformance	Incidence of defects that should not have occurred

Quality Drivers

Performance	Operational characteristics that distinguish product performance
Durability	Product life and ability to endure demanding use conditions

Quality Enhancers

Features	Number and type of options that can be added
Serviceability	Ease, speed, and cost of maintenance and repair

Quality Aesthetics

Appearance	The fit, finish, and appearance of a product
Reputation	The image created by the brand name or company

Product Quality Killers

Customers expect reliability and conformance to specifications. Whether they are buying a computer, an automobile, or a Boeing jet, customers expect the product to conform to the specifications that are basic elements of the product. For example, Nescafé creates different blends of coffee to match customers' taste preferences in different international markets. This is conformance to expectations (i.e., specifications). Customers also expect products to operate reliably. Companies such as General Electric, Motorola, and Honeywell have engaged in *six-sigma programs*. Six sigma is a statistical term referring to the probability of product failure. At two sigma, a business with one million products would experience 40,000 failures. At six sigma, the failure rate drops to as close to failure-free as one could expect to get. GE has spent $1 billion to convert all its divisions to six sigma principles. Higher conformance to specifications and fewer failures enhance customer retention and are also raising GE profitability.

Product Quality Drivers

Performance and durability are the workhorses of product quality. Improvements in steering, braking, and fuel economy have been key aspects of improved automobile performance. For example, BMW adds an extra coat of paint to its vehicles sold in Japan in order to meet the quality expectations of the Japanese luxury car buyer. Manufacturers who cannot keep pace with performance improvements will simply lose market share over time. Those who can lead with improved product performance will have created a position on a basis of product differentiation and competitive advantage. Intel, for example, seeks to stay ahead of competitors by continuously improving its products. For over three decades, Intel has followed *Moore's Law:* Every 18 months the operating performance per unit of space should double. This pursuit of performance has enabled Intel to dominate the market it serves, with an 85 percent market share. Durability is also a key component of product quality. Customers have expectations with respect to how long the product should last and how well it should stand up in normal usage. A business that fails to meet customer expectations with respect to durability will face difficulty in both attracting new customers and retaining existing customers. Durability is a common source of advantage in demanding industrial product use situations. For example, ESCO Corporation is a specialty steel manufacturer that makes wear parts for front-end loaders and buckets for mining and construction applications. With proprietary steel chemistry and product designs, ESCO is able to offer customers greater product durability that extends the life of its products and reduces the incidence of breakage in extreme earth-moving applications.

Product Quality Enhancers

A product that meets customer expectations with respect to conformance, reliability, performance, and durability can be differentiated with enhanced quality features. Additional options that can improve the eased use, safety, or enjoyment of a product can be important sources of product differentiation. Air bags, automotive entertainment systems, cruise control, and navigation maps are examples of features that have been added to automobiles to enhance their quality. Features, as a source of differentiation, become more important as a business serves more affluent segments of the market. These customers often want more than the basic elements of product quality. They are seeking enhanced quality in the products they purchase.

Serviceability is another quality enhancer. Products that are easier to maintain and repair save time and money. The Saturn was engineered to make automotive repair easier and less time-consuming, with a net result of lower repair costs. This design has also produced lower insurance costs due to lower-than-normal costs of repair in the event of an accident. Both lower the total cost of ownership for Saturn owners.

Product Quality Aesthetics

The appearance of a product and its reputation can also serve as sources of product differentiation. In Japan, the appearance of a product, or even of the package around the product, can have an enormous impact on the success of that product. For example, a British stereo manufacturer introduced its high-quality system into the Japanese market but failed because the box it was packaged in did not match the quality of the product it contained.

Likewise, the image a brand projects or reputation a company has established can be important in some markets. The quality of products such as Porsche, Rolex, and Chanel is judged not only on their functional characteristics but also on their aesthetic characteristics, which are derived from the image they project. A watch comparable on all seven other aspects of quality listed in Figure 7-9, but not made by Rolex, will fail to attract customers who value the Rolex name and the image it projects.

Service Differentiation

Service, as well as products, can be an important source of differentiation when it comes to positioning strategies. Nordstrom, FedEx, and Caterpillar are well-recognized businesses that have sought to attain a superior position in the area of service differentiation. Many competitors carry the same brand name products and can match the atmosphere found in Nordstrom stores, making Nordstrom's superior service a critical element in its positioning strategy. As with product quality, there are similar dimensions of service quality as outlined in Figure 7-10.

Service Quality Killers

One of the basic requirements of service quality is *service reliability*; classified in Figure 7-10 as a quality killer.[4] Customers expect such reliability first and foremost as a measure of service quality. For FedEx, the promise of *"when it absolutely, positively has to get there"* communicates its service position around reliability.

A second service-quality killer is *service assurance*, which includes the competence and courtesy of service personnel. Caterpillar has sought to strengthen its competitive position and customer benefits with a differential advantage in responsive service. Offering a 24-hour parts and repair service available anywhere in the world has helped Caterpillar differentiate itself from competitors and create a valued service benefit for Caterpillar customers. This creates a service quality assurance in that customers can expect the same quality of Caterpillar service worldwide.

Service Quality Drivers

Nordstrom has always sought to achieve an unparalleled service quality advantage. This position of superior service differentiates it from competitors by offering customers higher levels of service *performance* and *responsiveness*. Nordstrom is legendary in

FIGURE 7-10 DIMENSIONS OF SERVICE QUALITY

Quality Killers

Service Reliability	Ability to deliver the promised service dependably and accurately
Service Assurance	Employee competency with respect to knowledge and courtesy

Quality Drivers

Performance	Able to outperform competitors and customer service expectations
Responsiveness	A service obsession to get it right when things go wrong

Quality Enhancers

Extended Services	Extra customer services that enhance the ease of purchase
Customer Empathy	Individualized attention to customer needs

Quality Asthetics

Appearance	The décor and appearance of employees and facilities
Reputation	The reputation you build at a service-oriented business

delivering service at levels that go beyond customer expectations and demonstrating its commitment to get what the customer wants in a timely fashion. This may mean replacing a sweater that shrank in the dryer despite a clearly labeled warning to line-dry only. By going beyond customers' expectations of service in this way, Nordstrom delivers a greater customer value to target customers.

Service Quality Enhancers

Extended services and individualized customer attention (*customer empathy*) are other aspects of service quality through which a business can seek to build a differentiation advantage. For example, Marriott's Customer Relationship Marketing program focuses on individual customers' needs and preferences, to the extent of prearranging tee times for golf games. Such highly customized attention creates a differential advantage based on service quality. Nordstrom offers customers the services of a "personal shopper" who will meet with them and get to know their tastes in design and color and other shopping preferences.

Service Quality Aesthetics

The *appearance* and *reputation* of the service quality can also impact perceptions of service quality and differentiation. At Les Schwab Tires, a chain of stores in the Pacific Northwest, the nearest employee actually runs to meet every customer who drives up, and whenever service workers move around the shop, they run instead of walking. This gives the appearance of exceptional service quality provided by energetic employees who care about getting customers in and out of the shop quickly. Les Schwab's service reputation leverages a small difference in employee behavior into a large differential advantage in its service differentiation and positioning.

Brand Differentiation

In many consumer and business-to-business purchases, customers are influenced by the status of a brand name or by the assurance of a well-known company. Brands such as Lexus and Mercedes have strong associations with prestige or status. The importance of these brand benefits to many target customers enhances their positioning and differential advantage.[5]

Brand differentiation provides another way to position a business's products relative to competitors and to create incremental customer benefits and value, as illustrated in Figure 7-7. For example, Marriott estimated that adding its name to Fairfield Inn increased Fairfield Inn's occupancy by 15 percent. Kellogg found that in matched product tests, customer choice of corn flakes cereal increased from 47 percent, when the brand was not known, to 59 percent, when the Kellogg name was identified—and when Hitachi and a competitor jointly manufactured TVs in England, Hitachi sold its TVs at a $75 price premium and achieved a higher market share.[6] Each of these examples illustrates the importance of brand benefits to target customers and the brand equity these brand reputations create for the business.[7]

A strong brand enhances positive evaluations of a product's quality, maintains a high level of product awareness, and provides a consistent image or brand personality. A strong brand, such as Coca-Cola, extends each of these positive customer evaluations to brand extensions that include Coke Classic, Diet Coke, Caffeine Free Coke, and Cherry Coke. Brand differentiation can be an important source of differentiation and extend the positioning benefits of a core brand to many closely related flanker brands. However, there are limits to brand extensions.[8] At some point, it may be necessary to create new brand names and build another area of brand equity as Coca-Cola did when entering the sports drink market with Powerade and the fruit juice market with Fruitopia.

Low Cost of Purchase

Thus far, we have focused on the benefit side of differentiation. A business can also create a source of advantage with low price and, hence, lower the cost of purchase. Businesses with a low-cost advantage in markets in which price is an important determinant of customer value can utilize a low price as a basis for product positioning. However, in these market situations, a business cannot ignore product, service, or brand issues. A business must still meet customer expectations in these areas, even though the strength of its product position is built around a more attractive price.

Low-Price Position
For example, Wal-Mart utilizes low prices to create an attractive position relative to competing retail stores. With a low-price positioning strategy, Wal-Mart must achieve a lower cost of buying, inventorying, and retailing the products it sells. This positioning strategy requires Wal-Mart to continuously find ways to contain or lower costs in

order to maintain low prices as a source of competitive advantage while still meeting target customer needs for product, service, and brand. With this positioning strategy, Wal-Mart creates customer value and a competitive advantage by offering lower prices.

While Wal-Mart uses large assortments of brand name products and massive retail outlets, Trader Joe's is an upscale specialty food and wine store with below-average prices. With 200 stores and growing at 20 stores per year, Trader Joe's carries 2,500 items, most of which (80 percent) are private label products. The average grocery store carries 25,000 branded products and relatively few private label goods (approximately 16 percent). Wines at $2.99 are common at Trader Joe's, as is their promotion wine Two-Buck Chuck at $1.99. The Food Institute describes Trader Joe's as a "gourmet food outlet-discount warehouse." The main source of Trader Joe's advantage—low price—is not easily copied, being a combination of a low cost structure and thousands of personally developed relationships with private label producers all over the world.

Lower Transaction Costs

The total cost of purchase also includes transaction costs, as shown in Figure 7-8. These are costs associated with the acquisition of a product. A business can build a low-cost advantage and customer value by lowering these non-price costs of purchase. For example, American Hospital Supply found that $0.50 of every $1 a hospital used to buy hospital equipment was spent on acquiring and inventorying the equipment. In response, American Hospital Supply devised a computerized ordering and inventory management system that would lower a hospital's cost of acquiring and inventorying equipment by 50 percent. In lowering these transaction costs, American Hospital Supply created a greater customer value and developed a source of advantage that enabled American Hospital Supply to grow to become the market share leader in this market.

BRANDING AND BRAND MANAGEMENT STRATEGIES

To fully capture the total value of a product's positioning, it is important to brand a product in a way that communicates its intended positioning. A brand name gives an identity to a product or service, providing a way to quickly comprehend the brand's primary benefits whether rational or emotional.

Brand Identity

The successful management of brands is built around sound marketing practices. A business with a strong market orientation that has segmented its target markets and tracks customer behavior by segment is in the best position to build a successful brand.[9] An internally focused business simply does not have the market intelligence needed to build a brand identity that is meaningful to target customers. The first step in developing a brand identity is to define the desired product positioning and value proposition for a specific target market. Without these specifications, the branding identification process would quickly deteriorate into an internal process built around product features rather than customer benefits.

Brand Encoding

A great deal of strategy goes into the branding process and the creation of specific brand names.[10] Because there are a great number of options, we have created a brand encoding system to help understand how to encode a product's positioning into a brand name for a specific market and desired image. The encoding system is presented as a hierarchy of possible naming components that starts with the company name, followed by a brand name and further enhanced or modified by sub-brand names, numbers, letters, product names, and benefits. A brand can be as broad as a company name like Dell, as narrow as a specific version of a product like Microsoft Windows ME, or a brand name can be as abstract as Altoids.

Company brand names such as Nike and General Electric create an image and umbrella brand under which a wide range of products can be communicated to diverse product-markets. The Nike name carries an image of competitiveness and winning across product-markets that include track, golf, soccer, football, basketball, and many others. General Electric's image for reliability and good value reaches across light bulbs, appliances, plastics, medical systems, power generation systems, electric motors, transportation equipment, electrical distribution equipment, jet engines, credit, and other financial services. Companies such as Sony, Intel, and Ford have created specific brand names to supplement their company names and enhance the identity and position of their products.

Ford, for example, brands its cars as Ford Explorer, Ford Taurus, and Ford Mustang. Intel adds to its company name and brand name a product name to further distinguish its product positioning with Intel Pentium Processors, Intel Celeron Processors, and Intel Xeon Processors. Other companies such as Procter & Gamble use only a brand name like Tide, Cheer, Bold, Bounce, Gain, and Ivory Soap in their line of laundry soaps. In each case, some combination of elements from the brand-encoding system allowed these companies to achieve their desired product positioning for each brand while building a portfolio of brands that has both meaning and synergy.[11] A brand name may or may not use each of the elements in the code. Choosing which specific elements to include in a brand is a matter of determining which combination is most likely to exert the full power of a product position as presented in the following brand encoding strategies.

Company and Brand Name

This is the branding strategy used by many automobile companies. The following is Ford's branding strategy for a variety of its automotive products. Brands created under the Ford name include now well-known names such as Mustang and Explorer. As shown, these brand names were further enhanced with sub-brand names, letters, and numbers.

Company	Brand	Sub-Brand	Product	Letters	Numbers	Benefits
Ford	Escape					
Ford	Explorer	Sport Trac				
Ford	Lightning			SVT	F-150	
Ford	Mustang	Cobra		SVT		Convertible
Ford	Land Rover	Freelander				
Ford	Focus		Wagon	SE		

Brand and Sub-Brand Name

In 1846 Church & Dwight Co. began selling sodium bicarbonate to help with cooking under the brand name Arm & Hammer. For 120 years this was the only marketed use for Arm & Hammer baking soda. However, in more recent years Arm & Hammer has extended its product application to deodorizers (refrigerators, carpets, cat litter), personal care (toothpaste, antiperspirants, pharmaceuticals), household products (laundry detergents, air fresheners), industrial products (degreasing, cleaning, depainting), and agricultural products (feed ingredients). In each case, the core brand Arm & Hammer was retained and its image leveraged with the addition of sub-brands as illustrated here.

Company	Brand	Sub-Brand	Product	Letters	Numbers	Benefits
	Arm & Hammer		Baking Soda			
	Arm & Hammer	Vacuum Free				
	Arm & Hammer	Crystal Blend				
	Arm & Hammer	Peroxicare				
	Arm & Hammer	Home Alone Pads				
	Arm & Hammer	Super Scoop				
	Arm & Hammer	Ultramax				

Company and Product Name

General Electric serves a diverse set of product-markets that range from consumer goods to medical and industrial and financial services. The GE name and logo are key factors in communicating the company's long tradition of providing quality products and services at prices that deliver customer value. Within each of these major GE product lines, branding is enhanced with numbers and letters to further identify levels of performance and specification. However, General Electric has elected not to include the brands NBC and CNBC under the GE flagship brand. For strategic reasons, GE has preferred to minimize the association between GE and NBC and CNBC.

Company	Brand	Sub-Brand	Product	Letters	Numbers	Benefits
GE			Aircraft Engines			
GE			Appliances			
GE			Capital			
GE			Industrial Systems			
GE			Lighting			
GE			Medical Systems			
GE			Plastics			
GE			Power Systems			
GE			Specialty Materials			
GE			Transportation Sys.			
	NBC					
	CNBC					

Company, Brand, and Product Name

Intel encodes its brand names to include the company name, a unique brand name, and the product name. As the following shows, this helps Intel communicate the positioning of four microprocessor families (Celeron, Pentium, Xeon, and Itanium) while also branding a Micro-Architecture with NetBurst and a memory chip with StrateFlash. For its more complex products, Intel uses letters or letters and numbers to abbreviate the product name using names such as the Intel IXP 1200 Network Processor, Intel PCA (Personal Client Architecture), and Intel IEA (Internet Exchange Architecture). The Intel company name provides an umbrella brand name that communicates Intel's reputation for quality and innovation. The individual brand names enable Intel to position multiple products in the same markets. The addition of product names allows Intel to sell multiple products to the same customer without confusing the product application.

Company	Brand	Sub-Brand	Product	Letters	Numbers	Benefits
Intel	Pentium				4	
Intel	Xeon					
Intel	Celeron					
Intel	Itanium					
Intel	Centrino					
Intel	StrateFlash		Memory			
Intel	NetBurst		Micro-Architecture			
Intel				IXP	1200	
Intel				PCA		
Intel				IEA		

Company Name, Brand Name, and Number

Microsoft uses a variation of the Intel strategy of leveraging its company name and branding individual products. However, rather than using the product name, Microsoft uses numbers and letters to communicate versions of its software brands. For example, Microsoft Outlook Express 6 allows buyers and users to quickly identify the Microsoft product and its newness relative to older versions of the same brand. This strategy allows the brand to date itself, as in the case of Microsoft Windows 95, 98, and 2000.

Company	Brand	Sub-Brand	Product	Letters	Numbers	Benefits
Microsoft	Windows			NT		
Microsoft	Windows				98	
Microsoft	Windows			ME		
Microsoft	Windows				2000	
Microsoft	Windows			XP		
Microsoft	Office				2003	
Microsoft	Outlook Express				6	

Brand Name and Benefit

Braun has successfully branded the Oral-B toothbrush. Taking advantage of the well-known name and image for quality in the Oral-B brand, Braun extended the Oral-B brand name by including primary benefits that differentiate the brands. The Oral-B Ultra Plaque Remover is clearly targeted at customers seeking the benefit of plaque removal, which customers can quickly tell is different from the intended benefit of the regular Oral-B toothbrush.

Company	Brand	Sub-Brand	Product	Letters	Numbers	Benefits
	Oral-B					Cross Action Power
	Oral-B		Series		900	Advance Power
	Oral-B					Advance Power Kids
	Oral-B		Series		7000	Professional Care
	Oral-B	OxyJet Center				Professional Care
	Oral-B					Cross Action Vitalizer
	Oral-B	Advantage				Control Grip
	Oral-B					Indicator
	Oral-B	SATINFloss				
	Oral-B	Super Floss				

Brand Name Only

Procter & Gamble has long been known for its "brand-name-only" strategy. In markets served by multiple P&G brands, P&G Brand Teams work hard to maintain their unique product positions. For example, the following are the P&G brands positioned for the laundry soap market. Each brand has a unique focus and product-positioning strategy. Including the P&G name as a prominent component of the brand names could dilute the positioning of the individual product brands. Also, because the products are well understood and sold in specific retail locations, there would be little value in adding a product name, letters or sub-brand name. In the brand-name-only encoding strategy, the primary benefit is often embedded in the name to further communicate the desired product position of the brand.

Company	Brand	Sub-Brand	Product	Letters	Numbers	Benefits
	Tide					
	Downy					
	Gain					
	Cheer					
	Bounce					
	ERA					
	Febreze					
	Dreft					
	Dryel					
	Ivory Snow					
	Bold					

Brand Name Development

Perhaps a larger challenge than a specific branding strategy is coming up with a new brand name. Whether a new company name, brand name, or sub-brand name, there is the challenge of creating a brand name that has meaning with respect to the positioning of a company and/or umbrella brand as well as being short and easily remembered. Summarized here are four ways in which new brand name are created.[12]

1. **Functional/Descriptive Names:** Functional names are purely descriptive of what a product or company is or does. International Business Machines (IBM), Digital Equipment, and E-Trade describe what the product or company does and are functional names. Merrill Lynch, BMW, Dell Computer, and Hewlett-Packard (HP) are also functional brand names. Wal-Mart combines both the function and description with the use of morphemes or part words. Wal is a morpheme derived from the name of Wal-Mart's founder Sam Walton, and Mart is derived from market. The combined name describes an owner and a store—Wal-Mart.
2. **Invented Names:** There are two kind of invented names: those that are built from Greek or Latin words and morphemes and those that are poetic constructions based on the rhythm or experience of saying them. Nike is derived from Greek mythology, while Agilent and Alliant are invented names. Poetically created brand names include Oreo, Kleenex, Snapple, and Google. Google was actually derived from the mathematical term *googol*.
3. **Experiential Names:** These are company or brand names that create a direct connection to something real and that can be associated with a direct experience. Web portals Explorer, Magellan, Navigator, and Safari are examples of names created to subtly communicate the experience of surfing the Web. Big Bertha, Red Bull, Path Finder, and Silk Soy Milk are also brand names developed to elicit an experience.
4. **Evocative Names:** These are brand names created to evoke the positioning of a company or product rather than the product function or product experience. Examples include Yahoo!, Virgin Airlines, and Apple. United Airlines introduced Ted in 2004 to compete with low-cost airlines such as Jet Blue and Southwest. Ted is a morpheme of Uni*ted* as intended to evoke a friendly image while retaining a subtle association with United Airlines.

Creating a New Brand Name

Recognizing the various approaches to brand-name development, a business or management team ultimately needs to develop a specific name for a specific business situation. For example, Cisco Systems developed a software solution to streamline the complex processes of making a large information-processing purchase decision. Cisco's online product support helps customers sort out the many considerations, technical details, and suppliers, but more importantly, it helps specify the information-processing system that would be best for that customer's situation. To give this service an identity, Cisco Systems sought to develop a brand name for this customer solution.

Figure 7-11 shows how Cisco's customer problem, its product solution, and the resulting customer benefits could be distilled into several descriptive words and morphemes to serve as inputs for potential brand names. The goal is to create a brand name

FIGURE 7-11 DEVELOPING A BRAND NAME

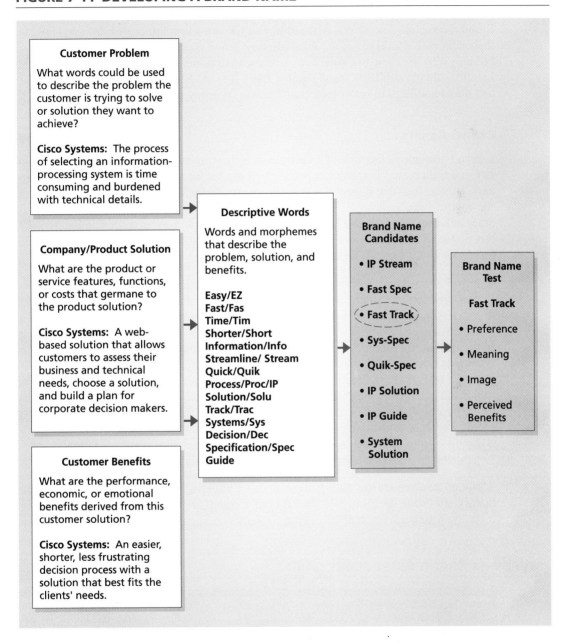

that either relates to the experience or evokes a positioning that is favorable to the product. Although many possibilities existed, Fast Track emerged as the most effective sub-brand name. The name conveys ease of use and infers the success of the user. Cisco's value proposition for Fast Track is: "*Your shortcut through the IP communications decision-making process.*"

BRAND EQUITY

Brand names like Coca-Cola, Microsoft, and GE are worth billions of dollars. How did they achieve this level of value? What are their brand assets? Do they have any brand liabilities? Why are some brands able to leverage their brand assets while others incur brand liabilities that lessen their brand equity? Let's first examine the concept of brand assets and brand liabilities to better understand how a company or brand builds brand equity.

Brand Assets

A brand, like any business with financial assets, has varying brand assets.[13] A brand such as Coca-Cola creates brand assets based on its market leadership and high level of awareness. Brand assets that impact brand value are also derived from an exceptional reputation for quality, brand relevance, and high levels of customer loyalty. Although a variety of other influences could create brand assets,[14] these five brand assets (shown in Figure 7-12) can be found to some degree in all of the top brand names such as Disney, Coca-Cola, Mercedes, Sony, General Electric, and many others.

■ **Brand awareness:** Companies with high brand awareness can more easily introduce new products and enter new markets, such as Nike with the Nike name and logo.
■ **Market leadership:** Market-share leaders such as Intel dominate the markets in which they compete.
■ **Reputation for quality:** A superior reputation for quality is a brand asset for companies such as Lexus.
■ **Brand relevance:** A brand must be relevant to consumers within a product-market to be a brand asset. Over the past 15 years, Lexus has gained brand relevance among luxury car buyers while Cadillac has lost brand relevance as the lifestyle and demographics of this market have changed.
■ **Brand loyalty:** For brands such as E-Trade, a high level of customer retention is a profitable brand asset that lowers marketing expenses and increases customer profitability.

Although there are several ways to measure these brand assets, one is with the Brand Asset Score Card shown in Figure 7-12. In this case, a brand is rated relative to the average brand in its competing market. Individual brand-asset scores can range from zero to 20. With five

FIGURE 7-12 BRAND ASSET SCORE CARD

Brand Assets	Below Average (0)	Somewhat Below (5)	About Average (10)	Somewhat Above (15)	Top Performer (20)	Brand Asset Score
Brand Awareness						
Market Leadership						
Reputation for Quality						
Brand Relevance						
Brand Loyalty						
Total Brand Assets						

assets, the overall brand-asset score ranges from zero to 100. An average brand would attain an overall brand-asset score of 50. Brands with large brand equity such as Coca-Cola, Microsoft, and GE should produce brand asset scores much greater than 50.

To understand how the score card would work, consider how you might have assessed each of the brand assets presented in Figure 7-12 for Cadillac and Lexus in 1990. Lexus was a relatively new brand, while Cadillac was the market leader with a 30 percent market share. Most luxury car buyers in 1990 would have rated Cadillac's brand assets higher than Lexus. If this analysis were performed again between 2000 and 2005, we would most likely see Lexus climb in brand assets and Cadillac slide in brand assets as its market share eroded to below 20 percent.[15] However, more recently Cadillac has been fighting back with new models and new advertising in an attempt to regain its brand relevance and reputation among luxury car buyers.

Brand Liabilities

Brands can also incur brand liabilities due to a product failure, a lawsuit, or questionable business practices. Prior to the Enron collapse, Arthur Andersen would have had relatively low levels of brand liabilities. Their involvement and questionable accounting practices led to considerable customer dissatisfaction and lawsuits, which in turn created brand liabilities that lowered Arthur Andersen's brand equity. At the same time, Arthur Andersen's brand assets were drastically reduced by declining market share, an eroding reputation for quality, and declining brand loyalty. The net result was a significant increase in brand liabilities and a corresponding reduction in brand assets. Although other brand liabilities could be considered, the following are five potentially harmful brand liabilities.

1. **Customer dissatisfaction:** Brands with high levels of customer complaint and customer dissatisfaction incur a brand liability that detracts from brand equity. Customer complaints in the telecommunication industry have created brand liabilities for some telecom companies.
2. **Environmental problems:** Brands associated with poor environmental practices may create a certain level of brand liability. The brand equity of many oil companies is lower when associated with oil spills or environmentally insensitive drilling practices.
3. **Product or service failures:** Product failures, like those experienced by Firestone Tires, result in brand liabilities that can potentially destroy a powerful brand.
4. **Lawsuits and boycotts:** Lawsuits and consumer boycotts create brand liabilities. Martha Stewart's lawsuit with regard to illegal stock trading tarnished the brand image of Martha Stewart. This created a brand liability that in effect lowers the brand equity associated with the Martha Stewart brand.
5. **Questionable business practices:** Questionable or unethical business practices that surface as negative news create brand liabilities. Nike, for example, lost some of its brand equity because of questionable working conditions at its foreign production sites.

As with brand assets, brand liabilities can be assessed using the Brand Liabilities Score Card presented in Figure 7-13. For most strong brands, brand assets will exceed brand liabilities. Using the Brand Liabilities Score Card one could make an assessment of Arthur Andersen before and after the Enron debacle. Again, although opinions will vary, most would find that their estimate of Arthur Andersen's brand liabilities increased after

FIGURE 7-13 BRAND LIABILITIES SCORE CARD

Brand Liabilities	Below Average 0	Somewhat Below 5	About Average 10	Above Average 15	Top Performer 20	Brand Liability Score
Customer Dissatisfaction						
Environment/Problems						
Product Failures/Recalls						
Lawsuits and Boycotts						
Questionable Practices						
Total Brand Liabilities						

the Enron scandal. Thus, for Arthur Andersen the Enron scandal resulted in a likely decrease in brand assets and a likely increase in brand liabilities, both contributing to a significant drop in brand equity.

Brand Equity

In a business, the owner's equity is the value of the owner's holdings in the company. It is determined by the difference between what a company owns in assets and what a company owes in liabilities. The larger the ratio of assets to liabilities the greater the owner's equity. As Figure 7-14 shows, brand equity can be assessed in the same way. To calculate

FIGURE 7-14 BRAND BALANCE SHEET AND BRAND EQUITY

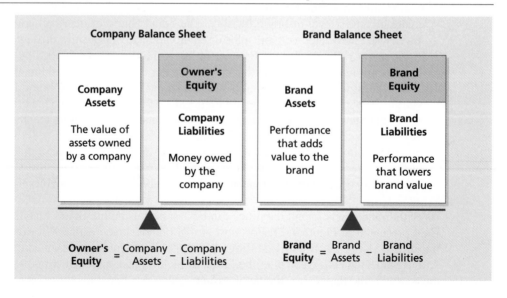

brand equity, simply subtract the total brand liability score from the total brand asset score. Tracking changes in brand equity over time is an important part of the brand-management process, because brand equity is not static.

For businesses such as Enron, Martha Stewart, and WorldCom, one can easily envision how brand equity quickly eroded as brand assets declined and brand liabilities grew. Likewise, it should be easy to comprehend how the brand equity of companies such as Dell Computer, Lexus, and Target has grown over the last 15 years as their brand assets grew without burdensome brand liabilities. In either situation, the brand-equity model can be a useful way to understand and manage a brand's equity.

BRAND AND PRODUCT-LINE STRATEGIES

The more products a business has to sell, the more ways it has to attract and satisfy potential customers. A broad line of products creates more selling opportunities for the sales force and channel partners. A business with a narrow line of products has to be more focused in order to be cost effective in its marketing efforts.

Because a broad product line provides a business with more potential customers and the potential to sell more to each customer, this type of marketing efficiency translates into more sales and higher levels of profitability. For example, in Figure 7-15, we can see that businesses with broad product lines are more profitable during the emerging and growing stages of a product life cycle than are businesses with a narrow product line.

FIGURE 7-15 BREADTH OF PRODUCT LINE AND RETURN ON INVESTED ASSETS

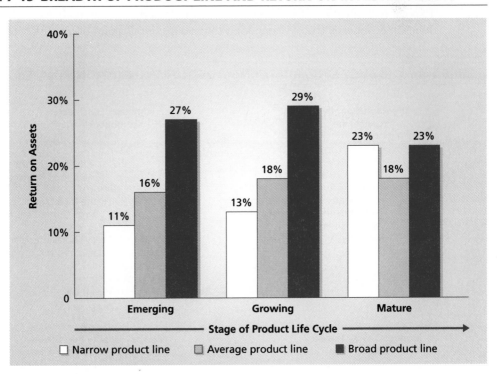

Thus, it is particularly important to expand a business's product line during these stages of the product life cycle. This is exactly what Microsoft did in the 1980s and 1990s in growing the computer market.

Product-Line Development

Quite often, a company will want to expand from one market segment into an adjacent segment in order to grow sales and profits. Product-line expansion requires considerable product differentiation and careful positioning because the same company is now going to ask for a different price for a different combination of product, service, and brand benefits. Toyota sequentially expanded its product line from a low product-price segment in the 1960s to the point where, today, Toyota offers a full line of automobiles, each with a different product-price position and unique brand name identity, as illustrated in Figure 7-16.

In the beer market, Anheuser-Busch's product-line strategy utilizes separate brand names for each of the several beer market positioning strategies it has pursued, as outlined in Figure 7-16. Each brand has a distinct product-price position that is attractive to different types of customers or different use situations. In recent years, Anheuser-Busch expanded its product line to the microbrew segment with the introduction of Michelob Hefeweizen, added Kirin to create an import brand position, and developed Michelob Ultra to create a product position with a low-carbohydrate beer.

Umbrella and Flanker Brands

An *umbrella brand* is the core product of a business such as Ivory (soap), American Express (credit cards), Betty Crocker (cake mix), Gerber (baby food), Kodak (film), and Johnson & Johnson (baby shampoo). From a consumer's point of view, the core product

FIGURE 7-16 PRODUCT LINE, BRANDING AND DIFFERENTIATION STRATEGY

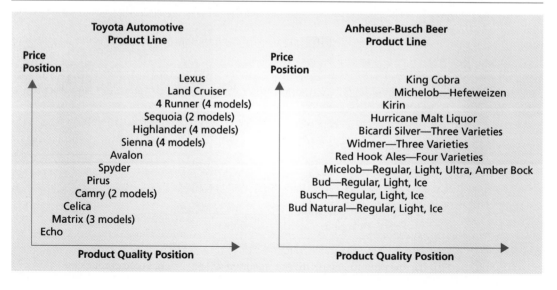

FIGURE 7-17 FRITO-LAY UMBRELLA AND FLANKER BRANDS

Frito's Corn Chips	Lay's Potato Chips	Ruffles Potato Chips	Cheeto's Cheese Snacks	Tostitos Tortilla Chips	Doritos Tortilla Chips	Rold Gold Pretzels	Granola Bars	Cracker Jack
Frito's Twist	Lay's Bistro Gourmet Chips Stax		Cheeto's Mystery Colorz Snacks		Dorito's Extremes Tortilla Chips			

is the most visible embodiment of the brand name. Accumulated exposure and experience with the core product solidifies a certain image and quality expectation. Umbrella branding involves the transfer of quality perceptions derived from a core product or brand to product line extensions that use the same brand name. The intent of umbrella branding is to enhance the effectiveness of marketing programs and to increase demand for product extensions by transferring brand awareness and perceptions of quality from the umbrella brand.[16]

For example, the Frito-Lay core brands capture 59 percent of the U.S. snack chip market. The sales growth of the Frito-Lay brands was largely due to the introduction of new flanker brands under the core brands of Fritos corn chips, Lay's potato chips, Cheetos, and Doritos as illustrated in Figure 7-17. These umbrella brands create a base from which to introduce flanker brands that enhance market penetration at a lower cost.[17] Summarized here are four ways a flanker brand benefits from a strong umbrella brand and how each of these benefits contributes to the profitability of the flanker brand.

1. **Brand awareness:** The high level of market awareness attained by the core brand creates an umbrella under which related products can be introduced at a much lower cost of advertising.
2. **Known quality:** The quality image of the core brand is transferred to brand-line extensions under the umbrella brand.
3. **Market reach:** Retailers are more inclined to give precious shelf space to well-known brands. As a result, brand extensions under these umbrella brands gain easier access to retail space.
4. **Product mix:** Brand extensions under the umbrella brand provide customers with more variety and the opportunity to buy variations of the core brand without having to switch to competing brands.

The purpose of brand and line extensions is to leverage the awareness and image of the flagship brand while, at the same time, not diluting its image or perceived quality. However, line extensions may not grow market demand and can cannibalize the core brand or other extensions while raising the total cost of marketing. Thus, careful product line accounting is needed to ensure that product-line extensions are profitable and, overall, that they incrementally improve the profitability of the entire product line.[18]

FIGURE 7-18 GARDENBURGER VERTICAL AND HORIZONTAL BRAND EXTENSIONS

Vertical Brand	Horizontal Brand Extensions				
	1	2	3	4	5
Extensions	Hamburgers	Chicken	Veggie	Meatless Meats	Dinners
1	Original	Chik'n Grill	Garden Vegan	Breakfast Sausage	Dinner Deluxe
2	Flame Grilled	BBQ Chik'n	Veggie Medley	Riblets	Crispy Pizza Nuggets
3	Santa Fe	Country Fried Chik'n	Savory Portabella	Meatballs	
4		Buffalo Chik'n Wings	Fire Roasted Vegetable	Meatloaf	
5				Sweet and Sour Pork	
6				Herb Crusted Cutlet	

Product-Line Extensions

Vertical Brand-Line Extensions

A successful brand can often be "franchised," meaning it can be extended to other versions of the product. This can be accomplished most easily with "vertical brand extensions" of the core brand. Gardenburger is a company that manufactures meatless products. Its core brand is shown in Figure 7-18 as the Original. Vertical brand names subsequently added to the basic Gardenburger brand name include Gardenburger Flame Grilled and Gardenburger Santa Fe. These vertical brand extensions provide variety for Gardenburger customers who may tire of the same taste of one product. It also may attract new customers from other meatless products or even customers trying meatless products for the first time.

Horizontal Brand-Line Extensions

Horizontal brand extensions within a product class are possible by adding complementary products. For Gardenburger, this meant adding horizontal product lines that included meatless chicken, sausage, ribs, dinners, and veggie entrees. Furthermore, a horizontal brand extension in veggie brands opened the door to additional vertical brand extensions. Each of these combinations leveraged the core Gardenburger brand while growing sales and profits.

New Product-Market Brand Extensions

Vertical and horizontal brand extensions provide excellent opportunities for growth within a given product-market. However, eventually a business will hit a point of diminishing returns and will need to examine the potential of its proven brand name in other product-market applications. Honda built a reputation in the automotive and motorcycle markets for reliable, high-quality products. This brand reputation allowed easy entry to other product-markets, often at a price premium. The Honda brand name was so strong that it was easily transferred to related product-markets such as lawn mowers, snowblowers, pumps, generators, skimobiles, and jet skis, as illustrated in

FIGURE 7-19 HONDA PRODUCT LINE AND LINE EXTENSIONS

Product Line	Product Line Offerings
Automobiles	Accord, Civic Sedan, Civic Coupe, Civic Hybrid, Insight, Odyssey, Pilot, S-2000
Motorcycles	Standard, Touring, Sport Touring, Sport, Crusier, Moto-Cross, Off-Road
Scooters	Silver Wing, Reflex, Elite 80, Metropolitan, Metropolitan II
Jet Skis	Aqua Trax F-12, Aqua Trax F-12X
All-Terrain Vehicles	Utility, Sport
Lawn and Garden	Lawn Mowers, Trimmers, Tillers
Snowblowers	Wheel-Drive, Track-Drive, Lightweight
Pumps	Construction, De-Watering, Multipurpose, Submersible
Generators	Handheld, Economy, Industrial, Super Quiet, Deluxe
Engines	GX Series, GC Series, Mini 4-Stroke

Figure 7-19. Each product-market had a "related relevance" to what the Honda brand name stood for in terms of quality and reliability and the benefits of Honda's core brand carried over to these new products.

Co-Branding

A successful brand can also be leveraged by entering another product-market with co-branding rather than creating a brand extension. One example is Yoplait yogurt's co-branding with Trix, a children's cereal, to create Trix Yoplait yogurt produced for children.[19] High awareness and brand preference for Trix among children quickly led to sales of Trix Yoplait yogurt with no advertising. Another example is General Mills' co-branding of Reese's Peanut Butter Cups with a new cereal called Reese's Puffs. The cereal carries all the imagery of the Reese's Cups.

Co-branding takes advantage of the potential synergy of two brands that share a common market space. Healthy Choice had many brand extensions in the frozen-food category. To enter the cereal market, co-branding with Kellogg's cereals saved considerable advertising money and provided easier access to cereal shelf space in retail stores. The composite product—"Healthy Choice from Kellogg's"—uses the Healthy Choice logo, colors, and packaging. Co-branding provided Healthy Choice with easy access to the already crowded cereal market, while it gave Kellogg's a credible product-line extension that included a dimension of weight loss and health, a product concept that had failed without the Healthy Choice name and credibility.

Trix Yoplait yogurt and Healthy Choice from Kellogg's are composite co-brands that merge two brands together. Co-branding can also include ingredient co-branding strategies. "Intel Inside" is a classic example of ingredient co-branding. The Intel microprocessor chip is an ingredient, a key component, of a personal computer. Intel's reputation for quality in personal computers adds perceived quality to the personal computer. Dell Computer with "Intel Inside" is a co-branding strategy that has helped Dell grow its sales of personal computers and helped Intel grow its sales of microprocessors. Using the "Intel Inside" logo on all personal computers using Intel microprocessors was a low-cost way to keep the Intel company name in front of personal computer customers.

Bundling and Unbundling Strategies

Products are often enhanced with additional features and services to provide customers with more complete solutions. Most personal computers are purchased with a variety of software packages to enable easier and faster usage of common programs such as word processing, spreadsheets, and Internet access. In other instances, customers may have designed their own specialty software and would seek to purchase a personal computer without this software (i.e., unbundled) in order to lower their total cost of purchase. Each of these product strategies can be used to further enhance a product's benefits or lower cost by removing product features and services.

Product Bundling

Bundling products serves to create a complete customer solution that has the potential to create a superior customer value and attract customers. Products such as living room sets, entertainment packages, and software offered with the purchase of computers are product bundles that have the potential to create a superior value (economic and perceived) for target customers. There are two approaches to product bundling.

A *pure product bundling strategy* involves the sale of two or more products at an overall price lower than the total price that would be paid if the products were purchased separately. Even when the products are offered individually at a discounted price that makes the total cost equal to the bundled purchase price, customers rate the bundled offering higher in perceived value.

A *mixed bundling strategy* offers the customer the opportunity to purchase each of the items separately at a sale price or bundled with an additional level of savings. There is evidence that when both options are available, customer perceptions of value exceed those produced with a pure bundling strategy.[20] In addition, a mixed bundling strategy has been shown to be more profitable than pure bundling strategies.[21]

Product Unbundling

Unbundling a set of products that is normally sold as an integrated bundle or system can also be desirable in attracting and satisfying customers. For many complex industrial and commercial purchases, customers may want to purchase individual products or components and integrate them into a certain configuration that best serves their needs.[22] In some instances, value-added resellers (VARs) fulfill this role. For specialized applications in architecture, agriculture, or chemical processing, VARs will purchase unbundled products and integrate them in a customized bundle that best suits the target customers' application. Hewlett-Packard may have an attractive product bundle, but it cannot meet the specific needs of all customers. By unbundling and selling individual products or component products to VARs and systems integrators, HP has been able to create value for its customers and sales growth opportunities for the business.

In the early evolution of a market, customer needs are generally less fragmented than in the later stages, and bundled product solutions are often very attractive. However, as markets grow and new customers enter, segments of the market emerge, and more customized product solutions are needed to satisfy different customers.[23] As a market matures, unbundling often becomes more important in attracting and satisfying customers.[24]

Product-Line Substitution Effects

Product-line additions can frequently have a substitution effect. This occurs when the new brand attracts new customers but also attracts customers away from the core or umbrella brand. Likewise, some new-brand customers may migrate to the umbrella brand or other brands in the product line as they become more familiar with the company's products.

For example, consider a well-known cracker with a retail price of $2.99 per box and wholesale price of $1.95 per box. As shown in Figure 7-20, customers attracted to the product line by the core brand will switch 10 percent of the time to the multigrain product and 25 percent of the time to the reduced-fat version of the core brand. Likewise, there is switching to other product line offerings among customers attracted to the multigrain or reduced-fat cracker. After this level of switching is taken into account, we can see that the primary demand of 50 million for the core brand is reduced to 35 million boxes. Both the flanker brands result in higher volumes as customers switch from the core brand to the flanker brands. However, despite some cannibalization of the core brand, the product-line extensions add to the sales and profits of the product line. Although the margin per box is lower for the flanker brands, the incremental demand created by the flanker brands creates a higher overall level of product-line profits.

FIGURE 7-20 PRODUCT-LINE SUBSTITUTION EFFECTS

Probability of Switching Between Brands

From - To	Core Brand	Multigrain	Reduced Fat
Core Brand	X	10%	25%
Multigrain	5%	X	20%
Reduced Fat	10%	5%	X

Area of Performance	Core Brand	Multi-grain	Reduced Fat	Product Line
Volume				
Primary Demand	50,000,000	10,000,000	20,000,000	80,000,000
Core Brand	32,500,000	5,000,000	12,500,000	
Multigrain	500,000	7,500,000	2,000,000	
Reduced Fat	2,000,000	1,000,000	17,000,000	
Net Volume	35,000,000	13,500,000	31,500,000	80,000,000
Wholesale Price per Unit	$1.95	$1.95	$1.95	$1.95
Sales	$68,250,000	$26,325,000	$61,425,000	$156,000,000
Variable Cost per Unit	$0.95	$1.00	$1.05	$1.00
Margin per Unit	$1.00	$0.95	$0.90	$0.95
Total Contribution	$35,000,000	$12,825,000	$28,350,000	$76,175,000

Product-Line Scale Effects

Although not immediately obvious, there is also the potential for scale effects with respect to fixed manufacturing expenses when operating below capacity in production and leveraging fixed marketing expenses associated with sales and distribution. In our example, we have extended the product-line profitability analysis to include these fixed expenses. First, assuming the business has excess production capacity, the flanker brands were added without additional plant and equipment. As illustrated in Figure 7-21, the $40 million in fixed manufacturing overhead can now be spread over more units (80 million vs. 50 million). This increases the gross profit of the core brand from $10 million ($50 million in total contribution minus $40 million in manufacturing overhead) to $36 million for the product line.

Also, some of the $10 million in marketing expenses can be shared with the flanker brands because no additional sales, customer service, or administration people have to be added to market the two flanker brands. The $10 million in fixed marketing expenses can now be allocated on a percentage of sales dollars to each of the brands. However, each brand still has some semi-variable marketing expenses that change with advertising and promotions. The net effect is a further increase in profitability from leveraging the use of excess production capacity and fixed marketing expenses that will need to be incurred with or without the flanker brands.

FIGURE 7-21 PRODUCT-LINE SCALE EFFECTS

Area of Performance	Core Brand	Multi-grain	Reduced Fat	Product Line
Volume				
Primary Demand	50,000,000	20,000,000	10,000,000	80,000,000
Core Brand	32,500,000	5,000,000	12,500,000	
Multigrain	500,000	7,500,000	2,000,000	
Reduced Fat	2,000,000	1,000,000	17,000,000	
Net Volume	35,000,000	13,500,000	31,500,000	80,000,000
Wholesale Price per Unit	$1.95	$1.95	$1.95	$1.95
Sales	$68,250,000	$26,325,000	$61,425,000	$156,000,000
Variable Cost per Unit	$0.95	$1.00	$1.05	$1.00
Margin per Unit	$1.00	$0.95	$0.90	$0.95
Total Contribution	$35,000,000	$12,825,000	$28,350,000	$76,175,000
Manufacturing Overhead	$17,500,000	$6,750,000	$15,750,000	$40,000,000
Gross Profit	$17,500,000	$6,075,000	$12,600,000	$36,175,000
Fixed Marketing Expenses	$4,375,000	$1,687,500	$3,937,500	$10,000,000
Variable Brand Expenses	$3,412,500	$789,750	$1,842,750	$6,045,000
Total Marketing Expenses	$7,787,500	$2,477,250	$5,780,250	$16,045,000
Net Marketing Contribution	$9,712,500	$3,597,750	$6,819,750	$20,130,000
Marketing ROS (%)	14.2	13.7	11.1	12.9
Marketing ROI (%)	124.72	145.23	117.98	125.46

These shared expenses often get overlooked, and when a brand appears to be producing a negative profit (net marketing contribution), a business may elect to remove that brand from the market. However, the total contribution may then drop (assuming it is positive), which contributes to fixed expenses in manufacturing and marketing. Product elimination decisions need to be done with care. Often the cost accounting used to produce product-line profitability statements includes allocations of fixed manufacturing expenses to a line of products, which can distort the stated profitability of any single brand or product.

■ Summary

For any specific target segment, a business needs to develop a tactical marketing strategy that involves positioning its product with respect to products and price and marketing its product with respect to promotion and place. This chapter focused on product position and product strategies, but a successful marketing strategy requires a highly integrated mix of product, price, promotion, and place. Product positioning and differentiation are key parts of a successful marketing strategy. How should a business position its products relative to customer needs and competitors? And what source of differentiation is needed to make this product position differentially superior to competitors' products?

Low-price differentiation is an important position to develop for businesses serving price-sensitive markets. However, lowering the customer's transactions costs can also be a valuable way to achieve a low-cost advantage. For markets in which differentiation is possible, a business could build its differentiation around a product or package advantage, service advantage, or an advantage in brand reputation. To be successful, the differentiation underlying the positioning strategy must be meaningful to target customers and sustainable (not easily duplicated by competitors).

A positioning strategy is further enhanced by the brand name used to identify a product. Because a company may have many products and serve many diverse markets, special care has to be given to how brand names are encoded to ensure both meaning and consistency across the product line. Commonly used brand-encoding systems include (1) company and brand name; (2) brand and sub-brand name; (3) company and product name; (4) company, brand, and product name; (5) company, brand name, and number or letter; (6) brand name and benefit; and (7) brand name only. Each of these brand-encoding systems has advantages and disadvantages with respect to distinctiveness, consistency, and communicating the product's positioning.

To grow, a business needs to leverage its product knowledge, production capabilities, marketing systems, and brand equity. Product-line strategies provide an excellent opportunity to grow and leverage current assets and expenses. Related product-line extensions that are built off an existing brand or a new brand are important ways to achieve profitable growth. Brands that are well-known for above-average quality create a basis from which to create flanker brands. However, one has to be mindful of sales cannibalization, damaging the image of the core brand, and the diminishing returns of adding a number of brands. Product bundling and unbundling are also product strategies that can enhance customer attractiveness in certain customer markets.

Finally, new-product development is an essential part of market-based product management. Without new-product success, a business's long-run survival is in question, as is its short-run ability to grow the business. The higher a business's percentage of new-product sales, the higher its level of real sales growth will be—and when new-product sales are also a source of relative competitive advantage, even higher rates of sales growth are achievable. A market-based business should manage the new-product development process on the basis of three important areas of input: customer, competitor, and technology. The goal is to develop a new product that is responsive to an unfulfilled customer need in a manner that is superior to what the competition is offering.

■ Market-Based Logic and Strategic Thinking

1 How did Intel's branding strategy help the company grow and maintain a dominant market share?
2 How would you evaluate the product-line positioning of Black & Decker relative to Sears in terms of customer choice and customer value? See Figure 7-3.
3 How does Starbucks' product-line positioning enhance both sales and profits?
4 How could a business with an attractive product position achieve a lower market share?
5 Why did Samsung's repositioning strategy yield higher sales and higher profits?
6 How would a business use the eight dimensions of quality differentiation in developing a product and package differentiation strategy?
7 How does a business such as McDonald's develop a positioning strategy around some aspect of service differentiation?
8 Why would a brand name such as Kodak, Disney, or Coca-Cola create customer value and provide a basis for product positioning and differentiation?
9 Why would the occupancy of a Fairfield Inn increase by 15 percent when the Marriott name is added to the building?
10 Why would a mere extension of a line of related products contribute to higher levels of profitability?
11 Why would a business use an experiential brand name versus an evocative brand name?
12 What are morphemes and how were they used in developing brand names such as InfoSeek, DuraFlame, and Compaq Computer?
13 What is the marketing logic that underlies Anheuser-Busch's product line and bundling strategy for the beer market?
14 What are the advantages of a product strategy involving a strong core brand with flanker brands? Under what conditions would this product-line strategy fail?
15 Why are vertical brand-line extensions less expensive than horizontal brand-line extensions?
16 How does a well-known brand help in the marketing and profitability of a flanker brand?
17 Why would a company like Ford co-brand with Eddie Bauer to create a unique brand of Ford Explorer within the Ford SUV product line?
18 How might product-line substitution effects contribute to the sales of Intel Pentium microprocessors when the Xeon and Celeron brands were introduced?
19 Frito-Lay introduced Stax to compete with Pringles in 2003. Assuming the company had excess production capacity, how would the profits of other chip products be affected by the success of Stax?
20 Under what conditions would the elimination of a flanker brand with a negative operating income result in lower overall operating income if eliminated?

Marketing Performance Tools

Each of the following **marketing perfor-mance tools** can be accessed by going to *www.rogerjbest.com* or *www.prenhall.com/best*.

The shaded cells are input cells. The non-shaded cells contain results calculated from your input values.

MARKETING PERFORMANCE TOOL—Impact of Product-Line Substitution

Product-Line Price Positioning

Price	Core Brand	Flanker A	Flanker B
$3.49			
$2.99	Core Brand	Multigrain	Reduced Fat
$1.49			
$0.99			
$0.49			
$0.00			

Probability of Switching Between Products

From - To	Core Brand	Flanker A	Flanker B
Umbrella	X	0.1	0.25
Flanker A	0.05	X	0.2
Flanker B	0.1	0.05	X

Product-Line Performance Impact

Area of Performance	Core Brand	Multigrain	Reduced Fat	Product Line
Volume				
Primary Demand	50,000,000	10,000,000	20,000,000	80,000,000
Core Brand	32,500,000	5,000,000	12,500,000	
Multigrain	500,000	7,500,000	2,000,000	
Reduced Fat	2,000,000	1,000,000	17,000,000	
Net Volume	35,000,000	13,500,000	31,500,000	80,000,000
Price per Unit	$1.95	$1.95	$1.95	$1.95
Sales	$68,250,000	$26,325,000	$61,425,000	$156,000,000
				Continued

Continued

Area of Performance	Core Brand	Multigrain	Reduced Fat	Product Line
Variable Cost per Unit	$0.95	$1.00	$1.05	$1.00
Margin per Unit	$1.00	$0.95	$0.90	$0.95
Total Contribution	$35,000,000	$12,825,000	$28,350,000	$76,175,000

This **marketing performance tool** allows you to estimate the sales and profit impact of a brand extension strategy. The data provided is from Figure 7-20. The shaded cells can be changed in doing the following application exercise. However, an entirely new example of your own can be input using the shaded cells.

Application Exercise: Using the data provided, change the switching probabilities to zero percent for all between-brand switching. How do the sales and profits change? Then, input your own assumptions about customer switching behaviors, treating Wheat Thins as the core brand, Wheat Thins Multigrain as flanker brand A, and Wheat Thins Reduced Fat as flanker brand B. How do the sales and profits differ from Figure 7-21?

MARKETING PERFORMANCE TOOL—Impact of Product-Line Scale Effects

Area of Performance	Core Brand	Multigrain	Reduced Fat	Product Line
Volume				
Primary Demand	50,000,000	20,000,000	10,000,000	80,000,000
Core Brand	32,500,000	5,000,000	12,500,000	
Multigrain	500,000	7,500,000	2,000,000	
Reduced Fat	2,000,000	1,000,000	17,000,000	
Net Volume	35,000,000	13,500,000	31,500,000	80,000,000
Price per Unit	$1.95	$1.95	$1.95	$1.95
Sales	$68,250,000	$26,325,000	$61,425,000	$156,000,000
Variable Cost per Unit	$0.95	$1.00	$1.05	$1.00
Margin per Unit	$1.00	$0.95	$0.90	$0.95
Total Contribution	$35,000,000	$12,825,000	$28,350,000	$76,175,000
Manufacturing Overhead	$17,500,000	$6,750,000	$15,750,000	$40,000,000
Gross Profit	$17,500,000	$6,075,000	$12,600,000	$36,175,000
Fixed Marketing Expenses	$4,375,000	$1,687,500	$3,937,500	$10,000,000
Variable Brand Expenses	$3,412,500	$789,750	$1,842,750	$6,045,000
Total Marketing Expenses	$7,787,500	$2,477,250	$5,780,250	$16,045,000
Net Marketing Contribution	$9,712,500	$3,597,750	$6,819,750	$20,130,000
Marketing ROS (%)	14.2	13.7	11.1	12.9
Marketing ROI (%)	124.72	145.23	117.98	125.46

This **marketing performance tool** allows you to estimate the sales and profit impact of a brand-extension strategy when taking into account manufacturing and marketing scale effects. The data provided is from Figure 7-21. The shaded cells can be changed in doing the following application exercise. However, an entirely new example of your own can be input using all of the shaded cells.

Application Exercise: Using the data provided, increase the variable cost for the multigrain brand until the net marketing contribution equals zero. How do overall sales and profits change? What would be the profit impact of eliminating the multi-grain brand product based on a variable cost estimated in above?

MARKETING PERFORMANCE TOOL—Assessing Brand Equity

Brand Assets	Below Average 0	Somewhat Below 5	About Average 10	Somewhat Above 15	Top Performer 20	Brand Asset Score
Brand Awareness						
Market Leadership						
Reputation for Quality						
Brand Relevance						
Brand Loyalty						
Total Brand Assets						

Brand Liabilities	Not a Concern 0	Minor Concern 5	Somewhat of Concern 10	Notable Problem 15	Major Problem 20	Brand Liability Score
Customer Dissatisfaction/Complaints						
Environment/Community Problems						
Product Failures/Recalls						
Lawsuits/Boycotts/Labor Problems						
Questionable Business Practices						
Total Brand Liabilities						

Brand Equity

	Brand Assets	Brand Liabilities
100		
80		
60		
40		
20		
0		

This **marketing performance tool** allows you to estimate a brand's brand equity based on your estimates of brand assets and brand liabilities. The shaded cells are the input cells used to compute brand assets and brand liabilities. You will have to graph the result using the chart provided to estimate the brand equity.

Application Exercise: Using a brand you are familiar with, estimate how the brand equity would have changed over a 10-year period. Estimate the brand assets and brand liabilities using the spreadsheets for the brand 10 years ago. Then print the results and plot the brand assets and brand liabilities and compute the brand equity.

Estimate the current brand assets and brand liabilities using the spreadsheets and print the results. Graph the brand assets and brand liabilities and discuss how brand equity has changed.

Notes

1. "The Top 100 Brands," *Business Week* (August 5, 2002): 95–99.
2. "Drills for All Reasons," *Consumer Reports* (November, 1997): 24–28.
3. David Garvin, "Competing on Eight Dimensions of Quality," *Harvard Business Review* (November–December 1987): 101–105.
4. Valarie Zeithaml, A. Parasuramon, and Leonard Berry, *Delivering Quality Service* (New York: Free Press, 1990): Chapter 1.
5. Bradley Gale, "Creating Power Brands," in *Managing Customer Value* (New York: Free Press, 1994): 153–174.
6. Peter Farquhar, "Managing Brand Equity," *Marketing Research* (September 1989): 24–33.
7. David Aaker, *Managing Brand Equity: Capitalizing on the Value of a Brand Name* (New York: Free Press, 1991).
8. Daniel Sheinin and Bernd Schmitt, "Extending Brands with New Product Concepts: The Role of Category Attribute Congruity, Brand Affect, and Brand Breadth," *Journal of Business Research* 31 (1994): 1–10.
9. D. Aaker, *Building Strong Brands* (The Free Press, 1996): 356–357.
10. D. D'Alessandro, *Brand Warfare* (McGraw-Hill, 2001).
11. S. Hill, C. Lederer, and K. Keller, *The Infinite Asset: Managing Brands to Build New Value* (Harvard Business School Press, 2001).
12. Igor International, *www.igorinternational.com*, "Name Development," (accessed 2004).
13. S. M. Davis, *Brand Asset Management* (Jossey-Bass, Inc., 2000).
14. K. Keller, "The Brand Report Card," *Harvard Business Review* (January–February 2000): 147–157.
15. C. Lederer and S. Hill, "See Your Brands Through Your Customers' Eyes," *Harvard Business Review* (June 2001): 125–133.
16. T. Erdem, "An Empirical Analysis of Umbrella Branding," *Journal of Marketing Research* (August 1998): 339–351; David Aaker, *Building Strong Brands* (New York: Free Press, 1995); P. Dacin and D. Smith, "The Effect of Brand Portfolio Characteristics on Consumer Evaluations of Brand Extensions," *Journal of Marketing Research* (May 1994): 229–242; A. Rangaswamy, R. Burke, and T. Oliver, "Brand Equity and Extendibility of Brand Names," *International Journal of Research in Marketing* (March 1993): 61–75.
17. M. J. Hatch and M. Schultz, "Are the Strategic Stars Aligned for Your Corporate Brand?" *Harvard Business Review* (February 2001): 129–134.
18. Bruce Hardle, "The Logic of Product-Line Extensions," *Harvard Business Review* (November–December 1994): 53–62.
19. D. Aaker, *Building Strong Brands* (The Free Press, 1996): 298–300.
20. Manjit Yadav and Kent Monroe, "How Buyers Perceive Savings in a Bundle Price: An Examination of a Bundle's Transaction Value," *Journal of Marketing Research* (August 1993): 350–358.
21. William Adams and Janet Yellen, "Commodity Bundling and the Burden of Monopoly," *Quarterly Journal of Economics* (August 1976): 475–498; and Richard Schmalensee, "Gaussian Demand and Commodity Bundling," *Journal of Business* 57(1984): 211–230.
22. Lynn Wilson, Allen Weiss, and George John, "Unbundling of Industrial Systems," *Journal of Marketing Research* (May 1990): 123–138.
23. Roger Best and Reinhard Angelmar, "Strategies for Leveraging Technology Advantage," in *Handbook on Business Strategy* (Boston: Warren, Gorham, and Lamont, 1989): 2-1-2-10.
24. Barbara Jackson, *Winning and Keeping Industrial Customers* (Lexington, MA: Lexington Books, 1985); and Michael Porter, *Competitive Advantage* (New York: Free Press, 1985).

CHAPTER 8

Market-Based Pricing and Pricing Strategies

rice is the most visible cost in any purchase, whether it is a new car, a computer, an insurance policy, a vacation, or a simple household cleanser. All customers are price sensitive to some degree. However, some customers are willing to pay more for extra benefits. These benefits can include reduced costs in other areas of product ownership. The costs of owning a product are much less obvious than its price. As shown in Figure 8-1, price is only the tip of the iceberg, and below the surface are many of the other costs of ownership. Market-based pricing considers the total value of ownership benefits and costs in determining the best price for a product.

FIGURE 8-1 PRICE IS ONLY THE TIP OF THE ICEBERG IN THE VALUE-PRICING EQUATION

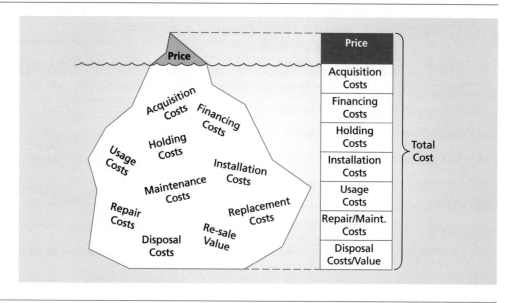

UNDERSTANDING LIFE CYCLE COSTS

A company will tend to remain focused on price until it begins to understand how customers acquire, finance use, maintain, and dispose or re-sell its product when compared to competing products. As you look deeper into the costs of ownership, you will likely find opportunities for customer savings and value creation. For example, Figure 8-2 is a life cycle cost analysis of a company's product that it was trying to sell into the automobile manufacturing market. This market is highly price competitive and customers simply do not pay price premiums. To win this business, the company was told it would have to offer a price below the current price of $2.00 per pound. This is where most businesses would focus on their price and terms in a effort to obtain this business.

FIGURE 8-2 LIFE CYCLE COST AND VALUE PRICING

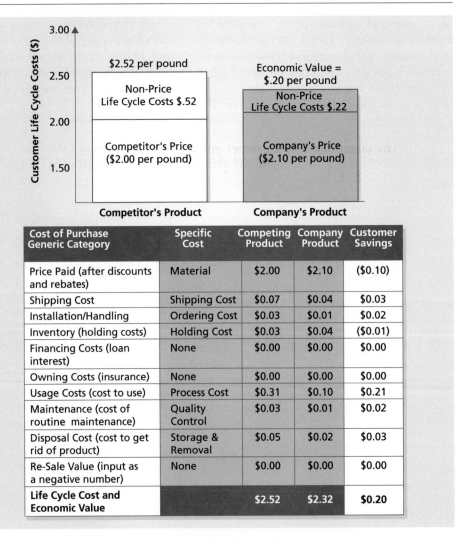

Cost of Purchase Generic Category	Specific Cost	Competing Product	Company Product	Customer Savings
Price Paid (after discounts and rebates)	Material	$2.00	$2.10	($0.10)
Shipping Cost	Shipping Cost	$0.07	$0.04	$0.03
Installation/Handling	Ordering Cost	$0.03	$0.01	$0.02
Inventory (holding costs)	Holding Cost	$0.03	$0.04	($0.01)
Financing Costs (loan interest)	None	$0.00	$0.00	$0.00
Owning Costs (insurance)	None	$0.00	$0.00	$0.00
Usage Costs (cost to use)	Process Cost	$0.31	$0.10	$0.21
Maintenance (cost of routine maintenance)	Quality Control	$0.03	$0.01	$0.02
Disposal Cost (cost to get rid of product)	Storage & Removal	$0.05	$0.02	$0.03
Re-Sale Value (input as a negative number)	None	$0.00	$0.00	$0.00
Life Cycle Cost and Economic Value		$2.52	$2.32	$0.20

However, in qualifying the material for use, this company looked more closely at how its product was used in comparison to the competing product. The cost comparisons in Figure 8-2 show that the competitor's product was harder to use, required more material per unit, had higher levels of waste, and required more quality control time. The order entry, shipping, and inventory costs were also higher, as were disposal costs due to more wasted material. The analysis showed that even with a 5 percent price premium ($2.10), customers could still save $.20 pound. Because this material was purchased in millions of pounds, this was a significant customer savings. The competitor would have to lower its price to $1.80 per pound to match this company's total life cycle cost per pound. Although it was a challenge to convince the automobile manufacturer, the company was able to win the business with a price premium. In the end, the customer benefited with a substantial cost savings and the company benefited with a higher margin product.

Unfortunately most businesses do not engage in sufficient customer and competitor analysis to understand all the cost drivers or the full value of their product. As a result, these businesses are more likely to engage in cost-based pricing. In the early 1990s, many computer makers used cost-based pricing to price personal computers.[1] This pricing process started with the cost of making a personal computer (purchased parts, labor, and equipment) and added on a desired profit margin to achieve a retail price, as illustrated in Figure 8-3. In this example, the cost to make a low-priced computer for the under-$1,000 segment of the PC market was $600. A desired profit margin of 25 percent was added to the cost to produce a price to retailers of $800. Retailers also used cost-based pricing and marked their cost of $800 up to a price of $940 to achieve a 15 percent profit margin. In this case, everybody should be happy: The target end-user customer got a personal computer for under $1,000, retailers obtained a desired margin of 15 percent, and the computer manufacturer achieved a desired margin of 25 percent.

FIGURE 8-3 COST-BASED PRICING VERSUS MARKET-BASED PRICING

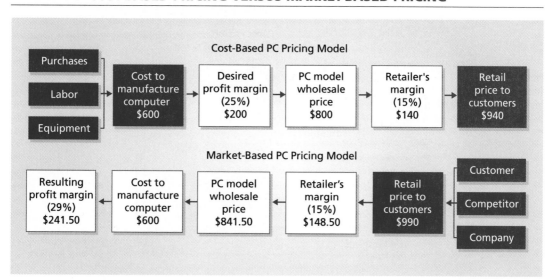

However, something is missing from this approach to pricing. First, cost-based pricing ignores what the customer would be willing to pay for a certain level of product performance. Second, this approach to pricing overlooks what the competition is offering relative to the customer's needs and price affordability. Recognizing these flaws in their pricing logic, many computer makers shifted from cost-based pricing to market-based pricing in the mid-1990s.

As shown in Figure 8-3, market-based pricing starts with the customer, the competition, and company positioning. Based on customer needs, price sensitivity, and competing products, a price is developed around a product's relative strengths to provide a better value than competing products. In this example, the customer would have paid $990 for the same computer based on its benefits and price relative to competing computers. Retailers would still want their traditional 15 percent margin, resulting in a market-based price of $841.50 from the PC manufacturer. At a cost of $600 per unit, the margin would be $241.50 per unit. This would be $41.50 higher than the margin obtained with cost-based pricing. In this instance, market-based pricing achieved a higher profit while delivering an attractive customer value. It may appear that market-based pricing is the preferred approach to pricing, but there are situations in which cost-based pricing may be a better approach depending on the market situation, as illustrated in Figure 8-4.

Cost-based pricing is the most commonly used approach to pricing in business.[2] This is largely because customer and competitor intelligence are hard to obtain and because cost-based pricing is relatively easy to do. One study found that over 60 percent of the businesses surveyed used cost-based pricing as their primary basis for setting price.[3] This is consistent with an ongoing worldwide study of over 25,000 managers from over 90 countries where 64 percent of those surveyed used cost-based pricing to set price. As shown, those in general management are more likely to endorse market-based pricing, while many in marketing management and other related job functions are more likely to use cost-based pricing.

FIGURE 8-4 PRICING ORIENTATION AND PRICING STRATEGIES

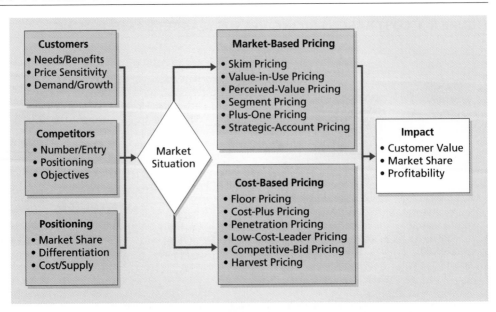

Managers in this study who used market-based pricing also had much higher levels of marketing knowledge and stronger market-oriented attitudes.[4]

Pricing Strategy	Senior Management	Marketing Management	Product Management	Sales/Sales Management	Marketing Communications
Market-Based	55%	37%	34%	31%	17%
Cost-Based	45%	63%	66%	69%	83%

MARKET-BASED PRICING

Market-based pricing requires extensive customer and competitor intelligence.[5] Without high levels of both, market-based pricing is simply not possible. This is why most businesses fall back into cost-based pricing as illustrated in Figure 8-5. A business with a strong customer orientation may believe it is using market-based pricing, but without competitor intelligence, the business cannot fully gauge its price position. Likewise, a business focused on competitors' pricing and positioning but ignoring customer needs will evolve into reactive competitive pricing. Thus, only businesses with a strong market orientation that focus on both customers and competitors have the possibility to engage in market-based pricing.

Market-based pricing starts with a good understanding of customer needs and the benefits a product creates relative to competitors' products.[6] On the basis of customer benefits, price is set relative to competition to create a superior value. In this way, price is set in the market, not at the factory or in the financial department. This section reviews the various market-based pricing strategies while the following section reviews commonly used cost-based pricing strategies.

FIGURE 8-5 CUSTOMER AND COMPETITOR INTELLIGENCE AND PRICING ORIENTATION

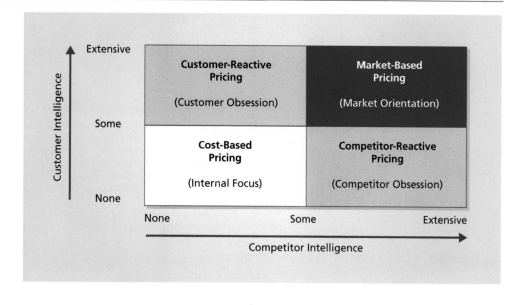

Skim Pricing

Skim pricing is most likely to occur at the early stages of the product life cycle, as illustrated in Figure 8-6. In some situations, a business holds a proprietary product advantage relative to competition because it holds a patent or the product has a unique capability. In such a case, a business will pursue a premium price strategy while still delivering superior customer value until competition can match its source of competitive advantage. For example, many prescription drugs are patented. Under the protection of a patent, the holder may charge higher-than-normal prices. During this period, the business is able to create a *price umbrella* because the competition cannot match the business's relative advantage.

But under what conditions is a skim pricing strategy likely to work? As summarized in Figure 8-6, when a business has a considerable, and sustainable, differentiation advantage in a quality-sensitive market that has few competitors and is difficult for competitors to enter, skim pricing is a viable market-based pricing strategy. When feasible, skim pricing allows a business to penetrate markets systematically as it adds production capacity. As the demand for a high-priced segment is saturated, price can be lowered gradually to attract more customers until prices reach a level affordable to most potential customers.

Value-in-Use Pricing

As a business moves into the growth stage of the product life cycle it will have to find a way to lower the cost to potential customers in order to attract their purchase volume. However, this does not necessarily mean lowering prices. By considering the total cost of ownership incurred by target customers, a business can utilize market-based pricing to produce an attractive savings (economic value) while maintaining a premium price. For example, in Figure 8-7, the price of a business's product is higher than the price of the competitor's product, but the customer's total cost of ownership is lower than with the

FIGURE 8-6 SKIM PRICING

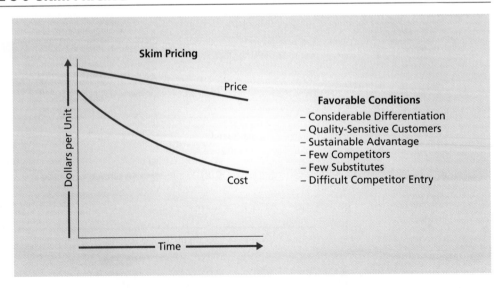

FIGURE 8-7 VALUE PRICING

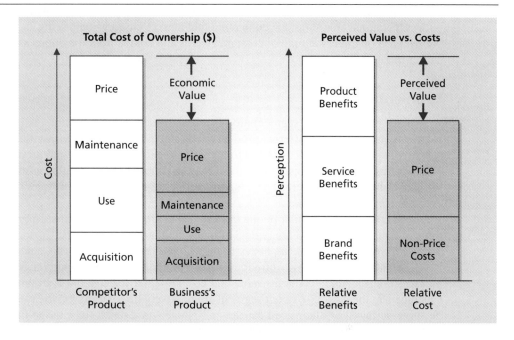

competitor's product. Because of lower acquisition, use, and maintenance costs over the life of the product, its *value in use* is higher than the competing product, and the customer saves money.

When using value-in-use pricing, the level of economic value and price should be set relative to what is an attractive savings to customers and should not be based on the cost of manufacturing and marketing the product. Customers are interested in savings or economic value, and the higher the savings, the more attractive the business's product. In market-based pricing, costs and margins are the business's problem, not the customer's. Chapter 4 discussed the various ways a business can lower the cost of ownership and, hence, achieve higher price levels while still creating a superior value for target customers.

Perceived Value Pricing

Some customer benefits are more difficult to quantify in terms of economic value, yet they have an important perceived value. Another approach to market-based pricing is perceived value pricing. As illustrated in Figure 8-7, the perceived benefits derived from the product, service, and brand (image or reputation) yield a certain level of total perceived benefits. The overall perceived cost of purchase is made up of the price paid, the terms of purchase, and any non-price costs that contribute to the total perceived cost of purchase. The net difference between perceived overall benefits and cost is perceived customer value. In this example, the strength of the business's overall benefits enables it to charge a price higher than the competition's (price premium) and still create a larger overall perceived value for customers. Chapter 4 provides a detailed discussion of how to measure perceived customer value and the various ways a business can improve its perceived benefits in order to obtain higher prices and still create a superior value when compared with competitors. One should keep in mind that market-based value pricing is only possible with a good understanding of customer needs and competitors' positions as presented earlier in Figure 8-3.

Segment Pricing

A primary goal of market segmentation is market-based pricing. Customers in different segments generally have different product needs and different price sensitivities. A price-sensitive segment would be attracted to low price regardless of additional product or service benefits. A quality-sensitive segment may pay more for the extra benefits (product, service, or brand) they desire. Thus, the market-based price could be different for different segments within a market.

Let's consider the cellular phone market. There are many potential segments, but the three outlined in Figure 8-8 are typical of many cellular phone markets. Customers in the *Staying Connected* segment are heavy users who use the cell phone in all aspects of their life. The package plan, which provides a fixed monthly cost for a wide range of usage, provides considerable economic value and cost certainty for customers in this segment. Customers in the *Use-As-Needed* segment are relatively heavy users but their usage could be sporadic based on their need for the cell phone. As a result their usage often varies from month to month. A flex plan best fits their needs because it provides for usage discounts during periods of heavy use. Finally, the *Security User* has low cell phone usage but keeps a cell phone for security reasons. This user is sensitive to the cost of cellular phone service but likes the security and convenience a cellular phone offers. For this segment, a security plan offers a low minimum monthly access fee but a higher usage fee. Because all three market-based price programs are available to any customer, we would expect customers in the various segments to prefer the market-based pricing alternative

FIGURE 8-8 SEGMENT PRICING

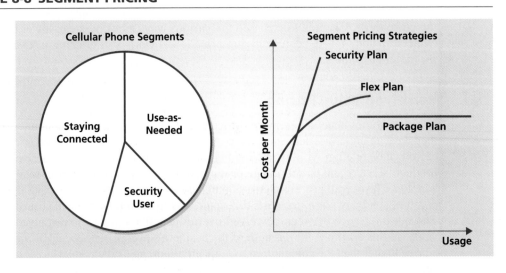

FIGURE 8-9 PRODUCT LIFE CYCLE PRICING STRATEGIES

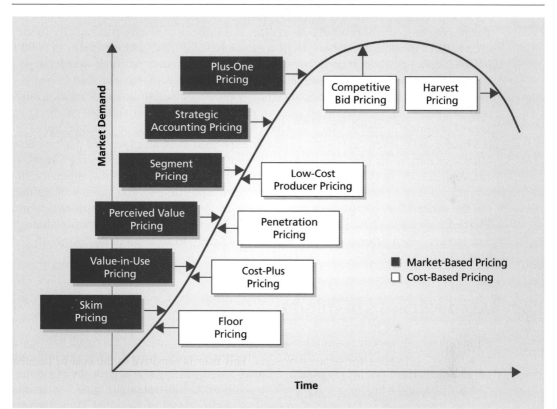

that best fits their usage patterns and price sensitivity. As shown in Figure 8-9, segment pricing is most likely to be used during the growth stage of the product life cycle.

Strategic-Account Pricing

Customers that are large and important to a business's sales and profits become strategic accounts. Pricing for strategic accounts is market-based and customized to the unique needs of the customer in the context of competitive market conditions. The market-based pricing perspective is also longer range and may include a pricing mechanism to adjust prices over a period of several years. A primary goal of strategic-account pricing is to maintain a strong and enduring customer relationship even when market conditions change. For example, in a B2B market sellers may be required to take a slightly lower price in a "seller's market" when average prices are generally high. Likewise, buyers may be asked to pay a slightly higher price in "buyer's markets" where average prices are generally low. This market-based price-sharing helps reduce large swings in margins while maintaining large volumes of the customer's business. Strategic account pricing will not work without a strong commitment to serving customer needs and a price that creates a superior value when compared to competitor's offerings.

Plus-One Pricing

As products mature in most competitive markets, businesses are able to emulate the best features of competitors' products. As a result, it is difficult to stand out as unique. To succeed in these markets, a business needs some source of differentiation in order to build a unique product position. It needs to establish a plus-one product position[7] in order to justify a market-based price with a slight premium relative to competing products.

A plus-one market-based pricing strategy product position is one in which a business can equal competitors on all areas of product and service quality but can find one area of meaningful performance in which it is clearly superior. For example, Volvo, in the luxury car market, must meet customer expectations in all aspects of performance but uses safety as its plus-one product differentiation strategy in achieving a market-based price relative to competing luxury cars. This is what makes Volvo uniquely different, and it is a central part of its product-price positioning and value proposition. On the other hand, Lexus uses performance as its plus-one pricing strategy, while Mercedes uses its reputation. As illustrated in Figure 8-9, a plus-one pricing strategy is a market-based pricing strategy that is most likely to be used in late stages of the product life cycle.

COST-BASED PRICING STRATEGIES

Although it may appear that market-based pricing is the preferred approach to pricing in a market-focused business, there are situations in which cost-based pricing may be an appropriate pricing approach. Market-based pricing starts with the customer, competition, and a business's competitive position, as illustrated in Figure 8-3. In this manner, price is set in the market to create a desired level of customer attractiveness and delivered customer value. In contrast, cost-based pricing starts with the cost of the product and a desired margin. On the basis of these requirements, a price is set and the product is sold to channel intermediaries who mark-up the price to a level that allows them to achieve a desired margin. This, of course, is the price the customer sees in the marketplace, as illustrated in Figure 8-3. In markets where product differentiation is minimal, cost-based pricing is often a reasonable alternative to market-based pricing.

Floor Pricing

Floor pricing is an internal, cost-based price computation based on a desired level of profitability. The floor price could be based on a desired margin or return on investment. As a result, floor pricing is often used in the early stages of the product life cycle (see Figure 8-9) when target customers are less price sensitive.

Consider a new product with an available production capacity of two million units per year. At that capacity the cost per unit is $5.00 and the fixed manufacturing expense is $5 million per year. The business is not interested in launching new products with less than a 30 percent gross profit. Given these financial parameters, a price of $10.70 per unit will yield annual sales of $21.4 million and a gross profit $6.4 million, a 30 percent gross profit margin.

$$\% \text{Gross Profit} = \frac{\text{Volume} \times \textbf{Price} - \text{Volume} \times \dfrac{\text{Unit}}{\text{Cost}} - \dfrac{\text{Manufacturing}}{\text{Exp.}}}{\text{Volume} \times \textbf{Price}}$$

$$.30 = \frac{2,000,000 \times \textbf{Price} - 2,000,000 \times \$5.00 - \$5 \text{ million}}{2,000,000 \times \textbf{Price}}$$

Price = \$10.71 per unit

A cost-based floor price of \$10.71 has nothing to do with what customers would pay for the product or what competitors are charging for a comparable product. However, the floor price of \$10.71 does serve the purpose of establishing the lowest price the business could charge and still make its financial objective of a 30 percent gross-profit margin.

Another common floor-pricing approach is based on return on investment or return on invested capital. Assume the same business wanted a minimum of a 30 percent pretax return on investment on the same project and required \$20 million in investment. In this case we need to include the operating expenses, which are estimated at \$2 million per year. Based on these financial parameters, a price of \$11.50 would be needed to achieve a desired pretax return on investment.

$$\textbf{Return on Investment} = \frac{\text{Volume} \times \textbf{Price} - \text{Volume} \times \dfrac{\text{Unit}}{\text{Cost}} - \dfrac{\text{Manufacturing}}{\text{Exp.}} - \dfrac{\text{Operating}}{\text{Exp.}}}{\text{Investment}}$$

$$.30 = \frac{2,000,000 \times \textbf{Price} - 2,000,000 \times \$5.00 - \$5 \text{ million} - \$2 \text{ million}}{20,000,000}$$

Price = \$11.50 per unit

Again, this price has nothing to do with market reality; it is an internally generated price that benchmarks what is needed to achieve a desired return on investment. If this price or a higher price cannot be obtained, the product will fail to earn the desired return on the \$20 million investment. Again, the floor price should not be used to set price; it should only be used to calibrate the lowest price at which a product can be sold and still meet the financial benchmarks set by the company.

Cost-Plus Pricing

Cost-plus pricing is also often referred to as markup pricing because the price is determined by using a standard markup on cost. For an internally focused business, cost-plus pricing is likely to be used in the early stages of the product life cycle as volume grows and the business's costs come down. The exact markup on cost will depend on the company and industry. However, channel intermediaries, who typically use cost-plus pricing, have standard markups that vary by industry.

For example, Figure 8-10 illustrates the cost-plus channel markups typically used in five different product-markets.[8] An average furniture manufacturer that sells to a wholesaler at a price index of 100 will see its furniture marked up by 38.9 percent to a

FIGURE 8-10 COST-PLUS PRICING AND CHANNEL MARKUPS

Business Sector	Manufacturer's Price Index	Wholesaler's Markup (%)	Wholesale Price	Retailer's Markup (%)	Buyers Price Index
Furniture	100	38.9	138.90	63.6	227
Gasoline	100	19.8	119.80	22.8	147
Groceries	100	23.5	123.50	28.5	159
Sporting Goods	100	34.8	134.80	57.8	213
Liquor	100	21.6	121.60	37.1	167
Average	100	27.7	127.70	38.8	177

price index of 138.9. At a wholesale index price of 138.9, the furniture is sold to furniture retailers who mark up the price by 63.6 percent. This result in a buyer's price index of 227, a price 2.27 times the manufacturer's selling price based on industry markup pricing in the furniture industry. Again, we should emphasize that this approach to pricing has little to do with customer needs, price sensitivity, or competitors' product and price positioning.

Penetration Pricing

Businesses focused on building volume may use a cost-based penetration-pricing strategy. As illustrated in Figure 8-9, this cost-based pricing strategy is most likely to be employed in the growth stage of the product where volumes are likely to grow fastest in response to lower prices. Thus, the primary objective of penetration pricing is to build volume that drives down cost as illustrated in Figure 8-11.

FIGURE 8-11 PENETRATION PRICING

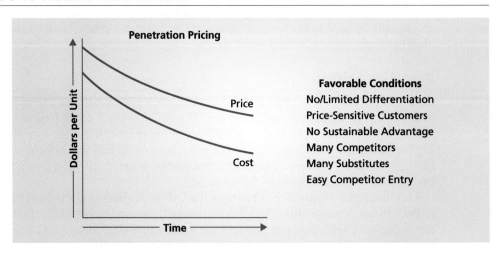

FIGURE 8-12 DRAM PRICE CURVE

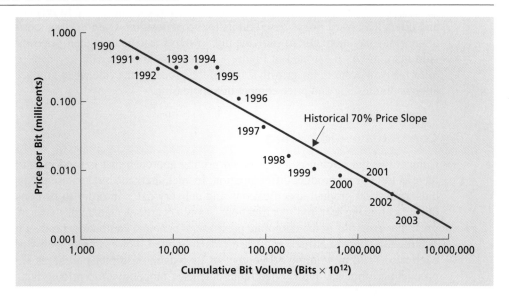

Cost-based penetration pricing is a mass-market strategy that is used most often when product differentiation is minimal, customers are price sensitive, many competitors or substitutes exist, and competitor entry is easy. The volume leader can often gain a cost advantage and continue to lower prices, discouraging competitor entry as well as encouraging competitor exit. The price of DRAMs (Dynamic Random Access Memory) is a good example of volume-sensitive pricing as illustrated in Figure 8-12. In this product-market, prices decrease by 30 percent every time cumulative volume doubles.[9]

A volume leadership position can enable a business to use penetration pricing to build market share and discourage competition from either entering the market or staying in the market. In this situation, the share leader is simply further down the cost curve and is able to price at a lower level and still maintain a desirable contribution margin. Thus, when cost reduction is volume sensitive and product differentiation is minimal, a penetration pricing strategy may be a viable path to market leadership and profitable growth.

Low-Cost Leader Pricing

The producers of BIC pens and lighters have always sought to have the lowest cost and a price that no competitor could get below. Likewise, from its beginnings Wal-Mart sought to be the low-cost leader in retail, and this was accomplished with a variety of management systems that lowered the cost of goods sold as well as lower operating expenses. A low-cost leader does not always have to be the volume leader. Although many companies may achieve a cost advantage based on volume and economies of scale, this is not required. There are even low-share businesses that have moved into the low-cost producer position.

Chi Mei, for example, is a low-cost producer of plastics and other chemicals. The company operates with a minimal sales force, minimal management staff, and no technical service. All aspects of its business are designed to maintain a low-cost leadership position. Although Chi Mei is not the share or volume leader, Chi Mei is the lowest-cost producer and offers the lowest prices based on its low-cost position. Even in situations where customers may pay more due to short supply, low-cost leaders base their prices on costs and slim margins. As illustrated in Figure 8-9, cost-based pricing by low-cost producers is most likely to occur in the growth stages of the product life cycle when product differentiation is diminishing and price competition increasing.

Competitive Bid Pricing

Competitive bid pricing is a cost-based pricing approach that is used in markets where there is little or no product differentiation. In such markets, bidders are prequalified and bids must meet product specifications and delivery dates in order to be considered. Of those meeting the required specifications, suppliers are selected on the basis of the lowest price. For example, in the corporate purchase of personal computers, product features are specified, bidders qualified, and price bids submitted. For example, Dell Computer has been successful in winning 50 percent of its bids in customer purchases with specific product performance and service requirements. Competitive bid pricing is a cost-based pricing strategy designed for this type of pricing.

Shown in Figure 8-13 is a ratio of price to cost called the bid ratio.[10] Alongside the bid ratio is a history of winning bids that the company obtained at different bid ratios. For example, a bid ratio of 1.2 (price is 20 percent over cost) resulted in winning bids 63 percent of the time. The probability of actually winning is also a function of the number of bidders. In this example, there are two bidders, and the probability of winning a bid with a 1.2 bid ratio is 0.40. The profit at this price level is $1 million, and the expected value, based on the probability of a winning bid, is $400,000. In this case, a bid ratio of 1.2 (with two bidders) is also the best cost-based price because it provides the highest expected value. Thus, in a given year, if the business bid 100 contracts in

FIGURE 8-13 COST-BASED COMPETITIVE BID PRICE STRATEGY

Bid Ratio	Percentage of Winning Bids	Probability of Winning*	Profit of Winning Bid (millions)	Expected Value	Cost-Based Pricing Logic
0.90	100	1.00	−$.05	−$500,000	A price
1.00	92	0.85	0	0	20 percent
1.10	80	0.64	+$.50	+$320,000	higher than
1.20	**63**	**0.40**	**+$1.0**	**+$400,000** ◄— cost offers the
1.30	21	0.04	+$1.5	+$60,000	best long-run
1.40	3	0.00	+$2.0	+$0	profitability.

*
$$\frac{\text{Probability}}{\text{of Winning}} = \left(\frac{\%\ \text{Winning Bids}}{100\%}\right)^{\text{No. of Bidders}} = \left(\frac{63\%}{100\%}\right)^{2} = 0.40$$

Expected value $= 0.40 \times \$1$ million $= \$400,000$

competition against one other bidder, and used a 1.2 bid ratio, it would achieve the best level of overall profitability for the year. Of course, as the number of bidders increases, the probability of winning decreases, and a lower bid ratio would be needed in order to maximize profits.

On the basis of this logic, we might expect a business to always use a certain cost-based price bid ratio, but this is not the case. For example, consider an aerospace contractor that is using a 1.2 bid ratio but has won more bids than expected and is now approaching full manufacturing production capacity. For the next bid, this contractor might purposely bid higher, knowing the chances of winning are lower. However, if the bid was won, it would be at a higher profit level and it would be worth the extra cost needed to complete another job while at full capacity. The opposite might also be true. If that contractor's capacity utilization is low, it may bid below the optimal bid price to improve its odds of winning. In these instances, volume is needed, and the business may forgo higher profits in exchange for a better chance of obtaining a certain volume of work.

Harvest Pricing

At the late stages of a product's life cycle, margins are often low and volumes flat or declining. The net result is poor profits with little prospect for improvement. Many businesses in this situation will use a cost-based harvest pricing strategy, as illustrated in Figure 8-9. Based on cost and the need for higher margins, the business will raise prices in anticipation of a reduction in volume. Subsequent cost-based price increases will result in higher margins as volume continues to fall. This sequence of cost-based price increases and volume reductions is normally continued until the business exits the market at a price customers simply will not pay.

However, there is an interesting twist to harvest pricing. In many instances a business will raise price to improve margins and expect to lose volume. This was true for a manufacturer of automotive components that raised prices 15 percent and lost 30 percent of its business volume. A subsequent price increase of 10 percent, however, resulted in a modest decrease of 1 million in volume while another 10 percent price increase a year later resulted in no decrease in volume. At this combination of price and volume, the business had uncovered a profitable niche market and managed price and volume to produce an attractive total contribution as illustrated in Figure 8-14.

FIGURE 8-14 HARVEST PRICING AND PROFITABILITY

Market Situation	Price	Volume	Sales	Unit Cost	Margin per Unit	Total Contribution
Late in life cycle	$10.00	10 million	$100 million	$10.00	$0	$0
15% price increase	$11.50	7 million	$80.50	$10.00	$1.50	$10.5 million
10% price increase	$12.65	6 million	$75.90	$10.00	$2.65	$15.9 million
10% price increase	$13.92	6 million	$83.49	$10.00	$3.92	$23.5 million

PRICING AND PROFITABILITY

Sales growth is an obsession in most businesses. Marketing and sales managers as well as general managers and CEOs generally believe that more is better: If those in marketing can deliver more volume, more market share, and more sales revenues, then we can grow profits. This may be true in many instances, but managers need to be especially careful when using price to achieve this objective. Let's examine a fairly common business situation.

The marketing and sales team of a business is challenged to grow sales revenues at a rate greater than 10 percent. Their product-markets are price sensitive and they judge a 10 percent price decrease would yield a 25 percent gain in volume. If this were achieved, sales revenues would go up 12.5 percent as shown in Figure 8-15. Furthermore, market share based on sales dollars would increase by 10 percent.

The problem with this sales-oriented scenario is that the strategy would lose money! As the analysis in Figure 8-15 illustrates, this lower-price strategy would grow sales revenues but lower profits. This is because the increase in volume (25 percent) is not sufficient to offset the reduction in margin (30 percent). The goal of a pricing strategy should be to make more profits—not more volume or more sales dollars. In this example a price strategy to grow sales 12.5 percent would lower total contribution by almost 12.5 percent. Because all other fixed manufacturing, marketing, and operating expenses are not likely to change, this price strategy to grow sales would lower overall profits. Marketing strategies like this that deliver superior sales growth but fail to contribute to profits will eventually bankrupt a company.

FIGURE 8-15 SALES OBSESSION VERSUS PROFIT ORIENTATION

Sales Obsession Performance Metrics	Original Situation	Growth Strategy	Percent Change (%)
Market Demand (millions)	200	200	0
Price (per unit)	$6.00	$5.40	−10
Volume (millions)	40	50	25
Market Share (units)	20%	25%	25
Market Share (dollars)	20%	22%	10
Sales Revenues (millions)	**$240**	**$270**	**12.5**

Profit Orientation Performance Metrics	Original Situation	Growth Strategy	Percent Change (%)
Price (per unit)	$6.00	$5.40	−10
Unit Cost	$4.00	$4.00	0
Margin per Unit	$2.00	$1.40	−30
Volume (millions)	40	50	25
Sales Revenues (millions)	$240	$270	12.5
Total Contribution (millions)	**$80**	**$70**	**−12.5**

Total Contribution

The objective of a pricing strategy should be to improve profits. Although growth in volume, market share, and sales sounds great, more is not always better. Any price change impacts both volume *and* margin. As shown in Figure 8-16, the goal in creating a pricing strategy should be to determine what price produces a combination of volume and margin that increases the business's total contribution. When the total contribution produced by a pricing strategy is lower, overall profits will also be lower because fixed costs are deducted from the total contribution.

The total contribution of a pricing strategy is equal to the unit volume sold times the margin per unit. For example, in the case study presented in Figure 8-15 the total contribution before the price change was $80 million. This was the result of a volume of 40 million units and a $2.00 margin per unit. The strategy to grow sales would produce a volume of 50 million units, but at a lower margin ($1.40 per unit). The result would be a gross profit of only $70 million ($10 million lower than the original level of business profits).

$$\textbf{Total Contribution} = \text{Volume (units)} \times \text{Margin (per unit)}$$
$$\text{(original situation)} = \quad 40 \text{ million} \quad \times \quad \$2.00$$
$$= \quad \textbf{\$80 million}$$

$$\textbf{Total Contribution} = \text{Volume (units)} \times \text{Margin (per unit)}$$
$$\text{(price strategy)} \quad = \quad 50 \text{ million} \quad \times \quad \$1.40$$
$$= \quad \textbf{\$70 million}$$

FIGURE 8-16 PRICE STRATEGY AND TOTAL CONTRIBUTION

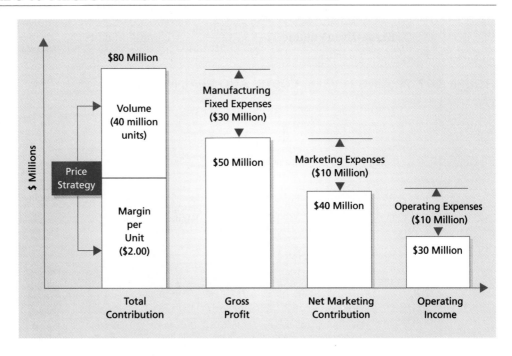

Price and Margin Erosion

The price paid by end users and the price a business actually receives are often quite different. Depending on channel strategies, price discounts, transaction costs, and the reality of getting paid, there is a large gap between the offered price and what we will call the "pocket price." As shown in Figure 8-17, price discounts given to channel intermediaries create levels of price reduction and potential margin erosion. Of course, when the cost of selling direct is greater than the margin given to intermediaries, the use intermediaries is more profitable. A variety of discounts can be offered to both intermediaries and end-user customers that further lowers price to an invoice price. After transactions costs are deducted, a net price is achieved. However, late payments, unpaid freight, and returns can lower the net price further to a "pocket price." When the variable cost sold per unit is deducted from the pocket price, we have the net margin per unit. As shown in Figure 8-16, when this margin is multiplied, we achieve a total contribution from which all other expenses must be deducted before a profit is obtained. Alternative marketing and distribution strategies, different pricing policies, and better management of payments and transaction costs offer many opportunities to reduce the lost margin that occurs in pricing.

Price-Volume Break-Even Analysis

Break-even analysis is often viewed as an accounting concept, but it is extremely useful in evaluating the profit potential and risk associated with a pricing strategy or any marketing strategy. For a given price strategy and marketing effort, it is useful to determine the number of units that need to be sold in order to break even; that is, to produce an operating income equal to zero.

$$\text{Operating Income} = \text{Volume} \times \text{Margin per Unit} - \text{Fixed Expenses}$$

$$0 = \text{Volume} \times \$2.00 - \$50 \text{ million}$$

$$\textbf{Break-Even Volume} = \frac{\$50 \text{ million}}{\$2.00 \text{ per unit}} = 25 \text{ million units}$$

FIGURE 8-17 PRICING LEVELS, COSTS, AND REAL MARGIN

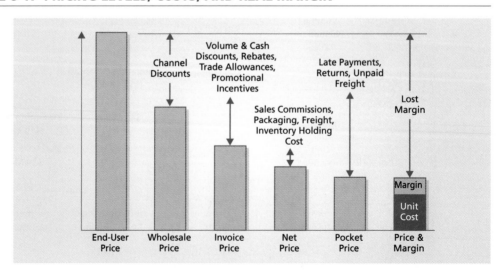

Price and Break-Even Volume

For example, in the business situation presented in Figure 8-16 the margin per unit was $2.00 and the total fixed expenses (manufacturing, marketing, and operating expenses) were $50 million. Sales of 25 million units would be required to break even. Break-even volume is the volume needed to cover fixed expenses on the basis of a particular margin per unit. Although break-even volume can be estimated graphically, as illustrated in Figure 8-18, it can be computed more directly with the following formula:

$$\text{Break-Even Volume} = \frac{\text{Fixed Expenses}}{\text{Margin per Unit}}$$

The lower the break-even volume is relative to manufacturing capacity or expected sales volume, the greater the profit potential.

Price and Break-Even Market Share

Because break-even volume is an unconstrained number, the reasonableness of the break-even volume requires additional considerations. Because market share is constrained

FIGURE 8-18 BREAK-EVEN VOLUME FOR A GIVEN PRICE STRATEGY

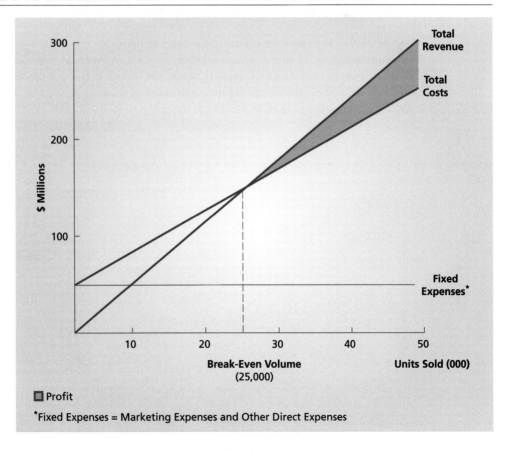

between zero and 100 percent, break-even market share provides a better framework from which to judge profit potential and risk. To compute the break-even market share requires only that we divide the break-even volume by the size of the target market, as shown next.

$$\text{Break-Even Market Share} = \frac{\text{Break Even Volume}}{\text{Market Demand}} \times 100$$

If the market demand for the product were 200 million units per year, then the break-even market share would be 12.5 percent when the break-even volume is 25 million units. In this case, the business has a 20 percent market share, which is 8.5 share points above breakeven. If the business's target share was 15 percent, then the risk of a loss is greater because the break-even share is close to the target market share.

PRICE ELASTICITY AND PERFORMANCE

Market demand and market growth are often dependent on price level. At high prices, many customers simply cannot enter the market, as described in Chapter 3. As the price of cellular phone services, CD players, and computers decreased, more customers entered these markets. In one sense, price regulates both the size of a market and how fast it will grow.

For example, Figure 8-19 shows how market demand for voice messaging (a telecommunications service) varies as a function of price. A business that wants to limit initial demand because of a lack of capacity to add the service may price the service at $5 per minute. This price produces an estimated demand of 9,000 customers in a particular geographic market. In addition, at this price, the price elasticity is −2.20, which means that for each 1 percent reduction in price, demand would grow by approximately 2.2 percent.

FIGURE 8-19 VOICE MESSAGING PRICE ELASTICITY OF DEMAND

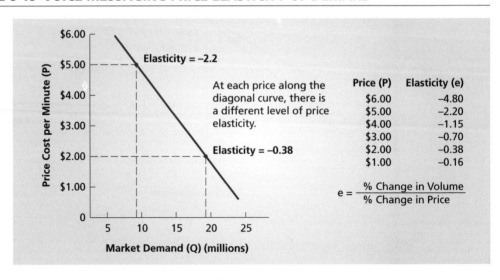

Therefore, a 10 percent price reduction from $5.00 to $4.50 should yield a 22 percent increase in customer demand (from 9,000 to 10,980).

A business might continue to lower price to grow demand, but when the price elasticity reaches -1.0, the sales revenue will have reached its maximum. At this point, price moves either up or down will result in lower overall sales revenue. This is the price point at which a nonprofit organization doing fund-raising events would be able to maximize the revenues received, if that is their objective. However, a business wanting to grow profits may price above or below this price point, in an effort to maximize profits.[11]

Inelastic Price Performance

As shown in Figure 8-20, when a price is inelastic, all aspects of performance are improved when prices are increased. Lowering price when it is inelastic will hurt sales, margins, and total contribution but increase unit volume, as presented in Figure 8-20.

For example, Yellow Pages advertising is known to be price inelastic, with an elasticity of approximately -0.7. What would be the consequence of a Yellow Pages business lowering prices on its $100 ads by 10 percent? Assume that the business normally sells one million of these ads and that its variable cost is $50 per ad. The results are a unit margin of $50, sales revenues of $100 million, and a total contribution of $50 million, as shown in the following.

Current Price Situation

Price per Ad = $100	Variable Cost per Ad = $50
Ad Volume = 1 million ads	Margin per Ad = $50
Sales Revenue = $100 million	Total Contribution = $50 million

FIGURE 8-20 PRICE ELASTICITY AND PERFORMANCE

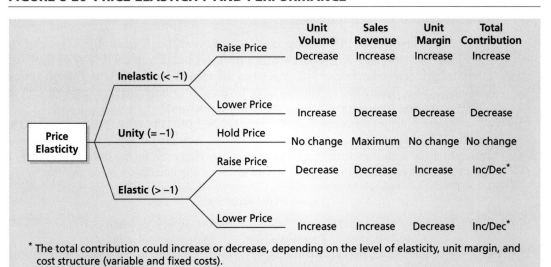

* The total contribution could increase or decrease, depending on the level of elasticity, unit margin, and cost structure (variable and fixed costs).

A decision to lower prices by 10 percent when the price elasticity is equal to -0.70 would produce the following performance:

Lower Price Strategy

Price per Ad = $90	Variable Cost per Ad = $50
Ad Volume = 1.07 million ads	Margin per Ad = $40
Sales Revenue = $96.3 million	Total Contribution = $42.8 million

As shown, a decision to lower price by 10 percent when prices were inelastic lowered margins by $10 per ad, lowered sales by $3.7 million, and lowered total contribution by $7.2 million, even though volume increased. This would have been a disastrous pricing decision. A business that did not know that its price was inelastic could easily follow a strategy of lowering prices in response to competitors or customer concerns about price.

The correct strategy in this case would be to raise price, because the price is inelastic. A strategy to raise price by 10 percent when the price elasticity is -0.70 would produce the following estimate of performance:

Raise Price Strategy

Price per Ad = $110	Variable Cost per Ad = $50
Ad Volume = 0.93 million ads	Margin per Ad = $60
Sales Revenue = $102.3 million	Total Contribution = $55.8 million

As shown, this strategy would increase margins by $10 per ad, sales by $2.3 million, and total contribution by $5.8 million. Knowing the correct direction to move the price improved this business's total contribution by 10 percent, while giving up 70,000 ads. Although there was a loss of unit market share (number of ads sold), dollar market share improved significantly.

Elastic Price Performance

Figure 8-20 also shows that pricing strategy is more difficult when prices are elastic. Although sales revenues will increase with a price cut and decrease with a price increase, the change in total contribution will depend on the level of price elasticity. Though a price may be elastic, it may not be enough so to produce a volume increase large enough to more than offset the margin decrease created by a price cut.

For example, let's assume that the price elasticity for the same Yellow Pages ad is -1.5. This is clearly an elastic price, and one that may lead many businesses to lower price to grow both unit volume and sales revenue. However, as the following shows, a strategy to lower price by 10 percent would lower total contribution by $4 million.

Lower Price Strategy

Price per Ad = $90	Variable Cost per Ad = $50
Ad Volume = 1.15 million ads	Margin per Ad = $40
Sales Revenue = $103.5 million	Total Contribution = $46 million

A strategy to raise prices by 10 percent when the price elasticity is equal to -1.5 would yield less ad volume and less sales revenue but would produce higher margins and a larger total contribution.

Raise Price Strategy

Price per Ad = $110	Variable Cost per Ad = $50
Ad Volume = 0.85 million ads	Margin per Ad = $60
Sales Revenue = $93.5 million	Total Contribution = $51 million

The biggest challenge in using price elasticities is not the calculations, it is estimating a value for price elasticity. However, every time a business changes its price, it has the opportunity to compute the actual price elasticity. However, because market conditions can change, the same price move can have different price elasticities. For example, if the ease of switching suppliers is average in a "buyer's market" where supply exceeds demand, price elasticities could be high as illustrated in Figure 8-21 and 8-22. However, if the market shifted to a "seller's market" during a period of short supply, the price elasticities could drop to much lower levels for the same product.

Ease of Switching

One dimension of price elasticity is the ease of switching. The easier it is for customers to switch suppliers of a product or to substitute products, the higher the price elasticity because customers can easily move to obtain lower prices. The level of product differentiation, cost of switching, and customer loyalty each impact the ease of switching as described in the following:

- **Product Differentiation**—The more unique a product is in its product and service benefits, the harder it is to replace with other products or substitutes. In markets where product differentiation is strong, price sensitivity is often lower.

FIGURE 8-21 FORCES THAT SHAPE PRICE ELASTICITY

Ease of Customer Switching	0	0.5	1	Score
Product Differentiation	Extensive	Some	None	0
Cost of Switching Suppliers	High	Modest	Low	0
Customer Loyalty	High	Modest	Low	.5
Ease of Switching Index				.5

Supply/Demand Conditions	0	0.5	1	Score
Supply Conditions	Short	Adequate	Excess	.5
Demand Conditions	Strong	Modest	Weak	0
Substitutes	None	Few	Many	.5
Supply/Demand Index				1.0

- **Cost of Switching**—The more expensive it is to switch suppliers, the harder it is for customers to switch suppliers when prices increase. Thus, higher switching costs generally result in lower price elasticities.
- **Customer Loyalty**—The more loyal a customer is to a brand or company the less likely they will switch suppliers when prices go up. When customer loyalty is low, however, the ease of switching is much greater and prices are more elastic. A manager can assess the ease of switching for a specific product-market by estimating levels of product differentiation, switching costs, and customer loyalty, and then calculating an Ease-of-Switching Index as shown in Figure 8-21. This would provide a rough estimate of one dimension of price elasticity using the guidelines presented in Figure 8-22.

Supply/Demand Conditions

In many markets supply generally outpaces demand. In the automobile market, for example, price elasticity is going to be higher because customers can easily get a comparable product from several sources. In markets where demand outpaces supply, as was the case for Chrysler's PT Cruiser, the price elasticity was much lower. The supply conditions,

FIGURE 8-22 GUIDELINES FOR ESTIMATING PRICE ELASTICITY

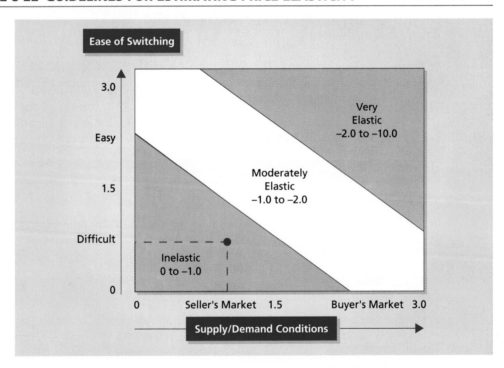

demand conditions, and substitutes each have an impact on price elasticity, as described in the following guidelines:

- **Supply Conditions**—In markets with excess supply, prices are generally more elastic. In short-supply situations, even in commodity markets, price increases can be inelastic.
- **Demand Conditions**—When demand is strong and growing, prices tend to be less elastic. On the other hand, in markets with weak or flat demand, prices tend to be more price sensitive.
- **Substitutes**—In markets with many substitutes, such as beverages, price sensitivity is high because there are many substitute products from which to choose. In many prescription-drug markets, there are few substitutes, which lowers price elasticity.

Using these guidelines and the scale presented in Figure 8-22, a manager can make a rough estimate of market conditions and how they will potentially impact price elasticity. Using this Supply/Demand Index along with the Ease-of-Switching Index, a manager would assess the price elasticity to be inelastic for this market situation. Of course, noting these conditions and calculating the actual price elasticity after a price change would provide a basis for revising Figure 8-22 to be more representative of a specific product-market.

PRODUCT-LINE PRICING

As a business adds more products to its product line, it enhances sales growth but also increases the chances of cannibalization of existing product sales. It is necessary to know both a product's price elasticity and the degree to which there is a cross elasticity with other products. Products that have a positive cross elasticity are substitutes; lowering the price of one product will decrease the demand for the other product. Products that have a negative cross elasticity are complementary products; lowering the price for one product will increase the demand for both products. Because the margins may be different for alternative products in a product line, one has to give careful consideration to any price change to ensure that the total profits are increased for the entire product line.

Pricing Substitute Products

In extending the product line of a business, one has to recognize that there will be some cannibalization when one product in the line may be substituted for another. For example, a business that offers both Yellow Pages advertising and direct-mail advertising would find that there is a cross elasticity of demand between the two of approximately 0.8. This means that if the business were to raise the price of Yellow Pages advertising by 10 percent, the demand for direct mail would go up an estimated 8 percent, assuming no change in direct-mail prices. The cross elasticity between these products and other media, such as newspaper, television, and radio advertisement, is less than 0.3. Thus, the rate of product substitution based on price change is much

FIGURE 8-23 PRICE AND CROSS-PRICE ELASTICITY OF COMPETING LAUNDRY DETERGENT BRANDS

Brand	Share (%)	Wisk	Tide	Surf	Era	Solo	Cheer	Bold-3	All	Fab
Wisk	22.7	−1.37	0.31	0.37	0.23	0.11	0.12	0.09	0.08	0.07
Tide	21.5	0.33	−1.39	0.37	0.23	0.11	0.13	0.09	0.08	0.07
Surf	19.5	0.48	0.46	−1.91	0.33	0.16	0.16	0.12	0.11	0.09
Era	13.5	0.36	0.33	0.39	−1.57	0.11	0.12	0.10	0.08	0.07
Solo	5.9	0.36	0.34	0.41	0.25	−1.78	0.13	0.11	0.10	0.07
Cheer	4.9	0.46	0.47	0.47	0.31	0.15	−2.20	0.12	0.13	0.09
Bold-3	4.4	0.49	0.44	0.49	0.34	0.18	0.16	−2.32	0.11	0.10
All	3.6	0.48	0.46	0.50	0.32	0.17	0.20	0.12	−2.36	0.10
Fab	3.6	0.50	0.50	0.49	0.33	0.16	0.17	0.14	0.12	−2.41

Elasticities: A1 percent price change in the brand column creates the percent change in market share for each row of brands.

less. Figure 8-23 shows the price elasticities and market shares for nine competing laundry detergents as well as their cross elasticities.[12] The results of this empirical study illustrate the price elasticity of each brand of detergent as well as the cross elasticity of competing substitutes. As shown, cross elasticity is much higher for higher-share brands.

To better understand the effects of product-line substitutes, let's examine two coffees sold in the same coffee shop. Figure 8-24 shows a regular (12-ounce cup) priced at $1.40 and a specialty coffee at $1.75 per cup. The regular coffee is price elastic (elasticity equal to −2) while the specialty coffee is inelastic (−.8). However, regular coffee customers are more likely to switch to specialty coffees when specialty coffee prices are lowered—in this case as the cross elasticity is 0.40. Specialty coffee drinkers are less likely to switch to regular coffee as the cross elasticity is 0.20. Although many pricing strategies could be tested, a 10 percent price increase in specialty coffees should increase the coffee shop's monthly total contribution from $21,750 to $22,565 as shown in Figure 8-24.

Pricing Complementary Products

Of course, products that are complements will also be affected by price change. Software and printers are products that complement personal computers. Therefore, the demand for these products varies with the price of personal computers. If the cross elasticity between PCs and spreadsheet programs were −0.6, then for each 1 percent change in the price of PCs, there would be a 0.6 percent change in the demand for spreadsheet programs. Thus, if computer industry prices decrease by 10 percent, the demand for spreadsheet programs should go up by 6 percent. Conversely, if the price of personal computers were to increase by 10 percent, the demand for spreadsheet programs would decrease by 6 percent.

FIGURE 8-24 PRODUCT-LINE IMPACT OF PRICE CHANGE WHEN PRODUCTS ARE SUBSTITUTES

From-To Price Change	Regular	Specialty 10%
Regular	−2.0	0.4
Specialty	0.2	−0.8

Before Price Change Performance	Regular	Specialty	Product Line
Volume (units sold)	25,000	5,000	30,000
Price per Unit	$1.40	$1.75	$1.46
Sales Revenues	$35,000	$8,750	$43,750
Variable Cost per Unit	$0.70	$0.90	$0.73
Margin per Unit	$0.70	$0.85	$0.73
Total Contribution	$17,500	$4,250	$21,750

After Price Change Performance	Regular	Specialty	Product Line
Volume			
Regular	25,000		25,000
Specialty	500	4,600	5,100
Net Volume	25,500	4,600	30,100
New Price	$1.40	$1.93	$1.48
Sales	$35,700	$8,878	$44,578
Variable Cost per Unit	$0.70	$0.90	$0.73
Margin per Unit	$0.70	$1.03	$0.75
Total Contribution	$17,850	$4,738	$22,588

To better understand the effects of product line complements, let's examine how coffee and pastries are sold in the same coffee shop. Coffee (12-ounce cup) is priced at $1.40 and food at $1.95 as shown in Figure 8-25. The coffee is a little more price elastic (elasticity equal to −2) than the food (−1.5). However, regular coffee customers are more likely to buy to food. Thus, any increase in coffee sales will also result in an increase in food sales in this case as the cross elasticity is −0.40. Additional food sales are less likely to result in increased coffee sales because the cross elasticity is −0.10. Although many pricing strategies could be tested, a 10 percent decrease in the coffee price would increase the sales of both coffee and food but result in a lower overall total contribution as shown in Figure 8-25.

FIGURE 8-25 PRODUCT-LINE IMPACT OF PRICE CHANGE WHEN PRODUCTS ARE COMPLEMENTS

From-To Price Change	Coffee −10%	Food
Coffee	−2.0	−0.4
Food	−0.1	−1.5

Before Price Change Performance	Coffee	Food	Product Line
Volume (units sold)	30,000	10,000	40,000
Price per Unit	$1.50	$1.95	$1.61
Sales Revenues	$45,000	$19,500	$64,500
Variable Cost per Unit	$0.75	$1.00	$0.81
Margin per Unit	$0.75	$0.95	$0.80
Total Contribution	$22,500	$9,500	$32,000

After Price Change Performance	Coffee	Food	Product Line
Volume			-
Coffee	36,000	400	36,400
Food	-	10,000	10,000
Net Volume	36,000	10,400	46,400
New Price	$1.35	$1.95	$1.48
Sales	$48,600	$20,280	$68,880
Variable Cost per Unit	$0.75	$1.00	$0.81
Margin per Unit	$0.60	$0.95	$0.68
Total Contribution	$21,600	$9,880	$31,480

Summary

Pricing is a critical part of customer value and business profitability. High prices are great for margins but could result in low customer volume if perceived benefits are less than perceived price. In competitive markets where product differentiation is feasible, market-based pricing presents a pricing logic designed to deliver high levels of customer value and business profitability.

Market-based pricing starts with customer needs, competitors' positions, and the business's product positioning, and works backward to margin. In contrast, cost-based pricing approaches start with the cost of the product and a desired margin and work forward to a market price. Cost-based pricing can lead to under- and overpricing in markets in which differentiation is possible. However, in markets in which differentiation is minimal and customers are price sensitive, cost-based pricing can be a viable approach to pricing.

Changes in price affect both volume and margin. A price decrease that grows volume and sales revenues but results in a decrease in total contribution adversely impacts a business's profits. The goal of any pricing strategy should be to grow or maintain profits. Therefore, it is critical to evaluate how total contribution will change with a price increase or decrease. Because the total contribution is the product of volume times margin, a change in price will affect both volume and margin as well as total contribution.

Because price affects margin and a certain level of fixed expenses is needed to achieve a certain level of market penetration, a break-even analysis is useful in assessing profit potential and risk. However, break-even volume, although a useful target, is not as useful in risk assessment as break-even market share. Because market share is constricted between zero and one (100 percent), it provides a relative index by which risk can be judged. Break-even market share enables a business to gauge profit potential and risk by looking at the difference between target share and the break-even market share. It also shows the feasibility of achieving a break-even volume within a market context.

Price-volume relationships are made more complex by varying degrees of price elasticity. Price elasticity is a measure of price sensitivity. When prices are inelastic, price increases result in a decrease in volume but an increase in sales and profits. A price decrease when prices are inelastic would result in higher volume but lower sales and lower profits. When prices are elastic, a price decrease will result in higher volumes and higher sales revenues. However, profits may go down if margins are low or up when margins are large. Price elasticities are not easy to estimate, and they vary based on a customer's ease of switching and a market's supply-and-demand conditions. Understanding these forces and tracking price elasticities that result from price changes allows a business to build a set of guidelines for estimating price elasticity.

Product-line pricing decisions are also complicated by cross elasticity. The price elasticity of demand for a given product may signal a particular pricing strategy. When cross elasticity exists between products, a business needs a more careful analysis of profit impact. The demand for products that are substitutes will change in the direction of the price change of the substitute. The demand for complementary products will change inversely to a price change in a complementary product.

■ Market-Based Logic and Strategic Thinking

1 Why would personal computer manufacturers shift from cost-based pricing to market-based pricing?

2 How does customer intelligence and competitor intelligence influence pricing?

3 Why might GE Aerospace use cost-based pricing instead of market-based pricing in developing a bid for a U.S. Air Force contract?

4 How would an earthmoving equipment manufacturer with superior productivity price its product using economic value?

5 How would you approach pricing the Lexus sport-utility vehicle? What elements of perceived value would be important in developing a market-based price?

6 Is Compaq pursuing a cost-based pricing strategy in the personal computer market? Why? What is the underlying pricing logic that supports Compaq's pricing strategy?

7 How does the three-segment–based price strategy for cellular phones described in the text contribute to the customer value in each segment?

8 When would a business use cost-based pricing?

9 How can a price decrease that increases volume and sales result in a profit decrease?

10 Explain how ease of switching and supply/demand conditions operate for an inelastic service such as a dentist and an elastic service such as a plumber.

11 In 2000, the market demand for personal computers was 129 million and the average price was $1,922. The average margin was 20 percent of sales. By 2003, prices dropped to an average price of $1,708 and demand grew to 161 million. Average margins slipped to 17 percent of sales. What is the price elasticity over this time period, and how did sales revenues and total contribution (volume $\times$ margin) change?

12 If coffee and doughnuts were both price elastic and also cross-elastic complements with the margin on doughnuts being much higher, how would you vary prices to increase overall profitability?

13 In Figure 8-24, why would a price increase for specialty coffee increase overall sales and profits?

14 How would Dell Computer use competitive bid pricing in responding to an insurance company's request for a quote on 1,000 PCs of a certain type?

15 Which pricing strategy would you have recommended for Gillette's Mach3 razor: skimming, competitive, or penetration? What factors and assumptions influence your choice of new product-price strategies?

16 Why is break-even market share potentially more valuable to a marketing manager than break-even volume?

Marketing Performance Tools

Each of the following **marketing performance tools** can be accessed by going to *www.rogerjbest.com* or *www.prenhall.com/best*. The shaded cells are input cells. The nonshaded cells contain results calculated from your input values.

MARKETING PERFORMANCE TOOL—Sales and Profit Impact of Price Elasticity and Price Change

From-To Price Change	Regular 0%	Specialty 0%
Regular	−2.0	
Specialty		−0.8

Before Price Change Performance	Regular	Specialty	Product Line
Volume (units sold)	25,000	5,000	30,000
Price per Unit	$1.40	$1.75	$1.46
Sales Revenues	$35,000	$8,750	$43,750
Variable Cost per Unit	$0.70	$0.90	$0.73
Margin per Unit	$0.70	$0.85	$0.73
Total Contribution	$17,500	$4,250	$21,750

After Price Change Performance	Regular	Specialty	Product Line
Volume (units sold)	25,000	5,000	30,000
Price per Unit	$1.40	$1.75	$1.46
Sales Revenues	$35,000	$8,750	$43,750
Variable Cost per Unit	$0.70	$0.90	$0.73
Margin per Unit	$0.70	$0.85	$0.73
Total Contribution	$17,500	$4,250	$21,750

This **marketing performance tool** allows you to estimate the sales and profit impact of different levels of price elasticity for two products with no cross elasticity. The "before price change" table allows you to compare the sales and profit impact for the Application Exercise presented here. The shaded numeric input cells can be changed in doing the following application exercise. However, you can create an entirely new example of your own by using all the shaded input cells.

Application Exercise: Using the data provided, estimate how sales and profits for regular coffee would change with a plus/minus 10 percent change in price. Decide which price change is the best. Then reset the regular coffee price change to zero. For specialty coffee, estimate how sales and profits would change with a plus/minus 10 percent change in price. Decide which price change is the best. Then reset the specialty coffee price change to zero. Finally, what would be the best price change for the product line, and how would sales and profits be affected?

MARKETING PERFORMANCE TOOL—Sales and Profit Impact of Price Change with Product Substitutes

From-To Price Change	Regular 0%	Specialty 0%
Regular	−2.0	0.4
Specialty	0.2	−0.8

Before Price Change Performance	Regular	Specialty	Product Line
Volume (units sold)	25,000	5,000	30,000
Price per Unit	$1.40	$1.75	$1.46
Sales Revenues	$35,000	$8,750	$43,750
Variable Cost per Unit	$0.70	$0.90	$0.73
Margin per Unit	$0.70	$0.85	$0.73
Total Contribution	$17,500	$4,250	$21,750

After Price Change Performance	Regular	Specialty	Line Product
New Demand			
Regular Coffee	25,000	0	25,000
Specialty Coffee	0	5,000	5,000
Net Volume	25,000	5,000	30,000
New Price	$1.40	$1.75	$1.46
Sales	$35,000	$8,750	$43,750
Variable Cost per Unit	$0.70	$0.90	$0.73
Margin per Unit	$0.70	$0.85	$0.73
Total Contribution	$17,500	$4,250	$21,750

This **marketing performance tool** allows you to estimate the sales and profit impact of different levels of price elasticity for two products that are substitutes. The "before price change" table allows you to compare the sales and profit impact for the application exercise presented here. The shaded numeric input cells can be changed in doing the following application exercise. However, you can create an entirely new example of your own by using all the shaded input cells.

Application Exercise: Using the data provided, estimate how sales and profits for regular coffee would change with a plus/minus 10 percent change in price. Decide which price change is the best. Then reset the regular coffee price change to zero. For specialty coffee, estimate how sales and profits would change with a plus/minus 10 percent change in price. Decide which price change is the best. Then reset the specialty coffee price change to zero. Finally, what would be the best price change for the product line, and how would sales and profits be affected?

MARKETING PERFORMANCE TOOL—Sales and Profit Impact of Price Change with Complementary Products

From-To Price Change	Coffee 0%	Food 0%
Coffee	−2.0	−0.4
Food	0.2	−1.5

Before Price Change Performance	Coffee	Food	Product Line
Volume (units sold)	25,000	5,000	30,000
Price per Unit	$1.40	$1.75	$1.46
Sales Revenues	$35,000	$8,750	$43,750
Variable Cost per Unit	$0.70	$0.90	$0.73
Margin per Unit	$0.70	$0.85	$0.73
Total Contribution	$17,500	$4,250	$21,750

After Price Change Performance	Coffee	Food	Line Product
New Demand			
Coffee	25,000	0	25,000
Food	0	5,000	5,000
Net Volume	25,000	5,000	30,000
New Price	$1.40	$1.75	$1.46
Sales	$35,000	$8,750	$43,750
Variable Cost per Unit	$0.70	$0.90	$0.73
Margin per Unit	$0.70	$0.85	$0.73
Total Contribution	$17,500	$4,250	$21,750

This **marketing performance tool** allows you to estimate the sales and profit impact of different levels of price elasticity for two products with complementary cross-price elasticity. The "before price change" table allows you to compare the sales and profit impact for the application exercise presented here. The shaded numeric input cells can be changed in doing the following application exercise. However, you can create an entirely new example of your own by using all the shaded input cells.

Application Exercise: Using the data provided, estimate how sales and profits for coffee would change with a plus/minus 10 percent change in price. Decide which price change is the best. Then reset the coffee price change to zero. For food, estimate how sales and profits would change with a plus/minus 10 percent change in price. Decide which price change is the best. Then reset the food price change to zero. Finally, what would be the best price change for the product line, and how would sales and profits be affected?

Notes

1. A. Cleland and A. Bruno, *The Market Value Process* (San Francisco: Jossey-Bass, 1996): 106; D. Kirk-patrick, "The Revolution at Compaq Computer," *Fortune* (December 14, 1992): 80–88.

2. P. Noble and T. Gruca, "Industrial Pricing: Theory and Managerial Practice," *Marketing Science* vol. 18, no. 3 (1999): 435–454.

3. G. Cressman, Jr., "Commentary on Industrial Pricing: Theory and Managerial Practice," *Marketing Science* vol. 18, no. 3 (1999): 455–457.

4. R. Best, "Marketing Excellence Survey," *www.MESurvey.com*: (accessed) September, 2004.

5. Michael Morris and Gene Morris, *Market-Oriented Pricing* (Lincolnwood, IL: NTC Business Books, 1990): 93–100.

6. R. Dolan and H. Simon, *Power Pricing* (New York: Free Press, 1966): 82–83.

7. California Technology Stock Letter (February 4, 1999): 4.

8. "Annual Statement Statistics," Robert Morris Agency, 1996.

9. Thomas Nagle and Reed Holder, *The Strategy and Tactics of Pricing* (Upper Saddle River, NJ: Prentice Hall, 1995): 199–206.

10. Gerald Smith and Thomas Nagle, "Financial Analysis for Profit-Driven Pricing," *Sloan Management Review* (Spring 1994): 71–84.

11. R. Dolan and H. Simon, *Power Pricing* (New York: Free Press, 1996): 222–241.

12. Gerard Tellis, "The Price Elasticity of Selective Demand: A Meta-Analysis of Econometric Models of Sales," *Journal of Marketing Research* (November 1988): 331–341.

CHAPTER 9

Marketing Channels and E-Marketing

D ow Corning has been the market leader in silicon technology applications for over 50 years. Its products span many market applications in electronics, construction, health care, and multitude of industrial applications. However, as some of its product-market applications reached the mature stage of the product life cycle they became less competitive. Dow Corning's full service consultative-engineering approach did not work in more mature, price-sensitive market applications. With some difficulty the company shifted to a set of new channel strategies which required radically different marketing strategies.[1]

Research on the market for silicon led to the identification of two market segments that could still be served profitably with the traditional Dow Corning marketing approach. As Figure 9-1 shows, the innovation/technology segment would be served directly by Dow Corning, while a mixed-channel strategy would be used to serve the service quality segment. These channel strategies were more appropriate for newer, high-growth market applications, but a different channel strategy and marketing mix was needed for the more price-sensitive segment. This would involve less sales and service and more competitive prices. This resulted in an e-marketing channel strategy which would be a more cost-efficient marketing channel. Because the e-marketing channel strategy was different from Dow Corning's core product positioning, the 400 silicon-based products targeted with the e-marketing channel strategy would be sold under a new brand name, Xiameter.

The Xiameter e-marketing channel offers customers online purchasing with the capability to compare prices with competitors' prices to ensure that customers get the lowest price available in the market at that time. Orders are placed online, and products are delivered with a guaranteed shipping date. Xiameter's success and profitability are directly linked to a cost-efficient, no-frills e-marketing channel.

For established businesses like Dow Corning, General Electric, and Charles Schwab, e-marketing provides an additional marketing channel for them to reach new customers and serve existing customers more efficiently. For these businesses, e-marketing channels leverage existing brand equity, supply-chain capabilities, and operating expenses already in place. In contrast, some new businesses have chosen to build their entire business model around e-marketing, using it as their primary means of building a brand, interfacing with customers, and delivering products. Businesses such as Amazon.com, E*Trade, and eBay were founded on the premise that e-marketing could be their primary marketing channel and a core component of their business model. The customer value these businesses create and the sales and profits they obtain are directly related to their successful management of e-marketing. The e-marketing channel is vital to the existence and survival of these companies.

FIGURE 9-1 MULTICHANNEL DELIVERY OF MULTIPLE VALUE PROPOSITIONS (VP)

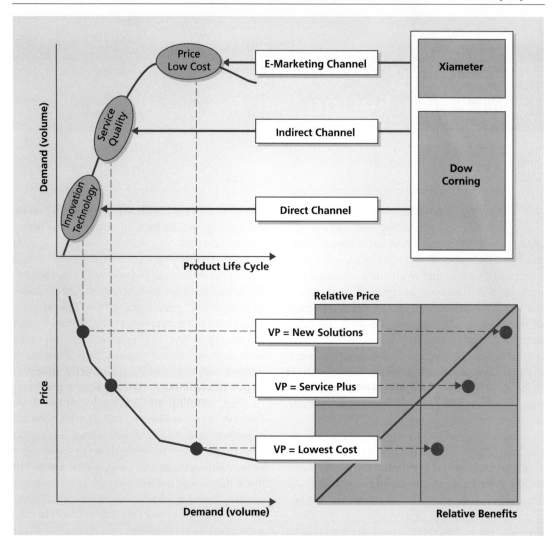

MARKETING CHANNELS AND CHANNEL STRATEGY

The choice and management of marketing channels directly impact three important areas of performance.

1. **Customer value:** Marketing channels can enhance or reduce customer value based on the service quality and the efficiency with which end-user customers are served.
2. **Sales revenues:** Marketing channels determine customer reach, which impacts sales to existing customers as well as sales to potential customers.
3. **Profitability:** Marketing channels have a direct impact on margins and marketing expenses and play a critical role in the profits that can be obtained in any given marketing channel.

FIGURE 9-2 PERSONAL COMPUTER MARKETING CHANNELS: DELL VERSUS HEWLETT-PACKARD

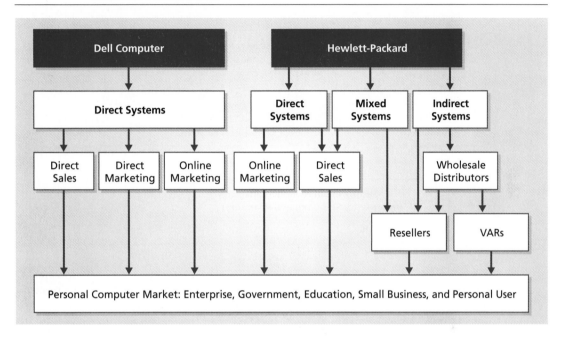

In the personal-computer market, a variety of marketing channels have emerged in an effort to reach and serve many different types of customers. As shown in Figure 9-2, Hewlett-Packard has built its business using a complex marketing channel system, relying heavily on a combination of direct and indirect marketing channels. In contrast, market leader Dell Computer has grown to the number one position by honing its direct marketing channel approach with direct marketing, e-marketing, and direct sales.

Marketing channels are a key component of a supply chain that links manufacturers with end-user customers. As illustrated in Figure 9-3, supply chain management involves the management of materials, information, and money that flow from suppliers to a business to marketing channel partners who provide the business's products to target customers. Companies such as SAP, which has established itself as a market leader in supply chain management, have developed systems to help businesses more efficiently manage supply chain functions such as order entry, inventory, and shipping between a business and its suppliers and channel partners.

Because many businesses sell through channel partners, they do not directly interface with the end-user customer. Customer relationship marketing (CRM) is a channel management activity that helps businesses establish one-on-one marketing relationships with customers, even when channel partners are needed to reach target customers. With the advent of Internet technologies and e-marketing channels, CRM allows a business to gain a much better focus on its customers' individual needs and preferences. Properly managed, CRM solutions help businesses better manage this process and improve customer satisfaction and retention.

Many different marketing channels can be used to connect businesses with customers. The purpose of this chapter is to understand how channel partners impact marketing channel

FIGURE 9-3 MARKETING CHANNELS AND CHANNEL ACTIVITIES

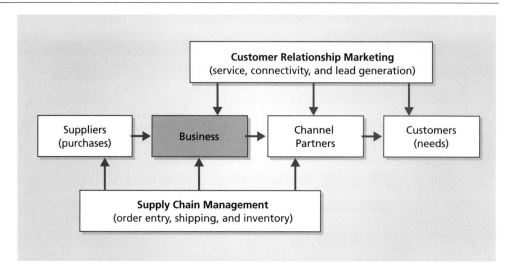

performance and the various marketing channels that can be configured to reach customers with different needs. We will also examine how marketing channels can serve as a source of competitive advantage.

MARKETING CHANNEL PERFORMANCE

Marketing channel performance is based on three things: customer reach, operating efficiency, and service quality. All three are needed for a customer-effective and cost-efficient marketing channel. If a business cannot reach potential customers, sales will not happen. If operations are not efficient, the cost to serve customers will be too high to be profitable. Without service quality, customer retention will suffer, even if customers can be reached effectively and served cost efficiently. All three components of marketing channel performance shown in Figure 9-4 must be operating at satisfactory levels for a marketing channel to achieve desired sales, profits, and customer satisfaction.[2]

FIGURE 9-4 OPERATIONAL COMPONENTS OF CHANNEL PERFORMANCE

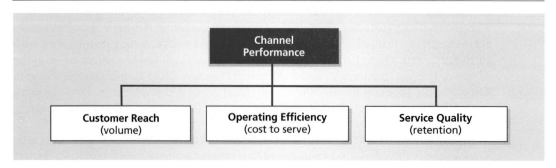

Customer Reach

One of the primary objectives of a marketing channel is to reach target customers. Of course, this has to be done in a way that is cost effective and provides the level of service quality sought by target customers. Every marketing channel differs in its structure and its ability to reach customers. With direct marketing channels, a company engages in direct contact with its customers. This can be accomplished with direct sales, direct marketing, telemarketing, and e-marketing. Indirect marketing channels include channel intermediaries such as wholesalers, distributors, retailers, original equipment manufacturers, and value-added resellers.

To illustrate the impact of marketing channels on customer reach and sales, let's examine how Dow Chemical modified its channel strategy for the sale of epoxies. The worldwide business-to-business (B2B) market demand for epoxy is approximately $5 billion. This market includes 2,000 customers, with 20 percent of them accounting for 80 percent of the purchases. For these 400 customers, the average revenue per customer is $10 million per year, and Dow Chemical serves this group of customers with a direct-marketing channel as shown in Figure 9-5. Although this marketing channel is cost effective and profitable, it could not be used to reach the 1,600 smaller epoxy customers who buy considerably less and are often geographically hard to reach.

In 2000 Dow Chemical launched e-epoxy.com, investing $2 million in an e-marketing channel in an effort to reach these 1,600 smaller customers in a cost-effective way. In the first 7 weeks online, e-epoxy.com attracted 200 new visitors per week and 100 repeat visitors per week. Two-thirds of the sales produced through this e-marketing channel were from customers who had never done business with Dow Chemical.[3] The end results were gains in market share, sales, and new customers.

The marketing channel with perhaps the most potential to expand customer reach is the e-marketing channel. The ability to reach a world of potential new customers at an

FIGURE 9-5 REACHING NEW CUSTOMERS WITH AN E-MARKETING CHANNEL

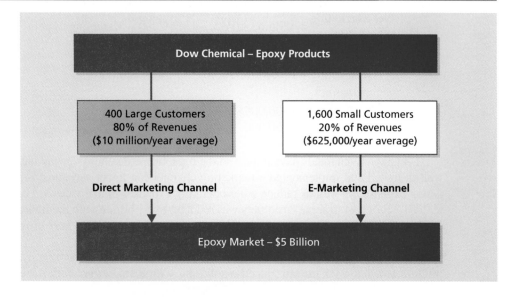

insignificant marginal marketing cost has led most businesses to invest to some degree in e-marketing. General Electric, for example, added an e-marketing channel to supplement its traditional marketing channels, much like Dow Chemical did with e-epoxy.com. GE saw immediate results as its e-marketing channel sales grew from $7 billion in 2000 to $14 billion in 2001. Much of this growth in e-marketing channel sales was attributed to new customers.[4]

Operating Efficiency

Marketing channels also vary in their cost structure. A direct marketing channel offers higher margins, but the company must bear the full cost of channel management and of marketing expenses. An indirect marketing channel has lower margins but lower costs of marketing and channel management. In this case, the channel intermediary receives a portion of the margin in exchange for distribution and carrying out some of the marketing channel functions.

In the following example, the net marketing contribution of each marketing channel is the same but the revenue and cost structures differ. Each channel produced unit sales of 100,000 units. The direct marketing channel had a higher margin per unit ($5.00) but higher marketing expenses ($250,000).The indirect marketing channel had a lower margin per unit ($3.00) and lower marketing expenses ($50,000). In this example, both channels produced the same marketing profitability.

$$\text{Net Marketing Contribution} = \text{Volume} \times (\text{Price} - \text{Unit Cost}) - \text{Marketing Expenses}$$

$$\begin{aligned}
\text{Direct Marketing Channel} &= 100,000 \times (\$10.00 - \$5.00) - \$250,000 \\
&= \$500,000 - \$250,000 \\
&= \$250,000
\end{aligned}$$

$$\text{Net Marketing Contribution} = \text{Volume} \times (\text{Price} - \text{Unit Cost}) - \text{Marketing Expenses}$$

$$\begin{aligned}
\text{Indirect Marketing Channel} &= 100,000 \times (\$8.00 - \$5.00) - \$50,000 \\
&= \$300,000 - \$50,000 \\
&= \$250,000
\end{aligned}$$

E-marketing channels have improved the operating efficiency of many businesses. A well-designed and implemented e-marketing channel can lower variable costs and marketing expenses as well as reduce other operating expenses in many cases. For example, in 2001, GE's cost to serve customers was reduced by $1 billion with the implementation of e-marketing channels. For many businesses, e-marketing channels have provided a low cost way to reach smaller, hard-to-reach customers.

Online buying also saved GE $1 billion on the purchase of goods and services in 2001. In 2002 Hewlett-Packard introduced e-sourcing with *b2eMarkets.com* for conducting electronic requests for information and requests for proposals and quotes. This has allowed HP to reduce costs and time in their procurement of products and services.

Service Quality

Every channel also has different levels of service quality. With direct marketing channels, companies have the opportunity to control service quality because they have the advantage of a direct customer interface. This allows for service enhancements, mass customization, and quick response to customer problems.

Indirect marketing channels remove the business from the end-user customer. As a result, they are dependent on channel partners to adequately deliver desired levels of customer service. Because indirect channel intermediaries often represent many different lines of products, their product knowledge and commitment to specific customer needs may not be as complete.

E-marketing channels that improve order fulfillment and track deliveries without multiple phone calls have the potential to lower cost and improve customer satisfaction. To further enhance e-marketing channels, CRM systems are designed to facilitate a one-on-one customer relationship with target customers. One of the primary goals of CRM is to identify problems, resolve them, and maintain a dialogue with customers as to how the company can improve its service quality.

ALTERNATIVE CHANNEL SYSTEMS

The first decision a business must make is whether to use a direct, indirect, or mixed channel system.[5] All things being equal, a business would generally prefer to sell and distribute directly to target customers, because this combination of channel and sales responsibility offers the most control and greatest potential for value-added sales and services. On the other hand, a business may not have the expertise or resources needed to fund and support a direct channel system and therefore might elect to reach target customers through an indirect channel system. A business may also need to use a combination of direct, indirect, and mixed channel systems in order to reach different target markets cost effectively and to deliver the service level expected by target customers. These three channel systems are shown in Figure 9-6.

Direct Channel Systems

As illustrated in Figure 9-7, a direct approach can include a direct sales force, direct marketing, telemarketing, online marketing, manufacturer's representatives, sales agents, or brokers. In each case, the business retains ownership of the products and responsibility for sales, distribution, service, and collection of payment for products sold.

Although a direct sales force offers the best opportunity for sales communication and customer interaction, it is often too expensive to reach target customers with a direct sales approach. The cost of direct customer sales contact is high and increasing. For example, the fully loaded cost (salary, benefits, and expenses) of a direct salesperson in many business-to-business markets can range from $100,000 to over $300,000 per year. One way to reduce these costs is by using manufacturers' representatives, sales agents, and brokers.

FIGURE 9-6 ALTERNATIVE CHANNEL SYSTEMS

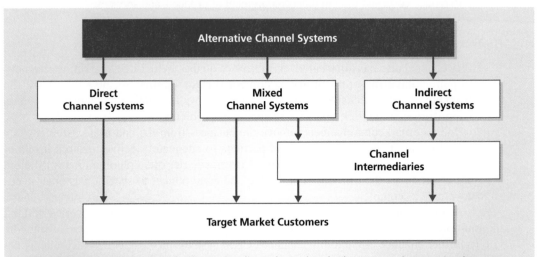

- **Direct Channel Systems:** Provide alternative direct channel and sales systems that require the business to retain ownership (title) of products sold and responsibility for delivery to customers and value-added functions desired by customers.
- **Indirect Channel Systems:** Provide varying degrees of sales and value-added functions while transferring ownership and responsibility for delivery to target customers to channel intermediaries.
- **Mixed Channel Systems:** Provide direct sales contact and technical support while the actual purchase is made at a channel intermediary who has taken title (ownership) of the products being sold.

These assume the selling responsibility for the business and are paid a sales commission only when a sale occurs. Direct marketing, which includes direct mail and catalog sales, offers a less expensive alternative, but the opportunity for sales communications is more limited. Telemarketing provides a greater opportunity for a sales communication but is more labor intensive and often more expensive than direct marketing. E-marketing channels, when implemented well, can greatly enhance customer reach, customer interactivity, online information searches, purchasing, and after-sale customer service. Online marketing channels can be efficient and offer greater opportunities for customer interaction in home shopping and Internet computer-based purchasing.[6] For maximum customer reach, online marketing is ideal. For example, the bookseller Barnes & Noble launched its online store in 1997, and in 7 years has attracted approximately 18 million customers in 230 countries.

Indirect Channel Systems

Because using a direct channel system is often expensive, it limits the number of customers a business can profitably reach. As a result, many potential customers who buy in smaller purchase amounts cannot be profitably served with a direct channel system. In these situations, a business has to at least consider using indirect channel systems. Indirect channel systems are inherently more complex, because they involve at least one intermediary who takes over both ownership of the product and the majority, if not all, of the control in both sales and distribution. As shown in Figure 9-7, an indirect channel

FIGURE 9-7 ALTERNATIVE B2C MARKETING CHANNELS

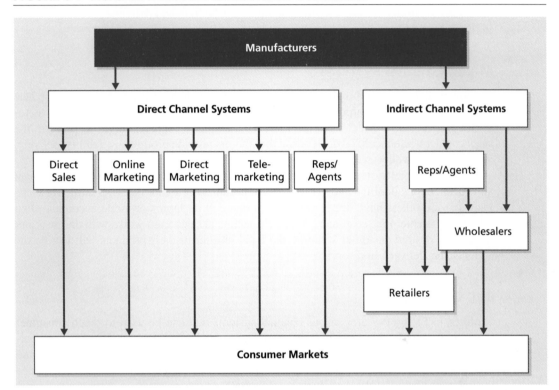

system could include retailers, commercial distributors (also called dealers), full-function wholesalers, and specialty wholesalers.

Retailers take over the sales and point-of-purchase distribution in consumer markets, and distributors or dealers assume this responsibility in business-to-business markets. Compensation for their services is usually in the form of a discount off the customer selling price. This discount can range from 10 percent to over 50 percent.

Wholesalers offer an intermediate point of sales and physical distribution between a business and retailers or dealers. There are full-function wholesalers who offer a full range of products and services (inventory, delivery, credit, and stocking) and limited-function wholesalers who offer a limited range of products and services. For example, a cash-and-carry wholesaler does not deliver the product or offer credit. In most cases, the discount offered to wholesalers is less than that offered to retailers or dealers, because the range of services is considerably less.

Value-added resellers (VARs) and original equipment manufacturers (OEMs) are unique indirect channel system alternatives in that they buy products, directly or indirectly, add value to them, and resell them. These alternatives will be discussed at greater length in the discussion of business-to-business alternative channels. E-marketing can also enhance or supplement existing channel systems, improving many interactions along the supply chain. Customers often gather information online and then buy the product from a wholesaler or retailer. Others may place orders online but take actual delivery at a retail outlet. E-marketing channels can also be used to help track orders, especially in complex industrial purchases where lead times can be long and deliveries complicated, as in the case of a Caterpillar grader or avionics for a Boeing jet.

Mixed Channel Systems

In some instances, a combination of direct and indirect channel systems provides the best way to reach and serve target customers.[7] For example, many industrial and business-to-business firms use a direct sales force or manufacturers' representatives to perform the sales contact while localized dealers and distributors provide product availability, delivery, and service, as well as terms of payment.

Mixed channel systems are particularly important when products are fairly technical and localized availability and service are important. For example, Microsoft, Hewlett-Packard, and others have direct sales forces that call on large corporate accounts, often referred to as enterprise customers. While the technical sales team works with the customer to create a desired customer solution, the local reseller of their products will handle the actual sales, delivery, and service.

B2C Channels

Outlined in Figure 9-7 are various channel systems that can be used to reach consumer markets. As shown, there are both direct and indirect channel systems. In consumer markets, businesses traditionally used indirect channel systems such as wholesalers and retailers to reach target customers effectively and cost efficiently. However, innovations in direct marketing, online marketing, and wholesale shopping have opened new direct business-to-consumer (B2C) channel systems that may be equally attractive. Direct marketing through consumer catalogs, direct-mail marketing, telemarketing, and electronic marketing have grown significantly in recent years and offer future growth opportunities with innovations in telecommunications. Catalog companies, such as Esprit, Eddie Bauer, and L.L. Bean, have had noteworthy success with direct consumer marketing. In contrast, companies such as Mary Kay Cosmetics, Electrolux, and Amway have used a direct sales approach to reach target consumers. In each case, a different direct channel system is required to effectively meet customer needs and to produce acceptable levels of profitability. The emergence of online retailing has opened up a new type of indirect B2C channel. Just as with physical retailing, online retailers buy their products from manufacturers or wholesalers and resell them to consumers via the Internet. Easy price comparisons and 24/7 shopping make online stores very convenient for consumers. This indirect channel works particularly well for standard products such as books or CDs where customers do not need to inspect before they buy.

B2B Channels

Software manufacturers, such as Adobe, serve both consumer and business customers. As illustrated in Figure 9-8, these companies use a direct marketing channel to reach and serve large enterprises such as *Fortune* 500 companies. To reach medium-sized to smaller businesses and individual consumers, these manufacturers use online marketing as part of their direct channel, but, to a greater degree, they use an indirect channel to reach these

FIGURE 9-8 MARKETING CHANNELS AND SALES SYSTEMS USED TO REACH SOFTWARE BUYERS

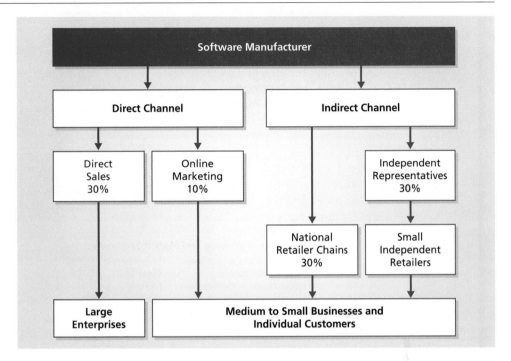

customers. As shown in Figure 9-8, software producers will sell direct to large national chains, but they use independent, commissioned representatives to reach smaller independent retailers. Each of the channels has different levels of cost, control, sales contact, and ownership.

As stated earlier, most businesses would prefer to sell and distribute with a direct channel system. This provides a greater degree of control and specialized knowledge that can be customized for the end customer. However, for industrial products, such as the one illustrated in Figure 9-9, only 25 percent of sales are via direct channel systems.[8] This percentage is partly the result of the cost of a business-to-business direct sales call, which ranges from $100 to over $300. In industrial markets, approximately 50 percent of all sales are derived from the combination of manufacturers' reps or sales agents and industrial distributors. For many inexpensive industrial and commercial products, wholesalers are used. In some instances, as in hospital supply products, the large hospital supply wholesaler may sell directly to hospitals and other medical institutions.

Unique to the business-to-business market, as outlined in Figure 9-10, are VARs and OEMs. VARs purchase a variety of equipment from several manufacturers and package them as a system. A VAR often provides the total system, as well as specialized services, to help the customer learn, use, maintain, and upgrade the system. For example, a VAR in the agricultural market may purchase computers, printers, modems, fax machines, and telecommunications equipment from several manufacturers, along with specialized software, to help farmers with crop rotation, fertilizing, planting, and water requirements.

FIGURE 9-9 CHANNEL SYSTEMS FOR A MANUFACTURER OF WELDING RODS

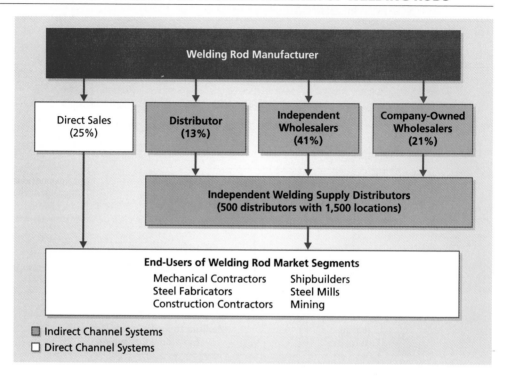

FIGURE 9-10 ALTERNATIVE BUSINESS-TO-BUSINESS CHANNEL SYSTEMS

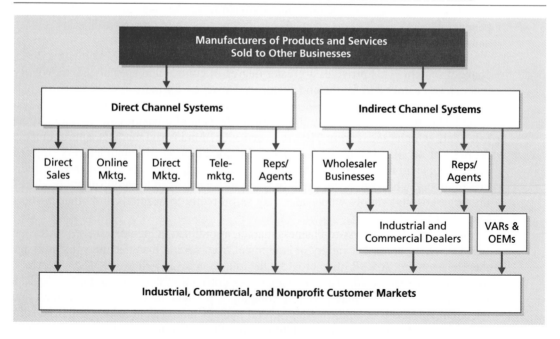

The agricultural customers could buy all these products separately, but they prefer to purchase a complete (bundled) system that is customized to their specific needs.

An OEM is similar but actually creates a new manufactured product. OEMs, such as Ford, IBM, or Caterpillar, buy component products from other manufacturers to incorporate into their products. For example, Ford does not manufacture tires; it purchases them from a tire manufacturer such as Firestone. Although Firestone operates primarily through company-owned retail tire stores, it also sells tires to automobile manufacturers, who provide another important, indirect channel sales opportunity. Likewise, IBM may buy disk drives from Seagate and computer chips from Intel, as well as make its own.

Virtually all B2B businesses now have some e-marketing capability. Many components of e-marketing are informational while others involve order placement. An excellent example of total commitment to an e-marketing channel is Dow Corning's as presented at the start of this chapter.

CHANNEL SYSTEMS THAT BUILD CUSTOMER VALUE

There are many alternative channel systems a business can use to reach target customers. To be successful, however, a channel system must enhance customer value by either increasing customer benefits or lowering customer cost of purchase, or both as shown in Figure 9-11.

Delivering Product Benefits

Because many products are perishable or easily damaged, it is important to select a channel that will be able to deliver a business's product to target customers in the form that meets or exceeds customer expectations. In selecting a particular channel system,

FIGURE 9-11 HOW MARKETING CHANNELS CONTRIBUTE TO CUSTOMER VALUE

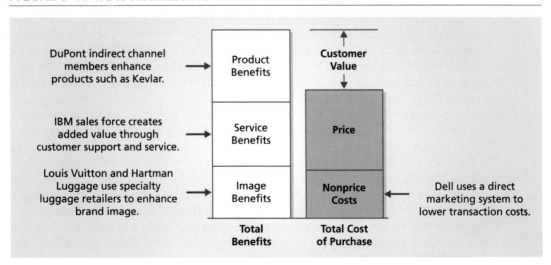

a business needs to consider how that channel system either enhances or detracts from the following product benefits:

- **Product Quality:** Can the channel system deliver the product with the quality level required and expected by target customers?
- **Product Assortment:** Can the channel system provide the range of products required in order to achieve a desired level of customer appeal?
- **Product Form:** Can the channel system provide the product, as it is needed, to both intermediaries and final customers?

In each case, a channel system is not a viable alternative if it cannot meet the product benefits sought by target customers.[9] Customers simply will not buy products that do not meet their buying needs. There are almost always competing alternatives, so customers will satisfy their buying needs by purchasing a competing product.

Delivering Service Benefits

Every channel has advantages and limitations with respect to service. The need for delivery, installation, training, technical support, repair, terms of payment, credit, and easy return are all service benefits that a business has to consider in selecting a particular channel system. To determine if a channel system is viable, a business has to consider the following questions with respect to a customer's service needs and expectations.

- **After-Sale Services:** What are the after-sale services that are critical to achieving total customer satisfaction with the product or service?
- **Availability/Delivery:** To what degree do customers benefit from quick access to goods or services and immediate delivery?
- **Transaction Services:** Can the channel system provide for the customer's credit needs, terms of payment, warranty, free-on-board (FOB) pricing, and return of faulty products?

Each of these service benefits can be critical. A business with a better product may not achieve market success if it fails to provide the service benefits required by target customers. To be successful in meeting customer expectations, a business has to make the product available at the target customer's desired point of purchase. In addition, it must meet or exceed each of its customer's product and service requirements, whether the customer is an end-user or a channel intermediary.

For example, let's consider how marketing channels add value to a fiber-cement siding product used in many residential homes. This siding product is made from a combination of paper and cement. As shown in Figure 9-12, these raw materials are needed at a low cost on a reliable basis in order to serve the growing market demand for fiber-cement siding. Manufacturers add roughly $.45 per square foot by transforming these raw materials into a semi-finished product. However, in this form, at the point of production, the product has no value to home owners. A marketing channel is needed to reach the end-user customer. Producers sell to wholesalers who have in place a system of distribution that reaches the many construction retailers around the United States. Wholesalers add $.10 per square foot to the price of the product in exchange for their logistic and distribution

FIGURE 9-12 HOW MARKETING CHANNELS ADD VALUE TO FIBER-CEMENT SIDING PRODUCT

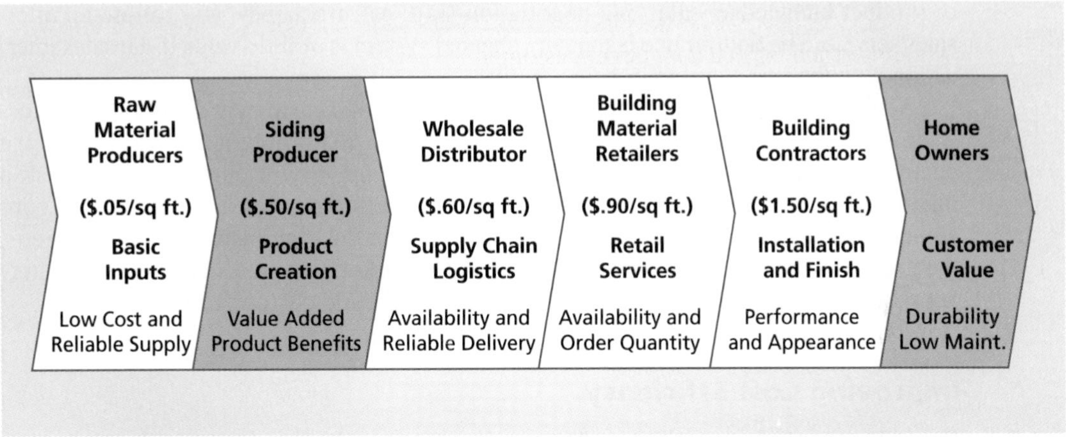

Raw Material Producers	Siding Producer	Wholesale Distributor	Building Material Retailers	Building Contractors	Home Owners
($.05/sq ft.)	($.50/sq ft.)	($.60/sq ft.)	($.90/sq ft.)	($1.50/sq ft.)	
Basic Inputs	Product Creation	Supply Chain Logistics	Retail Services	Installation and Finish	Customer Value
Low Cost and Reliable Supply	Value Added Product Benefits	Availability and Reliable Delivery	Availability and Order Quantity	Performance and Appearance	Durability Low Maint.

services. Construction retailers add $.30 per square foot in performing their role in offering localized inventory, desired purchase quantities, and customer service in the proper installation of fiber-cement siding. Contractors install the product, add trim, and paint the product to achieve the desired performance and appearance. The net result is a cost to home owners of roughly $1.50 per square foot of siding. The benefits far exceed this cost as fiber-cement siding is resistant to fire, bug infestation, and rot and often comes with a 50-year guarantee.

Building Brand Image

It is important to carefully consider how a channel system will affect the image of a product or manufacturer. Hartman Luggage, for example, manufactures a high-quality line of luggage and has a certain image for quality. Hartman is selective in choosing retailers who will support or enhance this brand image.

Likewise, Perfume de Paris manufactures and markets perfume at approximately one-third the price of Chanel and other higher-priced perfume products. It is important for Perfume de Paris to have its product sold through mass merchandisers who emphasize price, because mass merchandising is consistent with its target customer and product and price-positioning strategy.

Building Company Benefits

Overall benefits can be enhanced and contribute to building customer value with relationship marketing.[10] Direct channel systems offer the greatest opportunity for presenting product information, controlling the selling effort, and offering specialized selling skills. This opportunity to enhance the total benefits through personal relationships developed with customers or channel intermediaries can be important. Strong customer-firm relationships produce high degrees of commitment by both parties, and high commitment has the potential to enhance customer value.

When a business cannot directly interact with target customers, it must take care in selecting a channel system that will be capable of fulfilling these customer relationships effectively.[11] For a given product and customer, this selection may require a certain level of product knowledge, sales and negotiation skill, call frequency, and follow-up after-sales service. The bottom line is that any channel system is of little value if the sales interaction with the target customer is ineffective.

With an e-marketing channel, a business with 10,000 customers should look at customers not as a segment of 10,000 customers but as 10,000 segments, each with one customer. Today e-marketing channels can be extended with customer relationship marketing and the development of one-on-one marketing relationships. Whether a consumer business with thousands of customers or an industrial business with hundreds, the use of customer relationship marketing and e-marketing enables businesses to interact with customers, make customized offerings, and build customer loyalty.

Improving Cost Efficiency

By making a product readily available, a business can lower a customer's transaction costs. Customers have preferred points of purchase. If a business does not make products readily available at these points of purchase, it inherently raises the cost of the transaction. For undifferentiated products, this type of transaction cost is high. Customers will not make the effort to purchase the product if it is not conveniently available. On the other hand, the more differentiated a product and the greater its perceived value, the more willing the customer may be to incur this type of transaction cost.

Another way to affect customer value (total benefits less total costs) is to lower the cost of reaching customers. The more cost-efficient a channel system is, the greater is the opportunity to lower customer costs or to increase business profitability. An important marketing responsibility is to find and develop channel systems that are cost efficient while still delivering the benefits sought by customers.

It is often assumed that the more intermediaries there are in a channel system, the higher the total cost of purchase. In general, that assumption is not true, or that channel system would not exist. Consider, for example, the channel system presented in Figure 9-13, in which 100 manufacturers each contact 20,000 retailers once a month. In this channel system, there is a monthly transaction cost of $50 for order placement, handling, delivery, and billing. The net result is an industry that has an overall channel system transaction cost of approximately $1.2 billion, as shown.

When an extra layer (wholesalers) is added to the channel system, each of the 100 manufacturers can now sell each month to wholesalers at a cost of $25,000 per month, as illustrated in Figure 9-14. This cost is much higher because a great deal more merchandise is handled and delivered each month. In this channel system, the wholesalers need to then distribute to the 20,000 retailers each month. Their cost is $750 per transaction, which is also considerably higher because wholesalers are shipping a variety of products, because they represent a large number of retailers. As shown, in this channel system the wholesaler lowers the annual transaction costs to $210 million, or approximately $1 billion less than the channel system without a wholesaler function.

Although a business generally builds customer value through a combination of product, service, and image benefits and the cost of acquiring these benefits (price and transaction costs), any given channel system can enhance or detract from the delivered

FIGURE 9-13 TRANSACTION COSTS IN A CHANNEL WITHOUT WHOLESALERS

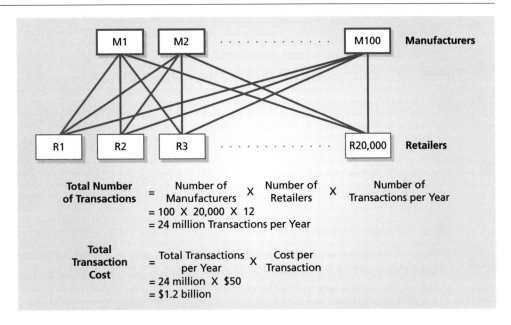

FIGURE 9-14 TRANSACTION COSTS IN A CHANNEL WITH WHOLESALERS

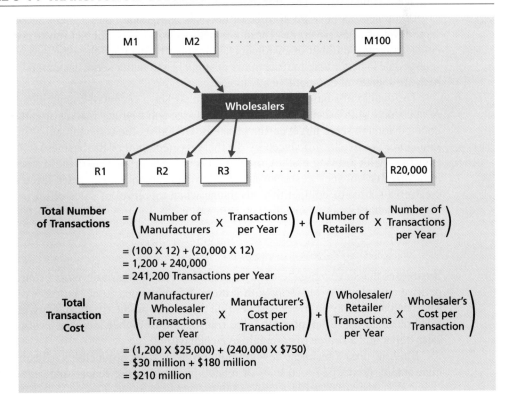

customer value. Thus, selecting a particular channel system requires both careful consideration of the benefits sought by customers and the cost of delivering them through a particular channel system.

CHANNEL SYSTEMS AND COMPETITIVE ADVANTAGE

Customer contact is essential for any sale to occur. This contact can take many forms, whether indirect or direct. For indirect channel systems, a business must have a sufficient number of outlets, whether retail or wholesale. For direct sales channel systems, a business must have a certain number of salespeople to establish and maintain a certain level of contact. Either can be a source of competitive advantage when done in a manner that creates value for customers and relative advantage over competitors.

Sales Force Advantage

When a direct channel system is selected as the best way to reach and effectively serve target customers, it is essential that a business have a sufficient number of salespeople. Assume that a business has 1,000 target customers and the required rate of customer contact for sales effectiveness and customer satisfaction is two customer visits per month. This translates into 24,000 customer contacts per year. Further assume that a salesperson in this particular industry can make three customer visits per day and has 4 days per week to make customer calls. This translates into a need for 38 salespeople.

If competitors have an average of only 20 salespeople, they cannot accomplish the same level of sales coverage. These competitors will either contact fewer customers or contact the same number of customers less frequently. In either case, the business with 38 salespeople is better able to reach more customers and better serve customers' needs, and both are sources of competitive advantage.

The quality of a business's sales force can also be a source of competitive advantage. A sales force with exceptional product knowledge and a strong market orientation is in a good position to serve target customer needs. Of course, the behavior and attitudes of the sales force are in part influenced by the market orientation of the business.[12] As a result, a business with a strong market orientation is in the best position to build customer relationships that enhance customer satisfaction and retention. The sales force is, in fact, creating a source of competitive advantage when this level of sales effort is valued by customers and cannot be matched by competitors.[13]

Sales Productivity

Businesses that have a high level of sales productivity can also develop a source of competitive advantage. A business with a more efficient sales force, in terms of sales per salesperson, will have a lower cost per sale than a less productive business with the same sales revenue. An efficient sales force translates into higher levels of profitability per sales dollar and a source of competitive advantage.

But how does a business develop high levels of sales productivity? Businesses with high-quality products, broad lines of related products, and efficient sales administrative systems produce high levels of sales per salesperson. High-quality products are easier to sell than are low-quality products, and they often have premium prices. A broad product line provides more sales opportunities per sales call—and the use of computers and other telecommunications systems has been shown to improve sales administrative efficiency and to allow for more time with customers.

Distribution Advantage

For markets in which indirect channel systems are the dominant channel system used to reach target customers, share of distributor outlets can be directly linked to market share. As shown in Figure 9-15, generally the higher a drug store's outlet share, the higher its market share. Empirical studies have shown that the relationship between outlet share and market share is nonlinear and generally S-shaped, as shown in Figure 9-16. A small distributor share produces proportionately smaller market shares. However, as outlet share grows, market share grows at a faster rate until it exceeds outlet share. Then, as outlet share continues to increase, the rate of market share growth decreases.

There are only a few cases in which extremely high outlet and market shares have been observed. The lower part of the curve, below a 50 percent outlet share, is well documented.[14] However, because market share must equal 100 percent when outlet share equals 100 percent, the upper half of the curve in Figure 9-16 can be extrapolated with some confidence. Recognizing this relationship, for markets in which indirect retail or dealer channel systems are required to reach and serve target customers, businesses with dominant distribution shares have a source of competitive advantage. Why? Because in any given market, there is a finite number of distributors, and fewer good ones. The business that dominates this channel system can control market access by blocking market entry because the number of available distributors or retailers is limited.

FIGURE 9-15 DRUG STORE CHAIN MARKET SHARE VERSUS OUTLET LOCATION SHARE

North American Drug Store Chains	Sales ($ billions)	Market Share (%)	Number of Stores	Outlet Share (%)	Sales per Store ($ millions)
Walgreens	$13.4	23	2,363	14	$5.67
Rite Aid	11.8	20	3,963	23	2.97
CVS	11.1	20	3,909	23	2.84
Eckerd	8.8	15	2,786	17	3.16
American Drug Stores	5.2	9	882	5	5.93
Longs Drug Stores	2.8	5	337	2	8.40
Shoppers Drug Mart	2.8	5	801	5	3.52
Jean Coutu	1.2	2	483	3	2.38
Phar-Mor	1.1	2	104	1	10.38
Medical Shoppe Int'l.	1.0	2	1,236	7	0.84
Total/Average	$59.2	100%	16,864	100%	$3.51

FIGURE 9-16 DISTRIBUTION OUTLET SHARE VERSUS MARKET SHARE

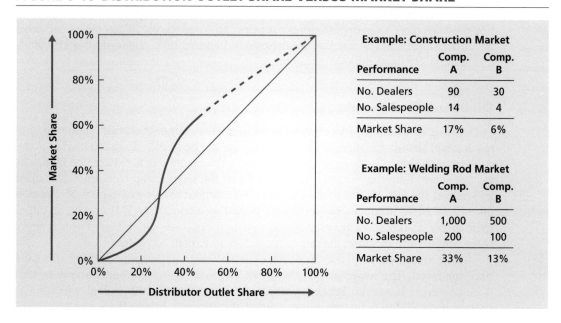

Example: Construction Market		
Performance	Comp. A	Comp. B
No. Dealers	90	30
No. Salespeople	14	4
Market Share	17%	6%

Example: Welding Rod Market		
Performance	Comp. A	Comp. B
No. Dealers	1,000	500
No. Salespeople	200	100
Market Share	33%	13%

PROFIT IMPACT OF ALTERNATIVE MARKETING CHANNELS

In determining the profitability of any channel strategy, several aspects of profitability come into play. The reach of a marketing channel will impact the volume obtained with that marketing channel, and net prices and marketing expenses also vary by type of marketing channel. As shown in Figure 9-17, direct marketing channels are able to capture most, if not all, of the end-user price. However, the cost of most direct marketing channels is generally higher because the business is responsible for selling, distribution, and payment. E-marketing is an exception. Once the online selling infrastructure in place, direct online sales can yield very high margins. For Office Depot, the world's second-largest online retailer in 2003, $2.6 billion in online sales suggests a highly profitable direct marketing channel. Office Depot operates 56 Web sites in 14 countries.

Mixed channels use a combination of direct sales and intermediary distribution. Although this lowers their cost of marketing (as a percent of sales), revenues derived from mixed marketing channels are lower because intermediaries take a portion of this price for their services. As shown in Figure 9-18, indirect marketing channels result in the lowest out-of-pocket marketing expenses. However, the net price derived from the use of indirect marketing channels is much less than other channel types because multiple intermediaries capture percentages of the end-user price in exchange for the channel services they provide.

Consider, for example, an electronic-components manufacturer who sells 100,000 units per year into a market in which it has a 5 percent market share. These sales are

FIGURE 9-17 CHANNEL MARGIN VERSUS CHANNEL MARKETING EXPENSES

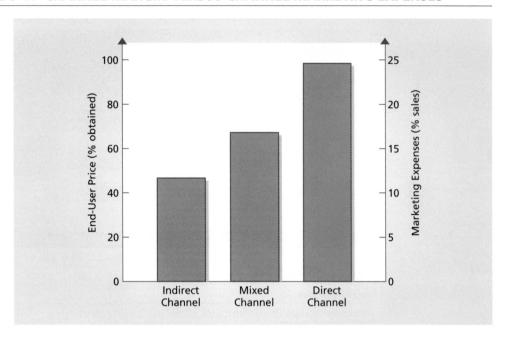

currently achieved with a mixed-marketing channel as shown in Figure 9-18. After discounting the end-user price to dealers (33 percent) who sell the product locally, and paying sales commissions to salespeople who call on end-users (10 percent), an invoice price of $18.09 is achieved. A direct marketing channel would bypass the dealer and an invoice price of $27 per unit could be achieved after paying a 10 percent sales commission. The indirect channel would not require a sales commission but would add a wholesaler to the marketing channel. The invoice price achieved by the manufacturer using an indirect marketing channel would be $15.08 as illustrated in Figure 9-18.

Although the net price and margins are lower using the indirect marketing channel, the cost of marketing is much less, as shown in Figure 9-19. The net margin is $4.08 per unit, but the marketing costs are only 5 percent of sales. The net marketing contribution using the indirect marketing channel is lower but the marketing productivity (479 percent) is much higher than the mixed-channel marketing productivity (278 percent). In contrast, the direct marketing channel offers higher net prices and net margins. Sales using the direct marketing channel are higher than sales obtained using the mixed marketing channel. However, the marketing expenses are much higher (15 percent of sales). Nevertheless, the direct marketing channel delivers a higher net marketing contribution, slightly less than twice the net marketing contribution currently obtained with the mixed marketing channel. However, to get this economic benefit will require spending more than twice what is currently spent on marketing channel expenses. The marketing return on sales (ROS) for the direct marketing channel is much higher

FIGURE 9-18 ALTERNATIVE CHANNEL MARKETING PROFITABILITY

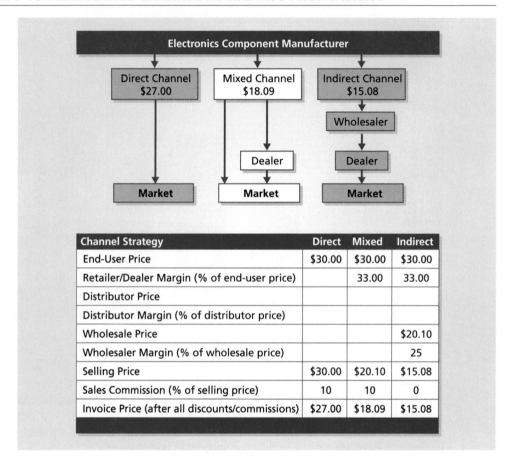

Channel Strategy	Direct	Mixed	Indirect
End-User Price	$30.00	$30.00	$30.00
Retailer/Dealer Margin (% of end-user price)		33.00	33.00
Distributor Price			
Distributor Margin (% of distributor price)			
Wholesale Price			$20.10
Wholesaler Margin (% of wholesale price)			25
Selling Price	$30.00	$20.10	$15.08
Sales Commission (% of selling price)	10	10	0
Invoice Price (after all discounts/commissions)	$27.00	$18.09	$15.08

(39.5 percent) than the marketing ROS for the mixed channel strategy (27.8 percent). The marketing productivity, however, for the direct marketing channel is slightly lower (264 percent vs. 278 percent).

The break-even analysis for each marketing channel strategy (also shown in Figure 9-19) provides a way to assess the profitability risk of each channel. The break-even volume is lowest with the indirect channel. Even though margins are lower in the indirect channel, the marketing expenses are much lower and hence, there is a lower break-even volume. However, the break-even price in the indirect channel is only $3.37 below the current invoice (net) price of $14.08. In the direct channel, there is a difference of $8.70 between the net price and the break-even price at a sales volume of 100,000 units. Although there are many trade-offs with respect to prices, sales, margins, and profits, the ultimate choice of a marketing channel will depend on the effectiveness of the channel in reaching customers and delivering value as well as the profit potential and available marketing resources.

FIGURE 9-19 ALTERNATIVE CHANNEL MARKETING PROFITABILITY

Channel Strategy	Direct	Mixed	Indirect
Invoice Price	$ 27.00	$ 18.09	$ 15.08
Transactions Costs (shipping, billing, etc.)	$ 5.00	$ 2.00	$ 1.00
Net Price	$ 22.00	$ 16.09	$ 14.08
Volume Sold (units)	100,000	100,000	100,000
Sales Revenues	$2,200,000	$1,609,000	$1,408,000
Variable Cost per Unit	$ 10.00	$ 10.00	$ 10.00
Margin per Unit	$ 12.00	$ 6.09	$ 4.08
Gross Profit	$1,200,000	$ 609,000	$ 408,000
Marketing & Sales Expense (% sales)	15	10	5
Marketing & Sales Expense	$ 330,000	$ 160,900	$ 70,400
Net Marketing Contribution	$ 870,000	$ 448,100	$ 337,600
Marketing Return on Sales (%)	39.5	27.8	24.0
Marketing Productivity (%)	264	278	479

Channel Strategy	Direct	Mixed	Indirect
Net Price	$ 22.00	$ 16.09	$ 14.08
Margin per Unit	$ 12.00	$ 6.09	$ 4.08
Marketing & Sales Expenses	$ 330,000	$ 160,900	$ 70,400
Break-Even Volume	27,500	26,420	17,255
Break-Even Price	$ 13.30	$ 11.61	$ 10.70
Net Price Premium Over Break-Even Price	$ 8.70	$ 4.48	$ 3.37

■ Summary

Regardless of how attractive a business's products or services may be, if the business cannot reach target customers with a desired level of services, it has little chance of marketing success. Customers have product and service requirements along with preferences of where to buy. Likewise, a business has image requirements and the need for sales effectiveness and cost efficiency. To be successful, a channel system must meet both customer and business requirements.

The biggest decision is whether to use a direct or an indirect channel system. In a direct system, the business retains ownership of its products and is responsible for many of the selling, delivery, warehousing, and transaction activities. Direct channel systems include direct selling, direct marketing, telemarketing, and the use of manufacturers' reps and sales agents. An indirect system takes ownership of the product and varying degrees of responsibility for selling, warehousing, delivery, and transaction activities. Indirect systems include different combinations of wholesalers and retailers in the consumer market. In the business-to-business market, indirect systems can also include different combinations of wholesalers and dealers, value-added resellers (VARs), and original equipment manufacturers (OEMs).

The biggest change in marketing channels is the use of e-marketing channels. For businesses like General Electric, it has leveraged their ability to reach customers and capitalize on existing brand awareness, order-entry systems, and operating expenses. For dot-com businesses like e-Bay, e-marketing is the primary marketing channel and a core element of their approach to serving customers. Without an effective e-marketing channel strategy, many dot-com businesses did not survive. Managed successfully e-marketing channels have proved to be an important marketing channel in both B2C and B2B markets.

In many instances, multitiered channel systems are more customer effective and cost efficient than direct systems. The belief that having more intermediaries in a channel system pushes up the cost, and, therefore, the price of a product, is not true. If a more efficient system were available, marketers would find it. However, rarely is one channel and sales system sufficient to reach all target customers—and, the greater a business's market coverage, with either a direct or an indirect system, the greater its market share. Thus, an important part of a profitable marketing strategy is a well thought-out and well-managed marketing channel strategy.

■ Market-Based Logic and Strategic Thinking

1 Why is it advantageous to view a combination of sales and channels of distribution as a channel system?
2 How has the use of a direct channel system helped Dell Computers grow over the last 10 years?
3 How has Compaq's channel system contributed to its growth over the last 10 years?
4 What is the difference between a direct and an indirect channel system? Why might a business use both?
5 What is a mixed channel system? Why would Microsoft's Office suite be marketed with a mixed channel system to large business customers?
6 What are the various direct sales and channel systems that could be used in the consumer market? How do they differ from the business-to-business market?
7 What role do online channel systems play in the way we buy airline tickets and stocks?
8 How does e-marketing help businesses reach customers, lower cost, and improve customer service?
9 What role do VARs play in business-to-business markets? How do they enhance customer value?
10 How does the use of multiple channel systems affect the growth of a business?
11 How does the use of a channel system either enhance or detract from customer value?
12 What specific factors need to be considered in selecting one channel system over another?
13 Why can a channel system be a source of competitive advantage?

14 What are some of the ways a channel system can be a source of advantage and contribute to a higher market share?

15 How can increased sales force quality and sales force productivity be developed into a source of competitive advantage?

16 How would you go about determining the profit impact of an alternative channel system?

Marketing Performance Tools

Each of the following **marketing performance tools** can be accessed by going to *www.rogerjbest.com* or *www.prenhall.com/best*.

The shaded cells are input cells. The non-shaded cells contain results calculated from your input values.

MARKETING PERFORMANCE TOOL—Channel Marketing Profitability

Channel Strategy	Direct	Mixed	Indirect
End-User Price	$30.00	$30.00	$30.00
Retailer/Dealer Margin (% of end-user price)		33.00	33.00
Distributor Price			
Distributor Margin (% of distributor price)			
Wholesale Price			$20.10
Wholesaler Margin (% of wholesale price)			25
Selling Price			$15.08
Sales Commission (% of selling price)	10	10	0
Invoice Price (after all discounts/commissions)	$27.00	$18.09	$15.08

This **marketing performance tool** allows you to estimate the invoice price and channel discounts and sales commissions for three different marketing channel strategies. Using the example presented in Figure 9-18, answer the following application exercise questions. The shaded cells can be changed in doing the following application exercise. An entirely new example of your own can be input using all the shaded cells.

Application Exercise: Using the data provided, what would be the invoice price in the indirect marketing channel if the business decided to bypass the wholesalers? Why would their channel marketing expenses be higher? How would the mixed channel invoice price change if dealers required a 40 percent margin instead of a 33.3 percent margin? Estimate how the net price would change for each channel if the sales commissions increased from 10 percent to 15 percent.

MARKETING PERFORMANCE TOOL—Channel Break-Even Volume/Price

Channel Strategy	Direct	Mixed	Indirect
Invoice Price	$ 27.00	$ 18.09	$ 15.08
Transactions Costs (shipping, billing, etc.)	$ 5.00	$ 2.00	$ 1.00
Net Price	$ 22.00	$ 16.09	$ 14.08
Volume Sold (units)	100,000	100,000	100,000
Sales Revenues	$2,200,000	$1,609,000	$1,407,500
Variable Cost per Unit	$ 10.00	$ 10.00	$ 10.00
Margin per Unit	$ 12.00	$ 6.09	$ 4.08
Gross Profit	$1,200,000	$ 609,000	$ 407,500
Marketing & Sales Expense (% sales)	15	10	5
Marketing & Sales Expense	$ 330,000	$ 160,900	$ 70,375
Net Marketing Contribution	$ 870,000	$ 448,100	$ 337,125
Marketing Return on Sales (%)	39.5	27.8	24.0
Marketing Productivity (%)	264	278	479

Channel Strategy	Direct	Mixed	Indirect
Net Price	$ 22.00	$ 16.09	$ 14.08
Margin per Unit	$ 12.00	$ 6.09	$ 4.08
Marketing & Sales Expenses	$ 330,000	$ 160,900	$ 70,375
Break-Even Volume	27,500	26,420	17,270
Break-Even Price	$ 13.30	$ 11.61	$ 10.70
Net Price Premium Over Break-Even Price	$ 8.70	$ 4.48	$ 3.37

This **marketing performance tool** allows you to estimate the sales and profit impact of three different marketing channel strategies. Also shown for each marketing channel strategy is the marketing ROS, marketing productivity, and break-even volume and break-even price. Using the example presented in Figure 9-19, answer the following application exercise questions. The shaded cells can be changed in doing the following application exercise. An entirely new example of your own can be input using all the shaded cells.

Application Exercise: Using the data provided in Figure 9-19, what would be the sales and profit impact of an indirect marketing channel if the business decided to bypass the wholesalers but required channel marketing expenses to be increased from 5 percent of sales to 10 percent of sales? How would the mixed channel strategy profits and break-even volume change if dealers required a 40 percent margin instead of a 33.3 percent margin? Then, estimate how the marketing ROS and marketing productivity would change for each channel if the sales commissions increased from 10 percent to 15 percent.

Notes

1. J. Nicholas DeBonis, Eric Balinski, and Phil Allen, *Value-Based Marketing for Bottom-Line Success*, (McGraw-Hill, 2003).
2. M. Understrom and T. Anderson, *Brand Building on the Internet*.
3. K. Schnepf, "Customers of Epoxy Resin and Related Products Find E-epoxy.com a Powerful Procurement Channel," *(www.dow.com-new/prodbus/2001)*.
4. J. Welch, *Jack: Straight from the Gut* (Warner Business Books, 2001): 341–351.
5. Kasturi Rangan, Melvyn Menezes, and E.P. Maier, "Channel Selection for New Industrial Products: A Framework, Method and Application," *Journal of Marketing* (July 1992): 69–82.
6. R. Oliva, "Painting with Business Marketers' Web Palette," *Marketing Management* (Summer 1998): 50–53.
7. F. Cespedes and R. Corey, "Managing Multiple Channels," *Business Horizons* (July–August 1990): 72.
8. Robert Haas, *Industrial Marketing Management: Text and Cases*, 4th ed. (Northridge, CA: Kent, 1989): 239; and Michael Morris, *Industrial and Organizational Marketing* (Old Tappan, NJ: Macmillan, 1988): 489–523.
9. Niraj Dawar and Philip Parker, "Marketing Universals: Consumers' Use of Brand Name, Price, Physical Appearance, and Retailer Reputation as Signals of Product Quality," *Journal of Marketing* (April 1994): 81–95.
10. James Anderson and James Narus, "A Model of Distributor Firm and Manufacturer Firm Working Partnerships," *Journal of Marketing* (January 1990): 42–58.
11. David Morris, "What's Old Is New in Relationship Marketing," *Marketing News* (February 1994): 4, 8; and Robert Robicheaux and James Coleman, "The Structure of Marketing Channel Relationships," *Academy of Marketing Science* (Winter 1994): 38–51.
12. Judy Siguaw, G. Brown, and Robert E. Widing, "The Influence of Market Orientation of the Firm on Sales Force Behavior and Attitudes," *Journal of Marketing Research* (February 1994): 106–116.
13. Robert Ping, "Does Satisfaction Moderate the Association Between Alternative Attractiveness and Exit Intention in a Marketing Channel?" *Academy of Marketing Science* (Fall 1994): 364–371.
14. Gary Lilien, Philip Kotler, and K. Moorthy, *Marketing Models* (Upper Saddle River, NJ: Prentice Hall, 1992): 434–438; P. Hartung and J. Fisher, "Brand Switching and Mathematical Programming in Market Expansion," *Management Science* (August 1965): 231–243; and Gary Lilien and Ambar Rao, "A Model for Allocating Retail Outlet Building Resources Across Market Areas," *Operations Research* (January–February): 1–14.

Marketing Communications and Customer Response

I n order to better understand customer response to marketing communications, a large nationwide department store conducted a careful study of customers' responses to a specific marketing communication effort. The target market was well-defined and the selected media was known to cover 75 percent of the target market. The campaign would feature specific merchandise known to have appeal in this target market. Full-page advertisements would run for 5 consecutive days in two daily newspapers, and radio spots would be aired on each day on two stations that would each run the ad two times daily in four time slots—early morning, mid-day, early evening, and late evening.

On each evening that the marketing communications were run, target-market customers were surveyed to determine their level of response. Shown in Figure 10-1 is the level of advertising awareness for each day of the 5-day advertising effort. Although the ad awareness grew to 68 percent by day 5, the majority of the ad awareness was attained by the third day (over 60 percent). Of the 68 percent who were aware of the marketing communication, only

FIGURE 10-1 ADVERTISING AWARENESS AND MESSAGE FREQUENCY

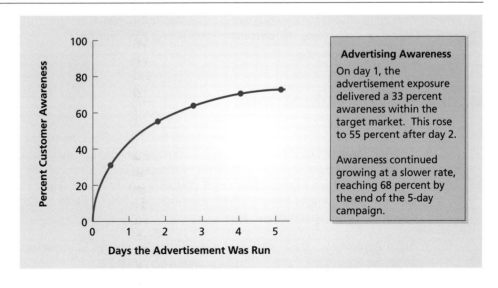

Advertising Awareness

On day 1, the advertisement exposure delivered a 33 percent awareness within the target market. This rose to 55 percent after day 2.

Awareness continued growing at a slower rate, reaching 68 percent by the end of the 5-day campaign.

FIGURE 10-2 ADVERTISING EFFECTIVENESS AND CUSTOMER RESPONSE

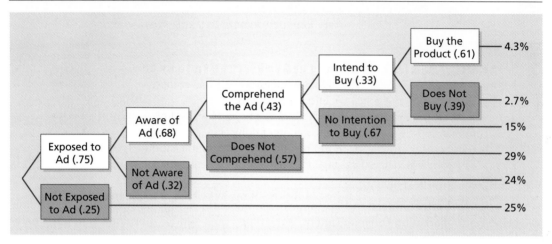

43 percent were able to accurately describe the ad content and store name as shown in Figure 10-2. Of these customers, a third stated an intention to respond to the marketing communications. Sixty-one percent of those intending to purchase the advertised merchandise actually made the purchase. The net result was that 4.3 percent of the target market took the intended action and made the specified product purchase as depicted in Figure 10-2.

When buyers were asked how they learned of the advertised merchandise, 46 percent mentioned newspaper A, 23 percent mentioned newspaper B, 18 percent said they heard about it from someone else, and 13 percent mentioned the radio. Perhaps more important was that the average purchase amount was $60, of which the advertised merchandise accounted for roughly half. Thus, the marketing communication drew 4.3 percent of the target market to the store to buy the advertised merchandise, but these customers bought an equal amount of non-advertised merchandise. The net result was a meaningful gain in net-marketing contribution.

MARKETING COMMUNICATIONS

The first job of a marketing communication is to build awareness: to inform customers of a business's products or services. Second, marketing communications needs to continually reinforce messages in order to maintain awareness. Third, it is often the job of a marketing communication to motivate a target customer to take action. Thus, there are three fundamental marketing communications objectives, any one of which can be the focus of a particular marketing communication.

1. **Build Awareness:** Build a level of awareness with respect to important information about the organization and its products and/or services.

2. **Reinforce the Message:** Sustain a desired level of retention with respect to image, key benefits, and name recognition over time.
3. **Stimulate Action:** Motivate target customers to take a specific action in a relatively short time.

Because message reinforcement and action can come only after a reasonable level of awareness, businesses need to first build awareness and comprehension before moving on to other marketing communications objectives.

As illustrated in Figure 10-3, there is a hierarchical set of customer response effects. Building awareness, comprehension, intentions, and action are major steps upward in the hierarchy of customer response. If a marketing communication fails to reach target customers (exposure, the first stage in the hierarchy), none of the customer response effects that follow are possible.

In this example, 37 percent of the target market were not reached with the marketing communication and therefore will not have a chance to become aware, comprehend, form intentions, or take action. Of the 63 percent of the customers who are exposed to the business's marketing communication, 54 percent can accurately recall seeing the marketing communication. This means that another 29 percent (the 46 percent who not aware out of the 63 percent who are exposed to the ad) are removed from further customer response because they do not fully comprehend the marketing communication content. Thus, the combination of target customers lost due to lack of exposure (37 percent) and awareness (29 percent) is 66 percent.

FIGURE 10-3 MARKETING COMMUNICATIONS AND CUSTOMER RESPONSE INDEX

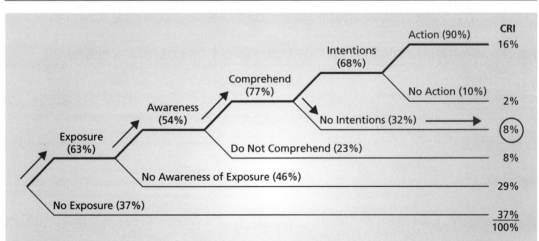

The overall customer response index for any combination of effects in the customer response hierarchy is the product of the proportions of individual effects that make up that combination. For example, the customer response index for customers who are aware of the communication (63%), comprehend its content (54%), but are *not* interested in the product or service (23%) is as follows:

CRI = % that are aware X % that comprehend X % that are not interested
    = 0.63 X 0.54 X 0.23
    = 0.08, or 8%

Of those target customers who were exposed and are aware of the ad, 77 percent adequately comprehend the marketing communication while 23 percent did not fully comprehend the ad content and its intended message. This creates an additional lost-customer response of approximately 8 percent. Of those who comprehend the ad, 68 percent intend to take a desired action. Thirty-two percent of those who comprehend the ad are not sufficiently motivated to take action, which creates another 8 percent loss in customer response. Target customers who intend to take action, but do not, create an additional loss of potential customer response of 2 percent. Finally, target customers who are exposed, aware, comprehend, intend to take action, and take the desired action produce a customer response of 16 percent. In order to achieve a higher overall level of customer response, a business would need to target specific stages in the customer response hierarchy in which to improve its performance.

STRATEGIES TO INCREASE CUSTOMER RESPONSE

Potential causes of poor customer response in the customer response hierarchy are listed in Figure 10-4. Low levels of target market reach (exposure) usually occur because the wrong media are chosen or media coverage is insufficient. Marketing communications play a major role in low levels of awareness and comprehension. Low levels of awareness can be caused by insufficient message frequency (not enough repetition) or poor ad content. Low levels of comprehension can also be the result of insufficient frequency or poor ad copy. Low levels of intention to act can be attributed to ineffective ad content and/or a weak value proposition. A failure to act could be the result of both ad copy and other influencing factors such as competitor actions or lack of service during order placement.

FIGURE 10-4 MARKETING CAUSES OF LOW LEVELS OF CUSTOMER RESPONSE

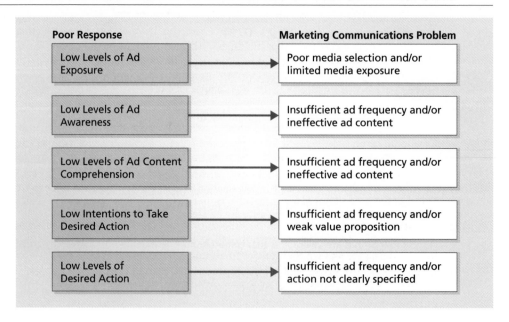

Correcting these problems is essential to improving overall customer response. For example, assume that for the situation presented in Figure 10-3, the business developed a more effective marketing communications strategy that increased awareness from 63 percent to 75 percent. This increase would translate into a potential increase in customer response index (CRI) from 16 percent to 19 percent.

$$\textbf{CRI} \text{ (current)} = 0.63 \times 0.54 \times 0.77 \times 0.68 \times 0.90 = 0.16$$
$$\textbf{CRI} \text{ (improved)} = 0.75 \times 0.54 \times 0.77 \times 0.68 \times 0.90 = 0.19$$

Assume, also, that because of improved ad copy the comprehension of its marketing communication was increased from 54 percent to 67 percent. The combined effects of increased awareness and comprehension resulted in a 50 percent increase in the overall CRI, from 16 percent to 24 percent, as shown here.

$$\textbf{CRI} \text{ (improved)} = 0.75 \times 0.67 \times 0.77 \times 0.68 \times 0.90 = 0.24$$

A well-positioned product with an attractive customer value (perceived benefits that are greater than perceived costs) and a strong marketing channel system will still not achieve full marketing success without a good marketing communications program. If target customers are unaware of a product and its benefits, cost, and value, there is little opportunity for purchase.

For example, Johnson Controls is a *Fortune* 500 business that serves a variety of markets, one of which is the commercial building services market. Johnson Controls has achieved an excellent reputation among customers. However, a market research study revealed a low level of awareness in the commercial building services market; customers mentioned Johnson Controls with disappointing frequency when asked to identify suppliers of this service.[1]

In response to this information, Johnson Controls developed the "Classic Buildings" marketing communication illustrated in Figure 10-5. These print ads were run in *Forbes, Fortune, Business Week*, and the *Wall Street Journal*, each of which reaches building and facilities managers (the target customers) in *Fortune* 1000 businesses. Nine months after the campaign, measurements were made. Unaided recall of Johnson Controls had increased by 30 percent. The marketing communication effort increased company awareness and helped pre-sell the company. Both effects contributed to an increase in sales.

The importance of building awareness and customer response is highlighted in Figure 10-6. For any level of awareness, the levels of comprehension, intention, and purchase are consecutively lower. Perhaps more important is the fact that the level of customer loyalty is lower still. Sustained profitability depends on customer retention, and each step up the hierarchy of customer response is a step toward profitability. In this example, we can see that 30 percent awareness results in a low level of customer loyalty. When awareness is built up to 80 percent, the subsequent customer responses and customer loyalty are higher. Awareness is the first step in new-customer acquisition. The higher the awareness for a product, the higher is the customer response and the higher the potential for customer retention. A 5 percent increase in retention produces a 25 percent increase in the lifetime value of a customer. Thus, building awareness is a first step in building profits based on brand and customer loyalty.

FIGURE 10-5 JOHNSON CONTROLS' "CLASSIC BUILDINGS" PRINT AD

STRUCTURALLY SOUND *with*

GOOD *fire* RESISTANCE

although LAWNCARE & GENERAL

GROUNDSKEEPING

COULD BE *upgraded.*

WHEN WE LOOK *at a* building, we see it as being more than simply steel, glass or brick. We see it as a total building environment.

That means comfortable indoor temperatures. Great lighting and truly balanced acoustics.

It also means the outside of the building. The landscaping, the groundskeeping. It means painting and cleaning. In fact, it can include security, and even food service.

We are, in short, committed to creating the ideal building environment.

One of the most economical and practical ways to achieve this is through outsourcing. Whereby you contract an outside company to perform everyday services that are quite separate from your core business.

With over 40 years of experience in integrated facility management, we have the skills to provide a complete range of services. From mail services to heating, ventilation and air conditioning to structural maintenance.

The savings are often quite dramatic. And, ultimately, outsourcing

lets you spend more of your valuable time doing what you do best.

As the experienced leader, we realize that any building, given the right kind of attention, can become more comfortable and productive. There is absolutely no reason why your business can't be as well.

Which is precisely why we have always been interested in improving life in the great indoors. Not to mention outdoors.

[EL CASTILLO, CHICHEN ITZA, *Mexico*]

JOHNSON CONTROLS

BUILDING CUSTOMER AWARENESS AND COMPREHENSION

Creating awareness among a large number of people is not the objective of most marketing communications. The objective is to create awareness among and communicate effectively to *target customers*. Even a memorable advertisement that is well-known among the general population is a failure if it does not achieve a high level of awareness and comprehension among target market customers.

Media Selection and Customer Awareness

As outlined in Figure 10-4, target customer awareness and comprehension are affected by media selection, message frequency, and ad copy. To reach target customers effectively, a business has to have a good understanding of their media habits. Do they watch television, and, if they do, which programs? Do they listen to the radio, and, if so, which stations and at what time? Which newspapers and which sections of the newspaper do they read? Which magazines do they subscribe to? How do they go to work, with respect to exposure to outdoor signage? Do they use the Yellow Pages? Are they Internet users or cable TV shoppers, or do they respond to direct-mail advertising? All of these questions must be answered in order to purchase the combination of media that will effectively reach as many target customers as economically possible.

FIGURE 10-6 ADVERTISING EFFECTIVENESS AND CUSTOMER RESPONSE

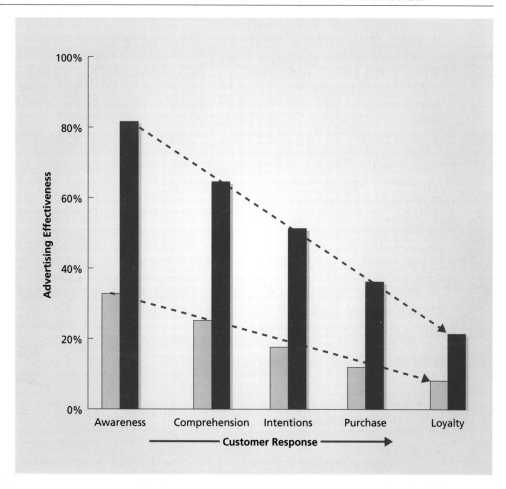

A key measure of effective media selection is *target market reach.* Target market reach is the percentage of target customers who will be exposed to the business's message given a certain combination of media. For example, a golf ball manufacturer wants to reach golfers. To do so, the manufacturer might advertise in print media such as *Golf Digest, Golf Magazine,* the *Wall Street Journal,* and *Business Week* and on television during golf tournaments. Through this combination of media, the manufacturer might, for example, be able to reach 63 percent of the golfers it considers target customers for its golf balls.

To get a target market reach greater than 63 percent would require the manufacturer to add media that reach target customers not reached with the current combination of media. If the incremental reach were more expensive than the incremental economic benefit derived from reaching these target customers, then the business would not seek to go beyond its current level of target customer reach.[2]

Message Frequency and Customer Awareness

Once a business has found the right combination of media to effectively reach target customers, the next question becomes how often the business needs to expose target customers to its message in order to achieve a certain level of awareness. Using too few messages may prevent information from getting through to target customers and will probably result in low levels of awareness and comprehension. On the other hand, too many exposures could irritate target customers and potentially have an adverse effect on retained information and perceptions of the ad, product, or company.

A few years ago AFLAC insurance had only 13 percent name recognition in the United States and was looking for an effective marketing communications campaign to cut through the clutter of mundane insurance ads and raise brand awareness. The company found what it was looking for and initially spent $35 million advertising it. The now infamous AFLAC duck led to more sales leads in the first 2 weeks of that year than in the previous 2 years combined, leading to record revenues. AFLAC's brand-name recognition skyrocketed to over 90 percent, and revenues grew 30 percent every year the campaign was run. However, after several years of hearing a duck screaming "AFLAC!" in various situations, many people were finding it irritating. At some point the positive impact of such repetition will turn into negative perceptions of the company.

Figure 10-7 shows how the frequency of print advertising by leading chemical companies affects the year-to-year change in ratings of company reputation. Leading chemical companies that advertise fewer than seven to twelve times per year in *Chemical and Engineering News (C&EN)* adversely affect their reputation, whereas those at higher levels of frequency positively affect their reputations.[3] For Amoco

FIGURE 10-7 ADVERTISING FREQUENCY AND AWARENESS IN A BUSINESS-TO-BUSINESS MARKET

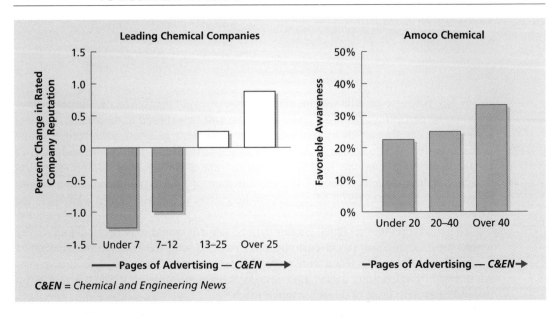

C&EN = Chemical and Engineering News

Chemical, the level of favorable awareness steadily increased with the level of message frequency in *C&EN*.

If Amoco Chemical were to stop its marketing communications, over a relatively short time its level of awareness would diminish. Shown in Figure 10-8 are the results of a classic study on message frequency and awareness.[4] In a "concentrated frequency" strategy, 13 consecutive messages were exposed to target customers over 13 weeks. As shown, the message awareness steadily increased each week until it reached its highest level in week 13. However, after week 13, no more messages were exposed to target customers for the remainder of the year and, as shown, the message awareness decayed back down almost to zero. This marketing communications strategy would be appropriate for building awareness and comprehension for seasonal products, political candidates, and special events.

The same message was also sent to a different group of target customers once every 4 weeks throughout the year in a "distributed frequency" strategy. These target customers also received 13 message exposures, but they were spread out over the entire year. In the 4-week period following each exposure, recall of the message decreased, but it did not go below the level prior to the last exposure. Hence, each additional exposure built from a higher base position—and, as shown, although this pattern of exposure frequency

FIGURE 10-8 MESSAGE FREQUENCY AND MESSAGE AWARENESS

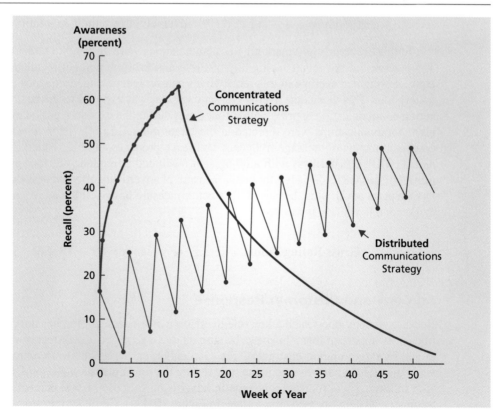

produced a longer-lasting effect, it never reached the highest level of awareness produced by the concentrated frequency effort. This approach to marketing communications would be appropriate in building and maintaining target customer awareness and comprehension.

In Figure 10-8, target customers were exposed to each of the 13 messages sent. A more typical situation is one in which target customers are exposed to only a fraction of the messages sent. So, for most marketing communications, there are more messages sent than received, as illustrated in the following:

Number Recalled	Proportion Recalling	Weighted Average
0	0.10	0.00
1	0.10	0.10
2	0.10	0.20
3	0.10	0.30
4	0.15	0.60
5	0.20	1.00
6	0.15	0.90
7	0.05	0.35
8	0.05	0.40
Total	**1.00**	**3.85**

In this example, eight marketing communications were directed to target customers. Ten percent did not recall seeing any of these ads, while 5 percent recalled seeing all eight. A weighted average of this recall yields an average message frequency of approximately four. This means the average target customer was exposed to the business's marketing communication approximately four times during the exposure period even though eight communications were directed at the target market. In television advertising, the combined impact of message frequency and reach produces an index called *gross rating points* (GRPs). A business with a 60 percent reach and a frequency of four produces an impact of 240 GRPs. This is a far better measure of advertising effectiveness than the dollars spent on advertising, because GRPs better measure how well the ad reached a target market and how often it was seen.

$$\textbf{Gross Rating Points} = \text{Reach} \times \text{Frequency} = 60 \times 4 = 240$$

Ad Copy and Customer Response

Because ad copy plays such a key role in creating awareness, comprehension, and intentions, it is important that a business be sure its message is accurately received and interpreted by target market customers. For Gardenburger, the stakes were extremely high when they ran an advertisement one time during the final episode of *Seinfeld*, at a cost of $1.5 million. This produced a change in advertising expense of 500 percent Therefore, testing the ad copy seemed appropriate. In Figure 10-9 is a Gardenburger story board that

FIGURE 10-9 GARDENBURGER TELEVISION AD STORY BOARD

was used to test the ad concept before it was developed. Once tested and refined, Gardenburger created the 30-second ad and ran it one time. The results were sensational! The Gardenburger ad reached 76 million people and store sales went up 328 percent from the same week 1 year earlier. Even though expensive, this marketing communications produced an increase in both sales and profits.

A highly memorable marketing communication that does not communicate the product and its benefits will fail to enhance interest in the product and will lower the overall level of customer response. Ad copy is best able to attract customers when it is based on customer needs and situations familiar to customers. It needs to integrate customer needs and situations with the product's benefits and business name.[5] If an ad is attractive but fails to create product interest, the ad copy is of limited value to the customer or to the business.

For example, Loctite once introduced a product under the brand name RC-601.[6] The ad copy was highly technical and targeted at production managers. The ad failed and the product failed. Follow-up customer research revealed that the target customers were really maintenance workers who detested technical data and liked pictures of how to do things. Based on the needs of this target customer, the product was re-named Quick Metal and launched with the ad copy shown in Figure 10-10. This ad copy served for both the direct mail piece and the advertisement. The results were phenomenal as Quick Metal achieved first-year sales at a level higher than any other new product in the company's history.

FIGURE 10-10 LOCTITE'S PRODUCT POSITIONING FOR QUICK METAL

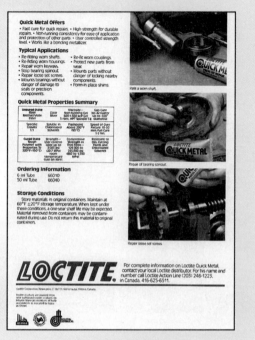

MESSAGE REINFORCEMENT

Although building awareness, comprehension, and intentions are critical to achieving a high level of target customer response, these levels will diminish, as shown in Figure 10-8, if the message is not continually reinforced. As presented earlier, Johnson Controls' marketing communications program improved ad awareness, but to hold or continue to grow a high level of awareness, a company would have had to continually keep the message in front of target customers.

Message Reinforcement and Pulsing

Maintaining a high level of awareness is expensive and requires new ad copy as the old copy begins to wear out. One approach to message reinforcement that maintains awareness, reduces copy wear-out, and is cost efficient is *pulsing*.[7] Pulsing involves the use of alternating exposure periods. An example of pulsing is a television advertisement that achieves 150 GRPs over a 4-week exposure period and is run in alternating 4-week periods. As shown in Figure 10-11, a certain level of awareness is built up during a 4-week exposure period; it then diminishes to some degree over the following 4-week period in which there is no message exposure, and then awareness is built up again in a subsequent 4-week exposure period.

If a business can maintain a desired level of awareness with pulsing, it can reduce the cost of advertising because there is no advertising expenditure in alternating nonexposure 4-week periods. A secondary benefit of pulsing is that it reduces the potential for copy wear-out due to overexposure to the same message. Because the marketing message is not seen on a continual basis, the ad copy's novelty and appeal wear out at a slower rate. Also, pulsing reduces the potential for overexposure, which can cause customer irritation and reduce ad effectiveness.

Heavy-Up Message Frequency

Because certain products can be purchased more readily at some times of the year than at others, a business may use a heavy-up exposure pattern to build higher levels of awareness, comprehension, and, it is hoped, interest in the advertised product or service. Figure 10-11 illustrates a heavy-up marketing communications program for a well-known brand that is

FIGURE 10-11 MESSAGE REINFORCEMENT STRATEGIES

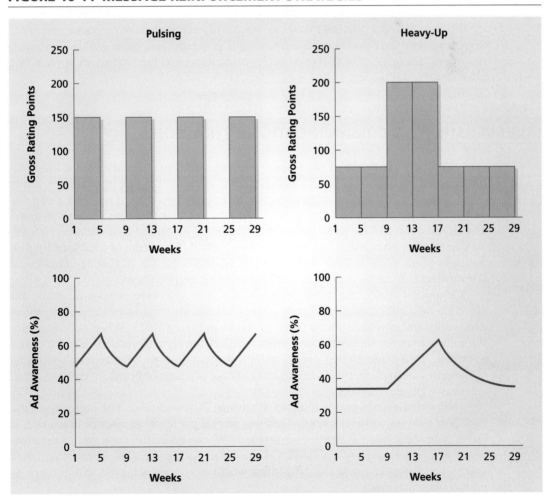

consumed most heavily in the summer. Many other exposure patterns are possible, but in this example, the business elects to maintain a certain level of base awareness throughout most of the year and to heavy-up its message frequency just before and during the prime buying period for this product. The business could also combine a heavy-up strategy for its primary promotion period and a pulsing strategy throughout the rest of the year.

STIMULATING CUSTOMER ACTION

Quite often, simply informing target customers and maintaining awareness are not enough to stimulate customer action. More is needed, particularly for new products whose benefits cannot be fully realized until they have been tried. For example, advertising copy that attempted to explain the benefits of the Post-it Note was simply not taken seriously by target customers.[8] After 18 months in four test markets, 3M's efforts to communicate the benefits of Post-it Notes led nowhere. A further complication was that 3M had a policy against giving away free goods on a new-product introduction. The marketing director opened a fifth test market to specifically get around the corporate policy and to generate trial purchase through a free sample program. This move enabled customers to discover the benefits of Post-it Notes by using them, and the product went on to be a great commercial success.

PUSH VERSUS PULL COMMUNICATIONS STRATEGIES

One almost always thinks of marketing communications as being directed toward customers, but an important aspect of marketing communications is communications directed toward channel intermediaries. Approximately one-third of marketing communications dollars is spent on customer advertising and two-thirds on sales promotions. The largest portion of the sales promotion expense (37 percent of total spending) is spent on intermediary promotions and the remaining portion (63 percent of total spending) on customer promotions. In total, approximately 63 percent of the marketing communications budget is spent on customers and 37 percent on intermediaries.

Customer-targeted marketing communications are *pull* type communications. The objectives of a pull-through marketing communication are to build awareness, attraction, and loyalty and to reduce search costs, as shown in Figure 10-12. When pull marketing communications are successful, customers will seek out certain products or services and, in essence, by the interest they create, pull the product through the channel. A pull strategy requires channel intermediaries to carry certain products or brands in order to attract and satisfy target customers.

Push communications are directed at channel intermediaries. The objective in this case is to motivate channel intermediaries to carry a particular product or brand and, in this way, make it more available to customers. When successful, push communications result in a wider range of availability, fewer stockouts, greater merchandising (shelf space), and a greater marketing effort than would have been achieved with little or no push communications.

FIGURE 10-12 PUSH–PULL (

Customer
Pull

Customer
Preference
• Awareness
• Attraction

C
• Con
• Effe

Customer Pull
Communication:

Communications Mix
Advertising
Sales Promotions
Catalogs
Direct Marketing
Telemarketing
Electronic Marketing
Public Relations

However, without continued reinforcem
from customers' minds and, eventual

There are many forms of cu
rebates, sweepstakes, gifts, and
program, it changed how c
Bean, Eddie Bauer, Spie
mailings to targeted c
ing on the Internet
tomer pull in the

Adverti

Unde
m

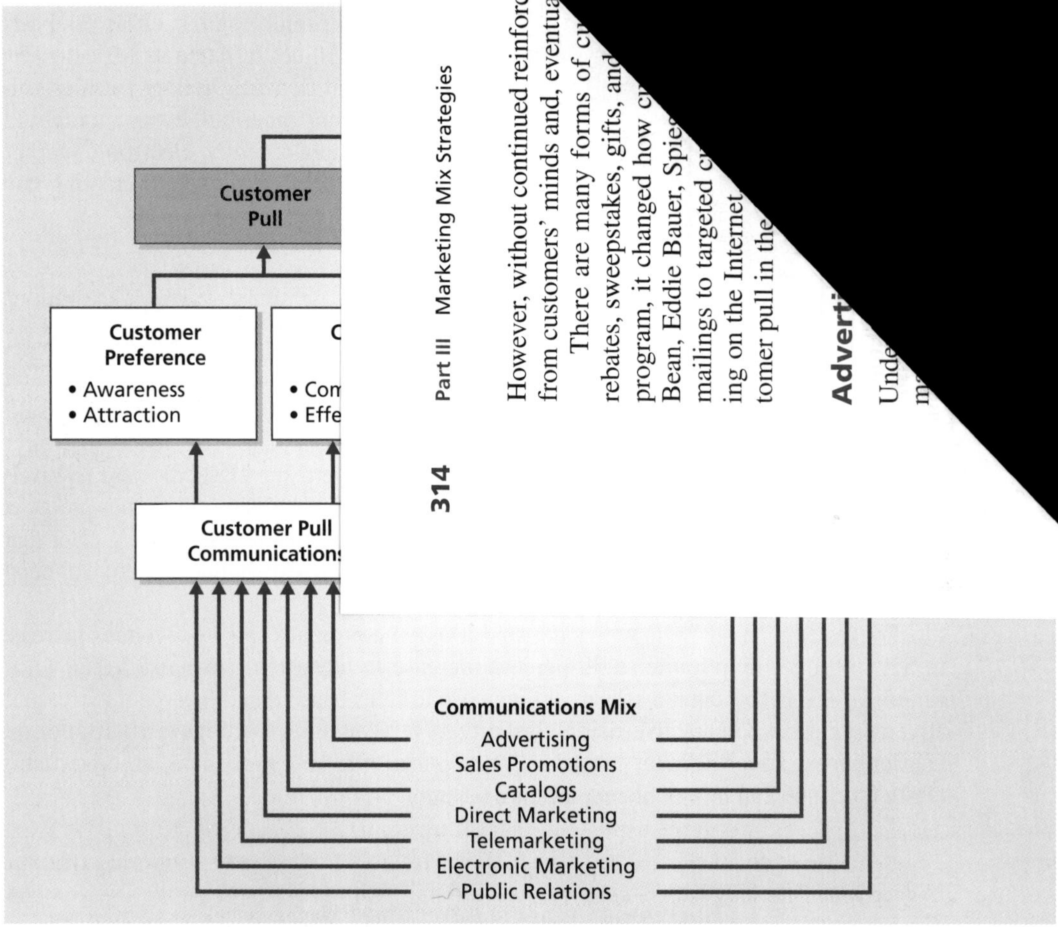

It is important, however, to understand that it is the combination of both push and pull marketing communications that creates the greatest impact on customer response and, therefore, market share gains.[9]

PULL COMMUNICATIONS AND CUSTOMER RESPONSE

As also shown in Figure 10-12, a wide range of alternative marketing communications can be used to create a communications mix designed to create customer pull.[10] To illustrate the power of media advertising, consider the fate of L&M cigarettes. Before cigarette advertising on television was banned, L&M had a 17 percent market share. After the ban, the decision was made to not advertise, because L&M management believed that other forms of advertising were ineffective. They were wrong, and today L&M is no longer on the market. The brand had good brand recognition and good customer pull.

...ent of the brand name and its positioning, it faded ...ly, from the marketplace.

...stomer-directed sales promotions, such as coupons, ...rewards. When United Airlines initiated its Mileage Plus ...stomers selected airlines and flights. Catalogs such as L.L. ...gel, and many others stimulate customer pull every month with ...stomers. Direct marketing and, more recently, electronic market- ...take a similar, but even more customized, approach to creating cus- ...marketplace.

...sing Elasticity

...rstanding the sales impact of marketing communications is important in market-based ...nagement. The responsiveness of consumers to advertising expenditures can be measured as advertising elasticity. One measure of advertising elasticity is the percent change in sales or volume per 1 percent change in advertising effort. Although there are considerable variations among products and market situations, short-run advertising elasticities are relatively small when compared with price elasticities. A study of 128 advertising elasticities produced an average advertising elasticity of 0.22, with very few advertising elasticities greater than 0.5. This means that for every 1 percent change in advertising expenditures, there will be an estimated 0.22 percent change in volume sold.[11]

For instance, a business with sales of $200,000 per month saw its revenues increase to $220,000 per month after a 50 percent increase in advertising expense as shown in Figure 10-13. In this case, a 10 percent increase in sales based on a 50 percent increase in advertising produced an advertising elasticity of 0.20, as shown in Figure 10-13. For the Gardenburger advertisement that aired once during the *Seinfeld* finale, an advertising elasticity of .66 can be calculated, as shown here:

$$\text{Advertising Elasticity} = \frac{\text{Percent Change in Sales (weekly)}}{\text{Percent Change in Advertising Expense (weekly)}} = \frac{328\%}{500\%} = .66$$

It is important to keep in mind that there are certain limits to what advertising can accomplish with respect to sales response at different stages of a product's life cycle. During the introductory stage, a business builds awareness, comprehension, and interest, but the market demand is small, and even when advertisements are extremely effective, only a limited volume and sales response are achievable.

FIGURE 10-13 ESTIMATING ADVERTISING ELASTICITY

Sales Revenue	Performance	Advertising Expense	Performance	Advertising
Before Advertising	$200,000	Before Advertising	$10,000	Elasticity
After Advertising	$220,000	After Advertising	$15,000	
% Change in Sales	10.0	% Change in Advertising	50.0	0.20

The growth stage of a product's life cycle offers the greatest opportunity for sales gains using advertising. A business that does not invest in advertising during this phase is missing its best opportunity to grow sales, because advertising elasticities will be greatest during this period. However, as a market matures, less new volume comes into the market, and the effects of advertising on sales response begin to diminish. Finally, in declining markets, a business needs to cut back on advertising because dollars spent on advertising produce little, if any, sales response.

Advertising Carryover Effects

In addition to a short-run advertising impact on sales response, advertising also has been shown to have a long-run carryover effect; that is, the advertising effort made in a given period will produce some additional sales response in subsequent sales periods. Advertising carryover coefficients range from zero to less than one, with the average carryover coefficient equal to approximately 0.5.[12] This means that in the period immediately following the ad effort, a 0.50 sales effect from the previous period will carry over. In the second period, the carryover effect of 0.50 is squared, and 0.25 of the sales response produced two periods earlier occurs, and so on, as shown in Figure 10-14.

For the Gardenbuger ad run on the *Seinfeld* show, assume that the carryover effect was 0.5. Recall the Gardenburger advertising elasticity was 0.66. This produced first-week incremental sales (sales above the norm) of approximately $1.5 million. With a 0.50

FIGURE 10-14 MEDIA ADVERTISING AND SALES CARRYOVER

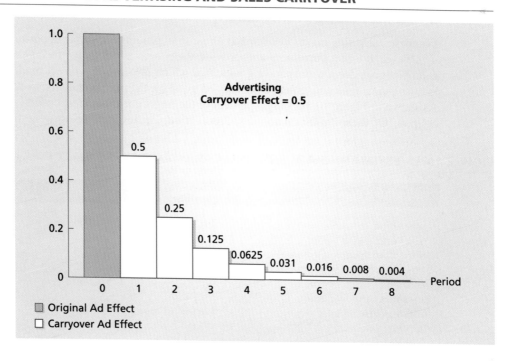

advertising carryover effect, the total impact of this ad expenditure effect is approximately $3 million, as shown here.

$$\frac{\text{Total Sales}}{\text{Effect}} = \frac{\text{Incremental Sales}}{(1 - \text{Carryover Effect})} = \frac{\$1.5 \text{ million}}{(1 - 0.5)} = \$3 \text{ million}$$

Thus, the overall sales response to the advertising effort would have been double the short-run effect as shown in Figure 10-14. Although there are statistical methods that can be used to estimate the carryover effect of a marketing communication, in Figure 10-15 we have laid out a simple method of estimating the next period's carryover sales. In this example, the sales were growing at 2.5 percent per month under normal conditions (normal advertising). With a 50 percent increase in the advertising effort ($10,000 to $15,000), the sales during the month of advertising increased by 10% percent above what would be expected. This results in an advertising elasticity of 0.2. However, in the month following the increased advertising effort, the sales were $5,000 above what would be expected. This 25 percent increase above normal sales represents an estimate of the carryover effect. Assuming it to be true, the full effect on incremental sales is $26,667. Thus, the marketing communications effort produced a period increase of $20,000 and subsequent sales of $6,666 over the next several months.

$$\frac{\text{Total Sales}}{\text{Effect}} = \frac{\text{Incremental Sales}}{(1 - \text{Carryover Effect})} = \frac{\$20,000}{(1 - .25)} = \$26,667$$

Direct Marketing Promotions

Database marketing makes customized direct-mail programs a viable opportunity to efficiently reach target customers and provide them with an incentive to take action. For example, consider a new sparkling wine, for which the producer direct mailed 100,000 known champagne consumers a $5 coupon good on the purchase of its sparkling wine. As shown in Figure 10-16, only 5 percent of the target customers responded by using the coupon. Of these 5,000 customers, 2,000 tried the new sparkling wine but did not

FIGURE 10-15 ESTIMATING ADVERTISING CARRYOVER SALES EFFECT

Advertising Period	Before Ad	Ad	After Ad
Advertising Expense	$10,000	$15,000	$10,000
Sales Performance			
Without Ad Spending Increase	$195,000	$200,000	$205,000
With Ad Spending Increase		$220,000	$210,000
Incremental Sales		$20,000	$5,000
Estimated Carryover Effect	0.25		
Total Incremental Sales	$26,667		
Carryover Sales	$6,667		

FIGURE 10-16 CUSTOMER RESPONSE TO A DIRECT MARKETING PROMOTION

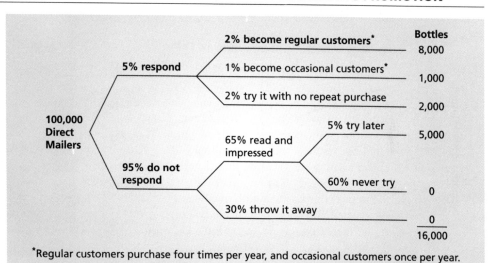

*Regular customers purchase four times per year, and occasional customers once per year.

repurchase; 1,000 used the coupon and became occasional buyers at the rate of one bottle per year; and 2,000 used the coupon and became regular purchasers at the rate of four bottles per year. Among the 95 percent who did not respond, 30 percent never opened the mailer and 65 percent opened it and were favorably impressed. Of these 65,000 customers, 5,000 purchased the product without the coupon at a later date. In total, 16,000 bottles of the new sparkling wine were purchased as a result of the direct-mail program, even though there was only a 5 percent initial response.[13]

Promotional Price Elasticity

The average price elasticity for consumer nondurable products is -1.76 according to a study of 367 brands.[14] However, the price promotion price elasticities for the three product categories shown in Figure 10-17 are considerably higher.[15]

   Assume the market demand for sparkling wine is 10 million bottles per month and that a particular brand has a 4 percent market share resulting in a unit volume of 400,000 bottles. Without advertising, this brand should experience a promotional price elasticity of -10. Thus, a 5 percent price promotion should yield a 50 percent increase in unit volume, from 400,000 to 600,000 per month, as shown here:

$$\text{Unit Volume} = (10 \text{ million} \times .04) \times [1 + (-10 \times -.05)]$$
$$= 400,000 \times 1.5$$
$$= 600,000 \text{ bottles}$$

   By combining a price promotion with advertising, the promotional price elasticity can be further increased, as shown in Figure 10-17. For example, the promotion price elasticity of sparkling wine increases to approximately -14 with the support of an

**FIGURE 10-17 PROMOTIONAL PRICE ELASTICITY WITH
                AND WITHOUT ADVERTISING**

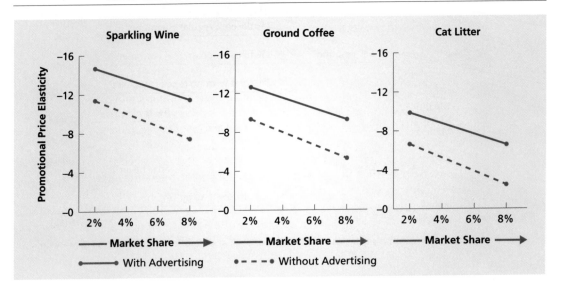

advertising campaign. This would produce additional unit sales of 80,000 with a 5 percent price promotion.

$$\text{Unit Volume} = (10 \text{ million} \times .04) \times [1 + (-14 \times -.05)]$$
$$= 400,000 \times 1.7$$
$$= 680,000 \text{ bottles}$$

In all three cases shown in Figure 10-17, the promotional price elasticity increased significantly with the use of advertising. For cat litter, this effect was very dramatic, doubling promotional elasticities. It is also important to note that the promotional elasticities decreased with the increase in market share.

Recognizing the high level of price sensitivity to promotions and the tremendous short-run revenue gain that can be achieved from a price promotion, one can understand why many companies have increased their use of them. However, a marketing strategy that seeks profitable growth must also produce a higher net marketing contribution. Thus, it is important in market-based management to also assess the profit impact of a marketing communications effort.

PUSH COMMUNICATIONS AND CUSTOMER RESPONSE

Marketing communications directed at intermediaries are designed as push communications; they stimulate intermediaries to engage in aggressive customer promotion efforts. As seen in Figure 10-12, the objective of push communications is to build greater product availability and marketing effort. Businesses that are aggressive in rewarding and supporting channel intermediaries are able to obtain more market coverage (number of desired distributors) than are nonaggressive businesses. This support provides several mechanisms to deliver effective in-store merchandising and marketing efforts of a business's products.

Trade Promotions and Customer Response

Trade promotions designed to stimulate purchase are common among businesses who sell their products through intermediaries. Quite often, trade promotions involve price reductions to distributors or retailers. The idea is that the price incentive will motivate the intermediary to push the product.

For example, assume that a normal can of orange juice concentrate costs $1.49 and the manufacturer offers a $0.20 discount to encourage the retail trade to push the sale of frozen concentrate. Assume also that the normal sales level is one million cans per month; the retailer margin is normally $0.19 per can; the manufacturer's sales and distribution costs are $0.15 per can; and each unit costs $0.50 to produce. In non-promotion months, the manufacturer would expect to make $650,000 in total contribution, as is shown here:

$$
\begin{aligned}
\begin{matrix} \text{Total} \\ \text{Contribution} \\ \text{(current)} \end{matrix} &= \begin{matrix} \text{Current} \\ \text{Volume} \end{matrix} \times \left(\begin{matrix} \text{Retail} \\ \text{Price} \end{matrix} - \begin{matrix} \text{Retailer} \\ \text{Margin} \end{matrix} - \begin{matrix} \text{Sales and} \\ \text{Distributtion Cost} \end{matrix} - \begin{matrix} \text{Unit} \\ \text{Cost} \end{matrix} \right) \\
&= 1{,}000{,}000 \times (\$1.49 - \$0.19 - \$0.15 - \$0.50) \\
&= 1{,}000{,}000 \times \$0.65 \\
&= \$650{,}000
\end{aligned}
$$

An important question for the manufacturer should be how much volume a trade promotion would have to produce to make a promotional period as profitable as a typical non-promotion period. With the discount, the manufacturer's net promotional margin per unit drops to $0.45 per can. As shown, the business would have to increase sales by 44 percent to 1.44 million cans in order to produce the same level of profitability.

$$
\$650{,}000 = \frac{\text{Promotion}}{\text{Volume}} \times (\$1.49 - \$0.19 - \$0.15 - \$0.50 - \$0.20 \text{ discount})
$$

$$
\$650{,}000 = \frac{\text{Promotion}}{\text{Volume}} \times \$.45
$$

$$
\frac{\text{Promotion}}{\text{Volume}} = 1.44 \text{ million units}
$$

Forward Buying and Customer Response

Trade promotions such as the one just described often result in forward buying by both customers and retailers. If the product is promoted effectively, customers will buy more during the promotion and will not have the same level of need in the following non-promotion period. the impact of customer forward buying was presented in Chapter 8 with the discussion of price promotions.

Retailer forward buying involves less buying before the trade promotion as well as buying more than is needed during the promotion to take full advantage of the discounted price. These aspects of retailer trade promotion forward buying are illustrated in Figure 10-18. As shown with a trade promotion, inventory is depleted before the promotion ends and more than replenished during the trade promotion.

The net effect of forward buying is that retailers are able to buy at lower prices for a period much longer than the promotion. One study found that 80 percent of the products purchased by retailers were purchased at promotional prices. Buying at promotional

FIGURE 10-18 RETAILER INVENTORIES AND FORWARD BUYING ON A TRADE PROMOTION

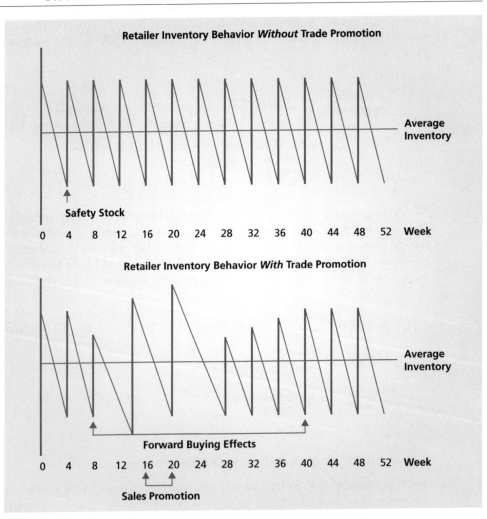

prices, of course, greatly affects the manufacturer's profitability. This combination of customer stockpiling (customer forward buying) and deal-prone shopping (switching from one deal to another) makes it difficult for manufacturers to make a profit on push sale promotions.[16]

Market Infrastructure and Push Communications

Figure 10-19 illustrates a communications market infrastructure that includes both end customers and intermediaries and non-market sources that influence them.[17] For example, marketing communications targeted at industry gurus, consultants, and financial analysts create secondary marketing communications that, in turn, influence the trade press, business press, and the general press. These non-market sources of influence, in turn, provide information to channel intermediaries and customers.

The solid lines in Figure 10-19 represent normal marketing communications targeted at customers or intermediaries. Dashed lines are indirect communications—the

FIGURE 10-19 MARKET INFRASTRUCTURE AND PUSH
MARKETING COMMUNICATIONS

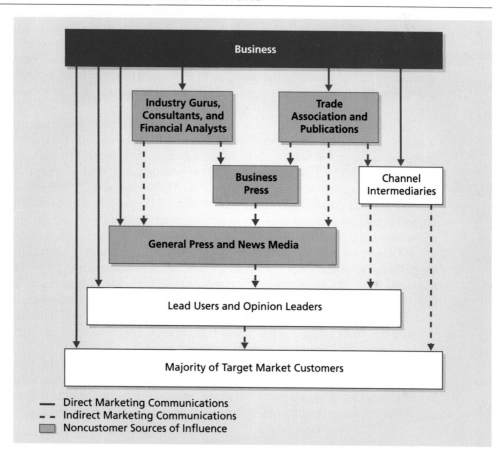

type of communications targeted at individuals and institutions that influence customers and channel intermediaries. Some of these indirect communications are *primary* communications (from the company to the source of the influence), and others are *secondary* communications (from one source of influence to another). Of course, one of the most important sources of secondary marketing communications is from lead users and opinion leaders who communicate by word of mouth to the larger market of target customers.

■ Summary

Without an effective marketing communications program, a marketing strategy will fail. Target customers must be made aware of the product and its benefits, be continually reminded of these benefits, and be stimulated to take action. Building awareness, message comprehension, and interest are essential phases in building a high level of customer response. The customer response index is a diagnostic tool to help a management team determine the sources of weakness in its marketing communications program.

To be effective and cost efficient, a business's marketing communications must reach target customers and deliver an adequate level of message frequency to maintain desired levels of awareness, comprehension, and interest. Pulsing enables a business to use alternate exposure periods to more economically maintain customer awareness and interest while reducing the problem of ad copy wearout. Heavy-up efforts enable a business to build awareness and interest to higher levels during seasonal buying periods.

To build market share, a business needs both pull and push marketing communications. Pull marketing communications are targeted at customers with the intent of creating enough awareness and interest to motivate customers to demand the business's product. This customer demand creates market pull on intermediaries who, in turn, want the business's products to satisfy this customer demand. Push marketing communications are directed at intermediaries, with the intent of pushing the product through the channel. The objective of push communications is to create greater availability of, interest in, and access to the business's products.

Although the sales response to a marketing communication is difficult to estimate, the customer response index, advertising elasticity, advertising carryover effects, and promotional price elasticity provide systematic methods for estimating this response. However, sales response should not be the primary objective of a marketing communication. For marketing communications designed to increase sales, it is more important to estimate the profit impact of that promotion. Many sales promotions are not profitable, but businesses are forced into them to minimize losses.

In most markets, there is a marketing communications infrastructure that includes customers, intermediaries, and non-market sources of influence. Some push through marketing communications are public relations–type communications directed at nonmarket sources of influence that, in turn, influence customers and intermediaries.

■ Market-Based Logic and Strategic Thinking

1 What role does message exposure play in the success of a marketing communication?

2 Why are customer awareness and message comprehension critical to the success of a marketing strategy?

3 How can interest in ad copy affect interest in a product and, subsequently, customer response?

4 When a business has an excellent marketing communications program and high intention to purchase, but a very low customer response, what kind of a marketing problem does it face?

5 When should a business use a combination of pulsing and heavy-up marketing communications?

6 Why is the message frequency for a marketing communication considerably lower than the number of messages sent?

7 Why will a business's market share be lower if it is not effective in both pull-through and push-through marketing communications?

8 At what stage of a product's life cycle is advertising elasticity likely to be highest?

9 How should the carryover sales effect of an advertising effort be used in evaluating the profit impact of the advertising effort?

10 What are the various behaviors that need to be tracked in order to evaluate the profit impact of a trade promotion?

11 How does the promotional price elasticity for a product change with advertising support? What effect does market share have on promotional price elasticity?

12 Why are the marketing communications infrastructure and public relations–type marketing communications important to the overall success of a marketing communications effort?

13 If advertising elasticity is so much smaller than promotional price elasticity, why should a business advertise?

14 How should a business use the advertising carryover effect in evaluating the sales response and profitability of a marketing communication?

15 Why are indirect sales promotions rarely profitable? If they are not profitable, why do manufacturers continue to offer them?

16 How does retailer forward buying affect trade promotion profitability?

Marketing Performance Tools

Each of the following **marketing performance tools** can be accessed by going to *www.rogerjbest.com* or *www.prenhall.com/best*. The shaded cells are input cells. The nonshaded cells contain results calculated from your input values.

MARKETING PERFORMANCE TOOL—Estimating Ad Effectiveness and Customer Response

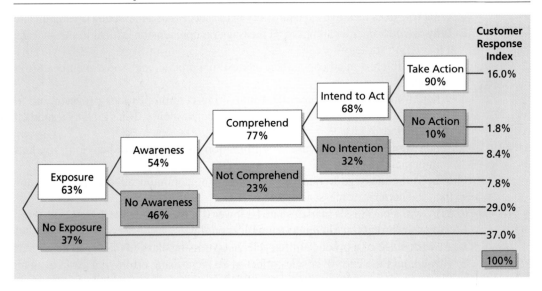

This **marketing performance tool** allows you to estimate the customer response for different levels of marketing communication effectiveness. The data provided is from Figure 10-2. The shaded numeric input cells can be changed in doing the following application exercise.

Application Exercise: Using the data provided, how would the results of this marketing communication change if advertising exposure was only 50 percent? Using the results provided, evaluate the impact on improving ad awareness from 68 percent to 75 percent. For future advertisements, would it be more effective to work on increasing comprehension by 10 points (43 percent to 53 percent) or to work in improving intentions to purchase by 10 points (33 percent to 43 percent)?

MARKETING PERFORMANCE TOOL—Estimating Advertising Elasticity

Sales Revenue	Performance	Advertising Expense	Performance	Advertising
Before Advertising	$200,000	Before Advertising	$10,000	Elasticity
After Advertising	$220,000	After Advertising	$15,000	
% Change in Sales	10.0	% Change in Advertising	50.0	0.20

This **marketing performance tool** allows you to estimate the advertising elasticity for a marketing communication effort. The data provided is from Figure 10-13. The shaded numeric input cells can be changed in doing the following application exercise.

Application Exercise: Using the data provided, how would the advertising elasticity change if the sales after advertising were $215,000 rather than $220,000? What level of sales increase would be needed to obtain an advertising elasticity of 0.33?

MARKETING PERFORMANCE TOOL—Estimating Advertising Carryover Sales Effect

Advertising Period	Before Ad	Ad	After Ad
Advertising Expense	$10,000	$15,000	$10,000
Sales Performance			
Without Ad Spending Increase	$195,000	$200,000	$205,000
With Ad Spending Increase		$220,000	$210,000
Incremental Sales		$20,000	$5,000
Estimated Carryover Effect	0.25		
Total Incremental Sales	$26,667		
Carryover Sales	$6,667		

This **marketing performance tool** allows you to estimate the advertising carryover effect for a marketing communication effort. The data provided is from Figure 10-14. The shaded numeric input cells can be changed in doing the following application exercise.

Application Exercise: Using the data provided, how would the carryover effect change if the incremental sales after advertising were $10,000 rather than $5,000? How would the new carryover effect (estimated in the previous question) impact the overall incremental sales of the marketing communications effort?

Notes

1. Betty Arndt, "Johnson Controls' 'Classic Buildings' Marketing Campaign—A Pre- and Post-Campaign Evaluation," in *Drive Marketing Excellence* (New York: Institute for International Research, 1994).
2. Peter Danaher and Roland Rust, "Determining the Optimal Level of Media Spending," *Journal of Advertising Research* (January–February 1994): 28–34.
3. David Bender, Peter Farquhar, and Sanford Schulert, "Growing from the Top," *Marketing Management* (Winter/Spring 1996): 10–19.
4. H. Zielske, "The Remembering and Forgetting of Advertising," *Journal of Marketing* (January 1959): 140; and J. Simon, "What Do Zielske's Real Data Really Show About Pulsing," *Journal of Marketing Research* (August 1979): 415–420.
5. Brian Wansink and Michael Ray, "Advertising Strategies to Increase Usage Frequency," *Journal of Marketing* (January 1996): 31–46.
6. Bill Abrams, "Consumer-Product Techniques Help Loctite Sell to Industry," *Wall Street Journal* (April 2, 1981).
7. Vijay Mahajan, Eitan Muller, John E. Little, and Hugh Zielske, "Advertising Pulsing Policies for Generating Awareness of New Products," *Marketing Science* (Spring 1986): 86–106.
8. Cliff Havener and Margaret Thorpe, "Customers Can Tell You What They Want," *Management Review* (December 1994): 42–45.
9. David Reibstein, "Making the Most of Your Marketing Dollars," *Drive Marketing Excellence* (New York: Institute for International Research, 1994).
10. Gary Lilien, Philip Kotler, and K. Moorthy, *Marketing Models* (Upper Saddle River, NJ: Prentice Hall, 1992): 329–356.
11. Gert Assmus, John Farley, and Donald Lehmann, "How Advertising Affects Sales: Meta Analysis of Econometric Results," *Journal of Marketing Research* (February 1984): 65–74.
12. Ron Schultz and Martin Block, "Empirical Estimates of Advertising Response Factors," *Journal of Media Planning* (Fall 1986): 17–24.
13. Stan Rapp and Tom Collins, *Maximarketing* (New York: McGraw-Hill, 1987).
14. Robert Blattberg and Scott Neslin, *Sales Promotion Concepts, Methods and Strategies* (Upper Saddle River, NJ: Prentice Hall, 1990): 356.
15. Albert Bemmaor and Dominique Mouchoux, "Measuring the Short-Term Effect of In-Store Promotion and Retail Advertising on Brand Sales," *Journal of Marketing Research* (May 1991): 202–214.
16. Robert Blattberg and Alan Levin, "Modeling the Effectiveness and Profitability of Trade Promotions," *Marketing Science* (Spring 1987): 124–46.
17. Regis McKenna, *The Regis Touch: New Marketing Strategies for Uncertain Times* (Reading, MA: Addison-Wesley, 1985).

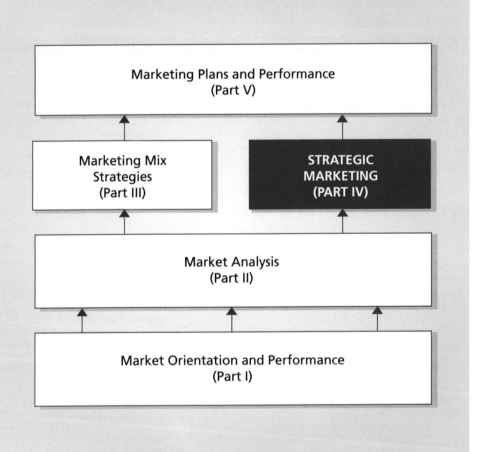

PART IV

Strategic Marketing

■ The concept is interesting and well-formed, but in order to earn better than a "C" grade, the idea must be feasible.
— *Yale University professor's comments on Fred Smith's thesis proposing the overnight delivery service known today as FedEx*

S trategic market planning sets the strategic direction for a business and plays a critical part in achieving a business's long-run objectives of sales growth, profit performance, and share position. Marketing mix strategies (covered in Part III) are more tactical, but essential to establishing desired target market positions and producing short-run growth and profit performance. Both impact growth, profitability, and share position. Long-run marketing strategies set the strategic direction, while short-run target market positioning strategies provide the marketing tactics needed to work incrementally toward long-run goals.

To facilitate the strategic market planning process, each product-market of interest is strategically assessed with respect to its market attractiveness and position of competitive advantage. Using these two dimensions of strategic opportunity and position, in Chapter 11 we present a method of building a strategic market-planning portfolio that includes all existing and potential product-markets.

The strategic market plans generated by the portfolio analysis can be either offensive or defensive. Offensive strategic market plans, presented in Chapter 12, are growth-oriented plans built around share penetration or market growth of existing markets or plans to enter new, existing, or emerging markets. Offensive strategic market plans are critical to business growth and future market position and profitability.

Defensive strategic market plans, presented in Chapter 13, are designed to protect market positions and profitability. Defensive strategic market plans can include protecting profitable market positions, reducing market focus to improve profitability, and harvesting and divestment strategies that will terminate with market exit. Defensive strategic market plans are critical to current share, sales, and profit performance.

CHAPTER 11

Strategic Market Planning

The General Electric Company (GE) has evolved from having a relatively concentrated focus on electrical products to having a diverse portfolio of product-markets, as shown in Figure 11-1. Today, the GE portfolio includes light bulbs, household appliances, medical systems, plastics, transformers, jet engines, financial services, transportation equipment, steam turbines, and broadcasting. However, each product-market in the GE portfolio is under continuous review with respect to share position, sales growth, and profit performance in an effort to meet shareholder performance expectations.

Jeffrey Immelt, the GE CEO to follow Jack Welch, used this type of strategic market planning portfolio to communicate to the investment community his vision for profitable growth. Through a combination of market development and company acquisition, GE pursues strategic market opportunities in its various businesses. Although all of GE's businesses have some level of projected sales growth, broadcasting and medical systems are strategically important for GE to achieve its targeted sales and profits in 2005. In broadcasting, for example, GE's subsidiary company NBC merged in 2004 with Vivendi Universal, a French media and telecommunications conglomerate, to become NBC Universal, one of the world's leading global media companies. This merger positioned GE for faster growth in the international entertainment market.

Successful companies such as General Electric, Procter & Gamble, and Hewlett-Packard achieve success year after year with a great deal of strategic market planning.[1] These businesses are committed to serving shareholders, and this requires continuous review of current performance, new opportunities, and funding and investment decisions that contribute to a balance of short- and long-run performance. Product-market diversification is one aspect of portfolio analysis and strategic market planning.

PRODUCT-MARKET DIVERSIFICATION

Diversification across product-markets adds two important advantages to the overall performance of a business. First, it reduces dependence on any single product-market. Second, by diversifying, a business can smooth overall performance with offsetting conditions created by the competitive conditions and product life cycles in different product-markets.

FIGURE 11-1 GE BUSINESS PORTFOLIO AND PROFITABLE GROWTH PLAN

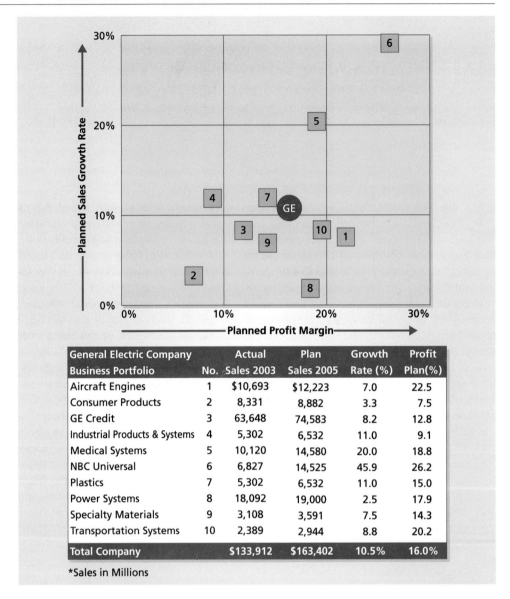

General Electric Company Business Portfolio	No.	Actual Sales 2003	Plan Sales 2005	Growth Rate (%)	Profit Plan(%)
Aircraft Engines	1	$10,693	$12,223	7.0	22.5
Consumer Products	2	8,331	8,882	3.3	7.5
GE Credit	3	63,648	74,583	8.2	12.8
Industrial Products & Systems	4	5,302	6,532	11.0	9.1
Medical Systems	5	10,120	14,580	20.0	18.8
NBC Universal	6	6,827	14,525	45.9	26.2
Plastics	7	5,302	6,532	11.0	15.0
Power Systems	8	18,092	19,000	2.5	17.9
Specialty Materials	9	3,108	3,591	7.5	14.3
Transportation Systems	10	2,389	2,944	8.8	20.2
Total Company		$133,912	$163,402	10.5%	16.0%

*Sales in Millions

For example, Figure 11-2 illustrates the overall sales of a business that is diversified across different product-markets. In product-market A, its core market, sales are growing at an average rate of 1.5 percent per year, but this growth varies from year to year because of economic conditions and competitive forces. Because the business is also positioned in two other, diversified product-markets, it is able to take advantage of offsetting product life cycles and competitive forces. Product-market B is growing at 4 percent per year and product-market C at almost 15 percent per year. Although sales in each of these two markets are much less than in the company's core market, product-market A, each contributes to overall sales growth and stabilizes performance.

FIGURE 11-2 PRODUCT-MARKET DIVERSIFICATION AND SALES PERFORMANCE

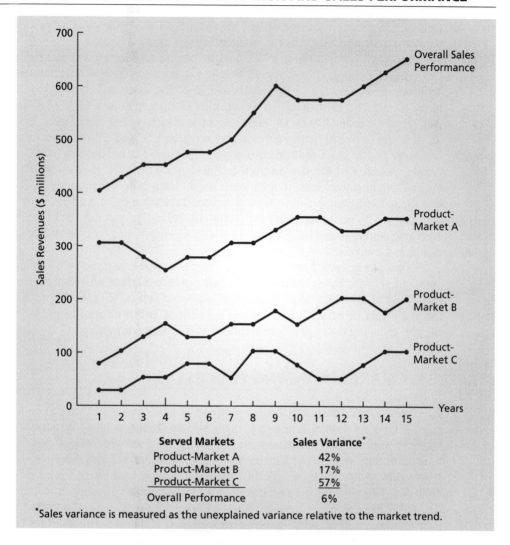

Served Markets	Sales Variance*
Product-Market A	42%
Product-Market B	17%
Product-Market C	57%
Overall Performance	6%

*Sales variance is measured as the unexplained variance relative to the market trend.

The unexplained sales variance over the time period shown for product-market A is 42 percent, and for product-markets B and C, 17 and 57 percent, respectively. When the sales performances of all three markets are combined, the offsetting effects created by different competitive conditions and product life cycles produce more consistent growth, with only a 6 percent unexplained variance in the sales trend for the time period shown.

TWO LEVELS OF DIVERSIFICATION

Product diversification provides one level of diversification. Obviously, the less dependent a business is on a single product, the less vulnerable it is to a major change in performance. For instance, Coca-Cola has a broad line of beverage products that serves virtually all world markets. For Procter & Gamble, diversification goes further, because P&G has developed product positions in widely diversified consumer household product-markets. General Electric, as discussed earlier, has expanded into a wide range of product-markets unrelated to its original electrical products.

Market diversification provides another way to achieve growth and risk reduction. DuPont, for example, has diversified across many markets that range from carpets to swimsuits and cookware with products such as Nylon, Dacron, Teflon, Lycra, Kevlar, and many others. This diversification has enabled DuPont to grow to a $50 billion company and yet not be dependent on any one product or market. In the early 1990s, US West split its company in two to better serve diverse markets. US West Communications remained in charge of the more mature core telecommunications businesses, while MediaOne Group was created to grow in high-technology markets. In the late 1990s, Hewlett-Packard pursued the same strategy when it split itself into two companies: an $8 billion test and measurement business named Agilent Technologies, and a $39 billion computer and imaging business that kept the name HP. This split enabled HP to move faster in emerging computer and imaging markets without abandoning its core product-markets in test and measurement.

Every product-market is eventually going to experience periods of economic recession and growth, but it is unlikely that all product-markets will experience the same conditions at the same time. Thus, participation in several diversified product-markets has the effect of offsetting economic conditions and product life cycle influences, thereby reducing the overall variability of business performance.

STRATEGIC MARKET PLANNING PROCESS

Each product-market in a business's portfolio in some way contributes to both the short-run and the long-run performance of the business—and, depending on current and future share position and performance, some product-markets will receive additional investment to grow or defend an important strategic market position. Other product-markets will be required to reduce focus in order to achieve a stronger competitive position and profit contribution with available resources. Still others may have resources withdrawn from them as a business begins to exit these product-markets. Because resources in any business are limited, a strategic market plan is needed to carefully map out its future share position, sales growth, and profit performance. A strategic market plan sets the direction and provides guidelines for resource allocation.[2]

In order to specify a strategic direction for a product-market and to allocate resources to obtain desired short- and long-run performance, a business needs a strategic market planning process,[3] as outlined in Figure 11-3. The first step in this process is a careful assessment of current business performance, market attractiveness, and competitive advantage for each product-market a business wishes to consider over a 3- to 5-year strategic market planning horizon. With this information, the business can perform a *portfolio analysis* to better understand the current position of each product-market and its performance. On the basis of the portfolio position of each product-market, a *strategic market plan* can then be specified with respect to a desired set of performance objectives.

However, to make the strategic market plan actionable, the business has to develop a marketing mix strategy in accordance with the strategic market plan and resources

FIGURE 11-3 STRATEGIC MARKET PLANNING PROCESS

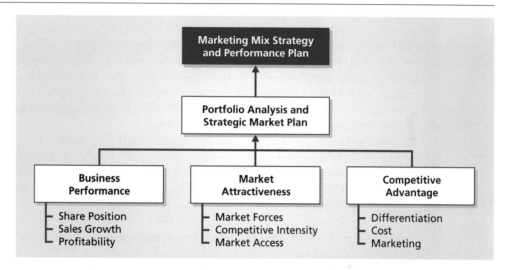

allocated. As the strategic market plan and a corresponding marketing mix strategy are rolled out over a planning horizon, a performance plan outlines the targeted short-run and long-run share position, sales growth, and profitability.[4] This chapter reviews the strategic market planning process and how it maps the short- and long-run performance of a business.

BUSINESS PERFORMANCE

Because each product-market can vary in attractiveness and competitive advantage, there can be a wide range of performance outcomes. The primary objective of a strategic market plan is to create a strategic direction and set of objectives for any product-market that affect three critical areas of business performance:

- **Share Position:** How will the strategic market plan contribute to the product-market's share and competitive advantage?
- **Sales Growth:** How much will the strategic market plan contribute to the business's sales growth?
- **Profit Performance:** How will the strategic market plan affect short- and long-run profitability and contribute to shareholder value?

The strategic market plan for any given product-market is intended to produce results in all three areas of business performance. One of the primary objectives of a strategic market plan is to make explicit how share position, sales revenue, and profit performance will change over time. For instance, a strategic market plan to *grow* share in a growing market will produce drastically different levels of performance than will a strategic market plan to *protect* market share in an increasingly competitive mature market.

MARKET ATTRACTIVENESS

The primary purpose of a strategic market plan is to provide a strategic direction from which to set performance objectives and guide the development of a tactical marketing mix strategy. This is an important step in the strategic market planning process, because it requires a careful examination of market attractiveness. This step allows a company to compare the relative attractiveness of different product-markets using a common set of attractiveness criteria. To facilitate this step in the strategic market planning process, we need a systematic way to assess market attractiveness.

To assess and index the attractiveness of a product-market, a business must ask itself, *"What factors make a market attractive or unattractive?"* Factors that typically shape market attractiveness include market size, market growth, competition, margin potential, market access, and fit with the company's core capabilities. These factors can be meaningfully grouped into three dimensions of market attractiveness: market forces, competitive intensity, and market access, as shown in Figure 11-4.

To create a measure of market attractiveness, each of these three dimensions can be weighted to reflect its importance in relation to the others. In the example presented in Figure 11-5, market forces and market access are both weighted at 30 percent of the total importance, whereas competitive intensity is weighted a little more heavily at 40 percent. Each dimension is further broken down into several factors that contribute to that particular dimension of market attractiveness. Each of these factors is also weighted to represent its relative importance within that dimension of market attractiveness.

By rating the attractiveness of each factor within each dimension, an overall index for market attractiveness can be created, as illustrated in Figure 11-5. The industry forces that influence market attractiveness may be different for each situation, so the factors in each dimension that are appropriate for your analysis may be different from the ones listed in Figure 11-5. Special care should be taken to ensure that all the underlying forces that shape market attractiveness are adequately represented, on the basis of market and profit performance.[5]

FIGURE 11-4 FACTORS THAT SHAPE MARKET ATTRACTIVENESS

FIGURE 11-5 MARKET ATTRACTIVENESS INDEX

Very Unattractive	Unattractive	Somewhat Unattractive	Somewhat Attractive	Attractive	Very Attractive
0	20	40	60	80	100

Market Attractiveness Factors	Market Attractiveness Rating	Relative Importance*	Market Attractiveness Score
Market Forces			
Market Size	80	40%	32
Rate Growth	60	30%	18
Buyer Power	40	30%	12
Market Forces Total			62
× Relative Importance of Market Forces		30%	18.6
Competitive Intensity			
Price Rivalry	40	40%	16
Ease of Entry	80	30%	24
Substitutes	60	30%	18
Competitive Intensity Total			58
× Relative Importance of Competitive Intensity		40%	23.2
Market Access			
Customer Familiarity	80	40%	32
Channel Access	100	30%	30
Sales Requirements	60	30%	18
Market Access Total			80
× Relative Importance of Market Access		30%	24.0
Market Attractiveness Index		18.6 + 23.2 + 24.0 = 65.8	

*Relative Importance sums to 100%.

In the example shown, each individual market attractiveness factor is rated from "very unattractive" (0) to "very attractive" (100) for a given product-market. This rating is multiplied by the relative importance of that factor to obtain a weighted individual factor attractiveness score. The sum of these individual scores for each dimension is computed and multiplied by the importance given that dimension. For example, market size is given a rating of 80 for attractiveness and is assigned 40 percent of relative importance within the market forces dimension. This method of indexing market attractiveness results in a score of 32 (80 × 40) for this factor. This score is added to the scores of the other factors in this dimension to arrive at a total factor-weighted score of 62. This is multiplied by 0.30, the relative importance weight assigned to the market forces dimension, to produce a weighted overall score of 18.6 for market forces. When this process is completed for all the market attractiveness factors and dimensions, an overall market attractiveness index of 65.8 is obtained.

COMPETITIVE ADVANTAGE

The process of developing a multifactor index of competitive advantage follows the same procedure. The first question is, *"What makes one business strong, with respect to competitive advantage, and another weak?"* In answering this question, many businesses will arrive at a list of factors that determine competitive advantage that can be categorized into three dimensions of competitive advantage: differentiation advantage, cost advantage, and marketing advantage. Each of these drivers of competitive advantage also has underlying forces that shape the business's competitive advantage,[6] as shown in Figure 11-6.

Each of the three dimensions of competitive advantage is assigned a relative weight, just as was done in determining market attractiveness. As with market attractiveness, for each of the underlying factors the relative importance within the dimension must be determined, as illustrated in Figure 11-7. Each factor must be assessed with respect to the competitive advantage of the business in its existing market or the potential position in new markets under consideration.

As shown in Figure 11-7, the competitive forces that shape a differentiation advantage for this business are relatively strong and make up more than half of the overall competitive advantage index of 54.8. The business's competitive advantage with respect to marketing advantage is weak (6.8). This is due to a lower dimension weighting (20 percent) and a lower factor rating. Overall, the business is midrange in terms of competitive advantage, with an index of 54.8.

PORTFOLIO ANALYSIS AND STRATEGIC MARKET PLANS

When combining the overall competitive advantage score with the overall market attractiveness score, we create a product-market portfolio. Each product-market served by a business can be placed in a portfolio such as the one shown in Figure 11-8. Product-markets strong in both market attractiveness and competitive advantage present the strongest portfolio position and the best opportunities for profit performance.[7] Having product-markets in this position usually leads to a strategic market plan to invest to protect this attractive position of advantage. For each combination of market attractiveness and competitive advantage, there is at

FIGURE 11-6 DETERMINANTS OF COMPETITIVE ADVANTAGE

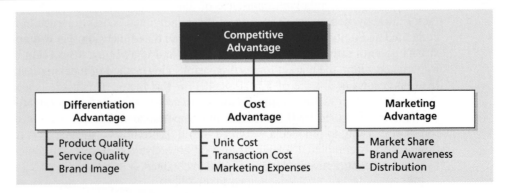

FIGURE 11-7 COMPETITIVE ADVANTAGE INDEX

Major Disadvantage	Definite Disadvantage	Slight Disadvantage	Slight Advantage	Definite Advantage	Major Advantage
0	20	40	60	80	100

Sources of Competitive Advantage	Competitive Advantage Rating	Relative Importance*	Competitive Advantage Score
Differentiation Advantage			
Product Quality	80	40%	32
Service Quality	60	30%	18
Brand Image	80	30%	24
Differentiation Advantage Total			**74**
× Relative Importance of Differentiation Advantage		40%	**29.6**
Cost Advantage			
Unit Cost	40	70%	28
Transaction Costs	60	20%	12
Marketing Expenses	60	10%	6
Cost Advantage Total			46
× Relative Importance of Cost Advantage		40%	**18.4**
Marketing Advantage			
Market Share	40	40%	16
Brand Awareness	40	30%	12
Distribution	20	30%	6
Marketing Advantage Total			34
× Relative Importance of Marketing Advantage		20%	**6.8**
Competitive Advantage Index		29.6 + 18.4 + 6.8 = 54.8	

*Relative Importance of sums to 100%.

least one strategic market plan to be considered.[8] Each of these strategic market plans is further explained in the following comments.

- **Invest to Grow:** This is an offensive strategic market plan to invest marketing resources to grow the market or a product's position in a market. For example, Dell Computer has invested heavily over the past 15 years to grow both the personal computer market and its market share in this market.
- **Invest to Improve Position:** This is an offensive strategic market plan that seeks to improve a business's competitive advantage in an attractive segment of the market. Lexus, Mercedes, and BMW have selectively invested to strengthen their competitive positions in the SUV segment of the automotive market. This is a segment that was growing in market attractiveness but each of these companies lacked a competitive product in this segment relative to market leaders.

FIGURE 11-8 PORTFOLIO ANALYSIS AND STRATEGIC MARKET PLANS

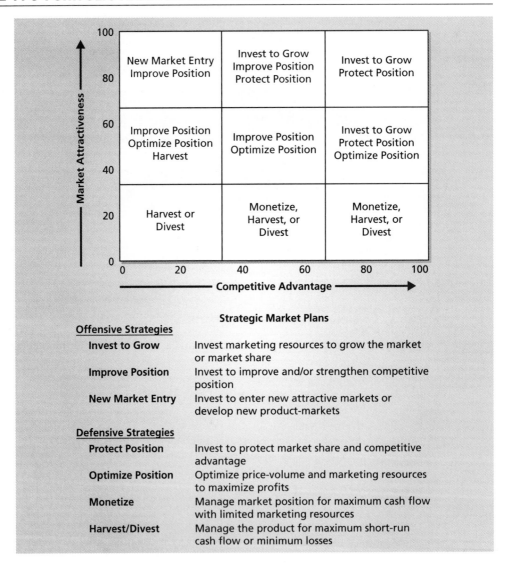

- **New-Market Entry:** This is an offensive strategy to enter new attractive markets. Toyota was among the first to enter the hybrid automotive market and plans to strengthen its competitive advantage in this market in 2005 with the addition of five new hybrid cars. New-market development strategies are required for many new product-markets, including flat-screen televisions, cellular phones, and DVD players. New-market development strategies require a large investment in marketing resources and will operate at a loss until market volumes reach breakeven levels.
- **Protect Position:** This is a defensive strategy to invest to protect an attractive market position in which the business dominates with respect to competitive advantage.

Gatorade in the sports drink market and Red Bull in the energy drink market both have market shares over 80 percent. Although these markets are attractive and growing, these products will come under increasing attack as new competitors enter the market.

- **Optimize Position:** This defensive strategy often occurs in the late stages of growth and mature stages of the product life cycle. When growth potential is limited and competitive position is set, businesses need to optimize the marketing mix to produce maximum marketing profits. This is the stage of the product life cycle were volumes are nearly at full potential and margins are still somewhat attractive. Additions to marketing resources can occur at a slower rate because the product-market is mature. A business using this defensive strategy can make a conscious effort to reduce its customer base in order to reach a more profitable level of business. Many banks have redefined their customer base by charging fees for small accounts that cannot be profitably served. As higher fees force many customers out, these banks are able to grow profits with a smaller, more focused customer base. When managed correctly, optimizing position at the later stages of the product life cycle should allow the product to produce its maximum profits.

- **Monetize Strategy:** This is a defensive strategy that occurs in less attractive markets in which a business has some level of competitive advantage. A monetize strategy means managing prices and marketing resources in a way that maximizes cash flow without exiting the market. Businesses in the cash flow mode often reduce terms of payment with credit card purchases, do not pay for shipping, and offer few customer services. Although price competitive, these business minimize their investment in these products and seek to get the maximum cash flow from their market position.

- **Harvest/Divest Strategy:** A harvest strategy strives to maximize profits and cash flow as a business slowly exits a product-market. Prices are increased to improve margins as volumes decline. In the short run, this produces higher levels of total contribution. Reductions in marketing expenses lower the cost of marketing. A divest strategy is best utilized when there is no prospect of short-run profits. Exiting the product-market is simply a way to cut losses quickly and reallocate marketing resources to more productive endeavors.

As shown in Figure 11-8, attractive product-markets usually warrant an offensive strategic market plan. Strategic market plans can vary from improving a business's competitive advantage in attractive market situations to entering a new market. In addition, there may be opportunities to help develop or grow attractive emerging markets in which the business has the potential for a strong competitive advantage.

On the basis of a portfolio analysis and performance objectives, a business selects either an offensive or a defensive strategic market plan. First, with respect to performance objectives, offensive strategic market plans are geared to deliver above-average performance in the areas of sales growth, share position, and long-run profit performance. Defensive strategic market plans are important in protecting important share positions and producing short-run profit performance, while also contributing to long-run profit. Strategic market planning requires a careful balance of offensive and defensive strategic market plans in order to meet short-run profit objectives and investor expectations while investing in the business to protect important strategic positions, as well as developing stronger share positions in existing or new markets.

Offensive Strategic Market Plans and Performance Impact

Because offensive strategic market plans are more growth oriented than are defensive plans, they are more likely to occur in attractive markets.[9] For example, consider Dell Computer, which grew from a college-dorm-room startup in 1984 to the number one position in global PC sales 16 years later. By 2000, Dell had attained 10.2 percent share in the market for personal computer market that was growing at a rate of 5 to 6 percent per year, amounting to sales of over $25 billion. Although industry margins were declining, Dell as the low-cost leader maintained higher-than-average margins and produced $5.2 billion in gross profit in 2000. With a more efficient marketing strategy, Dell produced a net marketing contribution of $2.8 billion in 2000. This equates to a Marketing ROS of 11.3 percent and Marketing ROI of 119 percent.

2000 Actual Performance

$$\text{Sales Revenue (2000)} = \text{Market Demand} \times \text{Market Share}$$
$$= \$248 \text{ billion} \times 10.2\% = \$25.3 \text{ billion}$$

$$\text{Gross Profit (2000)} = \text{Sales Revenue} \times \text{Percent Margin}$$
$$= \$25.3 \text{ billion} \times 20.7\% = \$5.2 \text{ billion}$$

$$\text{Net Marketing Contribution} = \text{Gross Profit} - \text{Marketing, Sales, \& Administrative Expenses}$$
$$= \$5.2 \text{ billion} - \$5.2 \text{ billion} = \$5.2 \text{ billion}$$

Figure 11-9 shows Dell's 2000 actual performance side-by-side with estimated results of a possible offensive and a possible defensive strategy, as well as the actual outcome for the fiscal year ending in 2004. An offensive strategy for Dell to continue to grow market share to 15 percent in an expanding market would present a bigger

FIGURE 11-9 ESTIMATED OUTCOMES OF ALTERNATIVE STRATEGIC MARKET PLANS

Dell Computer Actual vs. Planned Performance	Actual 2000	Offensive Plan—2004 Grow Share	Defensive Plan—2004 Hold Share	Actual 2004
Market Demand (billions)	$248.0	$310.0	$310.0	$290.0
Market Share (%)	10.2	15.0	10.2	14.3
Sales Revenues (billions)	$ 25.3	$ 46.5	$ 31.6	$ 41.4
Percent Margin (%)	20.7	18.0	18.0	18.2
Gross Profit (billions)	$ 5.2	$ 8.4	$ 5.7	$ 7.6
Marketing Expenses (% of sales)	9.4	9.4	9.4	8.5
Marketing Expenses (billions)	$ 2.4	$ 4.4	$ 3.0	$ 3.5
Net Marketing Contribution (billions)	$ 2.8	$ 4.0	$ 2.7	$ 4.0
Marketing ROS (%)	11.3	8.6	8.6	9.7
Marketing ROI (%)	119	91	91	114

strategic challenge. This strategic market plan would require Dell to increase its marketing resources from $2.4 billion in 2000 to $4.4 billion in 2004. Based on market growth and market share assumptions, sales were projected to grow to $46.5 billion. Margin erosion was expected to continue as PC prices fall, and margins in 2004 were forecasted to be 18 percent. If this held true, Dell's gross profit in 2004 would be $8.4 billion despite declining margins (from 20.7 percent in 2000 to 18 percent in 2004). The net result would be an increase in net marketing contribution of $1.2 billion. Decreasing margins would dilute marketing profits, as Marketing ROS in 2004 decreased to 8.6 percent and Marketing ROI decreased to 91 percent.

2004 – Estimated Performance of an Offensive Strategy to Grow Market Share

$$\text{Sales Revenue (2000)} = \text{Market Demand} \times \text{Market Share}$$
$$= \$310 \text{ billion} \times 15\% = \$46.5 \text{ billion}$$

$$\text{Gross Profit (2000)} = \text{Sales Revenue} \times \text{Percent Margin}$$
$$= \$46.5 \text{ billion} \times 18.0\% = \$8.4 \text{ billion}$$

$$\text{Net Marketing Contribution} = \text{Gross Profit} - \text{Marketing, Sales, \& Administrative Expenses}$$
$$= \$8.4 \text{ billion} - \$4.4 \text{ billion} = \$4.0 \text{ billion}$$

Although Dell's efficiency in producing marketing profits diminished as the PC market has approached the late stages of market growth, Dell's 20-year offensive strategy has positioned the company well for when the PC market matures and Dell will have to rethink its strategic market plan for the PC market.

Defensive Strategic Market Plans and Performance Impact

Defensive strategic market plans are designed to protect important strategic market positions and to be large contributors to short-run cash flow and profit performance. As shown in Figure 11-8, defensive strategic market plans are most likely to occur in attractive markets with strong competitive advantage or in unattractive markets with weak levels of competitive advantage.

As shown in Figure 11-10, defensive strategic market plans involve protecting or reducing the market position within existing markets.[10] Defensive strategic market plans can also involve monetizing for maximum cash flow or harvesting or divesting market share positions in existing markets.[11] As such, defensive strategic market plans are less likely to generate significant sales revenue growth except for a defensive strategy to protect (hold) share in a growing market. However, defensive strategic market plans are critical sources of short-run cash flow and profit performance, and in many ways, they define the business's current level of share, sales, and profit performance.

A great number of other factors may come into play in selecting one strategic market plan over the other, but let's look at an estimate of what Dell Computer's performance in 2004 would be if it had adopted a defensive strategic market plan to protect market share in the growing PC market. Using the same assumptions already made for market growth,

FIGURE 11-10 OFFENSIVE AND DEFENSIVE STRATEGIC MARKET PLANS

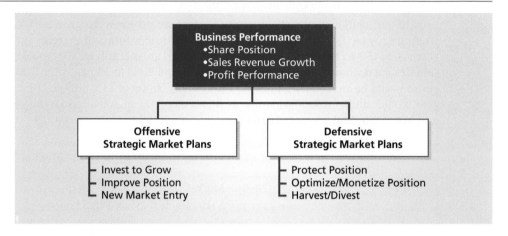

margin erosion, and marketing expenses as a percent of sales, a defensive Dell Computer strategic market plan to protect market share might produce the following estimate of 2004 performance, also shown in Figure 11-9:

2004 – Estimated Performance of an Defensive Strategy to Protect Market Share

Sales Revenue (2004) = Market Demand × Market Share
= $310 billion × 10.2% = $31.6 billion

Gross Profit (2004) = Sales Revenue × Percent Margin
= $31.6 billion × 18.0% = $5.7 billion

Net Marketing Contribution = Gross Profit – Marketing, Sales, & Administrative Expenses
= $5.7 billion – $3.0 billion = $2.7 billion

As the preceding shows, a defensive strategic market plan to protect market share might yield an estimated $6.3 billion increase in sales revenue and a decrease of $0.1 billion in net marketing contribution. Although many factors could keep these goals from being met, this strategy, if successfully implemented, would succeed in protecting a share position, growing sales revenue, and holding net marketing contribution close to its prior level.

Dell's decision to stay with an offensive strategy during a period of slower-than-predicted market growth allowed actual sales to grow to $41.4 billion and net marketing contribution to $4.0 billion, as shown in Figure 11-9. This produced a Marketing ROS of 9.7 percent and a Marketing ROI of 114 percent.

As the PC market enters the late growth stages of its product life cycle, Dell will have to consider whether offensive strategies can continue to be profitable. It may be that in the near future Dell will have to begin shifting to a defensive strategy to protect its market leadership position as the PC market matures.

MARKETING MIX STRATEGY AND PERFORMANCE PLAN

A strategic market plan is a long-term strategy with a 3- to 5-year time horizon and specific performance objectives. A market mix strategy is a short-term marketing strategy with a 1-year time horizon. A marketing mix strategy needs to be reviewed each year with respect to changing market conditions and adjusted accordingly to achieve the long-run performance objectives of a strategic market plan. In some instances, market conditions may change so much or so suddenly that the strategic market plan needs to be reassessed to determine if it remains the best long-run plan to achieve the business's performance objectives in a particular product-market.

Marketing Mix Strategy

Given a specific strategic market plan, a detailed tactical marketing strategy needs to be developed. This means developing a marketing mix strategy with respect to product positioning, price, promotion, and place. The degree to which the performance objectives of a strategic market plan are achieved depends on the effectiveness of the tactical marketing strategy designed to support this strategic market plan.

For example, Intel's strategic market plan to enter the low-end personal computer market required a different tactical marketing strategy from Intel's strategic market plan to defend its high-share position in more expensive microprocessors. Each required different types of products and pricing to achieve a position that would be attractive to target customers relative to competitors' product-price positions.

The strategic market plan sets the strategic direction and provides broad guidelines for resource allocation. However, the tactical marketing strategy is the workhorse that has to succeed for the strategic market plan to achieve both short- and long-run performance objectives. The right strategic market plan with the wrong tactical marketing mix strategy will not normally produce desired levels of performance.

Performance Plan

The performance objectives and conditions under which a business would use either an offensive or a defensive strategic market plan are very different. As outlined in Figure 11-11, offensive strategic marketing plans are geared to deliver above-average performance in the areas of sales growth, improved share position, and long-run profit performance. Defensive strategic market plans are important in producing short-run profit performance and protecting important share positions, and they also contribute to long-run profit performance and strategic position.

Offensive strategic market plans require investment for growth, which limits short-run profit performance while building sales revenue and improving share position. In the long run, a growth-oriented marketing strategy will shift from an offensive strategic market plan to a defensive strategic market plan. As shown, defensive strategic market plans are key sources of short-run profit performance but are not major contributors to sales revenue growth or long-run share and profit performance.

For example, consider Zi-Tech Acoustics, a $250 million engineering acoustics business. It manufactures and markets a variety of acoustic products to four distinct markets.

FIGURE 11-11 PERFORMANCE OBJECTIVES AND STRATEGIC MARKET PLAN

Performance Objective	Impact on Business Performance			
	Some	Moderate	Considerable	Substantial
Offensive Strategic Market Plans				
Short-Run Profit Performance	X	X		
Short-Run Share Position	X	X		
Long-Run Profit Performance			X	X
Long-Run Share Position			X	X
Long-Run Sales Revenue Growth			X	X
Defensive Strategic Market Plans				
Short-Run Profit Performance			X	X
Short-Run Share Position			X	X
Long-Run Profit Performance		X	X	
Long-Run Share Position	X	X		
Long-Run Sales Revenue Growth	X	X		

Figure 11-12 illustrates the market share, sales revenues, and net marketing contribution for the company and in each of the four product-markets it serves. A portfolio analysis based on market attractiveness and competitive advantage produced the product-market portfolio illustrated in Figure 11-13. Also shown in Figure 11-13 is a new market opportunity (M5) uncovered in the strategic market planning process. This analysis, along with the current performance with regard to share position, sales revenue, and net marketing contribution, led to the strategic market plans outlined in Figure 11-13 and described in the following:

■ **Market 1** is a mature market in which Zi-Tech will strive to protect share to maintain a net marketing contribution that produces over 50 percent of the overall net marketing contribution.
■ **Market 2** is mature, and management feels that a strategy to optimize Zi-Tech's position to more profitable would yield greater profits.
■ **Market 3** is attractive and growing. These conditions led to a strategic market plan to invest to grow market share.
■ **Market 4** is unattractive and declining; its competitive advantage is average. A harvest strategy would be designed to make a positive net marketing contribution in the short run but to be completely out of the market in 5 years.
■ **Market 5** is a new market opportunity uncovered by the strategic market planning process. Zi-Tech would like to enter this market. It will involve losses for the first couple of years, but by year 5, Zi-Tech hopes to produce a positive net marketing contribution in market 5.

A set of performance objectives was created for each market plan, as outlined in Figure 11-14. As shown, in the current year, Zi-Tech produced sales of $250 million in four product-markets. Three of the four product-markets were profitable, and the overall net marketing contribution was $43.5 million. On the basis of the strategic market plans and performance objectives created for each product-market, Zi-Tech hopes to grow

FIGURE 11-12 ZI-TECH CURRENT PERFORMANCE AND STRATEGIC MARKET PLANS

Portfolio Planning and Performance	Market 1 Growers	Market 2 Maintainers	Market 3 New Business	Market 4 In Trouble	Company Total
Strategic Market Plan	Protect Position	Optimize Position	Invest To Grow	Harvest Strategy	
Market Growth Rate (%)	3	0	17	−5	3.4
Market Demand (customers)	800,000	1,000,000	1,200,000	1,500,000	4,500,000
Market Share (%)	23	13	7	12	12.8
Volume	184,000	130,000	84,000	180,000	578,000
Revenue per Customer	$420	$450	$660	$325	$432
Sales Revenues	$77,280,000	$58,500,000	$55,440,000	$58,500,000	$249,720,000
Variable Cost per Customer	$250	$300	$440	$300	$304
Margin per Customer	$170	$150	$220	$25	$128
Gross Profit	$31,280,000	$19,500,000	$18,480,000	$4,500,000	$73,760,000
Marketing Expenses (% sales)	11.7	12.0	11.7	12.9	12.1
Marketing Expenses	$9,041,760	$7,020,000	$6,486,480	$7,546,500	$30,094,740
Net Marketing Contribution	$22,238,240	$12,480,000	$11,993,520	($3,046,500)	$43,665,260
Marketing ROS (%)	28.8	21.3	21.6	-5.2	17.5
Marketing ROI (%)	246	178	185	-40	145

FIGURE 11-13 ZI-TECH PORTFOLIO ANALYSIS AND STRATEGIC MARKET PLAN

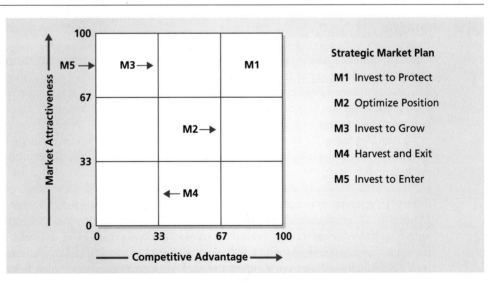

Strategic Market Plan

M1 Invest to Protect

M2 Optimize Position

M3 Invest to Grow

M4 Harvest and Exit

M5 Invest to Enter

FIGURE 11-14 STRATEGIC MARKET PLAN AND PERFORMANCE OBJECTIVES

Zi-Tech Acoustics				Revenue ($ millions)

Performance Objectives

Strategic Market Objective	Share Objective	Sales Revenue Growth	Profit Performance
M1 Protect	Hold	Minimal	Strong
M2 Max. Profits	Reduce	Decline	Improve
M3 Grow	Increase	Increase	Long Run
M4 Monetize	Reduce	Decline	Short Run
M5 Entry	Increase	Increase	Long Run

Revenue ($ millions)

	Current	2–3 Years	4–5 Years
M5		M5 (–$2)	M5 ($5)
M4	M4 (–$3)	M4 ($2)	M3 ($23)
M3	M3 ($12)	M3 ($18)	
M2	M2 ($12.5)	M2 ($14)	M2 ($15)
M1	M1 ($22)	M1 ($22)	M1 ($22)

(Net Marketing Contribution)

overall sales by $100 million to $350 million in 4 to 5 years. More important, the Zi-Tech performance plan projects net marketing contribution to grow from $43.5 to $65 million in 4 to 5 years.

If this strategic market plan is successful, Zi-Tech will have improved its strategic position in served markets while growing sales and profits over a 5-year period. In Chapter 16 we will look more closely at how this plan translates into shareholder value. However, a 40 percent increase in sales revenues and a 49 percent increase in net marketing contribution should contribute positively to the net profit and shareholder value.

■ Summary

Strategic market planning is a process. It involves assessing the market attractiveness and competitive advantage of the current situation along with business performance measures of share position, sales revenues, and profitability. This type of assessment is made for each product-market served by the business and for new market opportunities the business may want to consider.

From this assessment, a portfolio analysis is created based on two dimensions of performance: market attractiveness and competitive advantage. Each dimension is created with an index based on several underlying forces that shape it. Market attractiveness is indexed with respect to market forces (market size, growth, buyer power), competitive intensity (price rivalry, ease of market entry, substitutes), and market access (customer familiarity, channel access, sales force requirements). Competitive advantage is indexed with respect to cost advantage (unit cost, transaction costs, marketing expenses), differentiation advantage (product quality, service quality, brand image), and marketing advantage (market share, brand awareness, channel control). A strategic market plan is specified for each product-market the business serves or would like to consider entering in the future, based on the product-market's position in the portfolio.

The strategic market plan is a long-run, 3- to 5-year, strategic market objective that involves share position but has corresponding implications for short- and long-run sales revenue growth and profit performance. Strategic market plans can be offensive or defensive. Offensive strategic market plans involve market penetration strategies to grow share position, sales, and long-run profitability. Offensive strategies can include investing to grow, selective investment, market entry, and new-market development. Defensive strategic market plans involve protecting share, sales, and profits or harvesting strategies to exit markets while maximizing short-run profits. Defensive market strategies can include protecting or optimizing position for maximum profits, monetizing for maximum cash flow, harvesting, and divesting. The combination of strategic market plans (one for each product-market) results in an overall view of how the business will grow with respect to share, sales, and profits.

Although the strategic market plan for a given product-market sets short- and long-run goals with respect to market share, sales revenues, and profits, it does not specify how this performance will be achieved. Therefore, for each strategic market plan there needs to be a corresponding tactical marketing plan. The tactical marketing plan is a marketing mix strategy (product, price, place, and promotion) and resource allocation (marketing budget) that specifies the tactical details of how a given strategic market plan will be achieved. On the basis of these marketing tactics and the marketing budget, a 3- to 5-year forecast of market share, sales revenues, and net marketing contribution, a performance plan is created.

■ Market-Based Logic and Strategic Thinking

1 How does the level of product-market diversification affect sales growth and performance consistency?
2 Why would the overall variation in sales revenues over a 10-year period be different when comparing General Electric and Dell Computer?
3 What is meant by the "strategic market planning process"?
4 How is a strategic market plan different from a strategic market planning process?
5 How would you assess the attractiveness of a new consumer product-market for Procter & Gamble? Be specific as to what factors you would include in building an index of market attractiveness for a Procter & Gamble consumer market.
6 How would you assess the competitive advantage Procter & Gamble would have in a new consumer product-market? Be specific as to what factors you would include in building an index of competitive advantage for a Procter & Gamble consumer market.
7 Using the following information, create a portfolio analysis and specify a strategic market plan for a business that serves three product-markets.

Product-Market	Share (%)	Sales ($ millions)	Market Attractiveness	Competitive Advantage
A	10	$20	20	40
B	33	$50	75	80
C	5	$10	85	15

8   Using the information presented in question 7 and the added information that follows, create a 3-year performance plan with respect to market share and sales revenues for each product-market, given the strategic market plan specified. Also create a projection of overall sales for each year of the 3-year planning horizon.

Product-Market	Strategic Market Plan	Share Objective (%)	Market Demand ($ millions)	Market Growth (%)
A	Reduced Focus	5	$200	5
B	Protect Share	33	$150	7
C	Grow Share	10	$200	20

9   Under what conditions would a business specify an offensive strategic market plan?

10 Under what conditions would a business specify a defensive strategic market plan?

11 What role do offensive and defensive strategic market plans play in the short- and long-run performance of a business?

12 How would the sales and profit performance over a 3-year period differ between a business with only defensive strategic market plans and a business that has only offensive strategic market plans? Why is it important to have a balance of offensive and defensive plans?

13 Why is a tactical marketing plan for each strategic market plan an important part of the strategic market planning process?

14 How does a manager develop a tactical marketing plan and a marketing budget to achieve a specific strategic market plan?

15 How would the tactical marketing plan and marketing budget for a strategic market plan to grow market share (offensive) differ from those of a reduced focus strategic market plan to reduce share?

16 How does a business create a forecast of its future performance based on the strategic market plans for each product-market it intends to serve over a given planning horizon?

Marketing Performance Tools

Each of the following **marketing performance tools** can be accessed by going to *www.rogerjbest.com* or *www.prenhall.com/best*. The shaded cells are input cells. The non-shaded cells contain results calculated from your input values.

MARKETING PERFORMANCE TOOL—Market Attractiveness Index

Very Unattractive	Unattractive	Somewhat Unattractive	Somewhat Attractive	Attractive	Very Attractive
0	20	40	60	80	100

Market Attractiveness Factors	Market Attractiveness Rating	Relative Importance*	Market Attractiveness Score
Market Forces			
Market Size	80	40%	32
Market Growth	60	30%	18
Buyer Power	40	30%	12
Market Forces Total			62
× Relative Importance of Market Forces		30%	18.6
Competitive Intensity			
Price Rivalry	40	40%	16
Ease of Entry	80	30%	24
Substitutes	60	30%	18
Competitive Intensity Total			58
× Relative Importance of Competitive Intensity		40%	23.2
Market Access			
Customer Familiarity	80	40%	32
Channel Access	100	30%	30
Sales Force Capabilities	60	30%	18
Market Access Total			80
× Relative Importance of Market Access		30%	24.0
Market Attractiveness Index			65.8

*Relative Importance sums to 100%.

This **marketing performance tool** allows you to index the market attractiveness of a product-market or business situation. The data provided are from Figure 11-5. The shaded numeric input cells can be changed in doing the following application exercise.

Application Exercise: Using the data provided, answer the following questions. How would the market attractiveness index change if the weights for competitive intensity and market access were reversed? How would the market attractiveness index change if price rivalry was rated very attractive? Which single factor is to most damaging to the overall market attractiveness index (has the largest negative impact)?

MARKETING PERFORMANCE TOOL—Competitive Advantage Index

Major Disadvantage	Definite Disadvantage	Slight Disadvantage	Slight Advantage	Definite Advantage	Major Advantage
0	20	40	60	80	100

Sources of Competitive Advantage	Competitive Advantage Rating	Relative Importance*	Competitive Advantage Score
Differentiation Advantage			
Product Quality	80	40%	32
Service Quality	60	30%	18
Brand Image	80	30%	24
Differentiation Advantage Total			**74**
× Relative Importance of Differentiation Advantage		40%	**29.6**
Cost Advantage			
Unit Cost	40	70%	28
Transactions Cost	60	20%	12
Marketing Expenses	60	10%	6
Cost Advantage Total			**46**
× Relative Importance of Cost Advantage		40%	**18.4**
Marketing Advantage			
Market Share	40	40%	16
Brand Awareness	40	30%	12
Distribution	20	30%	6
Marketing Advantage Total			**34**
× Relative Importance of Marketing Advantage		20%	**6.8**
Competitive Advantage Index			**54.8**

*Relative Importance sums to 100%.

This **marketing performance tool** allows you to index the competitive advantage a business has in a specific product-market or business situation. The data provided are from Figure 11-7. The shaded numeric input cells can be changed in doing the following application exercise.

Application Exercise: Using the data provided, answer the following questions:

How would the competitive advantage index change if the weights for differentiation advantage and marketing advantage were reversed? How would the competitive advantage index change if service quality was rated as major advantage? Which single factor is most damaging to the overall competitive advantage index (has the largest negative impact)?

MARKETING PERFORMANCE TOOL—Strategic Market Planning Portfolio

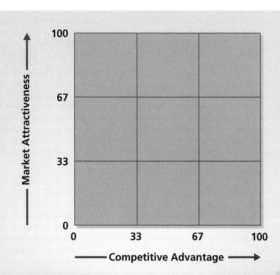

Strategic Market Plan	Current Year	Year 1	Year 2	Year 3
Market Growth Rate (%)		3.1	3.0	2.9
Market Demand (customers)	800,000	825,000	850,000	875,000
Market Share (%)	23	23	23	23
Volume	184,000	189,750	195,550	201,250
Revenue per Customer	$420	$420	$420	$420
Sales Revenues	$77,280,000	$79,695,000	$82,110,000	$84,525,000
Variable Cost per Customer	$250	$250	$250	$250
Margin per Customer	$170	$170	$170	$170
Gross Profit	$31,280,000	$32,267,500	$33,235,000	$34,212,500
Marketing Expenses (% sales)	11.7	11.7	11.7	11.7
Marketing Expenses	$9,041,760	$9,324,315	$9,606,870	$9,889,425
Net Marketing Contribution	**$22,238,240**	**$22,933,185**	**$23,628,130**	**$23,323,075**
Marketing ROS (%)	28.8	28.8	28.8	28.8
Marketing ROI (%)	246	246	246	246

This **marketing performance tool** allows you to evaluate the sales and profit impact of different strategic market plans over a 3-year period. The data provided are from Figure 11-12 and used to forecast the sales and profits for a protect position strategy for market 1. The shaded numeric input cells can be changed in doing the following application exercise.

Application Exercise: Using the data provided, answer the following questions. How would the sales and profits play out if there was no market growth? How would the sales and profits play out if there was 5 percent price erosion each year? How would the sales and profits play out if the business lost one share point each year over the 3-year planning period?

Notes

1. Michael Treacy and Fred Wiersama, *The Discipline of Market Leaders* (Reading, MA: Addison-Wesley, 1995).
2. Some analysts believe the guidelines of the market plan may lead to a strategic advantage. See David A. Garvin, "Leveraging Processes for Strategic Advantage," *Harvard Business Review* (September–October 1995): 77.
3. Roger A. Kerin, Vijay Mahajan, and P. Rajan Varadarajan, *Strategic Market Planning* (Boston: Allyn and Bacon, 1990).
4. Frances V. McCrory and Peter G. Gerstberger, "The New Math of Performance Measurements," *Journal of Business Strategy* (March–April 1992): 33–38.
5. Kasturi Rangan, Melvyn Menezes, and E. P. Maier, "Channel Selection for New Industrial Products: A Framework, Method and Application," *Journal of Marketing* (July 1992): 69–82.
6. L.W. Phillips, D. R. Chang, and R.D. Bussell, "Product Quality, Cost Position, and Business Performance: A Test of Some Key Hypotheses," *Journal of Marketing* 47 (January 1983): 26–43.
7. Michael E. Porter, *Competitive Advantage* (New York: Free Press, 1986).
8. David Aaker, "Formal Planning System," in *Strategic Market Management* (New York: Wiley, 1995): 341–353.
9. Thomas Powell, "Strategic Planning as Competitive Advantage," *Strategic Management Journal* 13 (1992): 551–558; Scott Armstrong, "The Value of Formal Planning for Strategic Decisions: Reply," *Strategic Management Journal* 7 (1986): 183–185; and Deepak Sinha, "The Contribution of Formal Planning to Decisions," *Strategic Management Journal* (October 1990): 479–492.
10. William K. Hall, "Survival Strategies in a Hostile Environment," *Harvard Business Review* (September–October 1980): 75–85.
11. Kathryn Rudie Harrigan, *Strategies for Declining Businesses* (Lexington, MA: Lexington Books, 1980); and Kathryn Rudie Harrigan and Michael E. Porter, "End-Game Strategies for Declining Industries," *Harvard Business Review* (July–August 1983): 111–120. Also see Katheryn Rudie Harrigan, *Managing Maturing Businesses* (New York: Lexington Books, 1988).

CHAPTER 12

Offensive Strategies

D ell Computer has been operating with an offensive growth plan since its inception. Dell was an early follower in the PC market when the market was relatively small in the late 1980s, striving to build share with its low-cost advantage and innovative marketing strategy. Over this past 15 years, Dell grew to $41 billion in sales, based on a combination of growing PC market demand and Dell's increasing market share. Even as PC prices and margins eroded, the growth in volume and low cost of marketing allowed Dell to enjoy profitable growth. However, the PC market is maturing, and Dell can no longer depend as much on market growth to provide increasing volume. Also, market share gains will be tougher in a mature market as competitors fight against any loss in volume or market share. Thus, Dell's strategic marketing plan for PCs may shift to a more defensive strategy as it strives to maintain a market leadership position and

maximize profits in a maturing market. However, to maintain double-digit growth rates for the company, Dell will need new offensive strategies.

As shown in Figure 12-1, Dell's PC sales in 2001 were 65 percent of its $31 billion in sales. The PC market was maturing and Dell's PC sales growth is projected to slow by 2006. To accomplish its objective of double-digit sales growth, Dell will put more marketing effort into the related market demand for servers, services, software, and peripherals. Growth in the non-PC sector of Dell's product portfolio is estimated to take Dell to $62 billion in 2006. At that time Dell will derive more than 50 percent of its sales from outside the PC market. Because these related segments are large, attractive markets in which Dell has relatively low market share, the opportunity for growth in these related markets should provide Dell with continued opportunity for rapid growth throughout this decade.

FIGURE 12-1 DELL COMPUTERS OFFENSIVE GROWTH STRATEGY

Product Portfolio	2001	2002	2003	2004*	2005*	2006*
Personal Computers	$20	$23	$26	$27	$29	$30
Servers/Storage	$5	$5	$7	$8	$9	$10
Services	$3	$4	$4	$5	$7	$9
Software/Peripherals	$3	$4	$4	$7	$10	$13
Total Revenues**	$31	$36	$41	$47	$55	$62
% Personal Computers	65	64	63	57	53	48

*Projected Sales
**Projected Sales made by Dell for 2004–2006

STRATEGIC MARKET PLANS

Many businesses such as Dell, Coca-Cola, Microsoft, Starbucks, Wal-Mart, and Intel experienced considerable growth in the 1990s. To grow so rapidly, these businesses had to implement a variety of strategic market plans that ranged from market share penetration to development of completely new products and entering new markets. In every case, their strategic market plans have addressed three basic performance objectives:

- **Share Position:** How will the strategic market plan contribute to the business's share position in served markets?
- **Sales Growth:** To what degree will the strategic market plan contribute to sales growth?
- **Profit Performance:** How will the strategic market plan impact short- and long-run profit performance?

Because resources are limited, a business needs a strategic market plan to carefully map out its future growth and profit performance.[1] Every strategic market plan a business develops will in some way affect both short- and long-run business performance in each of the three areas of performance identified. Depending on the situation, some will be offensive and some will be defensive strategic market plans.

Offensive strategic market plans are usually growth-oriented and are more likely to occur in the growth stage of a product-market life cycle,[2] as shown in Figure 12-2.

FIGURE 12-2 MARKET GROWTH AND OFFENSIVE AND DEFENSIVE STRATEGIES

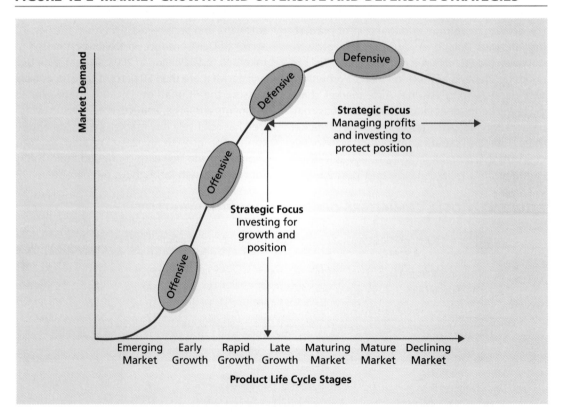

Offensive strategic market plans are designed to produce sales growth and improve share position and future profit performance. Defensive strategic market plans are more likely to occur in the latter stages of a product-market life cycle and are often designed to protect important share positions and be large contributors to short-run sales revenues and profits. This chapter examines various offensive strategic market plans, and Chapter 13 will present various defensive strategic market plans.

OFFENSIVE STRATEGIC MARKET PLANS

The combination of market attractiveness and competitive advantage creates a portfolio position for any given product-market.[3] As shown in Figure 12-3, attractive markets are most likely to warrant an offensive strategic market plan to improve competitive advantage and share position when the business's competitive advantage is average or below. These offensive strategies can range from growing the competitive advantage and market share in existing product-markets to entering a new market with no established share

FIGURE 12-3 PORTFOLIO ANALYSIS AND STRATEGIC MARKET PLANS

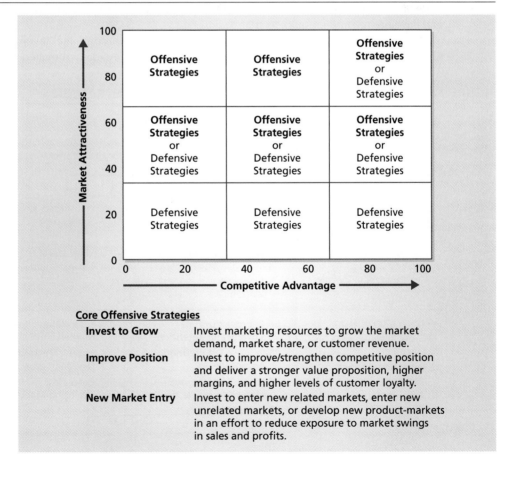

Core Offensive Strategies

Invest to Grow	Invest marketing resources to grow the market demand, market share, or customer revenue.
Improve Position	Invest to improve/strengthen competitive position and deliver a stronger value proposition, higher margins, and higher levels of customer loyalty.
New Market Entry	Invest to enter new related markets, enter new unrelated markets, or develop new product-markets in an effort to reduce exposure to market swings in sales and profits.

position. In addition, there may be an opportunity to use an offensive strategic market plan to help cultivate an emerging or underdeveloped market in which the business has established a strong position of advantage.

Of the six portfolio positions in which an offensive strategic market plan could be used, the three with average market attractiveness and the one with highest market attractiveness and highest competitive advantage could also use a defensive strategic market plan. In these portfolio positions, more information would be needed before one could select between an offensive or defensive strategic market plan. For example, an offensive strategic market plan may be warranted, given the business's sources of relative advantage. On the other hand, a defensive strategic market plan to protect the current position may be the best alternative for achieving desired performance objectives. In some cases a defensive plan is appropriate when the business chooses to optimize its market focus and attempt to minimize investment and capture more profits.

Offensive strategic market plans are fundamentally geared for growth and inherently involve strategies to penetrate or grow existing markets or to enter or develop new markets, as summarized in Figure 12-4. There is a wide range of potential offensive strategic market plans.[4] However, a logical place to start with offensive strategies is within *existing* markets. A business that has already established a working knowledge of customers and competitors, and has resources in place to serve existing markets, should seek to leverage its existing market position with an offensive strategic market plan to further penetrate and develop the product-markets it already serves.

Coca-Cola has been described as the "perfect growth company" even though it already commands a 50-percent market share of the worldwide carbonated soft drink

FIGURE 12-4 STRATEGIC MARKET PLANS AND OFFENSIVE STRATEGIES

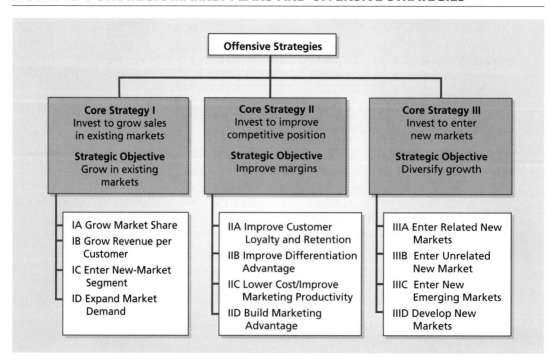

market. From the company's point of view, Coca-Cola represents only a 2-percent *share of stomach* on a worldwide basis. This point is further driven home in Coca-Cola's annual report, which features 47 empty Coke bottles and 1 full one. This way of thinking has enabled Coca-Cola to grow its volume at the rate of 7 to 8 percent, while PepsiCo, its chief rival, is growing unit volume at the rate of 1 percent per year. Clearly, Coca-Cola is challenging its marketing managers to think offensively and find ways to grow Coca-Cola's share of the beverage market.

OFFENSIVE CORE STRATEGY I: INVEST TO GROW SALES

As shown in Figure 12-4, four fundamental offensive strategic market plans can be used to increase a business's penetration of an existing market. These strategic market plans range from share penetration to growing market demand in markets served by the business.[5] A business can grow its market share, increase its revenue per customer, enter new market segments, or expand market demand and thereby create a bigger pie to grow share in. Because there are three offensive core strategies, each with four specific offensive strategies, we have numbered the offensive core strategies I, II, and III and each of the specific offensive strategies A, B, C, and D. There is no intended order of importance in this numbering system; it just helps keep track of the different types of offensive core strategies and their specific tactical strategies.

OFFENSIVE STRATEGY IA: Grow Market Share

One of the more obvious marketing strategies is to grow market share. However, many factors affect a business's ability to grow market share and profitability.[6] Its share potential is one consideration. To what degree has the business achieved its share potential? What factors driving share development need to be managed to grow share in a given product-market? Finally, will share growth actually contribute to profitability? Each is an important consideration in developing an offensive strategic market plan to grow market share.

In Chapter 3, we introduced the share development index (SDI) as the ratio of actual market share to share potential. The share potential of a business is based on what that business believes it should be able to achieve with a successful tactical marketing strategy, given the strength of its competitive advantage and marketing effectiveness in a given product-market. For example, in the following share-development path, a business estimates that it should perform at a 90 percent level in product awareness, 50 percent in product preference, 80 percent in intentions to purchase, 80 percent in product availability, and 70 percent in rate of purchase. Performing at these levels would produce a potential market share index of approximately 20 percent.

$$
\begin{aligned}
\text{Market Share Potential} &= \frac{\text{Product}}{\text{Awareness}} \times \frac{\text{Product}}{\text{Preference}} \times \frac{\text{Purchase}}{\text{Intentions}} \times \frac{\text{Purcchase}}{\text{Availability}} \times \frac{\text{Purchase}}{\text{Rate}} \\
&= 0.90 \times 0.50 \times 0.80 \times 0.80 \times 0.70 \\
&= 20.2\%
\end{aligned}
$$

If a business's actual market share were 8 percent, the business would be underperforming and, hence, would have a Share Development Index of 40.

$$\text{Share Development Index} = \frac{\text{Current Market Share}}{\text{Market Share Potential}} = \frac{8\%}{20\%} \times 100 = 40$$

This means that the business has achieved only 40 percent of its potential market share. Therefore, there is an opportunity to grow market share with a market penetration strategy.

To grow share, a business has to examine each area of performance along the share-development path with respect to its expected versus actual market performance. For instance, the business in the example expects to achieve 90-percent product awareness in its target market. If its actual target-market awareness were only 67 percent, this performance gap would prevent the business from reaching its full market share potential. Thus, to grow share when it is lower than its full potential, this business would need to examine key performance gaps in its market share response.

There is also the possibility that a business has reached its share potential but feels it can still expand its market share position with a new strategic market plan. For example, product improvements that are able to shift product preference from 50 percent to 70 percent would raise the market share potential (index) from 20.2 percent to 28.2 percent in the example presented. Of course, to achieve this level of share penetration, the business would have to adequately communicate and deliver these product improvements to the full satisfaction of target customers.

Perhaps the most important consideration in developing strategies to grow share is to make sure the planned share growth will be profitable. Some methods of growing share can actually result in a lower net marketing contribution, as illustrated in the Santa Fe Sportswear example in Chapter 2. Because market share is such a competitive metric, it is easy to get caught up in share wars without remembering to consider the unprofitable possibility of winning the battle for share but losing the war with respect to profits.

OFFENSIVE STRATEGY IB: Grow Revenue per Customer

Harley-Davidson derives 77 percent of its $4.1 billion in sales from the sale of motorcycles. The other 23 percent is growing as result of increased customer purchases of clothing, parts, and accessories. In clothing alone, Harley introduces 1,200 new items per year (excluding riding boots, baby clothes, and clothing for pets). The retail clothes are so important to communicating the brand that every dealership now has fitting rooms. This has allowed Harley-Davidson to grow revenue per customer from $10,540 to $13,630 per year. Even better for Harley-Davidson, the incremental sales of related products have much higher margins, build customer loyalty, and enhance their brand awareness and brand equity as wearers of the Harley-Davidson merchandise communicate their brand name.

As a business approaches 100 percent of its share development index, additional growth based on market share gains becomes increasingly difficult. Up to this point, share gains have been based on correcting ineffective tactical marketing strategies, improving competitive position, or adding to a business's marketing effort. However, there is also the opportunity to grow revenues with existing customers by growing the amount of revenue *per* customer. For example, McDonald's once sold a limited product line of hamburgers, french fries, and drinks. With product line extensions in hamburgers, chicken and fish sandwiches, and a line of breakfast products, McDonald's has been able to grow the average dollars spent at McDonald's by customers who already were McDonald's customers. Of course, these line extensions also attracted new customers to the fast-food industry and drew new customers from competing fast-food businesses.

For businesses with well known brand names, such as Kodak, Nike, Honda, IBM, and Disney, it is easy to introduce line extensions that leverage the awareness and image already created by their company reputation.[7] When Honda entered the lawn mower market in the early 1990s, the Honda lawn mower was immediately perceived by many customers as reliable and of high quality. These perceptions were created by Honda's success in automobiles, motorcycles, and other motorized products. The high level of name awareness also greatly assisted the company's quick penetration of this market. Many lawn mower customers were already owners of other Honda products. This level of awareness led Honda to build a growth strategy around the volume of Honda products purchased by existing Honda customers. This strategy is aptly expressed in Honda's marketing objective: *"Our goal is to have five Hondas in every garage."*

Obviously, few, if any, Honda customers would purchase five Honda automobiles. However, the Honda offensive strategic market plan is to capture the Honda car owner's purchase of lawn mowers, recreational vehicles (motorcycles, snowmobiles, jet skis, all-terrain vehicles, outboard motors), and portable motors and generators. In this way, Honda is growing its business by building the total ownership of Honda products among existing customers. A business's existing customer pool is a customer franchise that offers considerable opportunity for within-market sales growth.

Revenue per customer can also be built with a strategy to build price premiums. Businesses that enhance their products by adding value-added services or building a superior reputation for quality can charge higher prices than competing businesses and still maintain a superior customer value. General Electric's turbine engines command a premium price relative to competing turbines around the world. This premium is based on superior product quality, engineering and installation services, and a reputation for innovation and technology in the area of turbine design and development. In this way, GE is able to attain higher revenue per customer than many competing turbine manufacturers.

OFFENSIVE STRATEGY IC: Enter New-Market Segments

Another offensive growth strategy within existing markets is to enter a new customer segment within an existing market.[8] For example, as the personal computer market has grown, the under $1,000 personal computer segment has emerged. Intel, which did not have a product suitable for this segment, saw competitors such as Advanced Micro Devices take the lead in the under $1,000 segment. With demand in this segment growing faster than in any other segment, Intel responded with a new product designed for the price-performance needs of the segment. As shown in Figure 12-5, the Celeron chip provided PC manufacturers a low-cost Intel microprocessor for this segment. This offensive strategic market plan provided a new source of sales revenues and profitability for Intel.

FIGURE 12-5 INTEL NEW SEGMENT ENTRY STRATEGY

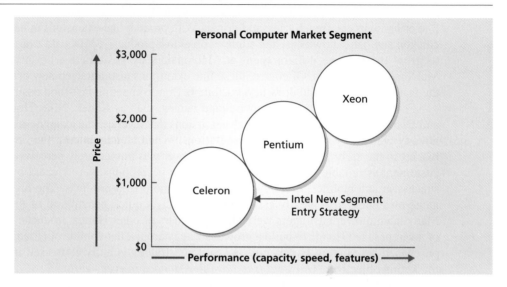

The vodka market is divided into four segments based on price and differences in taste, brand image, and packaging, as illustrated in Figure 12-6. Absolut Spirits had been successful in the premium vodka market segment and was number two in overall market share behind market leader Smirnoff. Although Absolut held a strong position in the $15 to $25 premium segment, it lacked market positions in the super-premium segment (over $25) and traditional segment ($10 to $15). This presented a good opportunity for growth as these segments were growing in market attractiveness. Gray Goose, a competitor's product in the super-premium segment, saw its United States sales increase from 100,000 cases to 1.4 million cases in 2003. To take advantage of these opportunities, Absolut Spirits introduced Level in the super-premium segment to compete with Gray Goose, Belvedere, and Ketel One. The company also positioned Danzka with unique packaging (in a metal container for faster chilling, shaped like a cocktail shaker) in the traditional segment at a suggested price of $13 to $14 per bottle.

OFFENSIVE STRATEGY ID: Expand Market Demand

At any given point in time, the number of customers in a market is finite. New customer growth strategies can focus on growing market demand by bringing new customers into a market. For example, the market for flat-screen TVs was 4 million per year in 2003. Although Sony and Samsung will battle each other for market share, their common offensive strategy is to grow market demand. They estimate that this market will increase to 14 million units per year in 2005 and 30 million in 2007. Clearly the world-wide market potential is well beyond this number. Thus, this type of offensive growth strategy is likely to serve them both well over the rest of this decade.

In Chapter 3, we introduced the concept of a market development index. This index is simply the ratio of current market demand to maximum market demand (the maximum number of customers possible for a particular geographic market scope). For example,

FIGURE 12-6 VODKA NEW SEGMENT OFFENSIVE GROWTH STRATEGY

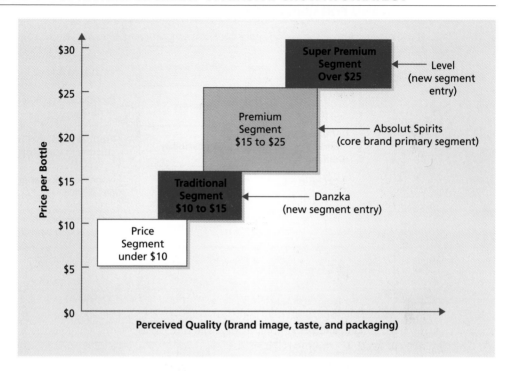

the market development index for the wireless phone market in the United States is estimated at approximately 33.

$$\begin{aligned} \text{Market} \\ \text{Development} \\ \text{Index} \end{aligned} = \frac{\text{Current Market Demand for Wireless Phones}}{\text{Market Potential for Wireless Phones}} \times 100$$

$$= \frac{140 \text{ million customers}}{180 \text{ million customers}} \times 100$$

$$= 77.8$$

This means that there are many potential customers who have not entered the market for various reasons. As shown in Figure 12-7, there are basically five market forces in the wireless phone market that limit market demand from reaching its full potential. Each of these forces must be addressed in strategic market plans to grow either the entire market or a specific segment within the market.

Marketing communications efforts can be used to address awareness and comprehension of benefits for the wireless phone market. Improving availability is a matter of adding more cell sites in geographic areas where potential demand justifies the investment. Compatibility, however, is more likely to be a product design issue. To improve compatibility, wireless providers have to better understand how customers

FIGURE 12-7 FACTORS THAT NEED TO BE ADDRESSED IN GROWING THE MARKET DEMAND FOR WIRELESS PHONES

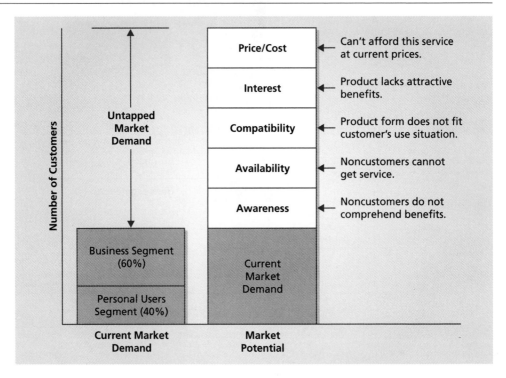

use wireless phones and design products to better serve those use situations. For example, a contractor on a construction site may need a more durable phone, whereas a salesperson may need more features to enhance sales productivity. Finally, because the ongoing cost of wireless phone service prevents many potential customers from entering the market, some wireless phone service providers have developed special usage rate pricing programs that make the price of service adjustable, based on level of usage. The net effect of these efforts is a new market demand of over 25,000 new customers per week.

OFFENSIVE CORE STRATEGY II: IMPROVE COMPETITIVE POSITION

In situations where a business is in an attractive market but with a weak or average competitive position, it may require an investment to improve competitive position. With an improved competitive position, a business has a better chance to achieve price premiums and high levels of customer retention. When this is successfully accomplished, a business is able to improve margins and net marketing contribution. As shown in Figure 12-4, there are four offensive strategies to improve competitive position, each of which is discussed in this section.

OFFENSIVE STRATEGY IIA: Improve Customer Loyalty and Retention

Businesses spend money to gain new customers in growing markets, but if they do not retain these customers, they will experience higher marketing expenses and lower marketing profits. The cost of acquiring a new customer is 5 to 10 times higher than the cost of retaining a customer. Furthermore, a 2 percent increase in loyal customers has been shown to lower marketing costs by 10 percent. An offensive strategy to increase customer retention and customer loyalty will have an immediate impact on marketing profits (net marketing contribution).

For example, in Figure 12-8 we can see that AT&T has 89.2 percent customer retention. With 21.9 million customers, this means AT&T lost 2.4 million customers in 2003. To hold its customer base at 21.9 million would mean acquiring 2.4 million new customers. Not only is this 5 to 10 times more expensive with respect to marketing expenses, but new customers often use less service. This means lower monthly margin per customer and higher marketing expenses. Improving AT&T's customer retention from 89.2 percent to 94.2 percent would increase the lifetime value of its customers by 25 percent. This is an offensive strategic investment that not only impacts short-term profits but greatly enhances future profits when a higher percentage of loyal customers can be retained.

OFFENSIVE STRATEGY IIB: Improve Differentiation Advantage

One of the major customer complaints in the wireless communications market is reliability. To address this problem and turn it into a differentiation advantage, Verizon Wireless created a team of 50 "road warriors" who each drive 100,000 miles annually (5 million miles in total) in specially equipped cars to test the reliability of Verizon's network against several competitor's phones. An onboard computer system makes synchronized inbound and outbound calls of $2\frac{1}{2}$ minutes each to the home office, with 15 seconds between calls. Besides connection quality, the sound quality is also checked by playing recordings of 20 phrases representing all sounds used in the English language. Verizon's computer system logs each call and uses a global positioning system

FIGURE 12-8 WIRELESS TELEPHONE CUSTOMER RETENTION

2003 U.S. Market Wireless Service Provider	Customers (millions)	Customer Retention (%)	Lost Customers (millions)
Nextel	12.3	94.4	0.7
Verizon	36.0	92.4	2.7
AT&T Wireless	21.9	89.2	2.4
Sprint	15.5	89.2	1.7
Cingular	23.4	88.8	2.6
T-Mobile	12.1	86.8	1.6
Other	27.2	NA	NA

to note the precise locations where problems occur. Gridlock produces the most severe test and is the best indicator of how well the system works. Verizon's efforts to improve reliability resulted in an increase in customer retention from 90 percent in 2000 to 92.8 percent in 2003. This was accomplished while growing their number of customers more than 15 percent per year.

To further enhance the differentiation advantage achieved through the actual improvement in reliability, Verizon has run an advertising campaign using this testing process as the theme. The simple statement "Can you hear me NOW?" is familiar to customers. This campaign has also raised the importance customers place on reliability when making a vendor choice. Overall, Verizon relies heavily on this source of differentiation because the company is not the low-cost producer.

OFFENSIVE STRATEGY IIC: Lower Costs/Improve Marketing Productivity

Sony found its profit margins were shrinking in consumer electronics as prices eroded faster than manufacturing costs could be lowered. Even with higher volumes, gross profits were in decline as margins dropped. To address this problem and restore margins to more acceptable levels, Sony examined its cost structure closely and identified a number of areas where costs could be cut. To promote standardization, the number of components used in Sony consumer electronics would be reduced from 840,000 to 100,000. To reduce material costs further, the number of suppliers was reduced from 4,700 to 1,000. Sony is also moving more production from Japan to China where the cost of labor is much lower and is adding more technology to its manufacturing processes. Overall, Sony estimates that these changes will reduce manufacturing costs by $3 billion.

A 3M business found that many of its distributors purchased below-average amounts and often were late in paying their bills. These distributors were moved to an online purchasing system where they had to provide a credit card number to initiate the purchase. This change left them somewhat dissatisfied, but they were told what they would have to do to improve their buying status. In the end, few customers were lost and this 3M business greatly reduced its marketing expenses and improved its cash flow. Both of these factors contributed to a higher level of net marketing contribution and to higher levels of marketing productivity (net marketing contribution per dollar of marketing expense).

OFFENSIVE STRATEGY IID: Build Marketing Advantage

Nautilus was a pioneer brand in the $5 billion home-fitness equipment market. The company's direct marketing approach was successful, but Nautilus had not responded to market trends that included more emphasis on cardiovascular equipment and a shift toward retail-store purchases. Although Nautilus could re-tool to produce new products, a shift from direct marketing channels and relying heavily on infomercials to selling through retail stores would be much harder. Because 80 percent of the $5 billion in sales in this market occurred in retail stores, these changes were essential. To close this gap and build a marketing advantage, Nautilus not only began selling though specialty sports equipment retailers, but has also sought to develop partnerships with Amazon.com, Costco, and The Sports Authority. These additional marketing channels improved Nautilus's competitive position by providing the company with a marketing advantage over its competitors.

Starbucks serves coffee around the world to about 20 million customers every week, who buy an average of between $3.50 and $4.00 per visit. While building an excellent brand with great perceived quality, the company will achieve sales growth with a marketing advantage in both number of stores and store location. Starbucks has been growing its number of retail coffee outlets by about 30 percent per year, expanding from 3,000 stores in 2000 to 7,500 in mid-2004. These 7,500 stores include 500 drive-through outlets in the United States and almost 1,800 coffee outlets in more than 30 international markets, most of which are even more profitable than the traditional U.S. coffee houses. This dominant advantage in store location has been a real growth engine, allowing Starbucks to sustain its remarkable growth despite industry downturns.

OFFENSIVE CORE STRATEGY III: ENTER NEW MARKETS

At some point, every business needs to examine growth opportunities outside the existing markets it serves.[9] This need can occur for three fundamental reasons: (1) the number of attractive market opportunities within existing markets may be limited; (2) new-market opportunities outside existing markets are simply more attractive in terms of meeting the business's overall performance objectives; and (3) a move to new markets helps diversify a business's sources of profitability and, hence, reduces variation in performance.[10]

As shown in Figure 12-4, there are four fundamental offensive strategic market plans for entering new markets. New-market entry strategies can include entry into established related markets that are similar to markets already served by the business, entry into established markets that are unrelated to markets served by the business, entry into new emerging markets, or entry into markets with considerable undeveloped market potential. Entry into established markets (related or unrelated) means competing with established competitors for existing market demand. On the other hand, entry into emerging markets requires significant investment to develop market demand, but often in the absence of competition.

OFFENSIVE STRATEGY IIIA: Enter Related New Markets

Not content to rest on its laurels with a 50 percent market share of the worldwide carbonated soft drink market, Coca-Cola is still seeking to grow market share by entering the $1 billion energy drinks market, illustrated in Figure 12-9. This is a related new-market entry strategy in the beverage category, which allows Coca-Cola to find new sources of sales growth while leveraging its core competencies and sources of competitive advantage.

K2 is best known as a ski manufacturer. Over a 10-year period, K2 steadily increased its share of the American ski market until by the mid-1990s, it became the market share leader. The American ski market is mature, and opportunities to grow sales through either market growth or increased market share are limited. This situation led K2 to a strategy of related new-market entry into the snowboard and in-line skate

FIGURE 12-9 NEW-MARKET ENTRY OPPORTUNITIES FOR COCA-COLA

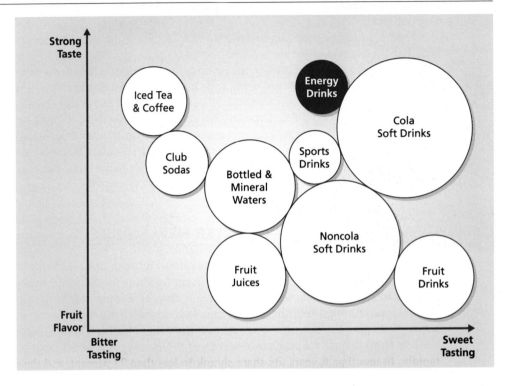

markets. K2 hopes to achieve significant sales revenue growth over the next 10 years as a result of this new-market entry strategy. K2's entry into these two related customer markets enables it to leverage its brand name awareness, reputation for quality, manufacturing and design expertise, and, in some instances, its existing marketing channel and sales systems. Each of these factors offers a variety of potential cost and marketing efficiencies.

There are instances in which entry into a new market can be blocked. Market entry can be difficult because of the cost of entry, technology requirements, or a lack of market access. In the telecommunications industry, these difficulties have led to many mergers, joint ventures, and strategic alliances among telecommunications, computer, and cable TV companies. In each case, partner companies provide related market expertise and leverage. By blending the strengths of businesses from two related markets, these new entities become potentially more complete businesses from which to build and market products that more completely serve and fulfill customer needs.

OFFENSIVE STRATEGY IIIB: Enter Unrelated New Markets

Westinghouse acquired CBS in the mid-1990s. The week before, Disney acquired ABC. The Disney acquisition was a *related* new-market entry strategy in which

Disney could leverage its name, reputation for quality, and creative and production expertise. In contrast, the Westinghouse acquisition was an *unrelated* new-market entry strategy that moved Westinghouse into the increasingly attractive communications market. Disney was leveraging its strength along with new-market access. Westinghouse was redefining itself by acquiring CBS in the hope of reshaping its competitive advantage in an increasingly attractive market. However, both of these businesses were pursuing new sources of market share, sales growth, and profit performance.

One of the primary advantages of an unrelated new-market entry strategy is reduced market dependency. Most markets go through temporary periods of expansion and contraction, and investments in unrelated businesses will have a smoothing effect on the revenues and profits of the combined portfolio of product-markets. For example, the residential construction market is a slow-growth market that fluctuates considerably with economic conditions. A manufacturer of earth-moving equipment for this market could reduce the magnitude of swings in performance by entering a market such as mining or agriculture that is unrelated to the residential construction market. In this way, variations in overall business performance could be minimized.

An additional advantage of market diversification is reduced vulnerability. If a business derives the bulk of its performance from one type of market, a major change in that market could threaten the company's performance, and, potentially, its survival. In the mid-1970s, the National Cash Register Corporation (NCR) was focused primarily on the cash register market and had over an 80 percent share of this market. When competitors entered with a new cash register technology, NCR's market share began to decline rapidly. In less than 6 years, its share shrank to less than 25 percent, and the company's survival was threatened.

Thus, there are three good reasons a business might pursue an unrelated new-market entry strategy:

1. **New Source of Growth:** New-market diversification offers the potential of adding to the business's sales growth and profit performance.
2. **Smoother Performance:** New-market diversification offers customer diversification, which can reduce the magnitude of swings in sales and profit performance.
3. **Reduced Vulnerability:** New-market diversification reduces market dependence and vulnerability, which better protects the business's performance and, in some instances, its survival.

Although these are important benefits, many businesses have failed to perform effectively in diversified markets and have retreated to their core markets. Mobil's acquisition of Montgomery Ward, Coca-Cola's acquisition of Columbia Pictures, and General Motors' acquisition of Data Information Services were each unsuccessful diversified new-market strategies. In each case, the new-market opportunities went too far from the marketing and business expertise and experience of the acquiring company. On the other hand, Phillip Morris's acquisition of the Miller Brewing Company, Pepsi's acquisition of Kentucky Fried Chicken, and Motorola's move into wireless communication products provided the advantages identified above while still leveraging their marketing and business expertise.

OFFENSIVE STRATEGY IIIC: Enter New Emerging Markets

As depicted in Figure 12-4, a business can grow by entering new emerging markets into which customers have not yet entered. Although considerably riskier with respect to profit performance, this strategy can enable a business to establish an early leadership position in the market. From this position, a business can influence product positioning and market growth.

High-technology markets have rapidly emerging market demand and relatively short product and market life cycles. Businesses in these markets need to move quickly to capitalize on emerging new market opportunities or they will completely miss this opportunity for growth.[11] The pioneer in these emerging new markets has the potential to achieve a competitive advantage if it can sustain its advantage in these early stages of market development.[12] When pioneers can establish a *dominant design*, a standard emerges that followers must follow in order to compete.[13] For example, VHS prevailed over Beta as the design standard in the early evolution of the VCR market.

As the market emerges, *early followers* enter the market. Early followers emulate the dominant design and enter the market after letting the pioneer invest in developing the technology, establishing the design standard, and initiating market development. Many Japanese companies use an early follower strategy. Comcast and Earthlink both entered the market for Broadband Internet market as early followers. CompuServe, Prodigy, and America Online established dominant positions in the dial-up Internet service market, but as the technology developed and the broadband market emerged, Earthlink and Comcast entered the market and capitalized on emerging new-market demand for high-speed Internet.

With rapid market growth, many customers are attracted to the market, and customer use and experience grow. It is during this phase of market development and growth, as customer needs become more salient and numerous, that segments begin to form. This growth attracts more competitors, many of whom will fill niche markets to serve the unique needs of a subset of customers.[14] This is a critical point for market leaders in emerging markets to develop multisegment solutions. Businesses that remain narrowly focused will see their market shares erode as new competitors deliver more attractive value propositions. Market pioneers who can sustain a market leadership position through this phase of market development are in the best position to achieve high levels of performance.[15]

OFFENSIVE STRATEGY IIID: Develop New Markets

Apple Computer's initial entry into the personal computer market was a market growth strategy that focused on the enormous untapped market potential of the personal computer market. Apple's philosophy was to bring computing power to the masses. The company's original positioning strategy for Macintosh was: "Only a few have the expertise to operate computers. . . . Introducing Macintosh, for the rest of the world." In the beginning, they had few competitors because they were addressing a market ignored by the major computer manufacturers. Only after Apple legitimized this market did competitors begin to flow to this untapped market.

Global markets such as China, India, and Africa make up over half the world population, yet many of the products manufactured for the United States, Western Europe, and more affluent Asian countries have not been formulated for these markets. Constraints due to price, use compatibility, and availability create a large untapped new-market potential for many products.

For example, many products need electricity, yet rural areas of underdeveloped countries cannot use electrical products because they do not have electricity. A company such as General Electric, which makes gas turbines for jet engines, has already adapted its expertise and technology in that area to enable a business (called a co-generator) to produce its own electricity and sell any excess to local utilities during periods of excess supply. GE has the capability of building electricity production on a small scale, thereby bringing many of its electrical products to consumers in remote locations around the world.

A growth strategy to develop an untapped new-market potential offers both high risk and the potential for high return.[16] Because the market is undeveloped, the cost of development can be significant even with a good customer solution. On the other hand, with few competitors, if any, a business has the opportunity to pioneer a portion of the market largely ignored by competitors. With a "first-mover" advantage, there is the potential to own the market until other competitors venture to enter. A company called Under Armour was launched in 1995 with $40,000 by a college student who maxed out five credit cards developing the market for special undergarments for athletes. By 2004, Under Armour had sales over $100 million, and companies like Nike and Adidas were looking to enter this new emerging market.

CHOOSING OFFENSIVE STRATEGIC MARKET PLANS

A business may pursue multiple offensive strategies, especially if growth plans are more aggressive. For example, Starbucks Coffee has an objective of becoming the world's most recognized and respected brand. To accomplish this, the company is implementing a wide variety of offensive strategic marketing plans and is growing rapidly. Figure 12-10 shows how Starbucks is using many different kinds of offensive strategic market plans to move toward its goal.

A market-based business will often find that it has more market opportunities than it has resources to fund. In that case, the business will have to prioritize strategic market opportunities on the basis of its performance objectives. A business with a short-run need for better profit performance would be inclined to select the share penetration strategy, shown in Figure 12-11, rather than a long-run market development strategy. The share penetration strategy is expected to produce $14 million in net marketing contribution in 5 years. The share penetration strategy offers immediate profit performance and a reasonable level of sales revenue and profit growth.

On the other hand, a business with a good cash position, but facing stagnant growth in maturing markets, might pursue the market development strategy presented in Figure 12-11. This offensive strategy would produce a $1.2 million negative net marketing contribution in the first year of a new-market development strategy. However, in 5 years, this strategy would be expected to produce $13 million in net

FIGURE 12-10 STARBUCKS' OFFENSIVE STRATEGIC MARKET PLANS

Invest to Grow in Existing Markets	Invest to Improve Competitive Position	Invest to Enter New Markets
Grow Market Share	**Customer Loyalty**	**Enter Related New Markets**
• Aggressive expansion of retail presence; 30% annual growth in number of coffee outlets to 7,500 in 2004.	• Starbucks Card fosters short-term customer loyalty. • Commitment to quality builds long-term customer loyalty.	• Wholesale Coffee Beans • Bottled Coffee Drinks • Premium Ice Cream • Premium Teas
Grow Revenue per Customer	**Differentiation Advantage**	**Enter Unrelated New Markets**
• Starbucks Card—Customers can prepay up to $500. • Wireless Internet access in 1,000 stores in 2003.	• Quality—Opened Agronomy office in Costa Rica to assist growers. • Netherlands roasting plant for fast transport across Europe.	
Enter New-Market Segments	**Cost/Marketing Efficiency**	**Enter New Emerging Markets**
• Adding drive-through outlets for higher volume and ROI than traditional coffee houses. • Wholesale coffee bean sales.	• Vertical integration from the plantations to the cup. • Drive-through outlets offer lower marginal cost.	
Expand Market Demand	**Marketing Advantage**	**Develop New Markets**
	• Large-scale retail presence at strategic locations. • International retail partnerships to become competitive quickly.	• Frappuccino reaches 7% of total revenues in its first year.

marketing contribution. Although riskier, this new-market development strategy could provide this business with needed growth and diversification into an attractive market. Thus, the selection of one offensive strategic market plan over another depends on the business's short-run profit needs, strategic position and resources, and opportunities for growth.

FIGURE 12-11 ALTERNATIVE OFFENSIVE STRATEGIC MARKET PLANS

Area of Performance	Share Penetration Strategy		Market Development Strategy	
	First Year	In 5 Years	First Year	In 5 Years
Market Demand	600,000	600,000	20,000	200,000
Market Share (%)	15	20	80	50
Market Growth Rate (%)	0	0	58	58
Target Volume	90,000	120,000	16,000	100,000
Revenue per Customer	$ 450	$ 450	$ 950	$ 450
Total Revenue (millions)	$ 40.5	$ 54.0	$ 15.2	$ 45.0
Variable Cost per Customer	$ 250	$ 250	$ 650	$ 200
Total Variable Costs (millions)	$ 22.5	$ 30.0	$ 10.4	$ 20.0
Margin per Customer	$ 200	$ 200	$ 300	$ 250
Total Contribution (millions)	$ 18.0	$ 24.0	$ 4.8	$ 25.0
Marketing Expenses (millions)	$ 7.0	$ 10.0	$ 6.0	$ 12.0
Net Marketing Contribution (millions)	$ 11.0	$ 14.0	–$ 1.2	$ 13.0

■ Summary

Businesses have a short-term obligation to investors to meet their financial promises of growth and performance. At the same time, they have an obligation to investors and employees to carve out a set of marketing strategies that will improve the position of the business in the long run. The purpose of strategic market planning is to examine the market attractiveness and competitive advantage of each market served by a business. On the basis of an assessment of this position, a strategic market objective is developed and resources are allocated accordingly. To accomplish these performance objectives, a business generally needs a combination of offensive and defensive strategic market plans.

Offensive strategies are more growth oriented and are more likely to occur during the growth phase of the product life cycle, while defensive strategies are more likely to be used in maturing, mature, and declining markets. Offensive strategies can be broken down into three core offensive strategies: sales growth, margin improvement, and diversified growth. Each of theses core offensive strategies has four specific strategies.

Offensive strategies for pursuing sales growth are focused on existing markets. Sales growth offensive strategies include: (1) increasing market share, (2) growing customer purchases, (3) expanding into new-market segments, and (4) efforts to expand market demand by growing market potential. Offensive strategies to improve competitive position with the objective of margin improvement are focused on existing markets and strategies that can improve profit margins. Offensive strategies to improve margin include: (1) increasing customer loyalty, (2) improving differentiation advantage, (3) lowering costs and improving marketing productivity, and (4) building a stronger marketing advantage. Offensive strategies with the goal of diversified growth are focused on new markets and strategies that can achieve sales growth outside the current market domain. Diversified sales growth offensive strategies include: (1) entering new related markets,

(2) entering new unrelated markets, (3) entering new emerging markets, and (4) developing new markets. A good mix of offensive strategic marketing plans is chosen by considering the expected impact of each strategy on short-term or long-run growth in revenues and profitability.

■ Market-Based Logic and Strategic Thinking

1 What is the difference between offensive strategic market plans and defensive strategic market plans?

2 Explain why a business might shift from an offensive strategy to a defensive strategy over the life cycle of a particular product.

3 How can a business meet short-run growth and profit performance targets and still invest in strategic market plans that are focused on long-run objectives with respect to share position, sales growth, and profit performance?

4 How has Harley-Davidson's offensive strategy to grow revenue per customer impacted its sales and profits?

5 How would a Nike offensive strategy to grow market penetration differ from a strategy to grow customer purchases (revenue per customer) in the under-18 female athlete market?

6 Why would Google use an offensive sales growth strategy to expand the Internet search market versus going for more market share of this market?

7 Why would margin improvement be an offensive strategy?

8 Why would AT&T's efforts to improve customer retention be an offensive strategy to improve margins?

9 Absolut Vodka entered two new market segments as part of an offensive strategy to grow sales. Explain the logic of this offensive strategy and why they elected to create new brand names for each segment shown in Figure 12-6.

10 Microsoft has developed a product called Meeting Pro to help facilitate the running of small business meetings. Although this is a value-added software product, Microsoft offers this product at no cost to Windows users. Explain how this is an offensive market share strategy.

11 Why are offensive strategies crucial for the long-run success of a business? What kind of offensive strategies could McDonald's use to ensure future growth in sales and profits?

12 Microsoft has developed a joint venture with Sony to develop an online alternative to the telephone. What type of offensive marketing strategy best describes this joint venture, and what would the expected short- and long-run performance objectives be?

13 How does a market penetration strategy to grow market share differ from a strategy to enter a new segment in the same market?

14 Why is a marketing strategy to grow customer purchases (revenue per customer) potentially more profitable than many other offensive marketing strategies?

15 Why would a business first pursue offensive marketing strategies to increase market share or grow revenue per customer rather than other offensive marketing strategies?

16 What forces limit new-customer growth within existing markets? How could a business grow market demand by addressing these forces?

17 What are the important differences between a related new-market entry strategy and an unrelated new-market entry strategy?

18 When would a business pursue an unrelated new-market entry strategy?

19 What is the advantage of growing market demand in a new, emerging market?

Marketing Performance Tools

Each of the following **marketing performance tools** can be accessed by going to *www.rogerjbest.com* or *www.prenhall.com /best*.

The shaded cells are input cells. The non-shaded cells contain results calculated from your input values.

MARKETING PERFORMANCE TOOL—Defensive Strategy

Strategic Market Plan (customers)	Current	Plan	Plan	Plan
Protect Share Strategy	Year	Year 1	Year 2	Year 3
Market Demand	1,000,000	1,050,000	1,100,000	1,150,000
Market Share (%)	10.0	10.0	10.0	10.0
Customer Volume	100,000	105,000	110,000	115,000
Customer Retention	0.90	0.90	0.90	0.90
Retained Customers	85,500	90,000	94,500	99,000
New Customers	14,500	15,000	15,500	16,000
Revenue per Customer				
Retained Customers	$500	$500	$500	$500
New Customers	$300	$300	$300	$300
Average Revenue per Customer	$471	$471	$472	$472
Sales Revenues (millions)	$47.10	$49.50	$51.90	$54.30
Percent Margin per Customer				
Retained Customers (%)	50.0	50.0	50.0	50.0
New Customers (%)	33.3	33.3	33.3	33.3
Average Percent Margin (%)	48.5	48.5	48.5	48.5
Gross Profit (millions)	$22.82	$24.00	$25.17	$26.35
Marketing Expenses				
Retention Cost per Customer	$25	$25	$25	$25
Acquisition Cost per Customer	$150	$150	$150	$150
Average Marketing Expense (% sales)	9.2	9.1	9.0	9.0
Marketing Expenses (millions)	$4.31	$4.50	$4.69	$4.88
Net Marketing Contribution (millions)	$18.51	$19.50	$20.49	$21.47
Marketing ROS (%)	39.3	39	39	40
Marketing ROI (%)	429	433	437	441

This **marketing performance tool** allows you to estimate the performance impact of an offensive strategy. The first table is a case situation for a business where the strategic market objective is to hold market share. This table is used to compare the performance impact of an offensive strategy. The second table can be used to input different offensive strategies in order to understand the performance impact when compared to the offensive strategy in table 1. The shaded numeric input cells can be changed in doing the following application exercise.

MARKETING PERFORMANCE TOOL—Evaluating Offensive Strategies

Strategic Market Plan (customers)	Current	Plan	Plan	Plan
Offensive Strategy to Grow Share	Year	Year 1	Year 2	Year 3
Market Demand	1,000,000	1,050,000	1,100,000	1,150,000
Market Share (%)	10.0	11.0	12.0	13.0
Customer Volume	100,000	116,000	132,000	150,000
Customer Retention	0.90	0.90	0.90	0.90
Retained Customers	85,500	90,000	103,950	118,800
New Customers	14,500	26,000	28,050	31,200
Revenue per Customer				
Retained Customers	$500	$500	$500	$500
New Customers	$300	$300	$300	$300
Average Revenue per Customer	$471	$456	$458	$459
Sales Revenues (millions)	$47.10	$52.65	$60.39	$68.61
Percent Margin per Customer				
Retained Customers (%)	50.0	50.0	50.0	50.0
New Customers (%)	33.3	33.3	33.3	33.3
Average Percent Margin (%)	48.5	47.6	47.7	47.8
Gross Profit (millions)	$22.82	$25.05	$28.79	$32.77
Marketing Expenses				
Retention Cost per Customer	$25	$25	$25	$25
Acquisition Cost per Customer	$150	$150	$150	$150
Average Marketing Expense (% sales)	9.2	11.5	11.3	11.0
Marketing Expenses (millions)	$4.31	$6.08	$6.81	$7.58
Net Marketing Contribution (millions)	$18.51	$18.97	$21.99	$25.19
Marketing ROS (%)	39.3	36	36	37
Marketing ROI (%)	429	312	323	333

Application Exercise: Using the data provided, answer the following questions: What would be the performance impact of a strategy to increase revenue per customer among retained customers from $600 to $700 while increasing the cost of retention from $25 to $50 per customer? What would be the performance impact of a strategy to hold share and improve customer retention from 90 percent to 92.5 percent? What would be the profit impact of a strategy to grow the market at 10 percent per year if it required the new-customer acquisition cost to increase from $150 per customer to $200 per customer?

Notes

1. David Aaker, "Portfolio Analysis," *Strategic Market Management* (New York: Wiley, 1995): 155–169.
2. Bernard Catry and Michel Chevalier, "Market Share Strategy and the Product Life Cycle," *Journal of Marketing* (October 1974): 29–34.
3. Philippe Haspeslagh, "Portfolio Planning: Uses and Limits," *Harvard Business Review* (January–February 1982): 58–73; and S. Robinson, R. Hichens, and D. Wade, "The Directional Policy Matrix Tool for Strategic Planning," *Long-Range Planning* (June 1978): 8–15.
4. David Aaker, "Growth Strategies," *Strategic Market Management* (New York: Wiley, 1995): 238–259.
5. Charles Lillis, James Cook, Roger Best, and Del Hawkins, "Marketing Strategies to Achieve Market Share Goals," in *Strategic Marketing Management*, H. Thomas and D. Gardner, ed. (New York: Wiley, 1985).
6. David Szymanski, Sundar Bharadwaj, and Rajan Varadarajan, "An Analysis of the Market Share-Profitability Relationship," *Journal of Marketing* (July 1993): 1–18; and C. Davis Fogg, "Planning Gains in Market Share," *Journal of Marketing* (July 1994): 30–38.
7. Daniel Sheinen and Bernd Schmitt, "Extending Brands with New Product Concepts: The Role of Category Attribute Congruity, Brand Affect and Brand Breadth," *Journal of Business Research* (September 1994): 1–10.
8. Gary Hamel and C. K. Prahalad, "Seeing the Future First," *Fortune* (September 5, 1994): 64–70.
9. Edward Roberts and Charles Berry, "Entering New Business: Selecting Strategies for Success," *Sloan Management Review* (Spring 1985): 3–17.
10. Richard Rumelt, "Diversification, Strategy and Profitability," *Strategic Management Journal* 3 (1982): 359–369.
11. G. Stalk Jr., "Time: The Next Source of Competitive Advantage," *Harvard Business Review* (July–August 1988): 41–51; and Thomas Robertson, "How to Reduce Market Penetration Cycle Times," *Sloan Management Review* (Fall 1993): 87–96.
12. William Robinson and Claes Fornell, "Sources of Market Pioneer Advantage in Consumer Goods Industries," *Journal of Marketing Research* (August 1985): 305–317; and William Robinson, "Sources of Market Pioneer Advantages: The Case for Industrial Goods Industries," *Journal of Marketing Research* 25 (1988): 87–94.
13. Roger Best and Reinhard Angelmar, "Strategies for Leveraging Technology Advantage," in *Handbook on Business Strategy* (New York: Warren, Gorham and Lamont, 1989): 2.1–2.10.
14. Vijay Mahajan, Subhash Sharma, and Robert Buzzell, "Assessing the Impact of Competitive Entry on Market Expansion and Incumbent Sales," *Journal of Marketing* (July 1993): 39–52.
15. Glen Urban, T. Carter, S. Gaskin, and Z. Mucha, "Marketing Share Rewards to Pioneering Brands: An Empirical Analysis and Strategic Implications," *Management Science* 32 (1986): 635–659.
16. Igal Ayal and Jehiel Zif, "Market Expansion Strategies in Multinational Markets," *Journal of Marketing* (Spring 1979): 84–94.

CHAPTER 13

Defensive Strategies

istorical share leaders such as General Motors, AT&T, IBM, and others have been under attack in their core markets for some time. For each, a loss on one share point is considerable in terms of sales revenues, net profits, and cash flow. Relatively new share leaders such as Intel, Cisco Systems, and Microsoft face the same challenge. These businesses, like other share defenders, are engaged in a battle to protect their share in the markets they serve.[1]

Intel is the worldwide market leader in the microprocessor market. For many years Intel has been able to maintain an 85 percent share in a growing market. A strategic market plan to invest to protect market share has provided continued growth in sales revenues despite increased competition. As shown in Figure 13-1, a protect position strategy maintained outstanding margins that allowed Intel to grow gross profits and marketing profits (net marketing contribution) over the 5-year planning horizon shown. Intel's cost of marketing, sales, and administration has historically been between 15 and 20 percent but was reduced to 14.3 percent of sales in 2003. Advertising expenses make up over 40 percent of the Intel marketing budget as it spends to maintain its brand awareness and brand equity. In 2003 this strategy produced a net marketing contribution of $12.8 billion, for a Marketing ROS of 42.4 percent. Because marketing expenses were managed to a lower level as a percentage of sales, Marketing ROI grew to 297 percent. This strategy and performance continues to contribute to increased earnings and shareholder value.

Businesses in less attractive markets or businesses with fewer resources may be forced to reduce share in an effort to find a more profitable combination of market share and profitability. Others may be forced to exit markets slowly with a harvest strategy or quickly with a divestment strategy. Each defensive strategy is intended to maximize or protect short-run profits or to minimize short-run losses. This chapter examines defensive strategic market plans and the role they play in achieving the short- and long-run performance objectives of a business.

FIGURE 13-1 INTEL STRATEGY TO PROTECT MARKET SHARE

Area of Performance	1999	2000	2001	2002	2003
Market Demand (billions)	$34.6	$39.6	$31.2	$31.5	$35.4
Market Share (%)	85	85	85	85	85
Sales Revenues (billions)	$29.4	$33.7	$26.5	$26.8	$30.1
Percent Gross Margin (%)	59.5	62.3	49.2	49.8	56.7
Gross Margin (billions)	$17.5	$21.0	$13.0	$13.3	$17.1
Marketing & Adm. (billions)	$ 4.7	$ 6.7	$ 4.5	$ 4.3	$ 4.3
Marketing & Adm. (% of sales)	15.9	19.9	16.8	16.2	14.3
Net Marketing Contribution (billions)	$12.8	$14.3	$ 8.6	$ 9.0	$12.8
Marketing ROS (%)	43.6	42.3	32.4	33.6	42.4
Marketing ROI (%)	274	212	193	207	297

DEFENSIVE STRATEGIC MARKET PLANS

A key part of Intel's long-run performance has been its ability to successfully implement a protect share strategy in the microprocessor market. Any degree of share erosion will lower unit volume, sales revenues, and net marketing contribution. However, a defensive strategy to protect share should not be misinterpreted to mean a hold resources constant strategy. To protect share in a market growing at 15 to 20 percent a year, Intel will have to continue its roll-out of new products and add to its marketing budget. Not doing either would almost guarantee erosion of Intel's market share position in the microprocessor market.

In general, businesses in high-share positions in growing or mature markets will use defensive strategic market plans to maintain cash flow that supports short-run profit performance and shareholder value. Without these defensive strategic market plans and their profitability, businesses would face a difficult short-run situation in terms of profit performance and would lack the resources to invest in growth-oriented offensive market opportunities.

For example, consider the business situation presented in Figure 13-2. Currently, the business is in four markets, one of which is losing money. The first market (M1) is a maturing market in which the business holds a high-share position. The business's strategic market plan for this market is to protect this high-share position. The second market (M2) is a slow-growth market in which this business's strategic market plan is to grow share. The third market (M3) is a high-growth market in which the business's strategic market plan is to protect its share position. Market four (M4) is losing money and has been determined to be unattractive. The strategic market plan for this market is to harvest share and maximize short-run profits as the business systematically exits the market. A fifth strategic market plan is to enter an attractive emerging market (M5) in which the business will lose money initially but which will be a good source of future growth, improved share position, and long-run cash flow.

FIGURE 13-2 STRATEGIC MARKET PLANNING AND PERFORMANCE

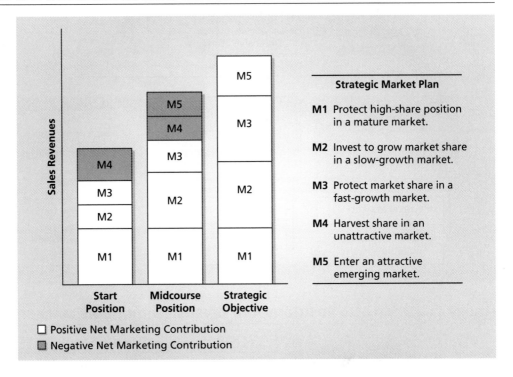

Strategic Market Plan

M1 Protect high-share position in a mature market.

M2 Invest to grow market share in a slow-growth market.

M3 Protect market share in a fast-growth market.

M4 Harvest share in an unattractive market.

M5 Enter an attractive emerging market.

□ Positive Net Marketing Contribution
▨ Negative Net Marketing Contribution

With these five market-based management strategies, this business hopes to grow revenue and profits through a series of strategic moves to protect, grow, or harvest market share.[2] Each strategic market plan plays an important role in the business's short- and long-run sales and profitability. For two of these markets, defensive strategic market plans are needed to protect the company's share position in different ways. One other market calls for a defensive strategy to harvest whatever profitability can be squeezed out of it.

The primary goal of a defensive strategy is to protect profitability and key strategic share positions that are worth the investment. A secondary goal of defensive market strategies is to manage the profitability of businesses that are moving beyond the potential for high growth or profitability. With these goals in mind, Figure 13-3 outlines defensive strategic market plans that may be appropriate in different situations.

As shown in Figure 13-4, certain portfolio positions, based on market attractiveness and competitive advantage, can lead to more than one possible defensive strategy. For example, a business with a strong competitive advantage in a fairly attractive market may find that protecting the share position might be appropriate, or it may choose to defend the market by optimizing or monetizing it. In all cases, defensive marketing strategies are focused on maximizing short-run profits and protecting or improving the overall strategic position of a business.

FIGURE 13-3 STRATEGIC MARKET PLANS AND DEFENSIVE STRATEGIES

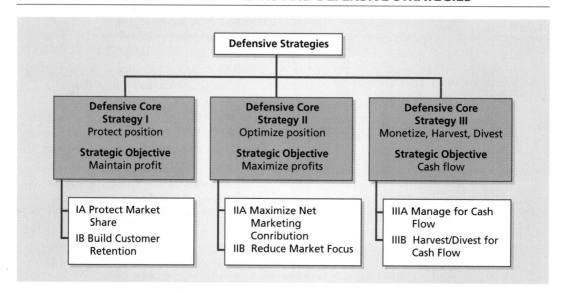

FIGURE 13-4 PORTFOLIO POSITIONS AND DEFENSIVE STRATEGIC MARKET PLANS

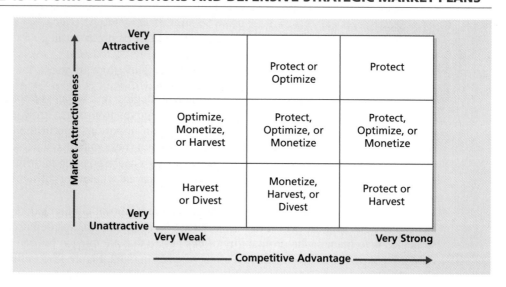

DEFENSIVE CORE STRATEGY I: PROTECT POSITION

In many competitive environments, whether sports or business, the best defense is an offense. Quite often businesses with a dominant share and strong position of competitive advantage are lulled into the delusion that they are undefeatable. Eventually, however, these businesses will be overtaken by more aggressive challengers if they are not careful. To hold a high-share position in an attractive, growing market, a business must continue investing aggressively in order to sustain its competitive advantage.

DEFENSIVE STRATEGY IA: Protect Market Share

Share leaders in many industries have market shares in excess of 50 percent. However, the conditions under which they have to defend their share positions can be drastically different. For example, Campbell Soup has a 60 percent share position in a mature American soup market; Gillette has a 70 percent share and is the share leader in the razor and blade market, which is also mature; and Kodak has more than a 60 percent share of the declining American film market. Their defensive strategies in slow-growing mature markets will be different from those of businesses with high shares in fast-growth markets. Intel, with an 85 percent share of the fast-growing computer market, and Microsoft, with a 95 percent share of the rapidly developing desktop operating-system market, will each have to exert greater marketing efforts to protect their high-share positions while their markets are still experiencing rapid growth. However, each has the same fundamental objective: invest to protect market share. Depending on the nature of the market situation, a defensive strategy to protect market share might take on different forms.

Investing to Protect Position in Growth Markets

Growth markets require a much greater marketing effort and more investment in new products to protect a share leadership position than do mature markets. The faster the market grows, the more marketing resources are needed to protect share. If a business does not invest to protect share in a growth market, its market share is almost certain to decline. Thus, growing markets create a much greater potential for share loss than do slow-growth markets. Hence, the resources needed to offset the effects of growth with a defensive strategic market plan to protect share must be much greater.

In the Profit Impact of Marketing Strategies (PIMS) database, the average business will experience approximately a –0.4 percent annual rate of market share change per 1 percent of market growth rate. This means that a business in a market growing at 10 percent a year will experience a 4 percent rate of share erosion if the effects of market growth are not offset by a defensive strategic market plan. Using this average, a business with a 20 percent market share in a market growing at a rate of 10 percent per year would experience an estimated share loss of almost 4 share points in 5 years if it did nothing to offset the negative impact of market growth. Of course, if the market were growing at 15 percent per year, the business would experience a much faster rate of share erosion, as shown in Figure 13-5.

Although the effects of market growth on market share change are likely to be different among industries, the differences are relatively small in reasonably diverse areas of business, as also shown in Figure 13-5. Thus, the impact of market growth on market share erosion is fairly uniform among different areas of business.

Investing to Protect a High-Share Position

Market share leaders such as Eastman Kodak, Campbell Soup, and Cisco Systems have strong share positions that generate considerable sales revenues and profits that directly affect the financial performance of these businesses. Hence, defensive marketing strategies to protect these high-share positions are critical to short-run profit performance and provide a major source of cash for investment in offensive marketing strategies for future growth and profit performance.

It is hard to imagine how having a large market share could be a handicap with respect to protecting market share. However, in the PIMS database, we consistently find

FIGURE 13-5 MARKET GROWTH RATE AND SHARE EROSION

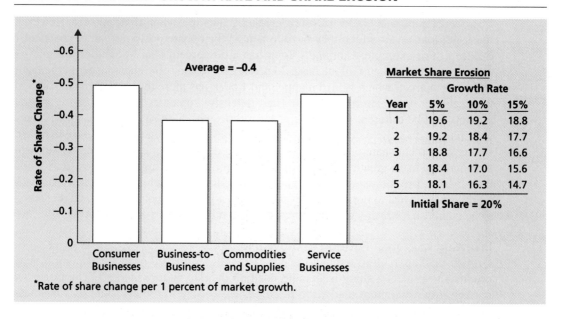

	Growth Rate		
Year	5%	10%	15%
1	19.6	19.2	18.8
2	19.2	18.4	17.7
3	18.8	17.7	16.6
4	18.4	17.0	15.6
5	18.1	16.3	14.7

Market Share Erosion

Initial Share = 20%

*Rate of share change per 1 percent of market growth.

an inverse relationship between market share change and size of market share. As shown in Figure 13-6, the average PIMS business would experience approximately a –0.08 percent rate of market share change per 1 percent of current market share. This means that a business with a 30 percent market share would experience a –2.4 percent annual rate of

FIGURE 13-6 MARKET SHARE EROSION AND CURRENT SHARE POSITION

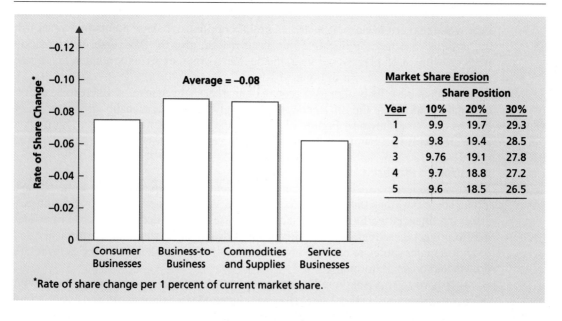

	Share Position		
Year	10%	20%	30%
1	9.9	19.7	29.3
2	9.8	19.4	28.5
3	9.76	19.1	27.8
4	9.7	18.8	27.2
5	9.6	18.5	26.5

Market Share Erosion

*Rate of share change per 1 percent of current market share.

share loss, which would lead to a 26.5 percent share loss in 5 years. A business with a 10 percent market share would never really feel this effect, because the size of its market share is much smaller, and its share would erode only to an estimated 9.6 percent in 5 years.

Thus, high-share businesses have to invest considerably more to protect share independent of other share-eroding market forces such as market growth, competitor entry, or competitor strategies. As one begins to comprehend the impact that high share and high-market growth rate have on eroding market share, one can better understand the market share losses experienced by Eastman Kodak, IBM, AT&T, General Motors, and other high-share businesses. And, as it is on market growth, the impact of market share on the rate of market share change is fairly consistent among diverse areas of business in the PIMS database, as illustrated in Figure 13-6.

To successfully defend high-share positions, businesses need to continuously improve their competitive advantage and marketing effort. Share leaders that make temporary cuts in marketing to improve short-run profit only hurt next year's profits with a reduced market share. Thus, share leaders must remain committed to (1) new-product development, (2) efforts to improve product and service quality at a rate faster than the competition, and (3) fully supporting the marketing budgets needed to protect a high-share position.[3]

Investing to Protect a Follower Share Position

Of course, not everyone can be a market share leader. Illustrated in Figure 13-7 are four market structures, each presenting followers in a different market share position. A business that is second in market share, but is a close follower (Market II in Figure 13-7), has an interesting strategic market decision to consider. Does this follower challenge the leader with an offensive share penetration strategy? Or does it protect its share position and maximize the profits that can be extracted from that share position? Depending on

FIGURE 13-7 MARKET STRUCTURE AND SHARE POSITION

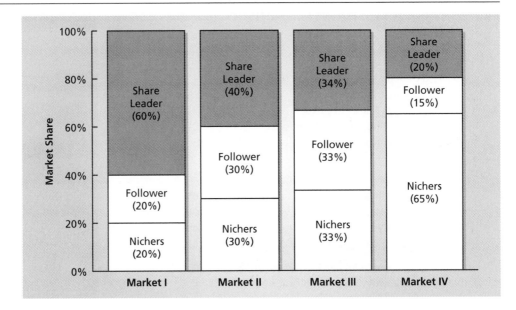

the strength of the share leader, the share leader's commitment to defending its share position, and the follower business's resources and short-run profit needs, either strategic market plan could be pursued. But what does a successful defensive follower strategy look like?[4]

Figure 13-8 profiles the average follower (number two share) business in the PIMS database that has achieved above-average profitability and the average follower business with below-average profit performance. With respect to competitive advantage, profitable share followers have higher relative product quality, which helps support higher levels of customer value, price, and unit margin. However, they also invest more aggressively in marketing as a percentage of sales as well as on a relative basis when compared with competitors. These effects produce a slightly higher share, which contributes to a higher level of capacity utilization.

These businesses also invest more in research and development (R&D) as a percentage of sales. This investment translates into a higher level of technological advantage that most likely can be traced back to higher relative product quality. Thus, profitable followers protect their number two share position with investments in both R&D and marketing. As pointed out earlier, without these types of investments, a business could not protect a share position, even in relatively slow-growth markets.

Investing to Protecting a Niche Share Position

The strategic decision whether to engage in a long-run offensive or defensive strategic market plan has to also be made by *niche* share businesses. For example, niche share businesses depicted in Figure 13-7 may elect to pursue offensive strategic market plans to challenge share leaders—or, perhaps the market situation would lead a business to pursue a defensive strategy to protect a profitable niche market. In many ways, a niche business is simply the share leader in a more narrowly defined market. Thus, share leaders, followers, and niche businesses could each pursue defensive strategies to protect their market share positions.

FIGURE 13-8 SUCCESSFUL VERSUS UNSUCCESSFUL FOLLOWER SHARE STRATEGIES

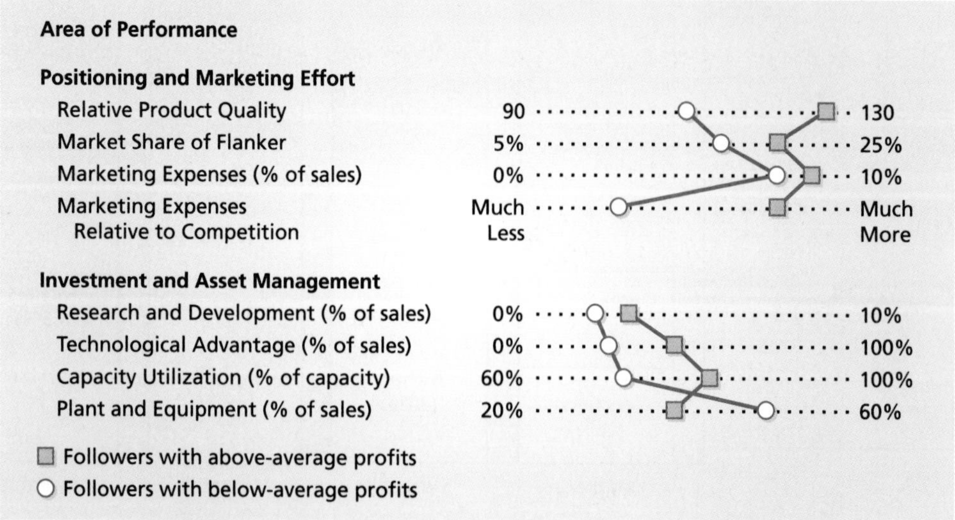

Area of Performance

Positioning and Marketing Effort

Relative Product Quality	90	130
Market Share of Flanker	5%	25%
Marketing Expenses (% of sales)	0%	10%
Marketing Expenses Relative to Competition	Much Less	Much More

Investment and Asset Management

Research and Development (% of sales)	0%	10%
Technological Advantage (% of sales)	0%	100%
Capacity Utilization (% of capacity)	60%	100%
Plant and Equipment (% of sales)	20%	60%

☐ Followers with above-average profits
○ Followers with below-average profits

A business that pursues a niche strategic market plan could be a small business with limited resources or a large business that has pursued a reduced-focus strategy within a larger market and still achieves high levels of profitability.[5] For whatever reason, the business could develop a dominant position in a niche market but still have an overall share of the market that is relatively small compared with that of the share leader. However, within its market niche, it is the share leader and has the same needs as share leaders in defending its share position.

Shown in Figure 13-9 are average profiles for profitable high-share and profitable low-share businesses. If you examine these two profiles closely, you will notice that there are only two areas of commonality: relative product quality and relative sales force expense. Having above-average product quality and above-average customer contact and market coverage are key success factors for both profitable high-share businesses and profitable low-share businesses.

However, to achieve above-average levels of profitability, low-share niche businesses need to focus in order to keep expenses low.[6] Their niche focus is most evident in their narrow product line, limited new-product effort, and limited advertising effort relative to competitors. In addition, relative prices are slightly below the average relative price index of 100. With an average relative price near 96, and relative product quality close to 123, these successful niche businesses create an attractive customer value as shown in the following:

$$\text{Customer Value} = \text{Relative Benefits} - \text{Relative Price}$$
$$+27 = 123 - 96$$

As shown in Figure 13-10, low-share niche businesses with above-average customer value are more profitable. As a matter of fact, a low-share business with above-average customer value is more profitable than a high-share business with below-average customer value. Thus, an important component of success for niche-share businesses is above-average customer value and sales coverage with a careful product focus.

FIGURE 13-9 MARKETING STRATEGIES FOR PROFITABLE SHARE LEADERS AND PROFITABLE LOW-SHARE NICHE BUSINESSES

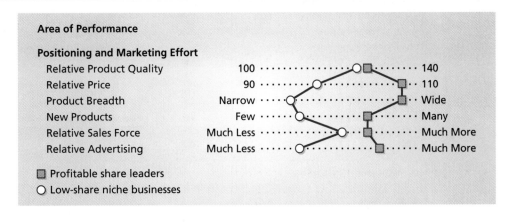

FIGURE 13-10 CUSTOMER VALUE, MARKET SHARE, AND PROFITABILITY

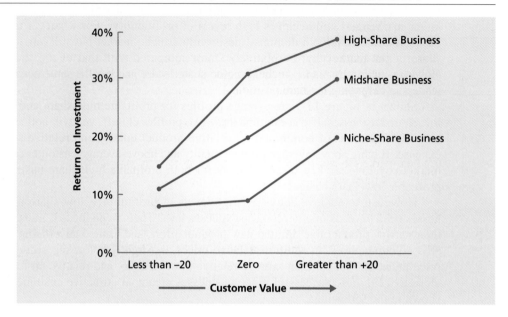

DEFENSIVE STRATEGY IB: Build Customer Retention

Protecting a valued share position is certainly a defensive strategy that is at the core of many successful businesses. However, the profit impact of holding a 30 percent market share can be quite different for high and low levels of customer retention.

For example, assume that two businesses each produce $400 of margin per customer the first year, but this margin grows by $25 per year for each year the customer is retained. Further assume that each business spends $500 to acquire a new customer and $100 per year to retain a customer. As shown in Figure 13-11, the business with 75 percent customer retention will retain the average customer for 4 years, whereas an

FIGURE 13-11 PROFIT IMPACT OF CUSTOMER RETENTION STRATEGY

| | 75% Customer Retention* | | | | 80% Customer Retention* | | |
Year	Net Cash	Discount Factor	Value	Year	Net Cash	Discount Factor	Present Value
0	−$500	1.000	−$500	0	−$500	1.000	−$500
1	+$300	0.870	+$261	1	+$300	0.870	+$261
2	+$325	0.756	+$246	2	+$325	0.756	+$246
3	+$350	0.658	+$230	3	+$350	0.658	+$230
4	+$375	0.572	+$215	4	+$375	0.572	+$215
5	0	0.497	0	5	+$400	0.497	+$199
	Net Present Value at 15% = +$452				Net Present Value at 15% = +$651		

* Customer Life = 1/(1 − Customer Retention)

80 percent customer retention rate will keep the average customer for 5 years. That's an extra $199 in discounted net cash flow.

This analysis demonstrates how a business that is able to build a higher level of customer retention can be more profitable than another business, even when both have the same market share. Whether a high-share market leader, a share follower, or a low-share niche business, a business can build profits with a defensive strategy to protect share while building customer retention.

DEFENSIVE CORE STRATEGY II: OPTIMIZE POSITION

Product-markets in late-growth and mature stages of their product life cycle need to be managed to optimize marketing profits. It is during the late stages of market growth that maximum market profits are obtained, as shown in Figure 13-12. As volume produced by market demand nears its maximum potential and margins are yet to be fully squeezed, a business is able to extract its highest level of gross profit. Because sales are slowing, investments in marketing expenses should also slow. Managed properly, this combination of volume, margin, and marketing expenses should yield maximum marketing profits over the product life cycle, as shown in Figure 13-13. Businesses that mismanage price and margin or over-invest in marketing at this point are likely to miss their best opportunity for profits.

FIGURE 13-12 PRODUCT LIFE CYCLE AND MARKETING PROFITABILITY

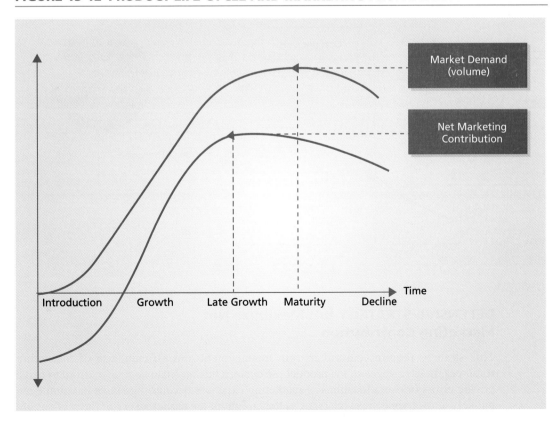

FIGURE 13-13 PROFIT LIFE CYCLE AND COMPONENTS OF MARKETING PROFITABILITY

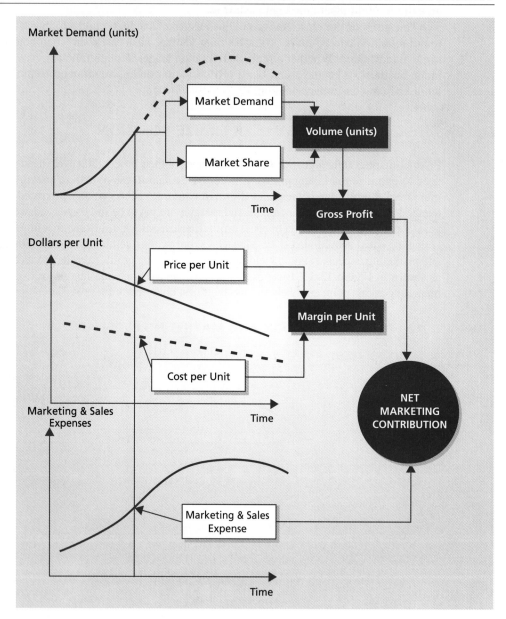

DEFENSIVE STRATEGY IIA: Maximize Net Marketing Contribution

This strategy requires careful margin management and efficient use of marketing resources. In later stages of the product life cycle, a business can no longer afford to make pricing errors or overallocations of marketing expenses because increases in volume are unlikely to overcome these mistakes as they might in the earlier stages of the product life cycle. Thus, the first step in optimizing net marketing contribution is optimal management of margin-volume rather than price-volume.

Price-volume strategies in the growth phase of the product life cycle were rewarded with higher volumes, sales, and marketing profits. However, in the later growth and mature stages of the product life cycle, lower prices, which mean lower margins, are not likely to produce higher volumes because market growth is limited and competitive reaction to losses in volume are likely to be substantial. Thus, the strategic marketing challenge is to find the right combination of margin and volume that yields the highest gross profit as shown here:

$$\text{Gross Profit} = \text{Volume (units)} \times \text{Margin per Unit}$$
$$= \text{Market Demand} \times \text{Market Share} \times (\text{Price} - \text{Variable Cost})$$

Proper margin management is the first step in successfully achieving an optimized position. For example, in the personal computer market, the price elasticity is close to -2 for most PCs. Margins for most PCs are 20 percent or lower. As the market for PCs matures, a business may need to rethink its pricing in order to optimize profits as market growth slows. Shown in Figure 13-14 is the profit impact of a 10 percent price decrease to grow

FIGURE 13-14 PROFIT IMPACT OF PC PRICE INCREASE

10% Price Decrease Area of Performance	Current	Proposed	Change
Market Demand	2,000,000	2,000,000	0
Volume	100,000	120,000	20,000
Market Share (%)	5.0	6.0	1.0
Price	$2,000	$1,800	($200)
Sales Revenues	$200,000,000	$216,000,000	$16,000,000
Variable Cost per Unit	$1,600	$1,600	$0
Margin per Unit	$400	$200	−$200
Gross Profit	$40,000,000	$24,000,000	−$16,000,000

10% Price Increase Area of Performance	Current	Proposed	Change
Market Demand	2,000,000	2,000,000	0
Volume	100,000	80,000	−20,000
Market Share (%)	5.0	4.0	−1.0
Price	$2,000	$2,200	$200
Sales Revenues	$200,000,000	$176,000,000	−$24,000,000
Variable Cost per Unit	$1,600	$1,600	$0
Margin per Unit	$400	$600	$200
Gross Profit	$40,000,000	$48,000,000	$8,000,000

volume and sales and an optimize strategy for a PC priced at $2,000 with a 20 percent margin in a market with a price elasticity of -2. As shown, the price decrease will produce a 20 percent volume increase, one point market share increase, and $16 million increase in sales revenues. In a sales-oriented culture, this strategy would be viewed as a great success. However, because of lower margins following the price decrease, this business will actually lose $16 million in gross profits.

An optimizing strategy to raise prices by 10 percent in a maturing market would result in lower volumes, lower market share, and lower sales as shown in Figure 13-14. Although these are not promising results, this defensive strategy will actually yield an $8 million *increase* in gross profits. If the strategic market objective is to optimize position in order to maximize profits, then a price increase is the best strategic market plan. Reduced spending on marketing and sales at this stage of the product life cycle could also improve marketing profits as shown here:

$$\text{Net Marketing Contribution} = \text{Gross Profit} - \text{Marketing Expenses}$$
$$= \text{Gross Profit} - (\text{Acquisition Costs} + \text{Retention Costs})$$

Because market demand is slowing, investments in marketing to acquire new customers should be reduced while a higher proportion of the marketing budget is focused on customer retention. Recall that acquiring a new customer costs 5 to 10 times more than retaining an existing customer, and as a market reaches its full potential, there are fewer customers entering the market. At this point, the business should be able to maintain market share of customers with a lower level of marketing expenses, assuming customer retention is at a good level of performance. Low customer retention at this stage of the product life cycle would make it impossible to achieve maximum marketing profits because the business would need to spend heavily on new-customer acquisition just to replace lost customers and maintain market share.

DEFENSIVE STRATEGY IIB: Reduce Market Focus

As shown earlier in Figure 13-4, a business may find itself in a portfolio position that can lead to more than one defensive strategic market plan. Should the business invest to strengthen its competitive advantage, allocate resources to protect its share position, or reduce its focus position within a market to maximize profitability? All can be viable strategic market plans, depending upon different market and business conditions.

A decision to pursue a reduced focus defensive strategy would be most appropriate when:

> There are not sufficient resources to invest to protect the current share position or when greater levels of profitability can be derived from a narrower, more selective choice of target customers.

Thus, a reduced market focus prescribes a defensive strategic market plan that involves narrowing market focus and trimming market share in an effort to improve profit performance. This approach may produce a reduction in revenue and marketing budget but higher levels of profitability as a percentage of sales.[7] As shown in Figure 13-15, the whole idea of a reduced focus is to become more efficient. In this illustration, a mass

FIGURE 13-15 SELECTIVE MARKET FOCUS, MARKETING RESOURCES, AND MARKETING PRODUCTIVITY

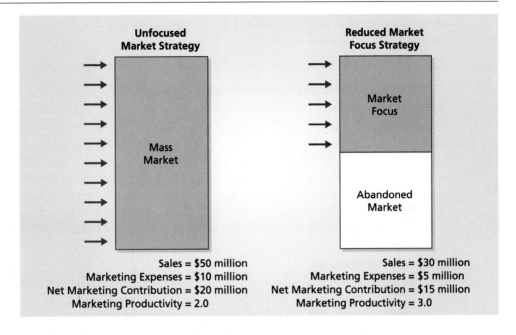

market approach is less efficient than a reduced market focus in terms of marketing productivity. Although sales and profits are reduced, a reduced focus is able to improve marketing productivity from $2 of net marketing contribution per dollar of marketing budget to $3 net marketing contribution. Thus, this business had to shrink to become more efficient in producing profits.

DEFENSIVE CORE STRATEGY III: MONETIZE, HARVEST, OR DIVEST

At some point in every product-market life cycle, markets will be less attractive and will need to be managed for short-run profits regardless of competitive advantage. In some mature or declining markets, an attractive cash flow can be managed for some time with a monetize defensive strategy. In other situations, the best defensive strategy may be a slow market exit (harvest strategy) or a rapid market exit (divest strategy). In each case, the defensive strategy is designed to maximize immediate cash flow.

DEFENSIVE STRATEGY IIIA: Manage for Cash Flow

In many mature markets, market demand can be expected to remain strong for many years. When an optimize position is not viable, a business may elect to remain in the market with a monetize cash flow strategy. This defensive strategy operates with minimal marketing resources and typically low prices. Many mature commodity products can be managed with competitive prices and sold with no sales or service. These products are not typically advertised and are often sold on a cash basis. The goal of a monetize strategy is to extract the maximum short-run cash flow from the market. At the point when this can no longer be accomplished at a desired level of cash flow, a business may elect to pursue a harvest or divest strategy.

DEFENSIVE STRATEGY IIIB: Harvest-Divest for Cash Flow

Portfolio positions that warrant a defensive strategy to exit from a market can lead to a harvest (slow exit) marketing strategy or to a divestment (fast exit) strategic market plan, as depicted in the portfolio model shown in Figure 13-4. When additional profits can be made with a slow exit, a harvest strategy can be a good source of short-run profits. If a business were losing money in a given market, it might be more inclined to pursue a quick market exit strategy and divest its share position as quickly as possible. In this case, a divestment strategy also improves short-run profits by eliminating a source of negative cash flow.

Harvest Price Strategy

The combination of unattractive markets and weak competitive advantage translates into both weak strategic position and potentially weak profit performance.[8] When a reduced focus strategy cannot produce desired levels of performance, an exit strategic market plan warrants consideration. However, rather than divest a share position and exit quickly, there are often good short-run performance opportunities offered by systematically raising prices and reducing marketing expenses.[9]

For example, consider the business situation, outlined in Figure 13-16, that faced a chemical business.[10] Two of five product lines were not covering their marketing expenses. With respect to portfolio position, the business had an average competitive

FIGURE 13-16 CHEMICAL BUSINESS PRODUCT-LINE PERFORMANCE

Area of Performance	Silicon Pigments	Primary Products	Special Products	Basic Colors	Color Enhancers	Overall Total
Market Demand (millions)	100	167	154	96	556	
Market Share (%)	10	12	13	26	9	
Unit Volume (millions)	10	20	20	25	50	125
Unit Price	$4.50	$2.80	$1.60	$0.80	$0.60	
Sales Revenue (millions)	$ 45	$ 56	$ 32	$ 20	$ 30	$ 183
Unit Variable Cost	$3.50	$2.00	$1.30	$0.70	$0.54	
Unit Margin	$1.00	$0.80	$0.30	$0.10	$0.06	
Total Contribution (millions)	$10.0	$16.0	$ 6.0	$ 2.5	$ 3.0	$ 37.5
Marketing Expenses (millions)	$ 2.0	$ 7.0	$ 5.0	$ 3.0	$ 4.5	$ 21.5
Net Marketing Contribution (millions)	$ 8.0	$ 9.0	$ 1.0	−$ .5	−$ 1.5	$ 16.0

advantage in an increasingly unattractive market. Senior management felt the best strategy would be to divest the business by selling it. However, they could not find a buyer, so they pursued a harvest price strategy.

The prices of silicon pigments, primary products, and special products were immediately raised 10 to 19 percent. At the same time, the prices of basic colors and color enhancers were raised 10 percent and then another 10 percent in 6 months. These changes resulted in an overall price increase of 22.5 percent for basic colors and 25 percent for color enhancers. In addition, marketing expenses were modestly reduced. The initial customer reaction was expected. There was an immediate reduction of 14 to 18 percent in the volume of silicon pigments, primary products, and special products. The customer exit for basic colors and color enhancers, with more aggressive price increases, was even greater, because as the volume for these two product lines decreased by 33 and 35 percent, respectively.

However, after 18 months, customer defection subsided. As shown in Figure 13-17, the increased prices offset some of the lost volume, because sales revenues decreased from $183 million to $170 million. More important, however, each of the product lines now produced a positive net marketing contribution. The overall net marketing contribution more than doubled, from $16 million to $36.1 million.

After attaining this level of performance, the business was successful in finding a buyer. One might wonder why the company would not retain the business after it became profitable. First, this level of profitability was still below the company average and, hence, a drain on overall profits and shareholder value. Second, and more important, this was an unattractive market, and the business wanted to redirect these resources into a better strategic market opportunity.

Harvest Marketing Resource Strategy

In many instances, a business may not be able to raise prices as a strategy to harvest share while maximizing short-run profits. A soft drink manufacturer's prices are difficult to

FIGURE 13-17 CHEMICAL BUSINESS PRODUCT-LINE PERFORMANCE

Area of Performance	Silicon Pigments	Primary Products	Special Products	Basic Colors	Color Enhancers	Overall Total
Market Demand (millions)	100	167	154	96	556	
Market Share (%)	8.6	10.3	10.7	17.1	6.0	
Unit Volume (millions)	8.6	17.2	16.5	16.4	33.3	92
Unit Price	$4.95	$3.20	$1.90	$0.98	$0.75	
Sales Revenue (millions)	$42.6	$55.0	$31.4	$16.1	$25.0	$ 170
Unit Variable Cost	$3.50	$2.00	$1.30	$0.70	$0.54	
Unit Margin	$1.45	$1.20	$0.60	$0.28	$0.21	
Total Contribution (millions)	$12.5	$20.6	$ 9.9	$ 4.6	$ 7.0	$54.6
Marketing Expenses (millions)	$ 2.0	$ 7.0	$ 4.5	$ 2.0	$ 3.0	$18.5
Net Marketing Contribution (millions)	$10.5	$13.6	$ 5.4	$ 2.6	$ 4.0	$36.1

alter in the end market. In such a case, a business can reduce the marketing resources it devotes to that product and its market share position. For example, Slice is a low-share soft drink with minimal marketing support. Its market share is less than 5 percent of the lemon-lime soft drink segment and well behind Sprite, which has a 56 percent segment share. Although Pepsi has examined different ways to either revitalize the brand or reposition it, its market share remains relatively stagnant. By not supporting Slice, the company is maximizing what profits it can take as Slice slowly exits the market.

In heavily advertised consumer goods markets, share erosion can be rather dramatic with major reductions in advertising budget. From the PIMS database, one learns that the rate of share change is affected by the rate of change in advertising budget. For example, the following shows the rate of share loss for a consumer product that experienced a 25 percent reduction in advertising budget for each of 3 consecutive years. In this case, a 10 percent market share would erode to 9.6 percent in 3 years.

$$
\begin{aligned}
\text{Market Share (3 years)} &= \text{Market Share} \, (1.00 + [0.05 \times \text{Change in Advertising Budget}])^3 \\
&= 10\% \times (1.00 + [0.05 \times -0.25])^3 \\
&= 10\% \times (1.00 - 0.0125)^3 \\
&= 10\% \times .96 \\
&= 9.6\%
\end{aligned}
$$

When advertising budgets are large, this can be a significant savings. As long as the product has an adequate profit margin, a business could improve short-run profits as it reduces marketing expenses and slowly loses market share. The profits taken in the short run from the harvested product would normally be reallocated to a more attractive product-market in which the business hopes to build a stronger share position and desired levels of profit.

Divest Market Strategy

One of the most difficult decisions any business faces is the decision to quickly sell off (divest) an unattractive product. In some instances, these are products that the company was built on, and it is difficult to let them go. In other cases, they are major investments that are hard to kill because of the money spent and the commitment made to make them successful ventures. As a result, businesses often hang on to unattractive market positions with weak or average competitive advantage far too long.

Figure 13-18 shows the portfolio of General Electric's clock and timer products as it existed in the late 1970s. Many of the products were in unattractive markets, had a weak competitive advantage, or both. GE divested the businesses shown and invested in the two that were in more attractive market positions. Eventually, these product-markets were also divested because they did not match the overall performance objectives of the company.

To divest a share position, a business can either find a buyer for the business or simply close down the operation and sell its assets. In most instances, the desired choice is to find a buyer. Selling generally yields a greater return and preserves the employment of those working in the business.

**FIGURE 13-18 GENERAL ELECTRIC DIVESTMENT STRATEGY FOR UNATTRACTIVE
PRODUCT-MARKETS**

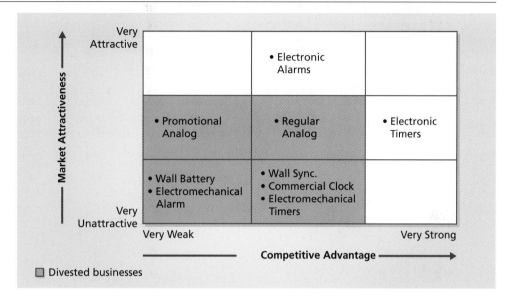

A divestment strategy, although desired, may sometimes not be feasible. For example, a business that has a 25-year commitment to produce a critical component for a government missile cannot easily exit the product-market; it has a responsibility to supply that product for the duration of the contract. Likewise, producers of pharmaceuticals or other life-supporting products may have a difficult time divesting a share position for either legal or ethical reasons. Also, a simple divest share position when no buyer is available can be difficult.

SELECTING A DEFENSIVE STRATEGY

Consider a business in a market with below-average market attractiveness and average competitive advantage that is making $25 million in net marketing contribution. This is a reasonably good profit performance, but an average competitive advantage in an unattractive market does not warrant an offensive strategic market plan to grow share. However, the share position is profitable enough to keep and, hence, a harvest market defensive strategy may not be appropriate. The choices left for this business are a protect-share strategy and a reduced-focus strategy.

As shown in Figure 13-19, if the business elected to pursue a protect-share strategy, it would have to invest in marketing and other business activities such as R&D to maintain its 30 percent share. Given these assumptions, it is estimated that the business could maintain sales revenues of $240 million over the next 3 years. A strategy of investing to protect share would produce $30 million in net marketing contribution. With marketing

FIGURE 13-19 SELECTING BETWEEN TWO DEFENSIVE MARKETING STRATEGIES

Area of Performance	Estimated Performance in 3 Years	
	Protect Share Strategy	Reduced Focus Strategy
Market Demand (000)	2,000	2,000
Market Share (%)	30	20
Unit Volume (000)	600	400
Unit Price	$400	$450
Sales Revenues (millions)	$240	$180
Unit Variable Cost	$300	$300
Unit Margin	$100	$150
Total Contribution (millions)	$ 60	$ 60
Marketing Expenses (millions)	30	20
Net Marketing Contribution (millions)	$ 30	$ 40

expenses also equal to $30 million, a protect-share strategy would yield a marketing productivity equal to 1.0.

The alternative defensive strategic market plan would be to reduce focus. This strategy would purposefully reduce the business's market share from 30 percent to 20 percent. However, the selective market focus strategy would yield a higher average price and unit margin and would require less in marketing expenses. The net result would be a $60 million reduction in sales revenue but an increase in net marketing contribution from $30 to $40 million. With marketing expenses of $20 million, this strategy would also result in a market productivity of 2.0, twice that of the protect-share strategy.

Overall, a business faces many market situations and a well-defined set of business objectives. Some performance objectives are short run, others are long run. Recognizing its performance objectives and its positioning in each of its markets, the business must put together a set of strategic market plans that will meet its performance objectives. Businesses will generally need a combination of offensive and defensive strategic market plans. Whereas offensive strategic market plans are geared for growth and improving share position, defensive strategic market plans are important sources of short-run profits and important in defending strategic share positions. Both are needed and play key roles in meeting a business's performance objectives.

■ Summary

Businesses have a short-term obligation to investors to meet their financial promises of growth and profit performance. At the same time, they have an obligation to investors and employees to carve out a set of strategic market plans that will improve the position of the business in the long run. The primary purpose of a defensive strategic market plan is to protect key strategic share positions while managing defensive positions to produce short-run growth and profits to meet the business's performance objectives.

Defensive strategic market plans play a critical role in the short-run profit performance of a business and in the protection of key strategic share positions that will support future profit performance. Strategically, important share positions require a defensive strategic market plan to protect share position. This can include a protect-share position in attractive markets in which a business has an average to strong competitive advantage. A protect market position defensive strategy can also include a strategy to improve customer retention, which, while maintaining a share position, can have a dramatic impact on profits with little or no change in sales revenue. A business may also use a reduced market focus strategy to more narrowly focus its resources in an effort to better defend a desired share position and improve the profits derived from this market.

To protect market share requires much more than a business-as-usual marketing effort. Market forces such as market-growth rate, market-share size, and competitor entry all create share-eroding forces that can cause share to decrease if not offset by improved competitive advantage or increased marketing effort. Declines in relative competitive advantage in the areas of new-product sales, product quality, and service quality can also contribute to market share erosion—and decreases in marketing effort in the areas of sales force and marketing communications will adversely affect defensive strategic market plans designed to protect an important share position.

In less attractive markets that are also maturing or mature markets where growth is limited and margins are reduced to low levels, a business may shift from an invest-to-protect defensive strategy to an optimize defensive strategy. A maximize-profits strategy could involve price increases to improve profits while sacrificing volume, share, and sales revenues, and/or reducing marketing expenses to a level focused primarily on customer retention. A reduced-focus strategy goes one step further in raising prices to drastically reduce market volume by focusing on certain customers in order to optimize profits.

In situations in which a business either is in an unattractive market or has weak competitive advantage, it may elect to use an exit strategic market plan. If the business is profitable and capable of producing good short-run profits, a harvest strategy would be used. A harvest strategy could involve raising prices or reducing marketing resources or both. This type of defensive strategic market plan enables a business to exit a market slowly while maximizing short-run profits. On the other hand, if a business is losing money or would like to free up resources at a faster rate, a divest strategy would be more appropriate. A divest strategy would normally seek to sell the business in order to maximize the value derived from the assets and goodwill created by the business. If there are no buyers, a business may simply have to use an accelerated harvest strategy. In some instances, a business may be prevented from exiting a share position because of legal or ethical considerations. Finally, companies tend to hold on far too long to businesses that should be divested. Holding on too long ties up resources that would otherwise be available to invest in offensive marketing strategies designed to improve sales revenue growth, share position, and future profit performance.

■ Market-Based Logic and Strategic Thinking

1 How do defensive marketing strategies contribute to a business's performance objectives (sales growth, share position, and profit performance)?

2 What are the differences between defensive marketing strategies and offensive marketing strategies?

3 Why is it more difficult to protect market share in a high-growth market than in a slow- or no-growth market?

4 Why do share leaders have to work harder than share followers to protect share?

5 What are some of the key aspects of performance that would enable a share follower to achieve the same level of profits as share leaders?

6 What aspects of positioning and marketing effort can be managed to achieve a high profit with a reduced-focus niche-market strategy?

7 Why should a reduced-focus niche strategy with above-average customer value deliver above-average profits?

8 How do defensive marketing strategies contribute to the long-run share position and profit performance of a business?

9 Compare defensive marketing strategies to protect a share position with strategies to exit a share position in terms of their contributions to short-run profit performance and the overall share position of the business.

10 Why would a business pursue a reduced market focus strategic market plan?

11 What is the primary objective of a monetize-strategic market plan?

12 Under what conditions would a business select an exit marketing strategy over a protect-share position strategy?

13 When should a business pursue a harvest-marketing strategy, and how could that strategy affect short-run profit performance?

14 When should a business pursue a divest marketing strategy, and how could that strategy affect short-run profit performance?

15 Why might companies continue to support businesses in harvest or divest share portfolio positions rather than harvest or divest them?

Marketing Performance Tools

Each of the following **marketing performance tools** can be accessed by going to *www.rogerjbest.com* or *www.prenhall.com/best*. The shaded cells are input cells. The non-shaded cells contain results calculated from your input values.

MARKETING PERFORMANCE TOOL—Defensive Strategy to Protect Share

Strategic Market Plan (customers)	Current	Plan	Plan	Plan
Invest to Protect Share	Year	Year 1	Year 2	Year 3
Market Demand	1,000,000	1,050,000	1,000,000	1,150,000
Market Share (%)	10.0	10.0	10.0	10.0
Customer Volume	100,000	105,000	110,000	115,000
Customer Retention	0.90	0.90	0.90	0.90
Retained Customers	85,500	90,000	94,500	99,000
New Customers	14,500	15,000	14,500	16,000
Revenue per Customer				
Retained Customers	$500	$500	$500	$500
New Customers	$300	$300	$300	$300
Average Revenue per Customer	$471	$471	$472	$472
Sales Revenues (millions)	$47.10	$49.50	$51.90	$54.30
Percent Margin per Customer				
Retained Customers (%)	50.0	50.0	50.0	50.0
New Customers (%)	33.3	33.3	33.3	33.3
Average Margin (%)	48.5	48.5	48.5	48.5
Gross Profit (millions)	$22.82	$24.00	$25.17	$26.35
Marketing Expenses				
Retention Cost per Customer	$25	$25	$25	$25
Acquisition Cost per Customer	$150	$150	$150	$150
Average Marketing Expense (% sales)	9.2	9.1	9.0	9.0
Marketing Expenses (millions)	$4.31	$4.50	$4.69	$4.88
Net Marketing Contribution (millions)	$18.51	$19.50	$20.49	$21.47
Marketing ROS (%)	39.3	39	39	40
Marketing ROI (%)	429	433	437	441

This **marketing performance tool** allows you to estimate the performance impact of a defensive strategy. The first table is a base case for a business situation in which the strategic market objective is to hold market share. This table is used to compare the performance impact of a defensive strategy. The second table can be used to input different defensive strategies in order to understand the performance impact when compared to the protect share strategy in the preceding table. The shaded numeric input cells can be changed in doing the following application exercise.

MARKETING PERFORMANCE TOOL—Evaluating Defensive Strategies

Strategic Market Plan (customers)	Current	Plan	Plan	Plan
Defensive Strategy	Year	Year 1	Year 2	Year 3
Market Demand	1,000,000	1,050,000	1,000,000	1,150,000
Market Share (%)	10.0	10.0	10.0	10.0
Customer Volume	100,000	105,000	110,000	115,000
Customer Retention	0.90	0.90	0.90	0.90
Retained Customers	85,500	90,000	94,500	99,000
New Customers	14,500	15,000	14,500	16,000
Revenue per Customer				
Retained Customers	$500	$500	$500	$500
New Customers	$300	$300	$300	$300
Average Revenue per Customer	$471	$471	$472	$472
Sales Revenues (millions)	$47.10	$49.50	$51.90	$54.30
Percent Margin per Customer				
Retained Customers (%)	50.0	50.0	50.0	50.0
New Customers (%)	33.3	33.3	33.3	33.3
Average Margin (%)	48.5	48.5	48.5	48.5
Gross Profit (millions)	$22.82	$24.00	$25.17	$26.35
Marketing Expenses				
Retention Cost per Customer	$25	$25	$25	$25
Acquisition Cost per Customer	$150	$150	$150	$150
Average Marketing Expense (% sales)	9.2	9.1	9.0	9.0
Marketing Expenses (millions)	$4.31	$4.50	$4.69	$4.88
Net Marketing Contribution (millions)	$18.51	$19.50	$20.49	$21.47
Marketing ROS (%)	39.3	39	39	40
Marketing ROI (%)	429	433	437	441

Application Exercise: Using the data provided, answer the following questions: What would be the performance impact of a strategy to hold share and improve customer retention from 90 percent to 92.5 percent? Assume the price elasticity in this market situation is −2. What would be the profit impact of yearly price increases of 2 percent over the 3-year planning period? Assume the market demand is declining by 5 percent per year (you will need to change market demand in both tables). What would be the performance impact of a harvest strategy where prices were increased 15 percent per year in a market with a price elasticity of −2?

Notes

1. Donald Potter, "Strategy to Succeed in Hostile Markets," *California Management Review* (Fall 1994): 65–82.
2. Sidney Schoeffer, "Market Position: Build, Hold or Harvest," PIMS Letter No. 3 (1978): 1–10.
3. Philip Kotler and Paul Bloom, "Strategies for High-Market Share Companies," *Harvard Business Review* (November–December 1975): 63–72.
4. Donald Clifford and Richard Cavanagh, *The Winning Performance: How America's High and Mid-Size Growth Companies Succeed* (New York: Bantam Books, 1985).
5. Carolyn Woo and Arnold Cooper, "The Surprising Case for Low Market Share," *Harvard Business Review* (November–December 1982): 106–113.
6. Robert Linneman and John Stanton Jr., "Mining for Niches," *Business Horizons* (May–June 1992): 43–51.
7. Robert Hamermesh and Steven Silk, "How to Compete in Stagnant Industries," *Harvard Business Review* (September–October 1979): 161–168.
8. V. Cook and R. Rothberg, "The Harvesting of USAUTO?" *Journal of Product Innovation Management* (1980): 310–322.
9. Kathryn Rudie Harrigan, "Strategies for Declining Businesses," *Journal of Business Strategy* (Fall 1980): 27.
10. George Seiler, "Colorful Chemicals Cuts Its Losses," *Planning Review* (January–February 1987): 16–22.

PART V

Marketing Plans and Performance

■ It is better to be prepared for an opportunity and not have one than to have an opportunity and not be prepared.
— *Whitney Young Jr.*
  1960s Civil Rights Leader, Executive Director of the Urban League, Dean of School of Social Work, Atlanta University

Given a specific strategic market plan and performance objectives, a marketing mix strategy and marketing plan must be developed and successfully implemented in order to move a business toward its planned performance objectives. Chapter 14 presents a process and structure for developing a marketing plan. Chapter 15 addresses implementation of a marketing plan and the various forces that affect the success or failure of a marketing plan. Ownership, commitment, performance measurement, adaptation, and resource allocation are important aspects of market-based management and successful implementation. Process market metrics such as customer awareness, customer perceptions of performance, trial usage, and customer satisfaction are key market-based performance metrics that are tracked, along with end-result metrics that generally measure profit performance. Finally, it is important that those in responsible marketing positions understand how marketing strategies individually and collectively affect net profit, cash flow, investment, and, ultimately, shareholder value. Chapter 16 carefully illustrates how each aspect of a marketing strategy ripples through the organizational maze of financial accounting to affect each aspect of profitability and, ultimately, shareholder value. Regardless of a business's assets, technology, and financial leverage, *there is only one source of positive cash flow, and that is the customer; everything else is expense.*

Building a Marketing Plan

Stericycle, Inc., is in the business of recycling medical waste. It provides a safe, cost-effective, and environmentally effective method for health care providers to dispose of their medical waste. From 1997 to 2000, Stericycle grew from a 5 percent market share to market leadership with 21.6 percent market share, as shown in Figure 14-1. In this expanding market, Stericycle continued to grow its market share to 22.7 percent by 2003.

FIGURE 14-1 STERICYCLE PERFORMANCE: 1997–2003

Area of Performance	1997	2000	2003
Market Demand (millions)	$1,000	$1,500	$2,000
Market Share (%)	4.6	21.6	22.7
Sales Revenue (millions)	$46	$324	$454
Percent Margin (%)	26.4	39.3	43.3
Gross Profit (millions)	$12.1	$127.3	$196.6
Marketing Expenses (millions)	$10.0	$59.5	$65.7
Net Marketing Contribution (millions)	$2.1	$67.8	$130.9
Operating Expense (millions)	$0.70	$4.5	$4.5
Operating Income (millions)	$1.40	$ 63.3	$126.4

☐ **Large Institutions** – Hospitals, Blood Banks, Pharmaceutical Companies
☐ **Small Institutions** – Care Facilities, Outpatient Clinics, Dentist, Medical Offices, and Vets

The market was also growing at a rate of 8 percent per year. The combination of market growth and share growth allowed Stericycle to grow sales from $324 million in 2000 to $453 million in 2003. Profit margins also improved from 39.3 percent in 2000 to 43.5 percent in 2003. This allowed gross profits to increase from $127.3 million to $196.6 million in 3 years.

This level of growth also required an investment in marketing. As shown in Figure 14-1, the marketing expenses grew sixfold from $10 million in 1997 to almost $60 million in 2000 but then grew at a slower rate to $65.7 million in 2003. As Stericycle's customer base has grown, the proportion of retained customers to new customers has increased. This has allowed the rate of marketing expenses to increase at a decreasing rate. The net result of this marketing effort was tremendous gain in net marketing contribution from $67.8 million in 2000 to $130.9 million in 2003. This allowed operating income to grow to $126.4 million (28 percent of sales) in 2003.

With limited resources and multiple market opportunities, Stericycle needs to build a marketing plan that will address both these segments in a way that capitalizes on opportunities to grow sales and profits in a growing market. The purpose of this chapter is to show how such a plan is created. First we will look at the process of building a marketing plan within the context of the market served by Stericycle, and then we will build a sample marketing plan for Stericycle, using publicly available information.

CREATIVITY VERSUS STRUCTURE

The market planning process is a delicate balance of creativity and structure. The opportunity to think creatively and explore market issues outside the realm of day-to-day business is an important part of developing a proactive marketing plan. On the other hand, a marketing plan has to have enough structure to ensure that it is comprehensive and accurate and that marketing strategies, resources, and performance objectives are credibly linked to the market situation.

Developing a marketing plan is similar to painting a picture. The creative use of light and color can make a picture interesting and appealing, but without some degree of form to add meaning to the composition, the picture may be intriguing but confusing. On the other hand, all form and no creative expression yields a sterile picture. The same is true for a marketing plan: Both creative insight and analytical structure are necessary to paint a meaningful picture of the market situation, marketing strategy, and logic-based path that connects desired performance objectives with marketing strategies.

Although a marketing plan is intended to help a business systematically understand a market and develop a strategy to achieve a predetermined set of strategic market objectives, there is a paradox between having no marketing plan and having a highly formalized marketing plan.[1] A business with no marketing plan completely forgoes the opportunity to uncover key market insights that are a direct result of the market planning process. At the other extreme, businesses with highly formalized processes often evolve to a level of filling out forms as a basis for a marketing plan.[2] Both extremes diminish the opportunity to uncover meaningful market insights.

What is needed is an open system that encourages exploration and creative insight and, at the same time, has a structure that ensures comprehensiveness and completeness.

With an open system, marketing planners should act as facilitators in the planning process rather than as developers of a marketing plan.[3] As facilitators, they facilitate acquisition of information, coordinate schedules, manage progress, and ensure that the business's mission, customers, and goals do not get lost in the planning process. Although there are recognizable organizational hurdles, in general, businesses that use a formal planning process are more likely to achieve improved performance than are businesses that have no formal plan.[4]

BENEFITS OF BUILDING A MARKETING PLAN

A good marketing plan is an essential part of a proactive market orientation. Businesses with a strong market orientation are in continuous pursuit of customer, competitor, and market intelligence and work cross-functionally to create value-added customer solutions. Although these activities are ongoing, important benefits result directly from the process of developing a marketing plan, as well as the successful *implementation* of the marketing plan.

Identifying Opportunities

It is not the *plan* itself, but the *process*, that helps a business uncover new opportunities and recognize important threats. A systematic evaluation of the market and internal capabilities provides an opportunity to step back from day-to-day tactical marketing decision making and take a broader, more comprehensive view of the market and business situation.[5] K2, a ski manufacturer, for example, has become the market share leader in the American market for skis. A systematic evaluation of the American ski market showed that it was a mature market and that additional share penetration would be difficult. However, while performing this situation analysis, K2 was able to more fully recognize the emerging markets in snowboards and in-line skates. This discovery, in turn, led to new market entry strategies that are intended to provide new growth, a more diversified strategic position, and new sources of profit.

Leveraging Core Capabilities

As K2 aggressively enters the snowboard and in-line skate markets, it will be able to leverage its brand name and awareness in closely related markets. K2 will also be able to leverage existing manufacturing and engineering expertise, as well as sales and distribution systems that currently serve the American ski market. Thus, an important benefit to a carefully thought-out marketing plan is the greater utilization of existing assets, business and marketing systems, and unique capabilities.

Focused Marketing Strategy

Most markets are complex aggregates of many smaller markets and market segments. These segments can be broken down further into smaller market niches. Without a good marketing plan, a business could find itself vaguely positioned in a variety of market segments. This situation could lead it in all directions in the search for customers without really being able to fully satisfy any of them.

A good marketing plan will delineate target customers such that the positioning strategy can be customized around the needs of the target segment and the marketing effort can be directed at these target customers. In this way, the marketing plan helps bring target customers into clearer focus. Charles M. Lillis, CEO of MediaOne Group, once stated: "I will know when our businesses have done a good job in market segmentation and planning when they can tell me who we should not sell to."

Resource Allocation

A well-defined target market focus is also cost efficient. If managers do not know who the company's customers are, they are going to spend a lot of time and money marketing to people who are not likely to buy, regardless of their marketing efforts. Or, if the customers do buy, they will be difficult to retain because the value proposition cannot deliver the customer satisfaction they desire. A good marketing plan will be more productive; it will take fewer dollars to accomplish performance objectives because there are fewer resources wasted on nontarget customers.

PERFORMANCE ROADMAP

A good marketing plan also provides a roadmap for both marketing strategy and expected performance. The marketing plan maps a business's projected market share, sales revenue, and profits over a specified planning horizon. This may sound like a fairly easy task, but the business world is complex with many factors affecting the situation, strategy, and resources needed. Market conditions are complicated and constantly changing with respect to customer needs, competitor structure and strategies, and the environment within which the market operates. In addition, market information is often incomplete or inaccurate or both.

The environment *within* a business can also make the market planning process difficult. Marketing strategies are often driven internally by short-run profit objectives rather than by market-based performance objectives. Further, resources are often not allocated on the basis of strategy needs and performance objectives, but by organizational needs, political processes, and short-run need for profits. These factors and others make meaningful marketing plans challenging to develop and successfully implement.

BUILDING A MARKETING PLAN: PROCESS AND LOGIC

A good marketing plan is the result of a systematic, creative yet structured process that is designed to uncover market opportunities and threats that need to be addressed in order to achieve performance objectives. As illustrated in Figure 14-2, the development

FIGURE 14-2 THE PROCESS OF BUILDING A MARKETING PLAN

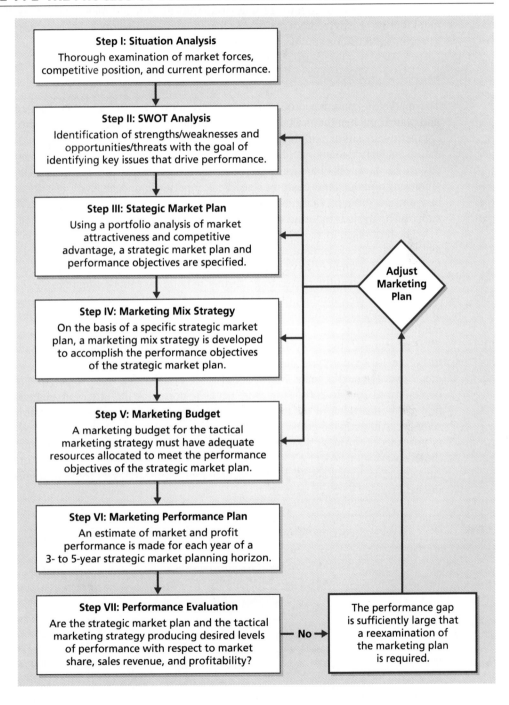

of a marketing plan is a *process,* and each step in the process has a *structure* that enables the marketing plan to evolve from abstract information and ideas into a tangible document that can easily be understood, evaluated, and implemented. This section is devoted to an in-depth discussion of each step in this process.

Step I: Situation Analysis

The marketing planning process outlined in Figure 14-2 starts with a detailed *Situation Analysis* of the market and business with respect to current market forces, the business's competitive position, and its current performance. The primary purpose of a detailed situation analysis is to uncover key performance issues that normally might go unnoticed in day-to-day business operations. First, we need to go deeper into the market and business situation to understand customer needs, competition, and channel systems, as well as business positioning, margins, and profitability, as outlined in Figure 14-3. A thorough situation analysis is required to uncover the key issues that affect performance.

The best place to start the situation analysis is with market demand. After a detailed analysis of market demand, we may find that the market is fully developed or that the total demand is small relative to the business's size and needs for growth. When this is the case, there may be little reason to go further in building a marketing plan for this product-market. Thus, an important place to start the analysis of a particular product-market situation is with an examination of the current market demand, maximum market potential, market growth rate, and factors limiting growth.

For example, the analysis of the market demand for medical waste recycling shown in Figure 14-4 would provide an excellent opportunity for Stericycle to grow sales revenues over the next 5 years. Market demand in dollar value was projected to grow by 25 percent from 2003 to 2006. However, just as important in this situation analysis would be how the dollar value of the market demand is projected to shift to the small institutions segment. Although the dollar value in the large institution segment is projected to grow, it is projected to grow at a much slower rate than in the small institution segment. Both these observations (derived from the situation analysis) would be critical in shaping a strategic market plan and designing tactical marketing strategies for both segments of the medical waste recycling market.

FIGURE 14-3 MAJOR COMPONENTS OF A SITUATION ANALYSIS

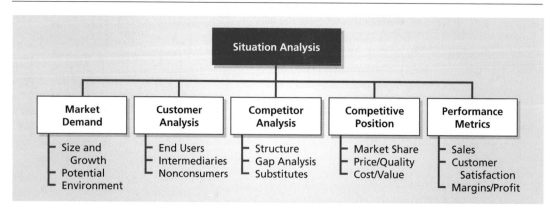

FIGURE 14-4 SITUATION ANALYSIS: MEDICAL WASTE MARKET DEMAND

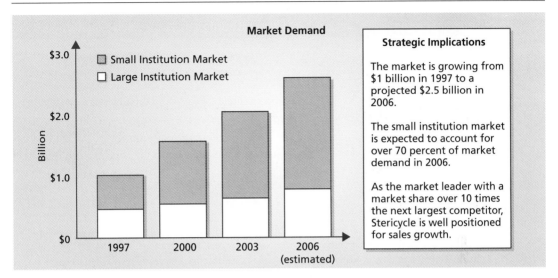

Market Demand

□ Small Institution Market
□ Large Institution Market

Strategic Implications

The market is growing from $1 billion in 1997 to a projected $2.5 billion in 2006.

The small institution market is expected to account for over 70 percent of market demand in 2006.

As the market leader with a market share over 10 times the next largest competitor, Stericycle is well positioned for sales growth.

Recognizing a good opportunity for growth and the segment differences uncovered in this portion of the situation analysis, Stericycle could further examine the needs and buying behavior of each segment to more completely understand the market situation. As shown in Figure 14-5, these segments are quite different in primary needs, price sensitivity, and experience in managing medical waste. There are also important differences in customer buying and, as a result, significant differences in revenue and margin per customer. These insights are a key part of the situation analysis. Without them, the business is likely to follow an internal strategy based on experience and management perceptions of market needs.

To complete this phase of the market planning process, we must comprehensively examine each of the situational forces outlined in Figure 14-3. When a comprehensive representation of the situation analysis is complete, it is time to move on to identifying and prioritizing key issues that affect the business's performance objectives (share position, sales growth, and profit performance).

The large institution market segment is smaller, is growing at a slower rate, is more price sensitive, and has much lower margins. This segment is also more concentrated with fewer customers. The small institution market segment is twice as large, is growing at twice the rate, and is less price sensitive with margins five times greater than those in the large institution segment. Also, Stericycle's product benefits and positioning better match the needs of the small institution customer.

Step II: SWOT Analysis

Perhaps the most difficult and elusive part of a marketing plan is the identification of key performance issues. A key performance issue is a problem or unaddressed opportunity that is an underlying cause that limits market or profit performance or both. In the process of sorting out key issues, it is useful to classify them as strengths and weaknesses or opportunities and threats. This is what is called a *SWOT Analysis*.

FIGURE 14-5 SITUATION ANALYSIS: MEDICAL WASTE MARKET SEGMENTS

Segment Profile	Large Institution	Small Institution
Value Driver	Low Cost	Value-Added Service
Primary Benefit	Low Price	Easy & Safe Waste Disposal
Price Sensitivity	Very High	Low
Demographics	Hospitals, Blood Banks	Physicians' Offices, Clinics
Waste Management Expertise	Above Average	Poor
Market Demand—2003	$500 million	$1,500 million
% Market Growth (next 3 years)	4.5	8
Number of Customers	16,667	1,060,000
Revenue per Customer	$30,000	$1,500
Percent Margin (%)	20	45
Margin per Customer	$6,000	$675

Strategic Implications: The large institution market segment is smaller, is growing at a slower rate, is more price sensitive, and has much lower margins. This segment is also more concentrated (i.e., fewer customers). The small institution market segment is twice as large, is growing at twice the rate, and is less price sensitive with margins five times greater than those in the large institution segment. Also, Stericycle's positioning better matches the needs of the small institution customer.

The SWOT analysis is critical in summarizing key strengths and weaknesses, as well as opportunities and threats. It is important in this process that there be a strong linkage between the situation analysis and the SWOT analysis. These must be interconnected, not separate and distinct, parts of the market planning process. The steps that follow will be only as good as the situation analysis and key performance issues that are uncovered in the situation and SWOT analyses.

Shown in Figure 14-6 is a SWOT analysis derived from a situation analysis of the medical waste recycling market and Stericycle's position and performance in it. As shown, there are several strengths, weaknesses, opportunities, and threats that Stericycle needs to recognize in building a marketing plan for the medical waste recycling market. It is important that the business also understand the degree to which each of these key issues affects key performance metrics. Because the key issues will be the primary guideline to developing a tactical marketing strategy, it is important that these issues be carefully specified and articulated. This step in the market planning process is critical in terms of the marketing strategy to be developed and the potential impact it has on performance.

Step III: Strategic Market Plan

On the basis of the insights derived from the situation analysis and SWOT analysis, a *strategic market plan* must be developed. The primary purpose of a strategic market plan is to provide a *strategic direction* from which to set performance objectives and guide the development of a tactical marketing strategy.[6] This is an important step in the

FIGURE 14-6 SWOT ANALYSIS: STERICYCLE MEDICAL WASTE MARKETS

Strengths	**Weaknesses**	**Strategic Implications**
– Market leader/well-known – Technology advantage – Many locations – 12 times larger than next largest competitor	– Not price competitive in large Institution market – Low margins in large Institution market	Stericycle is the technology leader and market leader with a market share 12 times larger than the closest competitor. Competitor exit will also aid share growth.
Opportunities	**Threats**	The best opportunity for profitable growth is in the small institution market segment.
– Growing medical waste market – Larger demand and faster growth in small institution market – Competitor exit should make it easier to grow share	– Increase in government regulation – Low margins in the large institution market – Patent expiration	Stericycle's key weaknesses are primarily associated with the large institution market segment.

market planning process because it requires a careful examination of market attractiveness and the business's competitive advantage based on the information provided in the situation analysis.

By analyzing the forces that shape market attractiveness and competitive advantage, the business can create a product-market portfolio. Each product-market opportunity can be placed in the portfolio, as shown in Figure 14-7. On the basis of the relative portfolio position, a long-run market share objective must be specified for each product-market.[7] The smaller, alternate care institutions are in an attractive market with an average position

FIGURE 14-7 STERICYCLE STRATEGIC MARKET PLAN

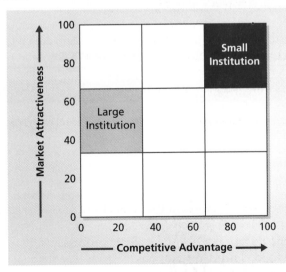

Strategic Market Plan

Small Institution: Grow Market Share
With a strong competitive position in an attractive market that is growing, marketing resources should be heavily weighted on this market segment.

Large Institution: Reduce Focus
With a weak competitive position and average market attractiveness, fewer marketing resources should be allocated to this segment and only profitable customers retained at desired margins.

of advantage. It represents the stronger strategic position and best opportunity for profit performance. This analysis and current performance indicate that an offensive strategic market plan to grow market share is appropriate.

The large institution segment is less attractive but is still above average in overall market attractiveness and competitive advantage. However, in this segment, a defensive reduced focus strategic market plan is more appropriate given limited resources and the profit potential of this segment.

Step IV: Marketing Mix Strategy

The next step in the marketing planning process is the development of a *marketing mix strategy* to put the strategic market plan into effect. Although the overall marketing strategy to protect, grow, reduce focus, harvest, enter, or exit a market position is set by the strategic market plan, more specific tactical marketing strategies need to be developed for each of the key performance issues. Each element of a marketing mix strategy is a specific response to a key performance issue that is identified within the context of the market situation. Thus, specific marketing strategies developed will be only as good as the key performance issues uncovered as an output of the situation analysis.

For example, given a strategic market plan to grow share in the small institution segment, Stericycle would need to develop a specific tactical marketing strategy. Outlined in Figure 14-8 is one approach to the marketing tactics that could be used to implement and achieve the performance objectives specified by this strategic market plan.

Note that the marketing mix strategy presented in Figure 14-8 is in direct response to key performance issues and is not vague. It is clear in its approach to addressing these issues and gives specific details with respect to target share, positioning, pricing, channel system, and the value proposition to be used in target market communications. This level of detail is required in order to evaluate the market and profit impact of this marketing mix strategy. A separate marketing mix strategy will also have to be developed for the large institution segment on the basis of its strategic market plan, key performance issues, and performance objectives. This marketing mix strategy is presented in the complete Stericycle Marketing Plan in this chapter's appendix on page 442.

FIGURE 14-8 STERICYCLE SMALL INSTITUTION SEGMENT STRATEGY

Small Institution Segment Strategy—Market Penetration	
Value Proposition:	Providing clinics and medical offices with safe and easy disposal of medical waste.
Positioning Strategy:	Recognized for outstanding service, unquestionable safety, and customer satisfaction while priced at a premium over lesser competitors.
Channel Strategy:	Direct waste removal and mail-in waste packages will be used to collect medical waste processed at the closest Stericycle medical waste processing location.
Share Objective:	Grow market share from 28.7 percent in 2003 to 30 percent in 2006.

Step V: Marketing Budget

Resources need to be allocated in a *marketing budget* based on the strategic market plan and the marketing mix strategy. Without adequate resources, the marketing mix strategies cannot succeed, and, as a consequence, performance objectives cannot be achieved. One cannot expect to grow share in the growing small institution segment without additions to the marketing budget. A reduced focus in the large institution segment should require fewer resources than a share growth strategy with respect to the marketing budget.

Specifying a marketing budget is perhaps the most difficult part of the market planning process. Although specifying the budget is not a precise process, there must be a logical connection between the strategy and performance objectives and the marketing budget.

There are three ways to build a marketing budget that is based on a specific strategic market plan and the marketing mix strategy designed to achieve the target level of performance. Each is briefly described with respect to Stericycle:

- **Top-Down Budget:** A new marketing budget based on projected sales objectives is determined, using past marketing expenses as a percentage of sales.
- **Customer Mix Budget:** The cost of customer acquisition and retention and the combination of new and retained customers are used to derive a new marketing budget.
- **Bottom-Up Budget:** Each element of the marketing effort is budgeted for specific tasks identified in the marketing plan.

Top-Down Budget

Stericycle's marketing expenses in 2003 were $65.4 million, and total sales were $453 million. Thus, the marketing budget was 14.5 percent of sales. This is a relatively high marketing budget as a percentage of sales but Stericycle is in a rapid-growth phase. If Stericycle's sales objective were $500 million in 2004, then a "top-down" approach would yield a marketing budget of $72.5 million in 2004 using 14.5 percent of sales for estimating the marketing budget.

Customer Mix Budget

Because the rate of new-customer acquisition can change the marketing budget required, the "customer mix" approach to funding the marketing budget is probably a better approach. Based on new customer growth, and assuming the acquisition cost per customer is five times the retention cost per customer, we estimate their acquisition cost to be $750 per customer and the retention cost $145 per customer. With these estimates, we can reconcile the marketing budget for 2003 as shown:

$$\textbf{Marketing Budget} = \begin{pmatrix} \text{Acquisition} & & \text{Number} \\ \text{Cost per} & \times & \text{of New} \\ \text{Customer} & & \text{Customers} \end{pmatrix} + \begin{pmatrix} \text{Retention} & & \text{Number} \\ \text{Cost per} & \times & \text{of Retained} \\ \text{Customer} & & \text{Customers} \end{pmatrix}$$

$$\textbf{Marketing Budget (2003)} = (\$750 \times 37,385) + (\$145 \times 257,350)$$
$$= \$28 \text{ million} + \$37.3 \text{ million}$$
$$= \textbf{\$65.3 million}$$

Stericycle had 275,230 customers in 2002. It retained 95 percent, or 261,469 customers, in 2003. Thus 13,762 of the 33,281 new customers are replacements for lost customers. The other 19,519 new customers produced incremental growth in Stericycle's customer base, sales, and profit performance.

If Stericycle wanted to grow its customer base to 313,500 in 2004 and retention remained at 95 percent, then the Stericycle would need to attract 33,488 new customers. Of these, 14,738 would replace those lost in 2003 (5 percent of 294,750) and the other 18,750 would be needed to achieve the target of 313,500 customers in 2004. Based on this customer mix and the cost of retention and acquisition, a marketing budget of $72.4 million would be needed as shown here:

$$\textbf{Marketing Budget (2004)} = (\$750 \times 19,738) + (\$145 \times 280,013)$$
$$= \$14.8 \text{ million} + \$40.6 \text{ million}$$
$$= \$55.4 \text{ million}$$

If Stericycle planned to grow overall by only 5,000 customers in 2004, they would need only 19,738 new customers to achieve this less ambitious objective. Because less marketing budget is needed for new-customer acquisition, this 2004 marketing budget would be $55.4 million. This is almost $8.4 million less than the marketing budget needed with a more aggressive growth objective. Thus, one can imagine how the marketing budget as a percentage of sales will decrease as new-customer acquisition slows. When this occurs, Stericycle's marketing expenses will be based primarily on customer retention.

$$\textbf{Marketing Budget (2004)} = (\$750 \times 33,488) + (\$145 \times 280,013)$$
$$= \$25.1 \text{ million} + \$40.6 \text{ million}$$
$$= \$65.7 \text{ million}$$

Bottom-Up Budget

A "bottom-up" approach would require specifying each marketing task and the amount needed to accomplish it given a particular strategic market plan and marketing mix strategy. For example, we can estimate the bottom-up 2004 marketing budget for a strategy to attract 40,000 customers and retain 285,000 in 2004:

$8 million	Marketing Management (marketing strategy, planning and administration)
$30 million	Sales Force (customer account managers)
$3 million	Technical Support (customer problem solving and technical training)
$12 million	Customer Service (inside sales and customer administration)
$3 million	Customer Safety Literature (how to handle medical waste)
$7 million	Promotion (free sample and trial programs)
$10 million	Marketing Communications (print ads, direct mail, and trade shows)
$73 million	**Overall Marketing Budget**

As shown, a bottom-up marketing budget provides a breakdown of specific expenses for marketing management, sales force, technical support, customer service, customer safety literature, promotional samples, and marketing communications. Each item in the marketing budget has a specific objective and cost based on the strategy to attract 40,000 new customers. In this case for 2004, this is an estimated marketing budget of $73 million.

When the new resources required are added to the existing base, a total budget for the marketing plan can be systematically derived. This bottom-up approach to setting the marketing budget is directly tied to a specific marketing strategy and performance objectives. Deviation from the resources required should be reconciled with the marketing mix strategy and the intended impact on performance. If insufficient resources are available to fund a proposed tactical marketing strategy, then the strategy must be revised to reflect how the available resources will be used to achieve a desired, though reduced, level of performance in share, sales, and profitability.

Step VI: Performance Timeline

Given an adequate allocation of resources, a *performance timeline* is critical in depicting performance levels for external market metrics and internal operating metrics over the planning horizon. This step must make explicit the timing of specific performance objectives (share position, sales revenue, and profit performance) so that the success or failure of the marketing plan can be evaluated. Performance metrics include external market metrics such as customer awareness, customer satisfaction, product availability, perceptions of product and service quality, and market share, as well as internal profit performance metrics such as sales revenues, contribution margins, total contribution, and net marketing contribution.

Marketing Profit Plan Metrics

In Figure 14-9 we have three approaches to building a marketing profit plan. Each has advantages and disadvantages. The *dollar metric* approach is the easiest because the information required is generally more available. A business more focused on volume may elect to build its marketing profit plan around a *volume metric*. Finally, a business that sells multiple products and services to customers may elect a *customer metric* for building a marketing profit plan. Any of these marketing profit plans could be expanded to include more details. However, Figure 14-9 provides an example of each marketing profit plan perspective for the planning period from 2003 to 2006.

The degree to which these estimates of projected performance are credible is directly related to the credibility of the key performance issues, strategic market plans, marketing strategies, and marketing budgets made to support specific tactical marketing strategies. If these linkages are not credible, then the numbers presented in the performance impact assessment are open to question.

Step VII: Performance Evaluation

Step VII, *performance evaluation*, involves the ongoing monitoring of market and profit performance, and comparisons with the performance timeline. If the marketing plan fails to meet the desired performance objectives specified as part of the strategic market plan, then the marketing plan has to be reevaluated with respect to all inputs used in the market planning process, as shown in Figure 14-2. These performance gaps require the business to consider several options. One is to reexamine the pricing, customer and channel discounts, unit costs, and the marketing budget to determine if, in fact, there are opportunities to improve performance.

A second alternative is to reexamine the entire marketing plan. Both the situation analysis and the key performance issues would be reviewed to see if there were alternative tactical marketing strategies that would work better in achieving the desired performance objectives. Whichever the case, a credible marketing strategy must be linked to the market situation, key performance issues, and available resources, and then linked to projections of external market metrics and internal profit metrics.

FIGURE 14-9 MARKET PROFIT PLANNING PERSPECTIVES

Marketing Profit Planning Perspective—Dollar Metric

Area of Performance	Base Year	2004	2005	2006
Market Demand (millions)	$ 2,000	$ 2,120	$ 2,350	$ 2,500
Market Share (%)	22.7	22.9	23.2	23.7
Sales Revenues (millions)	$ 454	$ 485	$ 545	$ 593
Percent Margin (%)	43.3	43.7	43.7	43.9
Gross Profit (millions)	$ 196.6	$ 212.2	$ 238.3	$ 260.1
Marketing Expenses (% sales)	14.4	13.6	13.6	13.0
Marketing Expenses (millions)	$ 65.3	$ 66.0	$ 74.0	$ 77.0
Net Marketing Contribution (millions)	$ 131.3	$ 146.2	$ 164.3	$ 183.1
Marketing ROS (%)	29.1	30.1	30.1	30.9
Marketing ROI (%)	201.0	221.4	222.0	237.8

Marketing Profit Planning Perspective—Volume Metric

Area of Performance	Base Year	2004	2005	2006
Market Demand (units millions)	15.95	16.95	18.80	20.00
Market Share (%)	22.7	22.9	23.2	23.7
Volume (units millions)	3.62	3.88	4.36	4.74
Price per Unit	$125.00	$125.00	$125.00	$125.00
Sales Revenues (millions)	$ 453	$ 485	$ 545	$ 593
Percent Margin (%)	43.5	43.7	43.7	43.9
Gross Profit (millions)	$ 196.9	$ 212.0	$ 238.3	$ 260.1
Marketing Expenses (% sales)	14.45	13.6	13.6	13.0
Marketing Expenses (millions)	$ 65.4	$ 66.0	$ 74.1	$ 77.0
Net Marketing Contribution (millions)	$ 131.5	$ 146.0	$ 164.1	$ 183.1
Marketing ROS (%)	29.1	30.1	30.1	30.9
Marketing ROI (%)	201.0	221.3	221.3	237.8

Continued

Marketing Profit Planning Perspective—Customer Metric

Area of Performance	Base Year	2004	2005	2006
Market Demand (customers)	1,323,000	1,415,000	1,567,000	1,667,000
Market Share (%)	22.7	22.9	23.2	23.7
Customer Volume	300,321	324,035	363,544	395,079
Revenue per Customer	$1,510	$1,500	$1,500	$1,500
Sales Revenues (millions)	$ 453	$ 486	$ 545	$ 593
Percent Margin (%)	43.4	43.7	43.7	43.9
Gross Profit (millions)	$196.8	$212.4	$238.3	$260.2
Marketing Expenses (% sales)	14.4	13.6	13.6	13.0
Marketing Expenses (millions)	$ 65.3	$ 66.1	$ 74.2	$ 77.0
Net Marketing Contribution (millions)	$131.5	$146.3	$164.1	$183.1
Marketing ROS (%)	29.1	30.1	30.1	30.9
Marketing ROI (%)	201.0	221.3	221.3	237.8

Of course, a final option is to refrain from pursuing this market opportunity further. It may be that none of the alternative marketing strategies considered can deliver the desired level of performance with credibility and confidence. When this is the case, the business is better off abandoning this market opportunity and allocating its resources and management time to other market opportunities.

SAMPLE MARKETING PLAN

To facilitate a better understanding of a marketing plan and the benefits of building one, a sample marketing plan for Stericycle is presented at the end of this chapter. The information used to construct the sample marketing plan shown here was taken from information publicly available in 1997, 2000, and 2003. All assumptions, inferences, analyses, and recommendations are the author's, not Stericycle's.

Because of space limitations, not all of the supporting assumptions, analyses, and interpretations of the information can be presented.

Step I: Situation Analysis

As shown in Figure 14-2, the first step in building a marketing plan is to create a situation analysis, which highlights external and internal forces that shape market attractiveness, competitive position, and current performance with respect to share position, sales revenues, and profitability. The following are the various situational forces used in building the situation analysis. As shown in the sample marketing plan, each important aspect of the current situation is presented in one page and the implications it has for strategy development are discussed. Outlined here is a brief summary of the situation analysis, the first six pages of the sample marketing plan.

- **Market Demand:** Presents the current and future level of market demand as well as Stericycle segment sales.
- **Market Segmentation:** Outlines a profile of each segment served by Stericycle with respect to segment needs, size, and growth rates, as well as revenue and margin per customer.
- **Industry Analysis:** Summarizes the industry forces that shape segment attractiveness and profit potential, and presents an overall index of industry attractiveness for each.
- **Market Share and Customer Retention:** Presents Stericycle's current level of market-share penetration and identifies the major forces that shape Stericycle penetration of this market.
- **Marketing Channels and Marketing Budget:** Illustrates the channel systems used to reach target segments and the breakdown of the marketing budget with respect to the costs of customer acquisition and retention.
- **Market and Profit Performance:** Presents the market share, customer retention, and lifetime value of each segment as well as sales, margins, and profits currently obtained from each segment.

More aspects of the situation and greater detail could have been developed and presented, but these situational forces and their respective strategy implications provide the basis from which to identify key issues that affect performance, which is the next step in the process of building a marketing plan.

Step II: SWOT Analysis

The SWOT analysis is a summary of the key strategy implications uncovered in the situation analysis. The various strategy implications are categorized as a strengths, weaknesses, opportunities, or threats so they can be more fully comprehended. Then, from this SWOT analysis, the most important issues need to be identified and described more completely. Among the strategy implications presented in the SWOT analysis, these are the issues determined to have the greatest impact on future performance. Thus, it is important that these strategic issues be highlighted and become a central focus of the strategy to be developed. For the Stericycle sample marketing plan, the following is a brief description of the SWOT analysis that is presented on page 7 of the sample marketing plan.

- **SWOT Analysis and Key Issues:** Summarizes the strategic implications uncovered in the Stericycle situation analysis and identifies key issues to be addressed in the strategies to be developed.

Recognizing both the information presented in the situation analysis and the strategy implications derived in the SWOT analysis, we next must develop a strategic market plan for each segment.

Step III: Strategic Market Plan

Stericycle faces two market opportunities: one in the large institution segment and the other in the small institution segment. Because the resources in most businesses are limited and market opportunities vary in market attractiveness and potential for competitive advantage, a strategic market plan needs to be specified for each market segment. This process follows and is presented on pages 8 and 9 of the sample Stericycle marketing plan.

- **Strategic Market Assessment:** Market attractiveness and competitive advantage criteria are specified and weighted with respect to importance. On the basis of these criteria, each market segment is assessed and indexed with respect to market attractiveness and competitive advantage.
- **Portfolio Analysis:** A product-market portfolio is created based on the market attractiveness and competitive advantage for each market segment.
- **Strategic Market Plan:** On the basis of the portfolio position, situation analysis, SWOT analysis, and resources, a strategic market plan is specified for each segment.

The strategic market plan for each segment sets a strategic direction and implicitly specifies the short- and long-run performance expectations for each segment. The next step in building a marketing plan is to develop a marketing mix strategy for each target market.

Step IV: Marketing Mix Strategy

The strategic market plan for each segment and the situation forces presented in the situation analysis were used to develop the marketing mix strategy for each market segment, presented on pages 10 and 11 of the sample Stericycle marketing plan.

- **Large Institution Segment Strategy: Reduced Focus and Monetize:** The marketing mix strategy (product, price, promotion, and place) recommended for this segment is a defensive strategy that involves selling to fewer customers but at desired margins. This is consistent with the strategic market plan specified for this segment and the situational forces presented in the situation analysis.
- **Small Institution Segment Strategy: Invest to Grow Share:** The tactical marketing mix strategy recommended for this segment is an offensive strategy to invest to build market share in a growing segment of the medical waste market. As such, the marketing mix is quite different from the one specified for the large institution segment.

Market Share Objective

Based on the two strategic market plans and their respective marketing mix strategies, a market share objective in created for each market segment. This is necessary for both developing the marketing budget and building the marketing profit plan for each segment. Marketing mix strategies provide the level of detail required to allow resource allocations in the marketing budget and to subsequently build a performance plan.

Step V: Marketing Budget

Producing a marketing budget is a critical step in building a marketing plan and one most businesses do not do a very good job of. Up to this point, the process of building a marketing plan was relatively free of risk and economic consequences. Now, it is time to resource each strategic market plan and supporting marketing mix strategy with a marketing budget. If this is not done correctly, the whole effort is subject to a higher probability of failure. The "customer mix" approach was used to develop the marketing budget that is summarized and presented on page 13 of the sample Stericycle marketing plan.

- **Marketing Budget:** On the basis of the market share objectives of each segment strategy and the respective costs of new customer acquisition and retention of existing customers, a marketing budget was created for each market segment over a 3-year planning horizon. The marketing budget for each segment is consistent with the market share objective for each segment over the next 3 years. Naturally, the large institution segment, with a reduced focus strategy, will require less marketing budget than the small institution segment, which hopes to more than triple its market share over the next 3 years.

Step VI: Marketing Performance Plan

The last page of the sample Stericycle marketing plan is a marketing performance. The plan outlines for each segment how market share, sales revenues, margins, marketing expenses, and profitability will evolve over the 3-year planning horizon. A brief description follows and is shown on page 14 of the sample marketing plan.

- **Marketing Profit Plan:** The current performance with respect to market share, sales, margin, marketing expense, and net marketing contribution is reported for each segment. Then, on the basis of the strategic market plan and tactical marketing strategy for each segment, a 3-year marketing profit plan is developed for the 3-year timeline.

    The performance timeline represents a close reconciliation between situation, strategy, and resource allocation. To the degree that this reconciliation is done accurately, the performance timeline provides a legitimate roadmap from which actual performance can be evaluated as the marketing plan is implemented over time.

Step VII: Performance Evaluation

The sample marketing plan built for Stericycle represents a strategic roadmap for navigation of two specific segment strategic market plans and tactical marketing strategies. As shown in Figure 14-2, after the marketing plan has been implemented, performance gaps are likely to emerge because of changing market conditions and the effectiveness of proposed marketing tactics. Addressing these performance gaps as they occur is a critical part of the marketing planning process. Modifying, adapting, or even abandoning the strategy for a segment are all part of the process of building and implementing a marketing plan. The next chapter is devoted specifically to successful implementation of a marketing plan.

■ Summary

A marketing plan serves as a roadmap. It carefully outlines where a business is, its desired destination (objectives), and the conditions it will face in its efforts to reach that destination. Understanding the market situation reveals a set of key issues that need to be addressed in order to reach the desired destination. Situation analysis and identification of key performance issues are key inputs to the marketing plan designed to accomplish a business's objectives.

The strategies developed in a marketing plan will not necessarily succeed just because they have been laid out. Resources in the form of people and money need to be allocated to implement strategies. If adequate resources are not available, attainment of a business's objectives may not be possible, and marketing strategies will have to be revised or abandoned. Thus, the process of developing a marketing plan is not that much different from planning an extensive vacation; it is just much more complex.

There are many benefits to a good marketing plan. The process of market planning can lead a business to discovery of new-market opportunities, to better utilization of assets and capabilities, to a well-defined market focus, to improved marketing productivity, and to a baseline from which to evaluate progress toward goals. There is a planning paradox, however. It goes without saying that those with no marketing plans severely restrict themselves in achieving benefits, but it is also true that those with too highly formalized marketing plans may also minimize their potential of achieving benefits. The business with no marketing plan will not see the market around them or the opportunities and threats that need to be addressed while pursuing a market objective. Businesses with highly formalized plans can evolve to merely filling in forms and can thereby miss the opportunity to understand the subtler aspects of the market.

Developing a marketing plan involves process and structure, creativity, and form. The process begins with a broad view of market opportunities that encourages a wider consideration of many market opportunities. For each market opportunity, a strategic market objective is set, based on market attractiveness and competitive advantage attained or attainable in the market. For each market to be pursued, a separate situation analysis and marketing plan is required. The situation analysis enables the business to uncover key issues that may limit performance. These key performance issues are the basic materials from which marketing strategies are built. Each aspect of the strategy must be scrutinized with respect to the market situation, key issues, strategies to address those issues, and the resources needed to achieve specific performance objectives. With the marketing strategy and budget set, an estimate of market and financial performance metrics must be projected over a specified time frame. If the marketing plan fails to produce desired levels of performance, the marketing strategy needs to be reexamined.

■ Market-Based Logic and Strategic Thinking

1 Why is a roadmap for a family vacation a good metaphor for the process of developing a marketing plan? What are the similarities and differences?

2 How would the process of developing a marketing plan help Stericycle achieve a higher level of sales growth and profitability?

3 Why would a business with a strong market orientation do a better job of creating a situation analysis than a business with a poor market orientation?

4 How could businesses engaged in no market planning or in highly formalized market planning both miss meaningful market insights?

5 How would a business with a sound market-planning process differ from a business with no marketing plan in the following:

> Discovering opportunities
>
> Leveraging existing systems, assets, and core capabilities
>
> Implementing a market-focused strategy
>
> Allocating resources
>
> Planning performance

6 Why does the first step in the market planning process involve a situation analysis?

7 What is the role of a SWOT analysis in the market planning process? What is the role of key issues in the SWOT analysis?

8 For each product-market opportunity, how is a strategic market plan determined?

9 How does the strategic marketing plan for a given product-market influence the marketing mix strategy for that product-market?

10 How are key performance issues identified in the SWOT analysis used in selecting a strategic market plan and building a marketing mix strategy?

11 Why is the development of a marketing budget so important to the success of the marketing plan?

12 What are the various ways one could develop a marketing budget for a given strategic market plan and supporting marketing mix strategy?

13 How should the resources needed to support a marketing plan be logically linked to the key issues, marketing strategies, and expected performance?

14 What is the purpose of the performance plan? What role should it play in the successful implementation of a marketing plan?

Marketing Performance Tools

Each of the following **marketing performance tools** can be accessed by going to *www.rogerjbest.com* or *www.prenhall.com/best*. The shaded cells are input cells. The non-shaded cells contain results calculated from your input values.

MARKETING PERFORMANCE TOOL—Marketing Profit Planning Perspective—Dollar Metric

Area of Performance	Base Year	2004	2005	2006
Market Demand (millions)	$2,000	$2,120	$2,350	$2,500
Market Share (%)	22.7	22.9	23.2	23.8
Sales Revenues (millions)	$ 454	$ 485	$ 545	$ 595
Percent Margin (%)	43.3	43.7	43.7	43.9
Gross Profit (millions)	$196.6	$212.2	$238.3	$261.2
Marketing Expenses (% sales)	14.40	13.60	13.60	13.00
Marketing Expenses (millions)	$ 65.4	$ 66.0	$ 74.1	$ 77.4
Net Marketing Contribution (millions)	$131.2	$146.1	$154.1	$183.9
Marketing ROS (%)	28.9	30.1	30.1	30.9
Marketing ROI (%)	200.7	221.3	221.3	237.7

This **marketing performance tool** allows you to estimate the sales and marketing profitability using a "dollar metric" planning perspective. The shaded numeric input cells can be changed in doing the following application exercise.

Application Exercise: What would be the impact on sales and marketing profits if Stericycle was not able to increase market share over this 3-year planning period? What would be the impact on sales and marketing profits if the market demand grew to $3 billion in 2006?

MARKETING PERFORMANCE TOOL—Marketing Profit Planning Perspective—Volume Metric

Area of Performance	Base Year	2004	2005	2006
Market Demand (units millions)	15.95	16.95	18.80	20.00
Market Share (%)	22.7	22.9	23.2	23.8
Volume (units millions)	3.62	3.88	4.36	4.76
Price per Unit	$125.00	$125.00	$125.00	$125.00
Sales Revenues (millions)	$ 453	$ 485	$ 545	$ 595
Percent Margin (%)	43.3	43.7	43.7	43.9
Gross Profit (millions)	$ 196.0	$ 212.0	$ 238.3	$ 261.2
Marketing Expenses (% sales)	14.40	13.60	13.60	13.00
Marketing Expenses (millions)	$ 65.2	$ 66.0	$ 74.1	$ 77.4
Net Marketing Contribution (millions)	$ 130.8	$ 146.0	$ 164.1	$ 183.9
Marketing ROS (%)	28.9	30.1	30.1	30.9
Marketing ROI (%)	200.7	221.3	221.3	237.7

This **marketing performance tool** allows you to estimate the sales and marketing profitability using a "volume metric" planning perspective.

The shaded numeric input cells can be changed in doing the following application exercise.

Application Exercise: What would be the impact on sales and marketing profits if price per unit decreased by $5 per year over the 3-year planning period? What would be the impact on sales and marketing profits if marketing expenses as a percent of sales increased from 14.5 percent to 16 percent?

MARKETING PERFORMANCE TOOL—Marketing Profit Planning Perspective—Customer Metric

Area of Performance	Base Year	2004	2005	2006
Market Demand (customers)	1,323,000	1,415,000	1,567,000	1,667,000
Market Share (%)	22.7	22.9	23.2	23.7
Customer Volume	300,321	324,035	363,544	395,079
Revenue per Customer	$1,510	$1,500	$1,500	$1,500
Sales Revenues (millions)	$ 453	$ 485	$ 545	$ 593
Percent Margin (%)	43.4	43.7	43.7	43.9
Gross Profit (millions)	$196.8	$212.4	$238.3	$260.2
Marketing Expenses (% sales)	14.40	13.60	13.60	13.00
Marketing Expenses (millions)	$ 65.3	$ 66.1	$ 74.2	$ 77.0
Net Marketing Contribution (millions)	$131.5	$146.3	$164.1	$183.1
Marketing ROS (%)	29.0	30.1	30.1	30.9
Marketing ROI (%)	201.4	221.3	221.3	237.7

This **marketing performance tool** allows you to estimate the sales and marketing profitability using a "customer metric" planning perspective. The shaded numeric input cells can be changed in doing the following application exercise.

Application Exercise: What would be the impact on sales and marketing profits if

Stericycle was able to add new services that increased revenue per customer to $2,000? How would marketing profits and marketing profitability metrics change if revenue per customer grew to $2,000 and margins increased to 50 percent?

Notes

1. David Aaker, "Formal Planning System," *Strategic Market Management* (New York: Wiley, 1995): 341–353.
2. Arie Rijvnis and Graham Sharman,"New Life for Formal Planning Systems," *Journal of Business Strategy* (Spring 1982): 103.
3. Henry Mintzberg, "The Fall and Rise of Strategic Planning," *Harvard Business Review* (January–February 1994): 107–114; and Benjamin Tregoe and Peter Tobia, "Strategy Versus Planning: Bridging the Gap," *Journal of Business Strategy* (December 1991): 14–19.
4. Thomas Powell, "Strategic Planning as Competitive Advantage," *Strategic Management Journal* 13 (1992): 551–558; Scott Armstrong, "The Value of Formal Planning for Strategic Decisions: Reply," *Strategic Management Journal* 7 (1986): 183–185; and Deepak

Sinha,"The Contribution of Formal Planning to Decisions," *Strategic Management Journal* (October 1990): 479–492.
5. Philip Kotler, *Marketing Management: Analysis, Planning, Implementation and Control*, 7th ed. (Upper Saddle River, NJ: Prentice Hall, 1991): 62–72.
6. Gary Hamel and C. K. Prahalad, "Strategic Intent," *Harvard Business Review* (May–June 1989): 63–75; and Michael Treacy and Frederic Wiersema, "Customer Intimacy and Other Value Disciplines," *Harvard Business Review* (January–February 1993): 84–93.
7. Rajan Varadarajan, "Product Portfolio Analysis and Market Share Objectives: An Exposition of Certain Underlying Assumptions," *Journal of the Academy of Marketing Science* (Winter 1990): 17–29.

Sample Marketing Plan

STERICYCLE MARKETING PLAN
2004–2006

Stericycle is the market leader with a 22.7 percent share of the medical waste removal market. stericycle is strategically positioned to dominate competition in the growing small institution segment.

This marketing plan reconciles important assumptions with strategic market objectives and a marketing budget needed to grow market share from 22.7 percent to 24 percent while increasing marketing profits by 33 percent over the next 3 years.

This marketing plan was written by Roger J. Best. It is intended as instructional material. The data used in this marking plan were taken from published sources but also include estimates and assumptions made by the author.

CONTENTS

SITUATION ANALYSIS

MARKET DEMAND

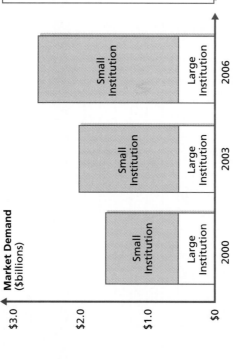

Market Demand
($billions)

- The market has grown from $1.5 billion in 2000 to $2 billion in 2003 and is projected to grow to $2.5 billion by 2006.

- The small institution market is growing faster (8 percent per year) and is projected to be a $1.9 billion market in 2006.

- The large institution market is growing at a slower rate (4.0 percent) and will decline to about 20 percent of market demand by 2006.

Strategic Implications: *The market is growing and Stericycle is well positioned for continued growth given its market leadership position.*

MARKET SEGMENTATION

Segment Profile	Large Institution	Small Institution
Value Driver	Low Cost	Service
Primary Benefit	Low Price	Easy & Safe Disposal
Price Sensitivity	Very High	Low
Key Demographic(s)	Hospitals Blood Banks	Physicians Offices/Clinics
Waste Management Expertise	Above Average	Poor
Market Demand—2003	$500 million	$1,500 million
% Market Growth (next 3 years)*	4.5 per year	8 per year
Number of Customers	16,667	1,060,000
Revenue per Customer	$30,000	$1,500
Percent Margin (%)	20	45
Margin per Customer	$6,000	$675

Large Institution Segment

- 25 percent of the market demand and lower market growth (4.5%).

- More price sensitive and lower percent margin.

Small Institution Segment

- Larger market demand and almost twice the rate of growth.

- Less price sensitive, more driven by service benefits.

*Market growth is primarily due to increased waste per customer rather than new customers entering the medical waste market.

Strategic Implications: *The small institution market offers the best opportunity for growth (volume) and profitability (margin). The large institution market is smaller, slower growing, and more price sensitive with eroded percent margins.*

INDUSTRY ANALYSIS

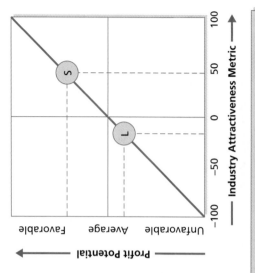

Segment Specific Competitive Forces	Relative Importance	-100	-50	0	50	100
Competitor Entry	0.20				S	L
Competitor Exit	0.05		L		S	
Qualified Substitutes	0.25				S/L	
Customer Buyer Power	0.15	L			S	
Supplier Power	0.05			L/S		
Price Rivalry	0.30	L			S	

Small Institution Market (S) = 47.5

Overall, a more favorable market segment based on competitive forces. Industry attractiveness index is 47.5.

Large Institution Market (L) = -15

Industry attractiveness slightly above average (score = -15). This market segment is less attractive due to customer buyer power and price rivalry.

Strategic Implications: The small institution market offers the best competitive environment. This makes it easier to achieve service differentiation and maintain good margins. To succeed in the large institution market would require a low cost producer strategy which does not leverage Stericycle's service differentiation advantage.

The industry analysis metric has six components. Each is measured on a five-point scale that ranges from unfavorable to favorable. The index above relates the industry analysis score with profit potential. As shown, the potential for good profits is far greater in the small institution market.

MARKET SHARE

Market Share Performance Metrics	Small Institution (%)	Large Institution (%)
Aware of Stericycle	80	95
Attracted to Service/Benefits	84	70
Price Is Acceptable/Good Value	75	25
Stericycle Available	58	80
Purchase Stericycle	95	30
Market Share Index	27.8%	4.0%

- Awareness of Stericycle is high in both markets. The Stericycle service is also fairly attractive in both markets.

- Price is a bigger issue in the large institution market because only 25 percent find the Stericycle service an attractive value at current prices.

- Availability is lower in the small institution market. This is largely due to not being able to reach smaller towns and rural areas.

- The rate of purchase is three times higher in the small institution market. This has a major impact on the overall market share index of the small institution market.

Market Share Index
Small Institution Market

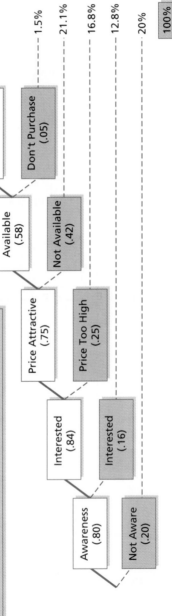

Purchase (.95)	27.8%
Don't Purchase (.05)	1.5%
Available (.58)	
Not Available (.42)	21.1%
Price Attractive (.75)	
Price Too High (.25)	16.8%
Interested (.84)	
Interested (.16)	12.8%
Awareness (.80)	
Not Aware (.20)	20%
	100%

Strategic Implications: *The biggest constraint to Stericycle's share growth in the small institution market is availability. Expanding locations and building awareness will drive Stericycle's market share. The large institution market is less attractive with respect to share growth because customers in this market find the price of the Stericycle service too high.*

MARKETING CHANNELS

COST OF MARKETING

Marketing Expenses (2003) Acquisition Cost	Marketing Budget
Number of new customers	37,385
Acquisition cost/customer	$750
acquisition cost (millions)	$28.0
Retention Cost	**$1.44**
Number of retained customers	257,365
Retention cost/customer	$145
Retention cost (millions)	$37.3
Total Cost of Marketing	**$65.3**

- Although Stericycle has a 95 percent retention, this still requires attracting 14,738 new customers to hold market share.

- Because the market is growing, this means attracting even more customers just to hold market share. The net result is a large portion of the marketing budget is devoted to attracting new customers.

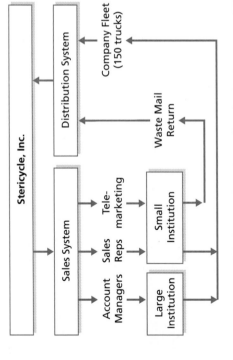

Stericycle, Inc.

Sales System — Distribution System

Account Managers — Sales Reps — Tele-marketing

Large Institution — Small Institution

Company Fleet (150 trucks)

Waste Mail Return

Strategic Implicattions: *Stericycle's cost of marketing is significantly higher in the small institution market for two reasons. One, there are more customers to sever, and hence, a much higher retention cost. Two, there are more new customers, and hence, a higher acquisition cost. Bottom line: the majority of the marketing budget is spent on customers in the small institution market.*

435

MARKET AND PROFIT PERFORMANCE

Market Performance	Small Institution	Large Institution	Company
Market Share (%)	28.7	4.5	22.7
Market Growth Rate (%)	8.0	4.5	5.0
Customer Retention (%)	95	86	95
Customer Life (years)	20 years	7 years	20 years
Financed Performance			
Sales Revenues (millions)	$431	$22.5	$453
Percent Margin (%)	44.50%	20.00%	43.28%
Gross Profit (millions)	$192	$4.50	$196.5
Marketing Expenses (millions)	$62.6	$2.70	$65.3
Net Marketing Contribution	$129.4	$1.80	$131.2

Small Institution Market
- Produces over 95 percent of the sales revenues.
- Produces 98.5 percent of the marketing profits.
- Achieves a 95 percent customer retention.

Large Institution Market
- Produces 5 percent of the sales revenues.
- Produces 1.5 percent of overall marketing profits.
- Achieves a 86 percent customer retention.

Strategic Implications: *The small institution market offers the best profitable growth; it is profitable and growing at a faster rate. The large institution market is operating above breakeven but does not possess the financial leverage to be as profitable as the small institution market.*

STRATEGIC MARKET PLAN

SWOT ANALYSIS

Strengths
- Market leader/well-known
- Technology advantage
- Many locations
- 12 times larger than the next largest competitor

Weaknesses
- Not price competitive in the large institution market
- Low margins/poor industry attractiveness in large institution market

Opportunities
- Growing medical waste market
- Larger market demand in small institution market
- Competitor exit should make it easier to grow share

Threats
- Increase in government regulation
- Patent expiration or infringement
- Large competitor entry through acquisition

KEY ISSUES

Stericycle is the technology leader and market leader with a market share 12 times larger than the next largest competitor.

The best opportunity for profitable growth is in the small institution market.

Stericycle's key weaknesses are primarily associated with the large institution market.

Strategic Implications: *The key issues can be directly linked to current positioning and performance. To the degree these issues are addressed in the marketing plan, Stericycle has the potential to achieve above-average levels of profitable growth.*

STRATEGIC MARKET ASSESSMENT

Market Attractiveness (influencing factors)	Relative Importance	Unfavorable 0	25	Average 50	75	Favorable 100
Market Size (volume)	30			L		S
Market Growth Rate	10		L		S	
Sustainable Margins	30			L		S
Industry Attractiveness	20		L		S	
Market Reach	10		L			S
	100					

Market Attractiveness
- Small Institution Market **Score = 92.5**
- Large Institution Market **Score = 40**

Competitive Advantage (influencing factors)	Relative Importance	Poor 0	25	Average 50	75	Strong 100
Product Advantage	20		LM			SM
Service Advantage	30		LM			SM
Price Competitive	25	LM			SM	
Reputation for Quality	5			LM	SM	
Marketing Advantage	20		LM			SM
	100					

Competitive Advantage
- Small Institution Market **Score = 89**
- Large Institution Market **Score = 20**

L = Large Institution Market   S = Small Institution Market

LM = Large Institution Market   SM = Small Institution Market

Strategic Implications: *The small institution market is a more attractive market and one in which Stericycle is able to leverage its competitive advantage. The large institution market is below average with respect to market attractiveness and well below average in competitive advantage.*

PORTFOLIO ANALYSIS AND STRATEGIC MARKET PLANS

Strategic Market Plans

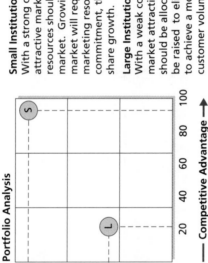

Portfolio Analysis

Small Institution Market (S) – Grow Market Share

With a strong competitive position in an attractive market that is growing, marketing resources should be heavily weighted on this market. Growing market share in a growing market will require more than the usual marketing resources. However, without this commitment, there is less chance of achieving share growth.

Large Institution Market (L) – Reduce Focus

With a weak competitive position and average market attractiveness, fewer marketing resources should be allocated to this market. Prices should be raised to eliminate unprofitable customers, and to achieve a more profitable combination of customer volume and margin per customer.

Strategic Implications: *The portfolio analysis yields two strategic market plans. In the small institution market, Stericycle should invest to grow market share in a growing market. In the large institution market, Stericycle should optimize its market position with profitable customers (reduce focus) and seek to maximize profits in this market.*

440

MARKETING STRATEGIES
AND
PERFORMANCE PLAN

SMALL INSTITUTION MARKET STRATEGY: MARKET SHARE GROWTH

Value Proposition . . . . . A Safe and Reliable Solution to Your Medical Waste Problems

Product Positioning

Provide above-average customer service, training, and quick response to problems. To enhance customer loyalty and effectiveness, waste management training will be provided along with an Excel-based software program to track customer waste management activities and problems.

Price/Customer Value

Prices will be 10 to 20 percent higher than competitors. However, because of superior product, service, and brand benefits along with a lower total cost of purchase, the customer value is intended to be very high.

Channel Strategy

Sales managers and sales reps will call directly on clients and set up training and service programs. Medical waste collection will be handled with direct pick up in high-volume locations and by waste return mailers for remote, low-volume customers.

Communication Strategy

Advertisements will be created for the small institution market that reflect their size, needs, and demographics. The value proposition will be central to all market communications.

Market Share Objective: *Our market share objective is to grow market share in the small institution market from 28.7 percent to 31 percent in 3 years.*

LARGE INSTITUTION MARKET STRATEGY: REDUCE FOCUS

Value Proposition . . . . . Safety and Service Can Save You Money

Product Positioning

Provide above-average customer service and quick response to problems. Get customers to look beyond price to the total cost of purchase (waste storage, pick up, cost of waste problems, administrative costs, etc.).

Price/Customer Value

Prices will be 10 to 20 percent higher than competitors, but demonstrate how Stericycle at a higher price saves the large institution customer money when they look at the total cost of purchase.

Channel Strategy

Account managers will call directly on large institutions and conduct a life cycle costs analysis (for those interested) and demonstrate economic value at higher prices. Medical waste collection will be handled with direct pick up.

Communication Strategy

Advertisements will be created for large institution market customers that reflect their size, needs, and demographics. The value proposition will be central to all marketing communications and built around economic value versus price.

Market Share Objective: *Our market share objective is to manage market share for maximum profits in the large institution market. This could result in further market share erosion from the current market share of 4.5 percent.*

MARKET SHARE PERFORMANCE METRICS

Shown here are market share performance metrics for the small institution market. The largest area of lost share is in availability (20.3%).

Market Share Performance Metrics	Small Institution Current (%)	Small Institution Plan (%)	Large Institution Current (%)	Large Institution Plan (%)
Aware of Stericycle	80	85	90	90
Attracted to Service/Benefits	84	84	80	80
Price Is Acceptable/Good Value	75	75	25	25
Stericycle Available	58	62	80	84
Purchase Stericycle	95	95	30	30
Market Share Index	**27.8%**	**31.5%**	**4.3%**	**4.5%**

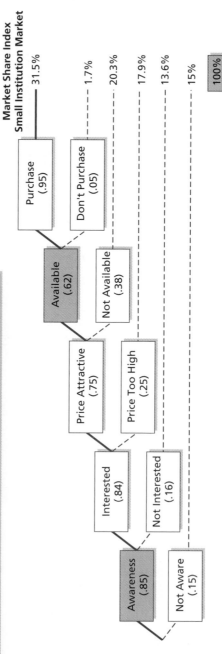

Market Share Index
Small Institution Market

Purchase (.95) — 31.5%

Don't Purchase (.05) — 1.7%

Available (.62)

Not Available (.38) — 20.3%

Price Attractive (.75)

Price Too High (.25) — 17.9%

Interested (.84)

Not Interested (.16) — 13.6%

Awareness (.85)

Not Aware (.15) — 15%

100%

Strategic Implications: *Gains in awareness and availability in the small institution market increase the market share index from 28.7 percent to 31.5 percent. Because this index is not a precise predictor of market share, the share goal for 2006 will be set a little lower at 30 percent. The share goal in the large institution market will remain at 4.5 percent but could fall due to price competition.*

MARKETING BUDGET

Customer-Based Marketing Expenses

Small Institution Market
- Acquisition cost per customer = $750
- Retention cost per customer = $135
- Total marketing budget will grow from $62.6 million in 2003 to 73.9 million in 2006.

Large Institution Market
- Acquisition cost per customer = $10,000
- Retention cost per customer = $2,500
- Total marketing budget will increase from $2.7 million to $2.8 million.

Small Institution Market	2003	2004	2005	2006
Market Demand (customers)	1,057,554	1,099,856	1,143,850	1,189,604
Market Share (%)	27.80	28.50	29.30	30.00
Total Customers	294,000	313,459	335,148	356,881
New Customers	37,280	34,159	37,362	38,491
Retained Customers (95%)	256,720	279,300	297,786	318,391
Marketing Budget (millions)				
Acquisition Cost	$28.0	$25.6	$28.0	$28.9
Retention Cost	$34.7	$37.7	$40.2	$43.0
Marketing Expenses	**$62.2**	**$67.9**	**$78.0**	**$86.8**

Large Institution Market	2003	2004	2005	2006
Market Demand (Customers)	16,667	16,834	17,002	17,172
Market Share (%)	4.50	4.50	4.50	4.50
Total Customers	750	758	765	773
New Customers	115	113	114	115
Retained Customers (86%)	635	645	651	658
Marketing Budget (millions)				
Acquisition Cost	$1.1	$1.1	$1.1	$1.1
Retention Cost	$1.6	$1.6	$1.7	$1.7
Marketing Expenses	**$2.7**	**$2.7**	**$2.8**	**$2.8**
Total Marketing Budget	**$65.3**	**$70.6**	**$80.8**	**$89.6**

Marketing Budget: *The majority of the marketing (95 percent) is devoted to the small institution market. The overall marketing budget will grow from $65.3 million in 2003 to $89.6 million in 2006. This is largely due to the rate of new-customer acquisition in the small institution market.*

MARKETING PROFIT PLAN

Small Institution Market	2003	2004	2005	2006
Market Demand (millions)	$1,500	$1,628	$1,766	$1,916
Market Share (%)	28.7%	29.0%	28.5%	31.0%
Sales Revenues (millions)	$431	$472	$521	$594
Gross Margin (%)	44.5%	45.0%	45.0%	45.0%
Gross Profit (millions)	$191.6	$212.4	$234.4	$267.3
Marketing Expenses (millions)	$62.6	$67.9	$78.0	$86.8
Net Marketing Contribution (millions)	$129.0	$144.5	$156.4	$180.5

Large Institution Market	2003	2004	2005	2006
Market Demand (millions)	$500	$520	$541	$562
Market Share (%)	4.6%	4.5%	4.5%	4.6%
Sales Revenues (millions)	$23	$23	$24	$25
Gross Margin (%)	20.0%	20.0%	20.0%	20.0%
Gross Profit (millions)	$4.6	$4.7	$4.9	$5.1
Marketing Expenses (millions)	$2.7	$2.7	$2.8	$2.8
Net Marketing Contribution (millions)	$1.9	$2.0	$2.1	$2.3

Overall Performance	2003	2004	2005	2006
Sales Revenues (millions)	$454	$495	$545	$619
Market Share (%)	22.7%	23.1%	23.6%	25.0%
Net Marketing Contribution (millions)	$130.9	$146.5	$158.5	$182.7

Marketing Plan Profit Impact: *If successful, this marketing plan will see net marketing contribution increase from $131 million (29 percent of sales) to $183 million (29.6 percent of sales). Marketing ROI (net marketing contribution divided by marketing budget) will improve from 200 percent to 239 percent.*

CHAPTER 15

Performance Metrics and Strategy Implementation

Nike is famous for innovation and its *"Just Do It"* marketing campaign—but this kind of marketing culture does not just happen. Nike's company culture motivates management behaviors that favor successful implementation of Nike strategies. For example, Nike's Eleven Maxims help Nike managers and all employees understand the Nike culture and approach to the business of marketing Nike.

1. It is our Nature to Innovate.
2. Nike is a Company.
3. Nike is a Brand.
4. Simplify and Go.
5. The Consumer Decides.
6. Be a Sponge.
7. Evolve Immediately.
8. Do the Right Thing.
9. Master the Fundamentals.
10. We Are on the Offense. Always.
11. Remember the Man (Bill Bowerman).

Nike's Eleven Maxims set a tone and style that favors successful implementations. This often requires high levels of persistence and adaptability as actual market conditions are likely to be different from those carefully articulated in a marketing plan.

A marketing plan provides a business with the roadmap it needs to pursue a specific strategic direction and a set of performance objectives. However, it does not guarantee that the desired performance objectives will be reached, any more than having a roadmap guarantees that a traveler will arrive at the desired destination. A marketing plan must be successfully implemented. Successful implementation is directly related to the marketing outline of a business or organization.

For example, a manufacturer of electric utility equipment engaged in an extensive market segmentation project in an effort to revitalize its sales and profitability. The effort revealed several market segments, all of which were reachable and judged to be attractive. A multisegment strategy was developed with separate segment strategies for each market segment. However, the sales force was divided into three sales regions and had not been part of the segmentation study and strategy development. The marketing manager knew that without their support and commitment this marketing strategy would fail.

To successfully implement this strategy, the marketing manager had to sell the strategy to three regional sales vice presidents. Two of the VPs agreed to implement the strategy, but one elected not to become involved. The results, shown in Figure 15-1, illustrate the importance of effective strategy implementation. In the two sales regions in which the marketing strategy was implemented, sales increased by 18 percent and 12 percent, in a market in which total demand declined by 15 percent. By contrast, there was only a 3 percent sales gain in the sales region that did not implement the marketing strategy.[1]

FIGURE 15-1 SALES IMPACT OF A SUCCESSFUL STRATEGY IMPLEMENTATION

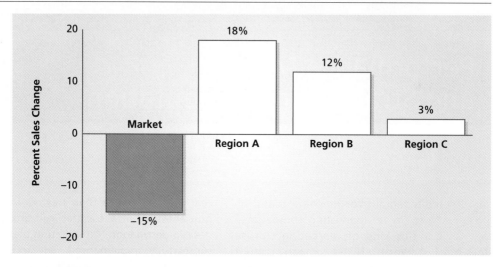

To achieve marketing success and reach target performance objectives, a business needs a good marketing plan and a well-executed implementation of the plan. A good marketing plan without a dedicated implementation effort will fail. This chapter will cover the forces that affect implementation of a strategy and a marketing plan, the importance of performance metrics, and the mechanics of a marketing plan variance analysis.

MARKETING PERFORMANCE METRICS

No matter how efficient a business's production operations, how expert its R&D, or how wise its financial management, if the customer doesn't buy or rebuy a business's products or services, marketing strategy will fail. As shown in Figure 15-2, market-based marketing strategies are designed to deliver customer satisfaction and retention. The degree to which a marketing strategy is successful will be detected first by market metrics that track customer satisfaction, retention, and perceptions of value; only subsequently will success or failure be observed in financial performance in the form of gains in revenue, total contribution, net profit, and cash flow. And, as shown in Figure 15-2, ultimately the results of a marketing strategy will affect shareholders in the form of earnings growth and expectations of improved future earnings.

The best the investment community can do is to report financial performance and expectations based on what the business says future performance will be. However, a business managed by a market-based management system is better able to detect and report future success by tracking market metrics, many of which lead changes in financial performance.

For example, an increase in the percentage of dissatisfied customers may not result in an immediate decrease in sales or net profits, for two reasons. First, dissatisfied customers often give a business a chance to correct the source of their dissatisfaction. Remedying

FIGURE 15-2 HOW MARKETING STRATEGY AND CUSTOMERS AFFECT SHAREHOLDERS

problems quickly and meaningfully can often translate into improved customer loyalty. Second, it often takes time for customers to make a change in product or supplier. Thus, there is often a time lag between customer dissatisfaction (a market metric) and sales decline (a financial metric).

To illustrate the importance of market metrics in market-based management and its profit impact, consider the example in Figure 15-3. In period I, the business had no customer dissatisfaction and net profits of $5 million on sales of $50 million. The total variable cost was $25 million and fixed expenses were $20 million. In period II, 10 percent of the business's customers became dissatisfied. In this example, however, the business did not have a market-based metric that tracked customer dissatisfaction. Thus, there would be no reason for concern because sales and profits were at a normal and expected level.

In period III, dissatisfied customers began to leave the business, and sales slowly declined. During this period, all fixed expenses remained the same, but there was less profit margin produced, and, hence, both sales and profits were down. The business took action in period IV by cutting marketing expenses in proportion to lost net income with the goal of returning net profits to their previous level. However, sales were still down, and, in period V, the business created a task force to investigate the problem. The task force found that the customers that had been lost had left because of a particular source of dissatisfaction.

In period VI, the business restored the marketing budget and added budget to correct the problem and to replace lost customers. There were no immediate sales gains, and net profit decreased because of the increased expenses. However, finally in period VII, the business was back to where it had been in period I; no customer dissatisfaction, sales of $50 million, and net profits of $5 million.

That sequence of events could easily have occurred over 3 to 5 years, but a market-based business would have detected the problem in period II and would have immediately

FIGURE 15-3 CUSTOMER BEHAVIOR, MARKET METRICS, AND PROFIT PERFORMANCE

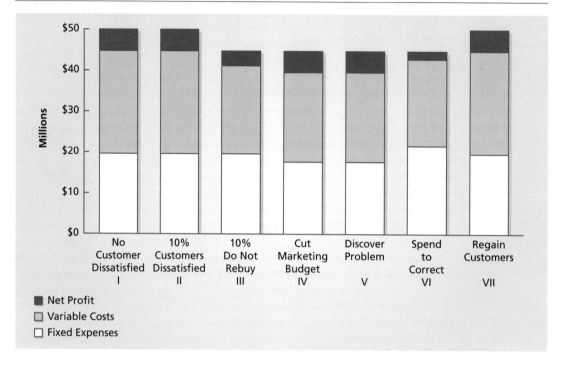

made corrections to restore customer satisfaction and retain its customer base. If the problem had been detected and corrected in period II, net profits over the seven periods would have totaled $35 million. The total in Figure 15-3 is $25 million. In other words, there were $10 million less in profit to reinvest in the business and contribute to earnings. In this way, stockholder value was diminished.

The purpose of this example is twofold: First, it points out the importance of market metrics that track customer behavior (remember, customers are the only source of positive cash flow). Second, it demonstrates that many market metrics are leading indicators of financial performance and are important market-based management tools that should contribute to better financial performance.

PROCESS VERSUS END-RESULT MARKET METRICS

Primarily, market metrics are ongoing measures of market performance. Because many market metrics precede financial performance, using them is critical to strategy implementation and financial performance. However, not all market metrics are leading indicators of business performance. There are process market metrics and end-result market metrics.[2] Both are important, but process market metrics are particularly important because they are also leading indicators of financial performance.[3] End-result market metrics correspond more closely to internal financial performance metrics.

Process Market Metrics

Customer awareness, interest, product trial, and customer satisfaction and dissatisfaction, along with perceptions of relative product quality, service quality, and customer value, all serve as process market metrics and leading indicators of end-result performance. Changes in each, positive or negative, precede actual changes in customer behavior. As a result, these in-process measures of customer thinking and attitude are important leading indicators of financial performance.

For example, perhaps customers are satisfied, but their perceptions of the value they derive from the product, relative to competing alternatives, are steadily diminishing. You may well have done nothing wrong to dissatisfy customers; the competition may have simply improved in delivering customer value based on a combination of total benefits and total cost. However, the net effect is that customer perceptions of the value created by the product have diminished. This change, in turn, opens the door to competitors' products that your customers may be inclined to try or purchase.

The whole purpose of process market metrics is to track customer perceptions and attitudes that precede changes in customer behavior and financial performance. For example, customer satisfaction is a process metric of considerable importance with many alternative measures.[4] As shown in Figure 15-4, measures of customer satisfaction can be broken down into different classifications. Very satisfied customers are loyal and buy in considerable amounts.[5] Merely satisfied customers are less loyal and more easily switch to competitors' products. Dissatisfied customers, of course, are likely to leave, although those who complain can be retained but remain vulnerable until the source of their dissatisfaction is adequately addressed. However, very few (less than 10 percent) dissatisfied customers complain,[6] and of those who do not complain, the majority stop buying from the business. Because most dissatisfied customers do not complain, a business may not know it has a problem. Eventually, these customers leave, and to maintain sales and profits, the business has to attract new customers. Businesses that use measures of customer satisfaction effectively have a process metric that enables them to take corrective action in order to avoid adverse effects on financial performance.

FIGURE 15-4 CUSTOMER DISSATISFACTION AND CUSTOMER EXIT

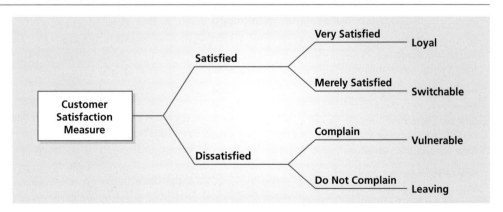

Thus, a market-based business with several process market metrics will detect early adverse changes in customer attitudes and perceptions. With an early warning signal, the market-based business can take corrective action before customers alter their purchase behavior. Without process market metrics, this problem may go undetected and unresolved until after declines in financial performance, as was illustrated in Figure 15-3.

End-Result Market Metrics

End-result market metrics include market share, customer retention, and revenue per customer. Each of these metrics occurs simultaneously with financial performance metrics. However, each provides a different set of performance diagnostic insights. For example, let's assume sales revenues are increasing and ahead of forecast, and financial performance is also better than expected. Most businesses would feel pretty good about their performance. However, if end-result performance metrics show that the business is losing market share in a growing market, and poor customer retention is masked by new customer growth, there should be concern. Without end-result market metrics, the business has only an internal measure of performance.

Even for a business that is not losing market share, poor customer retention has a powerful impact on financial performance, as illustrated in Figure 15-5. In this example, a business with a 20 percent market share and a 90 percent level of customer retention, produces 24 percent more net marketing contribution than the same business with an 80 percent customer retention.

Because existing customers generally spend more than new customers and the cost of serving an existing customer is less than that of acquiring and serving a new customer,

FIGURE 15-5 CUSTOMER RETENTION IS A KEY END-RESULT MARKET METRIC

Business Performance	80% Retention	90% Retention	Performance Gain
Customer Demand	1,000,000	1,000,000	None
Market Share (%)	20	20	None
Customer Volume	200,000	200,000	None
Revenue per Customer	$460	$480	+$20
Total Revenue (million)	$ 92	$ 96	+$ 4
Retained Customers	160,000	180,000	+20,000
Revenue per Customer	$500	$500	None
Cost per Customer	$200	$200	None
Margin per Customer	$300	$300	None
Total Contribution (million)	$ 48	$ 54	+$ 6
New Customers	40,000	20,000	−20,000
Revenue per Customer	$300	$300	None
Cost per Customer	$400	$400	None
Margin per Customer	−$100	−$100	None
Total Contribution (million)	−$ 4	−$ 2	+$ 2
Overall Total Contribution (million)	$ 44	$ 52	+$8 Million
Marketing Expenses (million)	$ 15	$ 16	+$1 Million
Net Marketing Contribution (million)	$ 29	$ 36	+$7 Million

the margin per customer is generally different. In this example, an existing customer produces $300 of margin per year, whereas a new customer results in a net loss of $100 per year. Retaining a larger percentage of existing customers improves total contribution and net marketing contribution even when an additional $1 million is added to marketing expenses for a customer retention program. Overall, the assets increase a little because higher revenues result in proportionately higher accounts receivable. However, return on assets still increases from 18 percent to over 30 percent.

Thus, the combination of market share, customer retention, and revenue per customer provides a totally different picture of performance than financial performance metrics. Both financial and market metrics are important, and each provides a different insight into business performance and successful implementation of a marketing plan.

SUCCESSFUL STRATEGY IMPLEMENTATION

Even if a flawless marketing plan could be developed, there would still be no guarantee that the marketing strategy and marketing plan would succeed in meeting the desired performance metrics. The marketing plan must still be successfully implemented. It is very difficult to implement a poor marketing plan, but it is still possible to fail to implement a good marketing plan. Shown in Figure 15-6 are three major forces that contribute to success or failure in implementing a marketing plan. As shown, each of these major forces has specific factors that contribute to the degree to which that force either positively or negatively affects the implementation of the marketing plan. Collectively, these factors will shape the behavior and organizational structure in a way that facilitates successful implementation.[7]

Owning the Marketing Plan

Perhaps the most common reason a marketing plan fails is a lack of ownership. If people do not have an ownership stake and responsibility in the marketing plan, it will be business as usual for all but a frustrated few. As shown in Figure 15-6, the ownership of a

FIGURE 15-6 SUCCESSFUL IMPLEMENTATION OF A MARKETING PLAN

market plan can be enhanced with detailed action plans, a champion and ownership team, compensation based on performance metrics, and top management involvement.

Detailed Action Plans

The development and use of detailed action plans may be the single most effective market management practice in determining the success of a marketing plan. A detailed action plan involves each aspect of the marketing strategy, but in greater detail with respect to specific actions that have to occur for the marketing plan to be implemented. Figure 15-7 outlines how a particular tactical marketing strategy within a marketing plan will be implemented. In this case, the strategy is broken down into five important action items, each of which must occur for this aspect of the marketing plan to succeed. As shown, for each of the five action items specified, an individual is assigned a specific responsibility, a measure or goal is delineated, and a time frame within which the action item should be completed is agreed upon.

Any number of action items could be added to this action plan, but the important point is that significant elements of this strategy have specific ownership. In this way, individuals have ownership and are accountable for implementing a portion of the marketing plan. Assigning responsibility enables a business to break the "business as usual" routine and fosters successful implementation of the marketing plan.

Champion and Ownership Team

Whereas laying out individual responsibilities in the detailed action plan is a way to get a wide range of people involved in implementation, every successful marketing strategy has a champion: a person who is devoted to the successful implementation of the marketing strategy and marketing plan. Although there is nothing wrong with having a single owner or champion, the creation of an ownership team can leverage the unique talents of multiple people and exert more organizational leverage than a single individual.[8] With a champion and an ownership team in place, the implementation process can stay on track even when some members of the team are gone for extended periods of time because of business trips, training programs, illness, or vacations.

FIGURE 15-7 DETAILED ACTION PLAN FOR A CHANNEL STRATEGY

Marketing Strategy To create adequate end-user product availability, 80 manufacturers' reps and 5 missionary salespeople will be used to sell and distribute our product to 5,000 industrial supply houses.

No.	Action Item	Responsibility	Measure	Time Frame*
1.	Identify target supply houses and establish contracts.	P. Elliot	5,000 Dealers	12 months
2.	Contact manufacturer reps.	T. Garcia	80 Reps	6 months
3.	Hire missionary sales force.	P. Wilson	5 People	3 months
4.	Develop rep training program.	S. Bradley	Program Pilot	6 months
5.	Develop dealer training program.	R. Otto	Program Pilot	6 months

*From time of implementation.

Compensation

Most people respond to financial rewards. Tying the compensation of those principally responsible for implementation of the marketing plan to performance metrics increases the incentive to successfully implement the marketing plan. Compensation can be tied to both external market metrics and internal financial metrics, which will be discussed later in this chapter. Market metrics are most important in the early stages of marketing plan implementation. Market metrics such as end-customer awareness and interest, product availability, and trial are market behaviors that must occur before financial metrics such as sales revenue, total contribution, net marketing contribution, and net profit can occur. The overall goal of compensation tied to market metrics is to create motivation and responsibility.

Management Involvement

Senior managers must stay committed to their involvement with the marketing plan and to their review of its progress. When top managers lessen the time available to review the marketing plan and performance, they send an implicit signal of lack of interest and support. This signal weakens the motivation of the ownership team and the chance for successful implementation.

Supporting the Marketing Plan

Though there are potentially many factors that could affect the degree to which a business is committed to a marketing plan, time to succeed, resource allocation, communication, and skills to succeed are critical.[9]

Time to Succeed

In many instances, commitment to a marketing plan weakens when financial performance is not on track. Without meaningful market metrics, a business may pull support for a marketing plan without knowing why it is not working. It may be that the marketing strategy and plan are good, but implementation has been poor. It may also be that the market metrics are on target but that it simply may take more time for financial metrics to respond to desired or target levels.

Time to succeed will, in part, depend on the marketing strategy and the nature of the market opportunity. A share penetration strategy in an existing market should take less time to succeed than a strategy to enter a new market that is undeveloped. In either case, the time to succeed, along with market metrics that signal progress, are important aspects of commitment to the marketing plan and successful implementation.

Resource Allocation

If the process and structure of marketing planning are followed as described in Chapter 14, the marketing plan should be allocated sufficient resources with respect to personnel and funding. If less than the required resources are reserved for the marketing plan, the chances for success are greatly reduced. Of course, if the resources needed are not systematically determined in the marketing planning process, it is even more likely that the marketing plan will be underresourced. (It is rare that marketing plans are overresourced.) Thus, an important step in successful implementation is to ensure that the resources needed are fully committed to support implementation of the marketing plan.

Communication

It is difficult to get support either internally, within the company, or externally, from the market, if the marketing plan and its strategic intent are not aggressively communicated. Although senior management and the market management team are likely to fully understand the logic and tactics of the marketing plan, others—in sales, customer support, manufacturing, and finance—may not understand the strategic objectives and marketing strategy being implemented. As a result, these employees, who may play key roles in successful implementation, will continue in a business-as-usual mode of operation. To facilitate communication and understanding, some businesses have created videos for employees describing strategic market objectives and the marketing strategy.

Internal communication of a marketing plan, including the specific role individuals within the business play with respect to the market plan, is critical. To the degree possible, these job functions should be integrated into detailed action plans, as described earlier. In this way, key individuals understand their roles and responsibilities in the successful implementation of the market plan.

External communication of the marketing plan is also critical. Each of the following groups must be made aware of different aspects of the marketing plan:

- **Target Customers:** Need to be made aware of the benefits of the product, the value proposition, and where the product can be acquired.
- **Channel Intermediaries:** Need to understand target customers, their profit potential, and inventory, sales, and service requirements.
- **The Trade Press:** Needs to be informed as to product benefits and availability of the product.
- **Market Influencers:** Must be informed. These could include consultants, financial analysts, or others who influence customers and channel intermediaries.
- **The General and Business Press:** Must receive news releases that can further communicate the market plan to potential customers, distributors, and investors.

Of course, the extent to which external market communications are engaged depends on the nature of the marketing strategy and product. A new product made to more effectively treat metal-working fluids in small machine shops would not interest most consumers, the general press, or even the business press. However, trade press publishers, consultants, the Environmental Protection Agency, and others may be interested in promoting awareness of a new product that greatly reduces the problems of disposal of hazardous waste, lowers the cost of disposal, and improves working conditions.

Required Skills

Do those implementing the marketing plan have the required skills to effectively implement the marketing plan?[10] For example, a bank wanting to improve customer satisfaction and retention may have to do some training to communicate new policies and customer-oriented employee attitudes. Two of the five action items detailed in Figure 15-7 involved training. For that marketing strategy to succeed, it was essential that manufacturers' reps and distributors were trained with respect to product knowledge, service requirements, how to sell the product, and how to explain the value derived from this product. Without a training effort, this strategy would likely not succeed.

In many instances, even members of the management team may need additional training to successfully implement the marketing plan. A business implementing a program to get more new product sales may need to provide some management training on the new product. Without the necessary skills, the management team might produce a meaningful objective but have no way of successfully accomplishing it.

Adapting the Marketing Plan

The marketing planning process does not stop when marketing plan implementation begins; it continues through strategy implementation. As do all systems, a marketing plan needs to be adapted to survive changing or unanticipated conditions. To survive, as well as to succeed, the marketing plan needs to be adaptive. Four factors that contribute to the adaptive nature of a marketing plan are continuous improvement, feedback measurements, persistence, and adaptive roll out of the marketing plan.

Continuous Improvement

A marketing plan that is not adapted to unexpected or changing market conditions will fail. Because market conditions are complex and changing, a business must be flexible in modifying its marketing plan to adapt to the changing market conditions. In many instances, these may be small changes, made in order to more finely tune the business's marketing strategy and value proposition. However, in some cases, a major shift in marketing strategy may be required.

The term *adaptive persistence* has been attributed to the success of many Japanese marketing strategies. One of Japanese management's greatest assets is their ability to adapt when a marketing plan is not working and to stick with it—to *persist*. The whole concept of continuous improvement is implicit in Japanese marketing plan implementation. Although the marketing plan sets the direction and provides the initial roadmap, once it is in place, the flexibility to adapt is an important aspect of continuous improvement.

Feedback Measurements

An essential element of any adaptive system, whether mechanical, electrical, or human, is feedback. Mechanical, electrical, and human systems have built-in sensors and feedback systems. Management systems also require measurements to provide a mechanism for feedback. Measurements of process-oriented market metrics play the role of a sensor in a marketing plan feedback system. These measurements signal the status of the marketing plan with respect to progress toward end-result metrics such as sales, market share, total contribution, and net profit.

Key process metrics that provide leading signals as to the success of the marketing plan and implementation include:

- Customer awareness, interest, intentions to buy, trial, and repeat purchase
- Intermediary market coverage, interest, support, and motivation
- Business responsiveness to customer inquiries and problems

Each of these market metrics has to reach an effective level of performance before financial metrics can begin to perform. The importance of market metrics is twofold. First, they provide an early signal as to the progress of the marketing plan. If market metrics are behind target performance levels specified in the marketing plan, then financial metrics and profit performance will be slower to materialize than projected. Second, the market metrics provide a signal as to which aspect of the marketing plan is not working. Is it the channel system, the communications strategy, or the product-price positioning strategy that is the cause of poor market performance? Each of these could trigger different strategies designed to better adapt the marketing plan to market conditions.

Persistence

Japanese companies are often cited as examples of successful marketing. However, rarely have Japanese marketing strategies worked initially. One of the great traits of Japanese managers is their inherent ability to adapt and persist throughout the implementation of the marketing plan. Japanese marketing managers remain committed to the strategic market objective and persist by adapting their market plans. Quite often, their marketing strategies need to be modified, but it is their determination to make them work that underlies the secret of their market success.

On the other hand, American managers are often quick to drop a marketing strategy and plan when it meets the first bit of resistance. Perhaps expectations of performance have been overstated—or time to succeed misspecified. Whichever the case, marketing strategies developed in a corporate office often lack the realism of the marketplace and may need to be adapted during implementation. Without a high degree of management persistence, there is little chance of successful implementation, particularly when aspects of the marketing plan need to be modified.

Adaptive Roll Out

A roll out is a gradual implementation of a marketing strategy that allows feedback and corrective adjustment. A roll out starts in a region of a broader market—the southwestern states, for example, after successful implementation, the strategy is refined and then rolled out to an adjacent region. This process of fine tuning the strategy continues until all regions of the market are served.

There are many benefits to a regional roll out as opposed to a nationwide launch, and it signals a business's marketing strategy to competitors as effectively. First, fewer resources are required in a small-scale regional launch of a marketing plan than in a nationwide launch. Second, problems with distributors, marketing communications, and product positioning can more readily be addressed and corrected on a small scale. Third, if the marketing plan is more effective than planned, additions can be made to production capacity without the potential of stockout and the loss of opportunities to capture customers when they want to buy. Fourth, even for a marketing plan that is tracking as planned on a regional basis, additional marketing insights will result that can be opportunistically integrated into the marketing plan as full marketing plan implementation is pursued. Fifth, the financial metrics generated from a successful roll out signal long-run profit potential and can be used to help fund the full introduction. Because of these benefits, many foreign competitors have used regional roll outs upon entering the American market.

Many American businesses do not want to take the time to engage in a corrective roll out of a marketing plan. However, it is rare that a marketing plan will succeed as conceived on paper. At risk are customers and distributors who might lose interest in the business's value proposition if it is ineffectively presented. In addition, the cost of a full-market introduction when things go wrong is enormous, even when customers and distributors are retained through the repositioning period.

Assessing Marketing Plan Implementation

Figure 15-8 lists the main ingredients of success in implementing a marketing plan and shows a profile of a business that worked to improve its marketing plan implementation. No single factor presented in Figure 15-8 will make or break the successful implementation of a marketing plan. However, when the sum of these factors is adequately addressed, the chances for successful marketing plan implementation are greatly improved. Although this business did not perform well on every factor, it performed much better than it had in past efforts. This level of implementation effort, along with a good marketing strategy and marketing plan, will enable the business to achieve a market success well beyond planned performance in a much shorter time than expected.

At the heart of successful implementation of a marketing plan is a business's market orientation. The greater the degree to which the business has built a market-based organization, the more likely is successful marketing plan implementation.[11] A market-based business with a strong customer focus and competitor orientation that works well across functions has a greater level of market sensitivity and urgency from which to both develop and implement a marketing plan.

FIGURE 15-8 AN ASSESSMENT OF MARKETING PLAN IMPLEMENTATION

Owning the Plan
- Detailed Action Plan   None ■ _ _ _ _ _ □ Extensive
- Ownership   None _ ■ _ _ _ _ □ Champion
- Compensation   None _ ■ □ _ _ _ _ Performance based
- Management Involvement   None _ _ _ ■ _ □ _ High

Supporting the Plan
- Time to Succeed   Inadequate _ ■ _ □ _ _ _ Sufficient
- Resource Allocation   Insufficient _ ■ _ □ _ _ _ Sufficient
- Communication Effort   None _ ■ _ _ □ _ _ Thorough
- Required Skills   Poor _ _ ■ _ □ _ _ Exceptional

Adapting the Plan
- Continuous Improvement   None _ ■ _ _ _ □ _ Ongoing
- Feedback Metrics   None ■ _ _ □ _ _ _ Extensive
- Persistence   None _ _ ■ _ □ _ _ Relentless
- Roll Out   Full Launch _ ■ _ □ _ _ _ Roll out

■ Past Efforts
□ Current Efforts

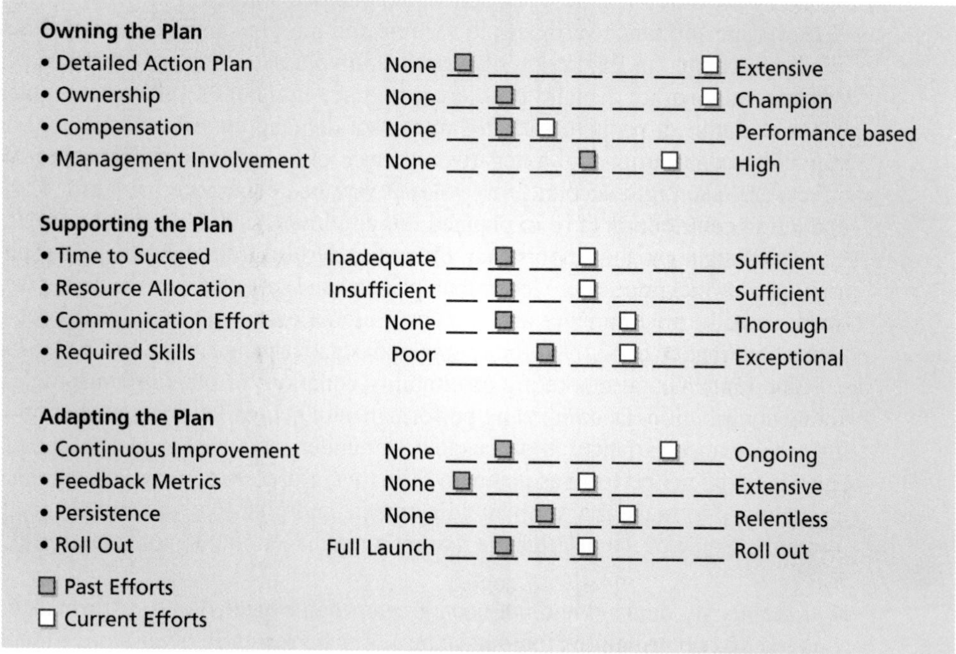

VARIANCE ANALYSIS: PLANNED VERSUS ACTUAL PERFORMANCE

In any planning activity, it is important to compare actual marketing results with planned results to see which variables contributed to the performance observed. If a business achieved the net marketing contribution performance (NMC) objective proposed in its marketing plan, this could be the result of all strategic variables performing as planned. On the other hand, over- and under-performance in different components of the net marketing contribution equation as shown could produce the same result. Variance analysis allows the company to isolate the components of marketing performance to understand better how each component contributed to the actual net marketing contribution.

$$\begin{aligned} \text{Net Marketing Contribution} &= \text{Volume} \times \text{Margin per Unit} - \text{Marketing Expenses} \\ &= [\text{Demand} \times \text{Share}] \times [\text{Price} - \text{Variable Unit Cost}] - \text{Marketing Expenses} \end{aligned}$$

Consider the business shown in Figure 15-9 with a marketing plan projected to produce $420,000 in net marketing contribution in year one of the plan. The actual NMC was $86,800 less than estimated in the marketing plan, shown also in the top tier of the diagram. What is the primary cause of this shortfall in performance? The second tier in the diagram shows variances between planned and actual volume ($V_a - V_p$), marketing expenses ($ME_A - ME_p$), and margin per unit ($M_a - M_p$). The volume sold was higher than planned, the unit margin was lower, and marketing expenses were higher. The $10,000 negative variance in NMC attributable to marketing expenses is easily determined by the difference between actual and planned marketing expenses ($ME_A - ME_p$). However, performance variances in volume and margin can be broken down further.

As illustrated in Figure 15-9, a variance in volume reflects any difference in planned versus actual market demand plus any difference in planned versus actual market share. In this example, a positive variance in market demand contributed $75,000 in extra net marketing contribution and a negative variance of $46,000 in market share. When these effects are taken into account, this volume variance contributed an extra $29,000 to net marketing contribution ($10 in planned margin times 2,900 more units sold).

The margin variance in this example is also derived from more than one source of performance. Actual prices were lower than planned and actual costs were higher than planned. In this case, the price variance and unit cost variance each had a negative impact on net marketing contribution of $52,900 for a combined negative variance of $105,800 in total margin.

The fundamental marketing profitability equation for planning purposes is net marketing contribution. Decomposing performance in net marketing contribution to underlying performance variances allows us to better understand what aspects of the plan worked and which did not perform as planned. With this information, a marketing manager is better equipped to make market plan adjustments and plan more accurately for future performance. Some of the insights the marketing manager could gain from this example are:

- If the market demand had not been greater than expected, the performance gap in net marketing contribution would have been much greater. In other words, there was a little luck involved.

FIGURE 15-9 VARIANCE ANALYSIS: PLAN VERSUS ACTUAL PERFORMANCE

Area of Performance	Plan	Actual	Variance*
Market Demand (units)	200,000	230,000	30,000
Market Share (%)	25.0	23.0	−2.0
Volume	50,000	52,900	2,900
Price per Unit	$16.00	$15.00	($1)
Sales Revenues	$800,000	$793,500	($6,500)
Variable Cost per Customer	$6.00	$7.00	$1.00
Margin per Unit	$10.00	$10.00	($2.00)
Gross Profit (millions)	$500,000	$423,200	($76,800)
Marketing Expenses % sales	10.0	11.3	1.3
Marketing Expenses (millions)	$80,000	$80,000	($10,000)
Net Marketing Contribution	$420,000	$333,200	($86,800)

*Actual-Plan

Net Marketing Contribution

$$NMC_{(actual)} - NMC_{(plan)}$$
$$(V_a \times M_a) - ME_a - (V_p \times M_p) - ME_p$$
$$(52.9\ k \times 8) - 90\ k - (50\ k \times 10) - 80\ k$$
$$\$333.2k - \$420\ k$$
$$= -\$86,800$$

Volume Variance
$$M_p(V_a - V_p)$$
$$10(52.9\ k - 50\ k)$$
$$= +\$29,000$$

Marketing Exp. Variance
$$(ME_a - ME_p)$$
$$= -(\$90k - \$80k)$$
$$= -\$10,000$$

Margin Variance
$$V_a(M_a - M_p)$$
$$52.9\ k(8 - 10)$$
$$= -\$105,800$$

Demand Variance
$$M_p \times MS_p(MD_a - MD_p)$$
$$10 \times 0.25(230\ k - 200\ k)$$
$$= +\$75,000$$

Share Variance
$$M_p \times MD_a(MS_a - MS_p)$$
$$10 \times 230\ k(0.23 - 0.25)$$
$$= -\$46,000$$

Price Variance
$$V_a(P_a - P_p)$$
$$52.9\ k(15 - 16)$$
$$= -\$52,900$$

Cost Variance
$$V_a(C_p - C_a)$$
$$52.9\ k(6 - 7)$$
$$= -\$52,900$$

V_p = Volume$_{(plan)}$ MD_p = Market Demand$_{(plan)}$ MS_p = Market Share$_{(plan)}$

V_a = Volume$_{(actual)}$ MD_a = Market Demand$_{(actual)}$ MD_a = Market Share$_{(actual)}$

P_p = Price$_{(plan)}$ C_p = Variable Cost$_{(plan)}$ M_p = Margin$_{(plan)}$

P_a = Price$_{(actual)}$ C_a = Variable Cost$_{(actual)}$ M_a = Margin$_{(actual)}$

ME_p = Marketing Expenses$_{(plan)}$ ME_a = Marketing Expenses$_{(actual)}$

- If the business had achieved its planned market share, the net marketing contribution shortfall would have been less than what it was.
- Higher cost per unit and lower unit prices than planned both contributed to lower levels of net marketing contribution.
- Higher marketing expenses than planned will have to be addressed in future profit planning.

FIGURE 15-10 VARIANCE ANALYSIS

Area of Performance	Plan	Actual	Variance*
Market Demand (units)	1,000,000	1,250,000	250,000
Market Share (%)	25.0	20.0	−5.0
Volume	250,000	250,000	0
Price per Unit	$450.00	$460.00	$10.00
Sales Revenues	$112,500,000	$115,0000,000	$2,500,000
Variable Cost per Unit	$200.00	$210.00	$10.00
Margin per Customer	$250.00	$250.00	$0.00
Gross Profit	$62,500,000	$62,500,000	$0
Marketing Expenses (% sales)	13.3	13.0	−0.3
Marketing Expenses	$15,000,000	$15,000,000	$0
Net Marketing Contribution	$47,500,000	$47,500,000	$0

*Actual-Plan

Net Marketing Contribution
$NMC_{(actual)} - NMC_{(plan)}$
$47.5 million − $47.5 million
$= 0$

Volume Variance
$M_p(V_a - V_p)$
$250(250\ k - 250\ k)$
$= 0$

Marketing Exp. Variance
$-(ME_a - ME_p)$
$= 15\ mil - 15\ mil$
$= 0$

Margin Variance
$V_a(M_a - M_p)$
$250\ k(250 - 250)$
$= 0$

Demand Variance
$M_p \times MS_p(MD_a - MD_p)$
$250 \times 0.25(1.25\ M - 1\ M)$
$= +$15.625\ million$

Share Variance
$M_p \times MD_a(MS_a - MS_p)$
$250 \times 1.25\ M(0.20 - 0.25)$
$= -$15.625\ million$

Price Variance
$V_a(P_a - P_p)$
$250\ k(460 - 450)$
$= +$2.5\ million$

Cost Variance
$V_a(C_p - C_a)$
$250\ k(200 - 210)$
$= -$2.5\ million$

A situation in which actual marketing profits are less than planned is likely to draw the attention of senior management. However, what about a situation in which there is no difference between planned and actual net marketing contribution, volume sold, or marketing expenses, as illustrated in Figure 15-10. Why worry? The marketing plan is obviously on track. A finance-oriented business would note that price per unit is $10 higher, but would also investigate the higher variable cost per unit. However, a finance-oriented business would rarely look beyond volume and would probably fail to recognize performance variances in market demand and market share.

A business that does not track marketing performance metrics such as market share and market demand will rarely discover its marketing plan is not working. In contrast, a market-based business that tracks market demand and market share would discover that the actual market performance in this case had major deviations from the marketing plan, although they netted out to zero. The variance analysis in Figure 15-10 illustrates the independent effects of variances in market demand and market share on net marketing contribution. This information alerts a business to the fact that there is an important performance gap in market share. It may be that with the market growing faster than expected, this business under-resourced its marketing expenses which was a potential cause of not achieving the intended share goal. With this variance analysis, we would expect a market-based business to recognize higher-than-expected market demand and to determine what is needed to achieve a target market share of 25 percent. Although performance variances in price and variable cost had a smaller impact on net marketing contribution, they also are still important in reconciling the accuracy of future marketing plans. From these examples, it should be clear that strategic market planning is incomplete without tracking performance metrics and doing variance analysis to determine how well the plan was implemented.

■ Summary

Developing a sound marketing plan is only the first half of achieving market success. The marketing plan must be successfully implemented. Without ownership, support, and adaptation, the marketing plan will fail. Detailed action plans, a market plan champion or ownership team, performance-based compensation plans, and top management involvement contribute to ownership of the marketing plan and provide a better chance for successful implementation.

Successful marketing plan implementation also requires time to succeed, sufficient resources, communication, and skills. In addition, numerous unanticipated problems and obstacles will arise during implementation. These require that marketing plans be adaptive. Continuous efforts to improve the marketing plan, based on feedback measures, are an important part of successful implementation. In addition, businesses that are persistent in adapting their marketing plans have a greater chance for success. A regional roll out provides a less expensive venue for adapting the marketing plan.

Performance metrics play a key role in marketing plan implementation. There are market performance metrics and financial performance metrics. Market metrics are external measures of market performance, such as awareness, customer satisfaction, and market share. Financial performance metrics are internal measures of performance such as unit margin, net profit, and return on investment. Market performance metrics, however, include both process metrics and end-result metrics. Customer awareness, perceived performance, and customer satisfaction are process performance metrics that occur ahead of end-result performance metrics such as sales, market share, net profit, and return on investment. Process market metrics play an important role in the early signaling of the success or failure of a marketing plan and its implementation effort.

Finally, an important part of assessing the success of a marketing plan is to understand which parts of the marketing plan performed as planned and which areas of performance did not. Variance analysis is a systematic assessment of each area of performance. While holding the effects of all other variables constant, a single variance between plan and actual performance can be assessed with respect to its impact on profits. This allows a manager to better understand what caused the performance. In some situations, large offsetting variances may be hidden behind overall variances that are small. A more precise understanding of how different areas of performance impact overall profit performance has the potential to reduce variances in future marketing plans.

■ Market-Based Logic and Strategic Thinking

1 Why is implementation as important as marketing plan development in achieving market success?

2 How do detailed action plans contribute to individual ownership of a marketing plan?

3 Why does a marketing plan need a champion or an ownership team?

4 How should a business tie compensation to successful implementation of a marketing plan?

5 Why is time to succeed an important element of commitment to a marketing plan?

6 What kind of signal is management sending when it does not have time to review a marketing plan and its performance?

7 What is meant by persistence in terms of commitment? What is meant by the term *adaptive persistence* as it is often used to describe the Japanese style of marketing plan implementation?

8 Why are continuous improvement and feedback measures important aspects of successful marketing plan implementation?

9 What are the advantages and disadvantages of a regional roll out of a marketing plan?

10 What role do resources, organizational communications, and training play in the support and successful implementation of a marketing plan?

11 Why are performance metrics important?

12 What is the difference between a market performance metric and a financial performance metric?

13 Why are process metrics an important part of the implementation process? What is the relationship between process metrics and end-result metrics?

Marketing Performance Tools

The following **marketing performance tools** can be accessed by going to *www.rogerjbest.com* or *www.prenhall.com/best*. The shaded cells are input cells. The non-shaded cells contain results calculated from your input values.

MARKETING PERFORMANCE TOOL—Variance Analysis

Area of Performance	Plan	Actual	Variance*
Market Demand (units)	1,000,000	1,250,000	250,000
Market Share %	25.0	20.0	–5.0
Volume	250,000	250,000	0
Price per Unit	$450.00	$460.00	$10.00
Sales Revenues (millions)	$112.5	$115.0	$2.5
Variable Cost per Unit	$250.00	$250.00	
Margin per Customer	$200.00	$210.00	$10.00
Gross Profit (millions)	$250.00	$250.00	$0.00
	$62.5	$62.5	$0
Marketing Expenses % sales	13.3	13.0	–0.3
Marketing Expenses (millions)	$15.0	$15.0	$0
Net Marketing Contribution (millions)	$47.5	$47.5	$0

*Actual-Plan

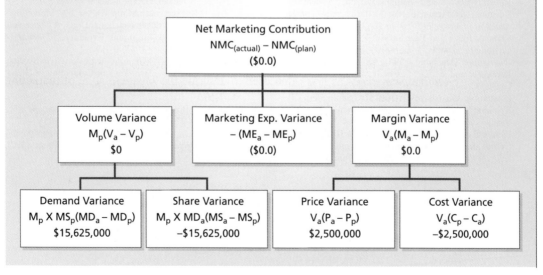

Net Marketing Contribution
$NMC_{(actual)} - NMC_{(plan)}$
($0.0)

Volume Variance
$M_p(V_a - V_p)$
$0

Marketing Exp. Variance
$-(ME_a - ME_p)$
($0.0)

Margin Variance
$V_a(M_a - M_p)$
$0.0

Demand Variance
$M_p \times MS_p(MD_a - MD_p)$
$15,625,000

Share Variance
$M_p \times MD_a(MS_a - MS_p)$
–$15,625,000

Price Variance
$V_a(P_a - P_p)$
$2,500,000

Cost Variance
$V_a(C_p - C_a)$
–$2,500,000

This **marketing performance tool** allows you to perform a variance analysis on marketing performance metrics obtained after implementing a marketing plan. The shaded cells are the input cells for the net marketing contribution equation. The variance between the planned and actual values for each performance component is provided along with the profit impact (the amount of variance in net marketing contribution). The current data from Stericycle's planned versus actual performance for 2003 are presented in Figure 15-10. New data can be entered in the shaded cells.

Application Exercise.   Using the data provided, set each area of performance in the plan column equal to the numbers shown in the actual column. This should create zero variance between plan and actual for all areas of performance. Now evaluate the impact of variances in market demand and market share by entering the planned market demand and market share data in the plan column. Evaluate how each variance in performance affected sales revenues and net marketing contribution. Then, set each area of performance in the plan column equal to the numbers shown in the actual column. This should create zero variance between plan and actual for all areas of performance. Evaluate the impact of variances in revenue per customer and variable cost per customer by inputting the planned values for revenue per customer and variable cost per customer in the plan column. Finally, evaluate how each variance in performance affected sales and net marketing contribution.

Notes

1. Dennis Gensch, "Targeting the Switchable Industrial Customer," *Marketing Science* (Winter 1984): 41–54.
2. George Cressman, "Choosing the Right Metric," *Drive Marketing Excellence* (November 1994), New York: Institute for International Research.
3. Robert Kaplan and David Norton, "The Balanced Scorecard—Measures That Drive Performance," *Harvard Business Review* (January–February 1982): 71–79.
4. Robert Peterson and William Wilson, "Measuring Customer Satisfaction: Fact or Artifact," *Journal of the Academy of Marketing Science* 20 (1992): 61–71.
5. Thomas Jones and Earl Sasser Jr., "Why Satisfied Customers Defect," *Harvard Business Review* (November–December 1995): 88–99; Frederick F. Reichheld and W. Earl Sasser Jr., "Zero Defections: Quality Comes to Services," *Harvard Business Review* (September–October 1990): 106–111; and Frederick F. Reichheld, "Loyalty-Based Management," *Harvard Business Review* (March–April 1993): 64–73.
6. Patrick Byrne, "Global Logistics: Only 10 Percent of Companies Satisfy Customers," *Transportation and Distribution* (December 1993); and Tom Eck, "Are

Customers Happy? Don't Assume," *Positive Impact* (July 1992): 3.
7. Nigel Piercy and Neil Morgan, "The Marketing Planning Process: Behavioral Problems Compared to Analytical Techniques in Explaining Marketing Plan Credibility," *Journal of Business Research* 29 (1994): 167–178; and Nigel Piercy, *Marketing Organization: An Analysis of Information Processing, Power and Politics* (Chicago: George Allen & Urwin, 1985).
8. Robert Ruekert and Orville Walker Jr., "Marketing's Interaction with Other Functional Units: A Conceptual Framework and Empirical Evidence," *Journal of Marketing* (January 1987): 1–19.
9. William Egelhoff, "Great Strategies or Great Strategy Implementation—Two Ways of Competing in Global Markets," *Sloan Management Review* (Winter 1993): 37–50.
10. Thomas Bonoma, *The Marketing Edge: Making Strategies Work* (New York: Free Press, 1985).
11. George Day, "Building a Market-Driven Organization," *Market-Driven Strategy* (New York: Free Press, 1990): 356–376.

Market-Based Management and Financial Performance

Businesses such as Disney, IBM, MBNA, Nordstrom, Ritz-Carlton, and Lexus have one thing in common: a passion for customer satisfaction. It is the core value that drives their business cultures and the marketing strategies that evolve. These businesses are also highly profitable, and for some time they have created value for customers, employees, and shareholders.

HOW TO OVERWHELM CUSTOMERS AND SHAREHOLDERS

The process starts with a strong market orientation and a passion for customer satisfaction, as illustrated in Figure 16-1. Although there are many ways to better serve customers in an effort to improve customer satisfaction, a business with a passion for customer satisfaction will start with its dissatisfied customers by encouraging them to complain.

Encouraging customer complaints is easier said than done. Most customers don't complain, for a variety of good reasons. A market-based business will develop proactive customer-satisfaction programs and systems to encourage customer complaint, and will measure their success by the rate at which they hear from dissatisfied customers. Capturing customer complaints provides a wonderful opportunity to discover and address sources of dissatisfaction. The most effective and lowest-cost customer research any business will ever engage in is hearing from dissatisfied customers.

However, a business with a passion for customer satisfaction will go further to understand customer needs, frustrations, and opportunities to create customer solutions that build higher levels of customer satisfaction. A day in the life of a customer is one way to further discover ways to build customer satisfaction. A day in the life of a customer is a *process*-focused, not *product*-focused, effort to understand how customers acquire, use, and replace products, and the sources of frustration that occur in these processes. The outputs of this effort are customer solutions designed to enhance customer satisfaction and improve customer retention, as shown in Figure 16-1.

With higher customer retention, a business can lower its cost of customer acquisition and improve its marketing productivity. Recall the common rule of thumb that it is five times more expensive to replace a customer than to retain one. Thus, higher customer retention means that fewer dollars of marketing budget are needed to maintain a certain level of market share. These gains drop to the bottom line, which contributes directly to improved net profits and shareholder value. In this last chapter, we make explicit the relationship between customer satisfaction and profitability and shareholder value, but also, in a broader sense, we demonstrate how every marketing strategy affects profits and shareholders.

FIGURE 16-1 HOW TO OVERWHELM CUSTOMERS AND SHAREHOLDERS

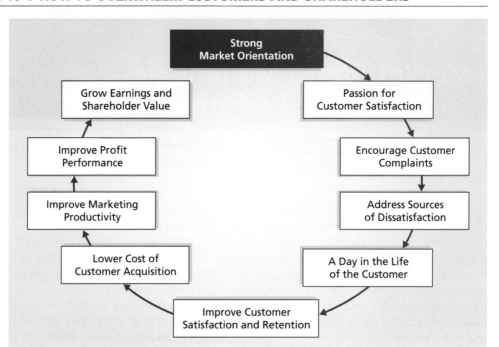

CUSTOMER SATISFACTION AND PROFITABILITY

The American Customer Satisfaction Index (ACSI) was developed by Claus Fornell at the University of Michigan Business School to measure customer satisfaction with goods and services available to household consumers in the United States. Research using these measures of customer satisfaction revealed that businesses scoring in the top 50 percent in customer satisfaction produced over 2.4 times greater shareholder value than businesses in the bottom 50 percent in customer satisfaction. Fornell explains the importance of the relationship between customer satisfaction and shareholder value in the following way:

> With few exceptions cash flows accrued from two sources: current customers and new customers. For most companies, the flow is much greater from the current customers. It is as simple as that. The satisfaction of current customers has a great deal of impact on shareholder value.[1]

To manage this process, a business must first understand its levels of customer satisfaction, dissatisfaction, complaint recovery, and customer retention, as well as the cost of customer acquisition. Figure 16-2 presents the current customer situation for AirComm, a wireless telecommunications business.

As shown in Figure 16-2, AirComm has achieved a 75 percent level of customer satisfaction, which translates into an 80 percent customer retention, given the rate at which AirComm recovers customer complaints and resolves dissatisfaction. At current levels of performance, 25 percent of AirComm's customer base is dissatisfied, but the business hears

FIGURE 16-2 AIRCOMM CUSTOMER SATISFACTION AND 80 PERCENT CUSTOMER RETENTION

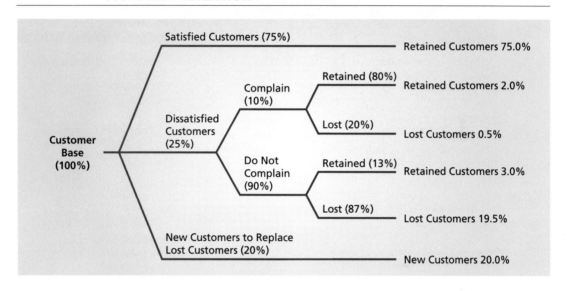

from only 10 percent of these dissatisfied customers. When AirComm *does* recover a customer complaint, it is able to retain 80 percent of these dissatisfied customers. The business loses 87 percent of those dissatisfied customers it *does not* hear from. Of course, this level of customer complaint recovery contributes to AirComm's overall level of customer retention.

At this level of customer satisfaction and retention, AirComm produces a net profit of $50 million on sales of $500 million, for a 10 percent return on sales. As shown in Figure 16-3, the major driver of profitability is the percentage of retained customers.

FIGURE 16-3 AIRCOMM PROFITABILITY AT 80 PERCENT CUSTOMER RETENTION

Area of Performance	Retained Customers	Lost Customers	New Customers	Overall Performance
Number of Customers	800,000	200,000	200,000	1,200,000
Revenue per Customer	$500	$300	$200	
Total Revenue (millions)	$400	$ 60	$ 40	$500
Variable Cost per Customer	$300	$200	$150	
Margin per Customer	$200	$100	$ 50	
Total Contribution (millions)	$160	$ 20	$ 10	$190
Marketing Expenses (millions)	$ 40	$ 10	$ 50	$100
Market Exp. per Customer	$ 50	$ 50	$250	
Net Marketing Contribution (mil)	$120	$ 10	−$ 40	$ 90
Operating Expense (millions)				$ 40
Net Profit (before taxes) (millions)				$ 50
Return on Sales				10.0%

Retention Cost = $50 per Customer; Acquisition Cost = $250 per Customer.

FIGURE 16-4 AIRCOMM PROFITABILITY AT 90 PERCENT CUSTOMER RETENTION

Area of Performance	Retained Customers	Lost Customers	New Customers	Overall Performance
Number of Customers	900,000	100,000	100,000	1,100,000
Revenue per Customer	$500	$300	$200	
Total Revenue (millions)	$450	$ 30	$ 20	$500
Variable Cost per Customer	$300	$200	$150	
Margin per Customer	$200	$100	$ 50	
Total Contribution (millions)	$180	$ 10	$ 5	$195
Marketing Expenses (millions)	$ 54	$ 6	$ 25	$ 85
Marketing Exp. per Customer*	$ 60	$ 60	$250	
Net Marketing Contribution (mil)	**$126**	**$ 4**	**−$ 20**	**$110**
Operating Expense (millions)				$ 40
Pretax Net Profit (before taxes) (millions)				$ 70
Return on Sales				**14.0%**

*Marketing expenses focused on customer retention were increased by 20% (from $50 to $60 per customer) in an effort to improve customer satisfaction and achieve 90% retention.

At an 80 percent level of customer retention, AirComm's retained customers produce $120 million in net marketing contribution, while customers who are lost and those who replace them produce a combined net marketing contribution of −$30 million.

Improving customer retention to 90 percent would improve overall net profits by $20 million, with no change in sales revenue. Retained customer profitability would improve modestly, but the greatest gain in profitability would be due to a lower cost of new customer acquisition. As shown in Figure 16-4, the return on sales is 14 percent with 90 percent retention, a healthy increase over the 10 percent return at the 80 percent level of customer retention.

HOW MARKETING STRATEGIES AFFECT PROFITABILITY

A passion for customer satisfaction is one way a market-oriented business builds superior profits. Businesses with a strong market orientation see current and potential customers as key sources of profitability, cash flow, and earnings. Customers, products, and assets are all important parts of business and business success, but only one of these actually produces money. Each is an important aspect of a business, and each needs to be managed on a day-to-day basis for a business to be efficient and profitable. However, financial reports and product-line income statements often dominate the thinking of a business that lacks a market orientation. Products will come and go; assets will be purchased and consumed, but the customer is the only enduring asset a business has. Keeping in mind that the customer is the only source of positive cash flow, it is the responsibility of those in marketing to understand how customers affect a business and its profitability.[2] This section addresses these issues in an attempt to bring into greater focus customers and the importance of their role in contributing to the profits of a business.

Customer Volume

Recognizing the customer as the primary unit of focus, a market-based business will expand its focus to customers and markets, not just products or units sold.[3] This is an important strategic distinction because there is a finite number of potential customers, but a large range of products and services can be sold to each customer. As shown here, a business's volume is its customer share in a market with a finite number of customers at any point in time, not the number of units sold.

$$\frac{\text{Customer}}{\text{Volume}} = \frac{\text{Market Demand}}{\text{(customers)}} \times \frac{\text{Market Share}}{\text{(percentage)}}$$

Figure 16-5 presents an overall flow chart of how market-based net profits are derived. Customer volume, at the top of this diagram, is derived from a certain level of customer market demand and a business's share of that customer demand. Without a sufficient volume of customers, net profit will be impossible to obtain. Marketing strategies that affect customer volume include marketing strategies that:

- Attract new customers to grow market share
- Grow the market demand by bringing more customers into a market
- Enter new markets to create new sources of customer volume

FIGURE 16-5 A CUSTOMER-BASED MODEL OF NET PROFITS (BEFORE TAXES)

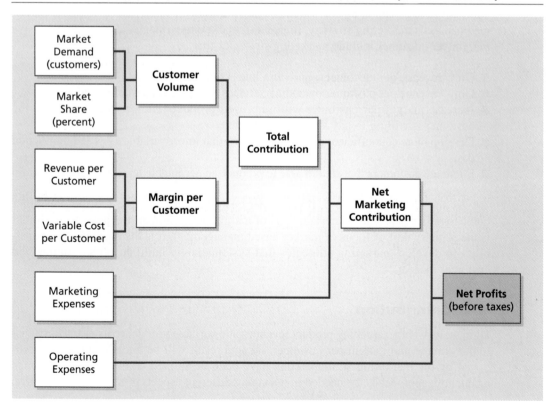

Each of these customer-focused marketing strategies affects net profits, invested assets, cash flow, and, as we will show later, shareholder value. Thus, a key component of profitability and financial performance is customer purchases and the collective customer volume produced. Without customer purchases, there is no positive cash flow or potential for net profits or shareholder value.

Margin per Customer

When customers decide to purchase an assortment of products and services from a business, the result is a certain revenue per customer—and, of course, a corresponding set of variable costs that go into each purchase and sales transaction must be taken into account to determine margin per customer:

$$\text{Customer Margin} = \text{Revenue per Customer} - \text{Variable Cost per Customer}$$

This measure of customer profitability, as shown in the preceding and in Figure 16-5, could be computed on a transaction basis, monthly or annually. The bottom line is that a business has to make a positive margin per customer or it will produce no profits and, therefore, no shareholder value. In many instances, new customers may produce a small or negative customer margin. Over time, we would expect a business to manage its marketing strategies so as to increase customer margin. If it does not, it has several alternatives to consider, one of which is to not continue to serve that customer as part of the business's marketing strategy. In general, marketing strategies designed to improve margin per customer include marketing strategies that:

- Grow revenue per customer by product-line extensions
- Grow revenue per customer by adding services that enhance customer value
- Increase margin per customer with improved products and services for which the customer is willing to pay a premium price
- Develop more cost-efficient marketing systems that lower variable sales and transaction costs
- Eliminate customers that are not able to produce an acceptable level of customer margin

As shown in Figure 16-5, revenue per customer and variable cost per customer come together to produce a certain level of margin per customer. Because the customer is the primary unit of focus of market-based management, it is the business's responsibility to develop marketing strategies that systematically build customer volume and customer margin.

Total Contribution

Ultimately, whether tracking product revenues and variable product costs or tracking customer volume and margin per customer, the end result will be a total contribution produced by the marketing strategies that have been developed and implemented. Once again, both approaches are needed in managing different aspects of a business. However, those in marketing should be more concerned with a customer perspective and how to develop marketing strategies that affect both customers and the total contribution of the business.

$$\frac{\text{Total}}{\text{Contribution}} = \frac{\text{Customer}}{\text{Volume}} \times \frac{\text{Customer}}{\text{Margin}}$$

As shown in Figure 16-5, the total contribution produced by a marketing strategy is the product of the customer volume it produces and customer margin derived from customer purchases. The total contribution produced by a marketing strategy is an important component in the profitability equation because from this point forward only expenses are introduced. Hence, building market-based strategies that increase total contribution is an important priority in developing marketing strategies that deliver profitable growth.

Net Marketing Contribution

All marketing strategies require some level of marketing effort to achieve a certain level of market share. Expenses associated with sales effort, market communications, customer service, and market management are required to implement a marketing strategy designed to obtain a certain customer volume. The cost of this marketing effort is shown in Figure 16-5 as marketing expenses and must be deducted from the total contribution to produce a net marketing contribution. This is the net contribution or dollars produced after the marketing expenses are deducted from the total contribution produced.

$$\frac{\text{Net Marketing}}{\text{Contribution}} = \frac{\text{Total}}{\text{Contribution}} - \frac{\text{Market}}{\text{Expenses}}$$

In effect, this is how the marketing function contributes to the business's profits. If the marketing team develops a marketing strategy that fails and, therefore, lowers net marketing contribution, then that marketing strategy has, in effect, lowered the net profits of the business.

Marketing strategies are generally designed to affect total contribution, whether by increasing market demand, market share, or revenue per customer, or by decreasing variable cost per customer. The net marketing contribution equation should make it clear that such strategies are profitable only if the increase in total contribution exceeds the increase in marketing expenses required to produce that increase in total contribution: that is, for a marketing strategy to improve profits for the business, it has to improve net marketing contribution.

Net Profit (Before Taxes)

Although marketing strategies contribute to net profits through net marketing contribution, net profits (before taxes) of a business are generally beyond the control of the marketing function or the marketing management team. Marketing strategies produce a certain level of net marketing contribution from which all other business expenses must be deducted before a net profit is realized, as illustrated in Figure 16-5. These operating expenses include fixed expenses, such as human resources management, research and development, and administrative expenses, and other operating expenses, such as utilities, rent, and fees. In most instances, there would also be allocated corporate overhead, which includes company expenses such as legal fees, corporate advertising, and executive salaries.

$$\begin{matrix} \text{Net Profit} \\ \text{(before taxes)} \end{matrix} = \begin{matrix} \text{Net Marketing} \\ \text{Contribution} \end{matrix} - \begin{matrix} \text{Operating} \\ \text{Expenses} \end{matrix}$$

However, there are instances when a marketing strategy can affect operating expenses. For example, a strategy to improve a product to attract more customers and build market share could involve research and development expenses to develop the new product.

HOW MARKETING STRATEGIES AFFECT ASSETS

Most businesses do not consider the impact marketing strategies have on a business's investment in assets. As will be demonstrated, the assets of a business are indirectly affected by marketing strategies. We will limit our discussion to accounts receivable, inventory, and fixed assets. These assets normally account for the majority of a business's investment in assets.

Investment in Accounts Receivable

We frequently do not think about the effect a marketing strategy can have on accounts receivable. Accounts receivable is the money owed a business and varies in proportion to sales revenues and customer payment behavior. As sales revenues increase or decrease, there will be a corresponding change in accounts receivable. In addition, customer payment behavior will determine the time customers take to pay for what they have purchased. For example, if customers take an average of 45 days to pay their bills, for approximately 12.5 percent of a year (45 divided by 365), customers are holding the business's money. If annual sales were $100 million, the accounts receivable would be approximately $12.5 million at any point in time.

$$\begin{matrix} \text{Accounts} \\ \text{Receivable} \end{matrix} = \begin{matrix} \text{Sales} \\ \text{Revenues} \end{matrix} \times \begin{matrix} \text{Percent Days} \\ \text{Outstanding} \end{matrix}$$
$$= \$100 \text{ million} \times 0.125 \ (12.5\%)$$
$$= \$12.5 \text{ million}$$

To put this in marketing terms, accounts receivable is a function of customer volume, revenue per customer, and customer payment behavior. When we state this relation in terms of marketing strategy, we can express accounts receivable in the following way:

$$
\begin{aligned}
\frac{\text{Accounts}}{\text{Receivable}} &= \frac{\text{Customer}}{\text{Volume}} \times \frac{\text{Revenue per}}{\text{Customer}} \times \frac{\text{Percent Days}}{\text{Outstanding}} \\
&= 20,000 \quad\times\quad \$5,000 \quad\times 0.125\ (12.5\%) \\
&= \$12.5 \text{ million}
\end{aligned}
$$

In this form, one can readily see how strategies that affect customer volume and revenue per customer also affect accounts receivable. In addition, the selection of target customers could be based partly upon their bill-paying behavior. Thus, a business may avoid customers who are slow payers, thereby lowering the level invested in accounts receivable. For example, about 3 percent of residential phone customers are labeled "movers and shakers." These are customers who run up large telephone bills but move on and shake loose before paying their bills. If these customers could be identified early, it would be wise to avoid them when possible.

In addition, a business's service quality also affects how fast customers pay their bills (and, hence, the level of accounts receivable). For example, consider how customer service affects the following customer payment behavior[4]:

- Eight out of 10 *Fortune* 500 companies report that the level of customer service they receive affects their decision to pay a bill on time.
- More than half of the *Fortune* 500 companies withhold payment from suppliers when they are dissatisfied with the level of service they have received.

Thus, a business with a strong market orientation and commitment to service quality and customer satisfaction is likely to be paid faster than businesses that deliver lower levels of service quality or customer satisfaction. In this way, the market orientation of a business affects the business's investment in accounts receivable.

Investment in Inventory

Many businesses are required to carry large inventories to adequately serve target customers. Long production runs and uncertain market demand often require a business to maintain a certain level of finished goods inventory. There are also work-in-process inventories (partially finished goods) and raw materials inventories. All these inventories are assets with market values.

As with accounts receivable, the size and value of inventories vary with sales revenues and target customer purchase behavior. As such, inventory at any time is roughly equal to total cost of goods sold times a percentage of days of inventory on hand. The need to have inventory on hand to cover an average of 30 days of sales would equate to 8.2 percent days of inventory (30 days divided by 365 days in a year). If the manufactured cost of goods sold for a year is $40 million, the average investment in inventory would be $3.28 million, as shown here:

$$
\begin{aligned}
\frac{\text{Inventory}}{\text{Investment}} &= \frac{\text{Total Cost}}{\text{of Inventory}} \times \frac{\text{Percent Days}}{\text{of Inventory}} \\
&= \$40 \text{ million} \times 0.082\ (8.2\%) \\
&= \$3.28 \text{ million}
\end{aligned}
$$

In terms of marketing strategy, the investment in inventory can be expressed as:

$$\begin{aligned}\text{Inventory Investment} &= \frac{\text{Customer}}{\text{Volume}} \times \frac{\text{Unit Cost}}{\text{per Customer}} \times \frac{\text{Percent Days}}{\text{of Inventory}} \\ &= 200{,}000 \times \$200 \times 0.082\ (8.2\%) \\ &= \$3.28 \text{ million}\end{aligned}$$

Once again, marketing strategies that affect market demand, market share, and the unit manufacturing cost will affect investment in inventory. Likewise, channel marketing strategies will affect investment in inventory. A shift from a direct sales and distribution system to a distributor channel system could lead to lower inventories as a business is able to shift inventory requirements to distributors and, hence, lower the business's investment in assets.

Investment in Fixed Assets

Fixed assets include investments in buildings, land, equipment, office furniture, and so on. Most of these assets are depreciated each year as business expenses, and, therefore, at least from a financial accounting point of view, lose value over time. However, the amount and value of fixed assets at any point in time is relative to sales volume. A marketing strategy to grow sales volume substantially in a growing market would typically require additional fixed assets to accommodate that volume increase.

Thus, fixed assets are a function of sales volume which, in turn, is a function of marketing strategies to grow customer volume or volume per customer or both. Most businesses have excess manufacturing capacity, which is a large component of fixed assets. A marketing strategy to grow volume, by growing customer demand or increasing customer market share, will increase capacity utilization. If the increased volume produced increases net profits, this marketing strategy will result in an overall increase in the business's return on assets, because no addition to assets was necessary. Naturally, in situations where fixed assets have to be added to accommodate growth, the investment in assets would be greater. A business that derives profits from an increase in volume has to have profits sufficiently large to produce a higher return on assets.

In general, most managers do not consider the impact of a marketing strategy on assets or return on assets. Although not scrutinized at this level, every marketing decision affects one or more of the return-on-asset components shown in Figure 16-6.

For example, consider a scanner manufacturer's marketing strategy to capture a significant share of the retail scanner market. The business knew that a major customer was price sensitive and that competitors would price aggressively to get this customer's volume. Recognizing the importance of price, the scanner manufacturer offered a price lower than competing offers but required full payment within 10 days, with no cash discount. Unit margins were lower, but the large volume captured produced a large total contribution, and, with a minimal investment in accounts receivable, the business produced a much higher return on assets. The net result was a marketing strategy that produced higher net profits and a lower level of investment, each of which contributed to an increase in return on investment.

FIGURE 16-6 A CUSTOMER-BASED MODEL OF RETURN ON ASSETS

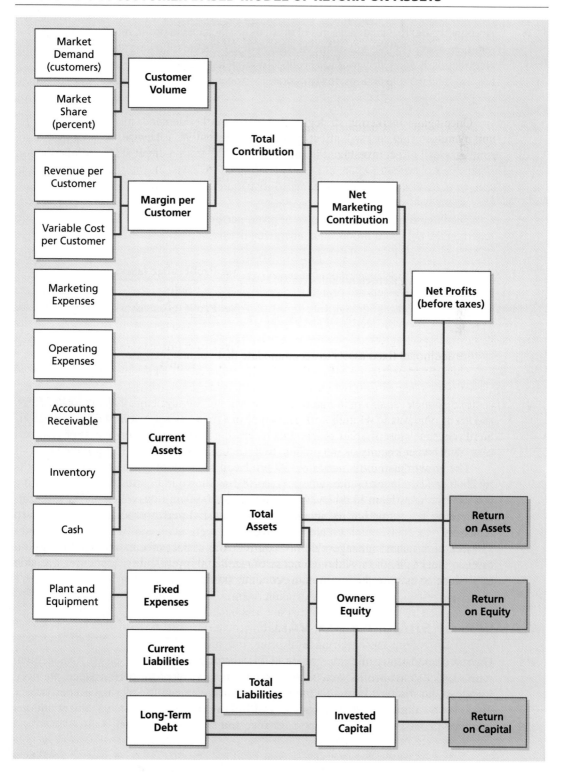

RETURN MEASURES OF PROFITABILITY

Accounting and financial measures of profitability include net profit, return on sales (ROS), return on assets (ROA), and return on equity (ROE). As the following shows, net marketing contribution is a key driver of net profits. To grow net profits in any given year, a business has two fundamental options: lower operating expenses or grow net marketing contribution.

$$\text{Net Profit (after taxes)} = \underbrace{\left(\begin{array}{c} \text{Customer} \\ \text{Volume} \\ \text{(new)} \end{array} \times \begin{array}{c} \text{Margin per} \\ \text{Customer} \\ \text{(new)} \end{array} \right) - \begin{array}{c} \text{Marketing} \\ \text{Expenses} \end{array}}_{\text{Net Marketing Contribution}} - \begin{array}{c} \text{Operating} \\ \text{Expenses} \end{array} - \begin{array}{c} \text{Interest} \\ \text{and} \\ \text{Taxes} \end{array}$$

The three fundamental measures of profit performance—ROS, ROA, and ROE—are based on the net profit produced in any given period:

$$\textbf{Return on Sales (ROS)} = \frac{\textbf{Net Profit (after taxes)}}{\textbf{Sales}}$$

$$\textbf{Return on Assets (ROA)} = \frac{\textbf{Net Profit (after taxes)}}{\textbf{Assets}}$$

$$\textbf{Return on Equity (ROE)} = \frac{\textbf{Net Profit (after taxes)}}{\textbf{Equity}}$$

For example, as shown in Figure 16-7, the sales of Stericycle in 1997 were $46 million and net income was $1.44 million. This resulted in a return on sales of 3.14 percent. In 1997, Stericycle had assets of $61.2 million that resulted in a ROA (return on assets) of 2.36 percent. With owner's equity of $45 million, ROE (return on equity) was 3.21 percent.

The growth plan introduced in 1997 produced tremendous gains in sales and profits by 2000 and continued on the same path to 2003 as shown in Figure 16-7. Net marketing contribution grew from $1.44 in 1997 million to $130.90 million, which played a significant role in the growth of net income. While financial performance metrics improved from 1997 to 2000, much greater improvements were achieved by 2003. This corresponded with much higher levels of Marketing ROS (28.9 percent) and Marketing ROI (199.2 percent). With this level of increased marketing profitability, Stericycle was able to produce an estimated $3 million in economic profit.

MEASURES OF SHAREHOLDER VALUE

Having demonstrated the importance of the customer and market-based management with respect to net profits, assets, and return measures of profit performance, we need to extend our discussion of how market-based management affects shareholder value.[5] To do so, we need to first develop a way of linking market-based management and net marketing contribution to profit performance and shareholder value.

FIGURE 16-7 STERICYCLE: MARKETING PROFITS AND FINANCIAL PERFORMANCE

Area of Performance	1997	2000	2003
Market Demand (millions)	$1,000	$1,500	$2,000
Market Share (%)	4.60	21.6	22.7
Sales (millions)	$ 46	$324	$ 453
Revenue per Customer	$1,075	$1,336	$1,510
Percent Margin (%)	26.4	39.3	43.4
Gross Profit (millions)	$ 12.1	$127.3	$196.6
Marketing Expenses (millions)	$ 10.7	$ 59.5	$ 65.7
Marketing Expenses (% sales)	23.3	18.4	14.5
Net Marketing Contribution (millions)	$ 1.4	$ 67.8	$130.9
Marketing ROS (%)	3.1	29.9	28.9
Marketing ROI (%)	13.5	114.0	199.2
Operating Expenses (millions)	$ 0	$ 45.7	$ 4.5
Operating Income (millions)	$ 1.4	$ 22.1	$126.4
Taxes and Interest (millions)	$ 0	$ 7.6	$ 60.7
Net Profit (millions)	$ 1.4	$ 14.5	$ 65.7
Balance Sheet Information			
Total Assets (millions)	$ 61.2	$597.9	$707.4
Total Liabilities (millions)	$ 16.2	$463.2	$299.6
Owner's Equity (millions)	$ 45.0	$134.7	$407.8
Invested Capital (millions)		$ 480	$ 570
Financial Performance Metrics			
Return on Sales (%)	3.1	4.5	14.5
Return on Assets (%)	2.4	2.4	9.3
Return of Equity (%)	3.2	10.8	16.1
Return on Capital (%)		3.0	11.5
Economic Profit (*)		($38.30)	$ 3.00

* Assume 11% cost of capital.

Return measures of performance such as ROS, ROA, and ROE, present an aspect of profit performance. Although these are important, shareholder value is more closely associated with earnings per share, economic value-added,[6] and price-earnings ratio. Each of these is briefly described here, and illustrated in Figure 16-8, for AirComm at the 80 percent level of customer retention.

- **Earnings per Share (EPS):** Net profit (after taxes) divided by the number of shares. For AirComm, a net profit (after taxes) of $3 million and 6 million shares translates to $0.50 per share.
- **Economic Profit (EP):** Net profit (after taxes) minus the business's capital investment times the cost of capital yields a measure of how much value it created by that level

FIGURE 16-8 AIRCOMM FINANCIAL PERFORMANCE: 80 PERCENT CUSTOMER RETENTION

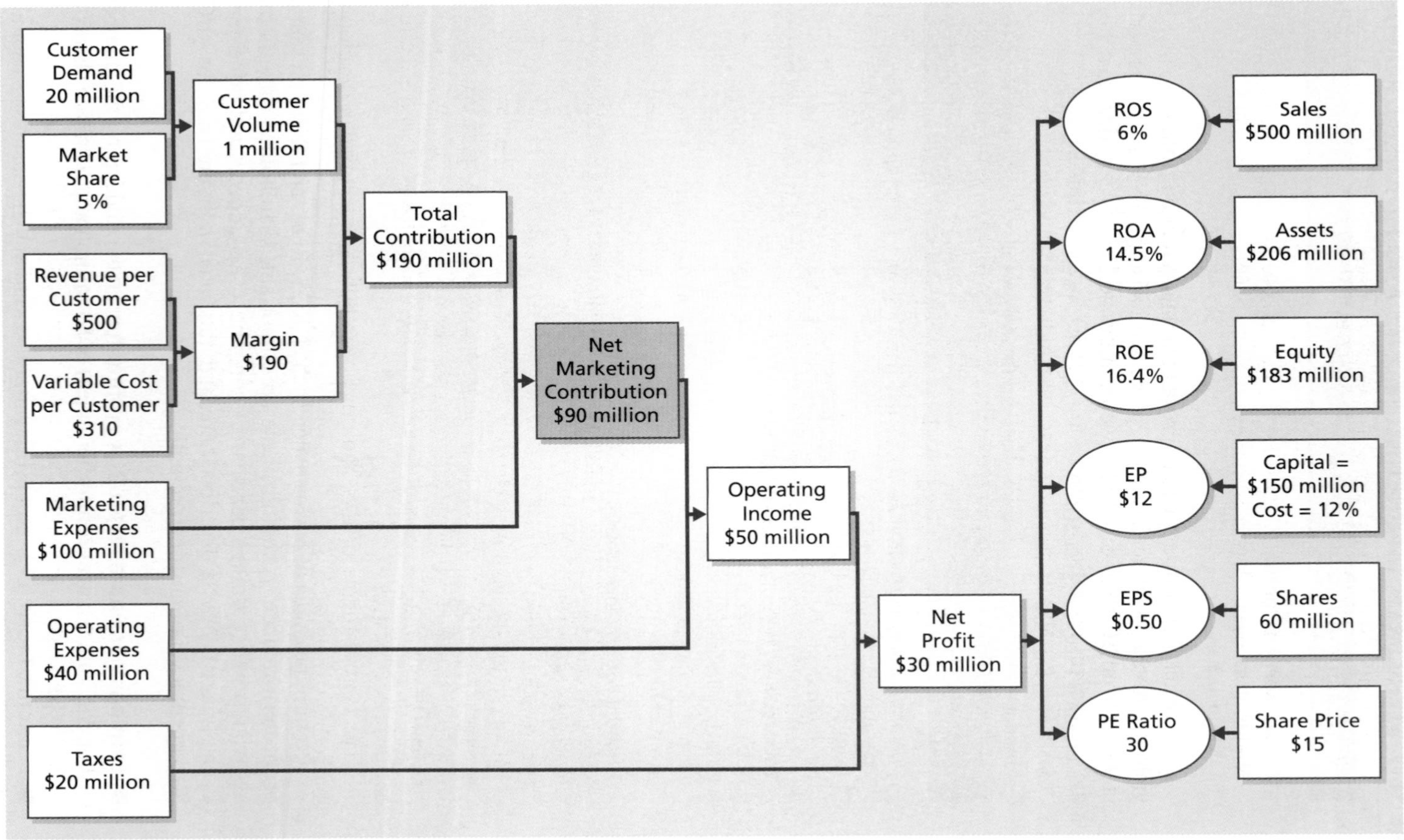

of net profit (earnings). For AirComm, a net profit (after taxes) of $30 million minus capital investment ($150 million) times the cost of capital (12 percent), yields an EP of $12 million.

■ **Price-Earnings (PE) Ratio:** The price of a share of stock divided by the earnings per share. For AirComm, the share price of $15 divided by its earnings per share of 0.50 yields a price-earnings (PE) ratio of 30.

A market-based strategy to improve customer retention from 80 to 90 percent would yield improved profit performance, as shown in Figure 16-9. Earnings per share would increase from $0.50 to $0.70, EP would improve from $12 million to $24 million, and the price-earnings ratio would drop from 30 to approximately 21—or, to maintain a price-earnings ratio of 30, share price would have to increase from $15 per share to $21 per share. As shown in Figure 16-10, net marketing contribution is the only positive source of earnings per share. When the AirComm net marketing contribution based on 80 percent retention ($110 million) is divided by 60 million shares, the net marketing contribution per share is $1.83. When operating expenses per share ($.47) and interest and taxes per share ($.46) are deducted from the net marketing contribution per share, the result is $.70 per share.

Thus, businesses with a strong market orientation and a passion for customer satisfaction and retention should deliver higher levels of profitability and shareholder value, even with no change in sales revenues.

MARKET-BASED MANAGEMENT

To be profitable, a business needs to achieve above-average market performance and operational performance.[7] In fact, market and operational performance are interrelated, as illustrated in Figure 16-10. A business with poor levels of customer satisfaction can expect sales to these customers to decline and the speed with which they pay their invoices to decrease. These businesses have to spend more marketing dollars in an effort to maintain a certain level of sales. The combination of these effects influences all aspects of financial performance shown in market and operational performance metrics.

The central theme of this book has been how a business can develop and deliver marketing strategies that:

■ Deliver high levels of customer satisfaction and superior customer value
■ Improve market position, sales, and profitability
■ Improve earnings and shareholder value

Market-based management, as shown in Figure 16-11, is at the base of a business with a strong market orientation. A strong market orientation translates into a strong customer focus, competitor orientation, and a team approach that cuts across organizational functions. The result is a market-based business that is in a strong position to develop and

FIGURE 16-9 AIRCOMM FINANCIAL PERFORMANCE: 90 PERCENT CUSTOMER RETENTION

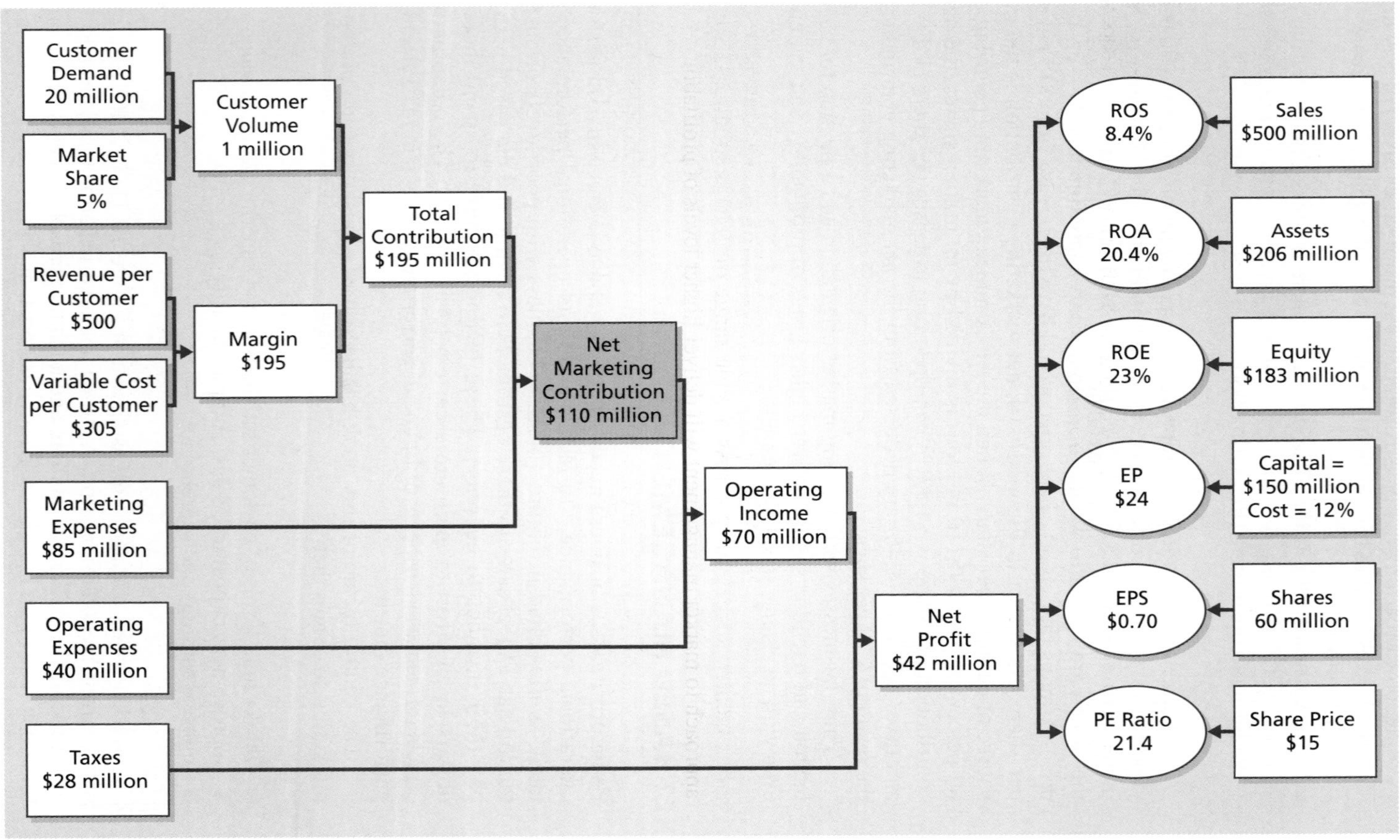

FIGURE 16-10 NET MARKETING CONTRIBUTION PER SHARE

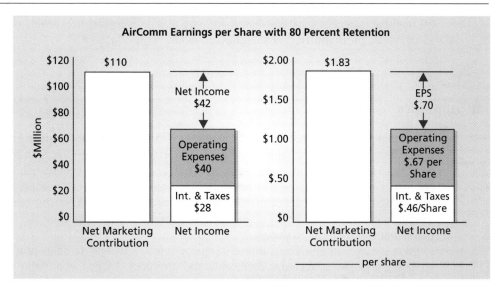

deliver market-based strategies designed to attract, satisfy, and retain customers.

deliver market-based strategies designed to attract, satisfy, and retain customers. Implemented successfully across a wide range of market situations, a market-based approach to market management will deliver higher levels of profitability, cash flow, and shareholder value than will a cost-based approach.

One should never forget that the only source of positive cash flow is the customer. Without customers, technology, assets, and management are of little value. The job of a

FIGURE 16-11 MARKET-BASED MANAGEMENT AND SHAREHOLDER VALUE

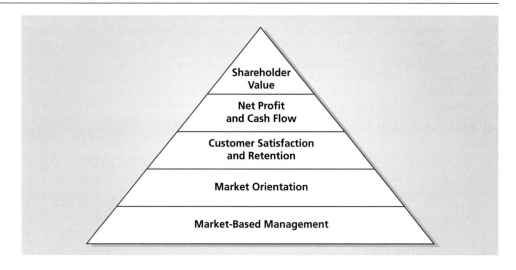

market-based business is to understand customers, competition, and the market environment within the context of the business's technology, assets, and management capabilities and to render a market-based strategy that delivers superior levels of customer satisfaction, profitability, and shareholder value.

■ Summary

Marketing strategies directly affect customers and sales revenues. However, they also affect margins, total contribution, and marketing expenses. These effects, in turn, lead to a net marketing contribution. Because operating and overhead expenses are beyond the control of marketing managers, net marketing contribution plays an important role in evaluating the profit impact of marketing strategies. Thus, throughout this book we have sought to determine the profit impact of a marketing strategy based on the level of net marketing contribution produced.

Marketing strategies also directly impact assets. Changes in sales produce corresponding changes in accounts receivable and inventory. Likewise, a major increase in volume based on a particular marketing strategy may require additional operating expenses and investment in fixed assets. Marketing strategies impact both the numerator of the ROA (return on assets) equation as well as the denominator. This presents a much broader view of the impact a marketing strategy has on a business's profitability.

The net marketing contribution for each product-market strategy contributes to both profit performance and shareholder value. Return measures of profit performance (ROS, ROA, and ROE) are driven by market performance and net marketing contribution. Shareholder measures of performance (earnings per share, EVA, and price-earnings ratio) are directly influenced by product-market performance and profitability.

Finally, it is the market orientation that is at the heart of market-based management. With a strong market orientation, a business will develop marketing strategies that are intended to attract, satisfy, and retain target customers. A market-based managed business should at the same time be evaluating alternative marketing strategies that contribute to the business's growth, short- and long-run profit performance, and strategic position. If successful, a market-driven business should deliver high levels of customer satisfaction, profitability, and shareholder value.

■ Market-Based Logic and Strategic Thinking

1 Why is it important for those in responsible marketing positions to understand the profit impact of marketing strategies?

2 What should be the role of net marketing contribution in the development of a marketing strategy?

3 Why is net profit often a misleading indicator of the profit impact of a marketing strategy?

4 How does a marketing strategy affect the assets of a business? Why should the accounts receivable and inventory change with a change in marketing strategy? When will the fixed assets change?

5 How does the net marketing contribution of a marketing strategy affect return on assets (ROA)?

6 How do investments in customer retention contribute to higher levels of profit performance?

7 Explain how the net marketing contribution of a marketing strategy affects return measures of profit performance.

8 How do changes in customer retention affect shareholder measures of performance such as earnings per share?

9 Explain how Stericycle's market share gain affected net marketing contribution, net profits, and return measures of performance.

10 Why should shareholders and Wall Street analysts be interested in a business's customer retention?

11 Why would two businesses with the same sales have different shareholder value if one had a 60 percent level of customer retention and the other 80 percent?

12 How would you use the net marketing contribution for each product-market to forecast earnings and earnings per share?

13 What role does net marketing contribution play in understanding the earnings level of a business?

14 How does the market orientation of a business affect customers, business performance, and shareholders?

15 Why should a market-oriented business with a passion for customer satisfaction produce higher levels of earnings per share and, therefore, have greater shareholder value than a business that is not market oriented?

Marketing Performance Tools

The following **marketing performance tools** can be accessed by going to *www.rogerjbest.com* or *www.prenhall.com/best*. The shaded cells are input cells. The non-shaded cells contain results calculated from your input values.

MARKETING PERFORMANCE TOOL—Marketing Profitability and Financial Performance

This **marketing performance tool** allows you to estimate the financial impact of marketing strategies. The gray numeric input cells can be changed in doing the following application exercise. Also new data can be entered into the shaded cells to examine how marketing profitability impacts financial performance.

Application Exercise: Using the data provided, answer the following questions:

How would net marketing contribution and financial performance change with a marketing strategy to grow sales by 10 percent? What would be the profit impact of a channel strategy that increased margins from 25 percent to 40 percent but required marketing expenses to increase from 9 percent of sales to 18 percent of sales? What would be the profit impact of a marketing strategy designed to reduce assets by 10 percent with a new channel strategy that lowered accounts receivable and inventories?

Notes

1. "Customer Satisfaction: The Fundamental Basis for Business Survival," *Siebel Magazine* (vol. 50, no. 1): 19–25.
2. Robert Kaplan and David Norton, "The Balanced Score Card—Measures that Drive Performance," *Harvard Business Review* (January–February 1992): 71–79.
3. Eric Hardy, "The *Forbes* 500's Annual Directory," *Forbes* (April 22, 1996): 232–278.
4. "Customer Service Impacts Cash Flow," *Positive Impact* (August 1993): 5–6.
5. Sidney Schoeffler, "Impacts of Business Strategy on Stock Prices," PIMS Letter No. 20 (1980): 1–9.
6. "Valuing Companies," *The Economist* (August 2, 1997): 53–55; Eric Olsen and Thomas Rawley, "Stock Prices Performance: Corporate Agenda for the 1980s,"

Journal of Accounting and Corporate Finance (Spring 1987): 3–15; Bill Birchard, "Mastering the New Metrics," *CFO: The Magazine for Senior Financial Executives* (October 1994); and Bill Barmhardt, "Chicago's Top 100 Companies," *Chicago Tribune* (May 15, 1995); Thomas Rawley and L. Edwards, "How Holt Methods Work for Good Decisions, Determine Business Value More Accurately," *Corporate Cashflow Magazine* (September 1993); and Bernard Reimann, "Stock Price and Business Success: What Is the Relationship?" *Journal of Business Strategy* (Summer 1987): 38–50.
7. Robert Hayes, "Strategic Planning: Forward in Reverse," *Harvard Business Review* (November–December 1985): 111–119.

GLOSSARY

acquisition cost The marketing expense to acquire one new customer.

adjacent segment strategy Segment strategies targeted at customers with slightly different needs than current customers.

advertising carryover effects Sales occurring after the period in which an advertisement was run.

advertising elasticity The percent change in volume per 1 percent change in advertising expenditures.

agents, brokers, and reps Salespeople who work for a business on a commission basis.

articulated market demand Current market demand based on articulated customer needs.

assets Cash, accounts receivable, inventory, plant and equipment, and other assets.

bottom-up marketing budget A budget based on the cost of each specific marketing task needed to implement a tactical marketing strategy.

brand assets Assets a brand can attain based on market leadership, awareness, brand relevance, reputation for quality, and brand loyalty.

brand encoding The process of branding products within a business based on a combination of company name, name, sub-brand name, number, letter, product name, or key benefit.

brand equity The attractiveness of a brand based entirely on its name and image.

brand image The perceived image of what a brand stands for in the mind of a target customer.

brand liabilities Liabilities a brand can incur based on customer dissatisfaction, environmental problems, product failures/recall, lawsuits/consumer boycotts, and questionable business practices.

brand management The process of naming products, managing brands, and brand-line extensions

to fully attain maximum brand equity and a brand's full profit potential.

brand personality The personality a brand takes on based on human personality characteristics.

break-even market share The market share needed to reach break-even volume.

break-even volume The unit volume at which total sales equals total cost.

capital Owner's equity plus long-term debt add up to the capital a business has invested in its business.

channel margin Margin required by a channel intermediary.

channel marketing expenses Marketing and sales expenses associated with a marketing channel.

channel partners Companies within a business's marketing channels that distribute, resell, or add value to a business's products and participate in the process of connecting businesses with end-users.

channel system A particular combination of distribution and sales.

cluster analysis A statistical method used to group customers based on similar needs into needs-based market segments.

co-branding Combining two brand names to create a new brand, such as the Eddie Bauer Ford Explorer.

company benefits The level of perceived benefit a customer attaches to a company or brand name.

competitive advantage A relative advantage one business has over another that is sustainable and translates into a benefit that is important to target customers.

competitive benchmarking Benchmarking a company outside an industry on a certain business practice in which the benchmark company is known for excellence.

competitive bid pricing Pricing a bid based on the historical success of past price-to-cost bid ratios and the competitive bid situation.

competitive performance metrics Marketing metrics that gauge the competitive position of a product or business.

competitive position A business's position relative to a benchmark competitor's position with regard to price, product quality, delivery, new product sales, and so on.

competitor analysis Benchmarking a key competitor with respect to important areas of performance.

competitor orientation The degree to which a business tracks competitors' strategies and benchmarks its performance relative to competitors.

competitor reactive pricing Setting price based on competitors' prices without knowing what customers need or would be willing to pay for a firm's product or service.

competitor response price elasticity The percentage change in a competitor's price per 1 percent change in the price of a business's product.

complementary products Products that are sold along with another product.

conjoint analysis (measurement) A statistical method for deriving the customer preferences for different levels of price and product performance.

cost advantage A sustainable lower cost relative to competition.

cost of capital The percentage paid (like interest) for capital (money obtained from investors and lenders).

cost-based pricing Pricing that is determined by a business's cost and margin requirements.

cost-plus pricing Price that is set based on the cost of the product plus a desired profit margin.

cross price elasticity The percent change in volume in one product when the price is changed 1 percent in another product.

customer focus The degree to which business seeks to understand customer needs and use situations, and tracks customer satisfaction.

customer life The number of purchase periods a customer is retained by a business.

customer's lifetime value The net present value of cash flows produced over a customer's life.

customer loyalty Customers are very satisfied, retained and would recommend a product or business to others.

customer loyalty index An index of customer satisfaction, retention and customer recommendation.

customer mix marketing budget A marketing budget based on the cost of new customer acquisition and retention.

customer performance metrics Marketing metrics that track customer satisfaction, retention, loyalty and customer value.

customer profitability Gross margin per customer minus the marketing expenses needed to serve a customer.

customer reactive pricing Setting price based on a thorough understanding of customer needs and price sensitivity but without taking into account competitors' prices and positioning.

customer relationship management A process devoted to developing and managing one-on-one relationships with target customers.

customer relationship marketing Marketing programs designed to personalize or customize a business's offerings to selected customers.

customer retention The percentage of customers retained from one purchase period to another.

customer satisfaction The degree to which customers are satisfied or dissatisfied with a business, product, or specific aspect of a product or service provided by a business.

customer satisfaction index An overall index of a business's customer satisfaction.

customer surveys Marketing surveys that track customer purchases, intentions to purchase, and performance perceptions.

customer terrorists Dissatisfied customers who seek to tell others of their dissatisfaction with a product, brand or company.

customer value Total benefits minus the cost of acquiring those benefits.

database marketing A database of customer purchases, preferences, needs, and demographics used in customized marketing communications, product offerings, and extra services.

day in the life of a customer A market-research approach that involves observing the process a customer goes through in acquiring, using, and disposing of a product.

defensive strategy (defensive strategic market plan) A long-run plan to protect or exit a market position.

demographic trap segmenting customers on the basis of demographics alone without considering customer needs.

differentiation advantage A sustainable product or service advantage that translates into a benefit important to target customers.

direct channel system A channel system that retains ownership of the product and requires management of its sales, distribution, and customer service.

discount factor The net present value of $1.00 when discounted from a particular point in time and at a particular discount rate.

discount rate A business's cost of capital.

discriminant analysis A statistical method that helps identify demographic characteristics that differentiate one needs-based segment from another.

distributors Intermediaries who take title (ownership) of a product and are responsible for its sale, distribution, and customer service.

divest market strategy A defensive strategic market plan to exit a market by selling or closing down a business.

dysfunctional product attributes Product attributes that cause customer dissatisfaction as well as attributes that are irrelevant in affecting customer satisfaction.

earnings per share Net profits (after taxes) divided by the number of shares held by shareholders.

economic profit Net income after taxes minus capital times the cost of capital.

economic value The value created based on the total cost of purchase of two competing products.

economic value-added Net profits (after taxes) minus the product of a business's investment in capital assets times its cost of capital.

e-marketing Electronic marketing using the Internet as a marketing channel.

empathic design process An observational approach to discovering customer problems, frustrations, and inconveniences in using a company's product.

end-result performance metrics Performance metrics that occur at the end of a normal accounting period.

evocative brand names Brand names designed to evoke a feeling or perception.

exit market strategies Defensive strategic market plans that specify a market exit strategy that can range from immediate exit with a divestment strategy to a slow exit with harvesting strategy.

experiential brand names Brand names that attempt to communicate the experience a customer will have with the brand.

experiment design A statistical method for understanding the influence of one variable, such as price, on another variable such as sales or customer preference.

external performance metrics Market performance metrics that track external performance with respect to market penetration, competitive position, and customer satisfaction.

factor analysis A statistical method for analyzing many variables in an attempt to reduce them to fewer performance dimensions.

firmographics Characteristics used to describe a business, such as size, financial position, years in business, type of business, number of locations, and so forth.

flagship brand The highest priced and quality brand in a business's product line.

flanker brand A product extension of a business's core brand.

floor pricing A price that is set on a financial requirement such as gross margin or return on investment.

focus groups A discovery method in which target customers are asked focused questions about a product or customer use situation.

forward buying The practice of buying a greater volume of a product when it is on sale.

frontal attack strategies Competitive strategies that directly attack a competitor's market share.

functional/descriptive brand names Brand names that describe the product or its owner, such as Dell Computer.

functional product attributes Product attributes that contribute to customer satisfaction.

generic product life cycle The product life cycle for a product category such as cereal or cars.

grow market share strategy A long-run offensive strategic market plan to grow market share.

harvest market strategy A defensive strategic market plan to slowly exit a market while maximizing profits.

harvest pricing Raising price in a series of steps in an effort to improve margins and maximize total contribution until the product exits the market.

heavy-up message frequency A period in which a business increases its advertising effort.

high potentials Profitable customers who are not loyal to a product or business.

horizontal brand-line extension Extending the brand to a line of related products.

horizontal market opportunity A market with closely related substitute products.

indirect channel systems Channels in which intermediaries take ownership of a business's product and the responsibility for its sale, distribution, and customer service.

industry analysis A structural analysis of a competitive environment based on competitor entry/exit, buyer/supplier power, substitutes, and competitive rivalry.

ingredient co-branding Adding a brand name to another product's brand like "Intel inside" on Dell and Compaq computers.

in-process performance metrics Performance metrics that occur during a reporting period and precede end-result performance metrics.

internal performance metrics Performance metrics that are internal measures of a business's operations.

in-the-box strategy Internal strategies that lack both customer and competitor intelligence.

invented brand names Brand names created from Latin or Greek words or partial words.

inventory turnover The number of times an inventory is sold per year.

Kano Method A process method used to uncover functional and dysfunctional product attributes that impact customer satisfaction and customer dissatisfaction.

knowledge advantage A business that possesses an advantage in both customer and competitor intelligence.

large-segment strategy A segment strategy that is focused on the largest market segment in a market.

lead-user analysis A process of studying how lead users (highly involved early users) use a product, the process offers insights into how a product can be improved or a new product developed.

life cycle cost analysis A process method for discovering the total cost of customer purchase that includes all costs over the use life of a product.

low-cost leader pricing The low-cost producer sets price based on cost in an effort to have the lowest market prices.

margin per unit The selling price of a product minus all the variable costs associated with producing, distributing, and selling the product.

market adoption forces Market forces that affect the rate of new-product adoption.

market analysis An external analysis of market demand, customer needs, competition, distributors, and environmental forces that influence market demand and customer behavior.

market attractiveness The relative attractiveness of a market based on market forces, competitive environment, and market access.

market-based management The commitment of a strong market orientation and management of markets that strives to deliver superior customer value and profitability.

market-based organization A business organized around markets with market units as profit centers.

market-based pricing Pricing based on target customer need, competitors' product position, and the strength of a business's product, service, or brand advantage.

market definition A specification of market scope that makes clear current and potential customers.

market development index The ratio of current market demand to market potential (maximum market demand).

market focus A business orientation that is focused on customers and competitors.

market infrastructure Channel intermediaries and channel influencers that shape opinions and communicate information about a business and its products.

market orientation The degree to which a business has a strong customer-focus and competitor orientation and works as a team across functions to develop and deliver a market-based strategy.

market penetration strategies Offensive strategic market plans designed to further penetrate existing markets or enter new markets.

market performance metrics Marketing metrics that track the attractiveness of a market.

market potential The maximum market demand that should occur when all potential customers have entered a market.

marketing profitability The net marketing contribution for a product, business, or company.

marketing profitability metrics Marketing ROS and Marketing ROI.

market segmentation Grouping customers into segments on the basis of similar needs and differentiating demographic characteristics.

market share The percentage of current market demand obtained by a business.

market share index A hierarchy of market share factors (such as awareness, availability, interest, intention to buy, and purchase) that results in an estimate of market share.

market vision A broad view of the market based on a fundamental customer need that goes beyond existing product solutions.

marketing advantage A sustainable advantage over competitors in either channels of distribution, sales force, or marketing communications.

marketing expenses All fixed expenses associated with selling, marketing, and managing of a marketing strategy targeted at a particular market.

marketing mix A combination of the 4Ps (product, price, promotion, and place) designed for a specific target market.

marketing planning process A process that starts with a situation analysis, which leads to a specific strategic market plan, tactical marketing strategy, and marketing budget, and results in a performance plan.

marketing productivity Dollars of net marketing contributions produced by a strategy per dollar of fixed marketing expenses.

marketing ROI The net marketing contribution divided by marketing expenses for a product, business or company.

marketing ROS The net marketing contribution divided by sales for a product, business or company.

mass customization An individualized marketing mix in which products, prices, promotion, and place are customized to the individual needs of a niche market or individual customers.

mass market A market that is not segmented and all customers and potential customers are treated as one.

mass personalization Individualized marketing communications that recognize individual customers by name, purchase behavior, needs and demographics.

message frequency The average number of times a target customer recalls seeing an advertisement in a given period of time.

mixed channel systems A combination of direct and indirect channel systems in which a business and intermediary perform different functions with respect to sales, distribution, and customer service.

monetizing strategies Strategies that minimize marketing investment and seek to maximize cash flow.

morphemes Parts of words that are used to create brand names.

multi-dimensional scaling A statistical method to help understand customer perceptions of competitors and their preferences for products.

Multi-segment strategy Two or more separate and distinct marketing mix strategies (4Ps) that are created for different needs-based market segments.

needs-based segmentation Market segmentation based on customer needs and/or the benefits they seek in satisfying a particular problem or buying situation.

net marketing contribution The total contribution produced by a marketing strategy minus marketing expenses needed to produce it.

net present value The value in today's dollars of a cash flow that occurs over time and is evaluated with a particular discount rate.

net profit Sales revenues minus all expenses including taxes and interest.

new-market entry strategies Offensive strategic market plans designed to enter new markets.

niche market (segment) strategy A small segment of a market that is often overlooked or ignored by large competitors.

nonprofit customers Customers who are not profitable and not loyal to a product or business.

oblique strategies Indirect, non-combative competitive strategies that lead competitors to follow a competitive move.

offensive strategies (offensive strategic market plans) Long-run plans (3 to 5 years) to penetrate markets or enter new markets.

one-on-one marketing Building one-on-one relationships with key customers a business wants to retain.

operating expenses Overhead expenses that are not the direct result of marketing activities.

operating income Sales minus all expenses before taxes and interest.

optimizing strategies Strategies that seek to optimize the marketing mix and marketing investment needed to maximize profits.

penetration pricing A low price strategy to achieve a high market share/high volume position.

perceived value pricing Pricing to create a greater customer value based on customer perceptions of product, service, company benefits, and the perceived cost of acquiring those benefits.

perceptual mapping A display of competing products based on their relative substitutability and customer ideal products based on their strength of preference for each competing product.

performance timeline A 3- to 5-year forecast of market and profit performance metrics.

plus-one pricing Adding at least one differentiating feature that allows a product to price slightly above competing products that lack this product or service feature.

portfolio analysis An evaluation of a product, market, or business with respect to market attractiveness and competitive advantage.

price-earnings ratio The price of a share of stock in a business divided by the business's earnings per share.

price elasticity The percentage change in unit volume for a product per 1 percent change in price.

price per unit The selling price of a product or service.

price premium The dollar amount, or percentage, by which the price of a product exceeds competing products.

prisoner's dilemma A price situation in which businesses are forced to follow downward price moves by competitors to remain competitive.

product adoption forces Product forces that impact the rate of new-product adoption.

product benefits The overall benefit a customer derives from the product performance and features.

product bundling Combining for sale two or more products at a total price that would be lower than the price paid if each product were purchased separately.

product differentiation The degree to which a business's product is meaningfully different and superior when compared by customers to competing products.

product-focused A business that is focused internally on product development and utilizes marketing primarily as an advertising and sales function.

product life cycle The life of a product as it progresses from introduction through growth, maturity, and decline.

product life cycle profit index An profit index based on the percentage of a business's sales at different stages of the product life cycle.

product positioning The manner in which customers perceive a business's product features and price in comparison to competitors' product features and prices.

product unbundling Offering for sale an individual product that is normally sold as part of a product bundle.

product-line extensions Products that are added to a product line under an umbrella brand that is well known and has an established reputation for quality.

product-line positioning A planned sequence of alternative product offerings that differ in product performance and price.

product-line scale The effect product line extensions or deletions have on the cost of producing and marketing a line of products.

product-line substitution The degree to which the sales of products are cannabalized with the addition of substitute products to the product line.

product-market This is a market definition that defines the specific market as a product is intended.

product-market diversification The degree to which a business has different products across different markets.

promotional price elasticity The percent volume increase per 1 percent price decrease during a price promotion.

protect strategies A defensive strategic market plan in which a business develops a marketing strategy to protect/defend its competitive position and market share.

pull communications Marketing communications directed at end-user customers in an attempt to motivate target customers to seek a business's products (i.e., pull the products through the channel).

push communications Marketing communications directed at intermediaries in an attempt to motivate them to push a business's product through the channel in an effort to reach target customers.

quality aesthetics Product and service attributes that impact the perceived quality of a product.

quality drivers The critical product and service attributes that drive customer perceptions of performance.

quality enhancers Extra product and service attributes that enhance customer satisfaction.

quality killers Product and service attributes that are expected to perform at a high level all the time.

reactive strategies Strategies based on either customer intelligence or competitor intelligence.

reduced market focus A planned reduction in market share by reducing focus to a smaller number of customers.

reference price A price point used by customers to evaluate the price of competing products.

regression analysis A statistical method used to analyze the relationship between a performance variable such as sales and influence variable such as price or advertising.

relative cost A business's cost per unit relative to a competitor's cost per unit.

relative market share A business's market share divided by the share of the market share leader competitor or next largest share competitor.

relative new-product sales The sales of new products introduced over the last 3 years divided by the new-product sales produced by a competitor over the same time period.

relative price A business's price divided by the price of a competitor or the average price of several competitors.

relative product quality An overall relative index based on customer perceptions when comparing a business's product against a competitor's product on each aspect of product quality.

relative service quality An overall relative index based on customer perceptions when comparing a business's service against a competitor's service on each aspect of service quality.

retention cost The cost of retaining one customer over a given period of time.

return on assets The net profit produced by a business divided by its total assets.

return on capital The net income after taxes produced by a business divided by its investment in capital.

return on equity The net profit produced by a business divided by its owner's equity.

return on sales The net profit produced by a business divided by its total sales.

sales revenue The price times the volume sold for each of the products sold by a company.

scanner data A tracking method that accounts for purchases by hour, day, or location.

segment attractiveness The attractiveness of a segment based on market forces, competitive intensity, and market access to a segment.

segment identification The demographics characteristics that distinguish a needs-based segment from other needs-based segments.

segment marketing mix strategy A marketing mix developed specifically for a target market segment.

segment marketing profitability The net marketing contribution a business derives from a particular market segment.

segment positioning The product-price position and value proposition developed specifically for customers in a given market segment.

segment pricing Pricing based on segment price sensitivity and customer need for additional product features and/or services.

segment strategy acid test A test to the segment product positioning strategy and value proposition that involves the proposed strategy and two competing alternatives.

served market demand The size of the target market to be served by the business.

service benefits The overall benefit a customer derives from the various components of service a business provides.

service differentiation The degree to which a business's service is meaningfully different and superior when compared by customers to competing products.

share development index The percentage of current market demand obtained by a business.

share follower The business with the second largest market share in a given market.

situation analysis An external analysis of market forces and internal analysis of business performance that are used to identify key performance issues and guide strategic market planning and development of tactical marketing strategies.

skim pricing A high price position that attracts a limited number of customers but is sustainable because competitors cannot match the business's competitive advantage and value proposition.

strategic account pricing A customer price that is negotiated and managed over several years with the intent of maintaining a close supplier-customer relationship.

strategic market definition A broad definition of market demand that includes the business's served market and relevant substitute product-markets.

strategic market planning The specification of a long-run (3- to 5-year) strategic market plan that will result in specific performance objectives with respect to market share, sales revenues, and profitability over the planning horizon.

strategy implementation The actions taken to implement, track, and adapt a tactical marketing plan derived from a specific strategic market plan.

subsegment strategy A further delineation of customers within a segment based on demographics or product usage.

substitute products Products that can be substituted for one another.

supply chain management Involves the management of the flow of physical materials, information, and money to and from a business and its suppliers and channel partners.

SWOT analysis A summary of strengths/weaknesses and opportunities/threats that are uncovered in a situation analysis.

tactical marketing strategy A 1-year marketing mix strategy (4Ps) for a particular target market and specific strategic market plan.

target market A collection of customers that the business has decided to focus on in building a marketing mix strategy.

team approach The degree to which a business works across functions as a team in creating and delivering market-based customer solutions and implementation strategies.

test market A test of a product in an isolated market in which sales can be tracked and evaluated to determine the impact of a new product or variation in the marketing mix.

top performers Customers who are profitable and loyal to a product, business, or company.

top-down marketing budget A marketing budget based on a certain percentage of sales.

total contribution Total sales minus total variable cost of sales.

trade-off analysis Customer preferences for different combinations of price, product, service, and company benefits.

transaction value The economic value a channel partner can obtain from transactions with a company based on margin per square foot inventory (square feet), inventory turnover, and marketing expenses.

two-tier marketing channel A channel and sales system that involves two or more intermediaries.

umbrella brand A core brand that is well known and under which brand extensions can be easily introduced.

unarticulated market demand Market demand that has not occurred because customers have not recognized (articulated) a need for a product or product feature.

underachievers Customers who are loyal but are not profitable or are minimally profitable.

unit volume vector A projection of volume sold in 3 to 5 years based on different combinations of market growth and market share.

untapped market opportunities The gap between current market demand and market potential.

value in-use pricing (value pricing) Pricing to create a dollar savings for a customer based on a lower total life cycle cost when compared to a competitor's total life cycle cost.

value map A graph of relative performance and relative price.

value proposition A short statement that communicates how a product or business creates value for target customers.

value-added resellers Intermediaries that buy products from several manufacturers and customize them for certain market applications.

variable cost per unit All of the variable costs associated with one unit sold.

variance analysis A breakdown of net marketing contribution based on actual and planned performance to better understand how a marketing plan achieved its results.

vertical brand-line extensions Variations in the brand that add more variety and options for customers.

vertical market opportunities Forward or backward integration along the supply chain that starts with raw materials and moves vertically through different stages of production, distribution, sales, and service.

volume The number of units sold for a particular product in a given period of time.

win-back customers Customers who stopped buying from a business but are won back at a later point in time.

CREDITS

Chapter 1

Page 18, Figure 1.11: F. F. Reichheld and W. Earl Sasser, Jr. "Zero Defections: Quality Comes to Services," *Harvard Business School Publishing* (September–October 1990).

Chapter 4

Page 98, Figure 4.2: Ad courtesy of the Weyerhaeuser Corporation. Page 105, Figure 4.7: Adapted from Forbis, John, and Nitin, Mehta. "Value-Based Strategies for Industrial Products," *Business Horizons* (May–June 1981) 32–42. Page 107, Figure 4.8: Ad courtesy of Sealed Air Corporation. Page 108, Figure 4.9: Ad courtesy of Rohm and Haas Company.

Chapter 5

Page 150, Figure 5.11: Advertising and photo courtesy of DuPont.

Chapter 6

Page 186, Figure 6.14: Source: PIMS Database, Strategic Planning Institute, Cambridge, MA. Page 186, Figure 6.15: Used with permission of US West Media Group. Page 189, Figure 6.18: Source: PIMS Database, Strategic Planning Institute, Cambridge, MA. Page 190, Figure 6.19: Source: Best, Roger J., Del I. Hawkins, and Charles M. Lillis, "Building a Value-Based Pricing Strategy," Working Paper (1994), University of Oregon. Page 191, Figure 6.20: Source (left side): Marketing Models by Kotler & Lilien, © 1992. Adapted by permission of Prentice Hall, Inc., Upper Saddle River, NJ. Source (right side): PIMS Database, Strategic Planning Institute, Cambridge, MA.

Chapter 7

Page 208, Figure 7.9: Source: Garvin, David. "Competing on Eight Dimensions of Quality," *Harvard Business Review* (November–December, 1987):101–105. Page 223, Figure 7.15: Source: PIMS Database, Strategic Planning Institute, Cambridge, MA.

Chapter 9

Page 289, Figure 9.15: Marketing Models by Kotler & Lilien, © 1992. Adapted by permission of Prentice Hall, Inc., Upper Saddle River, NJ.

Chapter 10

Page 304, Figure 10.5: Ad courtesy of Johnson Controls, Inc. Page 306, Figure 10.7: Adapted from Bender, David, Peter Farquhar, and Sanford Schulert. "Growing from the Top," *Marketing Management* (Winter/Spring, 1996):10–19. Page 307, Figure 10.8: Source: Zielske, H. "The Remembering and Forgetting of Advertising," *Journal of Marketing* (January 1959): 140. Page 309, Figure 10.9: Ad courtesy of Gardenburger. Page 313, Figure 10.12: Adapted from Reibstein, David. "Making the Most of Your Marketing Dollars," Drive Marketing Excellence, Institute for International Research, New York, NY, 1994. Page 318, Figure 10.17: Source: Bemmaor, Albert, and Dominique Mouchoux. "Measuring the Short-Term Effect of In-Store Promotion and Retail Advertising on Brand Sales," *Journal of Marketing Research* (May, 1991):202–214.

Chapter 13

Page 382, Figure 13.5: Source: PIMS Database, Strategic Planning Institute, Cambridge, MA. Page 382, Figure 13.6: Source: PIMS Database, Strategic Planning Institute, Cambridge, MA. Pages 384–385, Figures 13.8 and 13.9: Source: PIMS Database, Strategic Planning Institute, Cambridge, MA. Page 386, Figure 13.10: Source: PIMS Database, Strategic Planning Institute, Cambridge, MA.

INDEX